For Gwen, with
my very best,

A Woman of Valor

A Woman of Valor

A Woman of Valor

Clara Barton and the Civil War

STEPHEN B. OATES

THE FREE PRESS

NEW YORK   LONDON   TORONTO   SYDNEY   TOKYO   SINGAPORE

The Free Press
A Division of Simon & Schuster Inc.
1230 Avenue of the Americas
New York, N.Y. 10020

First Free Press Paperback Edition 1995

Printed in the United States of America

printing number
1 2 3 4 5 6 7 8 9 10

Library of Congress Cataloging-in-Publication Data

Oates, Stephen B.
  A woman of valor: Clara Barton and the Civil War / Stephen B. Oates.
    p.   cm.
  Includes bibliographical references.
  ISBN 0-02-874012-2
  1. United States—History—Civil War, 1861–1865—Medical care.
2. Barton, Clara, 1821–1912. 3. Nurses—United States—Biography.
I. Title.
E621 O24 1994
973.7'75—dc20   93-38830
                                                                          CIP

Frontispiece photo by Mathew Brady.
Courtesy of Library of Congress.

For Marie

"If I were to speak of war, it would not be to show you the glories of conquering armies but the mischief and misery they strew in their tracks; and how, while they march on with tread of iron and plumes proudly tossing in the breeze, some one must follow closely in their steps, crouching to the earth, toiling in the rain and darkness, shelterless like themselves, with no thought of pride or glory, fame or praise, or reward; hearts breaking with pity, faces bathed in tears and hands in blood. This is the side which history never shows."

Clara Barton

Contents

Foreword

*I*n this portrait of Clara Barton in the Civil War, I have referred to her as Clara, because that is how she was known to her family and friends. Calling her Barton makes her seem cold and distant, when she was anything but that: in the company of people she liked, she exuded a special warmth and had a relaxed informality about her. She was Clara. And this is the story of her Civil War, the war in the battlefield hospitals—now a bullet-ridden farmhouse, now a crumbling mansion, now a windblown tent—where she served as nurse, relief worker, and surrogate mother or sister, wife or sweetheart, to her "dear boys" who lay sick, wounded, and dying by her side. The Civil War was the defining event in Clara's life, shaping who she was and what she became. It gave her the opportunity as a woman to reach out and seize control of her destiny.

It is one of the most compelling stories I have ever encountered in all my years as a writer. It has a tragic national context, a sympathetic and original lead character, a wartime love affair with a married officer, powerful friendships and complex family ties, a sometimes antagonistic medical bureaucracy, obdurate male and female adversaries, plenty of battlefield action seen from a unique perspective, and a compelling plot: a passionate, driven, conflicted woman who overcomes "the fearful odds" against her, invades a man's domain, and helps change it dramatically.

To tell the story of Clara's Civil War, I have drawn heavily on the Clara Barton manuscripts, a good many of them never used before. Because Clara was in the storm, because she served near the battlefield of Second Bull Run, on the battlegrounds of Antietam, Fredericksburg, and Battery Wagner, and near the front during the Wilderness campaign and the siege lines of Petersburg and Richmond, I have tried to depict her in the swirling chaos of battle, to give some sense of what she expe-

rienced there and how it affected her, and to describe her important contributions to the Union war effort and to the liberation of her sex. This is, of course, a work of narrative nonfiction. Using authenticated details, I have tried to evoke Clara's wartime experiences through graphic scenes and images. I have tried to recreate a living woman in a living world, to simulate what it was like "to be there" with her as the war unfolded.

How I came to write A Woman of Valor *is a story in itself. For the past several years I have worked on a sweeping biographical history of the entire Civil War epoch, one that attempts to capture it through the intersecting lives of a dozen central characters. One of them was Clara Barton. Always fiercely independent, a dedicated loner, she refused to remain in my lineup. Every time I wrote something about her in conjunction with my other figures, I had the sensation that she was trying hard to keep me from knowing and understanding her. She would float into my consciousness without a face, for example, or give me the strange feeling that she was hiding from me somewhere in my study, or had just bolted out the door. At one point my computer abruptly malfunctioned and started throwing out an entire body of information— several months worth of work on Jefferson Davis. Nothing I punched on the keyboard could stop the machine from its insane mission to erace every trace of the Confederate president from its memory. All I could do was watch in despair. At first I blamed this on Davis's own stubborn pride, as if he were saying, "You're not putting me in a book with Lincoln or any other hated Yankee!" Later I decided it was Clara again, trying to sabotage my project in an effort to get out of it. Finally, submitting to her superior will, I put the biographical work aside and set out to write Clara's Civil War story by itself—and on a new computer, I might add. After that, she cooperated fully. I was helped to my decision by the remarkable details, so many of them never before published, that I kept discovering in the Clara Barton archives. Now I have told the story Clara wanted me to tell, speaking in an empathetic voice that attempts to understand and capture her in all her complexity, all her humanity. I hope she is not too disappointed with the result.*

PART ONE

The Search

Clara would never forget the day the Civil War first touched her personally. She was in Washington City, working as a copyist in the U.S. Patent Office, when she heard that something terrible had happened to the Sixth Massachusetts Regiment in Baltimore. A riot, someone said. The soldiers had been attacked while marching through the city en route to Washington, and the survivors were due in on the next southbound train.

Clara was "indignant, excited, alarmed." She was from Massachusetts—North Oxford, to be precise—and many of her childhood friends were members of the "old 6th Regiment." She hoped to God none of them had been killed or wounded. Anxious to help the soldiers somehow, Clara and her sister, Sally Vassall, joined a crowd of Washingtonians hurrying toward the Baltimore and Ohio Railroad Station. Clara walked with a resolute, flat-footed stride, her head erect, her eyes focused straight ahead. Her full name was Clarissa Harlowe Barton, and (she liked to point out) she was the daughter of Captain Stephen Barton, a veteran of the Indian wars in the old Michigan Territory. She was small, slender, and striking: only five feet tall, with silky brown hair parted in the middle and combed into a bun in the back of her head; she had a round face, a wide, expressive mouth, and exquisite, dark brown eyes. It was hard to tell her age; she looked to be in her late twenties but was actually thirty-nine. She was unmarried by choice and one of only a handful of women employed by the Federal government in Washington. In the current crisis, she was an ardent Republican and patriot—"from the bottom of my heart," she wrote a cousin, "I pray that the thing may be tested, may the business be taken in hand and proved, not 'if' we have a Government, but *that* we have one."

It was April 19, 1861, seven days after Confederate forces had fired on Fort Sumter in Charleston harbor and plunged the country into civil war. Since then, the pace of ominous events was almost too much to comprehend. Lincoln called up 75,000 volunteers to put down the rebellion in Dixie, Virginia seceded and virtually joined the Confederacy, and a menacing rebel army was assembling south of the Potomac. Defended by only a few ragtag volunteer companies, Washington City seemed vulnerable to attack and was prey to rumors of impending doom. Telegraphic dispatches indicated that the Sixth Massachusetts Regiment, the Seventh New York, and various other militia units were on their way to save the capital. But the latest intelligence—the mobbing of the Sixth in Baltimore—rocked Washington to its foundations.

Shortly after Clara and Sally reached the railroad station, the train from Baltimore came into view with blasts of its steam whistle. The crowd cheered as the locomotive rolled into the station belching smoke and ash, its boxed oil head lamp looming in front like a giant eye. As the wounded soldiers, more than thirty of them, were helped off the cars, Clara led several women forward to dress their injuries with handkerchiefs. Her indignation rose when she recognized a few of them; they were her old "schoolmates and playmates" from Worcester County. What was to be done with them? The Union Medical Department, so inadequate and understaffed that it could not cope with a riot, let alone a war, had no general hospitals in Washington or anywhere else. All it had were a few army post hospitals, and the largest of those had only forty beds and was located clear out in Fort Leavenworth, Kansas. The Quartermaster Department, which was responsible for constructing hospitals, was reluctant to do so on the grounds that they were expensive. "Men need guns, not beds," the quartermasters argued. Which was not much help to the wounded of the Sixth Massachusetts. Many of them found their way to the little infirmary on E Street, and Clara took a few others to her sister's house, where she bandaged their injuries and listened, transfixed, as they described their ordeal in Baltimore.

The first of four Massachusetts militia regiments mobilized in response to Lincoln's call for volunteers, the Sixth had enjoyed a rousing send-off in Boston two days before. There went the pride of the Bay State: swaying lines of infantry smartly clad in gray overcoats and armed with new rifles, heading south to defend the Union from the "traitors" in Dixie. Tumultuous flag-waving crowds greeted the regiment in Connecticut, New York City, and New Jersey. But when it reached Baltimore, a hotbed of secessionist sentiment, the crowds turned ugly. As the soldiers headed for Camden Street Railroad Station, where they would entrain for Washington, secessionist flags bristled on the sidewalks. "Kill the white niggers!" somebody shouted. "Hurrah for the Confederacy!" A mob of mutinous civilians pelted the soldiers with paving stones and then rushed their ranks. Drilled in street fighting, the Sixth fought back with rifle butts and bayonets. Finally, a column of troops opened fire, pouring volley after volley into the raucous crowd until it dispersed. When the riot was over, twelve civilians and four soldiers—the first battle casualties of the Civil War— lay dead in the streets.

As Clara mulled over the riot and the "great national calamity" now besetting the country, she thought: "I look out upon the same beautiful landscape—the same clear blue sky, the same floating clouds—the face of nature is unchanged—nothing there indicates that the darkest page in our country's history is now being written in lines of blood! But I turn and one glance on the *face* of *man* reveals the terrible certainty of some dark impending war." Yet this day, April 19, was the anniversary of the battle of Lexington and the shot "heard round the world," and Clara thought it "an omen of evil import to those who have dared to raise the hand of rebellion against the common country."

But all the omens seemed to bode ill for the Union. Demolition parties had burned the wooden railroad bridges west and north of Baltimore; by April 21 all rail and telegraph connections between Washington and the North were cut. The capital was isolated, trapped between hostile Maryland and secessionist Virginia. President Lincoln himself mounted "the battlements of the executive mansion," as one of his young secretaries put it, and scanned the Potomac through a telescope, searching for a sign of troop transports from the North. Beyond the Potomac, rebel flags could be seen flying over the buildings of Alexandria. The government was surrounded by its enemies. Right here in Washington, Southern sympathizers wore secession badges in the streets. As Clara observed, it was common "to see little spruce clerks and even boys strutting about the streets, and asserting that 'We had no Government,—it merely amounted to a compact but had no strength. Our Constitution was a mere pretense, and our government a myth.' " There were even disloyalists in the Patent Office where Clara worked. Two male clerks were particularly offensive in their protestations of support for the Confederacy. The damned traitors! It made Clara furious when they flaunted the very government that employed them. Those two would bear watching, she decided.

On Saturday Clara called on the Sixth Massachusetts, which had taken up quarters in the Senate Chamber since no barracks were available for them. The soldiers had fashioned beds on the carpeted floors, in the galleries, and out in the corridors. Clara found that they lacked the most basic necessities. Many of them had lost their baggage in Baltimore, and the militia officers did not know how to requisition government stores and supplies. Hearing that, Clara resolved to resupply the regiment herself. She marched home and emptied her drawers of thread, needles, thimbles, scissors, buttons, pins, strings, salves, and serving utensils and packed them all in "the largest market basket in the house." The next day, Sunday, she persuaded neighborhood grocers to sell her provisions, hired five blacks to carry them in wicker baskets, and led the parade up to Capitol Hill, where she distributed her stores to lusty cheers. One of the men had a two-day old copy of the *Worcester Spy*, which contained the first report of the regiment's history and journey to Washington, and the soldiers clamored for their benefactor to do them the honor of reading it aloud. Happily obliging, Clara strode to the vice-president's desk and read the story in her clear, soft, musical voice. "You would have smiled to see me and my audience in the Senate Chamber of the United States," she wrote a friend. "But don't tell us they are not determined—just fighting mad." She was certain that the rebels would attack Washington City within the next sixty days. "If it must be, let it come; and when there is no longer a soldier's arm to raise the Stars and Stripes above our Capitol, may God give strength to mine."

That same day, the flashy Seventh New York regiment reached Washington City and marched in perfect formation to the White House. The capital, it appeared, had been saved. Bands played, flags flew, brass howitzers boomed. Early the next morning came the Eighth Massachusetts and the First Rhode Island regiments. The Rhode Island troops were under the joint command of millionaire Governor William Sprague, who sported a yellow plume in his hat, and Ambrose Everts Burnside, a large, imposing man with impressive sideburns and whiskers that curled under his nose. Clara would come to know Burnside well enough in the hard days ahead. The Rhode Islanders found quarters in Clara's Patent Office, laying their bedrolls among the tables and displays of patented oddities. For weeks the regiments poured into Washington, camping in the Treasury Department, in warehouses, in the Center Market, behind City Hall, in the Navy Yard, on Franklin Square. "We are now an armed city," Clara wrote her friend and cousin, Elvira Stone. "Thirty thousand soldiers armed to the teeth, marching and counter marching drilling in squads, companies and battalions, the roll of the drums bursting upon your ears at almost every moment, the long lines of dark, dusty men, as some new

Regiment files up the Avenue, with their canteens and haversacks, and thousand bristling bayonets glimmering in the sun."

"I don't know how long it has been since my ear has been free from the roll of a drum," Clara wrote her father. "It is the music I sleep by, and I love it."

Clara had never before been so excited. She wanted desperately to enlist in the army, to serve the grand old flag as her "soldier father" had done. Yet it was impossible because she was a woman, and the army would tell her that a woman's correct sphere was the home. Oh, she knew the argument well. One day she would capture it perfectly in a bit of sarcastic verse: *Women*, men said, *would just be in the way. They didn't know the difference between work and play. What did women know of war anyway? What could they do? Of what use could they be? They would just scream at the sight of a gun, don't you see. Imagine their skirts among artillery wheels, and watch for their flutter as they flee across the fields. They would faint at the first drop of blood in their sight. . . . They might pick some lint, and tear up some sheets, and make us some jellies, and send on their sweets, and knit some soft socks for Uncle Sam's shoes, and write us some letters, and tell us the news. And so it was settled, by common consent, that husbands or brothers or whoever went, that the place for the women was in their own homes, there to patiently wait until victory comes.*

Clara hated that argument. She hated all restrictions on women because of their sex and thought them entitled to the same rights as men. She had rejected marriage, which she associated with death, and had turned her back on the idea of marriage and motherhood as the female ideal. She had become a single working woman, had taught school in Massachusetts, and had established the first public school in Bordentown, New Jersey. Then she had convinced male bureaucrats that she was competent and mature enough to work in the U.S. Patent Office. She had demonstrated that a woman could function quite ably outside the home, and she saw no reason why a woman of her qualifications and attributes wouldn't make a splendid soldier. Indeed, what man could surpass her? Thanks to the tutelage of her father and older brothers, she was a superb horsewoman and a dead shot with a revolver; she could consistently hit the bulls-eye of a target fifty feet away. She was physically strong, could handle a saw and a hammer, and could drive a wagon team. Indeed, her father had always told her that she was "*more boy than girl.*" Since childhood, she had idolized her warrior father, who had often treated her like a son destined to follow in his steps. A tall, lean man with large hands and a military bearing,

Captain Barton had enthralled little Clara with stories about his
wartime exploits with Mad Anthony Wayne in Michigan Territory, and
he had drilled her in military tactics. "We marshalled large armies, laid
in ambush, and fought sanguinary battles," she remembered. "I had no
end of camp material, but no dolls—I never had one." "Where other
little girls listened to fairy tales and mother Goose wonders, I sat on
my father's knee and asked for 'more stories about the war' and how
the soldiers lived." Most important: "I early learned that next to
Heaven our highest duty was to love and serve our country." And now,
in the worst crisis in its history, Clara ached to join the service and
fight for her country. "The patriot blood of my father," she said later,
"was warm in my veins."

But it made no difference to the U.S. Army: she was a *woman*, and
her place was the *home*.

True, some women were getting into uniform by masquerading as
men, but Clara was too inhibited to try that. Despite her soldierly
upbringing, she had a sense of propriety as a lady that held her back
like an iron hand. Her need to be a "lady" also stemmed from her
father: while treating her like a son, Captain Barton admonished her
always to act like "a proper little lady" and even forbade her to skate or
dance because "nice" girls didn't do that. As a consequence, Clara
grew up concerned with being ladylike at the same time that she identified with the male world of her father and excelled at "masculine"
endeavors. When she went to the firing range in Washington, for
instance, she was careful to have a male escort. This petite woman who
could ride and shoot like a man also took pains to maintain a fashion-
ably "feminine" appearance: her morning ritual found her dabbing
creams on her face, touching a little rouge to her cheeks, applying a
liner to her eyes, even covering up a rude strand of gray hair with
brown dye. She dressed in the complete paraphernalia of a lady, wore
hats and bonnets, cloaks and corsets, black veils and white linen collars, laced boots and cotton hose, tight-waisted jackets and round,
hooped skirts. The point was, Clara tried to be proper. No lady would
ever impersonate a man in order to become a soldier, so that option for
serving her country was out.

She did have another option that spring: Dorothea Dix was recruit-
ing women for her fledgling army nursing corps. This wasn't soldiering, but it was a way to serve the flag. What was more, Clara Barton
and Miss Dix had much in common: both were from Massachusetts,
both were strong-willed and unmarried, and both had been galvanized
into action by the Baltimore riot. Miss Dix, who for years had borne

her "battle flag of humanity" in behalf of the insane and the destitute in Massachusetts, was in New Jersey when she heard about the riot; she hurried to Washington and inspected the condition and accommodations of the men hurt in Baltimore. Sixty years old and tall, thin, and straight-backed as a general, she marched into the office of Acting Surgeon General R. C. Wood and told him bluntly that the Medical Department lacked adequate resources to fight a war. It had no hospitals, few surgeons, and no nurses beyond the soldiers detailed for regimental hospital service. "I propose," she said, "to organize under the official auspices of the War Department, an Army Nursing Corps made up of women volunteers." She had in mind something like Florence Nightingale's volunteer organization of the Crimean War in the mid-1850s. Acting as "General Superintendent of the Female Nursing Establishment" of the British Army's military hospitals, Nightingale and her brigade of female nurses had swept into the British army depot at Scutari, Turkey, and brought order, discipline, and cleanliness to the wretched Barrack Hospital there.

Dix's proposal to create a similar organization of nurses caused heads to shake all over the War Department, for military nursing in America was officially a male domain and had been for as long as the army bureaucrats could remember. Like Miss Nightingale, though, Dix was gifted with insatiable energy and an inability to take no for an answer. She promoted her cause everywhere in official Washington; she even went to see the president. Her persistence paid off: on April 23, Secretary of War Simon Cameron issued a directive appointing her to the War Department and announcing that she would help "the chief surgeon" organize military hospitals in Washington and appoint female nurses to help relieve suffering soldiers.

Dix's commission would not come through until June, but that did not deter her. She promptly sought the help of Dr. Elizabeth Blackwell, the first woman to earn a medical degree in America and the founder and head of New York's Infirmary for Women and Children. Dix also enlisted the aid of the newly formed Woman's Central Association of Relief in New York City, which, with Blackwell's assistance, set about screening applicants and working out a training program for female nurses at Bellevue Hospital. "No young ladies should be sent at all," Dix instructed the Woman's Central Association; only "those who are sober, earnest, self-sacrificing, and self-sustained; who can bear the presence of suffering and exercise entire self-control, of speech and manner; who can be calm, gentle, quiet, active, and steadfast in duty."

The news of Dix's appointment resounded in homes across the North. Since Lincoln's call to arms, thousands of women had felt the same urge to serve as Clara had. "Oh that I may have a hand or a foot or an eye or a voice, an influence on the side of freedom and my country!" cried Mary Livermore when the Sixth Massachusetts left Boston. In all directions, women did what they could within women's sphere: they flew flags, urged their men to enlist, cheered them as they left for the front. They formed scores of Soldiers' Aid Societies and set about assiduously collecting and forwarding supplies to Washington. Now Dix's appointment afforded them an opportunity to serve in the seat of war itself, and a "horde of eager women" flocked to Washington City, all clamoring to join Dix's corps and nurse and nurture the soldiers. None of them had any formal training, since America had no nursing schools at that time and nursing as a profession did not exist. Even so, the women thronging Dix's H Street headquarters had plenty of experience tending sick family members and neighbors, and they hoped to extend that experience to the nation's wartime hospitals. To Dix's horror, however, many of these would-be volunteers were young, attractive, and unmarried. What would the country say—indeed, what might *happen*—if she allowed such females to be placed in close quarters with a lot of soldiers? Dix promptly issued a bulletin to the press: "No woman under thirty need apply to serve in government hospitals. All nurses are required to be plain looking women. Their dresses must be brown or black, with no bows, no curls, no jewelry, and no hoops."

Clara never applied for Dix's nursing corps. Perhaps Dix's priggish requirements put her off. Clara, after all, was not "a plain looking" woman. Perhaps, too, Clara sensed that Miss Dix would be difficult to work for. One of her nurses, Mary Phinney von Olnhausen, commented that Dix was "a stern woman of few words." Others found her dictatorial and called her "Dragon Dix" behind her back. Clara disliked authoritarian women, and in any case she had an independent streak that caused her to shun women's groups and organizations. She was an ambitious loner, with a powerful need to get things done by herself. So she did not enlist in the army nursing corps. Let the "gentle, the quiet, and the plain" work for Dix, if they liked. Somehow, some way, Clara would find her own way to get into the war.

As Washington girded for war, Clara was shackled to her job as a copyist in the Patent Office between Seventh and F streets. One of the great buildings in Washington, made of white marble and covering nearly an entire square, the Patent Office housed a veritable museum of inventions and curiosities, ranging from Benjamin Franklin's printing press, George Washington's uniform, and the original Declaration of Independence, to a menagerie of "stuffed birds, beasts, fishes and insects," as Clara described it. Here, day after day, she toiled at her desk in the basement, preparing handwritten copies of patents, records, and annual reports at a salary, set by law, of eight cents per hundred words, not to exceed $900 per year. Her skill and speed with a pen were phenomenal: she could "reel off" ten thousand words of "bold round record" in a single day. Her productivity, however, was limited by the amount of work available.

When Clara first began working as a copyist in 1854, the Patent Office was the only government agency that employed women—four of them, counting Clara—within a public building in Washington. This was the innovation of Patent Office Commissioner Charles Mason, who thought that women made capable and efficient copyists. As far as her own appointment was concerned, Clara always claimed that she was the first female copyist to work "regularly" and to draw a salary under her own name, and that she was therefore something of a pioneer. According to her, the other female employees were substituting for disabled husbands or fathers and getting paid under the names of the men. However that may be, Mason was certainly impressed with Clara, so much so that he soon promoted her to "regular 'temporary clerk' " with an annual salary of $1,400, a phenomenal wage for a woman at that time (female bookkeepers, by contrast, earned around $500 a year; dressmakers in customers' houses, $300 a year; female teachers, about $250 a year; and female store clerks, $156 a year). Because she earned the same pay as men of her rank, Clara's male co-workers felt threatened. Fearful that her position and salary would establish a precedent and that women would soon replace them, they subjected her to what in a later day would be called sexual harassment. When she came to her desk in the morning, they glared and whistled at her and stooped to taunts and catcalls. They also impugned her character, spreading rumors that she was a "slut" with illegitimate "negroid" children. Such behavior got her "Yankee blood" up, she said, but she refused to quit; "there was a principle involved" and she was "determined not to yield it." She was also lucky that Commissioner Mason, a fair man relatively free of sexual prejudice, took her side. When one malcontent complained to him about Clara's "moral character" and insisted that she be fired, the commissioner demanded proof by five o'clock that afternoon. "But understand," Mason said, "things will not remain just as they are in this office. If you prove this charge, Miss Barton goes; if you fail to prove it, you go." When the deadline passed without the proof, the man went. And that put a stop to the harassment of Clara.

Clara lost her lucrative post in 1857 when the Democratic, pro-Southern Buchanan administration released her because of her political sentiments (she had boldly declared herself a Republican). She returned to Massachusetts and drifted aimlessly for three depressing years. For a time, she took art classes in Worcester but displayed such inaptitude for the paint brush that she gave it up. With no job and no place else to go, she retreated to North Oxford, to live with her father and her older brother, David, his wife, Julia, and their four children. Clara tried to be useful, helping Julia with the endless grind of household chores: she washed and ironed clothes, scrubbed floors, changed bedding, and sewed, all the while feeling "low spirited and discontented." She hated the role of domestic spinster. It hurt her pride. She felt right with herself only when she was independent and self-supporting, with a job and a purpose.

She tried desperately to find "something somewhere" she could do. She wrote letters in hopes of securing a position as a postmistress—the Post Office employed several hundred women in that capacity—but realized that the Buchanan administration would never give her anything. She did apply for a job with the Register of Deeds in Boston, only to be told that there was "no room for ladies." She also applied for a position as school administrator—she was certainly qualified, having established a public school in New Jersey—but was promptly rejected because of her sex. That kind of discrimination made her furious. "Were you in my place," she fumed to her nephew, Bernard Vassall, "you would . . . wish, and pine, and fret in your cage as I do, and if the very gentlemen who have the power could only know for one twenty-four hours all that oppresses and gnaws at my peace they would offer me something to do in accordance with my old *habits* and capabilities before I am a week older, but they will never know, and I shall always be oppressed no doubt."

The fact was, an educated, middle-class woman in antebellum America had almost no options for employment except for teaching. But Clara had no desire to return to the classroom. "I have outgrown that," she insisted. And anyway she thought that the salary of a female teacher—she had earned only $250 a year in New Jersey—was too pitiful to afford her a living. Which left her in limbo as far as meaningful work was concerned. "I am tired of doing nothing," she complained, am "nervous, and unhappy." Sometimes, she said, she "cried half the night." By June 1860, her distress had become so acute that she suffered an emotional and physical collapse. For two months, she convalesced in the care of friends in upstate New York, beset with thoughts of death, of laying down her burden at last. When that time came, she said, "it must be the sweetest hour of my whole existence."

Lincoln's victory in the 1860 presidential election sounded a trumpet of hope for Clara. A new Republican administration might reasonably be expected to offer her something,—at least an appointment as postmistress somewhere. Finally, in December, certain political friends interceded in her behalf and arranged for her reinstatement at the Patent Office. She did not get her old job back as a "regular 'temporary clerk' " but had to settle for the lower grade of copyist or "temporary writer," which entailed a considerable reduction in pay. Now she would earn from thirty-five to sixty dollars per month, depending on the amount of copying assigned to her. It was "mortifying," a mere "crumb" of patronage, but what choice did she have except to take what the men in Washington offered her?

When, with the outbreak of war, the Patent Office found itself short of funds and had to lay off employees, Clara was not among them. Neither, apparently, were the two Southern sympathizers she found so offensive. How they stayed on is not known. But Clara retained her post because she impressed and befriended the new Republican commissioner, D. P. Holloway, and because she knew how to survive in a male-dominated political bureaucracy: she had nurtured the support of the entire Massachusetts congressional delegation, including Senators Charles Sumner and Henry Wilson. Of them all, Wilson was her closest and staunchest "friend at court."

Clara had first met Senator Wilson in March, a few days after Lincoln's inauguration. She called on him in the Capitol—in the company of a nephew, of course, for a proper woman did not visit Capitol Hill without a male escort. The Capitol was under construction, as unfinished as the nation itself, with lumber and blocks of unhewn marble strewn about the grounds. A scaffold and a towering crane with steel ropes surmounted the uncompleted dome. Inside the building, Senator Wilson led Clara to a sofa in the reception gallery and "settled himself into a conversational posture," Clara said later, "which seemed to say 'let us talk.' " A stout, red-faced man with graying hair and lively eyes, Wilson exhibited an inexhaustible supply of good cheer. He smiled easily and often and was the very picture of the congenial gentleman. He talked, however, in a kind of broken, imprecise, slipshod style that betrayed his impoverished background. His father had been an alcoholic, his family exceedingly poor, his education limited, his early manhood spent apprenticed to a cobbler. Yet Wilson had overcome his hard-luck origins, had opened his own shoe business, entered politics as a champion of the workingman and an adamant foe of slavery, and risen high in the new Republican party.

He and Clara liked each other immediately. She found him uncommonly warm and sincere, and he was enthralled with her. Clara was a superb conversationalist; she liked nothing better than to engage a friend, man or woman, in an intimate discussion. She spoke with a solicitous smile, a sparkle in her dark brown eyes, and a relaxed informality that drew people to her. Republican Congressman Eli Thayer said that Clara had the "greatest faculty to make people talk" of anybody he knew. Wilson was so charmed that he was reluctant to part with her at the Capitol. Later the same day, he went to see her in her rooms on Seventh Street, made "some laughable apologies" for returning her call "so soon," said he planned to visit Boston on Monday, and asked if he might call on her again before he departed. "I did not object," she reported to Elvira Stone, and "*he called on me every day after I saw him until he left.*" Clara added, "(Oh yes he *is* married)."

Wilson was back in town by the end of April and hastened to pay his respects to Clara. "Oh I was so *glad* to see him," Clara wrote Elvira. He was "as good natured, full of fun and fight as ever," and "almost wild with delight at a prospect of an *opportunity* for our government to maintain her honor." Lincoln had called on Congress to convene on Independence Day, when the Republicans, thanks to the defection of Southern Democrats, would take over both houses and the chairmanships of all the important committees. Wilson was to chair the powerful Committee on Military Affairs. Surely in that capacity he could help Clara find a way to serve her country in the impending war, the greatest crisis in its young history. Until then, she had to endure the frustration of simply being an observer, circling important military events on her calendar.

In early May, Clara said good-bye to the Sixth Massachusetts, which had orders to join General Benjamin F. Butler's command in the Department of Annapolis, Maryland. It was sad news for Clara: she had given her "boys" much of her time, tending to their needs and joining in their discussions about the war and the great battle sure to be fought south of the Potomac. Among her favorites was handsome Horace Gardner, one of the wounded men she had helped after the

Baltimore riot. She had often "nursed" him while he convalesced in the E Street Infirmary. After his wound healed, he called on Clara in her apartment, and she enjoyed his company immensely. She thought him such a "splendid" young man. Visiting him and his comrades at the regimental quarters, Clara shook hands all around and brushed back her tears; she hated so "to let them go, poor noble fellows, they had come to seem like brothers, and indeed they had been brothers to us in our hour of need."

The next news she heard about the Sixth astounded her. In a surprise move without War Department authority, Butler struck at prosecessionist Baltimore, occupying it with his main force, including the Sixth Massachusetts, during a violent thunderstorm. The general said he intended to "bag the whole nest" of traitors in Baltimore, and that he did: he jailed prominent secessionists and confiscated more than 2,000 muskets sent up from rebel Virginia. Now Federal troops could pass unimpeded through this troublesome town, and the Union had its first war hero in the portly Butler, a well-to-do lawyer and a prominent Massachusetts Democrat who had favored Jefferson Davis for the presidency in 1860. Lincoln forgave Butler for acting without orders and appointed him a major general of volunteers, the first "political" general to achieve such a rank.

"I wept for joy when I heard of it all," Clara wrote a cousin in Worcester. She was terribly proud of the Sixth—"they so richly deserved the honor which is meted out to them—*noble old regiment they.*" She was impressed with Butler, too, and all the "laurels" he was getting for subduing Baltimore. The next Clara knew, he was assigned to command Fort Monroe on the tip of the Virginia peninsula, on the very rim of the hostile Confederacy. He made the news again when he refused to return three runaway slaves to their rebel owner. He pronounced them "contraband of war," and the name and the action stuck. Clearly this Benjamin Franklin Butler was a "comer"—somebody Clara might one day want to meet.

On May 20, the ax of war fell across Clara's family as it had so many others, North and South. On this day, North Carolina adopted an ordinance of secession—the eleventh and last state to do so—and Clara's oldest brother, Stephen Barton, Jr., found himself in the Confederacy. A prominent businessman, Stephen had moved to North Carolina several years before because of his asthma, hoping that a temperate climate would be better than the dampness and harsh winters of Massachusetts. He bought a tract of land and applied his hard Yankee business sense with a flourish, building up a successful manufacturing village he called Bartonsville on the west bank of the Chowan River, which emptied into Albemarle Sound. Bartonsville comprised a steam sawmill, a gristmill, a store, a blacksmith shop, and a machine and plow shop that manufactured 150,000 plow handles a year; the village had its own wharves, where steamboats stopped en route to and from the sound. Not all of Stephen's neighbors looked kindly on a Yankee community thriving in their midst, nor did they care for Stephen's politics. He made it clear that he was "a Union Democrat" and that he had no use for slavery. For that reason, he employed only white workmen he had imported from the North.

This much Clara knew from Stephen's letters before the war. Now that he was trapped in enemy country, she had no idea what evil might befall him. One day, to her surprise, his workmen turned up at her door in Washington, "a weary band of Yankees," as she described them later, who had survived "various detentions, hard usages, and petty robberies" to reach her. Stephen had ordered them north for their own safety but had refused to abandon Bartonsville himself, for fear that his property would be confiscated or destroyed. He had said something about hiring blacks to replace them, but that was all the workers knew. They were "penniless," Clara said later, and "I helped them home."

She would learn nothing more about Stephen until she read a notice about him in the *New York Tribune*. To Clara's horror, the report stated that eight or ten armed men called on him at Bartonsville and ordered him to clear out of North Carolina. Clearly "poor Stephen" was in danger, but Clara had no idea what to do or how to reach him. Her only hope was that Union forces at Fort Monroe might move down the coast and penetrate Albemarle Sound. If so, perhaps General Butler could find and get her brother out—if he were still alive.

By June, Union forces had moved across the Potomac, seized Robert E. Lee's mansion at Arlington, and captured Alexandria. Some 75,000 troops were now encamped on the hills around Washington City, and the Medical Department, with Dix's help, had established a few makeshift hospitals in hotels and churches in an effort to accommodate the sick. A naive optimism pervaded Washington, as men and women alike boasted that the war would be over in ninety days. It was the time of the "picture book war," when everyone was swept up in its glamour and pageantry: regimental bands played concerts and serenades; units drilled, raised flags, held dress parades; and military couples rode out to picnic and court at the Great Falls. "You couldn't discover from anything but the everywhereness of uniforms and muskets," wrote one of Lincoln's secretaries, "that we are in the midst of revolution and war."

The massive buildup, unprecedented in American military annals, created an administrative nightmare of the first order. The needs of 75,000 soldiers overwhelmed the small, understaffed Commissary and Quartermaster departments, and the camps were short of everything from uniforms to rations. Worse still, the crowded camps were incredibly filthy, with garbage scattered everywhere and pungent, fly-infested latrines laid out too close to cooking tents. As a consequence, disease broke out in epidemic proportions; entire units came down with diarrhea and dysentery, the most common affliction in the war. By June, 30 percent of the army was on sick call, and the military hospitals in Washington and Georgetown, overflowing with diseased and dying men, were dangerously short of medical supplies. The Soldiers' Aid Societies were doing all they could to relieve the want. The harried administration took an important step in June when it created a special civilian relief agency, the U.S. Sanitary Commission, which, as part of the War Department, set about promoting sanitation and hygiene in the army camps and coordinating the efforts of the Soldiers' Aid Societies. But in the early summer of 1861 none of it was enough. The Union's huge military machine, growing with daily arrivals of fresh troops, had outstripped the ability of the country to sustain it.

The critical shortages of supplies and medical stores afforded Clara a real opportunity to do something for the cause. If she could not *be* a soldier, she reasoned, she could at least do her part to *help* the soldiers. Independent as always, she became a one-woman relief agency, cooking food and buying stores out of her own salary and distributing them to the military hospitals and the hilltop encampments. She brought the soldiers tobacco and whiskey, pickled vegetables, homemade jellies, pies, and cakes to supplement the basic army diet of hardtack and salt pork. She had no qualms about distributing hard liquor. "Our men's nerves require their accustomed narcotics," she explained, "and a glass of whisky is a powerful friend in a Sun stroke, and these poor fellows fall senseless in their heavy drills." Clara's relief work proved time-consuming and expensive. "I have no time to write a military letter," she complained to a nephew. "I can only say that I spend all the time and money I can get on the troops."

She never went to the camps without a male escort or her fifty-year-old married sister, Sally Vassall. In the view of polite society, it was highly improper for an unmarried woman to visit an army camp alone. Any woman who defied that attitude risked being branded a whore or a concubine. Anxious to avoid gossip about her virtue, Clara usually rode out to the camps in the company of Dr. R. O. Sidney, an older gentleman and a clerk in the Post Office with a wife and family. Next to Wilson, he was perhaps her best male friend in Washington, someone she could count on to escort her to target practice as well as to the camps. As it happened, he was a native of Mississippi and the scion of slave owners; yet his mother had hated bondage and taught him that it was "a sin never to be tolerated in a Christian heart." In the 1850s, when his neighbors persecuted him because of his views, Sidney came north seeking "a home, among more congenial spirits." This inspired Clara to dub him "the very *Prince* of *Seceeders*—having seceded from his home state" and "adhered to our northern halls with a pertinacity worthy of a better cause than *secession*." He relinquished his medical practice and took a position at the Post Office as the clerk in charge of the New England Department, and became a man of "weight and note." Like Clara, he was "a most ardent admirer of our radical New England men" and considered Wilson in particular "a *glorious* fellow." Just where his wife and family were is unclear. What is certain is that he was lonely and complained of having few friends in Washington, and that he and Clara became extremely good friends. They enjoyed conversations in Clara's rooms on Seventh Street and took walks to the Long Bridge across the Potomac. In her letters home, Clara described Sidney as "a man—firm as a rock, and clear as a gem." He was her "*personal* and *especial* friend," for whom she entertained "an untold measure of esteem." One of her letters suggested that she treated him with such kindness and made him laugh so often that he declared himself "inexpressibly happy all the time." She paid him her ultimate compliment: she said she wanted him to meet her father.

By the summer of 1861, word of Clara's work with the soldiers had spread to her former homes in Massachusetts and New Jersey. Her friends shared news of her by letter and by word of mouth, and they took to sending Clara packages of delicacies and articles for the troops. Elvira Stone, Clara's cousin and confidante and postmistress of North Oxford, forwarded supplies collected by Clara's neighbors. Another longtime friend, Annie Childs, did the same with a group in Worcester. And Mary Norton, her best female friend, worked for Clara in Hightstown, New Jersey, where Clara had once taught school and lived with the Norton family. Clara established a network with her "dear sisters" by letter, thanking them profusely and explaining in detail what the soldiers required. Clara was a wonderfully descriptive writer; she had the ability to make her supporters feel as though they were with her in her work. Spurred on by their contributions, Clara devoted so much time to her relief operation that she often shirked her duties at the Patent Office. A male friend there, Edward Shaw, saved her job by working overtime at her desk, copying her assignments for her.

Clara still felt she wasn't doing enough. When an acquaintance returned from a visit to Fort Monroe and said that "the boys" there were suffering, Clara wanted to go and nurse them. But that meant taking to the field by herself, and she felt checked again by the iron hand of propriety. "Nothing but the fear of finding myself out of place or embarrassing others, restrains me," she wrote Mary Norton, "my heart is with them every hour and I only wish that my strength and labor might be."

As July approached, Washington was aswarm with politicians gathering for the special session of Congress, to begin on Independence Day. In the camps handing out stores, Clara saw them ride up in little cavalcades to review the troops, admire the bands, and call on General Irvin McDowell, commander of the field army. They reminded the general that rebel forces were encamped at Manassas Railroad Junction just twenty-five miles away. When was McDowell going to attack the "traitor" army, the politicians wanted to know, and march on Richmond? The *New York Tribune* had raised the cry "On to Richmond!" and it reverberated across the North. As if to urge the army on, Professor Thaddeus S. C. Lowe ascended above Washington in a hydrogen balloon, hoping to demonstrate its utility in military observation. The professor carried a telegraph connected by wire to the War Department, and Clara could see the balloon hovering over the city like a visitor from another world.

July 4 brought the noisiest Independence Day in memory. There was a "constant explosion of firearms, fireworks, shouting, and cries in the streets," wrote British journalist William Howard Russell. More than 20,000 New York soldiers paraded up Pennsylvania Avenue to the

White House, where Lincoln and doddering old Winfield Scott, the general-in-chief of the armies, looked on from a flag-covered platform. On Capitol Hill, talk of an impending battle buzzed in the corridors, and Lincoln sent over a rousing Independence Day message in which he promised to teach dissident Southerners "the folly of being the beginners of a war." That night, as Clara sat watching from the south steps of the Treasury Department, the army camps put on a grand display: large bonfires blazed against the night, and Clara thought their flames looked like "firing serpents leaping on the hillsides." Rockets burst overhead and roman candles shot up "burning blue." It was as if Washington's pent-up energy had exploded, lighting up the night sky from one horizon to the other.

By mid-July, the big battle, so long anticipated, seemed imminent. For two days, columns of troops, ambulances, and wagon trains clattered through Washington heading across the river. On July 16, McDowell and his staff, army medical director W. S. King, and more than 30,000 combat troops set out for Manassas Junction. Clara wrote to her father that they were "noble, gallant handsome fellows, armed to the teeth, apparently lacking nothing, waving banners and plumes and bristling bayonets." Yet the sight tugged at her heart, for she knew that "many a brave boy marched down to die."

A noisy crowd of politicians and reporters followed the army. Among them was Clara's friend, Henry Wilson, riding in a hired carriage filled with sandwiches. With so many of the soldiers gone, Washington was strangely quiet. Saturday, July 20, brought "rumors of *intended* battle" and contradictory accounts of enemy strength; one paper reported that the rebels were 80,000 strong. "My blood ran cold as I read it," Clara wrote, "surely they would never have the madness to attack, from open field, an enemy of three times their number behind entrenchments fortified by batteries."

But apparently McDowell did attack. All day Sunday, July 21, came reports of a battle raging in the woods along Bull Run, near Manassas Junction. Clara, putting her ear to the ground, could hear the distant rumble of cannon. Late afternoon dispatches indicated a great Union triumph, and "our city was jubilant," Clara wrote Judge Ira Barton, "rejoicing in the news of victory." But that night came shocking intelligence. The Grand Army was in retreat, with McDowell crying for General Scott to save Washington. Later reports were even more discouraging: the army had been routed at Bull Run, had overrun the crowd of civilians two miles in the rear, and all were fleeing back to Washington "in a perfect panic."

"All is quiet and sad," Clara wrote in her letter to Judge Barton, "and the mourners go about the streets," waiting for the return of their shattered army. It was an overcast night, with heavy clouds swirling across the moon, "forming a most fantastic mass of shapes in the sky," in the words of William Howard Russell. The lights in the White House and War Department burned all night. At dawn, with rain falling in torrents, the remnants of the army reached Washington City, creating colossal traffic jams at the bridges across the Potomac. Soldiers staggered into the city and collapsed on curbs and sidewalks, in gutters and doorsteps; some men were barefoot, others wrapped in blankets. Frederick Law Olmsted, general secretary of the Sanitary Commission, walked through "the streets of woe," and found men clustered together, sullen and feverish, with dirty, unshaven faces and bloodshot eyes. They had gone into battle on short rations, and the hungriest of them wandered from house to house begging for food.

All day Washington lay in dazed panic, expecting a full rebel attack, fighting in the streets, annihilation. Henry Wilson made it back, after a "memorable display of bareback equestrianship on a stray army mule." He told a friend grimly: "We want more men; we must go to work for them." Lincoln and the Congress agreed. That very day the government called up 500,000 three-year volunteers to save the country.

Stragglers and walking wounded reached the city, too, adding to the accumulation of stories about unmitigated suffering on the Manassas plains. The army had made almost no medical preparations before going into battle: medical director King, in the words of one expert, had "no plans, no organization, no enlisted personnel, no supplies, no ambulance corps." Riding over the battleground with instruments and dressing in his saddlebags, King had established a single field hospital for the entire army, this in the little church in Sudley, and had left everything else to divine intervention. Each regiment supposedly had its own surgeon and assistant surgeon, with regimental band members doubling as stretcher-bearers, but most outfits were appallingly short of medical equipment. The First Connecticut, numbering some 700 soldiers, had gone into action with a single ambulance, no stretchers, and no hospital stores.

What little medical arrangements there were evaporated when the army took flight, leaving more than a thousand wounded on the field to fend for themselves. Those who couldn't move lay where they fell, without water or shelter. Others with bones shattered, arms blown off, faces mangled, eyes shot out, scrotums and thighs ripped apart, managed to walk or crawl the entire twenty-three miles back to the capital.

Clara wrote to her father that it was her "painful duty" to report the disaster that had befallen the country. "This has been a hard day to witness, sad, painful and mortifying, but whether in the aggregate it shall sum up a defeat, or a victory, depends (in my poor judgment) entirely upon circumstances, vis. the tone and spirit in which it leaves our men, if sad and disheartened, we are defeated, the worst, and sorest of defeats, *if roused to madness, and revenge*, it will yet prove VICTORY,— But *no mortal* could look in upon this scene tonight, and judge of effects, how gladly would I close my eyes to it if I could. I am not fit to write you now, I shall do you more harm than good."

Clara was consumed with frustration and anger. More than ever she felt a need to do something. When she returned to the Patent Office, her frustration fixed on the two male clerks who had so loudly proclaimed their love for the Confederacy. With the defeated army still "thronging the streets," Clara went forthwith to Commissioner Holloway. If he would fire the two clerks, she said, she would be honored to do their work and donate their salaries—$1,600 apiece—to the government. Holloway was so impressed with Clara's spirit that he momentarily forgot her sex. "Good man!" he exclaimed. He was obliged to point out, however, that it was illegal for her to exceed her own salary. Still, he "wished to heaven there were some men" who felt as Clara did.

A few days after the battle, a train of two-wheeled ambulances clattered into town from the direction of Manassas. The Medical Department had dispatched them to collect the few hundred wounded remaining on the battlefield, and the civilian drivers told stories of grotesque sights out there: swollen corpses crawling with maggots and rotting in the July sun, parts of human bodies scattered about. In some ways, the dead were the lucky ones. The wounded had been dumped into the two-wheeled carts and hauled to Washington on a tortuous, bumping ride on rutted roads that made them scream in agony.

The ambulances deposited their cargo of wounded in extemporized hospitals in old warehouses, dilapidated churches, and schools. Another hospital was on the top floor of the Patent Office, in the uncompleted lumber room. Here crude tables had been "knocked together from pieces of the scaffolding," said a Dix nurse named Eliza Howland, and the wounded and sick were placed on them, six to a table. A system of pulleys hung from a top floor window, "and any time through the day, barrels of water, baskets of vegetables, and great pieces of army beef might be seen crawling slowly up the marble face of the building." In the cavernous lumber room, with tables stretching for what seemed half a mile, Dix's nurses worked side by side with surgeons and soldiers detailed for hospital duty, and Clara and other local women came every day to help out; Clara evidently did so in her spare time. They fed and washed the patients, spooned powders into their mouths, sang to them, wrote letters in their behalf, toiling up and down the endless rows of tables, saving some of the men, watching others die.

Miss Dix, efficient and indefatigable, hurried from hospital to hospital, giving orders to her nurses. In early August, the government started paying them a wage of $12.00 per month—their male counterparts received $20.50 per month—and army regulations established a ratio of one female nurse for every two male nurses in the military hospitals. Dix did not complain about the unequal pay based on sex, which was a common practice, but she complained fiercely about medical abuses and mismanagement. She scolded and snapped, ferreting out careless stewards, shirking or drunk physicians, and anyone who was rude to her nurses. When angry males questioned her authority, demanding, "Madam, who are *you* to dictate to me," Dix retorted, "I am Dorothea L. Dix, Superintendent of Nurses, in the employ of the United States Government."

Dix was equally hostile to independent women working in the hospitals outside her authority, and she shooed them out. Henceforth Clara could do little beyond bringing the patients her delicacies and refreshments. But she did lend a sympathetic ear, and their tales of suffering at Bull Run convinced her that the field was where she ought to serve, the field was where the pressing needs were. It was alarmingly clear, from what the wounded and the papers said, that many men had died at Bull Run for lack of simple care. More than anything, she wanted to go to the field in the next battle, "go to the rescue of the men who fell" and "work for them and my country." But that desire, strong as it was, warred with an equal desire not to embarrass her family by violating social mores and bringing a stigma to the Barton name. In the view of the army and the country, the battlefield was no place for a lady, or a woman of any kind. Not even Dix's nurses were allowed to accompany soldiers into the field. True, a couple of wives had ridden into combat with their husbands at Bull Run, but that was exceptional. The vast majority of army officers and politicians believed the battlefield was out of bounds for women, and nearly all "proper" women thought so, too.

*   *   *

By August, the army had a new commander, General George Brinton McClellan, a short, stocky man with a reddish mustache and a thick neck. He was four years younger than Clara and endowed with an arrogant self-confidence, certain that he was the chosen instrument of Providence to save the Union. He was a splendid horseman, and Clara often saw him riding through the streets astride a great black horse, followed by his staff and a small army of adjutants, orderlies, politicians, and reporters. With even the president deferring to him, McClellan mused that he had now become "*the* power of the land." The arrogant young general proved to be a brilliant organizer. In a matter of weeks, he had restored the discipline and the spirit of the army and given it a new name: the Army of the Potomac.

New units continued to pour into Washington, and Clara was usually at the depot to greet the soldiers with food and refreshments. Early August brought the Fifteenth Massachusetts Regiment, including a company from Oxford, the DeWitt Guards. One of Clara's nephews, Bernard Vassall, was second lieutenant of the company and looked dashing in his uniform. Other outfits arrived from New York, and Clara was delighted to find among them a few associates of her days at the Clinton Liberal Institute in Clinton, New York.

Clara fondly remembered the year she had spent as a student there in the early 1850s. Operated by the Universalists, the Clinton Liberal Institute was one of the few coeducational academies in the country, and Clara had plunged into her studies with uninhibited zeal, taking an overload of subjects and impressing her teachers and the female superintendent with her intellect.

Her studies had ended with the sudden death of her mother, and Clara had returned home to her father in North Oxford. Clara rarely mentioned her mother in her letters and diary, doubtless because she never felt close to her. Clara was the baby of the family, with four siblings a good deal older than she. Her sister Sally, closest to her in age, was eleven years her senior; David was thirteen years older, Stephen fifteen, and Dorothy seventeen. Clara's parents may not have intended to have another child, and may not have wanted Clara either. Certainly Clara felt neglected by her mother, Sarah, who left it up to her older siblings and her father to raise the "Tot," Clara's unfortunate family nickname. What was more, Sarah, though remarkably hard-working, was a profane woman with a ferocious temper. "She muttered and cursed her way around the house," one writer put it, "damning her lot and those about her." She had violent quarrels with Clara's father, Stephen, and those conjugal battles, full of shouts and recriminations, left Clara permanently scarred. As a little girl, she had nightmares and violent visions, once screaming in terror when clouds in the sky turned into giant, battling rams descending on her. She was "the troublesome child," as she put it, so insecure, so "abnormally sensitive" and shy, that the family became concerned; her mother, Clara remembered, doubted that much could be made of her. Clara attributed her painful shyness to her fear of "making trouble," of "doing something wrong." Of her childhood, she said, "I remember nothing but fear." She told Mary Norton, "I never had any childhood," and said that she survived those painful early years by knowing her "danger and weakness" and learning to be strong, "walk cautiously" and "always stand alone."

As she grew older, that frightened, hurt little girl remained inside her, and she suffered from recurring depressions. Sometimes she wished herself dead. "I see less & less in the world to live for," she wrote when she was thirty and teaching school in New Jersey. "I know it is wicked and perhaps foolish but I cannot help it. There is not a living thing but would be just as well off without me[.] I contribute to the happiness of not a single object and often to the unhappiness of many and always my own, for I am never happy[.] True I laugh and joke but could weep that very moment and be the happier for it. . . . How long I am to or can endure such a life I do not know."

Her parents' contentious marriage was probably a major reason Clara never married. Better indeed to stand alone than to be locked in mortal combat with a mate. Even so, Clara had her share of suitors who found her attractive, intelligent, and sensitive. Yet she turned down all marriage proposals. "Clara Barton had many admirers," explained a close friend, "and they were all men whom she admired and some whom she almost loved. More men were interested in her than she was ever interested in; some of them certainly interested her, yet not profoundly. I do not think she ever had a love affair that stirred the depths of her being. The truth is, Clara Barton was herself so much stronger a character than any of the men who made love to her that I do not think she was ever seriously tempted to marry any of them." This explanation was fair enough as far as it went. But Clara's friend overlooked the negative model of her battling parents and Clara's fear that surrendering to marriage would be the end of her independence.

Besides, her father was the most important man in her life. What other male could possibly measure up to him? Despite her unhappy childhood, Clara loved and respected her soldier-father, not only because he had showed her affection and told her war stories (and hence given her a degree of self-esteem) but because she thought him "entirely different in temperament" from her mother. In Clara's eyes, he was "a calm, reasonable, high toned moral man, also of great natural vigor and strength, athletic . . . in all things cheerful—generous & kind but very firm."

She loved her older brothers and sisters, too, for they had been like parents to her. Sally had taught her to read and spell before she was four and had introduced her to poetry. Brother Stephen had instructed her in mathematics and bookkeeping, and David had polished her horse riding skills. In return, she had often been the family nurse. From age eleven to thirteen, she had taken care of David through a dangerous and protracted illness that almost killed him, and she had periodically returned home to care for one or another sick relative.

In short, Clara's family ties meant everything to her; they made her feel needed, gave her a reason to live, became the "mate" she never had. She cultivated strong, loving relationships with her extended family, too, with a number of uncles, aunts, and cousins like Elvira Stone, Judge Ira M. Barton and his family, and with close female friends like Mary Norton and Annie Childs. And she was like a second mother to her several nieces and nephews, particularly Sally's youngest boy, Irving "Bubby" Vassall.

Irving was an intelligent, studious teenager with a keen interest in politics, and Clara enjoyed answering his questions and sharing his shrewd observations (he once noted that President James Buchanan had "a funny way of shutting one eye and cocking his head when he wishes to say something forcible"). She wrote Bubby long, affectionate letters imploring him not to study and think too hard lest it imperil his health. Alas, in 1858, while the Vassalls were living in Washington, Bubby came down with consumption; at one point he was so ill that he wrote Clara (who was then in North Oxford) that he was dying and that he loved her. The letter "unmanned me," Clara said, and she worried about "that poor dear child" so much that she developed crippling back pain. "None but our Heavenly Father ever knew how dear he has been to me," she wrote Mary Norton; "he has grown to be a young man, full of promise, noble and intellectual beyond all reasonable expectation, and even now he *is dying* in Washington." She could hardly bear to look at his letter. "Oh what a sad relic, and Mary you will not think me weak, if I tell you that I sat and wept the long night through and that now my tears are blinding me."

Clara did everything she could for her nephew; she wrote him letters telling him *"he must not give up."* She helped pay for his medical bills at the same time that she was sending money to a young female charge, an orphan, who was studying music in Boston. When he was nineteen, Clara sent him and Sally to Minnesota at her own expense, because its "clear, bracing air" was said to be good for consumptives. She went out with them to get them settled and returned to Washington late in 1859, so sick herself that she spent more than two weeks in bed, jocularly complaining that she had no one to depend on "excepting male friends and servants." She continued to send Bubby money and admonitions to remain in Minnesota, but he and his mother returned to Washington just before the war, with his health still tenuous. "But still we must hope," Clara wrote Mary Norton, "that time will work the [cure.]"

By 1861, Clara's father, now eighty-six, was also in failing health, and she worried about him constantly. David and his wife, Julia, were with him in North Oxford, and Clara kept in regular contact with them, monitoring her father's health by letter. When he seemed critically ill, Clara wrote Julia: "In thought and spirit I am in the room with you every moment. . . . I can *almost* see, and *almost* hear, and *almost* know, how it all is—between us seems to be only the 'veil so thin so strong,' there are moments when I think I can brush it away with my hand and look upon that dear treasured form and face, the earliest loved and latest mourned of all my life, sometimes I am certain I hear the patient's feeble moan, and at others above me the *clouds* seem to divide and in the opening up among the blue and golden, that loved face, smiling and pleasant, looks calmly down upon me, then I think it is all past, and my poor father is at rest." And yet she felt "a little of the old time hope—hope that he may yet be spared to us a little longer. . . . If my father still lives and realizes, will you tell him how much I love him and regret his sufferings, and how much rather I would endure them myself if he could be saved from them."

The old captain did pull through, and Clara wrote David that "I am so *glad* to know that he is better and even *gets into the kitchen*; that is splendid." "His recovery seems to be nothing less than a miracle," she wrote a cousin. There was "no estimating the strength of that 'iron constitution.' "

By September 1861, that iron constitution was failing again, and Clara was torn by conflicting loyalties. She wanted to be at her father's side—"I think of him every hour of my life and sometimes I think I cannot wait longer," she wrote Elvira—yet "the threatening aspect of things and the increasing probabilities of darkened scenes and bloody dangerous days" dissuaded her from leaving Washington City. McClellan was whipping the army into a superb fighting machine and would likely give battle soon. Even as Clara wrote Elvira, guns were thundering south of the Potomac. No one knew why, Clara said—maybe it was a salute to McClellan, maybe a skirmish, maybe the start of a campaign. If the latter, it was "the place of every loyal man and woman to stand the ground they occupy," she said; "if my countrymen are to suffer my place is with them, my northern brothers are here in arms danger and death staring them in the face and I cannot leave them."

Anticipating another battle, Clara stepped up her relief work: she advertised for supplies in the *Worcester Spy* and fired off letters to her many friends, asking them to send her "necessities" and "useful articles and stores" for the Massachusetts troops. When the soldiers advanced, they could take the supplies with them, thus avoiding the fiasco at Bull Run, where the soldiers had gone into battle short of almost everything.

McClellan, however, did not advance against the rebel army at Manassas. His army continued to drill and parade, drill and parade. October saw a fierce skirmish at Ball's Bluff on the Virginia side of the Potomac, but that was virtually all the fighting the Army of the Potomac did that entire fall. There was talk around town that McClellan might be a traitor, and a grim group of Radical Republican senators could be seen going regularly up to the White House. The young general hotly defended himself to reporters and politicians alike: he was preparing the army for a mighty victory, he said, but it was not yet ready for battle. Moreover, he was convinced that more than 130,000 rebels were entrenched at Manassas (actually there were about 34,000). Before he could advance, he needed 273,000 men. Only then could he attack Manassas, take Richmond, and win the war.

Clara's friend, Henry Wilson, supported McClellan and hastened to Massachusetts to raise additional recruits himself. He harangued crowds in Boston, crisscrossed the state organizing infantry and artillery units, and came back to Washington with the Twenty-second Massachusetts, some 2,300 strong, which was popularly known as "Henry Wilson's regiment." There were reports that Lincoln wanted to appoint Wilson a brigadier general, but Wilson declined to leave the Senate and his chairmanship of the Committee on Military Affairs. It was lucky for Clara that he remained on the Hill, as subsequent events were to prove.

When December came with the army still idle, Clara made a hurried trip to North Oxford to check on her father and strengthen her connections with the ladies of the area. It was a family reunion of sorts at the Barton farm just outside of town, for Clara had not seen her father's "loved face" and "treasured form" since the war began. What condition he was in is not recorded, but Clara doubtless gave the old farmhouse a thorough scrubbing. Florence Nightingale's *Notes on Nursing*, first published in 1859, taught Clara's entire generation of women that cleanliness was the key to successful home nursing.

At some point during her visit, Clara rode the train up to Worcester for a meeting with the "worthy ladies" of the city's "Ladies Relief Committee." A Mrs. Miller, the secretary, asked Clara: "Are our labors needed, are we doing any good, shall we work, or shall we forbear?" Clara urged them to continue working, and the committee agreed to send her supplies to distribute to Worcester County soldiers. In addition to her Worcester friend, Annie Childs, who sent her clothes and other supplies, Clara now had a full-fledged women's organization cooperating with her.

Her nephew Irving was visiting in the area, and he accompanied her when she started south with several large trunks full of stores. A couple of Worcester County outfits, the Twenty-first and Twenty-fifth Massachusetts regiments, were stationed at Annapolis, and Clara stopped off there to introduce herself and check on their needs before going on to Washington. When she presented herself at the headquarters of the Twenty-first, the officers clearly had heard about her. Colonel Augustus Morse, a "cordial, affable" man with raven hair and a full dress sword at his side, sprang from his seat with both hands extended. And Lieutenant Colonel Alberto Maggi greeted her with such a succession of bows and formalities that she was embarrassed. She had no idea, she said later, how to react to such extreme politeness, "till the clear appreciative, knowing twinkle of our 'cute' Major Clark's eyes set things right again." The officers invited her to share their dinner table, and Clara happily took her place between officers Morse and Maggi. She savored the meal and the company. This was where she belonged, where she felt most fulfilled, in the midst of such "good true men." After dinner, the officers took her to chapel, with virtually the entire regiment, a thousand strong, in attendance. The men, too, made her feel welcome. Because they treated her with respect, not once hinting that a military camp was out of bounds for her, Clara would always hold a special place in her heart for the officers and men of the Twenty-first. Indeed, it became her favorite regiment of the war.

Back in Washington City, Clara soon found herself inundated with boxes from the "patriotic ladies" of Massachusetts: boxes brimming with clothing and food, wine and whiskey, and medical stores such as lint for dressing wounds. The boxes filled her rooms and the surrounding garrets, until she had no more space to keep them. Accordingly, she rented part of a warehouse near Seventh Street and Pennsylvania Avenue and made it the headquarters of her one-woman distributing agency that functioned as "a link between home and the soldier."

In mid-December, Clara reported to Mrs. Miller that she had been "*more* than busy" unpacking cartons and distributing their contents to Massachusetts regiments. "I almost envy you ladies where so many of you can work together and accomplish so much, while my poor labors are so single handed." Even so, Clara's spirits were soaring. "I am the most happily situated at this present time than I ever was in all my life," she wrote her cousin Lucy; "i.e. the fewest annoyances, the most quiet and collected, the best able to mingle with and converse with my friends (if I had time)."

Inevitably, Clara encountered those who thought her work was superfluous. One official told her that the army was well supplied and didn't need the necessities and articles she took out to the camps. He had that on "proper authority," he told her, by which he presumably meant the War Department. He also said, "upon the same authority," that the army needed no more nurses, "either male or female."

"Well this may be so," Clara wrote Mrs. Miller of the Worcester committee, but she wished that her Worcester friends had been with her an hour before, in order to judge for themselves how adequately the soldiers were being cared for. Clara had seen a young cavalryman named Pollard, now under the care of his sister in the city, who had almost died in one of the area forts for want of food and medical treatment. "He had been attacked with ordinary fever 6 weeks before," Clara explained, "and had lain unmoved until the flesh upon all parts of the body which rested hard upon whatever was under him had decayed, grown perfectly black and was falling out, his heels had assumed the same appearance, his stockings had never been removed during all his illness and his toes were matted and grown together and are now *dropping off at the joint*, the cavities in his back are absolutely frightful." A civilian doctor who examined Pollard concluded that he was "*perishing for want of nourishment*—he had been neglected until he was literally starving." The regimental surgeon did come to see him and said that the regiment was short-handed since the assistant surgeon had been killed. He admitted that the men "had not received proper care" and said he was "very sorry." Pollard was to have three of his toes amputated, Clara reported, and was taking broths and soups and "a little meat," and would probably survive.

Had it not been for his sister, Clara believed, Pollard would have died, and the city papers would have been obliged to report, under the caption "Death of Soldiers," that "this soldier had *starved to death* through lack of proper attendance." It made Clara livid: "Ah men, all of our poor boys have not a sister within nine miles of them. And still it is said, upon authority, 'we have no need of nurses' and 'our army is supplied.' " How this could be, Clara failed to see. But she did know this: "If we New England people saw men lying in camp uncared for until their toes rotted from their feet, with not persons enough about them to take care of them, we should think they needed *more* nurses."

The U.S. Sanitary Commission thought the same thing, and it pressured the government to reform the chaotic army medical system, to build modern hospitals and field more surgeons and nurses. Goaded into action, the government did authorize the construction of two new pavilion hospitals, each holding 200 patients in well-ventilated wings fanning out from the center like spokes on a wheel. The government also empowered the Medical Department to hire a number of civilian surgeons to serve as acting assistant surgeons without military rank. These "contract" surgeons, "an anomalous civil element in a military establishment," as one woman described it, mainly ran the wards of the general military hospitals behind the lines, the same hospitals Dix was staffing with her female nurses.

Even with new hospitals and doctors, the army medical service was a disgrace. How else explain the cruel absurdity of what happened to Private Pollard? And his was not an isolated case. Exposed to the rainy cold of December, thousands of men lay sick and shivering in their tents, and the overworked regimental surgeons could do little for them. According to General Secretary Olmsted of the Sanitary Commission, the army's medical woes would never be solved until the entire Medical Department was reformed and reorganized. The main problem was the Medical Department's seniority system, which promoted army surgeons according to their years of service rather than their aptitude. As a result, the Medical Department, in the midst of a terrible national crisis, was run by a group of inept dotards who hadn't the faintest notion how to meet the needs of the Union's huge volunteer army.

The surgeon general, Clement Alexander Finley, personified all the evils of the system. When R. C. Wood had died early in the war, Finley had become surgeon general because he was the senior army officer in the medical service. Old Army to the core, he wore a cape and had a congenital dislike of change. He opposed an ambulance corps and disapproved of women nurses, and he devoted more energy to protecting his prerogatives than to relieving the suffering of the soldiers. It was "criminal weakness," warned General Secretary Olmsted, for medical responsibility to be entrusted to this "self satisfied, supercilious, bigoted blockhead, merely because he is the oldest of the old mess-room doctors of the frontier guard of the country. He knows nothing and does nothing, and is capable of knowing nothing and doing nothing, but quibble about matters of form and precedent." After Congress convened in early December, the Sanitary Commission lobbied energetically for reform of the Medical Department. The commission had a powerful friend in Henry Wilson, who agreed with its assessment and intended to promote legislation embodying its demands. It insisted that the "ossified" Finley be removed and the seniority system abolished; it also urged the government to create a corps of medical inspectors and to build an entire system of pavilion hospitals. Only then could the Medical Department adequately care for sick soldiers. Only then could it be prepared for the casualties of the next campaigns.

On Christmas day, 1861, Clara turned forty years old. She had the boundless nervous energy and trim figure of a much younger woman, and kept her shape by carefully watching her diet. Since her twelfth year, when she'd fainted at the sight of an ox being butchered, she had been a vegetarian, eating meat only when necessity or circumstances required it. Actually, she ate little of anything. Her small frame required only a couple of light meals a day. She had a tendency to gain weight and controlled it through protracted fasts. Irregular eating, however, made her constipated, a problem she struggled with much of her life. She told a physician later that she combated it "with daily enemas for twenty years." Clara was also extremely sensitive to stimulants of any kind. A half cup of coffee would almost intoxicate her. She could tolerate a little wine, which she enjoyed. But hard liquor, tea, hot chocolate—even a child's dose of medicine—made her perspire and feel clammy all over. She claimed she didn't need medicine anyway. She was "remarkably healthy and rugged," to use her words, was "firm as iron in muscle" and "athletic" and, in a day when diseases played havoc with people's lives, was rarely sick.

That could not be said of the Army of the Potomac, which suffered from an outbreak of typhoid fever that winter; 194 men died of it in December alone. Just before Christmas, McClellan himself came down with typhoid and spent a couple of weeks in bed, with the president, the Joint Committee on the Conduct of the War, and the national press waiting anxiously for every medical report from his doctors. Meanwhile, his enormous army lay all about Washington and Alexandria, largely inert. "The rebel army," wrote the wife of a judge, "threatens Washington, and still hopes to take it, whilst over three hundred thousand soldiers lie opposite them, idle and well-fed, with full pay, their families supported by public charity, their officers spending their time in reveling, flirting, and drinking."

Even so, Washington hummed with anticipation, for something big was in the air during the final days of 1861. On December 27, bewhiskered General Burnside came down from his headquarters at Annapolis, conferred with Lincoln, talked with the sick McClellan at his house, and took the train back to Annapolis, where an "amphibious division" of 12,000 men awaited his orders. The previous October, a joint army-navy expedition had embarked from Annapolis, sailed down the coast, and seized Port Royal, South Carolina, between Charleston and Savannah. Now Burnside and Union naval commanders were assembling a similar task force at Annapolis, and speculation had it that their target was the North Carolina coast, possibly Roanoke Island.

When Clara heard that, she could barely restrain her excitement. If Burnside drove inland, he might be able to liberate her brother Stephen at Bartonsville, and Clara's family would be united again. She pressed callers and scoured the papers for any news of the projected operation. She called it her "pet expedition," happily noting that it included the Twenty-first Massachusetts and three other Bay State outfits, among which were "upwards of forty young men" who had once been her pupils.

After the New Year, several former pupils, given a few hours of final leave, came to Washington to tell her good-bye. They sat in the parlor, Clara as animated as ever, her small hands folded in her lap, her dark eyes shining. She was proud of these young men. They looked so handsome in their new U.S. army uniforms—dark blue tunics, light blue trousers, and kepis or soft felt hats, which they had politely removed from their heads in Clara's presence. Just before they left, some of them gave her keepsakes to hold until they returned, or to send their families in case their names appeared on the "dead list" in the papers.

Clara struggled to keep her composure, she confided in Fannie Childs: "You know how foolishly tender my friendships are, and how I loved 'my boys.'"

The expedition departed from Annapolis on January 6 and 7, and a soldier reported to Clara that "the harbor was full, literally crammed with boats and vessels, covered with men, shouting from every deck." After he left, Clara wrote Fannie: "My head is just this moment full to aching, bursting with all the thoughts and doings of our pet Expedition—a half-hour ago came to my room the last messenger from them, the last I shall have in all probability until the enemies galling shot shall have raked through the ranks of my dear boys, and strewn them here and there, bleeding, crippled and dying." It was hard to believe: only a few years ago they were her "scholars," freshly scrubbed and eager to learn. Now they were soldiers on their way to "Southern Sands." What if they were killed and thrown into "a common trench unwept, 'uncoffined and unknown'"? She had heard that unidentified dead soldiers were buried that way. Should that happen to her former pupils, how would she know if they were dead? How would their families know?

For weeks, Clara's mind rode with those boys in the troop transports: she shared their mess, felt seasick with them, wondered where they would land and what battles they would fight. Reports indicated that the powerful flotilla, eighty ships in all, stretched out for miles as it headed southward in stormy seas. January 13 found it at Hatteras Inlet, off the North Carolina coast at Pamlico Sound. That put Burnside south of Albemarle Sound and about a hundred miles southeast of Stephen's place, situated on the Chowan River in Hertford County. Burnside's target appeared to be Roanoke Island, all right. Capturing it would give the North control of both sounds and put an end to rebel blockade running to and from their harbors. At the end of January, Clara wrote Fannie that she had received "no private returns from the 'Expedition' yet," but Colonel Morse had called on her with some news. Morse, now head of the post at Annapolis, had relinquished command of the Twenty-first Regiment to Lieutenant Colonel Maggi. The colonel told Clara that the *Baltic* would depart Annapolis that afternoon "to join them in their landing wherever it may be."

Meanwhile Clara toiled in "tedious labor" at the Patent Office, hardly able to control her pent-up energy. Evidently impressed with Clara as Mason had been, Commissioner Holloway gave her added responsibilities. "I have been a great deal *more* than busy for the past three weeks," she wrote Fannie, "owing to some new arrangements in the office, mostly, by which I lead the [Patent Office] Record, and hurry up the others who lag." After work, she made her rounds of the hospitals, calling first at the top-floor hospital in the Patent Office, now expanded into the outer room, where the nurses had set up camp beds between glass cases full of Patent Office paraphernalia. Here sick soldiers lay incongruously among balloons, mouse traps, patent churns, cog wheels, "and a general nightmare of machinery," as nurse Eliza Howland said.

At one of the hospitals, Clara found "a fine young man" who belonged to the "mess" of one of her army cousins, Leander Poor. The young man was sick with what the surgeons called "pleuritic fever." But he was feeling better now and believed he would be released soon. "Work and storm" kept Clara away from the hospital for three days. When she went back to see him on the fourth, he had died. "We bought him a grave in the Congressional Burying Ground," Clara wrote Fannie Childs, and gave him a proper military funeral. "Poor Fellow, and there he lies all alone. A soldier's grave, a sapling at the head, a rough slab at the foot, nine shots between, and all is over."

As Clara came and went in wartime Washington, she must have been amazed at how congested the city had become. An endless traffic of omnibuses, mule-drawn army wagons, cavalrymen on horseback, and military carriages churned through the muddy streets. The sidewalks thronged with soldiers and sailors and those who preyed on them: vendors hawking pornographic literature, prostitutes peddling their services, quacks advertising cheap cures for gonorrhea and syphilis. The city was crowded with contractors, too, all hoping to capitalize on the business side of war and secure a lucrative War Department contract for horses or equipment. Many of them were scoundrels and swindlers, selling the government huge quantities of rotten blankets, or tainted pork, or knapsacks that came unglued in the rain, or uniforms that fell apart, or hundreds of diseased and dying horses. Part of this was the result of maladministration in the overworked War Department, which had often ignored competitive bidding and purchased exclusively from favorite middlemen, many of them corrupt. Lincoln's capable new secretary of war, Edwin Stanton, who took office in January, promised to reform the War Office and drive away unscrupulous contractors. Even so, Clara wished her brother Stephen could be here to help. In this dark hour, she thought, the government could well use a skilled and honest businessman like him.

February came with electrifying intelligence from North Carolina. Stalled for two weeks by gale force winds, the Burnside expedition moved across Hatteras Inlet and bore down on Roanoke Island with all flags flying. On February 7, sixteen Federal gunboats routed a makeshift rebel fleet and shelled enemy shore batteries into submission. Some 7,500 assault troops then splashed ashore and the next day overwhelmed the rebel garrison, capturing more than 2,500 prisoners and thirty pieces of artillery. The Twenty-first Massachusetts fought brilliantly under Lieutenant Colonel Maggi, whose excessive politeness disappeared on the battlefield. With him in the lead, the Massachusetts men waded through a waist-deep marsh and near-impenetrable thickets that protected the rebel right flank, and seized a rebel battery there in a stirring charge with bayonets. The capture of Roanoke Island made a war hero of Burnside, who would dominate the headlines until Grant eclipsed him with a resounding triumph over Fort Donelson in Tennessee eight days later.

Clara was beside herself with the news from Roanoke Island. What she noted were the Union casualties: 37 dead and some 220 wounded or missing. And what of her boys? How many of them were in that number? She wanted more than anything else to be there with them, to nurse those who were hurt, hold those who were dying, identify those who were already gone. She had never felt so conflicted, had never struggled so hard with herself, "with the appalling fact that I was only a woman, whispering in one ear, and the groans of suffering men . . . thundering in the other."

She was near the limits of frustration when a letter reached her from North Oxford. It was from her nephew Sammy, Stephen's boy, and it was about Clara's father. "I sat up with Grandpa last night and he requested me to write to you and tell how he was," the letter said. "He takes no medicine, and says he will take no more. He is quite low-spirited at times, and last night very much so. Complains of pains in his back and bowels; said he should not stop long with us, and should like to see you once more before he died."

Clara made preparations to leave for North Oxford as soon as possible. A male friend in the Patent Office agreed to do her work for her, and in mid-February she took the train for home, heading in the opposite direction from Roanoke Island and the war front.

For Clara, it was a gloomy homecoming at the Barton farm. A blanket of snow lay over the surrounding fields and meadows, and a wintry wind pressed at the windows of the old farmhouse. Her father looked worse than she had ever seen him. His mind was still clear, but his body was failing him now, worn down by the ravages of age. He could eat nothing, "not a morsel of food," Clara wrote cousin Leander. All he could keep down was "a little milk and water." He had been sick so many times in the past few years but had always rallied. This time, it looked as if he might not make it, and Clara and the Barton family at North Oxford—David and his wife and children, Sammy and his mother, Elizabeth—prepared themselves for the worst.

The news from North Carolina, however, brightened the household considerably. Federal gunboats had penetrated Albemarle Sound, captured Elizabeth City, and sailed up the Chowan River far enough to burn Winton, only four miles south of Bartonsville. Could this mean that Burnside's expedition was actually destined for Stephen's place? It was an important manufacturing center, after all. Had the Bartons known in advance that the expedition would reach the Chowan River country, Stephen's son Sammy would have gone with it and made his way upriver with the gunboats. Sammy was anxious to leave now, and Clara thought that Colonel Morse, her friend at Annapolis, could get him passage to Roanoke Island, and that the Massachusetts officers there might help him persuade Burnside to send a force north to liberate Stephen.

As if these developments were not stunning enough, Clara actually received a letter from Stephen. How it got out of the Confederacy isn't clear—perhaps by way of the very gunboats that had so excited the family. "I am generally so busy that I get no time to be lonesome," Stephen reported. He spent most of his time with his hogs and cattle, seldom venturing from Bartonsville. While he had done "a very limited business" with his machinery this past year, he confidently expected "brighter prospects" in the area of Southern manufacturing. He said nothing about any violence committed against him by his neighbors and in fact made it clear that he intended to remain at Bartonsville.

Clara was shocked. Was Stephen doing business with the hated Confederacy? Did he think it was going to win the war? His letter made no profession of loyalty and patriotism to the Union. Did he share the rebel view that Lincoln was an abolitionist, a "Black Republican" tyrant out to destroy slavery and subjugate the South? Cut off and isolated as he was, Stephen was apparently oblivious of what the conflict was about, was ignorant of Lincoln's war objectives and the vast forces he had mustered to end the rebellion. Clara must set him straight. On March 1, she wrote him a long letter purporting "to give such opinions and facts as would be fully endorsed by every friend and person here whose opinions you would ever have valued."

First, she explained, the North was not waging an abolitionist war, as so many people of the South seemed to think. "Our Government has for its object the restoration of the Union *as it was*," she wrote, "and will do so, unless the resistance of the South prove so obstinate, and prolonged, that the abolition or overthrow of slavery follow as a consequence—never an object." Nor was the North trying to subjugate the South. "Both these ideas are used as stimulants by the Southern (mis) leaders, and without them they could never hold their army together a month. The North are fighting for the maintenance of the Constitutional government of the United States, and the defense and honor of their country's flag." Northerners, moreover, "would give their lives to save the Union men of the South. The North feel it to be a necessity to put down a rebellion, and there the animosity ends." This was an admirable summary of the Union war aims of 1861. Lincoln himself could scarcely have put them more plainly.

Second, Clara said, "We have now in the field between 500,000 & 600,000 soldiers" in all the war theaters. "We can raise another army like the one we have in the field . . . arm & equip them for service, and still have men and means enough left at home for all practical purposes. Our troops are just beginning to be effective, only just properly drilled, and are now ready to commence work in earnest or just as ready to lay down their arms when the South are ready to return to the Union as loyal and obedient states."

Third, "And this brings me to the point of my subject, here comes my request, my prayer, supplication, entreaty, command—call it what you will, only heed it, at once—COME HOME. Not home to Massachusetts, but home to my home—I want you in Washington. I could cover pages, fill volumes, in telling you all the anxiety that has been felt for you, all the hours of anxious solicitude that I have known in the last ten months, wondering where you were, or if you were at all, and planning ways of getting to you, or getting you to me, but never until now has any safe or suitable method presented itself." Now the Burnside expedition had "opened the way for your safe exit or escape to your native land, friends, and loyal government," and she urged him "to make ready" and when the opportunity came to "place yourself with such transportable things as you may desire to take on board one of our boats, under protection of our officers, and be taken to the landing at Roanoke, and from thence by some of our transports up to Annapolis, where either myself or friends will be waiting for you, then go with me to Washington and call your days of trial over."

Clara closed with a flourish: "I am a plain Northern Union woman, honest in my feelings, and counsels, desiring only the good of all, disguising nothing, covering nothing and so far, my opinions are entitled to respect, and will [I] trust be received with confidence. If you will do this as I suggest, and come at once to me at Washington, you need have no fears of remaining idle. . . . Washington had never so many people and so much business as now."

David loved Clara's letter. "I think it the best I ever heard," he wrote in a note to Stephen. "I most sincerely hope you will consider that as speaking my views and wishes a thousand times better than I could express them to you."

With the letters in the mail, Sammy set off on his lone mission to reach his father. Now all Clara and the remaining Bartons could do was hope and wait for news, as so many other families were doing in their stricken country.

In March, Clara left her father's bedside for a quick trip to Boston to see Governor John A. Andrew about one of her pressing concerns. Her friend and distant relative, Colonel Alexander DeWitt, a former congressman, went along as her escort. Standing before the governor in his office, Clara argued that a Massachusetts state agency ought to be established in Washington, to act as a distribution center for stores gathered by Bay State women for Massachusetts regiments. Clara's observation was that "a house of general distribution" such as the Sanitary Commission or the commissary department, charged with shipping supplies to all the battlefronts, was by definition an enormous concern "abounding in confusion." Therefore, she thought each state should establish in the vicinity of its greatest concentration of troops a depot of its own, to which supplies could be sent and through which they would be distributed. She had talked with various Massachusetts regiments about the need for a state agency, and they had petitioned the governor to establish one. Andrew was impressed with Clara's argument, and before long the state would open a distribution center in Washington along the lines that Clara proposed.

Clara found the governor a compelling man, despite his strange appearance. Pudgy and bespectacled, with curly blond hair, he possessed a large head and torso "out of proportion" to his short legs. Like Wilson and Sumner, he was a Radical Republican who argued that the war ought to be waged against slavery, too, and that the government should enlist black soldiers to help subdue the rebellion. With the war dragging on with no end in sight, Lincoln actually took a step in that direction. On March 6 he sent Congress a proposal for a gradual, compensated, state-guided emancipation program to commence in the loyal border and to be applied to rebel territory as it was captured. While nothing came of Lincoln's emancipation proposal, it was the first one a president had ever submitted to Congress in the history of the Republic and an indication that Lincoln was moving away from the limited war aims Clara had eloquently summarized for Stephen.

Back in North Oxford, Clara devoted herself day and night to her dying father. By mid-March, he could barely swallow cold water, yet he "lived and moved himself and talked strongly and sensibly and wisely as you have always heard him," Clara wrote Leander; "you will be gratified to know that he managed all his business to his entire satisfaction."

In his will, he left Clara a little land and a sum of money, which an executor would invest for her in a bank in Oxford. It hardly made her financially independent, but it did give her a cushion in case of an emergency, and she was most grateful. After she helped raise him up so that he could sign the documents, the old man said: "This is the last day I shall ever do any business—my work in this world is done."

He wanted to know about the war, though, so Clara read him the latest dispatches reported in the papers. As she did so, she became frustrated all over again. In distant North Carolina, Burnside's army invaded the mainland in mid-March and seized the important port of New Bern, on the Neuse River at the southern end of Pamlico Sound, at a cost of 90 killed and 381 wounded. At Burnside's request, a Massachusetts surgical team had gone to his army, which meant that it lacked adequate army doctors and was probably short of nurses as well. Now all of Clara's conflicted feelings were stirred up, and as she read Captain Barton the newspaper accounts of New Bern, she told him what was troubling her, opening up to the "soldier father" who had treated her so often like a son. She wanted to go to North Carolina, she told him, and nurse the wounded. But she was paralyzed with doubts. She was an unmarried woman. Surely he knew what soldiers thought of an unmarried woman in the field. She feared they would treat her like a camp follower, a prostitute. How could she go to North Carolina and maintain her dignity as a lady, a woman above reproach?

The old man raised himself up on his pillow and told her: "I know soldiers, and they will respect you and your errand." Even the roughest of them, he assured her, would show respect to a respectable woman. Then her father commanded her to go. He reminded her that she was "the daughter of an accepted Mason" and a Universalist and that it was her duty on both counts to "seek and comfort the afflicted everywhere." Above all, she was the daughter of a soldier and a patriot, and "he charged me with a dying patriot's love," Clara remembered, "to serve and sacrifice for my country in its peril and strengthen and comfort the brave men who stood for its defence."

That injunction freed Clara from the shackles of doubt. With her father's approval, she could challenge any attitude, go anywhere men were fighting. Yes, she could go to the front lines now, which was where she had wanted to serve from the first. She wrote a candid letter to Governor Andrew: "I desire Your Excellency's permission to go to Roanoke," by which she meant a letter of endorsement enabling her to nurse the Massachusetts troops in Burnside's command. She had reason to think that "our excellent Dr. Hitchcock," who had recently returned from Roanoke and carried much weight with the governor, would be sympathetic to her request. She should have proffered it weeks earlier, she admitted, but she had been called home to witness the final days of her "old Soldier father." When his "weary march" was over, her "highest duties" would close. "I would fain be allowed to go and administer comfort to our brave men, who peril life and limb in defense of the priceless boon the fathers so dearly won. . . . I ask neither pay or praise, simply a soldier's fare and the sanction of your Excellency to go and do with my might, what ever my hands find to do." She pointed out that forty of her former pupils were in Burnside's army. "I am glad to know that somewhere they have learned their duty to their country, and have come up neither cowards or traitors."

The day after Clara wrote Andrew, March 21, her father took a turn for the worse, and she and Julia Barton began a death vigil at his bedside. By five in the afternoon, he could no longer speak and tried to communicate to Clara by signs. Then at sixteen minutes past ten, "he straightened himself in bed," she said, "closed his mouth firmly, gave one hand to Julia and the other to me, and left us."

They buried him four days later, with the honors of a Freemason, down under the pines beside his wife, Sarah. Standing at his grave, Clara had never felt so alone. The person she most loved, her guide and her inspiration, was gone from this world, and she did not think she could bear the pain she felt in her heart. "The old soldier's heavy march is ended," she wrote cousin Leander, "for him the last tattoo has sounded, and resting upon the unfailing arms of truth hope and faith he awaits the 'reveille of the eternal morning.'"

In the evening after the funeral, a relative brought Clara a letter from Governor Andrew. Clara opened the envelope with great excitement. When she was ready to go to Burnside's division, the governor said, he would write her a letter of recommendation "with my hearty approval of your visit and my testimony to the value of the service to our sick and wounded."

No sooner had Clara received Andrew's endorsement than another letter came taking it away. A friend of hers named J. W. Fletcher had written Dr. Alfred Hitchcock in her behalf, thinking as Clara did that "our excellent" doctor would approve of her going to North Carolina. Hitchcock, however, did nothing of the kind. He scrawled across the back of Fletcher's letter, "I do not think, at the present time, Miss. Barton had better undertake to go to Burnside's Division to act as a nurse," and sent it to Andrew. The governor then forwarded it to Clara with the clear implication that he had changed his mind.

Clara was livid. She complained that Hitchcock had apparently formed "ludicrous opinions" of her as "a fussy unreasonable, meddlesome body." In a single devastating sentence, he rejected her patriotism, her credentials, and her heritage, because of the obnoxious male attitude that a woman on the battlefield would "just be in the way." Still, Clara had an injunction from her father; she *had* to serve. In desperation, she wrote directly to a captain in the Twenty-fifth Massachusetts, with Burnside in North Carolina. "I am a daughter of a soldier and a patriot," she asserted. Could he not find a "place" in that "treacherous soil" for her to be of use? She hoped he would let her come—"though it is little that one woman can do, still I crave the privilege of doing it."

But nothing worked out with him either, and Clara was back where she began as far as the war was concerned: in limbo. As if all this were not bad enough, a letter from Irving dashed her hopes that Sammy might reach Stephen through Burnside. Irving reported that Sam had been in Washington and gone to Baltimore but had found "no hope of proceeding on his voyage."

By the end of March, Clara was so hurt and disappointed that she decided not to return to Washington right away. She told Leander she simply "didn't feel ready." In a few days she took the train to Worcester, to stay a while with her cousin, Judge Ira Barton, and his wife, Maria. A tall, commanding figure with "Websterian" eyes, Cousin Ira had been a Massachusetts legislator and judge of the probate court and was an important man in Worcester County affairs. Clara had boarded with him and Maria in the late 1850s, and the "Barton Palace," situated in the sycamores across from Old South Church, had become something of a second home to her. Their daughter, Lucy, was married to a volunteer surgeon in the Army of the Potomac, and two of their sons, George and Edmund, were talking about enlisting as well.

From Washington, Irving sent "Aunty" Clara and cousin Elvira a series of long letters about the war. Clara always enjoyed his chatty, witty, and wonderfully opinionated letters. In his March letters, he discoursed on the "great naval engagement" between the ironclads, the *Monitor* and the *Virginia*, off Fort Monroe, opining that "hereafter wooden men of war will be unknown and the inventive faculties of the world will devise vessels so impregnable that naval engagements will be out of the question." He recounted McClellan's recent embarrassment at Manassas Junction. The general, well at last, had finally advanced against the rebel line there, only to find it abandoned. Irving supposed that "some of the spies in the War dept gave them notice and they commenced an evacuation." What would McClellan's next move be? "It would not be in the least surprising," Irving said, "if the whole Army of the Potomac except enough for the defense of Washington was suddenly thrown to the vicinity of Norfolk or perhaps landed at Aquia Creek" on the Potomac. Irving's prediction was amazingly accurate. The day after he wrote his letter, McClellan's army started embarking on troop transports at Alexandria. Their destination was Yorktown on the Virginia peninsula southeast of Richmond. "Stirring times are at hand," Irving wrote, "and if McClellan is a great General the rebels will be driven out of Virginia within a month."

On a personal note, Irving wrote Clara that he didn't think he could bear visiting North Oxford again. With Grandpa dead, "all that was ever pleasant was gone." He observed, "You must feel lonely there and anxious to get away," and he was right. Clara *was* lonely and anxious to get away, but to what? To her job in the Patent Office, her little distribution agency in the warehouse? She wanted to be *in the war*, yet the war was going on without her, all because of the atavistic attitude of an arrogant male surgeon. Yes, she felt left behind, like a powerful little eagle with her wings pinned to the ground. Here in North Oxford, a small town southwest of Worcester, the warfront seemed as distant and unreal as the stars. Oh, people talked about it constantly and worried about relatives and friends in uniform, and the women busied them-selves knitting socks, sewing articles of clothing, packing sheets and lint, to send in packages to the front, and occasionally men in blue uni-forms turned up on leave. But there was little else, in the cold and drizzle of early April, to remind Clara that the nation was at war. Events in Washington, battles in the East and West, were something that happened only in the newspapers.

And this the papers reported: in Congress, Clara's friend Henry Wilson had launched a furious legislative attack against slavery, argu-ing that it was "the heart, the brain, the soul" of the rebellion. That spring, Congress enacted two of his antislavery bills, and Lincoln signed them into law. One forbade the return of runaway slaves to their rebel masters. The other abolished slavery in Washington City, a move that aroused obstreperous opposition among proslavery Democrats, who howled that it was an entering wedge for national emancipation. Now the hideous slave pens Clara had seen in the nation's capital had become casualties of the war. Never again would human beings be bought and sold there.

With the Sanitary Commission cheering him on, Wilson also cham-pioned a bill to reorganize and remodel the Medical Department. The measure had the support of the president, Secretary of War Stanton, and General McClellan, which ensured its approval on Capitol Hill. As finally passed, the Medical Department reform act created a corps of eight medical inspectors charged with monitoring the sanitary condi-tion of the army, and it eliminated the accursed seniority system in favor of promotion on the basis of skill. Finley was out as surgeon gen-eral, replaced by Dr. William Alexander Hammond, a large, dark, authoritative man, just approaching thirty-five, who had given up a prosperous private practice to join the army as a surgeon. A man of "immense energy and capability," Hammond favored the building of more modern pavilion hospitals and promised an end to the chaos that had thus far characterized the efforts of his department.

And this the newspapers also reported: In the West, Grant won another impressive victory, near a little church called Shiloh in Tennessee. Farther south, a Union naval fleet captured New Orleans near the mouth of the Mississippi, and Benjamin Butler of Massachusetts took over the city with an occupying army. In the East, the Army of the Potomac had landed at Yorktown in what became known as the Peninsula Campaign. McClellan's plans called for him to dash boldly up the Peninsula, seize the rebel capital, and end the rebellion in a masterstroke. Predictably, however, he put Yorktown under a protracted siege when he could have overwhelmed its small garrison in a single offensive stroke. "I am greatly disappointed in McClellans tactics," Irving wrote Clara, "and such is the prevailing opinion here." McClellan was in a "very precarious" position off on the other side of Richmond, Bubby thought, and "it almost seems as if we are to have another Bull Run on a larger scale."

Clara was aroused by the developments on the peninsula, all the more so because of the role that Northern women were playing there. Because the army lacked an adequate ambulance system, the Sanitary Commission improvised a temporary hospital transport service for the campaign. It was the brainchild of Commission Secretary Frederick Law Olmsted, a short, slight, limping workaholic who liked to eat pickles with his coffee and who had authored popular books on the South before the war. As creative as he was energetic, Olmsted borrowed several old steamers from the government, refitted them as hospital ships, enlisted medical personnel, and dispatched them to the peninsula to lift off the wounded and sick from McClellan's army and bring them to general hospitals in Washington and other cities.

At Olmsted's invitation, some fifteen women enlisted in the transport service as "nurses at large, or matrons." These "lady superintendents" applied to the floating hospitals their considerable skills in running households: they organized the stores, took care of the sleeping and eating arrangements, supervised the cooking, and directed the cleaning details. They also exercised general supervision of the wards and the soldier nurses detailed to staff them. Among the superintendents were Katherine Prescott Wormeley, the daughter of a rear admiral in the British Navy, who headed the "Woman's Aid Society" of Newport; Georgeanna Woolsey and her sister, Eliza Woolsey Howland, of the prominent Woolsey family of New York City; and blond, blue-eyed Christine Kean Griffin, who had served as a hospital nurse the previous winter. Almira Fales of Washington, D.C., the wife of a second assistant examiner at the Patent Office, a mother who had given both her sons to the army, functioned as a transport nurse, treating every sick lad brought to her as "her boy." Other women served with distinction, too. Hard-working Helen Louise Gilson of Massachusetts, small, pretty, young, and unmarried—a Dix reject—was a nurse with her uncle's relief and medical unit, now affiliated with the Sanitary

Commission. And Eliza Harris, a pale woman with a low voice, attached herself to the big hospital on Fort Monroe, where she assisted surgeons in operations and invented "bully soup," a gruel made by mixing mashed army crackers, cornmeal, ginger, and wine in boiling water.

Numerous army surgeons and combat officers objected to women serving near the front lines, even if they did work under Olmsted's supervision and were confined to the hospital ships or Fort Monroe. But the women plunged into their work with alacrity and a growing sense of solidarity and purpose. Indeed, their presence on the peninsula posed the biggest challenge thus far to the male attitude, so frustrating to Clara, that women did not belong in a war zone. "We all know in our hearts that it is thorough enjoyment to be here," Katherine Wormeley wrote her mother. "It is *life*, in short, and we wouldn't be anywhere else for anything in the world."

Clara was too independent, too much of a loner, to enlist in the hospital transport service like Almira Fales, whom she knew through her husband. But the peninsula campaign did put the fight back in her, and she dreamed of serving the Potomac Army as an independent nurse, perhaps even as the head of her own hospital. Two of her relatives were with McClellan: cousin Leander Poor was a corporal of engineers, and Dr. Samuel L. Bigelow, cousin Lucy's husband, was a brigade surgeon in Fitz John Porter's division. Clara thought them "relations" enough to establish her right to take the field—if she could only find an army sponsor who would clear the way for her. On May 2, she wrote Leander, then at Yorktown, that she wanted to "come and have a tent there and take care of your poor sick fellows . . . now there is more seriousness than jesting in this suggestion, and I should go in *five* minutes if I could be told that I might,—when you get to be a general officer won't you call me into the service? I dare not ask the Dr. to give me a hospital for fear he doesn't like ladies but I know I should do my work faithfully, and don't think I should either run, or complain if I were left under fire."

After a month-long siege, McClellan finally captured Yorktown and proceeded up the peninsula with glacial speed, certain that ahead of him the rebels were massed like the Russians at Sebastapol. By the end of May, McClellan had reached the very gates of Richmond, all the while calling shrilly for reinforcements. On May 31 the rebels struck him at Fair Oaks, the first great battle of the campaign and in two days of fighting inflicted 5,000 casualties on McClellan's army, almost double the number lost at Manassas.

The army's medical director, surgeon Charles Stuart Tripler, established an evacuation hospital at White House Landing on the Pamunkey River and brought the wounded down from the battlefield in railroad freight cars. At White House, "a frightful scene of confusion and misery," contraband blacks employed by the army carried shrieking, shattered men onto hospital transports, unloading them wherever there was space. On the ships, teams of Sanitation Commission surgeons and nurses worked around the clock for three days, until the boats, bursting with wounded, at last pulled out for the North. At Fort Monroe, nurse Eliza Harris went aboard one hospital ship and could scarcely believe the scene before her. "There were eight hundred on board. Passage-ways, state-rooms, floors from the dark and foetid hold to the hurricane deck, were all more than filled; some on mattresses, some on blankets, others on straw; some in the death-struggle, others nearing it, some already beyond human sympathy and help; some in their blood as they had been brought from the battle-field of the Sabbath previous, and all hungry and thirsty."

The hospital boats created a sensation when they docked in Washington and other port cities like Baltimore and New York. No one had anticipated such casualties and such suffering. June brought a lull in the fighting, but the suffering continued unabated. Entrenched in low, swampy country in the rising heat of summer, the army was decimated by malaria and other debilitating diseases, and the floating hospitals now had to take off the sick with the wounded on their long, arduous trips to the North.

In June, Clara returned to Washington and her long-neglected job at the Patent Office. She was glad to find her warehouse full of boxes; her friends had not been idle in her absence. A box from Mary Norton's group in Hightstown, New Jersey, contained all manner of "treasures"—clothes, preserves, jellies, wines, shirts, sheets, and pillows—and Clara sent her thanks to Mary and "the noble ladies" of Hightstown. So many boxes came in the ensuing days that Clara had to rent another warehouse in which to store them. She dutifully donned her bonnet and visited the hospitals to distribute her "treasures." But she felt unneeded and unhappy, for the urban hospitals, including many new ones, appeared to be well supplied now.

According to medical reports, army hospitals were crowded that month with more than 10,000 cases of diarrhea and dysentery, malarial fevers, typhoid fever, and other disorders. Behind the statistics were scenes of human misery: wards reeking of vomit and pus and bloody excrement, men crying out in delirium, doctors and nurses struggling to save lives. The trouble was, they had almost no knowledge of the cause, transmission, and control of infectious diseases, which proved to be the Civil War's biggest killer. Doing the best they could with the medical wisdom of the day, physicians gave typhoid patients oral doses of turpentine, battled abdominal pain with applications of blisters and "hot fomentations," fought respiratory tract infections with "turpentine stupes," mustard and pitch plasters, and preparations of powdered blister beetles (a skin irritant) and croton oil (a counterirritant). If they heeded the advice of the Sanitary Commission, they treated severe headache victims by bleeding them with leeches.

To combat acute and chronic "diarrhea-dysentery," which afflicted and killed more Union soldiers than any other disease, military doctors prescribed a bewildering array of remedies, from opium (in the form of Dover's powder, laudanum, or paregoric) to copper sulfate, lead acetate, aromatic sulfuric acid, oil of turpentine, and various laxatives or purgatives—castor oil, Epsom salts, ipecac, sulfate of magnesia, and calomel (also called mercurous chloride). Except for the opiates, such "medicines" aggravated the condition horribly, sometimes with disastrous consequences. Calomel could produce ghastly side effects: profuse salivation with "the tongue protruding from the mouth," loss of teeth, and, in extreme cases, "mercurial gangrene," which caused "the soft parts of the mouth and cheeks" to rot and fall off in "a putrid mass." Yet calomel was a popular drug among military surgeons in the early years of the war.

To check malarial fevers, which were blamed on "bad air" or "noxious vapors" emanating from stagnant marshes and rank vegetation in the soil, Civil War doctors invariably prescribed quinine, the war's "wonder drug." It was so bitter tasting, though, that patients washed it down with a shot of whiskey, the war's all-purpose medicine. Severe malaria called for higher doses of quinine, which could produce giddiness, ringing in the ears, even deafness. For Civil War doctors, these were *good* signs, indicating that the drug was "pervading the system with its antidotal influence." To calm the feverish patient, the physicians would give him an opiate, now doubling as a tranquilizer. To control his diarrhea, they prescribed "mercurial remedies" followed by Epsom salts, which made "the fluxes" worse than ever.

If quinine treatment failed to check the fever, and sometimes it did, the malarial patient exhibited frightful symptoms that none who witnessed them would ever forget. According to medical records, the poor victim suffered from ever-worsening chills, diarrhea and abdominal cramps, "anorexia," vomiting, extreme thirst, jaundice, declining pulse, back pain, excruciating headaches (which might call for an application of leeches), and, in the disease's fatal stages, coughing, profuse sweating, "involuntary discharges," and delirium, until the victim lapsed into a coma and died.

The soldier afflicted with typhoid fever also got the quinine and whiskey treatment, this to check his fever. The oral doses of turpentine—a teaspoonful every hour or so—were supposed to control the intestinal disorders, the bloody diarrhea, colic, even intestinal ulcers, associated with the disease. Most Civil War doctors, said one, "regarded turpentine as little short of a sheet-anchor in the treatment of typhoid." Contracted by swallowing contaminated water or food, typhoid was highly contagious and the war's second most lethal disease. Some Union outfits became so badly infected that they were called "typhoid" regiments. Because Civil War doctors wrongly attributed this bacterial disease to environmental factors, to "miasma" or "malarial odor" in the air, "no care whatever was used in disposing of the bowel discharges from typhoid patients," a Civil War surgeon remembered, "and as flies were everywhere in great numbers, in warm weather, the wonder is we were not all infected; for there was nothing to prevent them from coming direct from the bowel discharges to our food." In June 1862, typhoid fever struck 751 men and killed 70 in the Army of the Potomac alone. In the next month, the toll would almost double.

On June 26 Clara wrote Julia about her hospital experiences, warning that "I *cannot* make a pleasant letter of this, *everything* is sad, the very pain which is breathed out in the atmosphere of this city is enough to sadden any human heart. 5000 suffering men, and room preparing for 8000 more, poor fevered, cut up wretches, it agonizes me to think of it. I go [to the hospitals] when I can." So many Union soldiers perished in the hospitals that there was no time for ceremonial funerals. Their bodies were dumped in plank coffins and taken by carts to makeshift burial grounds beyond the city. When Clara passed by the new Judiciary Square Hospital, she could see corpses laid out in a vacant lot and embalmers working on them.

At Mount Pleasant Hospital on top of Meridian Hill, Clara found a wounded "little boy" from Lowell, Massachusetts, a "tender" boy, just seventeen years old and the only child of his widowed mother. When Clara asked what he wanted, he said he would like to see his mother. He had enlisted and left for the army without telling her. Since his wound had healed, save for a little rheumatism, Clara persuaded the hospital's chief surgeon to discharge the youth and send him home rather than return him to the army. A few days later, he called on Clara to say good-bye. "I sent him on *to-night* to his mother as a Sunday present," Clara wrote Julia. "I am ungrateful to be heavy-hearted when I have been able to do *only that little.*"

Her heart grew heavier when fighting broke out anew on the peninsula. For seven straight days in late June and early July, Robert E. Lee, the new commander of the Army of Northern Virginia, pounded McClellan back from Richmond, and names like Mechanicsville, Gaines' Mill, Savage Station, White Oak Swamp, and Malvern Hill screamed in the headlines of the newspapers. In Washington City, Clara nervously searched the "Dead List" columns, dreading that she might find the names of one or more of her many friends on the Richmond front. Washington itself was transformed into a vast base hospital for the Army of the Potomac, which suffered a staggering 15,800 casualties as it fell back from Lee's relentless assaults. Day and night, crowded hospital ships arrived at the Sixth and Seventh Street wharves with blasts of their whistles. Stretcher-bearers unloaded the injured men in rotating lines, and Sanitary Commission workers served soup and coffee to those able to swallow. A convoy of ambulances, including some of the newer and more comfortable four-wheeled variety, conveyed the wounded to the various hospitals in Washington, Georgetown, and Alexandria.

"Oh these terrible days of fighting," Clara wrote Mary Norton, with McClellan's battered army huddled around Harrison's Landing, on the James River southeast of Richmond. "What suffering and want there must be soon . . . and Richmond still in the hands of the rebels, what shall we want to meet them with? 300,000 more to get ready—verily there is work to do." She told Mary about her hospital visits, so unfulfilling now, and then poured out all her pent-up frustrations. "I am sick at heart and yet not weak. I only wish I could work to some purpose. I have no right to these easy comfortable days and our poor men suffering and dying thirsting in this hot sun and I so quiet here in want of nothing, it is not rightly distributed, my lot is too easy and I am sorry for it."

When Clara wrote that letter, the new Army of Virginia was being organized between Washington and Richmond under the command of blustering General John Pope of Illinois. Word had it that Pope would march overland against Richmond and help relieve the pressure on McClellan. His immediate task was to concentrate his army of nearly 51,000 troops, who were scattered from the Shenandoah Valley clear down to Fredericksburg, on the Rappahannock River forty miles south-east of Washington.

The mobilization of Pope's army sparked Clara into action. Unlike the Army of the Potomac, far off on the other side of Richmond, this new army was accessible to her. When it began campaigning, she reasoned, it would need stores, and by July she had three warehouses full of them, plus the boxes in her apartment. All she lacked was the means to get them to the field, and she knew where to get the means: the quartermaster's office of the War Department. On July 11, clad in plain dress, Clara called at the office of Colonel Daniel H. Rucker, head of the Quartermaster Depot in Washington City, who sat at a desk behind a little fence with a gate. The room was full of male orderlies, and Clara waited nervously in a corner, watching Rucker. A professional soldier in his middle years, with a bearded face and heavy eyebrows, the colonel appeared "pressed and anxious and gruff." Clara was sure this rude man would send her away. Since childhood, she had suffered from attacks of "extreme bashfulness" in stressful situations, and one of those attacks was coming on now.

Presently, Rucker turned to her. "Well," he said crossly, "what do you want?"

Clara's composure crumbled. She started to cry.

"What's the matter?" he said, alarmed that he might have hurt her feelings. Clara wiped her tears away, struggling to control herself. "Don't cry," Rucker said more softly. "Come, sit down." He held the gate open, and she entered and took a seat. "Now tell me all about it," he said gently, as if speaking to a child; "what is it you want?"

Under other circumstances, his patronizing manner might have offended her. But she steadied herself and leaped at the opening he offered. "I want to go to the front," she asserted, meaning to the Army of Virginia.

Rucker understood perfectly well which army she meant. "The front!" he exclaimed. "That's no place for a lady; there's going to be a battle."

"But that is why I want to be there," Clara insisted. "I have no fear of the battlefield."

Rucker was incredulous. "Have you got a father or brother there?"

"No," she said, "I've got nobody there." A pause. "I have some things I want to take to the soldiers," she explained. "But I need wagons and a pass to get them there."

"What kind of things?" Rucker asked, his interest aroused.

Not just delicacies, she told him, but real food—pickled vegetables
and bread. She also had hospital supplies—bandages, salves, sheets,
bed shirts, and stimulants. When he asked where it all was, Clara
played her trump. "In my house, sir, and in three warehouses."

"Three warehouses! Heavens!" Rucker turned around and stared at
Clara in amazement. She sat there, triumphant, her tears gone now,
her eyes fixed on his. When she specified Fredericksburg as the place
she wanted to visit first, Rucker promptly wrote out an order providing
Clara with a wagon and driver to convey her supplies to the
Washington wharves. He signed a pass giving her transportation on
any government boat to and from Aquia Creek, an army port on the
Potomac with rail connections to Fredericksburg; Rucker then referred
the pass to General James S. Wadsworth, commander of the Military
District of Washington, who added his own authorization the same day.
Rucker even went to the Surgeon General's Office and returned with a
pass signed by Brigadier General Hammond himself. "Miss C. H.
Barton," it read, "has permission to go upon the sick transports in any
direction for the purpose of distributing comforts to the sick and
wounded, and nursing them, always subject to the direction of the
Surgeon in charge."

Clara left Rucker's office with her spirits soaring. She had broken
through the barriers of the male military bureaucracy and found a supporter in the army in Colonel Rucker, who was really a decent man,
she decided, and whose friendship she intended to cultivate as she had
Henry Wilson's. Now she could "work to some purpose" in this war. It
occurred to her, however, that the male administrators of the U.S.
Sanitary Commission might object to her taking supplies to the field,
or nursing independently on army hospital transports, on the grounds
that she was trespassing on their domain. To protect her flanks, she
called at the commission's headquarters in the Adams house on F
Street, persuaded the assistant secretary that her work was meant to
complement the commission's, and left with a letter of introduction,
which she could hand to Sanitary agents in the field: "Miss Barton proposes to devote herself, as an individual, to the same objects as those
which engage the Commission in its collective capacity, so far as
administering to the comforts of the sick and wounded soldier are concerned."

Before Clara could go to Pope's army, she needed to secure her supply lines from New Jersey and Massachusetts. On July 18 she
embarked on a whirlwind eleven-day tour across the two states. She
spoke with school committee members, women's aid societies, mayors,

and former army officers, and left her "arrangements" with them. On the way back, she stopped in Hightstown, New Jersey, long enough to dine with Mary Norton and her mother, caught an evening train crowded with soldiers, and reached Washington at dawn on July 29, exhausted but satisfied that she had strengthened her lifelines between the home and the field.

She also engaged two assistants: Anna Carver of Philadelphia, a prominent war worker, and Cornelius Welles, a one-time missionary in South America and an ordained Baptist minister. Welles had come to Washington under the auspices of the Free Mission Society and established and directed several schools for "contrabands." He was as serene a Christian as Clara had ever met. "Do you never have any doubts?" a friend once asked. "Never," he replied. "Why should I? I *know* that Jesus is my Savior." Secure in his faith and in himself, Welles had no trouble taking orders from a woman and told Clara he was eager to serve her "in any way."

On the morning of August 2, rumors flew about Washington that the Army of Virginia was fighting rebel infantry somewhere southwest of Manassas Junction, along the Orange & Alexandria Railroad. One rumor had it that "we are whipping them," Clara wrote cousin Leander; another that "they are whipping us. . . . But one thing I do suppose to be true, viz., that our army is isolated, cut off from supplies of food, and that we cannot reach them with more until they fight their way out." She wanted to go to Pope's army at once, but it was impossible until the rear lines were secure against rebel partisans. It irked Clara that certain people talked "like children about 'transporting supplies' as if it were the easiest thing imaginable to transport supplies by wagon thirty miles across a country scoured by guerrilla Bands." No one knew the condition of the poor soldiers, Clara told Leander, but she assumed "they must be dying from want of care, and I am promised to go to them the first moment access can be had."

Unable to stand idly by in Washington, Clara decided to take the field in the only direction open to her: Fredericksburg, on the Rappahannock River south of Washington, where General Rufus B. King's division was stationed, covering Pope's left flank. Using her permits from Colonel Rucker and General Wadsworth, she secured passage on a government tugboat, had her stores put aboard, and with Cornelius Welles and Anna Carver set off for Aquia Creek, thirty-five miles down the Potomac.

By the time she left, the situation in central Virginia had clarified. The rumors of battle turned out to be wrong, but three rebel divisions under Stonewall Jackson were reported to be at Gordonsville, south of Culpeper Court House, and Pope was preparing to march against them. The War Department ordered Burnside and McClellan to bring their forces home to cooperate with Pope, and the hospital transports evacuated the last of the sick and wounded from Harrison's Landing. The new medical director of the Potomac Army, Jonathan Letterman, had installed an ambulance system at long last, and there was no longer any need for the Sanitary Commission's improvised transport service and its lady volunteers. They had served at the front for only three months, but for Katherine Wormeley it had been "a lifetime."

"Our reign is over," Wormeley wrote Georgeanna Woolsey from her northbound transport.

The reign of Clara Barton, however, had just begun.

PART TWO

The Field

As the tugboat steamed away from Washington City, Clara and her assistants could see forts bristling with cannon and multitudes of white tents lining the banks of the Potomac. Presently, they came to Alexandria, a dingy, dilapidated town where George Washington had once worshipped in a small, brick church and where the infamous "Slave Pen" still stood, with a sign, "Rice & Co., Dealers in Slaves," hanging on its main entrance. Farther downriver, they passed Mount Vernon, George Washington's Virginia plantation, whose colonnaded, two-story frame house was said to be in the charge of a secessionist.

At last, the tugboat turned into Aquia Creek and docked at the wharves of a rude army supply base. After spending the night there, Clara's party rode a rattling train down to Falmouth Station on the northeast side of the Rappahannock. She called on the quartermaster at King's headquarters in the nearby Chatham House, a stately old brick mansion situated on a plateau near the river. The Yankees had captured the mansion when they invaded the area the previous spring, and they called it the Lacy House after its latest owner, J. Horace Lacy, a Confederate aide-de-camp who had been captured and imprisoned at Fort Delaware. The front windows of the house afforded a magnificent view of colonial Fredericksburg across the river, with its spired churches, cobbled streets, and neat, red-bricked houses. The next day Clara crossed into town on a suspension bridge and visited a hospital set up in a woolen factory. Here she witnessed her first amputation, an event she found too horrible to describe in her diary.

On August 4, she and her assistants were on hand at Falmouth Station when Burnside's legions arrived on flatcars from Aquia Creek and pitched camps in the woods along the heights. Now officially known as the Ninth Corps, comprising three full divisions, Burnside's command was on its way to join Pope by marching overland along the

57

Rappahannock River. Clara searched out the Twenty-first Massachusetts and had a happy reunion with her former pupils and the "cute" William S. Clark, now colonel and regimental commander.

Once her supplies were distributed, Clara hastened back to Washington to gather more and find out the latest news from the Army of Virginia; Welles and Anna Carver joined her a few days later. By then, Pope had concentrated his forces around Culpeper Court House, between the Rappahannock and Rapidan rivers. On August 9, Clara heard that a battle was raging south of Culpeper, but two anxious days elapsed before she could learn any details. Evidently a couple of Federal divisions, both in Nathaniel Banks's corps, had stumbled into Stonewall Jackson's infantry at the base of Cedar Mountain—also called Slaughter Mountain—and it was "truly named for the slaughter was tremendous on both sides," said a Union army surgeon. Indeed, Banks had lost more than a third of his men engaged. The medical director of the Army of Virginia, Surgeon Thomas P. McParlin, had established dressing stations near the battlefield and a main "clearing" or "evacuation" hospital up at Culpeper, on the Orange & Alexandria Railroad, where military trains could fetch the wounded back to Alexandria, a distance of some fifty miles.

Clara resolved at once to go to Culpeper. If the Cedar Mountain battlefield was anything like that at Bull Run, Union medical teams were likely short of everything from stimulants to ordinary bandages and salves, since the army was reluctant to send supplies forward during a campaign lest they be captured. When two officers warned her that "in all probability" she would be captured herself, Clara replied, "I fail to see any more danger to me than for our disabled men."

In fact, she faced considerable danger, for the war in central Virginia had turned brutal. Rebel partisans routinely shot Yankee noncombatants and soldiers alike. In retaliation, Pope punished rebel civilians with a vengeance: he confiscated their food and property and threatened to execute captured partisans, to arrest all "disloyal male citizens" within his lines, and to banish those who refused to take an oath of allegiance. And he vowed to treat those who returned as spies. Such measures had Lincoln's full approval. Indeed they reflected the decision of his government to wage a harsher war, to make rebel *civilians* feel the terrible consequences of supporting the rebellion. The new policy enraged General Robert E. Lee and Jefferson Davis, who damned the Yankees for waging "a campaign of indescriminate robbery and murder" and who threatened to respond in kind.

With the conflict entering a more vindictive and volatile stage, nobody in the Virginia war zone seemed safe, yet Clara wasn't afraid. On August 12, with Colonel Rucker's help, she secured an army pass from Pope's assistant inspector general in Washington authorizing her to take her stores to Culpeper by military railroad. Dressed in her battlefield "uniform,"—a bonnet, a red bow at the neck, a blouse, and a plain dark skirt—she sent Welles to Fredericksburg with one load of stores, and she and Anna Carver took another load downriver to Alexandria, Pope's busy supply base at the terminus of the Orange & Alexandria Railroad. With them was Gardner Tufts, head of the new Massachusetts state relief agency in Washington. At the depot, they found a train just in from Culpeper with 480 wounded, the first to be evacuated from the battlefield. Clara made arrangements to take the train when it returned on the morrow, and she and her co-workers spent a rainy evening loading her "precious freights"—stimulants, bandages, salves, and hospital clothing—into a boxcar.

Early the next morning the train pulled out with blasts of its whistle, and Clara was on her way to the battlefield at last. Having freed herself from her old constraints, she had never felt more needed and more exhilarated. She would show the government and the army that her supplies, her skill and energy, could make a difference in the battlefront hospitals. She would demonstrate that a woman could function quite ably in the field *without* male supervision.

As the train rocked through the countryside, the effects of war were visible everywhere: fences torn down, fields uncultivated, dwellings in ruins. All that morning and early afternoon, the train roared southward, past Bull Run and Manassas Junction—names with profoundly different connotations now, forever altered by the scourge of civil war—past Bristoe Station, Rappahannock Station, and Brandy Station, until at last the train pulled into the depot of Culpeper Court House at mid-afternoon. Here, at a makeshift relief station, several hundred wounded men lay under the blazing sun, awaiting evacuation by the train. There were no medical attendants in sight, and many of the wounded were dehydrated and groaning for water. Worse still, Clara noticed, their bandages were filthy. This was an *evacuation* area? How bad had it been on the battlefield itself? Well, at least these poor wretches were on their way to clean beds in the general hospitals in Alexandria and Washington. Hundreds more, Clara learned, lay all over Culpeper Court House, in churches, a tobacco factory, the Masonic Hall, private homes, and the few tents the army had brought to the field. Just as Clara had anticipated, the surgical teams had run short of everything, from bandages to salves and stimulants.

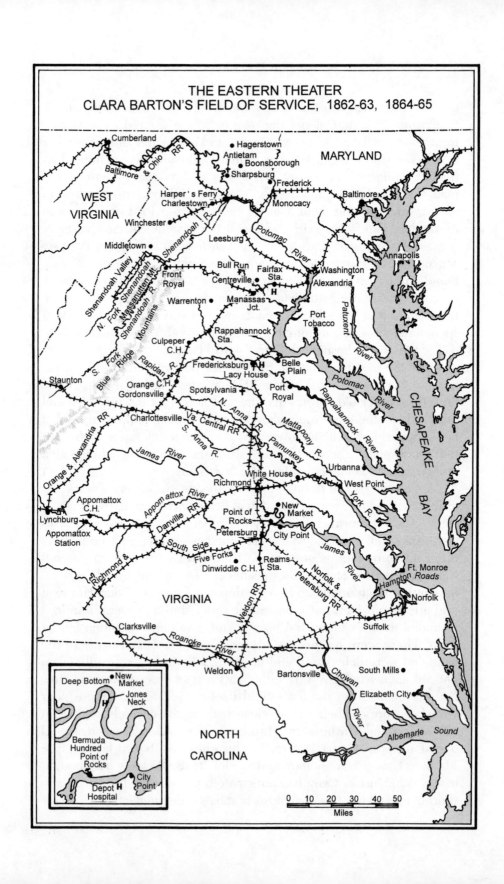

THE EASTERN THEATER
CLARA BARTON'S FIELD OF SERVICE, 1862-63, 1864-65

Cumberland

Baltimore & Ohio RR

WEST
VIRGINIA

Hagerstown
Antietam
Boonsborough
Sharpsburg
Frederick
Monocacy

MARYLAND

Baltimore

Harper's Ferry
Charlestown

Winchester

Middletown

Shenandoah R.

Annapolis

Leesburg

Potomac River

Shenandoah Valley
N. Fork Shenandoah
Massanutten Mt.
Shenandoah R.

Front
Royal

Bull Run
Centreville

Fairfax
Sta.

Washington
Alexandria

Warrenton

Manassas
Jct.

Port
Tobacco

Patuxent River

Culpeper
C.H.

S. Fork

Blue Ridge Mountains

Rapidan R.

Rappahannock
Sta.

Fredericksburg
Lacy House

Belle
Plain

Staunton

Orange C.H.
Gordonsville

Spotsylvania

Port
Royal

Rappahannock River

Potomac River

CHESAPEAKE
BAY

Orange & Alexandria RR

Charlottesville

Va. Central RR

N. Anna R.
S. Anna R.

James River

Mattapony R.

Pamunkey R.

Urbanna

White House
Richmond

West Point

York R.

Appomattox C.H.
Lynchburg
Appomattox
Station

Appomattox River

Danville RR

Point of
Rocks
Petersburg

New
Market

City Point

James River

Richmond &

South Side

Five Forks
Dinwiddle C.H.

Reams
Sta.

Ft. Monroe
Hampton Roads

Norfolk &
Petersburg RR

Norfolk

VIRGINIA

Weldon RR

Suffolk

Clarksville

Roanoke River

Weldon

Bartonsville

Chowan River

South Mills

Elizabeth City

NORTH
CAROLINA

Albemarle Sound

Deep Bottom
New
Market
Jones
Neck

Bermuda
Hundred
Point of
Rocks

Depot
Hospital

City
Point

0   10   20   30   40   50
Miles

Clara rolled up her sleeves and went to work. She acquired an army wagon and a four-horse team, courtesy of Colonel Rucker's Quartermaster Department, and set off through town to distribute her hospital stores. These were the first field hospitals Clara ever visited after a battle, and she was aghast. Men with arms and legs blown away, faces mangled, stomachs torn open, and intestines hanging out lay on the floors in their own filth and blood, crying out for water or a merciful bullet. Their wrecked bodies testified to the devastating power of the modern .58 caliber rifled musket, whose conical bullet, the minié ball, tore through human flesh, "shattering, splintering, and splitting" bones and joints. Cannons loaded with canister were even more destructive. When fired at charging infantry, the whirling iron balls blasted gaping holes in the ranks in a shower of blood, pieces of skin, decapitated heads, and other body fragments. Those who survived the battlefield and were taken to the hospitals faced a second war more deadly than the shooting war itself. Here the enemy was infection, contagious disease, and medical ignorance. Since nobody knew what caused infection, surgeons operated in coats stained with pus and blood, their hands unwashed, their scalpels, saws, forceps, bone pliers, and sponges merely dipped in pails of tap water before the beginning of the next operation. They sewed up wounds with undisinfected silk, and when they had trouble threading the needle, moistened it with their own saliva.

In such places, the death rate was appalling. Some 87 percent of the soldiers with "penetrating" abdominal wounds died; 60 percent of those with skull wounds, 62.6 percent of those with wounds to the chest, and 33 percent of those with shoulder joint wounds also died. The luckless soldier with a bone-breaking wound in the knee or ankle, or a severe gunshot fracture in the arm or leg, hand or foot, faced almost certain amputation—the best means the surgeon knew to save his life. Clara had seen an amputation in Fredericksburg, but that did not prepare her for what she witnessed in Culpeper. Here surgeons amputated limbs by the score, and soldier nurses tossed them out the door into hideous piles. An experienced surgeon could perform a typical "guillotine" amputation in a couple of minutes or so. First, his attendants placed the patient on the operating table and the surgeon put him to sleep with ether or chloroform. If both were lacking—and they often were in the Culpeper hospitals—the victim might get a shot of whiskey, or simply a slab of leather placed between his teeth, so that he could bite down on it when he started screaming. According to procedure, the surgeon would slice through the flesh with a razor-sharp knife, saw through the bone with a sharp-toothed saw, and snip off "jagged ends of bone" with pliers. Then he would place a clamp on the "spewing arteries," tie them with "oiled silk," apply a styptic, and dress the bloody stump, leaving it to heal "by granulation."

The odds of surviving an amputation were frightful. A man whose leg was sawed off at the hip stood only one chance in ten of living. The fatality rate for amputations at the thigh or the knee joint was more than 50 percent; for leg amputations as a whole, 34 percent; for shoulder joint amputations, 29 percent, for amputations of the upper arm, 25 percent; for ankle joint amputations, 7 percent; for amputations of the fingers or hand, 2.6 percent. All told, according to one authority, one-fourth of the wartime amputations resulted in death, "almost always of surgical fevers."

If the amputee survived the operation, he faced an uncertain convalescence, since his stump was bound to get infected. When an "odorless creamy pus" did appear three or four days after an amputation, Civil War surgeons pronounced it a *good* sign. They called it "laudable pus" and thought it nature's way of ridding the body of harmful tissue and thus a necessary part of the healing process.

It was beyond their understanding why infected stumps so often became gangrenous. "Hospital gangrene" turned the infected flesh into a black-green-purple-yellowish color and caused it to give off a sickeningly sweet stench that was overpowering. Harried surgeons tried to arrest gangrene with unsanitary knives, corrosive chemicals like nitric acid, and turpentine, charcoal, or chlorine. As the war progressed, a Union physician in the Department of the Ohio made the breakthrough discovery that bromine arrested hospital gangrene. An equally effective "medicine" proved to be the lowly maggot, which, by eating away the dead flesh, prevented the spread of infection and saved more than one life.

Clara was shocked at the filth in the Culpeper hospitals—their floors were slippery with blood, slime, and excrement. Since the overworked surgeons and attendants were too busy to clean the floors, Clara took care of that herself. She and her assistants would move the wounded to one side of the room and scrub the other side, then reverse the process. Clara even made bystanders help. At one hospital, a captain was dismayed to see her at work in such macabre surroundings. "Miss Barton," he told her, "this is a rough and unseemly position for you, a woman, to occupy."

"Is it not as rough and unseemly for these pain-wracked men?" Clara retorted.

Her take-charge attitude won her the admiration and friendship of Dr. James L. Dunn, a tall, blue-eyed Pennsylvanian serving as a brigade surgeon and acting division surgeon in General Franz Sigel's command. He had been in the Cedar Mountain battle, had witnessed the defeat of Banks's corps out there. His original outfit, the 109th Pennsylvania, went into the fight with 300 men and came out with 130—a casualty rate of 57 percent. "We lost almost all the staff officers myself being the only one unhurt," he wrote his wife. He and the other surgeons had done what they could for the wounded who lay on the battlefield but deferred major amputations until the injured could be removed to Culpeper, some eight miles to the north. Inadequate stretcher teams rescued as many as they could, dumped them into wagons, and brought them to Culpeper, where surgical teams went to work in earnest. In one twenty-four-hour stretch, Dunn alone performed twenty-two thigh amputations because of gunshot wounds to the knee, and too many amputations of the arm to count.

It was midnight when Clara appeared at Dunn's hospital with her four-horse team. She might well have blanched when she first saw him. Dressed in pantaloons, boots, and an old red shirt with the sleeves rolled up, he was "covered with blood from head to foot," as he described himself. When he said that he'd run out of every kind of dressing, Clara promptly replenished his supply from her wagon. "I thought that night," he wrote his wife later, "if heaven ever sent out a homely angel, she must be one, her assistance was so timely."

Clara toiled in the Culpeper hospitals for two days and two nights, going without sleep, seldom pausing to eat, as she scrubbed floors and handed out her bandages, salves, stimulants, and articles of clothing until not a single item was left. One of the last hospitals she visited was a house full of wounded rebels. Thinking her a local Virginian, they begged her for bedding and clothes. "I am from Massachusetts," she told them. Even so she gave them some of her remaining garments.

On August 15, exhausted and covered with grime, Clara and Anna Carver boarded a train for Washington. On the journey north, Clara closed her eyes in despair. Yes, she had found "an unoccupied place" to serve between the battlefield and the general hospitals in the rear. Yet the horrors of the field hospital service were too great for her to rectify by herself. She had witnessed unmitigated chaos at Culpeper Court House: no trained ambulance corps to retrieve the wounded, improvised hospitals short of basic necessities and filthy beyond description. What was more, she had begun "a course of labor," she said later, that required "sinews of steel and nerves of iron," and she wondered whether she had such sinews and nerves. The terrible sights and smells of the Culpeper hospitals haunted her all the way back to Washington City.

Over the next few days, she allowed herself little time to rest. She called at the office of Pope's medical purveyor, checked on the wounded at Alexandria, searched for Massachusetts men in the Washington hospitals. "Oh for time to breathe," she wrote Mary Norton. "I am *so tired.*" To keep stores pouring into her warehouses, Clara wrote a public letter addressed to "My dear Old Time Friend" and had it published in the papers. The letter was graphic, emotional, persuasive—and a fake. Purportedly written from Culpeper Court House, August 14, 1862, it began: "I am writing in the dreary midnight, among the painfully moving forms, scarce visible by the glimmering light, which shoots fitfully across some knitted brow or compressed lip, just serving to show from which victim the last half smothered sigh escaped . . . here, without a single convenience of life, without one cheering thought or view—my mind wanders out to you amid all the comforts of your invalid chamber at home." She reported that she and her assistant had come to Culpeper after hearing the first reliable news of battle. "From that hour there has come to neither of us a moment's rest; want and suffering lay on every side, our ample stores diminished with a rapidity truly appalling when we looked upon so many brave and noble patriots needing everything—possessing nothing. . . . A great proportion of the sufferers have been already sent to Alexandria and Washington. Still many remain who cannot be removed. . . . Would you know how our men bear their sufferings? Oh, how I wish I had words to tell you of all the patience, the nobility of soul, the resignation, and bravery of our gallant troops. Truly, a hospital after a hard fought battle, would seem the most unlikely place in all the world to inspire courage and ardor. But I gaze upon these men through blinding tears of admiration and respect, and sing in my heart, 'It is well to be a soldier.' "

It did not bother Clara that the letter was spurious. So what if she had violated factual truth by dating the letter from Culpeper? She was reaching for dramatic effect—for poetic truth. If the letter inspired women on the home front to work harder for the soldiers and the Union cause, then it served the higher purpose of national survival.

On August 18, the last trainload of wounded arrived from Culpeper, along with the news that Pope was abandoning his line there and pulling back north of the Rappahannock River, where he would await reinforcements from McClellan to help him stop the advancing rebel army. Two of Burnside's divisions under General Jesse L. Reno had already reached Pope after a hard march overland from Fredericksburg. Clearly another battle was imminent, and Clara made preparations to return to the field.

To those who cautioned her not to go, she would argue that women were "minute, intuitive, tender." Where were "such blessings" more needed than on the battlefield? To tell the truth, she was ashamed that she had let social mores and her accursed sense of propriety keep her from the field for more than a year. Henceforth, she intended to devote all her energies to her work there.

That decision, however, raised the problem of her job at the Patent Office. She approached Commissioner Holloway, explained what she planned to do, and asked if he could hold her job for her. She would not ask for a salary. An ardent patriot himself, Holloway not only gave her a leave of absence but insisted that she receive some compensation as special consideration for her work in behalf of the soldiers. With the commissioner's approval, Clara arranged with a Mr. Upperman to work as her substitute for half her salary, she to draw the other half. This would yield her an average of about twenty-five dollars a month, enough to pay the rent on her apartment and warehouse space and buy the few incidentals she might need in the field. Clara was grateful to Holloway, calling the arrangement "a noble gift of a noble friend" and her "charity fund in the field."

For the next several days, Washington was in a state of high tension as reports from the front indicated that the rest of Lee's army was racing north, probably to link up with Jackson and attack Pope before McClellan could reinforce him. At last, two corps from the Army of the Potomac reached Alexandria and set out for the front on trains provided by Colonel Herman Haupt, Lincoln's irascible but highly competent superintendent of military railroads. Alas, the Army of the Potomac had been obliged to leave most of its ambulances and medical stores behind and was ill prepared to care for its wounded in the coming battle. One division headed for the front without a single ambulance.

August 27 brought the ominous news that rebel cavalry and infantry had swung around Pope's army and captured his main supply depot at

Manassas Junction, confiscating tons of supplies, including numberless cases of chloroform. The infantry turned out to be Stonewall Jackson's corps, which meant that almost half of Lee's army was now between Pope and Washington. The rebels wrecked bridges and a stretch of the Orange & Alexandria Railroad, thus severing Pope's lifeline back to Alexandria and Washington. For the next couple of days, so many reports and rumors pummeled the capital that it was difficult to know what was happening. Jackson had apparently vanished, and the Army of Virginia had fallen back to Manassas, where freight cars and store-houses were still burning.

On August 30, a hot, humid Saturday, Clara heard that "Genl Pope was fighting on the old Bull Run battle ground, and had 8000 killed while the battle still went on." That afternoon, she could hear the rumble of cannon from the direction of Bull Run and smell the acrid scent of gunpowder on the wind. At mid-afternoon, a report from Pope appeared on the public bulletin board at the Treasury Department. It stated that he had fought a "terrific battle" the day before and had driven the enemy from the field but had suffered a staggering 10,000 casualties. If this report were accurate, Pope's losses already exceeded McClellan's in the first three engagements of the Seven Days Campaign. Today's fighting would only augment that number.

Because Pope's army was pitifully short of ambulances, the War Department pressed hacks, buckboard wagons, omnibuses, hay wagons, dogcarts, sulkies, and private carriages into service and dispatched them to the battlefield in the charge of civilian teamsters. At the same time, an appeal from Medical Director McParlin appeared in the papers and on hotel bulletin boards: "There is pressing need for the services of surgeons and nurses (male) to attend the wounded of the great battles that have taken place recently. We are requested by the War Department to call for such Volunteers from this point to repair at once to Alexandria, prepared to stay near the scene of action for some days at least." In response, hundreds of volunteers flocked to Haupt's Alexandria headquarters, demanding rail transportation to Manassas. While they waited, they helped themselves to bottles of hard liquor they had brought along as stimulants for the soldiers. By the time Haupt got them on their way at nine that night, they had degenerated into a drunken "rabble." None of them ever made it to the battlefield.

Clara, too, prepared to go to Manassas. She and two female friends spent all Saturday night packing her stores in boxes and barrels. Early Sunday morning, with a torrential rain falling outside, she dashed off a note to David and Julia:

Dear Brother & Sister
I leave immediately for the battlefield. don't know when I can return
If anything happens [to] me you David must come and take all my
effects home with you. Julia will know how to dispose of them.
Love to all
Your affectionate sister
Clara

By then, all Washington knew the terrible truth about the great battle fought at Bull Run on the previous day, Saturday, August 31: Pope had suffered a disastrous defeat at the hands of Lee and Jackson. As a consequence, the capital crawled with rumors of an impending attack. Refugees and escaped slaves reported grotesque sights at Manassas, a surreal landscape of shell fragments, wrecked gun carriages, shattered caissons and wagons, piles of dead horses, and human corpses strewn everywhere and emitting a putrefying gas. Thousands of wounded soldiers still lay on the rain-soaked battlefield. Thousands of others were scattered from an overburdened field hospital to the homes and churches of nearby Centreville, where Pope's army lay, too stricken to fight again. By dawn on Sunday, the field medical service was in chaos, as McParlin reported drastic shortages of surgeons, provisions, and hospital stores. "As I looked over the scene," he said later, "I felt impressed with a sense of how little could be accomplished at this hour."

To make matters worse, the civilian ambulance train, pressed into service on Saturday, had never reached the battlefield. Driven by civilian volunteers, many of whom had fortified themselves generously with liquor, the train got lost after crossing into Virginia and had wandered around half the night before turning up in Alexandria. The War Department ordered it back to Washington in disgust and sent out Medical Inspector Richard Coolidge to evacuate the wounded in whatever conveyances he could find. Coolidge reached Centreville at six on Sunday morning and started moving all the wounded and the field hospital teams southwest to Fairfax Station, on the Orange & Alexandria Railroad, where Haupt's trains could evacuate the wounded, hauling them back to Alexandria and Washington.

By 7:30 that Sunday morning, Clara had her boxes and barrels at the Washington depot, awaiting a train that would take her to Fairfax Station. True, Stanton had called only for male volunteers to help the army, but she ignored the qualification. Nobody had objected to her going to Culpeper, and she anticipated no interference now. In any case, she had her pass from Pope's inspector general tucked in her pocket. Nor was she going to the battlefield alone. In addition to Cornelius Welles, who had returned from Fredericksburg, Clara was accompanied by two new female assistants (Anna Carver was away): a Mrs. Morrell and Almira Fales, the wife of the Patent Office employee who had served on a hospital transport in the Peninsula Campaign. A tall, lean woman with blue eyes and strong arms, Fales told Clara, "I heard you were off for the fighting. I'd like to go with you."

Presently, a train arrived at the depot, and Clara and her assistants loaded her boxes and barrels into a boxcar and then climbed inside, Clara taking a seat on top of the boxes. At last, the train jerked forward in the driving rain, crossed the Long Bridge over the Potomac, roared down to crowded Alexandria, and then headed for Fairfax Station, sixteen miles due west. Inside their closed boxcar, swaying to the motion of the train, Clara and her cohorts had little idea what lay ahead of them. The fighting might well start up again in a tornado of violence that could consume them all. Before she left Washington City, Clara had had such a premonition of doom that she had written Mary Norton a quick note, telling her the same thing she had told David and Julia— "if by any *chance* I should not return, you will know where I *went* at least."

It was midmorning when the train ground to a halt at Fairfax Station. The door to Clara's boxcar slid open, and her co-workers climbed out into a misty drizzle. The opening was too high for Clara, and she had to wait until they fashioned steps out of blocks and empty boxes before she could get down. She stood there, awed by the spectacle in front of her: perhaps 3,000 wounded men lay beside the track and on a thickly wooded hillside, many on beds of hay, others on the wet ground. Surgeons with rolled-up sleeves and bloody aprons worked desperately on the worst wounded, leaving "ghastly heaps of cut off legs and arms" in their wake. Screams of raw pain swept across the assemblage in gusts. As male attendants started loading the wounded into freight cars of the waiting train, a small van of various horse- and mule-drawn vehicles came rolling over the crest of the hill, bringing more wounded from the battlefield, some eight miles to the west. Some of the so-called ambulances were old two-wheeled oxcarts, whose incessant jarring motion aggravated the suffering of their occupants beyond endurance.

Among the surgeons was Dr. Dunn, the tall Pennsylvanian who had admired Clara's work at Culpeper. He had been at Bull Run yesterday, at the large field hospital a mile from the lines, where about twenty surgeons had tried to treat more than 4,000 wounded. They had fled when the army retreated to Centreville, only to find themselves cut off by a rebel battery shelling the road. Dunn and several surgeons hid in the woods while another group pushed ahead. Dunn later heard that they were captured. His group had reached Fairfax Station at dawn and established the "evacuation hospital," such as it was, for there were no tents and no provisions at all. The doctor could barely restrain his joy when he saw Clara Barton standing on the train platform: she had come again to "supply us with bandages, brandy, wine, prepared soup, jellies, meals, and every article that could be thought of."

Clara quickly took stock. She and her colleagues were the only volunteers here. Many of the wounded were dying where they lay for want of care; most had had nothing to eat for days and were crying for food and water. Determined to keep as many alive as possible, Clara ordered a fire built and the food taken from her boxes and barrels. She reprimanded herself for not bringing enough utensils; there were only five tin cups, two water buckets, four bread knives, three plates, one camp kettle, and two lanterns for several thousand men. Next time she would know to equip herself better. She donned an apron, heated a kettle of soup, and waded into the sea of injured men with a pail of steaming liquid on one arm and things to eat in the other. She offered a spoon of soup here, a cracker with preserves there, speaking all the while in a soft, soothing voice. "I never realized until that day how little a human being could be grateful for," she said later.

By necessity, she tended to their wounds, too, functioning for the first time as a battlefield nurse. She was no stranger to disease. She had nursed her brothers and her father when they were ill and had taken care of her consumptive nephew. But nursing men with gunshot wounds, some so hideous it hurt to look at them, had to be learned on the job. And here, at this pitiful way station of damaged humanity, Clara learned. She made compresses and slings, applied tourniquets to bleeding stumps, replaced filthy bandages with fresh ones. She urged gasping men not to die, held their hands and stroked their foreheads, telling them as she had told Irving, "*you must not give up*," perhaps keeping some alive simply by the love in her voice. Yes, Clara loved these stricken soldiers. They were all her boys, and the sight of them—hurt, bleeding, some dying, others half demented with pain—pierced her heart. She realized that whatever she gave them would never be enough.

At one point, she noticed that a young man's chest was exposed through his torn shirt, and she knelt down to cover him. His right arm was terribly mangled. To her surprise, he threw his left arm around her neck and buried his face in her skirt. She took his blackened face in her hands. "Don't you remember me?" he asked. "I am Charley Hamilton who used to carry your satchel home from school."

Of course, she remembered him; he was her "faithful pupil!" Poor Charley, she thought. "That mangled right arm will never carry a satchel again."

As Clara and her colleagues "wept and worked" through the day, the number of wounded around them remained roughly the same. As fast as a freight car was filled on the tracks, another little convoy of wounded would arrive from the battlefield. The soldiers lay so close together, Clara said, that she and her fellow workers could scarcely move without stepping on "some poor mangled fellow" who would groan in pain. They broke open additional bales of hay and scattered it over the ground for the wounded to use as bedding. When night fell, the surgeons and nurses toiled on by the light of a few candles and Clara's two lanterns. They had to be careful, lest someone drop a candle, ignite the hay, and incinerate them all. At one point, it occurred to Clara what a dangerous place they were in. "We were a little band of almost empty handed workers," as she put it later, "literally by ourselves, in the wild woods of Virginia, with 3000 suffering dying men crowded upon the few acres within our reach."

About three in the morning, a surgeon approached Clara with a flickering candle in hand. "Lady," he said, "will you go with me?" As they made their way through the great carpet of wounded men, he explained that a mortally wounded soldier lay on another hill out there, crying for his sister. Several men had gone out to try to help him, but their presence seemed to make him worse. He thought perhaps she could comfort him.

"He can't last half an hour longer," the surgeon said; "he is already quite cold—shot through the abdomen—a terrible wound."

In a moment, Clara could hear him calling out: "Mary! Sister Mary!" Then: "I'm shot—I'm dying." She could see him now, stretched out on the ground, illuminated by the candles of perhaps twenty men. He was just a boy, hardly full grown; his hair was matted and wet, she noticed, and his eyes looked perplexed. Clara motioned the men away and knelt down beside him in the darkness. She kissed his forehead, then lay her cheek against his. She wanted to lie to the boy and say she was Mary, but there was no need. He thought she was Mary anyway. "Mary?" he said. "Have you come? I knew you would come." He added: "Now I'm not afraid to die." Then he ran his hand over Clara's face and through her hair, which had broken free of its fastenings and hung damply at her shoulders. He kissed her hair and thanked her for coming: "Bless you, bless you, Mary."

Clara sat on the ground, wrapped his feet in a blanket she had brought with her, lifted him into her lap, drew her shawl down around his shoulders, and gently rocked him to sleep. The morning found them that way.

When he woke, he seemed puzzled for a moment, then smiled, saying he knew before he opened his eyes that she wasn't Mary. Who was she? he asked. "Simply a lady," Clara said, who had heard he was wounded and had come to care for him. In fact, she was caring for a lot of men down at the railroad station. Would they take the wounded away? he asked. Yes, she said, the first train for Washington was almost ready to leave.

"I *must* go," he said.

"Are you able?" she asked.

Despite his terrible wound, he stood up with her help, saying that he had to get on that train, for he was his mother's only son and he wanted to be taken home, dead or alive. His name was Hugh Johnson, he said, and he was from New York. At his request, Clara wrote her name and a message on a letter from home he had in his pocket. If he died on the train, he said, they wouldn't throw him off and his mother would eventually get his body. But if he died out here in enemy territory, his mother would never find him. "I *must* go," he kept saying, as Clara helped him down to the station.

She laid him down, sought out the surgeon in charge of the train, and begged him to take "my boy" on board.

"Impossible," the surgeon said. "He is mortally wounded and will never reach a hospital—we must take those who have a hope for life."

"But you *must* take him," Clara said.

When the surgeon shook his head again, Clara tried another tack. Could the doctor guarantee that all on that train would live? she asked. "I wish I could," he said sadly. "They are the worst cases, nearly fifty percent must die eventually, of their wounds and hardships."

"Then give this lad his chance with them," Clara said; "he has given me good and sufficient reasons why he must go. And a woman's word for it, Doctor, you must take him."

Finally, he relented and motioned to some attendants. They put that "poor torn boy" on a blanket on the crowded train and gave him food and stimulants. Clara approached one of the attendants, a kindly looking man, and made him promise to take her boy, dead or alive, to the Armory Square Hospital in Washington—a clean new hospital on

Seventh Street, just a few rods on the other side of Pennsylvania Avenue from her apartment. Tell them, she said as the train pulled out, that he was Hugh Johnson from New York and to mark that on his grave.

All that Monday the trains came to carry off the wounded, and the van of oxcarts and wagons kept bringing more from Bull Run. The attendants transferred many of them directly to the freight cars, without giving Clara time to offer them nourishment. If this kept up, she feared that many men would die. Already weak from loss of blood and lack of food, they could not survive the long trip back to Washington without some sustenance. She approached the officers in charge about this "fearful emergency" and persuaded them to detain the ambulances at a certain point so that she could feed the wounded before they went on to the trains. Clara spent the entire day climbing up the wheel of every oxcart and talking to and feeding every wounded man with a spoon and an ever-replenished dish of food. When she ran short of food for the wounded, she and her co-workers gave them the meat from their own sandwiches.

It never occurred to her, she said later, how unladylike it was to be wading through the mud and climbing up on the wheels of wagons. At one point she ducked under six mules—three teams standing side by side—in order to take a flask of brandy to a soldier who had fainted from loss of blood beyond the last wagon. When she mounted the wheel of one cart and peered inside, she recognized with a start the face of another of her former pupils. "*Seven times*! in one train of ambulances I passed this ordeal," she told Mary Norton; "you will not wonder that my heart is sore."

In the afternoon, enemy cavalry appeared in the woods beyond the station, throwing the hospital workers into a panic. They feared a raid at any moment, feared that rebel horsemen would capture them and their suffering charges and send them all to the cruel prisons in and around Richmond. Their fears were not unfounded. Throughout the first year of the war, it was standard practice for both armies to capture and imprison enemy surgeons just like combat officers. In May 1862, Stonewall Jackson sought to end that practice: at the urging of his medical director, Jackson "unconditionally" released eight Union medical officers captured at Winchester, with the understanding that they were to proselytize for the release of rebel surgeons held prisoner in the North. Some time later McClellan and Lee agreed to treat medical personnel as noncombatants, but there was no such agreement between Lee and Pope or between the two rival governments. With the Union waging a harsher war in the summer of 1862, Union non-combatants did not expect the other side to fight with leniency.

All the wounded then in from the field were on a waiting train, and the danger of a calvary raid seemed so great that Almira Fales elected to leave with it, saying that she was only "going for stores." "I begged to be excused from accompanying her," Clara said a few days later, "as the ambulances were up to the field for more and I knew I would never leave a wounded man there if I knew it, though I were taken prisoner 40 times." So Clara remained at this hospital outpost, with the rebel army only a few miles away, and Welles and Mrs. Morrell stayed with her.

At six in the evening, a thunderstorm blew up, darkening the railroad station and the hills beyond. Lightning splintered the sky with peals of thunder. As if in answer, artillery sounded in the direction of Chantilly, six miles to the northwest. Clara and her co-workers heard it again, between claps of thunder: the unmistakable boom of artillery, followed by the rattle of musketry. No doubt about it: a battle had flared up in the storm. It began to rain in torrents, with a gusting wind that drove the rain across Fairfax Station in blinding swirls. The firing in the distance soon stopped, as if both sides lay chastened by the violence from above.

As night closed over Fairfax Station, the hospital team waited anxiously under the storm-tossed trees, fearful that the rebel army might break in upon them at any moment. At some point in the night, the van of ambulances materialized in the almost impenetrable gloom. How it found its way, Clara said, "no man knew." Another train stood on the tracks, ready to receive this latest batch of wounded. By now, Clara's helpers were worn out—they had not slept for thirty-six hours—and could scarcely go on. Mrs. Morrell finally collapsed from exhaustion and fell asleep on a pile of boxes. Driven by a fierce energy, Clara worked on virtually alone. She took army hardtack from the knapsacks of the wounded, pounded the crackers with stones, poured the crumbs into a mixture of whiskey, wine, and water, sweetened it with coarse brown sugar, and fed this concoction to the suffering as they were placed in the freight cars.

The departure of the train cleared off all the wounded for now, and as "the fire from its plunging engines died out in the darkness," Clara said later, "a strange sensation of weakness & weariness fell upon me almost defying my utmost exertion to move one foot before the other." A tent had been pitched for her on the hillside, and she made her way there in the rain, slipping and falling down again and again on the muddy slope. When she finally reached the tent, which was situated on a piece of flat ground, she found the floor covered with water. Too tired to care, she lay down in it, propping herself up with her left arm and resting her head in her left hand to keep the water out of her ears. In that awkward position, she drifted into the first sleep she had since awakening last Saturday morning, more than sixty hours before.

A little more than an hour later the rumble of wagons woke her with a jolt—it was the ambulance train again. Clara wrung the water from her hair and skirts and went forth again to do her work. The rain had stopped now, and the clouds were receding into "a distant corner," as she put it, where the lightning "was playing quietly by itself." The weather was clear and chilly and everything strangely quiet, she recalled, "save the ceaseless rumbling of the never ending train of army wagons, which brought alike the wounded, the dying and the dead."

On Tuesday, soldiers of two supporting divisions from the Potomac Army fell back through the hospital camp on their way to Alexandria. They brought disquieting news. Pope's Army of Virginia had abandoned Centreville and was in full retreat back to Alexandria and Washington. Soldiers, caissons, wagons, ambulances, refugees, escaped slaves—all clogged the Warrentown Turnpike in a mass of confusion. Worse still, rebel cavalry had again been spotted near Fairfax Station. "We knew this was the last," Clara said of the thousand wounded then at the way station. They must load them on the train as fast as possible and get out while they still could. The entire hospital crew pitched in, but lifting a thousand wounded men into boxcars could not be done in a hurry, and tension mounted as time slipped by.

At mid-afternoon, a mounted Union officer galloped up. "Miss Barton," he shouted. "It may be necessary to make a run for it. Can you ride?"

"Yes sir," she said.

"But you have no lady's saddle—could you ride mine?"

"Yes sir," Clara replied, "or without it if you have blanket and surcingle."

"Then you've got about another hour here," the officer said, and rode off.

Indeed, time was running out for the little band of workers at Fairfax Station. When a rebel sniper opened fire on them from the woods, they couldn't tell whether he was a partisan or an advance scout for the regular rebel army. Within the hour, the Union officer came galloping back. "Now is the time," he told Clara. "The enemy is already breaking over the hills—try the train—it will go through unless they have flanked and cut the bridge a mile or so above us. In that case, I have a reserve horse for you and you must take your chances of escape across the country."

At last, the train was ready to move. Mrs. Morrell was already with a group of injured in one of the freight cars. Dr. Dunn and the surgeons climbed into another as the conductor set the station afire so that the enemy could not use it. Clara and Cornelius Welles put the last wounded soldier on the last freight car, then leaped aboard just as the train steamed off. As it rounded a curve, Clara saw rebel cavalry dashing up to the burning station. Had the train been delayed a few minutes, she and Cornelius Welles would have fallen into rebel hands.

The train reached Alexandria at ten o'clock Tuesday night, September 2. At the depot a group of civilians waited with food for the wounded on board. "Oh! the repast which met those poor men at the train," Clara wrote later. "I stood in my car and fed the men till they could eat no more—then the people *would* take *us* home and feed us." After that, Clara made her way to Washington, somehow getting through the bedlam of wagons, caissons, and dispirited soldiers streaming in from the battlefield. Climbing the stairs to her rooms on Seventh Street, she sank into her bed and slept for twenty-four hours. Except for the nap in the flooded tent, she had gone without sleep from Saturday morning until late Tuesday night.

After she awoke, she went to the Armory Square Hospital on the other side of Pennsylvania Avenue, consulted the chaplain's record, and found on the last page the freshly written name, "Hugh Johnson."

"He died during the latter part of last night," the chaplain said. "His mother, sister, and a gentleman reached him some two days ago. They're now taking his body from the ward to be conveyed to the depot." He pointed out a window. Clara saw a coffin being lifted into a wagon; two women were standing beside it. She asked if the dear boy had had "his reason" to the end. Yes, the chaplain said. "And his mother and sister were with him two days?" she asked. Yes, he assured her. "There was no need of me," Clara said, sadly. "He had given his own messages."

Clara took his death like a soldier. Indeed cousin Leander Poor called and found her with "head, heart, and hands full of business, calm, methodical and cheerful." Clara said she felt "well and strong" and was ready to take the field again, whenever the army needed her. She had finally found her niche in the war, which was to "stand by the soldier between the bullet and the city hospital," as she put it later.

On Thursday, September 4, she wrote a long letter to her cousin,

Lizzie Shaver, describing her adventures at Fairfax Station. Since returning to Washington, she had found out what had happened at Chantilly during the thunderstorm. Rebel infantry had tried to flank Pope's battered army, but elements of the Ninth and Third corps had blocked their way. The Twenty-first Massachusetts had fought hard at Chantilly, suffering its worst casualties thus far. "The *Old 21st Mass.* lay between us and the enemy and they *couldn't pass*," Clara told Lizzie. But then she added, "God only knows who is lost." She was, she said, going to the hospitals now to search for her friends. "I have told you nothing of the old friends who met me among the wounded and dying on that bloody field. I have no heart to tell it today, but will some-time. . . . Oh, how I needed stores on that field. Two huge boxes from Jersey arrived today. I don't know where we shall need them next."

As Clara reported to Lizzie, Union forces were "all back again in the old places around the city—McClellan's Army is here again and he is in command of it all." And that he was. The Army of Virginia no longer existed. The War Department had consolidated what remained of it with the Army of the Potomac under McClellan's overall command, and McClellan was already at work reorganizing and disciplining his forces after the disaster of Second Bull Run. In six days of fighting, Pope had lost 16,000 casualties, including some 8,500 wounded—the Union's heaviest losses of any campaign thus far. To make room for the wounded, Surgeon General Hammond ordered 3,000 convalescent soldiers transferred to hospitals in Philadelphia. Even so, the wounded from Second Bull Run filled up all the hospitals in the Washington area and spilled over into the homes of "absent secessionists" in Alexandria. Even the Capitol became a temporary hospital for 2,000 wounded, who lay on cots in the rotunda, the corridors, and the great halls of the Senate and the House.

In the view of Surgeon General Hammond, Medical Inspector Coolidge, Olmsted of the Sanitary Commission, and everybody else with eyes to see, the Medical Department desperately needed an ambulance corps of trained personnel and a transportation system under its control (the ambulances still belonged to the Quartermaster Department). It was insane for the War Department to ignore the shortages of ambulances that had plagued relief efforts at Second Bull Run, or the outrageous behavior of the civilian teamsters hired to drive the vehicles that were available. This sorry and insubordinate lot stole blankets and food, drank up liquor intended for the wounded, and generally ignored their suffering charges in the back of the wagons. On September 7, Hammond sent a report to the War Department complaining bitterly about "the frightful state of disorder existing in the arrangement for removing the wounded from the field of battle. The scarcity of ambulances, the want of organization, the drunkenness and incompetency of the drivers, the total absence of ambulance attendants are now working their legitimate results. . . . The whole system should be under the charge of the Medical Department. An ambulance corps should be organized and set in instant operation."

But Henry Halleck, the current general-in-chief of the army, opposed an independent ambulance corps under the Medical Department, on the grounds that the current system was perfectly adequate, with the Quartermaster Department furnishing the ambulances and drivers. This fast-talking, chain-smoking Phi Beta Kappa objected to any "effeminating comforts" that might spoil the soldiers—even shirts and shoes. He sent Hammond's letter back to him with an emphatic NO scrawled on the back.

At that time, 600 Union wounded still lay on the Bull Run battle-field. An improvised train of hacks, omnibuses, ambulances, and other vehicles retrieved them on September 9—ten days after the battle had ended—and brought them back to Washington by moonlight.

"I am almost discouraged," surgeon Dunn wrote his wife from the National Hotel; "we are now back to where we started last spring, all the blood & treasure of the year lost, a magnificent army destroyed and nothing gained. The prospects look darker to me now than ever."

The prospects looked even darker when Lee's victorious army invaded Maryland, unleashing a late summer offensive that shook the entire North. By September 6, the rebels were near Frederick, and nobody could tell where they were headed—perhaps north into Pennsylvania. With uncustomary belligerence, McClellan ordered his army to march and promised to give "Bobbie Lee" the drubbing of his life. All through Friday and Saturday, soldiers tramped across the bridges into Washington and swung along Pennsylvania Avenue to the steady beat of drums, column after column of blue-coated veterans marching by with bullet-torn flags, their rifled muskets slung across their shoulders, 85,000 of them fanning out westward on various streets and roads. By September 8, the army was moving through Maryland in three parallel columns, with an enormous train of 3,000 wagons strung out for miles behind in a moving cloud of dust. The wagon train carried short rations and enough ammunition and forage for a week of campaigning, but it had few medical stores. Haupt's military trains were to furnish those and other supplies by way of the Baltimore & Ohio Railroad.

Still farther behind rolled a van of 200 ambulances, dispatched by the Quartermaster Department at the request of Jonathan Letterman, the dry, taciturn medical director of the Potomac Army. When McClellan had given the order to march, Letterman had leaped into action, vowing that the horrors of Second Bull Run would not be repeated in this campaign. In addition to requisitioning the ambulances from the quartermaster, he engaged seventy additional volunteer surgeons, requested that huge quantities of medical stores be sent out by rail, and took the field himself in the wake of the advancing army.

In her warehouse command post, Clara too prepared to join the campaign. As she said later, the terrible suffering at Fairfax Station had taught her "the folly and wickedness of remaining quietly at home" until the papers reported that a battle had been fought and that thousands of wounded needed medical care. This time, she intended to be *with* the army when it engaged the enemy, to have her stores where they were needed the most: on the battlefield itself.

All night September 9 she unpacked boxes of supplies from her supporters and arranged specific items for the field. As it turned out, she had immediate use for the two large boxes from New Jersey. Six others had arrived from the mayor of Worcester; her trip through New Jersey and Massachusetts in July was paying excellent dividends. But the unthinkable delayed Clara's departure. She felt weak and feverish and feared it was typhoid, perhaps contracted during her visits to the hospitals. She fought the fever with home remedies, soups and teas, and the sheer power of her will. She was determined not to get sick, vowing *I will not stay behind for this*.

On Saturday night, September 13, a messenger brought her a slip of paper from an anonymous friend in the army, who provided her with privileged information (she never revealed his name). *"Harper's Ferry,"* the note read, *"not a moment to be lost."* Earlier that Saturday, McClellan had come across a copy of Lee's marching orders, which revealed that he had divided his army and that a portion of it was closing in on the Union garrison at Harpers Ferry. McClellan had wired Washington in a burst of joy: "I have all the plans of the Rebels and will catch them in their own trap." He informed a subordinate that he intended to "cut the enemy in two & beat him in detail."

Clara must hurry if she was to reach the army before it started fighting. Ignoring her feverish condition, she rushed to Colonel Rucker's office—this "kindly" man had now become her "patron saint" in the army—and asked him for a wagon and permission to go to Harpers Ferry. He granted her that permission and promised to send her an army wagon and a team the next morning. But he cautioned Clara against taking female assistants with her. He had said this before, arguing that "no woman could stand what she could" and would become a burden. That contention overlooked the great physical stamina displayed by the women of the hospital transport service. Even so, Clara's experience at Fairfax Station inclined her to agree with the colonel. Almira Fales had deserted her, after all, and Mrs. Morrell had collapsed from exhaustion. This time, Clara would take only Welles and the driver Rucker assigned her.

The next morning, just as Rucker promised, a teamster called for Clara in a large covered wagon pulled by six mules. Welles was there, too, and they loaded up Clara's boxes, bags, and parcels, all carefully packed with everything from alcoholic stimulants, bandages, and dressing, to a grocery-store variety of pickled and canned foods and a large quantity of candle lanterns. Clara had not forgotten the harrowing experience with the naked candles and the hay at Fairfax Station. Dressed in her battlefield uniform, she climbed into the wagon seat with Welles, and the driver set the mules in motion. It was Sunday, and couples on their way to church saw a small, restless, bonneted woman ride by in a white-topped army wagon, sitting between a stout teamster and a serene-looking man.

They rode out of Washington on the route taken by McClellan and the Second and Twelfth Army corps, heading for Frederick, some forty miles northwest in rural Maryland. In Rockville and other villages along the way, Clara purchased a considerable quantity of fresh bread. When night fell, they camped in an open field, Clara sleeping in the wagon and the men in their blankets nearby. During the night, the distinct rumble of artillery kept waking her. It came from the west, in the direction of Catoctin and South mountains. Perhaps McClellan had already overtaken the rear of Lee's divided army. Clara would have to move faster on the morrow.

She had her crew up, breakfasted, and on the road before daylight. Their route took them through Hyattstown and Urbana, across the Monocacy River, and into Frederick. Here they learned that elements of the two armies had fought a battle on South Mountain yesterday and last night—this accounted for the artillery that had kept Clara awake—

and that the enemy had been driven from the field. Indeed, McClellan claimed "a glorious victory," and his Army of the Potomac was now pushing through the passes in pursuit of the retreating rebels. Meanwhile, Letterman's 200 ambulances had caught up with the army and were now conveying the wounded—some 1,800 of them—to field hospitals established by the medical director in and around Middletown, west of Frederick.

Clara also heard that the Confederates had wrecked the railroad bridge across the Monocacy River three miles south of Frederick, causing a monumental traffic jam, with civilian and army supply trains backed up for twenty miles. In addition to commissary and quartermaster supplies, Letterman's medical stores were on those trains. Now there was even more urgent need for Clara's supplies. As she pressed through Frederick, however, army hospital stewards stopped her and demanded all her bread for the wounded brought in from South Mountain. They had "orders," they asserted, to confiscate all the bread they could find. "I told them," Clara wrote Mary Norton later, "I was ashamed of both them and their order, they were on the R.R. had flour, ovens and people, go to work and *make* bread—hide that lazy order, and stop no mouthful of bread [from] going to the fainting men on the field." Clara added: "They did not get my bread."

From Frederick, Clara's party took the National Road west across Cactoctin Mountain and into a golden valley. When they reached Middletown, they stopped briefly at a roadside church and found it full of wounded men from South Mountain, which loomed in the west; they were "stretched on boards placed on the tops of the pews and covered with straw," as Clara said later. On their way again, heading for Turner's Gap in South Mountain, her party soon overtook "a solid moving mass" of covered supply wagons rolling along in the rear of McClellan's army, stirring up columns of dust as far as the eye could see. Following the huge supply train, they passed groups of sick and wounded Union soldiers lying by the roadside; the sight of those "pale haggard wrecks" moved Clara so much that she handed them slices of her bread. They told her that the hardest fighting the previous day had taken place at Turner's Gap—the road would pass right through it— and that General Jesse L. Reno had been killed. The Twenty-first Massachusetts was part of his division. God knew how many of Clara's boys lay dead up there.

When Clara reached the mountain pass, she gazed over an actual battlefield for the first time in her life. Along the roadside and wooded fields lay "a mingled mass of stiffened, blackened men," she wrote later, "horses, muskets, bayonets, knapsacks, haversacks, blankets, coats, canteens, broken wheels and cannon balls which had done this deadly work—the very earth plowed with shot." Bodies lay so thick that the wagon actually ran over some of them. "Shocked and sick at heart," Clara ordered the wagon to stop, and she and Welles climbed down and walked over the battlefield, searching, she said, for "some poor wretch in whom life had still left the power to suffer." They found nobody alive save for some civilians digging graves. It seemed to Clara that the sights at Turner's Gap moved the very trees to weep, for she saw drops of dew fall on the torn bodies beneath them.

She could take comfort from one thing, though. Since all the wounded had been cleared from the field, Letterman's ambulances were operating with an efficiency unprecedented thus far in the war.

Just as Clara and Welles returned to their wagon, they noticed a large drove of army cattle moving up the road. The officer in charge rode up to the party, exchanged introductions, and told Clara: "That house on the lower side of the road under the hill has been taken as a Confederate Hospital and is full of wounded rebels. Their surgeons have come out and asked me for meat—saying that the men will die for lack of animal food. I am a bonded officer and responsible for the property under my charge—what can I do?"

As much as she hated treason and opposed the Confederacy, her instincts were to help the suffering, regardless of which uniform they wore. "You can do nothing," she told the officer, "but ride on ahead. I am neither bonded nor responsible."

After he left, Clara spotted a big white ox that had strayed from the herd. She ordered her men to drive the animal to the rebel hospital and leave it there without a word. "The last I saw of the white ox," she remembered, "he had gone completely over to the enemy and was reveling in the tall grass about the house."

Clara's party set out again, heading down the western side of South Mountain in the wake of the wagon train. She was appalled at the growing number of stragglers they passed. She feared it meant that the Army of the Potomac lacked the confidence and spirit to destroy Lee's forces once and for all. From what the laggards told her, the army had swung left at Boonsboro and was marching on Sharpsburg some six miles to the south, near the Potomac River. There were reports that one force of rebels had captured Harpers Ferry and that the rest of Lee's army was drawn up in a defensive line at Sharpsburg, waiting to give battle.

That afternoon, Clara could hear artillery fire off to the south, and she urged her team on lest the battle start without her. Yet it was impossible to get around the huge train in their front. Every time they tried to pass the rear wagons, they were crowded into the ditch. Clara knew that the supply train, to avoid capture, would stay far in the rear once the fighting began. Her mission was "to bridge that chasm" between the supply wagons and the battlefield, to be there with her stores *when* her boys were fighting and dying. Yet unless she did something drastic, she would be trapped in the rear with the train.

Now was the time to test the mettle of her two male helpers. After the wagon train pulled over for the night, Clara allowed her men a few hours of rest. At one o'clock in the morning—it was now September 16—she roused and fed them and pressed her wagon forward for the rest of the night, passing ten miles of parked vehicles. By dawn, they were up with the horse-drawn artillery, heading along the Boonsboro Turnpike toward Sharpsburg. Twelve hours later, they finally reached the army, which was spread out south and north of the turnpike.

As it turned out, McClellan had fought no battle yet. Convinced that the rebels at Sharpsburg outnumbered him, he'd decided against attacking until the bulk of his infantry and artillery were up. To his soldiers, it did seem as though Lee's entire army was deployed in front of the town, for thousands of rebel campfires glowed menacingly in the night.

Moving along a narrow back road, past the smoke of countless Union campfires, Clara found Burnside's Ninth Corps, including the Twenty-first Massachusetts, bivouacked on the left side of the Union line, in a hollow near a little creek called Antietam. The air was "soggy" and difficult to breathe, she said later; "it was all used & made fetid by this press of human beings & animals." As her helpers prepared for the night, she felt an "impending sense of doom" hanging over the encampment. Everyone here thought the fighting would begin at dawn, and their campfire talk was subdued. Tired and feverish, Clara prayed for strength to meet the "terrible duties" ahead. As far as she knew, she was the only woman in this vast assemblage of men. Tomorrow she would go into battle with them—she would "see the Elephant," as the soldiers called the experience of combat—and she might well be killed. She hoped she would be brave like her father, and if she were killed, it was a price she gladly paid for the salvation of her country.

During the night, it started to rain. Inside her wagon, with a blanket pulled around her, Clara awaited the dawn.

*   *   *

At 3 A.M., September 17, intermittent firing broke out somewhere along the line. Aroused by the gunfire, Clara left the wagon and climbed to the top of a nearby hill, where she peered into the gloom through her field glass. The rain soon stopped, but it was too dark and misty to see anything. There it was again—firing off to her right. Had she seen the flashes of guns in the blackness? The wait for dawn was interminable. Even with the first perceptible gray of light, it was hard to see anything because of the accursed mist. Suddenly, a cannon boomed somewhere. Then artillery of both sides exploded into action with thunderous salvoes. Along the heights to Clara's right, seventy-five Union field pieces belched fire and smoke: twelve-pounder brass Napoleons, three-inch ordnance rifles, and huge twenty-pounder Parrott rifles, all hurling projectiles at rebel positions. Clara had never experienced such violence. The concussions of the guns deafened her. Shells and solid shot shrieked and hummed overhead and struck with such force that the ground trembled. Now the musketry was picking up, too, and coming from the far right of the Union line, held by General Joseph Hooker's First Corps. *There*, Clara told herself, *that is where the battle is beginning. There I'll be needed first.*

She raced back to her wagon. Welles and her driver were up and ready to go. They took a narrow lane that wound steeply up from the hollow to the crest of a wooded height, from which Clara, peering through her glass, could make out the spires of Sharpsburg and the crackling fire of musketry and flashes of cannon along the Hagerstown Pike to the north. The sun was burning off the mist now, and a little church was visible west of the road, standing out sharp and white against the trees. The battle lines appeared to reach from north of the church back across undulating fields all the way to Antietam Creek southeast of town. Right now, all the fighting was going on beyond that church, in stands of timber east of the Hagerstown Pike.

How to get over there? Clara must have acquired a map, because her party took a back road off the Boonsboro Turnpike—this was the Keedysville Road—that led across the Antietam at an upper stone bridge and wound past numerous farms in the woods northeast of Sharpsburg. At some point, they linked up with an infantry column on the way to support Hooker and followed it down a crude lane called the Smoketown Road, which led south toward the fighting. Soon they encountered groups of walking wounded heading for the rear. Most of them belonged to Mansfield's Twelfth Corps, which had gone forward to reinforce Hooker. Old General Mansfield had been shot in the stomach—a mortal wound—and carried to the rear, and Hooker, too, had been wounded and taken from the field. According to the injured men filing past Clara's wagon, chaos reigned on the battlefield ahead. Hooker's corps had been shattered in a wild, ferocious fight in a cornfield and the woods around it, and the Twelfth Corps was barely holding on with the help of a powerful line of artillery, which stretched from the Hagerstown Pike eastward across the Smoketown Road. Surgeons had converted farmhouses, barns, and other dwellings into field hospitals, and stretcher-bearers had plunged into the Cornfield and the East and West Woods—the names given to the morning's battleground—where 8,000 dead and wounded Federals lay in blasted heaps.

Around 9:00 A.M., Clara's party came to an old barn partially hidden in a cornfield just northeast of the main battleground. Driving through the tall corn, they found some 300 wounded men lying around the barn, too injured to move. "Here is where we are needed," Clara said, and she had her men unhitch the mules and unload her supplies. A quick look around told her that they were virtually on the frontlines: she could see a Union battery on a hill perhaps an eighth of a mile away, with Federal infantry standing under the cover of the guns as if anticipating a rebel attack. Beyond the trees to the south, the battle had flared up again. Clara could hear men screaming over the roar of gunfire.

Soon more wounded arrived at the old barn in the cornfield. "We were entirely surrounded," Welles said, "by those whose wounds were of the most ghastly and dangerous character, legs and arms off, and all manner of gaping wounds from shell and minnie balls." Clara looked about for the surgeons. Were there no surgeons here to treat these men? Her teamster found a farmhouse hidden in the corn and ran back to tell Clara that "they are there, the tables and surgeons." Grabbing an armload of stimulants and linen bandages, she made her way to an old stone dwelling, with an upper story and a broad veranda. Later identified as the rented farmhouse of one Sam Poffenberger, it was situated in "a slight hollow," Clara remembered, "under the lee of a hill," which sheltered the bottom floor from enemy shells and bullets.

To her surprise, Dr. James Dunn was standing in the dooryard; he was absolutely amazed to see her. "God has indeed remembered us," he said. "How did you get from Virginia here? So soon? And again to supply our necessities!" At seven that morning, the doctor had gone into battle with his brigade, which belonged to General George S.

Greene's division of the Twelfth Corps. The brigade had crossed the Smoketown Road and tramped through the nearby fields, only to collide with a line of rebels in the East Woods. Dunn and another surgeon had taken refuge behind this knoll and with other medical personnel had transformed the old farmhouse into a field hospital to treat the wounded from the Twelfth and the First corps.

They were in dire straits, he told Clara. "We have nothing but our instruments and the little chloroform we brought in our pockets. I have torn up the last sheets we could find in this house, have not a bandage, rag, lint or string. And all these wounded men bleeding to death."

"See here," he said, and he led Clara to the porch, where surgeons were operating on four chloroformed soldiers lying on makeshift operating tables, with an inevitable pile of arms and legs nearby. The soldiers' raw wounds were bandaged with corn leaves. "That is how desperate we are," Dunn said. Clara set her supplies down and replaced the corn leaves with linen, thinking that "never before had linen looked so white or wine so red."

The farmhouse was full of wounded men awaiting operations, and Clara set about comforting them with single-minded intensity. She "toiled as few men could have done," said one witness, "stanching wounds which might otherwise have proved fatal, administering cordials to the fainting soldier, cheering those destined to undergo amputation, moistening lips parched with thirst," and closing the eyes of the dead.

The farmhouse was so close to the battle lines that it was under fire much of the time. Rebel shells burst overhead, crashed into the surrounding trees, even exploded among the wounded men and soldier-nurses outside the barn. Stray bullets struck the upper floor of the old farmhouse so often that it was soon riddled with holes. Oblivious of the shells and bullets, Clara worked on sheer adrenaline, now at the farmhouse, now back at the barn where so many of the wounded had already died. In the yard, a man lying on the ground asked her for a drink of water. As she raised his head with her right hand and held the cup to his lips with the other, she felt a sudden twitch of the loose sleeve on her right arm; the soldier sprang from her hand and fell back, quivering. A bullet had ripped through her sleeve and struck him in the chest, killing him instantly. Clara was so profoundly shaken that she would never mend the hole in her dress.

Assisted by a dozen soldiers, who had volunteered their help, Clara and Welles moved as many wounded as possible inside the barn, so as to protect them from random shots. Just outside the barn door, a young man pulled at Clara's skirt. He had been shot in the cheek—the bullet was lodged there—and it burned so badly he couldn't stand it. She started to go for a surgeon but he said no, he would have to wait his turn for such a minor wound, and he begged Clara to cut the bullet out herself. She shrank from doing that. She had never severed human flesh before, she said, and anyway it would hurt him too much.

"You can't hurt me," he insisted. "I can endure any pain your hands can create."

Reluctantly, Clara took out her pocket knife. As she did so, another wounded man, an orderly sergeant shot through both thighs, raised himself with a desperate effort and dragged himself over to Clara. He said, "I will help do that," and held the young man's head in his hands while Clara cut the bullet out of his cheek, then washed and dressed the wound. "I do not suppose a surgeon would have pronounced it a scientific operation," she said later, "but that it was *successful* I dared to hope from the gratitude of my patient."

When Clara returned to the barn a little later, the orderly sergeant was weeping. Had his exertion been too much for him? she asked. "Oh no, no, madam," he said. "It is not for myself." He pointed to another wounded fellow just brought in. "This man is my comrade, and he tells me that our regiment is all cut to pieces, that my captain was the last officer left, and he is dead." He muttered, "God: what a costly war."

By late morning, "a savage continual thunder" sounded beyond the trees south of the Poffenberger farm. Some 1,800 yards away, at a sunken road between the Hagerstown Pike and Antietam Creek, two Yankee divisions battled rebel infantry and artillery in an inferno of violence that sucked everything into it for hundreds of yards around. On that grim battleground, solid shot gouged holes in the land; horses without mounts came bounding out of the smoke; long columns of foot soldiers swayed back and forth in deadly combat, their muskets blazing and clanging, their screams wavering in the wind. Smoke and dust swirled up from the struggling mass until it obscured the sun.

The fighting that morning produced so many wounded that virtually every farmhouse, barn, shed, corn crib, and manger along the entire Union line was bursting with them. All the improvised hospitals suffered shortages of food and medical supplies save the one at Sam Poffenberger's farm where Clara Barton had come. By early afternoon, the line of wounded around the Poffenberger farm "stretched out for five miles," Clara said later, and her food supplies were running out.

When her helpers reported that their bread and crackers were gone, Clara said, "Open the wine and give them that. And God help us." The first nine boxes of wine were packed in sawdust. But to Clara's astonishment, the last three boxes contained sifted cornmeal. In the damp stone kitchen at the rear of the farmhouse, she found a large kettle, built a fire, and made cornmeal gruel, which her men and the soldier-assistants distributed to the wounded. When that was gone, Clara and her companions searched the cellar and found three barrels of Indian meal and a bag of salt with the mark of the rebel army on them. They carried the confiscated provisions back up to the kitchen, where Clara made "gruel, gruel, gruel." By then, her hair was disheveled and her face covered with soot and dirt. Yet the men deferred to her as they would to a superior officer, as she handed them bowls of gruel for the long line of wounded outside. Among them were "quite a number" of injured Confederate officers who had been captured. "They were amazed at the kindness of northerners," Welles said a few days later, "particularly at a Massachusetts lady devoting herself to them as freely as to her own neighbors."

By noon, the fighting had died out in this sector of the field. The battle appeared to have shifted southward to Burnside's front at the Lower Bridge. During the afternoon, the medical director of the Twelfth Corps reassigned Dr. Dunn to another hospital. His departure left only a chief surgeon and a handful of assistant surgeons and male nurses at the Sam Poffenberger farm. Because none of the surgeons was available, Welles himself had to operate on one young man, hardly more than a boy; a bullet had shattered his right leg below the thigh and lodged in his other leg. Almost delirious with pain, he begged Welles to extract the ball, and Welles did so. "I wish I could pay you," the lad said. "I cannot, but God can—God *will*."

About 4:00 P.M., rebel artillery opened a fierce cannonade on the Union right, perhaps to clear the way for an infantry attack. Clara was in the Poffenberger farmhouse when the salvoes began. Shot and shell rained down on the federal artillery position nearby and struck all around the farmhouse, too, in a hurricane of noise that made the ground shake. Within moments thirty-four Federal guns opened up in response. It was "the most terrific artillery duel I ever heard," Clara said later. "The tables jarred and rolled until we could hardly keep the men on them." One barrage was so terrifying that all the male doctors and nurses ran away except the chief surgeon, who was attempting an operation at one of the tables.

Clara shouted over the noise: "Can I assist you?"

"Can you stand it?"

"Oh, yes," she assured him proudly.

In the midst of that "frightful firing," Clara chloroformed the wounded soldier and held him and the table securely while the surgeon completed the operation. But "the smoke became so dense," she recalled, "as to obscure our sight and the hot sulphurous breath of battle dried our tongues, and parched our lips to bleeding."

Soon the rebel cannons stopped firing—silenced by the superior firepower of the Union guns—and this part of the field fell strangely quiet. The battle raged on at the other end of the field, where Burnside's Ninth Corps had finally got across the Lower Bridge and had advanced against Sharpsburg itself, only to be struck by rebel reinforcements from Harpers Ferry and swept back to Antietam Creek. By 4:30 or 5:00 P.M., the battle was over, fought to a draw, with both armies hemorrhaging where they lay, too battered to continue. The sun shone "blood-red" over the smoking battlefield, where some 12,400 Yankees and 10,300 rebels had been killed, wounded, or captured in what would go down as the bloodiest single day of combat in American military history.

At the Sam Poffenberger farmhouse, the chief surgeon was still operating in the waning light. Although his male assistants had returned now, it was Clara who toiled at his side, with her ears ringing, her mouth tasting of gunpowder, and her hands raw. She was proud that she had stood her ground during the cannonade while all the male assistants had run away. So much for the popular belief that a woman would only "be in the way" on the battlefield, would faint at the first sight of blood, and would flee from gunfire with her skirts fluttering. That she had disproved that notion gave Clara great satisfaction.

When night fell, Clara went down to the barn and had her lanterns lit and hung inside, so that Welles and her men could see as they tended the wounded there. Then she returned to the farmhouse, where she found the chief surgeon in a "dark, dank" room, sitting at a table where a single candle burned. His head rested on his hand.

Clara put her hand on his shoulder. "You are tired, Doctor?"

"Tired!" he said, raising his head. "Yes, I am tired—tired of such heartlessness, such neglect and folly. Here are at least 1000 wounded men—terribly wounded, 500 of whom cannot live till day light without attention, and that 2 inches of candle is all the light I have or can get—what can I do?" The doctor lay his head back on his hand.

"Get up, Doctor," Clara said. "I want to show you something." She took him by the arm and led him to the door, pointing in the direction of the barn, where candle lanterns glowed in the waving corn.

The doctor couldn't believe his eyes. "*What is that?*"

"Lanterns," Clara said. "I brought 4 boxes of them. The men will be here in a few moments to light the house. You will have plenty of light. Don't despair in your good work, Doctor."

He stared at her, too dumbfounded to speak. Soon Clara's lanterns lit up every room in the farmhouse; they hung on the veranda, sat on the stone fence in the yard, hung over mangers and corn cribs, illuminating every place where the surgeons and soldiers were ministering to the wounded. Throughout that long night, Clara assisted the chief surgeon as he operated on soldiers, removing bullets and cutting off limbs; he was so busy he never did thank her for the lanterns.

Meanwhile Welles and her soldier-volunteers, thirty of them now, walked down the long line of wounded outside, feeding them from buckets of warm gruel. "We could not think of rest," Welles remembered, "for all around us were dying men, calling for water, for friends, for God to deliver them from their miseries; some of them with the whole thigh shot off, some with both arms off, some with bullet[s] through their chest."

At dawn, Clara and Welles checked on the hundreds of wounded they had been feeding. Welles said that almost half of them had died during the night. They went on to the battlefield itself, to the woodlots and the infamous Cornfield, which looked as though it had been struck by "a storm of bloody hail," as one soldier said. It was only now, as they gazed over the battlefield, that Clara and Welles learned what "a fearful cost" the Union army had paid at Antietam. A multitude of corpses were becoming black and bloated under the sun; many were mangled beyond recognition as human. Here and there in the rubble lay disembodied heads, their eyes eaten out by maggots and flies. "There are hundreds of horses too," a Connecticut soldier wrote, "all mangled and putrefying, scattered everywhere! Then there are the broken gun-carriages, and wagons, and thousands of muskets, and all sorts of equipments, the clothing all torn and bloody, and cartridges and cannon-shot, and pieces of shell, the trees torn with shot and scarred with bullets, the farm-houses and barns knocked to pieces and burned down, the crops tramped and wasted, the whole country forlorn and desolate."

The two armies agreed to a temporary truce so that they could clear the wounded and bury the dead. In all directions, burial details began their grisly work, piling corpses in carts and putting them in crude

graves. Already the smell was unbearable, and some of the men vomit-
ed as they collected the bodies. Here and there, Welles said, "a dozen
of the same company" were "laid in a row together, to be buried on the
field side by side." He and Clara walked over to the rebel side of the
field, which was "heart-sickening," Welles recalled, "but little seemed
to be done towards gathering them up for burial. The rebels whom we
saw were, without exception, the most forlorn, wretched, hungry-look-
ing beings we ever saw. The appearance of all, both officers and men,
was uniformly ragged and dirty, many barefooted, some bareheaded,
and all with *dirty shirts.*"

While Union workers buried their dead, Letterman's ambulances
were gathering up the wounded remaining on the field. By nightfall,
all of them would be in, a testament to the efficiency of the Letterman
system. The medical director had seen to it that each division had an
ambulance train, with an officer in command who answered to him.
Each ambulance team consisted of a driver and two soldiers chosen by
the Medical Department and drilled by specially selected line officers.
Although the number of ambulances had swelled to about 300 by late
arrivals, they were too few to transport nearly 10,000 wounded back to
larger evacuation hospitals in the rear, from which they would be sent
to Washington, Baltimore, Philadelphia, and other cities. Even so, the
Union field service would remove the wounded from Antietam far
faster than from any previous battlefield.

Having roamed over the entire field, Clara and Welles returned to
the Sam Poffenberger farm and girded themselves for another day of
killing. But neither army fired a shot that day. McClellan, still convinced that Lee outnumbered him (it was actually the other way
around), issued orders for his army to hold the ground it occupied. The
general might have won a victory the previous day had he not held an
entire corps in reserve in case he had to retreat. Now he seemed determined to lose whatever opportunity remained to destroy Lee's army,
and bitterness and disappointment spread through the Union ranks.
On September 19, with McClellan doing nothing to stop him, Lee
evacuated Sharpsburg and slipped across the Potomac into Virginia. "If
we had followed up our victory on the next day," Dr. Dunn wrote his
wife, "there would have been no southern army for we would have
killed or captured the whole of them. Why this was allowed McClellan
only knows."

As far as Dunn was concerned, Clara Barton had performed her
duties at Antietam better than McClellan had performed his. She had

supplied one of the Union's seventy-one field hospitals herself and had functioned brilliantly as an independent battlefield nurse. Clara was probably the only Northern female nurse and relief worker who served on the battleground itself, tending to troops under enemy fire. Her courage challenged received notions of military heroism, which conjured up an armed male leading a glorious charge or demonstrating uncommon valor in killing the enemy. Like Dunn and the other surgeons she assisted, Clara showed a different kind of courage, unarmed courage, in the hell of combat. As armed men set about killing and maiming one another, Clara tried to save lives, to help put smashed bodies back together, with no weapons but her hands and a soothing voice. She brought compassion and love to the rage and hatred of battle. "In my feeble estimation," Dunn wrote his wife, "Gen. McClellan, with all his laurels, sinks into insignificance beside" Clara Barton. Dunn thought her "the true heroine of the age, *the angel of the battlefield.*"

A day or so after the battle, Clara was making soup at one of the other farmhouse hospitals, with her sleeves rolled up and the bottom of her skirt raised and pinned about her waist, when a Wisconsin surgeon sought her out. He gave his name as F. H. Harwood and said he had "a peculiar case" that demanded a "woman's work." Leaning close to Clara, he whispered that he had just spoken to a wounded girl lying in an open shed hospital down the road; she was wearing a Union uniform, was shot in the neck, and was a little frantic, wild really, and wouldn't let him or any other man touch her. Could Clara help?

With one hand raised above her face and the other trying to undo the pin at her back, Clara replied with a single word. "What?"

"Yes," he said, "a girl, if there's any truth in signs and words combined."

Clara instructed Harwood to bring the girl to Clara's covered wagon, which was parked down the lane. When he and some soldiers did so, Clara spoke to the young woman, who was hardly more than sixteen. She gave her name as Mary Hartwell, though she was called Mary Galloway, after her stepfather. It was easy to see how Mary could be mistaken for a young man. She was dressed in a blue uniform, had a slender figure, and wore her hair cut short. She spoke in a clear, musical voice, her blue eyes wide with fright, for she was terrified that she was going to die. Clara spoke softly to her as she examined the wound in her neck and looked at her back. Then Clara climbed out of the wagon and summoned Dr. Harwood with a frown. She, too, was afraid that Mary would die.

"The ball has gone into the upper part of the chest and hasn't come out," Clara said, "but come in and see for yourself. She is composed and quiet now."

Inside the wagon, Mary lay with blankets and pillows under her back and head. "I suspect," Clara said, "the left arm is a little stiff from the effects of the ball which, you see, has penetrated just here, a little to the left side of the neck." Sure enough, Harwood found a "little round, blue-dyed hole, with the lips turned in, not a particle torn, a puncture."

He asked Clara, "Have you examined the back?"

"I have," she said, "but there is no bruise or discoloration; only a slight swelling."

Harwood turned Mary over and found the swelling near the inner border of her right shoulder blade. He thought it a miracle that the bullet had passed from the left side of her neck to the right side of her back without "cutting some vital organ" and killing her instantly. He told Mary he must operate at once, even though he hadn't an ounce of chloroform.

"Will I die, doctor?" she asked.

It was a wonder she wasn't dead already, he replied. "Now listen: The ball lies just under the skin on your back, and, with a very small cut, which you will scarcely feel, it will almost pop out like shelling peas." It wasn't that simple. When Harwood opened her flesh with his scalpel, he found that the bullet had severed a small fragment of her rib bone. "A little re-adjustment of the forceps," he said later, "and I was in possession of both ball and fragment of bone." If she cried out from the pain, he did not record it.

Later, when the two women were alone, Mary told her story in full. Evidently Clara relayed it to surgeon Harwood, who later published the story—and Clara's role in it—in his own account of Antietam. A resident of Frederick, Maryland, Mary had come to Antietam looking for her lover, a young lieutenant in the Third Wisconsin named Harry Barnard. They had first met when his regiment had occupied Frederick in the fall of 1861. The regimental officers had billeted in Mary's house, and she and the young lieutenant had fallen in love. Later, when the Third Wisconsin came through Frederick at the start of the Antietam campaign, Mary and young Barnard spent a few fleeting hours alone together. Then he marched away with his regiment, heading for South Mountain and Antietam. Frantic with grief and long-ing, Mary searched through her stepfather's storeroom—he was "a sporting man," a gambler and swindler—and she found a box full of Union uniforms. Donning one of them, she left that night and caught up with the rear of the Potomac Army, asking everyone she passed where the Third Wisconsin might be. Finally, claiming to be the regi-ment's hospital steward, she attached herself to an ambulance in the army's ambulance train and rode across South Mountain after the bat-tle there. At Antietam on the day of the battle, Mary somehow linked up with General William F. "Baldy" Smith's division as it moved to the right of the Union line. All that violent morning, she ran from unit to unit asking about the Third Wisconsin. She crossed the Hagerstown Pike when the rebels opened their last artillery bombardment on that end of the field. With guns thundering nearby, Mary crouched behind a fallen tree in "a bushy hollow." When she raised her head, a bullet struck her cleanly in the neck. She crawled farther down into the ravine and into some sheltering shrubs, where she lay more than thir-ty-six hours before Union soldiers found her. Believing her a wounded infantryman, they brought her to a farmhouse hospital on the Union right, leaving her in the open shed where Dr. Harwood found her.

Clara looked after Mary until she was well enough to be taken back to Frederick. The young woman was quite beside herself, since neither of them had found out anything about the fate of Harry Barnard. Whether he was dead or alive, no one seemed to know.

On September 18, the day after the battle, William Platt, Jr., arrived with the first of several supply trains sent out by the U.S. Sanitary Commission. Two days later the railroad bridge over the Monocacy River was finally repaired and the army stores were on their way as well. Meanwhile other men and women volunteers reached Antietam, some to nurse the wounded, others to give out their own supplies. Mary W. Lee of the Philadelphia Refreshment Saloon was there, dis-tributing home-made apple dumplings. Mrs. Lee appears to have reached the rear of the army the night before the battle—the same time Clara did—having ridden in with the Seventy-second Pennsylvania. The next day, she stationed herself on the Boonsboro Turnpike, behind the lines, and handed out bread and cups of water to the walking wounded streaming back from the battlefield. Eliza Harris, of hospital transport fame, arrived at Antietam the day after the

battle and worked with four other women in an evacuation hospital at
Smoketown. And Anna Holstein of Montgomery County, Pennsylvania,
came to Antietam with her husband, after a long struggle with her conscience. Her experience paralleled Clara's. When the war began, she
had felt "an uncontrollable impulse *to do*, to act; for *anything* but idle-
ness when our country was in peril." Her chance came when her husband and six women from her neighborhood headed for Antietam to
help care for the wounded. "But craven-like," she said, "I shrank
instinctively from such scenes, and declined to join the party." When
her husband returned and related how badly the soldiers were suffering, Anna threw off her constraints, helped collect "a car load of boxes,
containing comforts and delicacies for the wounded," and took them to
the battlefield. Like Clara, Anna Holstein experienced an epiphany in
the field that changed her life. "The *first* wounded and the *first* hospitals I saw I shall never forget, for then flashed across my mind, '*This* is
the work God has given you to do,' and the vow was made, 'While the
war lasts we stand pledged to aid, as far as in our power, the sick and
suffering. *We* have no *right* to the comforts of *our* home, while so many
of the noblest of our land so willingly renounce theirs.'"

With her own supplies depleted and so many other volunteers on
hand, Clara no longer felt needed. Worn down from work and lack of
sleep, she succumbed at last to the typhoid fever she had held at
bay. Her assistants fashioned a bed out of an old coverlet in the bottom of the wagon, and Clara lay there, desperately sick, as they set
out for Washington. All she remembered about the trip was that the
wagon "jogged" her for eighty miles. When she got home and looked
in the mirror, her face, she said, "was the color of gunpowder, a deep
blue."

For days she languished in her room. "Have I told you how sick I
am?" she managed to write Mary Norton. "A typhoid fever has been
staring me in the face for the last two weeks, and I have fought it as the
most desperate enemy I could have, and I trust to compel a surrender,
but I scarce know myself. I am from 15 to 20 lbs less than when you
saw me—but I shall regain that again when I can eat once more. . . .
When I think what I have been through I wonder that I have as much
strength as I have, but I shall never fail while this war lasts—my
strength will be as my day, and I shall be able to serve faithfully to the
end—To meet and cross and work at every Battlefield from Cedar
Mountain to Sharpsburg is no light labor and I should be ungrateful to
complain if my strength failed a little sometimes but it is only for a little, in two weeks I shall be strong and well as ever."

*   *   *

While Clara convalesced, the war took a dramatic new turn. On September 22, Lincoln issued the Preliminary Emancipation Proclamation, announcing that on January 1, 1863, he would free all the slaves in the rebellious states. This portentous decree promised to convert the conflict into a "remorseless revolutionary struggle"—the very thing Lincoln had warned against the previous year. Yet with the war dragging on with no end in sight and the casualties mounting beyond anyone's wildest speculation, Lincoln embraced this and other harsh war measures in a desperate effort to suppress the rebellion and end the killing.

Clara favored the projected new policy. If Southern resistance became "obstinate and prolonged," she had told Stephen, the abolition of slavery might "follow as a consequence." And that consequence, as Lincoln said, was at hand. Indeed, the war was growing into something larger, mightier, and more profound than the limited war of 1861, with repercussions beyond comprehension for all those swept up in its flames. In all of this Clara saw the hand of God, shaping events to suit His own designs. Indeed, she believed that Providence had ordained Lincoln's election, had "appointed" him to "meet this crisis." And if Lincoln now met it by abolishing slavery, Clara believed it was God's will working through him.

On October 9, she felt well enough to distribute goods to the sick and wounded in Alexandria. Colonel Rucker provided a special steamer for her passage to Alexandria and an army ambulance with a driver to carry her out to Camp Misery, a convalescent camp established in August for semi-invalids from the general hospitals, whose beds were needed for the Antietam wounded. The camp was a catchall for undesirables, too, "a sort of pen," as one man put it, "into which all who could limp, all deserters and stragglers, were driven promiscuously." By October, more than 10,000 luckless souls were confined in this reeking purgatory. They lived in dirty, floorless tents, mostly without blankets, and were poorly clad and racked by malnutrition and disease.

The Sanitary Commission and Christian Commission sent Camp Misery what supplies they could spare, and now Clara came to do her part. She spent "a most laborious day," she wrote Mary Norton, "examining and distributing among the Camp and Hospitals, not reaching home until near 11 o'clock at night." Despite Washington's neglect of Camp Misery, Clara had nothing but praise for the government. "I dont know how I should succeed in my work without the full cooperation and kind care of the Government,—they not only never deny me a request but try to anticipate my wants and necessities."

By mid-October, Clara was ready to rejoin the Army of the Potomac, still encamped on the Antietam battlefield. Anticipating her needs, Colonel Rucker sent her a message: "They will fight again. Can you go—and what transportation do you want?" Clara replied: "Yes I can go, and I want 3 six mule army wagons with good drivers." In a display of confidence, Rucker furnished her *four* army wagons and a four-wheel ambulance, plus five men to drive them, including the ambulance driver who had conveyed her around Alexandria. The four teamsters assigned to the wagons, Clara noted, were stout, rough men who had served throughout the Peninsula Campaign. With Welles and Clara's nephew Sam, who would go along as her assistants, they set to work loading the wagons with the biggest quantity of supplies Clara would take to the army thus far. Among the boxes was a supply of fine liquor donated by the surgeon general himself.

On October 21, Clara's wagon train set out on the road to Antietam "in the sun and dust" of a hot afternoon. Right away her four new drivers caused trouble. Indignant that they had been put in the charge of "*a lady*," they challenged her authority, pulling over for the night at four in the afternoon. Clara singled out their leader, George, a gnarled man with coal-black hair and eyes, and insisted that they push on until after dark. George consulted with the others, who cracked their whips "as a kind of safety valve to their smothered indignation," Clara said. Grumbling, they drew their teams back onto the road. But to annoy her, they perversely drove long past sundown, ignoring her repeated orders to stop. At nine that night, weary of their fun, they finally turned into a dark field to make camp.

Clara resolved to shame them with kindness. With the help of her ambulance driver, James, she made a fire of fence rails and then prepared coffee and supper, which she laid out neatly on a cloth on the ground, and had James fetch the men. Slowly, a little sheepishly, they took the places Clara assigned them. Then she sat down and politely ate and talked with them as if nothing had happened. The men were stunned. Later, after she had cleaned the dishes and was sitting by the dying fire, they approached her and stood "with the red glare of the embers lighting up their brown hard faces" while George spoke for them.

"We come to tell you that we're ashamed of ourselves," he said with difficulty. "We never seen a train under charge of a *woman* afore, and we couldn't understand it, and we didn't like it, and we thought we'd break it up, and we've been mean and contrary all day, and said a good many hard things, and you've treated us like gentlemen. We hadn't no right to expect that supper from you," he went on, "and it makes us ashamed, and we've come to ask your forgiveness." He promised they would not give her any more trouble. As for her being a woman, they would "get accustomed to that."

Clara assured them that she had no hard feelings, that as long as she had food, she would share it with them, that if they were sick, she would nurse them, and that at all times, she would treat them as gentlemen. "When I saw the rough woolen coat sleeves drawing across their faces," she said later, "it was one of the best moments of my life."

When she was ready to sleep, George hung a lighted lantern from the top of her ambulance, arranged a few blankets inside for her bed, helped her up the steps, and buckled the canvas down on the outside. When she awoke at daybreak the next morning, she smelled the aroma of burning chestnut rails and boiling coffee. George greeted her with a bucket of fresh water and announced that "breakfast was ready." She never had to cook for the men again.

When the party reached Frederick, they found it swarming with quartermaster and medical personnel. It was not only the army's advance supply base but also the center of several overcrowded military hospitals. Here 62 surgeons, 15 medical cadets, 22 hospital stewards, and 539 nurses cared for several thousand men too sick or too badly wounded at Antietam to be evacuated by military train to the general hospitals in Washington and other cities. Clara visited one of the Frederick hospitals and found herself in an enormous room containing about a hundred patients, some lying still, others tossing about, still others muttering and groaning in pain. One man made a terrible outcry and rose up in bed despite the efforts of a nurse and two surgeons to restrain him. Clara went over and read the card at the head of his bed: "H.B., 3d Wis." She could scarcely believe her eyes. *This was Harry Barnard, Mary's beau.* He had a nasty wound in his left arm, and it was apparently gangrenous. Clara asked the surgeons what they intended to do with him. The arm had to come off, they replied, or he would die. But Barnard, delirious from fever and pain, called out, "No, no, I want Mary—I want Mary!"

"Let me talk to him a minute," Clara said. As the men moved off, she bent over Barnard and said, "My good man, I know where Mary is.

If I bring her here will you let the doctors cure your poor arm?" At this, he calmed down and finally agreed. Clara went away, found the Galloway residence, and returned with Mary, who was thin and pale from a recent bout of sickness. When she saw Barnard, she had to struggle to keep from bursting into tears. Knowing she must be brave, she spoke encouragingly to Harry, and he took her hand with his well one and held tight as she continued to talk with tears in her eyes. Finally he accepted the medicine offered by the surgeons and drifted off to sleep. While he was unconscious, they cut and sawed off his infected arm. When he woke, his "wildness" was gone and he lay quietly, with Mary at his side. Clara left them that way, hopeful that with luck and proper treatment he would survive. His empty coat sleeve, she believed, would be his badge of honor, "a grander trophy" than all the medals and medallions that generals won and hung up "in government halls."

On October 26, Clara's little cavalcade overtook the Army of the Potomac as it was crossing the Potomac River at Berlin. After sitting at Antietam for more than a month, McClellan had finally set out after Lee, thanks to the constant prodding of the president. Apparently McClellan hoped to outflank Lee, who was reported to be in the mountains at Martinsburg, Virginia, and cut him off from his communications with Richmond. But no one in the army knew for sure because of McClellan's penchant for secrecy.

Burnside's Ninth Corps led the advance, and Clara's train linked up with it as it moved along Lee's flank down the eastern side of the Blue Ridge Mountains. As she rode along in her ambulance, Clara had never been happier. The days were cool and bright—splendid marching weather—and she loved the sounds of tramping feet, the jingle of cavalry, and the swirl of dust against the sky. She loved the sight of bewhiskered General Burnside, riding by on Major, his favorite horse, and flashing his winsome smile. She loved the camps at night, when the glow of campfires lit up the forest tops and the soldiers sang the stirring lyrics of "John Brown's Body," their favorite song.

> *John Brown's body lies a-mouldering in the grave*
> *Glory, Halle, Hallelujah!*
> *He's gone to be a soldier in the army of the Lord*
> *Glory, Halle, Hallelujah! . . .*

They'll hang Jeff Davis to a sour apple tree
Glory, Halle, Hallelujah! . . .
Now, three rousing cheers for the Union
Glory, Halle, Hallelujah!

Then the voices rang out:

John Brown's Body lies a-mouldering in the grave
While we go marching on!

More than anything else, Clara loved associating with these common soldiers. There was "something sublime" about them, she said later. She shared their army rations—usually moldy hardtack crackers and salted meat hardly fit to eat—and served them some of her jams and marmalades. Indeed, Clara identified so strongly with the soldiers that she considered herself one of them. "I am a *U.S. soldier*," she said repeatedly, and the Army of the Potomac "is my own army." By dint of her extraordinary will, she had become in a figurative sense what she had wanted to be from the start.

Because Clara shared their experiences and yet always maintained her "womanly dignity," she won the affection and respect of the hardened veterans of the Ninth Corps. Her father had been right: soldiers would respect a woman in the field who respected herself. The Twenty-first Massachusetts, with which she spent much of her time, even named her a "daughter" of the regiment and held a dress parade in her honor. As Clara stood at attention, the soldiers marched by to the tuck of drum, with flags and banners flying high and rifles gleaming in the firelight. Afterward, the men called lustily for a speech, which Clara gave, with embarrassment. Later the regimental historian paid her the ultimate compliment. Clara Barton, he wrote, was "a 21st woman to the backbone."

Clara basked in the attention. What was more, nursing men and dispensing gifts from home gave her a sense of control and power she had not known was possible. She had deliberately sought responsibility, had now found it, and it afforded her deep personal satisfaction. As she later admitted, she believed that she had "a selfish" right to tend to the soldiers' needs. For the first time in her life, she felt truly complete and fulfilled.

Still, soldiering had its downside. When the army ran into freezing rain and snow flurries, Clara's hands turned raw and burned from the cold. By November 1, one of her fingers had become acutely inflamed.

It hurt so badly that she had to take a dose of narcotics, despite the terrible side effects that had on her. She might have gone to Dr. Dunn for help, but her friend was not with the army as it marched through Virginia; his outfit was stationed near Harpers Ferry. In fact, she would not see him again during the course of the war.

Finally, a brigade surgeon lanced Clara's felon with a knife. He did so "on the field," she later boasted to some lady supporters. The operation didn't help: the inflammation spread until her entire hand was swollen and throbbing with pain.

On November 7, the army reached Warrenton, some fifteen miles west of Manassas Junction, during a driving snowstorm. Here, to the shock of almost everyone in the army, McClellan was relieved of command and Burnside appointed in his place. Lincoln himself had ordered the change because he thought McClellan was afflicted with a chronic case of "the slows." The general had moved with such caution that Lee was able to send a portion of his army to Culpeper Court House, which put it roughly between McClellan and Richmond. At the same time, Lee left part of his army in the Shenandoah to threaten McClellan's communications. Worse, McClellan never revealed any plan of battle, and Lincoln doubted that he had one. So McClellan was out, never to have another command, furious and bitter at the meddling politicians in Washington. "Good bye, lads," he told an honor guard, and was gone.

So Burnside was commander now—"Old Burny," who sputtered that he wasn't fit to lead a whole *army* but vowed to do it somehow. He tried with all he had to come up with a plan that would appease Lincoln and defeat Lee, who thus far seemed to have an uncanny ability to read the minds of the Yankee generals who fought against him. Already exhausted from work and worry, his good humor gone now, Burnside reorganized the Army of the Potomac into three Grand Divisions under William B. Franklin, Joseph Hooker, and Edwin V. Sumner respectively, and sent his troops marching southeast along the Rappahannock. Their destination was Fredericksburg, the old colonial town Clara had visited on her first trip to the field.

At Warrenton Junction, Clara and Sam parted with the army in order to accompany a contingent of 1,400 sick soldiers back to Washington City by the railroad. By then, Clara was a sick soldier herself. In addition to her swollen hand, which had all but disabled her, she suffered from "dogwood poisoning," contracted from a large evening campfire. According to Sam, the smoke from the dogwood irritated Clara's face. By the time they reached Washington, her face was so badly swollen she couldn't see out of one eye.

Clara had entrusted her wagon train to the care of General Samuel D. Sturgis, a divisional commander in the Ninth Corps of the Right Grand Division, and planned to rejoin Welles and her men as soon as possible. While she nursed herself in Washington City, Burnside's army reached Falmouth, on the opposite side of the Rappahannock from Fredericksburg, apparently with the idea of crossing the river and cutting Lee off from Richmond. But Burnside had to wait more than a week before pontoon bridges could be brought up, and the delay gave Lee enough time to hurry down to Fredericksburg and block Burnside's advance. That intelligence plunged official Washington into despair. When a delegation of Western women called at the White House and asked Lincoln for a word of encouragement, he replied, "I have no word of encouragement to give."

In early December, Clara received an urgent message from Welles, who was with the army at Falmouth. "We need more liquors and something to eat. Your place is here." Clara didn't need the reminder. By December 7, bad hand or not, she was on her way to Aquia Creek with a fresh load of supplies, including a number of pillows. The weather was bitter cold, and patches of snow were visible on the banks of the Potomac as the government steamer bore Clara southward. When she reached Aquia Creek, she found herself at a huge army supply base, with numerous transports and steamers anchored in the river and warehouses and sheds dotting the wintry shoreline.

To Clara's "great joy," she discovered that her Worcester friend, Major Hall of the Twenty-first Massachusetts, was now a quartermaster here. They had a long "*home* chat" that evening, and the next day he put her and her supplies on a military train for Falmouth Station, fifteen miles away. As the train roared southward, Clara gazed on a desolate countryside, the result of two years of unrelenting warfare by both sides. Before the war, this had been fertile farm and plantation country. Now many of the mansions were wrecked or burned out; cabins, barns, and fences had been torn down for firewood, and all the livestock consumed or driven off. Union axmen had chopped down all the trees along the route in order to meet the demands of a huge army in the field and of the supply base at Aquia Creek. The devastation had been bad when Clara visited the area in August, but nothing she'd seen matched the bleakness out there now.

At last the train pulled into Falmouth Station, situated a mile or so east of the Lacy House and the Rappahannock River. As her supplies were being unloaded, Clara looked out over a sprawling "canvas city"—the tents of the Potomac Army—which stretched from the hill-top mansions in back of the station to the riverfront village of Falmouth, a mile or so off to the northwest. Here, in snow-covered encampments, more than 110,000 soldiers awaited battle orders, with 150 pieces of artillery lined up on the higher ground above the river, ready to back them up. On the opposite side of the Rappahannock, along the heights behind Fredericksburg, lay the rebel army, prepared to dispute any move Burnside made to cross the river. Soaring over the Union camps were two large, black observation balloons, whose freezing occupants were trying desperately to ascertain rebel troop strength across the river.

An ambulance picked up Clara at the railroad station, courtesy of General Samuel D. Sturgis, and brought her to his tent headquarters on the grounds of the Lacy House, locally known as Chatham. Welles and her teamsters had tents here too. The general had looked after them, just as he had promised. Clara was extremely fond of Sturgis. As she said later, he was unusually sensitive to her position as an unaffiliated, unmarried woman in the field and gallantly offered her his "protection" against potential critics among the army brass. The general had strong opinions about certain ill-starred generals. "I don't care for John Pope one pinch of owl dung," he liked to say about the former commander of the now defunct Army of Virginia. A native of Pennsylvania and a West Point classmate of Burnside, Sturgis had curly hair, a mustache, and a heavy Vandyke beard. His division, which included the Twenty-first Massachusetts, had fought well at South Mountain and had led Burnside's assault on the Lower Bridge at Antietam in some of the hottest fighting of the battle.

That evening Sturgis treated Clara to supper, and afterward his troops gave her "a splendid serenade," as she wrote a friend. "I don't know how we could have had a warmer 'welcome home,' as the officers termed it." The army assigned her a room in the Lacy House, which she shared with a woman, presumably another volunteer, whom she identified only as a "Miss G." Word of Clara's arrival spread through the army, and she received a steady flow of callers, including several generals and the "very neighborly" Colonel Clark of the Twenty-first Massachusetts.

Clara insisted that she preferred "a good tent, floor and stove" to "a room in a rebel house and one so generally occupied." General Sumner, commander of the Right Grand Division, made his headquarters in the Lacy House, as did several other staff and combat officers, and Clara's cherished Ninth Corps had camps all about the neighborhood. She had been in the old brick mansion last August, and it looked as stately as ever, despite the barren, desolate plateau surrounding it. Built in 1771 by William Fitzhugh and named after William Pitt, earl of Chatham, it had passed through three generations of slave-owning country squires and stood as a symbol of a once-flourishing plantation culture now fighting for its survival. There were nine commodious rooms, including a great front hall and an impressive dining room with a fireplace and a high ceiling. The front of the mansion, which faced the Rappannahock and Fredericksburg, had a fine two-story veranda with a gable roof. Cabins for slaves were located in the rear, and beyond lay the fields they had once been forced to till from sunup to sundown.

Burnside's headquarters was a mile away, at the Phillips House, which afforded a sweeping view of the entire area, but he often held conferences with his generals at the Lacy House. Clara liked Burnside. She thought he had an "honest heart and a genial face," even if he betrayed the strain he was under. The commanding general was hard at work day and night, trying to devise some plan of action to make up for the blunder with the pontoon bridges. As of December 8, however, none of the officers and men to whom Clara spoke had any idea what Burnside intended to do. In fact, Burnside did not appear to know either. Two generals who called on Clara that day had entirely different views as to "the future programme," and Burnside himself stood in front of her door for a long time; "but to my astonishment," Clara said, "he *did not express his opinion*, Strange!"

The next day brought warmer weather, which melted the snow and turned the roads and camp grounds into oozing mud. With Welles and her teamsters, Clara spent the next couple of days wading through the mud from one regiment to another and handing out delicacies from the women at home. At one point, a Federal band started playing on the Falmouth side of the washed-out railroad bridge. A number of officers and men gathered round, cheering as the band ran through such tunes as "The Star Spangled Banner" and "Hail Columbia." Then it stopped, as though expecting a reaction from the rebel soldiers across the river. Getting none, the band played "Dixie," and both sides cheered.

Clara found the Twenty-first Massachusetts encamped a mile and a half up from the river, with the rest of the Second Brigade of Sturgis's division, and delighted in the stories her boys had to tell. When the regiment had arrived on the Rappahannock, several hundred rebels stood watching on the opposite river bank, and the Bay State men engaged them "in spicy repartee and generally good natured defiance," in the words of the regimental historian. The rebels made repeated references to the two Bull Runs, and the Union boys asked "how they liked South Mountain and Antietam." The two sides even hurled challenges and matched up regiments to fight one another in "the supposed" approaching battle.

Clara also made the rounds of Letterman's new divisional tent hospitals, impressive clusters of canvas around Falmouth Station and the Phillips and Lacy houses. The system of divisional hospitals, installed by Letterman in October, replaced the practice of improvising hospitals in farmhouses, barns, sheds, and corncribs and allowing any regimental surgeon to operate wherever he found himself. Each division, comprising three or four brigades (or twelve or more regiments), now had its own medical staff, including a surgeon in charge, three operating surgeons, and nine assistant surgeons, in addition to male nurses detailed from the line. When the fighting began, regimental assistant surgeons were to establish dressing stations at the front, where they would apply emergency aid to the wounded before sending them to the divisional hospitals in the rear, where the major surgical teams remained. Here was a real system, for a change. What was more, the army now issued tents and medical supplies on a brigade basis so as to avoid the extraordinary waste and inefficiency of past campaigns. Field relief agents of the U.S. Sanitary Commission were on hand, ready to distribute supplies when they arrived from its Washington warehouses.

Letterman had refined his ambulance system, too, making certain that drivers and stretcher-bearers were soldiers permanently detailed from the line and trained for the sole purpose of removing wounded from the field. Under Letterman's regulations, each regiment of 500 men or more had three ambulances to accompany it into battle, and they were under the exclusive control of a permanently detailed lieutenant. With the new hospital system and some 1,000 ambulances on hand from the Quartermaster Department, the army's field medical service promised to work smoothly in the coming campaign, thanks to the imagination and pertinacity of its medical director.

Even so, Clara felt there was still a place for her as a volunteer nurse, and so did her many army friends. Once Burnside moved against the rebels, there could be more than one battle, in which case the casualties could be worse than those at Antietam. In that event, the dressing stations at the front, not to mention the divisional hospitals in the rear, would be swamped and would have need of Clara. She would be able to serve again.

On December 9, there was much activity at the Phillips House. Generals Sumner, Hooker, and Franklin went up there to see Burnside and left with what was apparently a plan of battle, and other officers came and went throughout the day. That night in the Lacy House, Sumner conferred with his officers in a heated "talk around," as one man termed it, and the next night Burnside held a council of war there. Word swept through the camps that the army would move at dawn on the morrow, December 11. It would cross the river right at the town— Lee wouldn't expect that, Burnside hoped, and would be caught by surprise—and the Grand Divisions would drive him from the heights. There was a lot of spirited, often bitter opposition to the plan, but Burnside had his way. The engineers would start throwing pontoon bridges across the river before first light.

That night Clara was so excited she couldn't sleep. At two o'clock in the morning, she went outside and stood alone in the yard of the mansion. The moon shone brightly through a haze and cast moving shadows across Fredericksburg on the opposite bank. Tomorrow, her boys would try to cross that river and take that town, and all she could think was, "Thy will O God be done." Here and there campfires glimmered in the darkness, and she could hear sentries moving about somewhere near. The thousands of shelter tents seemed "dark and still as death" to her, and for a fearful moment she thought she could hear "the flap of the grim messenger's wings" as he selected tomorrow's victims as they slept. And she thought sadly, *Sleep, my weary men. Rest for tomorrow's battle. Enjoy your dreams tonight, of your sister, or wife, or mother. They might live to dream of you, cold, bloody, and lifeless; but this could be your last dream, soldier, so dream it well.*

She returned to her quarters. Still too aroused to sleep, she wrote Elvira Stone about this moonlit night opposite Fredericksburg—about the sleeping encampments and the winged touch of death hovering near. As she wrote, she noticed that the light still burned in General Sturgis's tent. Was he writing "a last farewell" to his wife and children? Had he felt the grim messenger's touch?

"Already the roll of the moving artillery is sounding in my ears," Clara concluded in her letter to Elvira, "the battle draws near, and I must catch one hour's sleep for tomorrow's labor."

But there was to be little sleep this night. At about 3:00 A.M. the banging of hammers sounded from the riverfront; the engineers of the Fiftieth New York were throwing pontoon bridges across the Rappahannock.

Daybreak, December 11, found Clara on the second-story veranda of the Lacy House, where she had a commanding view of the activity along the river on this cold, foggy morning. Twin pontoon bridges were about half completed a little upriver from the Lacy House, but rebel sharpshooters in Fredericksburg's riverfront opened fire on the Union engineers, driving them back to the cover of the shore. In a moment, a handful of engineers ran out to the end of the bridges and tried to attach another boat and hammer planks down on it, and again rebel gunfire cracked and blazed along the misty shoreline, forcing the engineers to retreat. This time some of them were hit, and they slumped to the plank walkway or toppled into the murky river. Clara saw their bodies floating downstream—death's first victims this day. Again, the engineers dashed out on the bridge, and again a flurry of musket balls sent them running back.

While this deadly ritual was going on, thousands of infantry—most of the Second and Ninth corps—and several batteries waited on the grounds of the Lacy House and the broad plateau surrounding it. General Darius N. Couch, commander of the Second Corps, stood on the riverfront shouting orders; he was a slight man and a year younger than Clara. The rest of the army stood in "great solid squares" for about three miles along the low hilltops in back of the mansion, along with endless parks of ambulances and commissary, ordnance, quartermaster, and regimental white-topped wagons, all arranged with precision in closed squares. It was "the most impressive exhibition of military force, by all odds, which I ever witnessed," said a rebel officer in awe.

But this huge force, more than 100,000 combat troops, could go nowhere until the bridges were completed, and that seemed unlikely unless the rebel snipers could be silenced. When the fog lifted, the gunfire from Fredericksburg grew so hot that Clara found herself under fire on the Lacy House veranda; it was a wonder she wasn't hit. Bullets struck the windows and doors of the mansion and ripped into men in the ranks below her. Mesmerized by the battle taking shape, Clara seemed unaware of the bullets whizzing around her. In the yard below, a courier handed a directive to General Henry J. Hunt, chief of artillery, from Burnside's headquarters at the Phillips House. Hunt turned and repeated the order to his men: "Bring the guns to bear and shell them out." From experience, Clara knew what was coming and hunkered down on the veranda. In a moment, 179 guns opened up along Stafford Heights and in the yard of the Lacy Mansion; twenty- and twenty-four-pounder Parrotts, four and a half–inch siege guns, Rodman three-inch rifled cannon, and twelve-pounder Napoleons hurled "a cyclone of fiery metal" at Fredericksburg, in the words of rebel General James Longstreet. As shot and shell struck the town, Clara saw roofs collapse, walls and chimneys cave in, buildings blow apart, timber and bricks explode through the air, and houses burst into flame, sending up geysers of black smoke against the sun. Never, not even at Antietam, had she witnessed such destructive force. For two hours the cannonade went on, so thunderous that the Lacy House shook beneath Clara's feet. And all the while, high above the rear of the Union army, floated Burnside's observation balloons, "like two great spirits of the air attendant on the coming struggle," said a rebel officer.

When the barrage ended early in the afternoon, the engineers scur- ried back out on the bridge to resume their work, and the rebel snipers opened fire again. How had they survived the bombardment? The town was wrecked and ablaze "in every quarter," Clara noticed. Below her, a soldier said, "The cellars are filled with sharp-shooters—and our shells will never reach them." Confusion reigned on the Lacy plateau as the enemy rifle fire continued to exact its toll. Then an officer cried: "Man the boats!" The infantry was going across to drive the rebels out. The Seventh Michigan of the Second Army Corps leaped into scows intended for the pontoon bridges, and the engineers climbed in, too, and started rowing the infantrymen across the river, with rebel bullets kicking up the water all around them. The boys in the boats cried: "Row! Row!" And the soldiers on land cheered and echoed them: "Row! Row!" Some of the Michigan men sprawled backward, struck by minié balls, whose "tearing, whirling, splitting action" ripped them apart. First one boat and then another reached the bluffs, momentarily out of sight of the enemy riflemen in the buildings above. The rebels ran out to the edge of the bluffs and fired down point-blank at the men in blue as they jumped into waist-deep water and fought their way up the bank, some jerking backward with gaping holes in them or parts of their heads blown away. Somehow the Michigan men made it to the top of the bluffs and the rebels retreated to their barricades, from which they kept up a steady fire.

Now the Nineteenth and Twentieth Massachusetts regiments went across in support, and the combined regiments drove the rebel sharp-shooters back into town in savage house-to-house fighting. Soon the engineers were able to finish the bridges across the Rappahannock, and some of the wounded, including wounded rebel prisoners, walked or were carried across to the Lacy House, where a dressing station had been established. Clara went downstairs to help, found a dying young rebel officer among them, and did her best to comfort him, too. She noticed with a start the faces of her teamsters beside her. The rough men who a few weeks before had "flushed with indignation at the very thought of being controlled by a woman" were now assisting her with the injured.

Meanwhile, more Federal infantry crossed the river, and a desperate fight was going on for control of the town. At one point, a courier dashed across the bridge and rushed up the steps of the Lacy mansion with a message for Clara. It was from brigade surgeon J. Calvin Cutter of the Ninth Corps, who had gone into town with Letterman to set up dressing stations for the wounded. "Come to me," it said, "your place is here." Clara knew old Dr. Cutter well. He had enlisted as the regimental surgeon of the Twenty-first Massachusetts and had seen his share of death and misery in the North Carolina campaign, at Second Bull Run, and at Antietam.

As Clara started to leave, the dying rebel officer tried to stop her. "Lady," he said, "you have been very kind to me," and he told her what a few hours ago he would never have revealed to any Yankee. "The whole arrangement of the Confederate troops and artillery is intended as a trap for your people. Every street and lane of the city is covered by our cannon. They are concealed, and do not reply to the bombardment of your army, because they want to entice you to cross. When your entire army has reached the other side of the Rappahannock, and attempts to move along the streets, they will find Fredericksburg only a slaughter pen. . . . Do not go over, for you will go to certain death."

But Clara went anyway, and her teamsters and Cornelius Welles followed her. They crossed the swaying bridge under enemy fire, "the water hissing with shot on either side," she said later. Just as the rebel officer had warned, enemy artillery opened up a withering fire on the Yankee infantry trying to take the town. At the end of the pontoon bridge, a Federal officer helped Clara over the debris. As he did so, an exploding shell fragment tore away part of her skirt and his coattail, then rolled along the ground a few yards away "like a harmless pebble upon the water." In the next instant, a solid shot passed over them with a *whish* and struck a Federal horseman riding by; the horse leaped in the air and rolled into the dirt with his "gallant rider" not thirty feet from where Clara was standing.

Clara thanked the officer for helping her and strode into the burning town with her male assistants. They found Dr. Cutter at a dressing station, where the wounded were getting emergency aid before the trained ambulance teams bore them to the divisional hospitals in the rear. At the dressing station, Clara helped set up a huge soup kitchen for the wounded. "Oh what a days work was that," she exclaimed later. But her exhilaration turned to sorrow when the kind officer who had helped her at the bridge was brought to the station, dead.

The battle for Fredericksburg raged around Clara until seven o'clock that evening, when the rebels finally abandoned the town and retired to the main enemy line on the ridges to the west and southwest. By then, two other pontoon bridges were completed, and all the next day, December 12, the Army of the Potomac filed across into smoking Fredericksburg and onto an open plain below the town. The residents had long since fled, and the Yankee soldiers set about looting their homes; they smashed "rebel" pianos, tossed books, glassware, and furniture into the streets, shattered pier glass mirrors with musket butts, dumped barrels of molasses and flour on the rugs, and slashed family portraits with bayonets; some even dressed up in women's clothing and cavorted in the streets. Horrified, General Couch posted provost guards at the bridges to keep looters from escaping to the rear and had other guards confiscate a huge pile of booty from the grumbling soldiers, who were left to wonder why the rebels had not disputed their crossing that day. As units made camps in the streets, the 300 men of the Fifteenth Massachusetts, an all-Worcester regiment, decided to sleep in feather beds for the first time in eighteen months. According to the regimental historian, they carried a hundred feather beds into the streets, arranged them in a row, and lay down in them "fully equipped, boots and all."

Clara spent much of that day back in the Lacy House, which the Second Corps medical director designated as a branch hospital for his corps. Here she nursed "the sadly wounded of the brave Michigan 7th" and others who had fallen in battle the day before. Aware of how difficult it was to maintain accurate medical records during a campaign, Clara tried to keep track of the men who died in the Lacy House, scribbling hasty notes in her pocket diary as to the manner and time of their deaths, their units, and where they were buried. No man was going to end up in an unknown grave and lost to his grieving family if she could help it. She even recorded the vital details of a wounded rebel prisoner: "Capt. Thomas Wm. Thurman Co. D 13 Miss. Decatur Miss. leg amputated. Parents in Georgia. 23 yers. old."

Of all the young men in the Lacy House that day, none impressed her like Wiley Faulkner of the Seventh Michigan. Shot through the lungs in the boat crossing and apparently dying, he sat in a corner, propped up against the wall; it hurt him too much to lie down. He told her his name and residence with great difficulty, and she stopped now and then to see how he was. He couldn't swallow anything and breathed so painfully that she feared he would die at any moment. When the stretcher-bearers tried to remove him so as to make room for more wounded from the town, he refused to budge and clung to his pitiful spot in the corner.

Old General Sumner, white bearded and white haired, still had his headquarters in the Lacy House. He had such a booming voice that his soldiers called him "Bull" or "Old Bull Head," and Clara could hear him bellowing a good deal that day, for Burnside had ordered him to remain on this side of the river rather than to go with his men. As for "Old Burny," the commander had worked out a battle plan for the next day that soon had the entire army astir: it called for his Grand Divisions to launch simultaneous frontal assaults against Lee's positions on the heights beyond Fredericksburg. Sumner's Grand Division, comprising the Second and Ninth corps (and most of the Massachusetts troops), was to attack an elevation called Marye's Heights directly west of town. Clara could see the hill clearly from the Lacy House. On its crest stood a menacing line of artillery and a picturesque mansion with white columns, a symbol of the hated rebel cause.

Clara had heard that J. Horace Lacy, the most recent owner of the Lacy House, was up there in the hills with Lee's army, and it was true. After spending time in the Federal prison at Fort Delaware, he had been exchanged for a Yankee prisoner at Aiken's Landing on the James River; he had rejoined the rebel army in Richmond and on December 10 had reached the hills outside Fredericksburg, bearing dispatches for Lee. During the Federal bombardment the next morning, Lacy was at Lee's command post, which, Lacy said later, afforded them a clear view of his mansion, whose porches were full of Union officers and "gayly dressed women." In all likelihood, only two women were at the Lacy House that morning: Miss G. and Clara Barton, the latter standing by herself on the second-story veranda. As Lacy told the story, a rebel artillery commander requested Lacy's permission to scatter "the unbidden guests" at his mansion, and Lacy asked Lee "to authorize the

fire of the heavy guns, which would have laid Chatham to the dust."
But Lee refused to permit this "unnecessary effusion of blood," thus
sparing Clara Barton and everyone else at the Lacy House that day.

Dawn, December 13, the day of battle, came with a fog so thick that it
reduced visibility to fifty yards. In the Lacy House, Clara was already
at her nursing duties, dressed in a simple black print skirt and a tightly
laced jacket—her battle uniform. She checked on Wiley Faulkner and
found "the poor boy" still alive, as if by a miracle. The fog was so heavy
that Clara could not see the spires of Fredericksburg, much less the
Union's military preparations for the coming assaults. But the commo-
tion of moving troops made "an indistinct murmur," one witness said,
"like the distant hum of myriads of bees."

At about ten in the morning, the sun brushed the fog away, revealing a spectacular panorama on the plain below Fredericksburg, where
Franklin's Grand Division was deployed in assault columns, with battle
flags fluttering and polished arms shining in the sunlight. While these
Federals prepared to attack the Confederate right, the Second and
Ninth corps were lining up in the streets of Fredericksburg itself, all
eyes fixed on Marye's Heights and the open plain between them and
the town. The Union infantry would have to cross that plain to reach
the Heights, which meant that they would be exposed to rebel artillery
fire from the crest.

Soon Union artillery behind the Lacy House opened fire on the
rebel lines, and enemy field pieces returned the fire, sweeping the
Union positions with a murderous cannonade. The rebel gunners
hadn't found the range yet, and some of their shots accidentally struck
the Lacy House, showering debris on the wounded and medical personnel inside. In the midst of that fierce bombardment, Clara brought
out a box of fruit a little girl had sent to her, and "while the house was
rocking and tottering to its foundation, with the terrible recoil of our
own guns, and the enemies solid shot and bursting shell were plough-
ing the ground all around us killing wounded men at the door, I
opened little Mary's box of delicious fruit and cut the apples in quarters and divided them among the poor suffering men."

As Clara stood near the eastern entrance, a shell exploded among
the reserve soldiers on the grounds outside. One man fell down with
blood spurting from his ankle; a shell fragment had severed an artery.
His comrades dragged him inside the mansion and laid him on the

floor beside Clara, who promptly tied her handkerchief into a tourniquet and wrapped it around his leg to stop the flow of blood. Later,
when she walked by him, the soldier grabbed the skirt of her dress and
whispered, "You saved my life." He kept saying that every time she
came near him or glanced his way. *You saved my life.*

When word came that the battle had begun, Clara crossed the pontoon bridge into shell-torn Fredericksburg. Many of her boys would be
killed and horribly wounded this day, and she intended to be there for
them in the dressing stations. As she made her way through the streets,
infantry assault columns tramped by on their way to the plain outside
of town. She was the only woman in Fredericksburg, and in all the
tumult, the veteran provost marshal general, Marsena Rudolph Patrick,
mistook her for a resident who had refused to leave town with all the
others; he thought that the rebel bombardment had driven her into the
streets. "You are alone," he said, "and in great danger Madam—do you
want protection?" Clara thanked him, turned to the passing soldiers,
and said she was "the best-protected woman in the United States." The
soldiers nearest her understood her meaning and said, "That's so, that's
so," and gave a cheer. The next line picked up the cheer, and the next,
and it swept through the ranks until everyone was cheering. Doubtless
they thought a victory had already been won. General Patrick removed
his hat and said as he rode away, "I believe you are right, Madam."

The cheering stopped abruptly when the soldiers reached the plain
and charged forward against the rebel positions on Marye's Heights.
To Clara's horror, a sheet of flame rose from a stone wall along the base
of the hill, and volleys of musketry and canister cut huge swaths
through the charging Yankee lines. My God, those boys were being cut
to pieces! The noise was so deafening that it was impossible to hear
anything else. Bullets hissed in the air; solid shot struck the ground
and bounded and leaped rearward; shells exploded in whirlwinds of
dust and debris. The most terrible of all was the canister: tin cans
loaded with iron balls and fired from field pieces like giant shotgun
shells. The canister struck the attacking Yankees like invisible whirling
blades, annihilating entire sections of the front lines and spattering the
rear columns with blood, brain matter, and fragments of bone, muscle,
and skin. But they were brave, these Union boys: brigade after brigade
of them pushed on toward the Heights, shouting at the tops of their
lungs, their faces and bodies turned sideways as if to breast a storm,
until they disappeared in a boiling maelstrom of smoke and flame.

Clara was stunned. So was General Couch, whose brigades led the assaults. Watching from the courthouse cupola, he cried out, "Oh, great God! see how our men, our poor fellows, are falling!" The rebel positions were clearly impregnable. It was sheer murder to hurl any more infantry against them, yet that was precisely what the Yankee generals did. Now three more brave brigades dashed suicidally toward the flaming stone wall, only to disintegrate like the others. By now, the plain was covered with bodies and parts of bodies. In the swirling smoke, Clara could see the survivors huddled against a slight rise in the ground perhaps 200 yards from the rebel infantry, scarcely daring to move lest snipers pick them off.

And still the assaults continued. In the afternoon, the Twenty-first Massachusetts marched forward with the other regiments of its brigade. Clara's "dear boys" were going into action now, and she watched with dread in her heart as they dressed ranks and started forward with their colors snapping. When a rebel battery opened fire on them, the head of a tall soldier flew from his body and rolled along the ground. "While the horrid red fountain was still spouting from the neck," said the regimental historian, "our well-ordered line was sweeping forward on the double-quick, under the best directed artillery fire that we had ever suffered or seen." Three times the colors of the Twenty-first went down in the smoke, only to rise again each time. As the regiment neared the stone wall, Sergeant Thomas Plunkett was carrying the flag when a shell exploded almost on top of him, shattering both his arms, wounding him severely in the chest, and killing three of his comrades. Somehow Plunkett was still standing. To keep the flag from falling to the ground, he planted a foot against the bottom of the staff and held the pole against the bloody stump that had been his right arm. Crying out, "Don't let it fall Boys, don't let it fall," he stood in that hail of bullets, refusing to go down until another soldier took the national banner now soaked with his blood. The survivors of this charge found shelter behind the little rise of land where so many others lay, while rebel shot and shell roared over them with a shuddering *whoosh*.

The Union assaults on Marye's Heights, which went on through the wintry afternoon, left some 900 dead and 7,000 wounded on that murderous plain; another 3,000 fell in the fighting south of town, and hundreds of men were missing. Letterman's stretcher-bearers brought back many of the wounded in a display of remarkable courage under fire. Others, bleeding and in shock, managed to walk, stumble, or crawl back on their own. The injured and dying filled up the courthouse and every church, warehouse, school, store, house, street, and ravine in Fredericksburg, where they cried for water, for a blanket, for chloroform or whiskey or God to put them out of their misery.

This was Clara Barton's Civil War—the war against death in the battlefield dressing stations. Driven as never before, she seemed a ubiquitous presence, now in a church, now a home, now the courthouse, holding some battered boy to her chest, wiping the brow of another. At one point, a shell struck the door of a room in which she was working. "She did not flinch," Welles reported, "but continued her duties." With the battle still raging, the stretcher-bearers brought in Private Plunkett, and Clara was at his side when the surgeons removed what remained of his arms, pared off the ragged bone ends and sockets, applied a powerful styptic to stanch the flow of blood, and sutured and dressed the stumps. Someone, perhaps Colonel Clark, showed her the flag Plunkett had kept from falling to the ground—his blood "literally obliterated the *stripes*," she said later.

Dusk brought a deafening silence to the battlefield. The dead and wounded were strewn everywhere in the wreckage; it was difficult to tell them apart. A thousand corpses were piled up in a "hideous heap" near the infamous stone wall. One observer reported that men lay "in every conceivable posture, some on their backs with gaping jaws, some with eyes as large as walnuts, protruding with glassy stare, some doubled up like a contortionist, here one without a head, there one without legs, yonder a head and legs without a trunk, everywhere horrible expressions, fear, rage, agony, madness, torture, lying in pools of blood, lying with heads half-buried in mud, with fragments of shell sticking in oozing brain, with bullet holes all over the puffed limbs."

Colonel Joshua Chamberlain of the Twentieth Maine heard a "cacophony" of groans and yells rising from the wounded who lay out there in a near-freezing wind. It was "a wail so far and deep and wide," the colonel said, that it pierced his heart. In his sorrow, he thought he heard a fluttering window shade saying, "*Never—forever; Forever— Never!*" in a woeful refrain. Then he saw "through the murk the dusky forms of ghostly ambulances gliding upon the far edge of the field, pausing here and there to gather up their precious freight; and the low-hovering half-covered lanterns, or blue gleam of a lighted match, held close over a brave, calm face, to know whether it were of the living or the dead."

All night the lights burned in the dressing stations of Fredericksburg. All night the ambulances clattered across the pontoon bridges, taking wounded back to the divisional tent hospitals and the well-lit Lacy House. All night the streets teemed with walking wounded, stragglers, and the remnants of regiments. All night fires smoldered in the rubble of blasted buildings and blinds flapped in the wind, and a sleepless Chamberlain kept hearing the melancholy refrain *"Never— forever; Forever—Never!"*

During the night, Captain Joseph Hamilton came across Clara as she was tending to fifty wounded men; Hamilton said they were "almost frozen." Surgical aid was impossible before daylight, so Clara had her male assistants light fires, dismantle a chimney, heat the bricks, and place them around the wounded men to keep them warm until the surgeons could help them.

The next day, Sunday, an officer ran up to her with great urgency. One of his men lay in a church across the street, shot in the face; he was suffocating from his own dried blood, the officer said. Clara seized a basin of water and a sponge and hurried to the church, where she found the man among scores of other wounded. Inured as she was to macabre sights, Clara blanched when she saw his face. It was "one solid crust," she remembered, "for any human appearance above the shoulders it might as well have been any thing else as a man." She knelt beside him and sponged the crust gently, wiping away the obstructions until at last she gazed on the features of a human face, disfigured from the wound, but a face all the same. Then she recognized him. It was Nathan J. Rice, the former sexton of her Universalist church in North Oxford, where in her youth she had learned "that of all that He has made nothing shall be lost, but that at some day in some way it shall be raised to His Glory."

That same Sunday, at a war council at the Phillips House, Burnside announced his intentions to renew the assaults the next morning. He had watched the battle yesterday through his field glass on the roof of the mansion, apparently impervious to the slaughter at Marye's Heights for which he was responsible. "It's all arranged," he told his generals; "we attack at early dawn, the Ninth Corps in the center, which I shall lead in person." Had that happened, Clara's "pet" corps would likely have been annihilated. But Sumner, Franklin, and Hooker all held that a renewal of the battle was out of the question; the assaults yesterday had failed; the troops were too exhausted and dispirited to fight again. After the conference, Baldy Smith, commander of the Sixth Corps, found Burnside alone, pacing up and down in great distress. The full realization of yesterday's calamity had finally dawned on him.

"Oh! those men! oh! those men!" When Smith asked what he meant, Old Burny pointed across the river, "Those men over there! I am thinking of them all the time."

On Monday, both sides agreed to a truce, and burial parties set to work digging mass graves for the discolored corpses littering the field. The wreckage on the battlefield was almost beyond description: "limbs flung from their bodies and half trampled into the bloody mire," wrote Joshua Chamberlain; "horses, cannoneers, dismounted guns, splintered ammunition chests, crushed wheels, overturned carriages, the tongue erect in air, the pole-yokes swinging gibbet-like on high, looming suddenly on you with a shuddering light." Many of the Union bodies were naked, their uniforms and shoes now the property of the victorious rebels. That night, in the middle of a terrible storm, the Army of the Potomac evacuated Fredericksburg and recrossed the Rappahannock, carrying all the remaining wounded with it. Letterman's medical service had performed brilliantly. Within twenty-four hours after the fighting had ended, the ambulance teams had removed virtually all the wounded from the field. In every other respect, however, the battle was an unmitigated disaster for the North. Total Union casualties came to 12,653 killed, wounded, and missing— more than had fallen at Antietam. By contrast, the rebels lost about 5,200—proof of their impregnable defensive positions. The Union casualties should have alerted everybody involved to the insanity of massed infantry assaults against a fortified enemy armed with the rifled musket and deadly artillery. But not even Lee would learn from the Union's folly at Fredericksburg.

Clara came back with the army that stormy night and took up her station at the Lacy House, the Second Corps' branch hospital. The Second Corps suffered the heaviest casualties in the army; the First Division alone lost 2,032 men of 5,006 engaged. Some 280 wounded of the Second Corps were officially listed as being in the Lacy House, but the actual count was considerably more. "I cannot tell you the numbers," Clara later wrote a Soldiers' Aid Society, "but some hundreds of the worst wounded men I have ever seen" lay in all nine rooms of the Lacy House and in a few surrounding tents. They "covered every foot of the floors and porticos," Clara remembered. They "lay on the stair landings" and under all the tables. "A man who could find opportunity to lie between the legs of a table thought himself rich," she said; "he was not likely to be stepped on." Five men had even been stuffed onto the four shelves of a common cupboard.

There were so many wounded that a group of late arrivals had to be left on the cold, muddy ground for lack of shelter. Clara took them warm drink, and a man with a shattered leg said that he remembered her from Second Bull Run. He'd been wounded there, too, and she had fed him while he lay in a wagon at Fairfax Station. He would never forget what she did for his group that Monday night after Fredericksburg. Once again, she instructed her men to heat bricks from a torn-down chimney, wrap the wounded in blankets, and keep the hot bricks around them all through the night.

In the Lacy House, meanwhile, operating surgeons were hard at work in every room, extracting bullets and sawing off limbs, which they threw out the front door. Walt Whitman, who visited the Lacy House while Clara was there, described the hideous sight that greeted him: "at the foot of a tree, immediately in front, a heap of feet, legs, arms, and human fragments, cut, bloody, black and blue, swelled and sickening—in the garden near, a row of graves."

With Welles and her teamsters, Clara established a soup kitchen on the Lacy House grounds and set to work feeding the broken men inside. They had to step carefully, for the floors were slippery with blood. As the surgeons performed amputations, Clara or an assistant was quick to put her pillows under the bloody stumps and offer swills of liquor when the patients awoke, screaming from pain.

The scenes Clara witnessed here would haunt her through all her remaining years. There was the delirious officer, fatally wounded, who confused her for his wife. There were the last of the soldiers retrieved from the field, "half skinned, with frozen legs & arms," who couldn't bear her heat applications until she had administered heavy doses of the surgeon general's liquor. There was Lieutenant Edgar M. Newcomb of the Nineteenth Massachusetts, who lay on a couch hemorrhaging from his wounds, with his stricken brother Charlie at his side. Clara knelt beside him, too, and she and Charlie sang hymns and quoted scripture, and when the dying young man confused Clara for his mother, she "kindly favored the illusion," Charlie remembered, "by shading the light." At last, after hours of agony, Lieutenant Newcomb died. "When I rose from the side of the couch," Clara said later, "I wrung the blood from the bottom of my clothing before I could step, for the weight about my feet."

And there was the young man who kept saying "you saved my life" whenever she came near him. And finally there was Wiley Faulkner, who was still clinging to his corner when Clara returned from Fredericksburg. When she checked on him at one point, he seemed not to be breathing; she thought "the poor boy" had finally died. When the stretcher-bearers brought in another wounded man, they could not find a space for him in the mansion. They asked Clara if they could remove the boy in the corner, who looked dead. Clara relented with a sigh, but when the stretcher men started to lift Wiley Faulkner, he opened his eyes. He was still alive, and he refused to be moved.

Through the snow and winds of those December days, Clara lived out of her tent in the yard and worked in that forlorn mansion, watching, grief-stricken, when the stretcher-bearers carried one of her *"dear"* boys away to the burial ground. All her motherly instincts found an outlet with them; they were all her family, and she could scarcely bear their suffering. At times, in her tent late at night, she did not think she could stand another hour in that house. But somehow she always found the strength to go on, drawing on reserves of energy she did not know she possessed. At dawn, she would suppress her tears, tie her hair up, and go forth again to nurse her *"dear"* soldiers.

By now, Clara and Miss G. were no longer the only women volunteers at the Lacy House. After the battle, Eliza Harris and two co-workers came to help. Anna Holstein, abiding by her vow at Antietam, also showed up after the battle and served in the tent hospitals of the Second Corps, where she read scripture to the suffering. Isabella Fogg and Sarah P. Edson labored at Falmouth as well. But none of them, brave and irreplaceable as they were, could claim Clara's distinction: she had been the only volunteer female nurse and relief worker in Fredericksburg during the battles of December 11 and 13. Thus far, she had made the battlefield hospital of the Eastern Theater her special domain.

At one point after the battle, the flap to Clara's tent opened, and there stood Henry Wilson, stocky and ruddy faced, his piercing eyes fixed on Clara's. Distressed about the disaster at Fredericksburg, the senator was here to check on the condition of the army himself. He stayed two days, and what he saw reinforced his view that the army needed more combat troops. As chairman of the Senate Committee on Military Affairs, Wilson was prepared to "draft every last man who could carry a musket." He and his Radical Republican colleagues wanted the president to enlist black soldiers, too, not only Northern free blacks, but also slaves in the Confederacy—the very blacks Lincoln had promised to free on New Year's Day. Thousands of former slaves fighting for the Union would hurt the South irreparably and hasten an end to this terrible war, so Wilson and the Radicals had repeatedly told Lincoln. The senator hoped that the president would go through with his promise to issue an emancipation proclamation. In his recent message to Congress, Lincoln hadn't mentioned it. Some conservative Republicans warned him that his emancipation plans were reckless and divisive, and angry Democrats threatened to move impeachment proceedings if he struck at slavery. Bidding Clara farewell, Wilson hurried back to Washington to make certain that Lincoln did not waver in his resolve.

On December 16, the army began evacuating the wounded from the hospitals around Falmouth Station, hauling them by train to Aquia Creek and then by hospital transport back to Washington. Many of them suffered terribly on the railroad journey, for they had to ride in small, open platform cars in freezing weather. They were better treated at Aquia Creek, where a Sanitary Commission relief station gave them blankets, shirts, and woolen drawers, along with hot meals and concentrated milk.

While evacuations went on at the Lacy House, Clara made hot toddies for her patients, to ease their pain on the ambulance ride to the railroad station. She promised to visit them in the Washington and Alexandria hospitals, but it broke her heart to tell them good-bye. The young soldier who kept saying "you saved my life" went off with one group, but Clara had been so busy and tired that she had forgotten to get his name or give hers. And Wiley Faulkner was still alive, thanks in large part to Clara's care and protection. By the time the ambulance came for him, he was "a mere little white bundle of skin and bones," as she described him later. As the stretcher men covered him with a blanket for his journey, Clara slipped into his blouse a bottle of "milk punch"—a potent mixture of eggnog and rum or sherry, the only nourishment he was able to take.

On Christmas day, Clara's forty-first birthday, the stretcher-bearers came for Sergeant Plunkett. Clara, Colonel Clark, and the rest of the Twenty-first escorted him to Falmouth Station, where the colonel gave an emotional farewell talk before they lifted Plunkett onto the flatcar of the waiting train. Only after the last of the wounded left two days later did Clara and her assistants take down her tents—all her stores were gone now—and secure a pass from General Sturgis for their return to Washington.

Their boat docked at the Sixth Street wharf on the last day of 1862, and Clara waded through ankle-deep mud to a streetcar for the ride home. As she climbed the long flight of stairs to her rooms, she could not get her mind off the "fires of Fredericksburg" and the endless suffering she had witnessed there and at the Lacy House. In her rooms, "cheerless, in confusion, and alone," she barely noticed an unopened box standing in the middle of the floor. Suddenly "a new sense of desolation and pity and sympathy and weariness" swept over her, and she sank down on the box and wept.

Later in the evening, when she felt better, she opened the box and found an amazing surprise: hoods, gloves, collars, pairs of boots and shoes, handkerchiefs, skirts, and a lovely dress—all for her personal wardrobe, a note said, "*From friends in Oxford and Worcester.*" Examining the dress, Clara recognized the work of her cousin and friend, Annie Childs. Yes, Clara thought, "Annie's scissors shaped and her skillful fingers fitted that." What "dear, kind friends" they all were, and she started crying again. This was such an inspiriting show of appreciation for her labors. Her friends knew that she lacked the time to make clothes for herself or the money to have them made. "I was not alone," she realized, "and then and there I rededicated myself to my little work of humanity, pledging before God all that I *have*, all that I *am*, all that I *can*, and all that I *hope* to be, to the cause of *justice* and *mercy*, and *patriotism*, my *country* and my *God*."

On New Year's Day 1863, Lincoln issued the Emancipation Proclamation and changed the course of the war profoundly and irrevocably. The proclamation not only made a promise of freedom and justice to black Americans; it also announced that the army and navy would accept black volunteers, and Governor Andrew made arrangements for the creation of an elite, all-black Massachusetts regiment that would prove to the country that black men could make splendid soldiers. Henry Wilson, for his part, was disappointed that Lincoln's proclamation had exempted the loyal slave border. Nevertheless, he extolled the edict. Indeed, said his early biographers, no one on Capitol Hill received it with "more joy" than the Massachusetts senator. For Clara, the proclamation was further manifestation that God was working through Lincoln to effect a "vast" and "mighty" change in their war-rent country.

With the army in winter quarters at Falmouth, Clara spent the short days of January gathering stores for the next campaign and "seeing and answering everybody," as she wrote Mary Norton. To her astonishment, she found that her work at Fredericksburg and Antietam had made her a celebrity. Officers saluted her on the sidewalks. A parade of soldiers called on her to pay their respects. Wilson told her that "*our cause ought not to fail*" with patriots like her serving it, and Senators Benjamin F. Wade and Schuyler Colfax held a reception in her honor at the house they shared. "I had only time to lay aside my army jacket, make myself presentable, and appear," Clara said. "Oh, the crowd and the wonderful evening." A few days later Colfax sent her a kitten with a bow about its neck. It was the perfect gift for Clara, who loved cats and no doubt set up military quarters for her new pet in the kitchen.

Because of her growing fame, Clara's Washington friends decided it was time she had her picture taken. They "waylaid" her one day and took her to Mathew Brady's National Photographic Art Gallery on Pennsylvania Avenue between Sixth and Seventh streets. In the top floor studio, or "operating room," Clara posed like a soldier in front of Brady's exploding camera. But the resulting photograph appalled her, for it exposed how exhausted and thin she was from months of campaigning and her bout with typhoid fever. "It looked like death on the pale horse," she told Mary Norton, "and I suppressed the issue."

In her "campaign diary," Clara carefully noted to which hospitals the "men of Lacy House" had been taken. Many of them were at Lincoln Hospital, one of the modern pavilion designs that had largely replaced the dilapidated, improvised hospitals of 1861. Clara jotted down information on missing soldiers, too. "Lieut Joseph P. Robinson (brother of Capt. Robinson at 6th St. Wharf.) in 32nd Mass. Regt 'find him,'" read one such entry, apparently recorded on the run. And she continued to keep track of the Massachusetts dead, in case their families should write her for information: "J. Allen of New Bedford, member Co. C U.S. Engineers, died at the Arsenal, Washington D.C., Jan 9 1863. Buried in the Congressional burying ground in burial Site No. 81."

One day a message came to her from Lincoln Hospital, saying that the men of Ward 17 wanted to see her. When she arrived there, seventy wounded soldiers saluted her, some standing, others rising feebly from their beds, and gave her three rousing cheers. All of them had left their blood at Fredericksburg, all had been at the Lacy House, all had been bandaged and fed by Clara's hand, and all loved her. To them "Miss Barton" was the outstanding nurse of the war, and their hurrahs moved her to her depths. Then a young man with a bright complexion came forward. "I am Wiley Faulkner of the 7th Michigan," he said. "I didn't die and the milk punch lasted all the way to Washington."

Not long after that, as she sat in her room contending with a mass of accumulated correspondence, Clara heard a limping footstep in the hallway and then a rap at her door. When she opened it, she was surprised to see a young man leaning on his crutch. It was her "hero of the *four words*," who said again, "You saved my life."

Sergeant Plunkett, of regimental colors fame, credited Clara with helping to save his life when the surgeons amputated the remnants of his arms, and he turned naturally to her when he ran into bureaucratic difficulty with the War Department. The sergeant had been taken to Armory Square Hospital and had recovered enough to go home, though his shoulders and chest were still swathed in bandages. Plunkett's brother had come down from Massachusetts to get him but had been blocked by military red tape and indifference at the crowded War Department. Nobody there would even listen to their story, the brother explained, let alone honor their request for a furlough. Sergeant Plunkett said he felt like a prisoner.

Clara took the Plunketts straight to the Capitol to see Henry Wilson. When he met them in the waiting room, looking "ruddy and busy," Clara said, "Mr. Wilson, permit me to introduce you to Sergeant Plunkett of the Massachusetts Twenty-first."

"How do you do, Sergeant?" Wilson said, instinctively extending a hand.

It was an embarrassing moment; Wilson apparently hadn't caught the full meaning of Plunkett's bandages. "You will pardon the Sergeant for not offering you a hand," Clara said; "he has none."

"No hands!" Wilson exclaimed. "No hands!! My God; where are they?"

In fact, the sergeant had no *arms*. When Clara recounted how they had been "shot off in Fredericksburg" while he carried the flag, Wilson's lips trembled. "What does the Sergeant want?" he asked.

"He wants to go home," Clara said; "his brother is here waiting to take him; they cannot reach the War Department."

"I can," Wilson said.

"He must have a furlough, not a discharge," Clara explained; "he will need his pay till he has his pension. Here is his application." She handed Wilson the paper.

"I will see to that," Wilson said, and turned to Plunkett. "You will go home Sergeant."

At ten o'clock that evening, Wilson called on Clara at her boarding-house. He had been to the War Department, he said, and "the Sergeant can go home to-morrow." He paced relentlessly back and forth for a few moments, then sat down by her writing table and put his head on his hand, visibly upset. "My God!" he said. "What a price!! Liberty should be the most precious of all things attainable by man." Yet "nothing—no, not all else together—is so dearly bought." What did he mean? He meant brave Union boys like Plunkett fighting and getting crippled or killed in order to save the Union's system of popular government and the beacon hope of liberty it held out to oppressed people everywhere. He meant black Americans, too, many of whom would soon be fighting and dying for liberty in the Union army. As he talked on in his rambling manner, he referred to the loss of courageous men on both sides and the skill of the rebel commanders. And this in turn reminded him of the desolation of the war, which he had seen firsthand at Fredericksburg. "And where is the end?" he asked Clara. "It is darker now than three years ago; where and *what* will be the end?" Then, abruptly, her "dear friend" seized his hat and left her, plunging out into the dark and muddy street, heading for his hotel for a long night's work.

The next day Sergeant Plunkett went home, but without his arms he faced an uncertain future. Later Clara wrote Wilson's Senate military committee, recalling Plunkett's heroism at Fredericksburg and asking that it grant him more money than the pension due him as a sergeant, since he would have to hire an attendant to feed him.

That January, everybody at Medical Department headquarters was praising Letterman for his achievements at Fredericksburg, which marked the end of the chaos that had plagued the Medical Department in the first year and a half of the war. The department now had 2,000 commissioned surgeons in command of almost 10,000 medical personnel, plus access to thousands of horse-drawn wagons and ambulances. The only problem was that the wagons remained the responsibility of the Quartermaster Department, and the men of the ambulance service were still soldiers detailed from the line. The surgeon general and his medical officers, backed up by the Sanitary Commission, argued that the collection and care of the wounded would be more efficient if the Medical Department had its own independent ambulance corps, consisting of men specially recruited and trained for ambulance service. In January, the Medical Department's friends on Capitol Hill, Henry Wilson chief among them, promoted legislation that would permit the Medical Department to enlist up to 12,000 volunteers and up to 500 commissioned officers to serve exclusively in an ambulance corps under its control. Clara lent her support to the proposed bill, writing Wilson that an independent ambulance corps would be an improvement over "the imperfect system now in operation." But Stanton and Halleck objected to a Medical Department ambulance corps as "impractical," and the bill was never reported from committee. Worse still, Secretary of War Stanton and Surgeon General Hammond were now locked in a bitter feud over this and other medical matters that only hurt the Union cause and the soldiers who served it.

In mid-January, Colonel Rucker informed Clara that the Army of the Potomac was about to move out again and that the War Department expected a battle. He wanted her to return to the field if she were able. He provided her with bread, meal, flour, two new tents, and a new stove—the weather was bitter cold in Virginia—and told her to telegraph him for anything else she might need. Clara thanked him warmly. But finding herself short of medical supplies (bandages, chloroform, opiates, and the like), she prevailed on Wilson to help her procure them from the surgeon general, who had, after all, given her that "fine lot of liquors" she had distributed at Fredericksburg. She also asked that Wilson arrange for her to "draw articles desired from the Medical Purveyor from time to time as I may need them."

This was a significant new step for Clara, who until now had relied almost exclusively on women's aid societies for her supplies. Now she was asking Wilson to make her an unofficial relief worker for the War Department. She assured her "old-time friend" that whatever the medical purveyor gave her would be "prudently and properly applied." Had she the money to buy medical stores, she would not ask the government for them, "or if I were able to sit quietly down in the midst of all the suffering and desolation around me without even attempting to relieve my portion of it, then I would not ask. This my nature forbids."

On January 18, Clara and Welles returned to the army, in time for a new campaign devised by Old Burny to recover the glory lost at Fredericksburg. On the morning of January 20, buglers blew colors, and Clara saw her army off, as column after column headed upriver with the idea of crossing the upper Rappahannock and turning Lee's left flank. But that afternoon a hard rain started to fall in the Falmouth-Fredericksburg area. By dusk the storm had developed into a freezing, wind-whipped downpour. "It was surely the stormiest night I ever knew," Clara wrote Mary Norton. The wind blew so hard that Clara's tent billowed and popped all night, but fortunately for her the ropes held. In the morning, with the storm still raging, Clara nursed a fire in her "little chimney stove presented by Col. Rucker" and had 120 sets of mittens—gifts from the ladies of Worcester—sent by wagon to the Twenty-first Massachusetts Regiment, which was on picket duty at the Lacy House. "I have no idea how long I may remain," Clara wrote Mary Norton. "I wait either for another battle, or winter quarters."

As it turned out, the howling storm wrecked Burnside's advance. By morning, the roads were "rivers of deep mire," as one soldier said, into which sank the entire army: troops, cannon and caissons, ambulances, supply wagons, horses, mules, everything. To make matters worse, Burnside directed that rations of whiskey be issued to the ranks, and many of the men got drunk. A couple of rival regiments even started fighting one another in a liquor-induced "free-for-all." On the hills across the river, rebel soldiers taunted the brawling Yankees, and one held up a sign that read "THIS WAY TO RICHMOND." To deepen the insult, the sign pointed the wrong way.

Somehow the army extracted itself and limped back to Falmouth and into winter quarters. The soldiers called it Burnside's Mud March and wondered whether there was "some destructive fate" hovering over the Army of the Potomac. To compound their misery, the cold, damp campgrounds and filthy winter hovels in which they lived bred infectious diseases in epidemic proportions. "I do not believe I have ever seen greater misery from sickness than now exists in the Army of the Potomac," reported Medical Inspector Thomas F. Perley. Small wonder that desertions that winter rose to a record high.

In January, several Dix nurses turned up at Aquia Creek, ostensibly to care for the sick and wounded sent back to Washington on army transports. But some of those nurses went ashore, too, and found themselves so close to rebel lines that none dared to make a fire. One young woman claimed that she "drank water from holes made by the horses' feet in the mud; it tasted good and sweet." If the brackish water had any side effects, she did not record them.

For Clara, the appearance of Dix nurses in the field was an ominous development. Not only was Miss Dix attempting to extend her sphere of influence; she was also on a campaign to exclude all unaffiliated female nurses like Clara from medical service, especially in the Washington-Virginia theater, where Dix could exert her authority directly. What was more, Clara faced formidable competition from the U.S. Sanitary Commission and its field relief workers, who distributed supplies raised by its thousands of regional and local affiliates. Among them was the New England Women's Auxiliary Association, ably led by Abby May and a group of "the most gifted and intellectual women of Boston." By January 1863, fifty-two towns in Massachusetts alone were sending supplies to the Women's Auxiliary, which then forwarded them to the Sanitary Commission's central office in Washington. As one Boston woman said, the Women's Auxiliary was doing all it could to mobilize the energies of "the loyal women of our land, that nothing may be lost to the common cause." Thanks to its contributions and those of affiliated groups across the North, the Sanitary Commission's storehouses in Washington soon "overflowed with plentiousness."

As an "independent Sanitary Commission of one," as an army surgeon described her, Clara had to compete with this huge national organization for the donations of northeastern women, and she also had to compete with the Sanitary Commission's relief workers in the field. This posed a troubling question: was the independent nurse and relief worker in the eastern theater no longer needed? Clara wasn't prepared to concede that yet, not when her own network of suppliers now included women and women's groups in New York and Pennsylvania, as well as New Jersey and Massachusetts. In fact, a pile of unanswered letters from them demanded Clara's attention, and on January 23 she abruptly returned to Washington to tend to that crucial correspondence and keep her support network intact. She intended to replenish her "haversack," too, and return to the army as soon as possible.

There was another reason for Clara's abrupt return. She lost her devoted assistant, Cornelius Welles, whose health was impaired from months of arduous labor in the field; he had irreversible heart disease, as it turned out. With the Army of the Potomac inactive for the winter, he was anxious to return to teaching black folk in Washington. A "large colony of the fragments of [black] families," as he described them, had come there from Fredericksburg, and he now devoted himself to teaching them and their children in his "contraband" school in Washington. "I find that my scholars here are rejoiced to know that I am again to take charge of the class which has of late greatly increased," Welles wrote his spiritual brethren.

Clara respected Welles and hated to lose him. Indeed, what was she to do without him? She could not, dared not, return to the field without a male companion. She wasn't worried about what the soldiers might think; they already respected her. What concerned her was the male sanitary agents, supply officers, and other army bureaucrats she often had to deal with. They might frown on an unmarried woman in the field by herself and complain to the War Department. To be sure, she had friends there who respected her and her work. But she also knew that General-in-Chief Halleck disapproved of women being in the field in any capacity. She didn't want to give him or anyone else an excuse to cut her off from Rucker's Quartermaster Department or ban her from the field entirely.

Apparently Clara told Henry Wilson about her problem, and he solved it himself. Without telling her, he put her brother David's name before the Senate, recommending a commission for him as assistant quartermaster with the rank of captain. Wilson's idea seemed to be that as assistant quartermaster David could work for her within the army, arranging for her to draw supplies from the Quartermaster Department and from the medical purveyor. Wilson also hoped that David could be assigned to Clara as her "companion and protector" in the field.

When Clara learned of David's nomination, she was overjoyed. "I know how my brother's name came before the Senate," she wrote Wilson, "and the arrangement was so completely what I needed,—would so facilitate my movements,—increasing my usefulness, and relieve me at once of all that I have ever found unpleasant in my field labors,—viz.—the necessary contact with strangers upon business matters, that I found myself instantly shorn of any words suitable for a reply." As for David, "I am confident that he will accept the position if offered him, for *my sake*, if upon no other consideration." She added that she was about ready to return to the field, "and *nothing* could so entirely conduce to my comfort, welfare, safety and efficiency, as that my brother, (if so it is to be) be as speedily assigned as possible, and thrown there with me,—the sooner this were accomplished, the sooner I could go to work, in *earnest*."

It didn't daunt Clara, a woman of illimitable energy, that David was fifty-four years old, with a wife and four children, and that he was in questionable health, suffering as he did from frequent "bilious" attacks. In her mind, he would make a good quartermaster; he had a way with horses and ran a thriving mill business in North Oxford. She waited impatiently for the Senate to confirm his appointment, without bothering to get his permission or even to inform him about his nomination.

But the engines of government worked slowly, even in wartime, and a month elapsed before Clara read in the *Washington Chronicle* of February 20 that David's commission had been confirmed and forwarded to the president. Only then did she tell her brother what was going on. "I have only to beg you that you will accept the position," she wrote him in haste, "and make ready to come and enter upon your duties when the papers assigning you to your post shall reach you." His pay would be about $130 a month—a considerable sum compared to the private's paltry pay of $13 per month—and would commence on the day of his acceptance. In a follow-up letter, Clara explained: "Your rank, a Capt., will I think entitle you to the charge of the Q.M. Dept. for a Division, and make you a staff officer. This Dept. provides for the quarters and transportation of the Army; storage and transportation of all supplies; army clothing; camp and garrison equipage, cavalry and artillery horses; fuel, forage; straw; material for bedding and stationery." She assured him, in case he had reservations, "It is not a dangerous position as the Q.M. has no call to be in advance at all, but it is in my estimation the most desirable position in the army." It was certainly "the most desirable" for Clara, since it would put David in an advantageous position within the army. It occurred to her, however, that his wife, Julia, might not appreciate David's military appointment. She added, "I wanted to write Julia and tell her that I am not to blame for getting her husband away, it is the U.S. Senate."

She also dashed off a letter to Elvira, her cousin and North Oxford postmistress, telling her about David's commission and urging her to see to it that he accepted "without hesitation." "The object," Clara pointed out, "was to make him a companion and protector for me, so far as possible for him to be with me, and I regard it as one of the most considerate, delicate and withal, generous compliments, which could have been paid me, from even so high a source."

Her scheming paid off, for David accepted his position and forwarded his papers to Rucker. Clara then took steps to have David stationed with Rucker in Washington. In fact, she drafted the letter David sent to the colonel asking for the assignment. Once David had learned his duties, she intended to get him reassigned to the field with her. Whether that would be with the Potomac Army or some other command, she did not know.

The Army of the Potomac, in the meantime, rocked with incriminations over the infamous Mud March, with subordinate generals quarreling violently with each other and with Burnside. Finally, Lincoln had taken all he could stand. He relieved Burnside and appointed "Fighting Joe" Hooker of Massachusetts to command the Potomac Army and lead it forward to victory. But winter storms dumped snow on Washington and northern Virginia, and Hooker could not go forth. "The Army of the Potomac," wrote one of Lincoln's secretaries, "is for the present stuck in the mud, as it has been for much of its existence."

In Washington, meanwhile, Clara devoted herself to her mountainous correspondence. "I am buried some hundreds deep in unanswered letters," she wrote Elvira. "Correspondence runs sadly behind hand when one goes to war I find." The vast majority of her donors knew her only by reputation—a reputation she had assiduously cultivated through her letters that appeared in the press, and she did her best to thank each of them. An indefatigable letter writer, Clara could reel off eight or ten long missives in a single day. Her letters weren't just written; they were *inhabited*, filled with poetic flights of description and an overriding sense that she and her backers were making history. She emphasized how much she was their representative on the battlefield, a conduit between them and their sons and husbands in uniform. This was "the broad platform upon which we meet, the very groundwork of our faith. It is a sisterly kindness which bids you seek me out and essay to fill my hands, which get so often, and sometimes so fearfully emptied." Their special relationship was indeed a sisterhood, forged by the demands of "a fratricidal war" and the hope of a better tomorrow. This war, Clara wrote one supporter, "not only opens coffers which never opened before, but hearts as well, dark shadows lie upon the hearth stones, but if in contrast the fading embers of humanity and brotherly love glow with a new radiance, it shall not at last have been in vain."

Occasionally her letters revealed a lighter side, for Clara had an unusual sense of humor too often suppressed by the weight of war. When a Mrs. Stout sent her a dressing gown for her personal wardrobe and said that Clara appeared to be "like other people," Clara replied that occasionally she was the opposite of other people. "Sometimes I have a hearty 'cry' over something that other people don't think worth noticing, and then again I laugh till the tears come, while those around look grave and don't see any thing in particular to laugh at—that's all the difference I believe." She made light of her small physical size. Because the clothes sent to her from strangers always seemed to fit, Clara had concluded that she was "just as big as every body else."

That raised the matter of her "new friend," the robe from Mrs. Stout. "Here I sit at my table," Clara told her, "in a most beautiful, charming brown dressing gown which I never heard of till an hour ago, and it wraps just as closely and lovingly, and wears just as easily, as an old tried friend who had been the companion of my joys and sorrows for years. . . . We were wondrously surprised at each other when we met, of course, but the little note of introduction which it bore, was *magic*; we understood each other at a glance, and with a kiss for the sake of the dear ones it had left, we became friends, *inseparable* while a thread of either of us remains."

Clara reserved her most intimate letters for her friend Mary Norton, who sent her a steady flow of supplies from her Soldiers' Aid Society in Hightstown, New Jersey. While Clara was older than Mary, they shared a common trait: they were spouseless, childless women in a world that regarded such a state as an aberration. They had met at the Clinton Liberal Institute in the 1840s, and Clara had lived with Mary and her family for about seven months in 1851–1852, residing in a room at their farm near Hightstown; Clara was then teaching school at nearby Cedarville. Mary was an effervescent young schoolteacher, and Clara enjoyed being around her. They shared a love for poetry, went on sleigh rides and trips together, and confided in one another about their romantic interests. Clara had enjoyed a courtship with Mary's brother, Charley, even though he was ten years younger than she.

But early in 1852 Clara fell into a protracted depression, perhaps triggered by a broken love affair with a young farmer. "I am so weary of all that's so wrongly called life," she confided in her diary; "am more and more certain every day that there is no such thing as true friendship at least not for me and I will not dupe and fool myself with the idle vain hobby longer. . . . I can see no possible satisfaction or benefit arising from *my* life."

Her malaise, however, went deeper than a broken relationship. It was the malaise of a lonely, thirty-year-old woman who, despite her excellence as a teacher, still had not found her true vocation and felt unfulfilled. Clara tried to suppress her feelings and wear a smile, but that only made her sadder. "True I laugh and joke but could weep that very moment and be the happier for it," she wrote in her diary. " 'There's many a grief lies hid not lost, / And smiles the least befit who wear them most.' " She knew this "repining" didn't help matters but couldn't stop "thinking it." Then she would try to pull herself together. "I will indulge in such useless complaints no more for the present, but commence once more my allotted task and cover neath smiles and pleasant words all."

Beneath the smiles, Clara was extraordinarily sensitive and easily hurt. By the time she left Hightstown in 1852, she and Mary had drifted apart—whether because of Clara's despondency, a misunderstanding, or something else is not clear. But a few years later, when Clara was back in North Oxford, they reconciled by letter. "Dear Mary," Clara wrote her in 1859, "it grieves me to hear you ask if I have forgiven you. I always forgave you child. I have no doubt that I was most to blame, in one respect I certainly was for I was older and should have had better judgment. It was strange that we who loved each other so much should ever become estranged."

By the Civil War, Mary was Clara's closest female friend—her "dear darling sister." On her trips home, Clara often stopped in New Jersey to see Mary. She also wrote her friend long, affectionate letters about her war work and her concerns for Stephen and Irving. When Clara returned to Washington after the Mud March and learned that Irving was ill again in North Oxford, she asked Mary to send him "a little

tiny" box of peach preserves. "Please do this for *my* little *pilgrim*,"
Clara said, "and I will go and care for *your soldiers*." Mary did send
Irving some preserves, and Clara took time away from her "business"
correspondence to write Mary a glowing seven-page letter that illuminated their special friendship and Clara's sense that here, in this cruel
war, she had finally found herself.

"You dont know all the good you are doing in this world, dear
Mary," Clara said, "and I dont want to tell you too much of it for fear
the fit will take you to do nothing but good. Now I dont want you to
become a devotee, and a martyr to other peoples necessities and suffering.

"I wish you to aid others where you can as comfortably as not, but
never lose sight of your own points of happiness—in short I dont want
you to be *too good*, for I expect to spend a great many days with you
yet, somewhere, and I want you to be as wildly joyous as ever, and as
wickedly mirthful as I am, and I really believe I am a great deal more
so, and not half as statue like and staid as when in the old time days of
school marm dignity you knew me *more*, but not as *well* as now.—I
think my associates did not quite get at my real character then,—the
under currents were strong. I did not quite know their strength . . . or
where they would lead, or where come out to the surface and I was a
little afraid of them myself and tried to cover them, I imagine,—but
now, I am better acquainted with me—and do not seem so formidable,
and mysterious as of yore, and sometimes I am mischievous and enjoy
others vexations, so dont you get too good or you will be no companion
for me."

As for her war work, Clara assured Mary: "I am so happy in doing
any little things I am able to, and glory so in any trifling sacrifice I am
called to make that I frequently think I ought to be the happiest person
in the world—and indeed Mary I think I become happier every year of
my life, notwithstanding this terrible war which would crush me to my
grave if I could not labor in it.

"It is easy to tell you (only another part of myself) how I appreciate
your thoughtful care and how I love you for it."

In March, David's fate took an unexpected turn when the War
Department assigned him not to Colonel Rucker's office in
Washington but to the Tenth Army Corps, which was stationed at Port
Royal, South Carolina, in the Department of the South. David was to

report to army headquarters on Hilton Head Island as soon as he could make his arrangements. To poor David, it seemed as if he had been posted on the moon. Hilton Head was situated some sixty miles down the coast from Charleston and what seemed a million miles from Massachusetts and his wife and children. Horrified, he hurried to Washington in late March, in hopes that his sister could get his orders changed. When that proved impossible, as she later claimed, his "family held me responsible for his personal safety in a deadly climate and insisted upon my accompanying him."

When she thought about it, though, Clara liked the idea. She wasn't "*very* particular" where she went, as she told Judge Barton, as long as it was the field. And there were compelling reasons for her to go to Hilton Head. It was far away from Dix's reach—about as far as Clara could get. Moreover, she learned from her War Department connections that army and navy forces in the Department of the South were planning a joint campaign to seize Charleston, a great blockade-running rebel port and the birthplace of secession. Here seemed a promising theater for her nursing and field relief operation. She hated to abandon her cherished Army of the Potomac, especially her "old pet" Ninth Corps, but she was ready for a new adventure.

She talked the matter over with David and agreed to go with him. Accordingly, she put through a formal request to the War Department, asking for permission to serve in the Department of the South and rehearsing her contributions to the Union cause from the Baltimore riot to Antietam and Fredericksburg. "I believe my services have been faithful, I know they have been laborious and appreciated. I have chosen my own position and I believe maintained it, which has been to stand by the soldier between the bullet and the city hospital. I trust I have never shrunk from duty or danger, and never shall while this terrible war lasts . . . and for certain reasons I now desire to go to Port Royal and would most respectfully ask your honored Dept. permission to do so and to take with me or have sent on to me such supplies as I may find necessary for the comfort of the suffering and the needy."

Rucker and her other friends in the War Department interceded in her behalf, and on March 27, 1863, an order came through on the authority of Secretary of War Stanton himself: "The Quarter Master, Col. Rucker, will issue transportation to Clara H. Barton from Washington to Port Royal SC. via New York. She is ordered to report at Port Royal as a nurse." In short, she was going there under the auspices of the War Department. She wasn't an official government nurse—unlike Dix's women, who received twelve dollars per month and one meal a day from the government, Clara would get no emolument for her services. But Stanton's approval did appear to grant her a semiofficial status outside Dix's authority. Indeed, Miss Dix would probably have had a fit had she known about it.

Major Edward Preston, a provost marshal, certainly believed that Clara was going south in an official capacity, and he said so in a letter of introduction he wrote for her: "The bearer Miss Clara H. Barton visits the Tenth Army Corps for the purpose of attending personally to the wants of wounded soldiers. She has rendered great service in all the great battles that have been fought in Virginia for the last six months. She acts under the direction of the Surgeon General, and with the authority of the Sect. of War. The smoke of battle, the roar of artillery and the shrieks of shot & shell do not deter her from administering to those who fall. She will explain all to you and I trust be able to do much good in the coming battles. Here she is highly respected and all bestow upon her much praise."

Armed with that glowing endorsement, Clara "made great haste to get ready" for her bold new adventure, sleeping little in forty-eight hours. She arranged for her nephew Sam, now a clerk in the surgeon general's office, to handle her business correspondence and forward her supplies from Washington. On March 30, departure day, Clara's friends insisted once again that she have her photograph taken at Brady's studio. She finally consented. But when Brady forwarded the photograph to her later, she declared it a "horrorgraph" and "suppressed" it as she had the other. "I was thin jaded hungry," she wrote Mary, "and hadn't been asleep for 48 hours and I looked as cadaverous as an owl in long days when mice are scarce."

That same March 30 General Sturgis called to tell her good-bye. As it turned out, Burnside and the entire Ninth Corps were on their way to the Department of the Ohio, comprising Kentucky and four midwestern states, which eased Clara's regrets about leaving the Potomac Army for Hilton Head. Sturgis said he was glad to get out of Hooker's army; he thought it was going to "get whipped again." "Genl Sturgis has sound judgment respecting the relative strength of bodies of troops," Clara wrote Judge Barton, "but I hope he mistakes this time."

That evening Clara and David entrained for New York City, where they intended to book passage on the government steamer *Arago*. In the city, however, they learned that the *Arago* would not depart for four more days, on a Saturday; so they took rooms at the Washington Hotel, where Clara wrote Judge Barton that they had left in such haste that she'd had no time to send home for anything. She needed a bottle of

"Mills Mint Specific" for her hair. "Being out in the field and looking at battles dries my hair and makes it fall," she explained. Could her cousin Ned express a bottle to her in New York before Thursday?

On Friday she received an unexpected caller. It was Sergeant Plunkett, and he had splendid news: he was "the fortunate recipient" of $4,000 from charitable donors, half of the money coming from the "Brokers Exchange" alone. Clara was delighted for "poor" Sergeant Plunkett; she thought that sum would go a long way toward paying for an attendant to feed and otherwise care for him.

On Saturday, April 4, the *Arago*, with Clara and David Barton on board, steamed out of New York City harbor and headed south in a rough sea, with angry gulls in pursuit. In the "ladies' cabin," which lurched and rolled with the waves, Clara made conversation with a Mrs. Van Wyke, whose military husband was stationed at Port Royal. The papers had reported some naval maneuver against Charleston, which convinced Clara that a battle was pending and that she was indeed going to an active and significant theater of the war. With "a few more such demonstrations," she believed, "the old city will surrender without resistance."

She was excited about another possibility, too. She hoped that the Union's coastal operations might somehow put her in contact with Stephen in North Carolina, if he were still alive. The Bartons hadn't heard a word from him for more than a year, and his silence worried them terribly and invited all manner of morbid speculations.

The *Arago* steamed steadily southward, passing off the North Carolina coast. The weather grew warmer. Clara was now farther south than she had ever been in her life. As the transport droned on, pushing the empty horizon ahead of it, David must have felt as though they were steaming toward the end of the world.

PART THREE

Hilton Head
and Battery Wagner

On Tuesday afternoon, April 7, the *Arago* reached Hilton Head, a low, flat, sandy island off the South Carolina coast. To the north, just across Port Royal Sound, lay St. Helena, Port Royal, and Parris islands. The Beaufort River divided the latter two islands and wound up past Beaufort, an old planters' town with spectacular magnolias and mansions with verandas around them and low slave barracks in the rear. The Sea Islands and their accessible harbors served as a military base for the South Atlantic Blockading Squadron under Rear Admiral Samuel Francis du Pont and the Union's Tenth Army Corps under General David Hunter.

As the *Arago* entered Port Royal Sound, passing the outer beach of Hilton Head, Clara could see huge stumps of live oak trees protruding from the sand, and fine plantation houses standing farther inland with rows of cedars and live oaks leading up to them. Presently the steamer bore down on a crude dock leading out to the channel from a busy military post, consisting of barracks and frame houses on stilts and an impressive, two-story manor with the Union flag snapping overhead in the ocean breeze. An incongruous signal tower, apparently added to the top of the manor after the Union occupation, resembled a miniature medieval castle.

The headquarters and ordnance and supply depots for the entire department, the post was heavily fortified against enemy attack. From the ocean beach to the east, a line of earthworks, palisades, and artillery stretched upland along the harbor. As Clara learned later, more entrenchments and batteries guarded the southern tip and the western side of the island, facing the rebel-held mainland. "The whole work," said an army chaplain, "was immense, elaborate, scientific, expensive, and strong."

When the *Arago* dropped anchor, a tug pulled alongside and a man leaped aboard with stunning news. A flotilla of nine Union ironclads, followed by transports loaded with infantry from Hilton Head, had steamed up the coast to attack Charleston harbor. "The first gun is to be fired upon Charleston this P.M. at three o'clock," the man said. Clara drew her watch; it was exactly three o'clock. "I felt as if I should sink through the deck," she wrote in her diary. "I am confounded. Literally speechless with amazement!" She had had a hunch that she was heading for a battle, and she was right. It was as if she had an inner compass unerringly pointing her in the direction of trouble. "I am no fatalist," she said, "but it is so singular."

Clara and David rode the tug to shore and immediately reported for duty at the headquarters of Lieutenant Colonel John J. Elwell, chief quartermaster of the Department of the South. But Elwell was not in his office in the mansion with the odd-looking signal tower. They found him in his quarters in a nearby bungalow, confined to his bed with a broken leg, and something about him—his vulnerability perhaps—touched Clara. He was a courtly gentleman in his early forties, tall and well built, with rich brown hair worn somewhat long in the back, a nose that sloped just over his mustache, and gentle gray eyes.

He apologized for not being "in the very best of condition." He had broken his leg when his horse fell through a bridge and plunged into a steep gully, throwing him savagely to the ground and fracturing both bones in his right leg just above the knee joint. As Elwell looked over their papers, David expressed his anxieties about serving down here, far away from his family, in what was probably a very unhealthy place. According to Clara, the colonel "spoke in the most consoling manner to David in reference to his fears and promised to be his friend." Then the colonel read Clara's letter of introduction from Major Preston. Very, very impressive. Since he was temporarily out of commission, he directed the Bartons to Assistant Adjutant General Charles G. Halpine for anything they might need, saying in a note to Halpine that he might be familiar with Clara's work, for she had been much in the Washington area of the war. "She is the American Florence Nightingale," Elwell asserted, "& has without a doubt seen more battlefields than any American woman."

Clara told Elwell that she wanted to go to Charleston as soon as he could arrange transportation for her. When she learned that only about 10,000 troops had followed the monitors into battle and that the enemy supposedly numbered many more than that, she was appalled. She was used to campaigning with the Army of the Potomac, which at one point after Antietam had numbered more than 130,000 men. She thought the

Tenth Corps far too small to establish a beachhead at Charleston and feared high casualties, which was all the more reason for her to go there. Elwell promised to see about getting her a pass, and Clara and David made their leave.

The next day they moved into temporary quarters, and David was assigned to help Captain Samuel Lamb, a pleasant fellow from Beverly, Massachusetts. Clara soon discovered that Hilton Head specialized in *"polite* warfare," as she described it to Mary Norton, "for it is a most 'civilized' and 'enlightened' place to say nothing of its being decidedly *fashionable,* and *splendidly gay*." Several officers had brought their wives to stay with them; General Hunter's wife lived with him in the house with the signal tower and was reported to be as good a shot with a pistol as the general was. On the beach, Clara saw "ladies and girls" riding horseback in all directions, and she thought it a strange sight indeed for a war zone.

Charming, young looking, and unmarried, Clara created quite a stir among the wifeless officers and men on the island. Several officers sent her bouquets of flowers—magnolias, orange blossoms, and roses—along with invitations to go horseback riding. But she had no time for such frivolous pursuits, not with a battle about to break out at Charleston. Her place was there, with the wounded and dying.

When Clara pressed Elwell about the pass, however, the colonel was not "quite inclined" to let her go to a battlefront. But finally he relented, and a conditional pass came through from General Hunter himself. "Our fleet is battering away at Fort Sumpter and Fort Sumpter returning about ten to one, and Charleston laughing at the fun no doubt," Clara wrote Mary Norton. "I join them by invitation of Genl. Hunter whenever the right time comes, if ever." She added: "I have little or no confidence in the success of this expedition and never have had. I wish I could see it in some brighter light, but it is not given me to do so."

Her pessimism was justified. Two days later, on April 11, the troop transports from the Charleston expedition reached Hilton Head, "much to the consternation of every body" there, Clara said. Soon the harbor was teeming with ships, waiting to unload their human cargo at the rickety dock, which could accommodate only one large ship at a time. The first ship pulled up to it, and soldiers streamed off carrying their rifles and camp gear. "All sorts of rumors were afloat," Clara wrote in her diary, "but the one general idea seemed to prevail that the expedition had 'fizzled.' . . . All seem disappointed & chagrined, but no one is blamed. For my part I am rather pleased with the turn it has taken, as I had thought from the first that we had 'too few troops to fight, and too many to be killed.' I have seen worse retreats than this one."

All the next day troops disembarked from the transports and made campfires around the military village. It was a fine, warm day, and the crackling fires reminded Clara of "the old soldier times" on the march with the Army of the Potomac. But in truth she was in a glum mood, for no one knew when there would be another campaign. "A dull life," she wrote in her diary, "and to little purpose only for the thought that the Lord knows best."

On April 13 General Hunter paid Clara a visit. He was an impressive-looking man, with piercing little black eyes that opened wide when he was excited. An outspoken old warrior and abolitionist, he had abolished slavery in his department back in May 1862 and had also recruited a black regiment among the local "contraband." One company, under the command of a black man named John Brown, was the first Union black outfit to see offensive action, doing so in a skirmish with rebel guerrillas. Hunter's abolition order got him into trouble with Lincoln, who promptly overruled it because it violated administrative policy. Lincoln also refused to sanction Hunter's black regiment, and eventually most of it disbanded. Even so, to use Clara's words, this old-line cavalry officer had caught the "great drift" of the Civil War before the president had. A few months later, in fact, Lincoln came around to Hunter's position on emancipation and black soldiers.

Clara and the general had a pleasant conversation, during which he gave her his view of the Charleston fiasco. To get at the city, he said, the navy had to destroy or neutralize Fort Sumter in the middle of the harbor and knock out the rebel shore batteries, especially those on Morris Island. But when the Union ships had steamed into Charleston Harbor with their eleven- and fifteen-inch guns blazing, rebel gunners had sunk one monitor and damaged four others in the first hour of combat, proving that the unwieldy ironclads were no match for heavily armed forts. Hence, it had been "impracticable" to renew the attack the next day, Hunter said, "and as he had only 10,000 troops to meet 50,000," he had withdrawn his troops. In fact, the rebels had nowhere near that many men in all of South Carolina. Like McClellan, Hunter and his army colleagues were afflicted with an exaggerated notion of rebel troop strength bordering on paranoia. In any case, Hunter said, the attack had been strictly a naval operation. His troops had gone along only to occupy Morris Island after the navy captured it.

So Charleston remained in rebel hands, and blockade runners continued to dash in and out of the harbor, eluding du Pont's blockading squadron. Secretary of the Navy Gideon Welles upbraided du Pont for withdrawing after a "single brief effort" and tarnishing the reputation of the Union navy. Washington wanted Charleston harbor closed, and if du Pont couldn't do it, the navy would find somebody who could.

Clara disagreed with Washington's view. "The possession of that City," she wrote Mary Norton, "is not of sufficient importance to justify the loss and sacrifice of human life incident upon its capture if indeed it can be done against all their fortifications and in their entrenchments. I would hit them where the armor was not so impenetrable, or the skin so thick—it can be done, and *will be*—so dont feel mortification at the want of success of that Expedition, rather let reason and cool judgment and humanity rule—and say it was best—*for it was*." As for Hunter and du Pont, "they are *above question*, and their *loyalty* not to be argued, they have grown old in the service of the country and in the discharge of their duties and it is not for us who have only *patriotic desire* and *national pride* and *good will* to match all these, to advise or criticize or decide over their gray heads." Clara added: "I flatter myself that I am getting to be a good soldier and learning to *obey* without complaint which is one of the first important lessons to be learned in the service."

In a recent letter, Mary had expressed concern about Clara's safety on the battlefield. "I thank you darling for all your kindly solicitude," Clara wrote her now, "and I will not 'make light of it,' because I happen to be so supremely *safe* at this moment. I know I *am* sometimes where it is very dangerous, but I have been mercifully spared, and protected. . . . No dear sis I will never be fool hardy, for I am too anxious to live to do my duty to others for that, even if I had no other desire, but I have, my life is not a burden that I should seek to throw it away, it is dearer than ever to me now, not only for what I may *do*, but for what I possess in the choice *glorious* class of friends who are circling around me a wall of living strength and beauty and loveliness."

Among Clara's glorious new friends was Captain Samuel Lamb, whom David was helping out. When Clara learned that he was the scion of the Lambs of Charlton, Massachusetts, she was astonished. His father had been the Barton family physician, she said, which in her opinion made the captain "a kind of relative." As it happened, Lamb had a wife named Sarah and two grown sons. Even so, he gave Clara bouquets of beautiful flowers and spent a good deal of his leisure time with her.

They went on early morning horseback rides along the beach, with Clara sitting properly sidesaddle. Since she had neglected to bring a riding outfit, she wore an "old extemporized rig"—a blue jacket with brass buttons and an "alpaca skirt." Sometimes they rode as far as the Drayton plantation, eighteen miles away, trotting through avenues of magnificent trees, with mocking birds trilling in them. They visited the Union pickets and once let their horses fly at a gallop, covering five miles in twenty minutes. Then they waded a deep creek and rested in the woods, where Clara held the horses' reins while the captain picked a basket of flowers for her.

Clara was extraordinarily fond of Captain Lamb, but their relationship was strictly platonic. She wrote cousin Annie that he was "so good and so modest and well bred and social and high-minded" that his acquaintance would afford pleasure to anyone. His twenty-year-old son, Frank, arrived on "the Head" in late April, with an appointment as "chief telegraph operator" for the entire Department of the South. "We think this rather advanced for a lad of scarcely 20," Clara wrote Mary Norton.

Meanwhile Clara and David moved into a suite of rooms next to Colonel Elwell's quarters, with Clara thinking that she was "only the other side of a pine board from him." On the day of the move, the weather was miserable, with rain and a furious wind lashing the island and waves thundering against the shoreline. Their new quarters consisted of two fourteen-foot rooms, each with a pine-wood floor, a fireplace, a door opening into a long hallway, and a rain-spattered window. David took the bedroom and Clara the parlor, where her army trunk doubled as her bedstand. Standing near her window was a solid mahogany table trimmed in brass, with a heavy top made of "black Egyptian marble." "We are most kindly cared for," Clara wrote in her diary that day, "the col has just sent in a stuffed rocking chair to me, which I fear he might need himself."

In her "grotesque" little room, Clara entertained a steady flow of visitors, men "of the highest order of intellect," she noted, "and accustomed to all the luxuries of social life, from private soldier to major Generals." A group of soldiers even serenaded her one midnight and left her a bouquet of flowers in the hall. In addition to Captain Lamb, her regular callers included Dr. John J. Craven, medical purveyor of the Tenth Corps, and Colonel Charles H. Van Wyck, commander of the Fifty-sixth New York, whose wife had arrived with Clara on the *Arago*. To Clara's delight, the colonel possessed "a most refined and delicate poetic taste." There was little to read at the post, so they repeated from memory "old scraps of poetry, alternately one *playing* that he had a real book of poems" while the other listened. They remembered so many poems that it seemed they had an entire *"library"* at their disposal.

Clara, David, and the two Lambs formed a "mess" together and shared their meals. She wrote Mary Norton that they had a lovely new kitchen with "a nice charcoal range and a dining room as cool and neat as if in N.J. & N.E. we have all descriptions of vegetables up to watermelons and you would smile to see *us soldiers* eating our dinners from the whitest of linen table covers with *silver knives & forks* but so it is."

The ocean was just three rods from Clara's front door, and she was quite mesmerized by the beauty of the beach, especially at night when she sat at her window. "The white sand glistens like frost," she said, "and lies in the moonlight at night like huge sheets and piles of driven snow."

The army barracks, Clara's included, were long, low, wooden structures, whose furniture had been confiscated from manor houses on the island. Indeed, Clara learned that Hilton Head and the other Sea Islands had once been the home of a flourishing plantation culture. The Beauforts, Rhetts, Barnwells, Fripps, and Coffins had all lived here, and the luxury cotton raised on their fertile estates had commanded high prices in New England and Europe. Many of the great planters had been secessionist fire-eaters, too, and hot-headed advocates of civil war. But when Union warships and occupation troops had seized the islands in November 1861, the planters had fled to the mainland with their house slaves, abandoning their estates and most of their field hands. After that, the islands became a refuge for escaped slaves from the mainland, and abolitionist volunteers, responding to a call from the Union commander on the islands, had come down to manage the abandoned estates, educate the blacks in "the rudiments of civilization and Christianity," and put them to work in the fields for pay. It was called the Port Royal experiment. Once Lincoln had decided to issue an emancipation proclamation, in August 1862, he authorized Union recruiters to enroll black men on the sea islands into the First South Carolina Infantry (Colored), under the command of a fiery abolitionist minister from Massachusetts, Thomas Wentworth Higginson. Lincoln's Emancipation Proclamation of January 1, 1863, publicly recognized the employment of black soldiers and officially freed all the slaves on the Sea Islands.

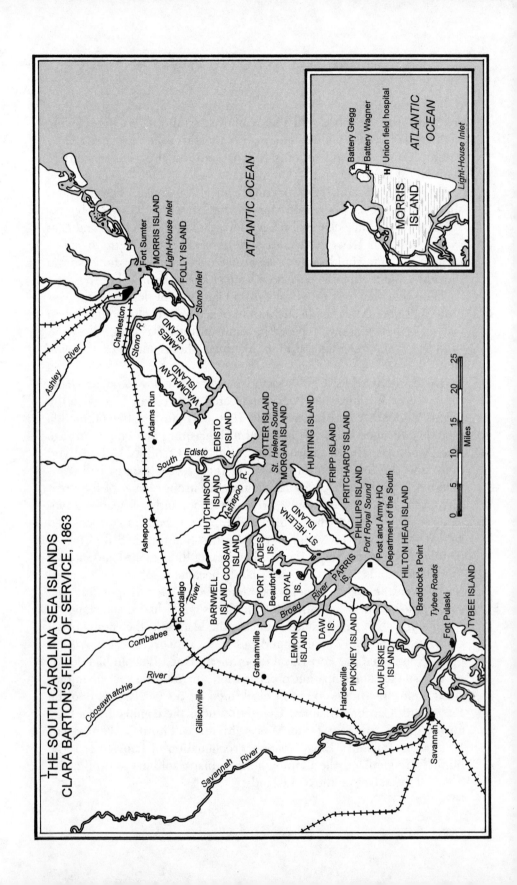

THE SOUTH CAROLINA SEA ISLANDS
CLARA BARTON'S FIELD OF SERVICE, 1863

Clara had seen some of the brutal effects of slavery in Virginia: the impoverished slave shacks behind the plantation mansions, the ragged clothes and haunted faces of slave refugees. Even so, she was ill prepared for what she found on the Sea Islands, here in the Deep South, where slavery had always been cruelest. Most of the blacks here had been field hands, driven like oxen by the slave driver's whip from dawn to last light, six days a week. Their endless, back-breaking labor, poor diets, and wretched living conditions had exacted a terrible toll on them, physically and psychologically. Many were bent and crippled, with the light long since gone out in their eyes. Abolitionist agents were shocked at their "abject" and "dismal" appearance and docile behavior and recoiled at their stories of white cruelty and abuse. That the blacks had survived at all was something of a miracle and a tribute to the strength of their survival mechanisms: the family and the slave church. Many of them had resisted slavery—had protested, fought back, or run away—and all nursed long-repressed feelings of hostility toward their former masters. Many of the them spoke an unfamiliar dialect; none could read or write English, and their illiteracy troubled Union authorities clear up to Washington. How, they questioned, could such people survive in free society? With government approval, many Northern women, black and white alike, volunteered to teach the "freed" people on the islands and opened schools for them on abandoned plantations. One such missionary was Charlotte Forten, a sensitive, idealistic young black woman from Philadelphia. When Clara came to Port Royal, Charlotte was teaching liberated slaves on St. Helena Island—"in the very heart of Rebeldom," as she put it. "I do not at all realize yet that we are in S.C.," Forten wrote in her diary. "It is all a strange wild dream, from which I am constantly expecting to awake."

Clara met one of the other missionary teachers in Colonel Elwell's quarters. Her name was Mary Gage, and she and her mother, Frances, had come down from Ohio to help instruct the blacks on Parris Island. Clara found Mary "a charming young lady," and promised to visit her and her mother. Perhaps inspired by Mary's work, Clara started teaching a group of "colored boys" to read, organized black women into a washing detail, and gave the more needy families food and clothing from her own supplies.

During those desultory April days, Clara lavished most of her attention on her bed-ridden neighbor, Colonel Elwell. She thought him a truly extraordinary man. Before the war, he had tried his hand at various professions in his home state of Ohio. A graduate of the Cleveland

Medical College, he had practiced medicine for nine years. He had
served a term in the Ohio legislature, taken up law and built up a
respectable practice, and then turned to academe, serving as professor
of "medical jurisprudence" at the Ohio and Union Law College and
Western Reserve Medical College. Yes, it was strange to find a physi-
cian-lawyer-professor from Ohio serving as chief quartermaster on a
South Carolina island, but that was the war for you. He had a nice
laugh.

He was also married, with a loyal wife named Nancy and children
awaiting him back in Cleveland.

Nevertheless, Clara was irresistibly attracted to this kind, "manly
man." He was a wonderful raconteur and conversationalist, and
between them flowed a steady hum of warm and witty chatter. She
brought him flowers and made a sock for Dr. Craven to put on his leg,
and her diary entries glowed with accounts of their time together.
"Called again on the Col. in the evening had a most delightful chat,
was the happiest for it, he is so calm and Christian like." "As usual his
mind was clear as a silver star and pure as white sand and we had a
long and pleasant chat." "Received a most beautiful note from the Col
before breakfast. What a life, and I am fearful that I ought to be in
some other quarter although 'whatever is, is right' I know." One April
evening they "conversed a long time on old battle scenes," Clara
describing her war experiences and the colonel recalling the time he
had "seen the Elephant," in the 1862 battle of Secessionville, on James
Island just south of Charleston.

At some point, Elwell came down with yellow fever and was so sick
it seemed that he might die. Clara scarcely left his bedside, and her
expert nursing helped him recover. Elwell would never forget the way
she cared for him when he lay in "that dark dismal back room," burning up with fever. She was so "tender, and considerate," he said later;
her very presence brightened the room for him.

By April 28, Clara noted in her diary, Elwell's leg was well enough
for him to get out of bed. It hadn't healed properly, though, and he
couldn't flex or fully extend it and had to hobble about on crutches.

With the colonel at least up and about, Clara decided to visit Mary
and Frances Gage on Parris Island. Captain Lamb went along, and they
found the Gages on a plantation situated in "a little paradise of flowers," as Clara put it. She and Frances had a long, intimate conversation,
and Clara was impressed by her "excellent judgment" and "correct and
large views." Now fifty-four years old, this compassionate, eloquent,
loving woman had fought all her adult life against slavery and discrimi-

nation against women. As a girl, she had endured the taunts of her Ohio schoolmates because of her sympathy for runaway slaves who came through their neighborhood. She often went to the cabins where they were hiding and felt their hurts as though they were her own. At age twenty, she married James L. Gage, a lawyer and like-minded abolitionist. While raising eight children, Frances not only "waged moral warfare" against slavery but rejected the notion, as she put it, that "a woman's true province" was "at home by the sick bed & cradle & in the domestic employment of the kitchen." She demanded the ballot for women and equality before the law for all citizens, regardless of sex or color. Her outbursts stirred up a lot of resentment among her neighbors, who dismissed them as examples of her "craziness." But she refused to be silent. She went on to become a prominent speaker and leader in the woman's rights movement, presiding over the Fourth National Woman's Rights Convention in Cleveland and serving as an elected vice-president of every annual convention from 1854 until the Civil War; she championed the cause in her temperance lectures, published poems, and articles for the *Ohio Cultivator* and the *Ohio Farmer*. An unflagging optimist, she believed that "good men are everywhere acknowledging our chains" and that "a better time" was coming for the oppressed of the land. To a feminist friend, she stressed a crucial point: "Let the mothers of our country train their sons to think & feel right & all will be well."

After the Gages moved to slaveholding Missouri, Frances took "the platform amidst hissing, and scorn, and newspaper vituperations, to maintain the right of woman to the legitimate use of all the talents God invests her with; to maintain the rights of the slave in the very ears of the masters." She suffered for her temerity in speaking out: three times great fires swept through the family property, infernos that Frances blamed squarely on antiabolitionist and antifeminist "incendiaries." The Civil War found the Gages back in Ohio, where Frances, signing her name as "Aunt Fanny," edited the "Home Department" of the *Ohio Cultivator* while caring for her husband, whose health had steadily declined. Four of their six sons enlisted in the Union army, and Fanny, too, yearned to help the cause. When she learned about the Port Royal experiment in the autumn of 1862, she gave up everything—her lecturing and writing, a sick husband, the other children—and came down to help the Sea Island blacks adjust to freedom. The Union military governor was so impressed with her talents that he appointed her general superintendent of the plantations on Parris Island, and her daughter Mary joined her there the following spring.

Clara spent three days with Fanny Gage, whose lively wit, poetic bent, and love for conversation matched Clara's own. They picked blackberries, which were as "dense as a black velvet carpet," and visited other plantations, where the blacks were raising rice, corn, cotton, and sweet potatoes under Fanny's supervision. By now, the magnolias and orange trees were budding white blossoms and sweetening the air with a rich fragrance, and Clara and Fanny walked together through a "sea of bloom" and out over the fields to the ocean. They could see a steamer lying off the island, men fishing with a net, and the *Arago* moored at the dock, and they listened, transfixed, to the unforgettable trills of mockingbirds as they soared and swooped overhead.

Clara's visit marked the beginning of a loving friendship with Fanny and Mary Gage, who often called on her at Hilton Head. Both Gages found Clara a kindred spirit and admired her war work, and the admiration was mutual. Clara was soon calling Mary her best young female friend and Fanny her "dear *womanly* friend." Clara was especially impressed with Fanny's intelligence. "Her reading and vigor of mind are remarkable," Clara wrote in her diary, "she is a powerful woman, and wins very much my affection."

It was John Elwell, though, who captured Clara's heart. "He is *my friend*," she wrote Mary Norton. "I could not tell you in a day all the good noble manly Christian qualities he possesses; the rare combination of intellect, scholarship, business talent, spirit and gentleness, firm like a man and tender like a girl." If anything, Elwell cared even more deeply for Clara. Yes, he was married and had children, and yes he mentioned how devoted his wife was to him. But alone, far away from her on this tropical island, he fell in love with Clara Barton. He adored everything about her: the "glow of the eye, and flush of the cheek, and strength of step." She was his "best" friend and "companion."

He had a volume of Elizabeth Barrett Browning, and they recited poetry to one another and had stimulating discussions about literature. They laughed together, wept together, and worried about the war together. At some point that spring, they began expressing their passion physically. Elwell later admitted that he loved her "all the law allows (and a little more perhaps)." With Elwell, Clara willingly violated Victorian propriety, which demanded that a lady be chaste, especially if she were unmarried. So much the proper lady in other respects, she refused to be a prude about sexual matters, as long as they were handled discreetly.

To avoid pregnancy, the lovers could avail themselves of various contraceptive methods then in vogue. Contraceptive manuals of the day highly recommended that the woman use a postcoital douche of cold water or solutions of "white vitriol," sulfate of zinc, chloride of zinc, or sulfate of iron, administered by a syringe. "Immediately after sexual intercourse," advised an 1855 pamphlet, "let the female arise, fill the syringe with cold water, and, placing herself over the basin, introduce the syringe the whole length, and inject the cold water, with moderate force, into the vagina, or birth place. Repeat the operation several times in quick succession, until a slight chill, or sensation of cold is experienced. . . . If these instructions are faithfully carried out, you need have no fears that you will become pregnant."

The contraceptive literature also recommended one of various "pessaries" or "intravaginal" devices. The most popular appears to have been a piece of soft sponge, soaked with "a weak solution of sulphate of iron" or the like, and inserted into "the upper part" of the vagina before intercourse, with a piece of ribbon or silk string attached to the sponge so as to remove it afterward. The sponge pessary, an 1856 manual claimed, "is an effective preventive," if followed at once by a vaginal wash. Condoms for men, called *baudruches* or "French secrets" and made of oiled silk or India rubber, were also available in Civil War America; an industrious chief quartermaster like Colonel Elwell would have had the resources to acquire as many "French secrets" as he desired.

He and Clara wrote one another intimate notes, and he called her "Birdie" and "My Pet" and asked if he might visit her "nest." The notes suggest that they would spend part of the night together, either in Clara's "nest" or his. Since his room was next door to hers, they had no trouble being discreet. "My Dear Sister," he wrote her after one tryst. "I did have a fine sleep last night! How could it be otherwise? That was one of the golden hours of life to me," which could never be forgotten in the future. "Ah! the *future*!—the great future. How it opened to us! I cannot forget the expression of your face while we were talking. It was the expression of happiness—the deepest happiness! not the evanescent flush of joy, but the deep realization of what only comes to us now and then. Was I mistaken? was it not a reflection of what I felt in my own heart? I think not.

"You touched one spring that I supposed was hidden—it must be.

How came you to find it in one situated as I am?—in the Army—in the rough and tumble life of the Quartermaster Dept.?"

Clara wrote him a similar note in the glowing aftermath of a night together. "*Sunrise* at the east window," it read. " 'Oh what a glory doth this world put on! . . . The great warm yellow sun throws back his sheets of blue and gold, and rises from his billowing bed dripping light and beauty, and commences his journey of gladness and joy to scatter his golden smiles among the darkened homes of the children of the earth. . . . All nature murmurs a blessing for cares extended and joys conferred, may not *my* great thanks be joined in the great hymn to the giver of gifts—who has not only vouchsafed me these great *general* blessings, but wrapped about me the kind arms of loving *ones*, who take up his great work of love and carry it out in detail, providing for my every want, cheering my every hour, sustaining my hopes, strengthening my purposes, blessing my life.

"There, in my quiet 'nest,' *spread all over with down* filled with *happy memories* I have only to sit in my cozy nook looking out upon the face of all this beautiful nature, and *be thankful*—thankful for *all*; but not the least, is the sweet consciousness that one may think and act, and be, what nature designed and still *be understood*, that one may love and trust a friend and still be known as only loving and trusting."

She concluded: "Such are you my friend making life to me. I am a stronger, happier woman for having known you, and in my heart of hearts I feel that to the latest hour of my life I shall bless god for having given me *John Elwell for my friend*."

She signed the note "Birdie."

He often signed his notes "John Boy," and in truth there was a little boy inside him who needed and depended on a woman's love, first his wife's and now Clara's. "My Birdie," he wrote in one note, "I have had a tough day—when may I retreat to the Bird's nest & rest my head? I am tired—I am a child—Many years ago I had a mother & what a relief to go to her in my trouble and lay my head on her lap—and then I had a wife,—always troubled to see care upon my brow—I have no mother & my wife can't come to me. So here I am a poor child—homeless, motherless, wifeless. I'm tired—when may I come to my Bird's nest?" He signed one such note "Your Child."

The hurt little girl inside Clara opened up to John Boy's pleadings, and it gave an intensity to their passion unlike anything either of them had ever experienced. She told him that she would never forget their "loving hours" together. "When my life has grown long and dark and broken and I turn back and lift the shaded folds one by one, I shall *know these months* by the bright golden threads of smiles and sun-beams that my generous friend has helped me to weave." Elwell felt the same way about his "darling" Clara. He told her that the memory of holding her in his arms would shine "for ever and ever."

They went on outings together—as much as Elwell's bad leg would allow. Once they took a trip to Port Royal and got caught in a storm. Frightened by the thunder and lightning, Clara hid in a *"powder maga-zine,"* and the sight of her amused Elwell so much that he broke out laughing. On Hilton Head, when Clara's "elegant friend" was not hob-bling about attending to his quartermaster duties, they took carriage rides together. They would drive down the beach almost to Braddock's Point on the southwestern tip of the island and return through the live oaks for an intimate supper of turtle soup. Sometimes they made love on those outings down the shore. "John Boy will be busy an hour or so," Elwell wrote her; "then look out for the carriage. John. Remember the bedding."

He could not bear to be apart from her. "Shall we take another of those pleasant rides my dear Sister?" he asked in one note. "I have been hard at work, but a rest of a couple of hours has done something for me. Our time is precious, and I do not know how to forego your companionship for two or three hours." He worried about her con-stantly. "Sister Clara—you have not been to supper and don't want any taken to you. What is the matter? Have I made you sick? I hope not. I cant love you sick—unless I see you tonight I shall not sleep a wink, perhaps." He signed the message: "Your Child, John."

Clara replied: "My dear brother, I am *not* sick *nothing is the matter*, and *how* did *you* know that I was not *at* supper." She added, "I will call and set matters right in about half an hour."

One night, after she slipped away to her room, he sent her a tender message. "This has been so beautiful an Evening. I expect to dream about it (again good night)."

No matter how much they loved and needed one another, they accepted boundaries to their relationship. She made no effort to win him from his wife, nor did he offer to leave her for Clara. When Clara gazed at the ocean beyond her window, she thought the waves were whispering in chorus, "Thus far shall thou go and no farther!"

One day she found him looking sad and asked what was troubling him, and he admitted that it was his "anniversary week." Clara was not one to be jealous. "He is so sensitive and delicate I almost fear to speak to him on some points," Clara wrote in her diary, "and yet I do not fear."

*   *   *

Still, in her moments alone that spring, Clara felt guilty that she was
not in the field, and she felt even worse when a report came that the
Army of the Potomac had gone into battle again. There was little military activity in this theater, and she saw no way that she could reach
Stephen in North Carolina. How could she remain here without "some
object"? Although she loved John Elwell, she had her work to do in
this war, and it wasn't getting done on Hilton Head. "All things conspire to give me an impression that this is not a sphere of usefulness
for me," she wrote in her diary. "I begin to think that I must return on
the Arago."

In early May her cousin Leander Poor arrived on Hilton Head with
a quartermaster appointment, and he was a relief compared to David,
who had done little but complain about his job since he and Clara had
arrived. Cousin Leander brought news that Hooker was fighting desperately in Virginia, and Clara regretted missing the opportunity to
accompany her army into combat. On May 8 rebel pickets on the
South Carolina mainland shouted across the river that "*Hooker was
whipped*," and subsequent news bore them out. As General Sturgis
had predicted, Fighting Joe Hooker had gone down to defeat, at a
place called Chancellorsville, and the wings of some "destructive fate"
continued to hover over the Army of the Potomac. "God is great; and
fearfully just," Clara wrote in her diary; "his ways are past finding out."

For two weeks, Clara vacillated about leaving Hilton Head. "Still
unsettled," she recorded on May 11. "My inclination says go." A few
days later she learned that a Federal steamer named the *Ranger* had
arrived from North Carolina and was soon to return. She was thrilled
to learn that one of the officers had been up the Chowan River, had
stopped at Bartonsville, and had actually talked to a Union man who fit
Stephen's description. Clara resolved to go to North Carolina on board
the *Ranger*, but when she talked with Elwell about a pass, he answered
with "a most emphatic 'no.' " The *Ranger* was not seaworthy, he said,
and he would never forgive himself if Clara sailed away on "such a
craft." He seemed so distressed and hurt by the possibility of her leaving him that Clara couldn't bring herself to protest. She simply wrote a
letter to Stephen, which Captain Griffin agreed to deliver if he saw her
brother again.

So it was settled: she would stay here with Elwell. "God's will not
mine be done," she recorded the next night, during a thunderstorm; "I

am content, how I wish I could always keep in full view the *fact* . . . that God orders all things precisely as they should be, all is best *that is*."

The next morning, a Sunday, brought a note from Elwell: "My Dear Sister, shall we take a ride this fresh beautiful Sabbath morning? I would like to. The storm is over and it is so bright and new. God is abroad this morning. Let us go out and meet him. Thine, John." And they did go out and meet Him, taking along a volume of Lyman Beecher's sermons to read together.

On May 27 a violent storm lashed the islands with heavy rains and gale force winds, and the waves crashed against the ocean shore of Hilton Head with a primal fury. At noon, to Clara's surprise, Frances Gage turned up at quartermaster headquarters: she had left Parris Island in the middle of the storm, setting out in a dugout with a crude sail and a couple of black oarsmen. The little dingy had almost sunk in the storm; the wind tore the sail to shreds, and the waves tossed the boat violently about. It was a wonder they hadn't capsized and drowned. Dripping wet and exhausted, Frances had bad news to report from home: her husband was dangerously ill, and she must go to his bedside. Mary, however, would stay on Parris Island. Two days later, after the weather had cleared, Frances hugged Clara good-bye and left for home on the *Arago*. Clara watched the steamer recede until it was just a black speck on the horizon and then was gone.

On June 3, at the invitation of a Mrs. Lander, a young friend of General Hunter, Clara and Elwell attended a dinner party at her temporary residence in Beaufort. An officer met them at the boat with a four-horse carriage and conveyed them to Mrs. Lander's home. Here an officer gave Clara a gift of a lovely pocket Bible as a token of esteem for her gallant service. "I do not deserve such friends as I find," Clara wrote in her diary.

Dinner was served at two o'clock, and among the notables on hand was Colonel Higginson. It was the first time Clara had met the commander of the First South Carolina Infantry (Colored). He was tall and animated and a physical fitness enthusiast—he ran everywhere, did calisthenics, and liked to play something comparable to touch football. Before the war, he had won fame as a militant abolitionist and a backer of John Brown's raid at Harpers Ferry.

At dinner, the *New York Tribune* correspondent, a Mr. Page, told everyone that he had seen Clara at work at the Lacy House during the battle of Fredericksburg. He had also seen her in town on the day of the assaults on Marye's Heights. He described how Provost Marshal Patrick had "remonstrated" with Clara about staying in town; the old gentleman had expected her to be shot at any moment, Mr. Page said.

The dinner guests talked at length about the black soldiers on the islands. The Second South Carolina Infantry (Colored) had been organized under Colonel James Montgomery, an intense, religious man who had ridden with John Brown in Bleeding Kansas. On this very day, in fact, the outfit was on a raid up the South Carolina mainland. Another black regiment had just reached the islands from the North: the Fifty-fourth Massachusetts Volunteer Infantry, under the command of twenty-five-year-old Robert Gould Shaw. This was the showcase black regiment raised under Governor Andrew's authority to demonstrate to skeptical whites that black men could make excellent soldiers. Frederick Douglass, the great black leader, had helped recruit men for the regiment, and two of his own sons had signed up. Lincoln's black volunteers were nothing if not courageous, inasmuch as the rebel South had vowed to execute all black men captured in blue uniforms. Wrote a young corporal of the Fifty-fourth: "There is not a man in the regiment who does not appreciate the difficulties, the dangers, and maybe ignoble death that awaits him, if captured by the foe, and they will die upon the field rather than be hanged like a dog."

After the dinner at Mrs. Lander's, Clara and Elwell went for a carriage ride in the neighborhood. They passed splendid two-story mansions with expansive, landscaped yards—symbols of what they hoped was a dying way of life. At one plantation, Clara wrote in her diary, "We saw the most beautiful grove of live oaks I ever imagined," with "pendant moss hanging from branches like the drapes of death, so dark and so mournful." As they turned to go, the sun was just setting behind a distant hedge and throwing shafts of light through the dense shade of the oaks.

Back at Mrs. Lander's, they spent the evening on the veranda with various officers, wives, the *Tribune* correspondent, and other guests, while a regimental band serenaded them. The main topic of conversation was Montgomery's raid up the Combahee River. One report credited Harriet Tubman with the idea of the raid; the famous black abolitionist and Underground Railroad conductor was now living in Beaufort and helping the former slaves, nursing soldiers, and serving as an unpaid spy and scout for the Union army. Before the raid, she had reconnoitered rebel defenses along the Combahee, and when Montgomery and 300 infantry and artillery men started upriver on two steamers (this was the night before Mrs. Lander's dinner party), Tubman went along as their pilot. They burned rebel cotton and rice fields and destroyed a pontoon bridge and other property, all reported to be worth several hundred thousand dollars, and returned to Beaufort with more than 700 "contrabands" liberated from rebel plantations. Montgomery's soldiers, all former slaves, "fought well and did not lose a man, but killed and wounded a number of the enemy"—so said the officers on Mrs. Landers' veranda the evening after the raiders returned. The next day Clara saw the blacks brought back from the mainland and was shocked at how degraded and hopeless they appeared. "The negroes were of all ages, sizes & complexions," she wrote a cousin later, "but most of them worthless in any country, only as subjects for missionary labors, and candidates for eternity."

At Colonel Higginson's invitation, Clara visited the camp of the First South Carolina, and she thought that the blacks were "a fine" group of soldiers and that the colonel had "every mark of a humane gallant officer." Inside the colonel's tent, a copy of Victor Hugo's *Les Misérables* and writing utensils lay on his table, next to an imposing piece of "secesh" furniture, a sort of bureau. Clara delighted in conversation with Higginson and his mild and courtly surgeon, Dr. Ruggers, and felt indebted to them for many happy moments of "choice entertainment."

Perhaps at Dr. Ruggers's suggestion, Clara visited General Hospital Number Ten for Colored Troops and there met Susie King Taylor, a slender, dark-skinned fourteen-year-old who was married to a soldier in the First South Carolina regiment. Born a slave on a plantation near Savannah, Susie was raised by her grandmother and taught to read and write by her master's daughter. When the First South Carolina was organized, she joined up as an army laundress. She also taught many of the black soldiers how to read and write, and she nursed them when they were sick. She could fire a rifled musket and take one apart and put it back together as expertly as any soldier.

Clara was "very cordial" toward her, Susie remembered, and they toured the hospital together. As Clara moved from bed to bed, she showed a special concern for the black patients, touching their cheeks and soothing them with her soft, musical voice. "I honored her for her devotion and care of these men," Susie said later.

*   *   *

A few days after the trip to Beaufort, Elwell took his first horseback ride and returned to his duties full time. Although he discarded his crutches, he still couldn't fully extend the injured leg and walked with a painful limp. He could sit a horse very well, though, and he and Clara took long rides together, cantering along the smooth white beach with the empty ocean stretching out beyond them to the very rim of the world. They dismounted to gather watermelons, plums, huckleberries, and blackberries for their table. The blackberries ran up trees as high as sixteen to eighteen feet, and they picked those they could reach from their horses. They liked to ride back to the base along a scenic trace called Moss Lane. At sunset they might take a long stroll along the beach, and people who saw them there—two figures silhouetted in the dying light—might have thought them a strange-looking couple, for Elwell stood a foot taller than Clara and outweighed her by almost a hundred pounds.

For restless Clara, though, the idyllic life with Elwell was beginning to wear thin. She felt increasingly guilty about spending her time "to little purpose." What right did she have to such peaceful bliss in the midst of a monstrous civil war? She complained to Mary Norton that she had three occupations on the islands—"eating, sleeping, and riding"—and that she really ought not to stay a day longer. "It is a great change for me, and not near as welcome a mode of life as following an army train with the guns ahead." Frustrated and guilt ridden, she came down with excruciating pain in her legs and in one of her ears; she lay in bed, unable to sleep, with Elwell and Captain Lamb watching over her. Two days later, she felt a little better and went riding with Elwell, only to return "almost exhausted," with her ear hurting worse than ever.

She felt a good deal better when Elwell told her that Union siege guns were being sent up to Folly Island near Charleston harbor. This development was clearly linked to recent command changes in the Department of the South. By June, Washington had had enough of du Pont and Hunter. Almost two months had elapsed since the failure of du Pont's expedition, and the rebel flag still flew over Charleston. Indeed, Montgomery's occasional raids against the mainland were the only Union military activity in the department. On June 3 the secretary of the navy relieved du Pont and turned the South Atlantic Blockading Squadron over to Rear Admiral John A. Dahlgren, a slender six-footer. On the same day, the War Department also relieved General Hunter and gave overall command of the department to a younger and more aggressive man, Brigadier General Quincy A. Gillmore, who reached Hilton Head nine days later. This balding, bewhiskered young general cut a striking figure. A graduate of West Point and a former instructor of engineering there, he was considered the best military engineer in the Union army. Thus far, his outstanding achievement in the war was the bombardment and capture of Fort Pulaski at the mouth of the Savannah River, which demonstrated that rifled cannon were brutally effective against "masonry fortifications." If Gillmore, an expert engineer, was sending siege guns north to Folly Island, it could only mean that "we are to have some demonstration up the coast above," Clara noted with rising excitement, and she remained alert to any scrap of information about possible troop movements.

In late June Clara received a letter from an editor friend named T. W. Meighan, a former soldier, who thought the government "too weak" to win the war and favored peace with the rebels at any price. Beyond Meighan, thousands of Democrats were clamoring for peace for the opposite reason: they thought that Lincoln was setting himself up as a dictator. With the war grinding endlessly on, Washington had resorted to another harsh war measure, a conscription law, which shattered what remained of the bipartisan coalition Lincoln had forged at the beginning of hostilities. By mid-1863, thousands of Democrats were in open revolt against administration policies, denouncing the president as an abolitionist tyrant who was dragooning white men into fighting a war for slave liberation. In the Midwest, dissident Democrats launched a peace movement to throw "the shrieking abolitionist faction" out of office and negotiate a peace with the Confederacy on any terms.

For his part, Meighan urged Clara to use her influence to help bring about an immediate end to the war and the killing, and on June 24 Clara responded in a long political letter, full of her special brand of wit and irony. "I am a *U.S. soldier*, you know," the letter began, "and, *as I am* merely a *soldier*, and *not* a *statesman*, I shall make no attempt at discussing *political* points with you." Then she proceeded to discuss those very points, demonstrating her political shrewdness, precisely where she stood on the war, and her unwavering support of Lincoln. "Where you in prospective see peace, glorious coveted peace, and rest for our tired armies, and home and happiness and firesides and friends for our war worn heroes, *I* see only the *beginning of war*, when we should make overtures for 'peace upon any terms,' then I fear would follow a code of terms to which no civilized nation could submit and present even an honorable existence among nations."

"God forbid" that she should wish for the death of one more man, or the desolation of another home. Like so many others on both sides, Clara had long since lost her romantic notions of war. They had died among the corpses and in the grotesque hospitals at Second Bull Run, Antietam, and Fredericksburg. Indeed, she had grown to hate the brutality of war, even as she realized how necessary the war was to save the nation and how glad she was for the chance to serve. "Out amid the smoke and fire and thunder of our guns, with only the murky canopy above, and the bloody ground beneath, I have wrought day after day and night after night, my heart well nigh to bursting with conflicting emotions, so sorry for the *necessity*, so glad for the *opportunity* of ministering with my own hand and strength to the dying wants of the patriot martyrs who fell for their country and mine—If my own life could have purchased theirs how cheerfully and quickly would the exchange have been made."

Yet, however catastrophic the war had become, Clara would never ask the president to sue their enemies for peace. The rebels were the ones who had broken the peace in the first place and "without cause." They now cried that they wanted independence. "They always *had* their independence till they madly threw it away; if there *be* a chain on them today it is of their own riveting."

Clara was not blind to the errors of the "ruling powers" in Washington. "I grant that our Government has made mistakes, sore ones too in some instances, but ours is a *human government*, and like *all* human operations liable to mistakes." If the government was " '*too weak*' to act vigorously and energetically," she wrote, then it ought to be strengthened until it could. When it won the war, *then* would come a proper end to the killing and "the peace we all wait for as kings and prophets waited, and without which, like them, we seek and never find."

In closing, she begged Meighan's pardon, pointing out bitterly that as a woman she wasn't supposed to have an opinion on "this strangely knotted subject," so "clearly" out of her line. "My business is stanching blood and feeding fainting men; my post the open field between the bullet and the hospital. I sometimes discuss the application of a compress or a wisp of hay under a broken limb, but not the bearing and merits of a political movement. I make gruel—not speeches; I write *letters home* for wounded soldiers, not political addresses—and again I ask you to pardon, not so much *what* I have said, as the fact of my having said anything in relation to a subject of which, upon the very nature of things, I am supposed to be profoundly ignorant."

* * *

By June 25, most of the troops stationed on Hilton Head had left on troop transports, destined, Clara heard, for Folly and Edisto islands near Charleston. She did not know what the troop movements portended, but she hoped it was a campaign. The idle days were getting on her nerves.

June 26 brought distressing news from the North: the rebels had invaded Pennsylvania, and Lincoln had called up 100,000 militia to help repel them. But no news came about the fate of the Army of the Potomac. For all Clara knew, a showdown battle might already be raging somewhere in Pennsylvania and the war racing toward a dramatic conclusion. Damn being stuck on this island, with only an occasional ship from the North to bring news from the outside world.

The principal action in this theater came from the sky: on June 28 another storm broke over the islands, with terrific thunder and lightning. The wind blew down many tents at the camp of the Fifty-fourth Massachusetts regiment on St. Helena Island. Clara heard that lightning killed one man and injured nine others in contiguous camps.

Like Clara, the men of the Fifty-fourth were restless and eager for combat. Not long after their arrival, they had accompanied Colonel Montgomery and his "contraband" regiment on a raid up the Altamaha River in Georgia. According to Colonel Shaw, commander of the Fifty-fourth, Montgomery argued that "praying, shooting, burning & hanging are the true means to put down the Rebellion." Supported by two gunboats, Montgomery and his men plundered and burned Darien, Georgia, an abandoned river port and the antebellum home of several wealthy planters. The contrabands were delighted to strike their former masters any way they could, but Shaw and the men of the Fifty-fourth did not view such raids as manly and honorable warfare. They wanted to do battle with rebel soldiers, to demonstrate to the white world that black troops were not inferior. Colonel Shaw told Brigadier General George C. Strong, commander of the First Brigade of Seymour's Division, that his regiment was ready for a real battle. "He seems anxious to do all he can for us," the colonel wrote Governor Andrew, "and if there is a fight in the Department will no doubt give the black troops a chance to show what stuff they are made of."

Meanwhile Clara continued her three occupations on Hilton Head: eating, sleeping, and horseback riding twice a day. After the evening ride, she might slip into Elwell's room and "stay late." One time, she noted, "he came home with me." On July 1, she went riding with "a

party of military men" out along the Braddock Point Road. Someone
made a remark that reminded her how "happy" she was on Hilton
Head, and it made her feel guilty again. She must, she thought, give up
the "gentle care" she enjoyed here and return to the "stern duties of
life." That realization caused her to weep as she rode along, and she
feared she was "poor company." Night fell, and they rode by moonlight
until another thunderstorm blew up—"the clouds followed a thunderstorm such as I had never seen," she wrote later. They tried to outride
the storm, but it caught them at Sally Point and soaked their clothes
and saddles. When they finally reached the post, Clara was still distraught, telling herself, *I must get out of here and return to the stern
duties of life.*

But no sooner had she resolved to leave than rumors swept through
the post that something was afoot involving Folly and Morris islands.
On July 3 Captain Lamb himself departed for Folly Island. So did
thousands of troops stationed on the other islands. "I begin to feel that
we are to have work in our department," Clara told her diary. On July
6 Elwell confirmed the rumors. Now a prominent member of
Gillmore's staff, he told Clara that the general was "pushing his whole
dept, troops being called from all quarters and moved on through."
From what Elwell could tell, Gillmore intended to concentrate his
forces—11,500 infantry troops and 98 pieces of artillery—on Folly
Island, a flat sandbar situated south of Morris Island. This was to be
done swiftly and secretly, in order to catch the rebels by surprise. Once
the infantry was in place on Folly Island, Gillmore would launch a
three-step campaign against Charleston, to begin with the seizure of
Morris Island at the gates of the rebel harbor. The rebel batteries there
protected Fort Sumter and the harbor entrance. After silencing those
guns, Gillmore planned to pulverize Fort Sumter with his rifled cannon, whereupon Dahlgren's warships could pass south of the fort, away
from the enemy batteries on Sullivan's Island, and shell Charleston
into submission, thus closing one of the Confederacy's great blockade-
running ports.

Clara was impressed with Gillmore's aggressiveness. The expedition
was "planned and sent off in an incredible short space of time," she
wrote Elvira, "but Gen'l. Gil[l]more is a *live* Genl. and *acts* more than
he talks." Eager to get into the fight, Elwell made arrangements to go
to Folly Island, and Clara persuaded the colonel to take her with him.
Elwell might well have had reservations about the love of his life going
into combat, but he did not risk an objection. He even provided her
with an ambulance to carry her cache of supplies, forwarded from

Washington by her nephew. Fitted out with a bed and cooking wares, which Elwell had borrowed from the Commissary Department, the ambulance was to double as Clara's "house."

Early in the morning of July 9 Clara and Elwell left Hilton Head on the monitor *Canonicus*. In addition to the ambulance, they took their saddle horses for any hard riding that might be called for. According to cousin Leander, Clara thought it was "like going into a wilderness, as she knew not *where* or *how* she was to be located."

It was noon when the *Canonicus* reached Folly Island, the embarkation area for the attack on Morris Island, just to the northeast. Several transports, anchored outside the bar, were busily unloading troops. To the north, beyond Folly Island, lay the gray outlines of James Island and beyond that the city of Charleston. Off to the right, at the northeastern end of Folly Island, forty-seven Union mortars and field and siege artillery lay concealed behind thick undergrowth and sand hills, all pointing across Lighthouse Inlet toward the rebel lines on Morris Island. Viewed through a field piece, Morris Island appeared to stretch about four miles northward toward Charleston harbor. According to a Union engineer, the island had once been "a quarantine burying-ground" called "Coffin Land." Gillmore planned to attack this wind-blown sandbar at dawn the next day. To confuse the enemy, General Alfred H. Terry advanced on James Island with almost 4,000 men, including the Fifty-fourth Massachusetts, and Higginson's First South Carolina regiment set out to wreck the railroad bridge across the Edisto River.

According to Clara, the *Canonicus* helped move troops across the bar at Folly Island all afternoon. She could see white tents on the beach a half mile or so behind the point batteries; the tents constituted a field hospital, established by her friend, Dr. John J. Craven, now functioning as chief medical officer for the Morris Island campaign. Clara's own ambulance and driver and the two riding horses were put ashore and apparently left at the beach hospital. At 3:00 A.M., the last of the troops landed by the lamps of the *Canonicus*, and Clara, Elwell, and a retinue of orderlies and reporters on board caught what sleep they could.

A little after daylight, July 10, "one sullen shot announced to us that the 'ball was opened,' " Clara scribbled in her diary. She and Elwell raced up to the deck and saw shells from the Union artillery bursting

on the rebel entrenchments and sand batteries at the southern end of
Morris Island. Soon four Union monitors steamed up abreast of Morris
Island and opened fire on the largest of the rebel sand forts, a formida-
ble and ominous looking earthwork situated at the northern end of the
island. The exploding shells kicked up geysers of sand and smoke in
and around the earthwork. Somebody said that that was Battery
Wagner—the center of the enemy's defenses on Morris Island and (in
Gillmore's view) the key to Sumter and Charleston.

Not far from the *Canonicus*, Clara noted, rowboats loaded with
Union troops "lay hidden by the lushes and thickets" behind the
Federal land batteries. At 7:00 A.M. she pointed at some "moving
objects" among the trees—"and *lo! our troops were leaping* from the
boats like wildcats," Clara wrote later, "and scarce waiting to form, on
they went, in one wild charge, across the marsh and up the banks, and
onto the entrenchments, and almost in a breath, up rose the *Old Flag*,
and the ground was ours."

The day was already miserably hot, with hardly a cloud to shield the
men from the broiling sun. They pushed on now, advancing up Morris
Island against "a hot fire" from Battery Wagner and Fort Sumter out in
Charleston harbor. "The brave old Fort opened with an energy and
spirit worthy of a better cause," Clara said. Red bursts of fire and
plumes of smoke leaped from Sumter, and balls came hissing down on
the thundering ironclads and on the Union infantry advancing up the
beach on Morris Island. By midday, Clara wrote, Sumter "was sending
up columns of white smoke which glistened in the sunlight like waving
towers of silver." The most accurate enemy fire came from Battery
Wagner, whose guns struck Dahlgren's flagship monitor sixty times. At
three in the afternoon, something that resembled a floating rebel battery—so Clara described it—came down between Sumter and Fort
Moultrie and joined in the duel against the monitors, dealing out shot
from "one most terrible gun." The Union ironclads returned the fire,
and Clara could see their shells skimming off "the tips of the waves at
every breath."

By nightfall, the Union infantry held three-quarters of Morris
Island, and all the rebel defenders had retreated inside Battery
Wagner. Clara described what happened that night in a letter to Elvira:
"While all were tired and hot and faint with the terrible days work in
such a scalding sun, and such a climate, what should happen as if
Heaven sent, but that the little steamer which came for our wounded
should bring us the *glorious, glorious* news" that Vicksburg had fallen
to Grant and that Lee's army had been "defeated and largely captured"

at Gettysburg in Pennsylvania. Clara was so happy that she shook
hands all around. *"The brave old Army of the Potomac victorious at
last,"* she said to Elvira. "Dear Old Army God bless every veteran in its
war worn ranks." The news, she added, had an electric effect on
Gillmore's troops. "They were no longer tired, or hungry or faint, neither could they talk, but just shouted and wept. Oh these are glorious
days, and the sunlight is breaking through. I begin to see some
prospect of rest for these tired armies, some husbands and fathers left
to the waiting wives and little ones at home."

It was dawn, July 11, a Saturday. From the deck of the *Canonicus,*
Clara and Elwell could see Battery Wagner clearly through a field
glass. Stretching across the island from the ocean on the east to a line
of marshes on the west, the sand fortress gave the appearance of "a
succession of low, irregular sand-hills," as Gillmore described it.
Wagner was strongly constructed, though, with sloping ramparts reinforced with palmetto logs, double bastions, traverses, and merlons.
Eight of its cannons—thirty-two-pounder carronades and twelve-
pounder mortars—were trained on the only infantry approach to the
battery, the narrow beach to the south. Gillmore himself conceded that
enemy gunners could sweep that sandy passageway with both "an enfilading and a cross-fire of artillery and small-arms." It seemed impossible for foot soldiers to take such a powerful stronghold, yet an infantry
assault was precisely what Gillmore ordered for this morning.

    With Clara and Elwell watching on the *Canonicus,* Brigadier
General Strong, a young West Pointer, formed a battalion of the
Seventh Connecticut into an assault formation, with the Seventy-sixth
Pennsylvania and the Ninth Maine in support. The units could be
identified by the regimental flags carried by the color bearers. Strong
gestured toward Battery Wagner and led his men forward in his stock-
ing feet. It was an old-fashioned infantry charge with fixed bayonets,
and the sheer audacity of it appeared to catch the rebel defenders off
guard. The Connecticut battalion made it over the outer works, leaped
across a moat in front of Wagner, and scrambled up to the crest of the
parapet itself. The Federals huddled against the outside of the wall; if
they raised their heads, rebel riflemen shot them in the face.

    Suddenly the rebel cannon exploded into action, pouring whirling
volleys of grape and canister into the advancing support troops. It was
a sickening sight—reminiscent of the horrors of Marye's Heights—as

the deadly shrapnel tore men to shreds and dissolved the supporting units into eddies of confusion. Under that withering fire, the surviving support troops fled to the rear. Without support, the Connecticut battalion had to retreat, too, only to be cut to pieces as it ran back through that storm of hot metal. The battalion lost 103 of the 196 men who went into action. All told, 339 Federals were killed, wounded, or captured.

Yet Gillmore remained convinced that the sand battery could be taken. Remembering how he had reduced Fort Pulaski with artillery, he resolved to bombard Wagner with heavy artillery and then send in another infantry charge. Under his orders, fatigue parties dug a line of trenches across the width of the island, within 1,350 yards of Wagner; then they started hauling up forty-one pieces of artillery to install in them, a task that would consume all of the following week. Gillmore guessed that about 1,600 rebels manned the battery. Surely, he believed, his forty-one pieces of artillery, including some of the most powerful siege guns ever employed in warfare, would smash up Wagner, disable its cannon, and kill so many of the rebel riflemen that his infantry would be able to capture the battery with relative ease.

Actually, at its peak strength, the rebel garrison numbered about 1,300 men. Even so, it was stronger than it looked to Gillmore through his field piece. Unknown to him, the rebels had added bombproof shelters capable of protecting a thousand men from artillery fire. They had also constructed a parapet across the rear, which made it a "closed" battery, to guard against a surprise Yankee attack from the north.

Dr. Craven, meanwhile, had established an excellent field medical service to care for the Union wounded. After the assault of July 11 had failed, ambulances transported the most seriously injured to the beach hospital on Folly Island, where they were loaded on hospital transports for the trip back to Hilton Head. Then Craven had the hospital tents brought to Morris Island and deployed in the dunes along the shore, at a point about a mile and a half from Wagner. Putting Dr. Martin S. Kittinger of the 100th New York and two other surgeons in charge of this "front hospital," Craven set up an ambulance line that ran along the outer beach, under cover of the sand hills, up to within a half-mile of Battery Wagner. His careful preparations indicated that he anticipated heavy casualties when Union infantry next tried to carry the enemy stronghold. With his approval, Dr. Marsh of the Sanitary Commission and his male agents put up a supply tent nearby and went to work disseminating Sanitary stores.

On July 12 Clara went ashore with a pass from Gillmore himself. The pass stated that "Miss Barton, Hospital nurse authorized by the Pres. of the U.S. will receive all facilities within our lines." Elwell went with her, but his leg hurt him so much that he had to walk with a cane. To Clara's surprise, she recognized a surgeon in one of the tents, a Dr. Day who had served with her on previous battlefields. When she entered his tent, he was delighted to see her and took both her hands in his. "I said yesterday that you would be here," he told her, "have you forgotten Antietam and South Mountain and 2nd Bull Run, come in— come in!!" They talked and reminisced, and then he took her around to see the wounded in the hospital tents. Later in the day, Elwell told her good-bye. He was going back to Folly Island, the Tenth Corps' supply base, to attend to his quartermaster duties. But he was in such pain that he needed help to mount his horse.

The next day, Clara returned to Folly Island and brought her ambulance and saddle horse across to Morris Island on a pontoon bridge that had been erected over Light House Inlet. As she rode past the war-torn Beacon House, shells from Fort Sumter screamed overhead and struck the ground with shuddering impact. The rebel gunners were apparently trying to hit the Federal line of communications back to Folly Island. When Clara reported for duty at the beach hospital, Dr. Craven cleared a tent for her, and she had her supplies and bed put inside. Then she went to introduce herself to Dr. Martin Kittinger, co-director of the field hospital.

A thirty-six-year-old bachelor, Kittinger suffered from chronic bronchitis, which he'd contracted in the field and which had grown worse during a stint as a rebel prisoner near Richmond in 1862. He had been paroled at City Point, Virginia, and had returned to active duty despite the burning pain in his lungs. Since then, a constant hacking cough left his voice low, husky, and hoarse. From the start, he and Clara liked and respected one another. He had no problem with the presence of a woman on the battlefield—Clara was the only female nurse on Morris Island—and they established a cordial and efficient working relationship.

Later, in a letter to her cousin, Lizzie Shaver, Clara jotted down her impressions of this strange island. "It is a narrow strip of pure glistening white sand," Clara wrote, "without a tree, or many shrubs, no tall vegetation to wither and decay in autumn." To the west, beyond the narrow beach, lay Vincent's Creek and a line of marshy swamps, and farther on another creek and inlets that separated Morris Island from James Island. To the east lay nothing but "blue and boundless ocean,"

Clara wrote, and the "views are grand beyond description, the water is as romance could paint it, and literally filled and flowing with phosphorescent light. The breakers come in not infrequently eight feet high, and eighty rods long, one unbroken line of swelling surge, like a beautiful water fall, until it breaks with its own mighty weight, and in an instant the whole smooth swell is transformed into one long whitened sheet of dashing spray and all day the clear breeze from these rolling waters sweeps across the whole island, thru every camp and hospital, leaving no particle of miasm, or anything unhealthy."

For the next few days, soldiers came to the hospital suffering from all manner of wounds and ailments. Some had been shot by rebel snipers or had collapsed from heat exhaustion while digging the trenches for the artillery. Others came down with chills and fevers, which Clara thought had been contracted on the Sea Islands, from the "miasmic vapors" that rose from their thick vegetation. This was a standard diagnosis for her day: all the medical texts blamed malarial fevers on "miasmas emanating from stagnant waters" and vegetation. Nobody knew that the common mosquito carried the deadly malarial infection.

On July 16, sitting on the floor of her tent, Indian fashion, and using a box as her desk, Clara dashed off a note to Judge Ira Barton. From the front of her tent, she wrote, she could observe the Union military preparations for the coming battle. "Directly up the beach to our left as we face the sea is Fort Wagner, before which our troops are fortifying and entrenching with incredible speed. Our pickets lie directly under the gun and a raised head or hand is a certain mark for the sharpshooter. A little to the right lies the Monitor, a little further on two more, then a war sloop, then the Paul Jones, then 2 more men of war, with the springtide of yesterday the Old Iron Sides worked over the bar and took her place a little to the right of the 'Paul Jones' looking like a small village in herself with all her guns, rigging and sea of heads, a little off the outside [of] the bar lies the Wabash." Clara thought the wooden screw frigate *Wabash* "the handsomest ship" in the fleet; it rode the water "just like a swan." Armed with one 150-pounder Parrott, one 30-pounder Parrott, one ten-inch gun, and forty-two nine-inch guns, it was a veritable floating fortress.

On that same July 16, word reached the hospital that General Terry's command had fought a sharp skirmish with the rebels on James Island and that the *Canonicus*, with Elwell on board, had gone to help evacuate the division and bring it to Morris Island for the attack on Wagner. Correspondents would later describe what happened on James Island that day: some 2,200 Confederates, supported by 12-

pounder Napoleons, mounted an attack against Terry's position, but three outpost companies of the Fifty-fourth Massachusetts contested the rebel advance with expert fire, giving the Tenth Connecticut enough time to fall back from a dangerously exposed position and join the rest of Terry's division as it formed in line of battle. The rebels came on with their artillery booming, but the Yankees repelled them with a combination of musketry and artillery fire, driving them off in considerable disorder. The Fifty-fourth Massachusetts Volunteer Infantry, in its first battle as a regiment, had acquitted itself well in its "baptism of fire." "It is not for us to blow our own horn," wrote a regimental corporal; "but when a regiment of white men gave us three cheers as we were passing them, it shows that we did our duty as men should."

Later that day, the *Paul Jones*, a "double ender" armed with a 100-pounder Parrott and several lighter cannon, opened fire on Battery Wagner. Determined to get a closer look, Clara mounted her horse, rode past the Union trench line, and headed directly toward the rebel fort, with the colors of the Confederacy flying defiantly over it. As she rode, some of the shells from the *Paul Jones* fell short and burst on the beach just in front of her. She stopped within 450 yards of Wagner, and peering at it through her field glass, she saw figures moving about on the parapets and the muzzles of enemy cannon aimed in her direction. As if by a miracle, no snipers fired at her. She raised the glass and gazed at Fort Sumter out in the harbor: it looked like a pile of malignant rock with the rebel flag flying over it, too. Then she swept the glass around to the northwest. Beyond the low hills of James Island, she could see the church spires, magnificent homes, and public buildings of Charleston etched against the sky. Then, noticing a thunderhead gathering on the horizon, she turned her mount and rode back down the beach to the field hospital. She seemed utterly oblivious of the danger she had been in. In her diary, she recounted this reckless ride up to Wagner as matter of factly as if it had been an afternoon canter on Hilton Head.

At the invitation of the skipper of the *Philadelphia*, she ate dinner on board and then returned exhausted to her tent. Just as she was taking off her skirt, two surprise visitors arrived at her tent: Mary Gage and Mrs. Lander. Young Mrs. Lander had a habit of lecturing people, and she gave Clara one of her "characteristic speeches," demanding that she leave this dangerous position and return to ship. "I said I *would not go*," Clara recorded in her diary. Mary Gage said she wouldn't go either; she intended to stay with Clara, and Clara was glad to have her.

After Mrs. Lander departed, Clara sent for her mail and found among her letters one from brother Stephen at Bartonsville. She was so excited that she neglected to mention in her diary a word of what Stephen wrote.

The next day, Clara and Mary gave the hospital patients the only food Clara had left, hardtack softened with water. She admitted that the crackers were "a little wormy." Sometime that day a letter came from John Elwell, apologizing to his "dear Clara" for not being able to tend to her "comfort." He had been "almost overwhelmed with work," he said. She couldn't imagine how much so. But he regretted that he had left her so "destitute" of supplies, and he promised to do better by her. He reported that he had seen to the removal of Terry's division from James Island and that all forces were to be concentrated on Morris Island. "Everything is going most encouragingly," Elwell said. "Who cannot afford to work,—to suffer and to die if need be for such a consum[m]ation of our long struggle."

Word reached the beach hospital that the Union trench line was complete and all the artillery in place. The battle for Battery Wagner would commence on the morrow. That night a thunderstorm struck, and Clara and Mary lay awake as the rain pounded against their tent and thunder cracked overhead with flashes of lightning. It was as if God Himself were raging and weeping in the heavens, in anguished anticipation of the human violence about to begin below.

By morning, July 18, the weather had cleared, and the two women stood on the bluff outside their tent, spellbound by the tableau before them. The ironclad *New Ironsides*, five wooden gunboats, and five low-riding monitors with their single turrets lay off Morris Island, ready for battle. Those ships were armed with some of the heaviest guns in the Union navy. The *New Ironsides* alone carried two 150-pounder Parrotts, two 50-pounder Dahlgrens, and fourteen eleven-inch rifled cannon. The federal trench line stretching across the beach sheltered fifteen eight-inch, ten-inch, and thirteen-inch siege mortars and twenty-six rifled cannon behind low parapets. The gun crews stood ready with ammunition and cut fuses, awaiting the order to open fire.

At exactly ten o'clock in the morning, the land-based artillery and the warships opened up on Battery Wagner with thunderous salvoes. The concussions were so powerful that the two women on the bluff had to clamp their hands against their ears. Mortar shells climbed high overhead trailing smoke from their burning fuses and fell on the enemy fort in spectacular explosions that shook the ground. The *New Ironsides* poured forth almost continuous volleys of eleven- and fourteen-inch shells that rolled over the sea and struck the sloped walls of Wagner, glancing upward and exploding above and inside the fort. From where Clara and Mary stood, the enemy parapets seemed to disappear in huge geysers of smoke and sand, rising and falling with every shell burst. It appeared that nothing could survive such destructive violence. At one point, Union guns were hurling twenty-seven shells a minute at the rebel battery. One shell severed the halyards on the flagpole, and the rebel colors fell to the parapet. The Federals, believing it a sign of surrender, broke out in cheers. But in a moment a lone figure mounted the parapet and held the flag in that violent mayhem until his comrades fashioned a new pole for it. Then they ran the flag up again, and it snapped in the wind as defiantly as ever.

By then, Wagner's gunners were firing back. So were the rebel batteries on Sullivan's and James islands, Fort Sumter, and Battery Gregg at the northern point of Morris Island. Enemy shells exploded on the beach in malevolent bursts and splashed in the water near the blazing warships. At the height of the cannonade, with smoke clouds hanging over the ships and the island, General Gillmore and a retinue of Federal commanders and reporters hurried to a high point within Union lines called Lookout Hill. Here the officers studied the stricken battery through their field glasses.

At four in the afternoon, the firing from Wagner stopped, and the fort lay silent in floating clouds of smoke. When Clara peered at it through her field glass, she saw no sign of movement anywhere. But the parapets, though marked and potted with shell holes, appeared miraculously intact, a tribute to the ability of a quartz sand fortification to absorb the most terrible punishment modern artillery could inflict on it.

General Gillmore swept the parapets with his glass, too, then huddled in council with the officers of his First Division. Clara could make out Brigadier General Truman Seymour, commander of the division; Brigadier General Strong, head of Seymour's First Brigade, who had led the first assault on the battery; Colonel Haldiman S. Putnam, commander of the Second Brigade; and Brigadier General Thomas G. Stevenson, commander of the Third Brigade, which included the Twenty-fourth Massachusetts. The officers could be seen gesticulating and pointing at Wagner, apparently arguing. General Seymour seemed particularly adamant.

The group broke up, and the brigade officers returned to their commands, which were waiting back down the beach. The Union ships and batteries were still firing on Wagner, and word spread quickly that an infantry assault would commence at twilight, when the tide would be out and the assault troops could not be clearly seen by the enemy batteries on James Island and on Sumter. Gillmore and Seymour appeared convinced that the Union bombardment had softened up the battery enough that it could be taken by frontal assault. Indeed, Seymour boasted that his command could "run right over it." Putnam informed his brigade that he disagreed. "I told the General I did not think we could take the fort so; but Seymour overruled me. Seymour is a devil of a fellow for a dash." Putnam added, "We are going into Wagner, like a flock of sheep."

To get a better view of the attack, Clara and Mary Gage hastened across the beach to Lookout Hill, where reporters were still congregated. At about five in the afternoon, they saw Colonel Robert Gould Shaw, a slender young man, report to General Strong, nod emphatically, and then head back down the beach to his regiment, which had just arrived on the island. Presently, the Fifty-fourth marched smartly up the beach, heading for the line of Federal artillery. As the blacks stepped along in perfect cadence, rebel batteries on James Island opened fire, and solid shot struck the sand and ricocheted over their heads, or bounced along the beach just ahead. But the blacks remained in good order, as proud a body of fighting men as Clara and the crowd on Lookout Hill had ever seen. At one point, the flag bearers rolled in the colors so as not to attract the attention of rebel gunners. But an officer shouted something, and the flags unfurled again and fluttered in the breeze as the regiment approached the Union line.

On Lookout Hill, located near the Federal batteries, Clara and the other observers had a commanding view of the Union brigades now forming into assault formations behind the artillery. The Fifty-fourth, 600 strong, marched to the front of the line, formed in double rows behind their young white colonel, and lay down with bayonets fixed to their muskets. This caused great excitement on Lookout Hill, for the blacks were clearly going to lead the attack. Behind them stood the other five regiments of Strong's brigade, with the four regiments of Putnam's brigade in support—white boys from Massachusetts, Connecticut, Maine, New Hampshire, New York, Ohio, and Pennsylvania. A total of 5,000 crack infantry would make the assault, with another 1,000 men—Stevenson's brigade—held in reserve. The soldiers stood in a "solid phalanx," as Clara described it, that stretched for a mile down the beach.

At about seven o'clock the Union artillery and warships stopped firing, and a strange silence settled on the island. All told that day, Federal guns had hurled an estimated 9,000 shells at Battery Wagner in what was perhaps the war's most vigorous barrage thus far. As the sun was setting behind James Island, General Strong, wearing a yellow handkerchief around his neck, rode to the front of the attacking columns with his aides and orderlies. He spoke to the Fifty-fourth from horseback: "Boys, I am a Massachusetts man, and I know you will fight for the honor of the State." He cautioned them to use only their bayonets. "Don't fire a musket on the way up, but go in and bayonet them at their guns."

By Clara's watch, it was 7:45 P.M. when the men of the Fifty-fourth stood up and dressed their lines. "Forward!" Shaw cried, and the Fifty-fourth Massachusetts stepped out with bayonets thrust forward and flags snapping in the breeze. They streamed past the Union batteries and headed up the thin strip of beach, with the darkening ocean on their right and Wagner looming ahead. In a moment, the beach became so narrow that the companies on the right found themselves marching in ankle-deep water. When they were within 200 yards of Wagner, shot and shell came hissing through the sky and struck the beach ahead of the regiment, indicating that the rebel batteries on Sumter and on James and Sullivan's islands had spotted it. Worse still, Wagner suddenly awakened with cannon bursts, and "a sheet of flame, followed by a running fire, like electric sparks, swept along the parapet," remembered Captain Luis Emilio. The Union bombardment had not silenced Wagner after all.

Clara was mesmerized. "The scene was grand beyond description," she wrote later. "A long line of phosphorescent light streamed and shot along the waves ever surging on our right. A little to [our] left marked that long dark line, moving steadily on—pace by pace—across that broad open space of glistening sand." Clara could hear the thud of rebel canister hitting the assaulting troops. Transfixed with horror, she watched as the black soldiers ran toward the fort now, Colonel Shaw in front with his drawn sword whipping the air. He led them into the moat in front of the rampart connecting the two bastions of the fort, scrambled up the banks, and clawed his way up the side of the rampart while artillery and muskets flashed, casting the scene in a pulsing light. Shaw was the first to reach the top of the rampart, and Clara could see

him standing alone, his sword pointing at the sky, in a surreal maelstrom of whirling iron and lead so loud and brilliant it seemed as
though the world were coming apart. Then he disappeared in a swirl of
smoke.

The blacks clambered up the wall after him, some leaping back from
point-blank musket fire and tumbling down its bloody slope.
Silhouetted against the sky stood a rebel stripped to his waist, firing
down at the oncoming blacks until he pitched backward, shot dead.
"Our men are on the parapets!" Clara exclaimed. Indeed, the color
bearers had planted both the regimental flag and Old Glory on them,
as white rebels and black Federals dissolved into fierce hand-to-hand
combat all along the crest. The blacks fought with bayonets and rifle
butts, the rebels with gun rammers, handspikes, and muskets, in a
swirling free-for-all against the exploding night. Some Federals leaped
inside the battery, only to run into a murderous fire from the rest of the
garrison, perhaps a thousand men, who had survived the day-long
Union bombardment inside the fort's bombproof shelters. Within minutes after it had reached the enemy rampart, the Fifty-fourth disinte-
grated in the face of superior numbers and firepower.

By now, the supporting columns should have gone forward, but for
lack of a coordinated plan of attack, they started late. By the time
Strong got them in motion, the Fifty-fourth's survivors were already
falling back down the rampart, leaving a number of prisoners behind.
Some of the blacks tried to make a stand at the bottom of the outside
wall, but the rebels lobbed lighted shells and hand grenades down on
the blacks, blowing many of them apart.

Meanwhile, Strong's five white regiments had swung to the right of
the Fifty-fourth's line of attack and charged the battery's southeast bastion, which blazed with musketry and artillery fire. Elements of two
Union regiments pierced the bastion but could not hold on when the
rest of the brigade fell back in great disorder, and no support came
from Putnam's regiments, which were waiting for Seymour's order to
advance.

Incredibly, the general who had argued so vehemently for a frontal
assault gave no command to Putnam until he learned that Strong's
brigade had been repulsed. Only then did Seymour order the colonel
to join the attack. For the third time, Union infantry dashed across the
killing beach, through the enemy's enfilading and cross fire. They
charged into the disputed southeast salient, climbing over sandbags
and traverses into an even deadlier three-way fire from the front and
the right and left flanks.

It was then that Clara noticed Colonel Elwell standing with Gillmore and his staff at the Union trench line. "My God," Elwell cried, "our men are being slaughtered." Bareheaded, he struggled onto his horse and spurred it furiously toward the battery, with his cane in his hand and his "long hair streaming in the wind." Clara was horrified. As a member of Gillmore's staff, he wasn't supposed to be in the attack (she was right: Gillmore was also stunned that his chief quartermaster should charge off like that). Clara saw the horseback figure reach the southeast bastion of Wagner, trot along the wall, then turn and gallop back through enemy fire, bearing a desperate message to Gillmore. "More men!" Elwell shouted. "Putnam is in the fort and says he must be reinforced!"

Then Elwell wheeled about and raced back toward Wagner, only to be shot from his horse about 150 yards from the southeast bastion. *No!* Clara instinctively started running toward him, her tiny feet churning in the sand. But he was moving now; she could see him crawling toward her, with solid shot striking the beach and bullets humming hatefully in the wind. He remembered that he retreated "in a most unmartial manner on my hands and knees spread out like a turtle."

Evidently she met him on the beach and tried to help him back to the Union lines. Still under fire, they crawled past corpses and badly wounded men along the shore. They came across Colonel Alvin C. Voris, commander of the Sixty-Seventh Ohio of Putnam's Brigade, lying in his own blood with a nasty wound in his side, his bright hair "dabbling in the sand," as Clara put it. He was unconscious but still breathing. Clara covered his wound with a makeshift bandage and bathed his face, urging him not to die and doubtless assuring him that Union stretcher-bearers would soon be along.

When she and Elwell neared the Union trenches, a couple of soldiers came out to get him and took him back to the hospital in the dunes, where the surgeons bandaged his wound. For his part, Elwell was amazed at Clara's courage; indeed he believed her "insensible to fear." Thinking him in good hands now, she turned back up the beach to help the other wounded. A war correspondent reported seeing her on the battlefield. "There, with the shot and shell flying and whispering about her, we find this noble and heroic Worcester woman stopping over the wounded soldier, tenderly administering to our brave men wounded." An admiring soldier later claimed that she was "the only woman present" on the Wagner battleground—he didn't see Mary Gage—"and through her untiring efforts many a soldier was returned to his wife and family and many a soldier boy to his poor mother."

Meanwhile, support troops from Stevenson's brigade had set out for Wagner, but there was nothing left to support. The assaults had all been repulsed, and survivors, both black and white, were falling back in the night, with clouds darkening the heavens. "They mowed us down like grass," was the way a black soldier put it. Even in the darkness, rebel gunners continued to blast the battleground with shells and canister; the cannon flashes lit up the beach and the clouds. Into that deadly fire went Union ambulances and stretcher-bearers, assisted by Dr. Marsh's Sanitary team and several Pennsylvania companies. Clara directed them to where Voris and so many others lay in the wave-washed sand. Sometime after 9:00 P.M., Mary Gage joined Clara, and they moved from body to body, calling to the stretcher-bearers when they found someone still alive. They discovered one officer, delirious with pain, lying among his dead boys. "Bury me here friends," he moaned, "here in the sands, right where I fell." The two women moved on to a group of wounded and dead of the Fifty-Fourth Massachusetts, and Clara would never forget what she witnessed. "I can see again the scarlet flow of blood as it rolled over the black limbs beneath my hands," she wrote later, "and the great heave of the human heart before it grew still."

When the ambulances had collected their first load of wounded, some of the drivers broke under the enemy shelling and ran their teams back to the beach hospital, their passengers screaming in agony. Clara and Mary also hurried back to the hospital, where Dr. Kittinger and his fellow surgeons were operating in tents lit with lanterns. "The sands about our hospital tents grow red with the blood of our wounded and slain," Clara said, as the ghostly ambulances came and went throughout the night. One black man brought to her had a gaping wound in his chest. Apparently he was one of several members of the Fifty-fourth who had been a slave; all the others were Northern free blacks. As Clara washed and covered him, he was very brave, saying of the rebels: "They too many for us this time." He knew he was dying, he told her, but he thanked God that his children would be free. What he said reminded Clara that on Morris Island—for the first time, she thought—the black man had been "permitted to strike a lawful, organized blow at the fetters which had bound him body and soul." Actually, black soldiers had struck a similar blow at a couple of earlier, less spectacular battlegrounds in the West.

All through "that fearful night," Clara and Mary Gage tended the wounded men brought in from the battlefield, offering a kind word here, a little water there. Under Dr. Craven's supervision, two hospital steamers evacuated 496 of the more severely wounded that night alone. From time to time, Clara checked on Elwell, who lay asleep in one of the hospital tents. When he awoke, he said later, "a dear, blessed woman was bathing my temples and fanning my fevered face. Clara Barton was there, an angel of mercy doing all in mortal power to assuage the miseries of the unfortunate soldiers."

"It seemed as if day light would never come," Clara noted. When it did come, it revealed a hideous sight: Dead men, black and white, littered the beach for almost a mile. At Wagner, dozens of corpses, many dismembered, were stacked up in the moat and along the parapets. A Southern officer admitted that some of the black corpses had been desecrated, but he insisted that it had been done "almost exclusively" by "the more desperate and lower class of our troops."

Both sides withheld their fire that day, and under a scalding sun burial parties went about the work of counting and covering the dead. At Wagner, the rebels dug a ditch and flung Shaw and twenty dead blacks into it. When a Union truce party asked for Shaw's body, the rebel commander supposedly remarked, "We buried him with his Niggers."

Only when the Federals tabulated their casualties did they realize the full magnitude of the fiasco. Of the 5,000 men engaged, 1,515 of them, including 111 officers, had been killed, wounded, or captured. At the southeast salient, every Union field officer had fallen except one. Colonel Putnam had been killed with the back of his head blown off. General Strong had been fatally wounded. General Seymour himself and several regimental commanders had all been wounded. The Fifty-fourth Massachusetts had lost 272 men, including its colonel, a casualty rate of 40.5 percent. Approximately 44 of them had been killed or mortally wounded, 29 had fallen into rebel hands, and 49 were missing and presumed dead, either killed in action or shot after trying to surrender.

The responsibility for such losses fell squarely on the shoulders of General Gillmore, who, thinking that Wagner had been reduced like Fort Pulaski, had ordered the assaults without any plan or specific instructions to his brigade commanders. Despite his brilliance as an engineer, Gillmore apparently did not realize that a fortification made of quartz sand could withstand a great deal more punishment than a brick-and-mortar structure like Fort Pulaski. In his "delusion" that

Wagner was largely immobilized, he had allowed his brigades to go forward piecemeal into the slaughter.

Although the numbers of men engaged and lost were only fractions of those at Antietam, Fredericksburg, and Gettysburg, Battery Wagner was nevertheless "one of the most terrific battles of the war," as a Union participant rightly said; "the fierce fighting and heroism at Wagner was not excelled upon any battlefield in the War."

Many Union men fought and died bravely at Battery Wagner, but the regiment that won the highest accolades was the Fifty-fourth Massachusetts. "They moved up as gallantly as any troops could," said General Strong before he was fatally injured, "and with their enthusiasm they deserved a better fate." Their gallantry had a profound impact on white public opinion, prompting the *New York Tribune* to describe Wagner as the black man's Bunker Hill. Lincoln, too, was proud of the Fifty-fourth and publicly praised his black soldiers for "fighting with clenched teeth, and steady eye, and well poised bayonet" to save the Union, while certain whites strove "with malignant heart" to hinder it.

Clara also perceived the significance of what the Fifty-fourth had done at Battery Wagner. She said later: "I can never forget the patient bravery with which they endured their wounds received in the cruel assault upon Wagner, as hour after hour they lay in the wet sands, just back of the growling guns waiting their turn for the knife or the splint and bandage, not a murmur, scarce a groan, but ever that patient upturning of the great dark eyes, to your face, in utter silence, which kept one constantly wondering if they *knew* all they *had done*, and were doing? and whenever I met one who was giving his *life* out with his blood, I could not forbear hastening to tell him lest he die in ignorance of the truth, that he was the soldier of Freedom he had sought to be, and that the world as well as Heaven would so record it and among them all."

At the beach hospital, Clara pitched a kitchen tent behind her sleeping tent, and she and Mary prepared what food they could find for their patients. For the next few days, the hospital boats evacuated the remaining wounded and took the blacks to the "colored" hospital at Beaufort and the whites to Hilton Head. Clara saw Elwell off with a sad good-bye. He promised to write her when he got back to their island home. She looked after a young Rhode Island artilleryman with such affection that he could not bear to leave her. "My Baby as I told him, so young, but brave," Clara scribbled in her diary. "Hand burned, arm broken three times, little finger blown off, wept because I could not go in the boat with him,—from Lonsdale. I wrote to his father."

Meanwhile, General Gillmore revised his strategy for getting at Charleston. Conceding that Wagner could not be carried by infantry assaults across the beach, he elected to put both Wagner and Fort Sumter under siege. To bring the Federal guns within range of Sumter, situated in the harbor north of Morris Island, Gillmore's men had to dig three more siege trenches that ran parallel with the one already in operation; each of the trenches would advance the Union line ever closer to Wagner until with the fourth it was only 300 yards away. These trenches, called "saps," were narrow and deep and protected by parapets, and in them were mounted 200- and 300-pounder rifled Parrotts and other formidable siege guns that had been hauled up from the rear. It was hazardous labor for the Union "sappers"—those digging the trenches. They were exposed to constant shelling from Wagner and Sumter and from the rebel guns on James Island. Working day and night, Union engineers and soldiers, including the men of the Fifty-fourth Massachusetts, forced their way slowly toward Wagner, digging to water level and throwing up embankments of sand and of earth and timber carried by hand from the rear.

Digging by day was the most dangerous, since rebel sharpshooters, firing Whitworth rifles mounted with telescopic sights, could hit a man 1,300 yards from Wagner. If anything, the Union sappers feared mortar shells even more. Fired from rebel batteries with a delayed report, they climbed across the sky in an arc, appeared to poise for an instant over the Union lines, and then burst into fragments, which rained down on the sappers in a deadly shower, killing or maiming those who could not get out of the way. To compound their misery, the average daily temperature was almost one hundred degrees Fahrenheit, and the scorching heat and the tormenting flies and sand fleas all took their toll.

During one artillery bombardment, Clara went to the front trench to see if anyone was hurt. Shells were exploding all around, throwing sand and debris on the infantrymen who lay in their rifle pits. These were men of the Tenth Connecticut under the command of Lieutenant Colonel Robert Leggett. Shouting over the racket of the shells, "Captain, this is the hottest place I was ever in," Leggett set out to find his commanding officer and get permission to fall back out of artillery range. At that instant, a soldier remembered, a huge shell exploded nearby, and "we saw the ugly fragments of iron tearing up the earth, raising clouds of dust as they sped on their awful work." When the dust clouds cleared, Clara spotted Colonel Leggett lying in the sand with his leg blown off at the knee. She sprang to his side, tore off some of her clothing, fashioned it into a tourniquet, and used it to tie off "the bleeding fragments," which stanched the flow of blood. Two stretcher-bearers materialized at her side and carried the unconscious colonel back to the hospital, with Clara following. A surgeon who examined Leggett said he was too weak to endure an operation. "He's dying, past being helped," the surgeon said, and walked away. Clara, however, refused to give up on the colonel and took care of him herself, bathing his face in water and calling him her "poor sufferer" and beseeching him not to die. To everyone's astonishment, he regained consciousness—brought back from the edge of oblivion, it appeared, by Clara's ministering. Gazing at her face, Leggett whispered that he couldn't believe he was alive, that it was a miracle, and that it was all due to Clara and that he would never, never forget it and that she was an angel.

The surgeons moved his tent close to Clara's, so that she could look after him. Even though he suffered from "chills & fever," often shaking violently through the night, he was "one of the most contented happy fellows I ever saw," Clara told David. He was playful, too, even flirtatious. While she sat under the raised part of his tent, writing to David, Colonel Leggett was "peeping" out at her and laughing.

The trench digging and the bombardments continued through the rest of July and into August. Like her "little army," Clara endured the infernal racket of the guns and the hot winds that whipped sand into her eyes. She remembered weeks "of weary siege *scorched* by the sun—*chilled* by the wave *rocked* by the tempest. Buried in the shifting sands—*toiling* day after day in the trenches,—with the angry fire of 5 forts hissing thru their forts during every day." The constant shelling kept her awake at night, and the lack of sleep wore her down. She wrote Elvira: "You cannot forget the fact that possibly each shot as it falls upon your ears has sent some poor fellow to the earth writhing in agony."

Clara rarely left the hot hospital tents, to which, day and night, came a steady stream of victims, men ripped apart by bullets or shell fragments or felled by sunstroke or heat exhaustion. Two men of the 100th New York were so badly hurt from a shell burst that Clara for a moment thought that death would be merciful for them. "One the leg blown off at the knee," she noted, "the other with his face cut, completely open from ear to nose, like a butchered hog." Dr. Kittinger,

Clara Barton circa 1850 or 1851, at about age twenty-nine. In these years, searching for meaning to her life, Clara suffered from recurring depressions, sometimes wishing herself dead. Yet she cultivated strong, loving relationships with her father, her brothers and sister, and her nephews and cousins. *Library of Congress*.

Clara Barton circa 1865, photographed by Mathew Brady. Clara "suppressed" earlier war photographs by Brady because she thought them unflattering (she pronounced one a "horrorgraph"). The pose here shows her loving, compassionate side, the side that made her such a remarkable nurse to her "boys" in battlefield hospitals. *Library of Congress.*

Henry Wilson of Massachusetts. A stout, red-faced man with graying hair and lively eyes, this powerful senator served as Clara's "friend at court," securing appointments and military passes for her. *Library of Congress.*

Stephen Barton, Sr. Clara idolized her "soldier father" and wanted to be a soldier like him. He taught her that "next to Heaven our highest duty was to love and serve our country." *Library of Congress.*

Sarah Stone Barton. Clara never felt close to her mother, who had a ferocious temper and left the raising of Clara up to her father and older brothers and sisters. *Library of Congress.*

Stephen Barton, Jr. Clara's oldest brother owned and operated a manufacturing village, Bartonsville, in eastern North Carolina. For three and a half years, Clara worried about Stephen's fate inside the Confederacy. *Library of Congress.*

David Barton. Clara's older brother taught her to ride horses and throw a ball like a boy. From age eleven to thirteen, she nursed him through a protracted illness. During the war she persuaded him to accept a commission in the quartermaster department, with the idea of getting him assigned to her in the field. *Library of Congress.*

Irving "Bubby" Vassall, youngest son of Clara's sister, Sally. Bubby suffered from tuberculosis, and Clara did everything she could for her nephew, loving him as though he were her own son. Later in the war he served as a clerk in the Massachusetts state relief agency in Washington. *Library of Congress.*

Samuel "Sam" Barton, Stephen's son. In 1861 Clara's nephew tried unsuccessfully to reach his father in North Carolina; by 1863 Sam was a clerk in the Surgeon General's office. *Library of Congress.*

Elvira "Vira" Stone. Clara's unmarried cousin served as postmistress of North Oxford and helped a local Soldiers' Aid Society raise supplies for Clara's one-woman relief agency. *Library of Congress.*

Rear of the Samuel Poffenberger farmhouse. During the battle of Antietam, Clara brought much needed hospital stores to this improvised Union field hospital and nursed countless wounded soldiers brought there from the battlefield. The farmhouse was situated so close to the battle lines that it was often under fire. Photographed by Brad H. Keller from an original photo by Fred W. Cross. *Courtesy Antietam National Battlefield, U.S. National Park Service.*

Lane leading from the Poffenberger farmhouse to the barn, where many other wounded were taken. "We were entirely surrounded," said Cornelius Welles, "by those whose wounds were of the most ghastly and dangerous character." Just outside the barn door, Clara removed a bullet from a young soldier's cheek with her pocketknife. Photographed by Brad H. Keller from an original photograph. *Courtesy of Antietam National Battlefield, U.S. National Park Service.*

Antietam, September 17, 1862. This "pencil and Chinese white drawing" by Alfred R. Waud shows citizen volunteers helping the wounded on the field of battle. The surgeons on the left have just completed an amputation. Clara witnessed similar scenes at the Sam Poffenberger farmhouse hospital. *Library of Congress.*

coughing constantly from aggravated bronchitis, operated on both of them. "I covered them with rubber blankets," Clara recorded in her diary, "it rained and was cold. I was astonished to see how comfortable they seem after dressing and being laid away. I went in with the doctor to see them in the evening, both sleeping."

Apparently the two men recovered enough to be evacuated. Another shellfire victim, however, was not so lucky. As Clara wrote Elvira, the "poor fellow, when carefully removed from the ambulance in the darkness of midnight, among the breakers of the surging sea, and the glimmering light on the dim lanterns fell on his quiet face, it revealed no contortion, no sign of agony, only the great gash where the spirit had passed out."

When the stretcher men brought in a wounded Pennsylvanian and laid him on the operating table, Clara tried to soothe him, for his left hand and right arm were terribly mangled. Seeing her, he made an involuntary motion to reach out with a hand, but both hands "dangled" helplessly by his side, Clara recalled, "looking as if the flesh and bones had been scooped out . . . it was a piece of shell of course." The surgeons cut off his left hand at the wrist and his right arm at the shoulder. The poor fellow had a wife and five small children, and Clara had no idea how they would manage. She was so kind to him that he begged her, "If only you will use your influence *to keep me here*, not have me taken away."

Then there was George Peets of Bridgeport, Connecticut, whose legs were both crushed and who was in such pain that he often did not sleep for thirty-six hours at a stretch. And yet he never complained. "I think our soldiers are brave and patient men," Clara wrote David, and "worth taking care of." She reported that her big tent was getting a floor this day. "I can live here as well as any where, and I do enjoy it because I know I am welcome, and sometimes I think I confer *some* happiness."

She sent a loving letter to Elwell, telling him how much she missed him and describing her hospital experiences. Back came a response from Elwell, thanking her for her letter. "It seemed so fresh from your inner nature—it was from the serene deep, where only I have drank. The voice and fragrance of love, kindness and regard, this little letter throws off when you are living in such confusion and discomfort—harried and worried every moment. . . . It has given to the cord that has been steadily tightening between us since we met, *another* tie."

He reported that he had reached Hilton Head "much used up," but after a two-day sleep he felt rested and strong enough to resume his

quartermaster duties, which entailed supervising the flow of supplies—forage and coal in particular—from New York through Hilton
Head to Morris Island. It was a demanding and worrisome responsibility, he told her. "A failure on my part to keep up a full supply of the articles named and many others would be more disastrous than the enemy
cannon. I am expected to do this and do it I will."

Although Clara did not say so in her letter to Elwell, there was
much about the Tenth Corps commissary department that angered her.
Her own supplies were exhausted, and she and her soldier comrades
were suffering from inadequate rations. They subsisted on what she
called "salt junk"—"old beef of such hardness and saltiness as you
never dreamed of," she told Elvira—and hardtack crawling with
worms and covered with mold. As she told Henry Wilson later, they
were "the mouldiest, wormiest crackers I had ever seen an army
insulted with." The constant traffic of ships brought only guns and
ammunition and timber, she complained. As a result, each soldier on
the trench detail had to work sixteen hours out of every twenty-four
with only "a little piece of salt meat and four wormy crackers in his
pocket—and a canteen of warm water." Such treatment, she contended, was inexcusable.

Indeed, conditions on Morris Island were so harsh that Clara had
sent Mary Gage back to Hilton Head. Now the only female nurse at
the hospital, Clara worked on mechanically, with "the shelterless sands
of Morris Island for my bed, my drink the tide water that leaked
through the loose sands of the little island fast becoming a crowded
cemetery, my shade from a scorching August sun, the friendly clouds
that scud between us, my light at night the moon, a dying camp fire,
and the long glowing trail of fire that followed the deadly track of the
enemies shell that hissed and shrieked and burst above us. My *employment*—Ah: that is the only bright spot. God be praised that he selected
my hands to perform that labor."

About mid-August, after the completion of the third parallel trench,
Clara had a nasty dispute with Dr. Samuel A. Green of Massachusetts
that brought an end to her labor. When Green, in temporary command
of the island's hospital service, learned that Clara's cooking and sleeping tents were government issue, he confiscated them for hospital use.
Already worn down from exhaustion and lack of sleep, Clara was
deeply hurt. Where in God's name was she supposed to sleep? on the
naked sand? At once she sent word to Elwell about what had happened. When Elwell confronted Green by letter, the doctor claimed
that he'd taken only her kitchen tent, for which he had been "receipt-

ed, and was responsible." But that was not so; he had seized her sleeping tent as well, on the grounds that a hospital tent was not to be used
for private quarters. The episode upset Clara so profoundly that she
could never talk about it without becoming empurpled with rage. A
year later, she told Henry Wilson that "a worthless, pain saving greedy
surgeon (and my cheeks burn while I write it) from Massachusetts, by
mere accident in rank in temporary charge of the island, too indolent
to provide comfortable quarters for himself, *got a QM to receipt for
mine and took them from me,* leaving me again at the mercy of the elements, which, together with my incessant toil in a short time brought
me [down] with acute disease."

It had happened to her before, this falling ill after an authoritarian
male had mistreated her. Back in the early 1850s, she had persuaded
the authorities of Bordentown, New Jersey, to build a new public
school with her as principal. But public opinion would not accept a
woman in that role, and the school board hired a male principal in her
place and demoted her back to the classroom. The principal proceeded
to treat Clara with disdain; she claimed he persecuted her. Shocked at
the prejudice of her neighbors and the behavior of her "superior,"
Clara suffered a breakdown in her health. She grew feeble and lost her
voice entirely. Only after resigning and moving to Washington City did
she recover.

Now, on Morris Island in the summer of 1863, it happened again.
After "six weeks of unremitting toil," she wrote a few months later, she
had been driven from her tents by the "selfish *cupidity* or *stupidity* of a
pomp[o]us staff surgeon with [a] little accidental temporary authority."
Exposed to the elements and enervated with rage and hurt, she fell ill
with acute dysentery and lay on a makeshift couch in one of the hospital tents. She was so sick with diarrhea and fever that she was sure she
would die and the morning sun would fall on her "dead face along with
the ghostly soldiers brought out for burial."

Somehow word of her illness got back to Elwell. Alarmed, he con-
tacted quartermaster officials on Morris Island, and they put her on a
ship for Hilton Head. Sick though she was, she resisted so vehemently
that she had to be carried "almost by force," Elwell said later. It was
August 18, and the siege of Fort Sumter had already begun, with
Union mortars and other artillery throwing 450 shells a day at what
remained of the rebel fortress. On board the departing ship, Clara was
burning up with fever, so much so that she was hardly aware of the
bombardment. The guns boomed far away, beyond the rim of her
ebbing consciousness.

* * *

For five days, Clara lay ill at Hilton Head, with a post physician, Colonel Elwell, David, cousin Leander, and Captain Lamb and his sons all hovering near. She couldn't leave her bed or eat anything, and Leander feared they were going to lose her. But on August 23, she began to come around. When a young relative, apparently stationed on the island, called on her that day, he found her sitting in an army chair and eating a little. According to her relative, Colonel Elwell sat beside her, joking "that it was the opinion of the chief Quartermaster that she was *playing* sick and she wouldn't be permitted to *play* possum much longer."

Clara was grateful to her male friends for treating her "tenderly." They attended to her every want, she wrote Elvira. "My slightest suggestion is law." She confided in the men about the ugly tent episode, and before long it was common knowledge throughout the Department of the South. Lieutenant Colonel James Hall, the provost marshal, wrote her a letter of apology, saying that the affair was "a piece of petty spite and unmanly persecution. . . . I am sorry for the sake of the dept. that so unmanly an affair should have happened, & hope that the disgrace of it may be with those who are really responsible, and not with the dept. as such, for I can assure you that you have many warm and appreciative friends who will not permit such acts to go unrebuked. . . . I find that officers in the subsistence department have hospital tents issued to them for their private quarters, and fail to appreciate the relative propriety of this course & that concerned in your case."

By August 27, Clara felt like "her old self" and announced that she would return to Morris Island as soon as she received permission. Within a few days, she felt well enough to go riding with Elwell, but her mind wasn't with him. It was on the terrible cannonading then taking place on the Charleston front. Sometimes her thoughts drifted back to the Army of the Potomac, or to the Ninth Corps, which was then campaigning with Burnside in eastern Tennessee. "Happy as I am in my friendly relations," Clara wrote Elvira, "I pine at the thought of 'the rough old fighting fields' of the Potomac and the West, and often thru the long dark night I wake and wish me there."

In early September, she received a letter from Elvira reporting that a young woman wanted to join Clara as her assistant. "She is filled with patriotism and a desire to do more than her position here at home gives her a chance to do," Elvira said. "She is very desirous to go & be useful somewhere in the Army but would like most to come to you[.] I really wish she might come."

Clara replied with an empathic no. "It will be necessary for me to say, as I have at least a hundred times before under similar circumstances that the nature of my position admits of no lady assistant, my own *conscience* would not admit of it. How could I answer to myself if I permitted a young lady to leave home and loving friends to come to me, knowing nothing of the horrors and dangers of field life and place herself unsuspectingly in the immediate jaws of death—a mutilation worse than death,—how shall I answer to those *friends*?!" It was one thing for young women to serve in the general hospitals in the cities, or in the field hospitals after a battle, as they had done at Chancellorsville and Gettysburg. But it was quite another to stand with Clara in the kind of hellish combat she had experienced. In her letter to Elvira, she went on at some length, explaining more fully than in any previous letter her conception of her singular role in this war. "My position is one of my own choosing, full of hardship, and fraught with danger, one that I could not have chosen if I had had father, a mother, a husband, a child, or even brothers or sisters whose interests centered at all in me, in whose home or family circles my absence would leave a vacuum. . . . I am singularly free,—there are few to mourn for me, and I take my life in my hand and go where men fall and die, to see if perchance I can render some little comfort as the wife or mother would if she could be there. I know nothing of permanency, nothing of remuneration, but *give* all I have of time strength and means—and give it directly to those who need, and reserve nothing to even help *sustain* an assistant if I had one."

Perhaps there was another reason Clara objected to a young assistant. As ambitious as she was altruistic, Clara did not want to share her position with anyone else, especially a young woman who was a potential rival. Yes, she admitted to Elvira, Miss Mary Gage had joined her on Morris Island for a week or two, but Clara had sent her home as soon as possible. "I may take an old colored woman with me for a servant," she added, "but this is all I dare risk."

According to Leander, the servant was "an intelligent colored woman whom we call *Aunt Betty* or *Aunty*." Clearly Clara thought "Aunt" Betty was strong enough to endure "the horrors and dangers of field life," perhaps because she had survived the horrors of slavery.

It was Colonel Elwell who finally arranged for Clara to return to Morris Island. She would go "beautifully supplied" with cooking utensils and with a promise that "spacious tents" were awaiting her,

Leander reported to Elvira. Her friend, Lieutenant Colonel Hall, had seen to the tents—had in fact worked out with Dr. Kittinger and Dr. Green their exact location at the hospital on Morris Island. But just when everything had been arranged, a certain Colonel Morgan complained that Clara's tents were located too near his own. Clara was incredulous. How could anyone be that narrow-minded and obsessive about his territory? Indignantly, she told everybody that she would not return to Morris Island unless she could be assured that her tents were not encroaching on the "rights" of others. She was not going to be humiliated again.

Clara had a powerful weapon with which to force the officers into line: her store of supplies. She informed them that she had "many articles" from benevolent societies in the North that would delight the suffering soldiers on Morris Island. In fact, her supply tents were bulging with "a large accumulation of stores," and more were on the way from her "generous" friends in Worcester.

One of Clara's defenders in the army, impressed by her supplies and the support she had in the North, railed against those who thought her work of little value—those who believed that "a poor private" should be allowed to die without her attentions and sympathy. "Let it not be said," he warned, "that she was compelled to go into some other department to dispose of her gifts for the want of a piece of ground to pitch her tents. Our soldiers require her attentions as much as any other department, and perhaps more so."

In a few days, Captain Lamb brought Clara a reassuring letter he had received from Lieutenant Colonel Hall. "I have just seen Dr. Kittinger who says come," Hall said in reference to Clara. As for her tents, "the location chosen & arranged is excellent & interferes with no one, and if any selfish creatures annoy her, there will be a fuss. . . . Miss Barton has friends & influence far beyond any of those who give her present annoyances. She is indeed engaged in a noble service and because [of] a few selfish and narrow minded persons among her, she must not be driven from her purpose."

By September 6, Clara was ready for a triumphant return to Morris Island. She heard that a fifth parallel trench had been completed and that Gillmore had put Wagner itself under siege, hoping to silence it by an overpowering mortar bombardment. That very evening, the steamer *Nelly Baker* arrived from the front with the electrifying news "in effect that Wagner is silenced," said one man, "and will be stormed tomorrow morning." Clara realized that she must hurry if she was to get back to Morris Island before the fighting ended.

Accompanied by Betty, who would function as her cook, Clara left for Morris Island the next day, with Elwell, Lamb, and Leander seeing her off. "To *think* of establishing one's self in range of hostile guns and administering comfort to the wounded and solace to the dying may be romantic," Leander wrote Elvira, "but it requires the heart and nerve that Clara alone of a thousand possesses to calmly meet the stern realities." While he overlooked Betty's own bravery in going with Clara, Leander suggested a profound truth about Clara: it was only when she met "the stern realities" that she was really happy.

Her return on September 7 was somewhat anticlimactic, since the rebels during the night had evacuated both Battery Wagner and Battery Gregg, leaving Morris Island in Union hands. A Pennsylvania veteran pronounced the siege "the most remarkable in history, for difficulties of a character generally regarded [as] insurmountable." As Clara learned, the bombardment of September 5 and 6 had gone on for forty-two consecutive hours. At daybreak on the fifth, seventeen siege and Coehorn mortars had opened fire on Battery Wagner, lobbing shells over the heads of Union sappers, who were huddled in a front rifle trench within one hundred yards of the sand fort, with Old Glory flying overhead to mark their position. Ten light siege guns swept the rear approach to the battery, while fourteen heavy Parrott rifles thundered away at its bombproof shelter, their shells (in the words of one man) darting "like lightning" in their "mission of death." When night fell, Union engineers lit huge calcium lights near the battery, and their glare, said a rebel colonel, brought out "every detail of our works as in the noonday." "As a pyrotechnic achievement alone," said Gillmore, "the exhibition at night was brilliant and attractive, while the dazzling light thrown from our advance trenches, the deafening roar of our guns, and the unswerving peals from James Island added sublimity and grandeur to the scene. The imagination was beguiled and taken captive, and all the cruel realities of war were for a time forgotten in the unwonted excitement of this novel spectacle."

At dawn on September 7, three Union assaulting columns stormed the battered ramparts of Wagner, only to find it abandoned. Looking around, they discovered torpedoes planted in the sand outside the fort, which guarded the approaches, and old-style boarding pikes along its outer edge. According to the chaplain of a Rhode Island artillery unit, the spears had "edged or bladed hooks set in hard wood handles, making a *chevaux-de-frise* of steel blades." A New Hampshire soldier described what they saw inside: "Dead bodies long unburied, heads, arms, feet (with the shoes still upon them), lay strewn all about—the

stench was almost unbearable." General Gillmore walked around
inside the battery, then wrote General Halleck that "Fort Wagner is a
work of the most formidable kind. Its bomb-proof shelter, capable of
holding 1,800 men, remains intact after the most terrible bombardment to which any work was ever subjected."

It had taken nearly two months for Gillmore's army of 11,000,
backed up with heavy artillery and a powerful fleet, to advance 1,350
yards from his first trench to the northern end of the island and drive
off some 1,500 rebels, including the garrison at Battery Gregg. He
had lost 2,318 men in the campaign. And to what end? True, Fort
Sumter was now only "a confused mass of crumbling débris," as rebel
general P.G.T. Beauregard put it, but rebel infantry burrowed into the
rubble still held it against Yankee attack, and its big guns had all been
removed and mounted elsewhere in the harbor. Protected by a ring
of batteries, Charleston was still a rebel city—and likely to remain
that way.

Two days after Clara reached Morris Island, Union sailors tried an
amphibious assault against Sumter, only to be driven back by small
arms fire at a cost of 127 casualties. Clara hoped that the Union would
make no further effort to take that recalcitrant fort. "It will all come in
time but I hope without the loss of another life," she wrote Amelia
Barton. "Fort Sumpter has cost enough already."

Clara paid a visit to Battery Wagner and walked around inside, collecting empty shell casings and some solid shot and other items of
interest. Outside the walls, skulls lay partially covered in the sand—it
was impossible to tell whether they were Union or rebel skulls. In
either case, they were hideous to look at, with their hollow eyes and
smiling jaws.

Later Clara penned a solemn benediction to the Morris Island campaign: "We have captured one fort—Gregg—and one charnel house—
Wagner—and we have built one cemetery, Morris Island. The thousand little sand hills that glitter in the pale moon light are a thousand
headstones, and the restless ocean waves that roll and break upon the
whitened beach sing an eternal requiem to the toil-worn, gallant dead
who sleep beside."

On September 15, Clara received a letter from General Gillmore's
headquarters. It had been dictated by the general and signed by his
assistant adjutant general:

The Brig. Gen. Commanding is informed by the Medical Officer in
Charge of the hospital on this island that your services will be no longer
required in connection with the hospital in the field, as the sick and
wounded are not to be retained here but will be sent immediately to
Beaufort. I am instructed to say that the General appreciates the value
of your kind offices to the sick and wounded soldiers, and the benevo-
lence which has led you to sacrifice so many comforts by residing here
at the actual scene of conflict, but in view of the crowded condition of
the island and the many inconveniences which such a residence must
entail, he deems it best that you should remove to Beaufort, where he
will provide for you a comfortable dwelling.

Clara could not believe this letter. She had been *ordered* off the
island. She spotted the evil hand of Dr. Green in the reference to "the
Medical Officer in charge of the hospital." How she detested that men-
dacious and mean-spirited man. That Gillmore should side with Green
against her was more than she could bear. After all she had done for
the army and its medical service, this was the thanks she got? A dismissal from the commanding general? She took it as a rejection, and it
hurt her to the quick. If Gillmore thought she was some frail creature
who could not endure hardship, he did not understand her at all.
Three months later, she was still mortified. "After four weeks of suffering most intense," she wrote, "I rose in my weakness and repaired
again to my post, and scarcely were my labors recommenced when
through the same influence or *no* influence brot to bear upon the Genl
commanding I was made the subject of a general Order, and commanded to leave the Island, giving me three hours in which to pack,
remove, and ship, four tons of supplies with no assistance, that they
knew of but one old female negro cook. I complied but was remanded
to Beaufort to labor in the hospitals there with this portion of the
Order."

She did go to Beaufort, did try "to labor in the hospitals there," but
found them closed off to her. The Sanitary Commission kept all the
hospitals well supplied, she was told, and they had no need of Clara's
stores. Worse still, she encountered imperious Mrs. Lander, who
informed her that Miss Dix held "supremacy over all female attendants
by authority from Washington." Indeed, Mrs. Lander claimed that Dix
had authorized her to keep all unaffiliated nurses out of the Beaufort
hospitals. Horrified that the arm of Miss Dix had reached clear down
to the Sea Islands, Clara felt rejected again. The arrogance of young
Mrs. Lander only deepened her pain.

Finding "each hospital labeled—no admittance—and its surgeons bristling like porcupines at the bare sight of a proposed visitor," Clara sailed back to Hilton Head and wrote General Gillmore "a full explanation" of her position. Her letter brought a sharp response in which, according to Clara, Gillmore called her "humanity to account for not being willing to comply with his specified request, viz to labor in Beaufort hospitals."

"How in reason's name was I 'to labor there,' " Clara recalled bitterly; "should I prepare my food and thrust it against the outer walls, in the hope it might strengthen the patients inside, should I tie up my bundle of clothing and creep up and deposit it on the door step and slink away like a guilty mother and watch afar off to see if the masters of the mansion would accept or reject the 'foundling'. If the Commanding General in his wisdom, when he assumed the direction of my affairs and commanded me where to labor had opened the doors for me to enter, the idea would have seemed more practical. It did not occur to me at the moment how I was to effect an entrance to these hospitals, but I have since thought that I might have been expected to watch my opportunity some dark night, and STORM them, although it must be conferred that the popularity [of] this mode of attack was rather on the decline in this Dept. at that time, having reached its height very soon after the middle of July."

In Clara's mind, she had never been so humiliated, had never felt so depressed. When she tried to think through her predicament, she had no idea what to do or where to go.

She drifted through the fall in a haze of horseback rides and social functions—now a dinner party on the *Arago*, now a deer hunt on a neighboring island. She wrote Amelia Barton, Sammy's wife, that the weather on Hilton Head was cool enough for a fire in the fireplace and that the days passed, one like another, "all bright, clear, and cool." She complained about "all the dust, sand, flies, fleas, mosquitoes, and regular army officers which infest this depot." "There is no war news, no news of any kind, in this Dept.," she wrote Mary Norton. "We are waiting for something to 'turn up.' "

Elwell, for his part, was overjoyed to have his "Pet," his "Dear Birdie," back with him on Hilton Head. He sent her tender notes reminding her that "I not only tell you everything but I believe I *show* you everything." Clara thanked her "friend" for doing so, but her passion for him was waning. She made no diary entries that fall about Elwell's brilliance and charm and rarely sent him a note. The longest note she wrote him was not about intimate matters between them but about the need for military schools for women, which clearly derived from an earlier discussion about women in war. "I have an idea that the elevation, and character, and education of woman, has something to do even with the *military* world," her note stated. If the United States desired to maintain military supremacy for future wars, she argued, it ought to establish "*military academies* for its *women*—for the *daughters* who will one day become the *mothers* of its armies—they should be active, and brave, and strong and fearless, capable of understanding the plan of a campaign,—but *women*, ay! *ladies* still—and the soldier boy, the *natural soldier* of such a mother, would be worth just one thousand drilled dough heads, who had merely, without foundation— been run through 'West Point.' " This was not "a state of things" she necessarily preferred, "for I *love peace*." Yet it was a "fact" that woman "has just so much to do with the creation of warriors and raising of armies,—It will not be simply because our *men* have been trained and drilled in the field that the *next* generation will find us with a better army than *this*." The mothers must "become soldiers too," she contended, "and for the sake of my country in its future, *God Bless the man* who sustains the women that follow their husbands to the field."

Plainly, Clara saw herself as the model for the soldier mother of the future. Swept up in her argument, she signed the note with a formal flourish: "Clara Barton."

By October 1863, Clara's best friend on the Sea Islands was fifty-five-year-old Fanny Gage, Mary's mother. During one of their frequent visits together, Fanny recounted her own ordeal after she had left Hilton Head the previous May. When she reached her home, her husband, James, had died; she saw to his burial, lectured on the freedmen in the East, and then returned to the Sea Islands just after the July 18 assaults on Battery Wagner. She learned that the Sixty-second Ohio, containing many recruits from her home neighborhood, had been in action there. "Scores of young men I have known for years, dead," she noted with tears burning her eyes. When she visited a hospital ship full of wounded from the Wagner attack, she vowed that "only for *the dying and the suffering* I would be cheerful." She served a stint in the hospitals, then returned to Parris Island, where she resumed her superin-

tendency and enjoyed a reunion with her daughter Mary, who recounted what she and Clara had done on Morris Island, apparently pointing
out that Clara had been under fire. After Clara returned to Hilton
Head, she and Fanny started seeing a great deal of one another.

Both women were hurting—Fanny because of the death of her husband, Clara from the fiasco on Morris Island—and they reached out to
one another in their pain. For her part, Clara had never met anyone so
caring and giving as Fanny. And Fanny greatly admired Clara too. In
fact, she thought her younger friend had accomplished more on the
battlefield than had any other woman of the war.

On Parris Island, they took long walks in the gathering autumn,
talking about the war and reminiscing about their faraway homes. As
they strolled across the great lawn of the plantation, "the pine dew"
dripped on them from the canopy overhead, and acorns fell like rain.
Sparrows and mockingbirds swarmed among the magnolias and live
oaks, and the blacks down in the vale often sang their favorite spiritual,
"O, Lord! remember me." When the two women reached the beach,
Fanny pointed out how the waves came "dancing to the shore like
maidens in their glee" and played together on "the whitened sand."

Fanny soothed Clara's hurt feelings and drew her out of her depression over the Gillmore episode, out into the sunlight of her love. For
Clara, Fanny was like a mother, showing her the warmth and care she
had never received from her real mother. Indeed, she called Fanny her
"dear adoptive mother," and Fanny addressed Clara as "my dear darling daughter." They came to love one another as deeply as two human
beings could—theirs was a friendship that would last "to the death," as
Fanny said later.

They shared a love for poetry, too, and wrote tender poems to one
another. One of Clara's read:

> Aunt Fanny dear in your kind care
> My very heart lies sleeping
> My bread and butter, flour & pans
> They all are in thy keeping.

Fanny wrote this poem to Clara during a visit on Hilton Head:

> Your kindness & care will I fear never let
> me that I am not a debtor to thee. . . .
> And should ever a dark cloud of blue rest
> Above thee

And you look over the past days for something to cheer
Just think for a moment how dearly I love thee
And thank thee for all thou hast done for me
here.

And in a lighter vein:

I know not dear Clara the language of flowers,
But I do know they brighten this good world of ours. . . .
But I did not sit down to write words like this
But to send you a "Howdey" and offer you a kiss
And to tell you how truly I love you dear, always
But sure, 'mid the cares, & the toils of the day.

Fanny could gently tease her "friend loved so dearly":

Think of this noble, generous, self-poised woman
So nobly here and free
That it seems a sacrilege to call her human frettings about a flea

On Parris Island one day, Clara and both Gages, Fanny and young Mary, got to talking about great poems and poets. Clara remarked that William Cullen Bryant's poem, "Death of the Flowers," had been running through her thoughts since the beginning of autumn. "It's so beautiful," she said, "that I never can recall the precise arrangement of the words any more than I can the exact features of a perfectly beautiful face." Mary said she had the same difficulty, but luckily she had a copy of Bryant with her. She fetched it, and she and Clara tried to commit the poem to memory: Clara would memorize several lines and repeat them aloud, and then hand the volume to Mary, who would do the same. But they took so long and made so many mistakes that Fanny grew impatient, dismissing their efforts as "school-girl recitations." She asserted, Clara recalled, that "she could make poetry faster than we could learn it after it was already made for us." To prove it, Fanny dashed off a poem, "October Days in So. Carolina Dedicated to Miss. Clara Barton 1863," celebrating Fanny and Clara's walks among the live oaks and "broad magnolias" in a soft and sighing wind. The poem recalled a black man singing, "Oh, Lord! remember me," while he worked in a sea of cotton. "Upon its snowy heaps are found no blood / Stains black and grim / The dark hands labor cheerily, God has remembered him." Clara and Mary were impressed, and Fanny thought enough of the poem to submit it to the *Anti-Slavery Standard* in Washington, which published it as "Autumn Days in South Carolina," a poem "Dedicated to Miss Clara Barton, the Heroine of the Potomac."

Clara wrote Mary Norton that she wished she had "the talent" to compose such "good things." She added: "I see enough to write from and about, but alas! the *more I see the less time* I have to write it, even if I had the talent."

Fanny Gage was not just a loving friend to Clara but a mentor and teacher as well. She told Clara about her abolitionist and feminist work before the Civil War, describing how she had been jeered for advocating "Justice to the negro" and "Justice to women" in public forums. Fanny made Clara aware that the problems of women and blacks were similar, since both were oppressed groups. Indeed, like Sarah and Angelina Grimké, Elizabeth Cady Stanton, and other woman's rights advocates, Fanny had first been an abolitionist and, in the process of trying to free the slaves, had helped begin the struggle for women's rights. In fact, presiding over an Ohio woman's rights convention in 1851, Fanny Gage had defended Sojourner Truth when the black abolitionist and orator had turned up at the convention. Horrified, some of Fanny's white colleagues warned her: "Don't let her speak, Mrs. Gage, it will ruin us. Every newspaper in the land will have our cause mixed up with abolition and niggers, and we shall be utterly denounced." Believing that abolition and woman's rights were interconnected, Fanny granted Sojourner Truth permission to address the assembly. "Look at me! Look at my arm!" Sojourner Truth said, exhibiting her muscles. "I've plowed and planted and gathered into barns, and no man could head me—And aren't I a woman?" Fanny herself told the convention that all women must "with one united voice, speak out in their own behalf, in behalf of humanity." If they did that, "they could create a revolution without armies, without bloodshed, that would do more to ameliorate the condition of mankind, to purify, elevate, ennoble humanity than all that has been done by reformers in the last century."

In their long discussions on Parris Island and Hilton Head, Fanny converted Clara to the cause of woman's suffrage and full equality before the law. Indeed, Clara became a committed feminist who shared her mentor's belief that women must "stand for the Right," must "Be bold, be firm, be strong" in demanding the same rights that men enjoyed.

Under Fanny's influence, Clara also developed a new regard and

sympathy for the freedmen. She listened intently when Fanny spoke
about the damage slavery had done to blacks, especially those on the
Sea Islands; yet despite their terrible hardships, she thought they
showed so much hope, were such good, decent folk with a hunger to
know and a real capacity to be self-supporting. The problem, she said,
was that until they developed that capacity, they were utterly dependent on the North. She talked increasingly about the need to stamp out
racial prejudice, rally public opinion behind Lincoln's Emancipation
Proclamation, convince Northern whites that they should help the
freedmen.

Now that Fanny had made Clara more racially conscious, she
became distressingly aware of the "thousands of old, sick, lame worn
out and helpless men, women and children" who, despite the efforts
of Northern philanthropy, lived and worked on St. Helena Island "in a
state of near destitution." That autumn, a smallpox epidemic swept
through this impoverished population "with almost the terrors of the
Plague," as Clara put it. She wanted to go to them yet dared not do so
lest she contract the dread disease and infect the soldiery on Hilton
Head. No matter; the army quarantined the entire island as far as military personnel and other whites were concerned, making it impossible for her to go. Desperately wanting to do something for the blacks,
she boxed up "some tons of clothing and comforts" from her own supplies and persuaded a black man named Columbus Simonds of Port
Royal to take them to St. Helena. A former slave, Simonds had taught
himself to read and write and had served as General Hunter's servant.
Gladly obliging Clara, he landed her supplies "silently from little
boats up the mouths of the creeks" on St. Helena and distributed
them himself.

The blacks were so grateful that they begged Simonds to let them
send Clara something in return. "I told them," Clara recalled, "they
might pick me up some pretty sea shells from their beautiful beach,
and if they could, conveniently, they might trap me a few singing birds,
that I would take home and present to the friends of their people at the
north." She did not indicate whether they acceded to her request. But
Simonds did write her a letter, and she sent it to the editors of the
American Baptist with a note that indicated Fanny Gage's influence.
Simonds's letter, Clara said, gave evidence "of the strongest character,
if more were wanting—of the faithful, grateful, true and simple hearted, christian nature of the African. . . . Whiter blood than theirs has
often failed to exhibit traits as high and noble."

*   *   *

In October, Clara spent several days packing her collection of Wagner "trophies" for shipment to Judge Ira Barton in Worcester. Annie Childs had written her that Worcester County was to hold a benefit fair for the soldiers, and Clara hoped the items could be auctioned off. In an accompanying note to the judge, she pointed out that they included "rebel 'shell' and 'shot' " from the various forts and batteries in and around Charleston harbor, plus a rebel torpedo and a John Brown pike—it was so labeled—that Colonel Elwell had given her.

According to Clara, the pike had been found inside Wagner and turned over to the colonel. How it got there was a mystery. When Brown attacked Harpers Ferry in 1859, he brought along almost a thousand pikes with which to arm the slaves. After the raid failed, Virginia secessionist Edmund Ruffin sent a John Brown pike to each of the slave state governors, including Governor William H. Gist of South Carolina, as an example of the violence he could expect from the hated Yankees. Now, ironically, one of those pikes had turned up in Clara's hands. It was a double irony, since in late 1859 she had actually objected to Brown's raid and sympathized with Southerners in their efforts to defend themselves against outside provocation. Clara had paraphrased Lincoln when she said of Southerners: "They are the same that people the world over are and would be under the circumstances." (Lincoln had said earlier: "They are just what we would be in their situation.") The war not only ended Clara's sympathy for the South but also sealed the doom of slavery—or so she and Fanny hoped. Indeed, the war converted Clara, as it had Lincoln and thousands of other Northerners, to Brown's own vision that slavery must be removed by the sword.

As for the rebel torpedo, Clara assured Judge Barton that the cap had been removed. Someone had found it buried at Wagner, "with the fingers of a dead Confederate soldier tied to the cap, but fortunately so much time had elapsed that the decaying flesh gave way on his being removed and the intended explosion prevented." She cautioned the judge that the torpedo, the pike, and the other items were strictly "for the benefit of the soldiers if anything be realized from them." If they weren't sold for that purpose, she preferred that they be donated to the American Antiquarian Society in Worcester, "as it occurs to me that in time they would become both interesting and valuable."

Clara's war trophies, filling five boxes, did arrive in Worcester in time for the fair. Elvira wrote Clara that she and Irving attended it and saw "the rebel torpedo contributed by Miss Clara Barton" on exhibit in the "curiosity room." But the relics were not put up for sale. Clara could not fathom why the fair administrators kept them. She joked that "perhaps they contemplate fortifying the city" against an enemy attack "and want them for ammunition."

In this period of enforced leisure, Clara realized that her wardrobe was ill suited for social occasions on Hilton Head. Her few clothes were in tatters, and she prevailed on Annie to make or buy some new things for her. She would very much like a black riding dress and one of those small hats Annie admired and some "checked poplins," which were said to be in fashion this autumn, and "a pair of slate colored corsets and a doz. linen collars" and even "a new black veil" to replace her old one, which had grown "a little rusty." Since Clara always wrote her letters with an eye toward eventual publication—was she not making history in her war work?—she became concerned lest these mundane wants become public. She warned Annie: "You must hold this letter very private, only making *verbal* extracts[;] it is so trifling and all about *dress* that it will not be interesting, or creditable."

No sooner had she written Annie about her need for a hat than one arrived from an older male admirer, who had apparently been unsuccessful in wooing her. The hat was "a very pretty (and I suppose fashionable) one," Clara wrote Annie sarcastically. "From one of my *crutched silver haired friends* who remembered gratefully the hour of his disaster. It is rolled at the sides, with a long black feather lying over the top etc. etc. is that the style?"

The end of October brought her an entire box of clothes from "dear Annie." Among the many exquisite items were cuffs and corsets and "a most beautiful" dress, which was "a most capitol fit," Clara wrote her, save that she needed another inch of "chest room." She thought she could correct that by enlarging the seam at the bottom of the waist and wearing a "stomacher"—a *white* stomacher, "they are so neat"—with a few buttons left open. "It is true that I have expanded a little," Clara admitted, "but the size of the neck and arm sizes are just right, so I am no larger generally and do not weigh more than formerly. I think my back is narrower, they all tell me so, and that I am more erect. I am sure I dont know, but I do know that if you will make my measure 24 instead of 23 inches [in the waist] and let it all be on the fronts, you could not improve it further for me." She also preferred her dresses shorter than the fashionable hoops that reached to the heels—"you know I am very unfashionable particularly in this regard generally wanting my dresses to the bottom of my cavs when no one else wore them so."

As for the cuffs on the dress just received, they "are splendid, just what I *thought* I *wanted* but I never saw them before, just the thing for the '*saddle*,' the '*parlor*' I don't know anything about, but I should think they would be beautiful there too. . . . The corsets are the prettiest form I ever wore by far and just a fit."

Still another box of soldiers' gifts had come from the Worcester Aid Society, and it made Clara feel guilty about not being in the field to distribute them. She wrote to the society through Annie Childs: "Oftener than I could wish, my heart sinks heavily, oppressed with the fear, that I am falling far short of the fulfillment of life's duties, but if ever there chance to be a time when I come nearly up to the measure, no one, not even myself knows how much of it is due to the kind hearts that never forget, and the willing hands that never weary, if with all this to sustain me I am doubly culpable."

But where could she fulfill "life's duties"? Back in Washington? The Army of the Potomac had fought no major battles since Gettysburg and appeared as inert on the Virginia front as Gillmore's Tenth Corps was on Morris Island. Neither place promised much for her. In November she sought Elwell's counsel, sending a terse note next door: "Reply to my question if I ought to remain in the Dept through the winter or return to Washington."

Back came a two-and-a-half page response. As to her question, Elwell said, "I don't know—I can't know nor can you, yet. It seemed clear to you that you should come here and I have no doubt it will be equally clear to you when duty calls you away from here—I think so. God who seemed to direct you here & me here, I think, will tell us when he wants us to go away." His advice was to "work and listen for the voice that will call you to a new field when your work is done here" and try to be "happy." "You are very dear to me and I use no idle words . . . one that is so considerate, so kind, tender, and patient, can only be dealt with frankly and generously."

She confided in Elwell that she would like to return to Morris Island but feared that Gillmore would refuse to give her a pass, would reject her again. Elwell, who had been in contact with Gillmore, tried to soothe her: "Don't feel bad—all is right—all will be right—Genl Gillmore feels most kindly to you—he will set this matter all right tomorrow—he will write to you and he will invite you to Folly Island. Now do believe when I say, Genl Gillmore is not disposed to interfere with what you think to be your duty."

The next day, as Elwell promised, a pass came from Gillmore authorizing Clara to visit Morris and Folly islands. He even attached a courteous note. But Clara resented and distrusted the general so much that she was reluctant to go, although she wanted to.

She was more confused when Frances Gage announced that she was going back to the North to plead the cause of Southern blacks on the lecture circuit. In a whirlwind of conflicting emotions, Clara finally decided to stay in the Department of the South. Clara's brother David, however, made arrangements to go with Fanny, evidently securing a furlough so that he could visit his family. As far as Clara was concerned, it was just as well that he would be gone for a while. He had done little except complain—about his health, the weather, and his job, despite the fact that his duties were "very light, and without responsibility," as a relative on the island said. He was a burden to everyone—to Captain Lamb and especially to Clara—who had found him of no use to her, since he had stayed behind in "creaturely comfort" while she had toiled on Morris Island.

On November 11 or so, Fanny and David left on a steamer bound for New York, and Clara felt lonely and empty. Mary Gage had elected to stay with her, and Clara was glad for the company. With Fanny gone, Mary was her "most intimate lady friend here." But Mary could not fill the void caused by Fanny's departure.

Shortly thereafter, Dr. Marsh and his fellow agents of the U.S. Sanitary Commission invited Clara to return to Morris Island and (in her words) "take charge of what they as men could not." Clara knew what they meant. Only a female nurse could care for a dying soldier as if she were his mother or sister. And there were other things only a woman could do. As an Ohio surgeon explained it, he could amputate a soldier's leg, but he could not bring himself to write his wife and tell her how her husband had died and ask her to kiss their daughter for him. This was what Dr. Marsh and his assistants wanted Clara to perform in the hospital on Morris Island.

She was inclined to accept, but Captain Lamb and her other male friends on "the Head" tried to dissuade her. Elwell had changed his mind and wanted her to stay, too, on the grounds that nothing was likely to happen in the Morris–Folly Island sector during the winter. The plain truth was that he did not want to be apart from her. When Clara announced her intention to go, the colonel called it her "Folly Island folly" and joined in the chorus of dissent among her friends.

Clara wrote a long letter to Mary Norton asking what she should do. "My friends here at the Head are trying to keep me from going to Morris Island this winter now that there is so little doing there, and to coax me off the notion, they have built me a most beautiful suite of rooms. . . . Oh such a splendid view of the whole bay and all the shipping of Port Royal and they send me the most splendid horses to ride, and *manufacture* wants—I am confident of it—here on the island for me to attend to— and then I think perhaps I ought to remain with them unless the troops move. . . . So what shall I do?—and I know you will tell me to remain at Hilton Head and keep comfortable this winter. Well, I dont know—perhaps I ought—but will watch and see and tell you."

As it turned out, she went nowhere that November except to St. Helena Island for Thanksgiving. The Seventh Connecticut was stationed there, "a fine regiment," Clara wrote Mary Norton, "the one that led in the reduction of Ft. Pulaski." It had also seen action on the Charleston front and in November had been transferred back to St. Helena, now apparently free of the dreaded smallpox. The wives of several officers were with the regiment, and Clara had become friends with the women, especially the colonel's wife, Harriet Foote Hawley. A cousin of Henry Ward Beecher, the famous New York minister, Harriet was "a splendid little lady," Clara said, "full of wit and spirit." For the past year, she had been a missionary teacher among the blacks in Beaufort and had been a frequent visitor at the hospitals there and on Hilton Head, where she had met and befriended Clara. "Hatty" Hawley and the other regimental wives invited Clara to spend Thanksgiving day with them, and Clara replied with alacrity: "Wind and weather permitting I hope to 'get permission to come over and play with you.' "

Traveling alone, she took a steamer across the bay and spent a delightful·Thanksgiving with the regiment. While the soldiers feasted on ten roast pigs, Clara, the wives, and the colonel and his staff enjoyed a delicious turkey dinner. "After dinner the horses were brought up and the ambulances manned or womaned or both," Clara recalled, "and off we started on a voyage of discovery over the island, the main road of which leads directly to the Beaufort ferry a most splendid Island it is[;] our ride lasted till dark—we gathered autumn leaves and keepsakes of all kinds and returned to camp laden, then I called for my *carriage* and came home by moonlight across the bay as smooth as a piece of glass."

On December 2 guns boomed all over Hilton Head in celebration of glorious news from the West: General Grant had defeated the rebel Army of Tennessee in the battles of Lookout Mountain and Missionary

Ridge near Chattanooga, and the rebels had fallen back into Georgia. "We have quite a little rejoicing over the good fortunes of our distant brothers in arms," Clara wrote in her journal. "Heaven grant us strength and spare us Grant, till the end come[s], and the purpose be accomplished."

Meanwhile, her days continued to drift without purpose. As was her habit when inactive, she wrote long entries in a journal, chronicling her boredom and lecturing herself that somehow, some way, she must make her days " *'tell'* to more purpose." She described how the mornings were "bright purple" now, with frost covering the ground and the dock, which glittered in the sunlight "like a huge bar of silver running into the sea." She recorded a stimulating visit from a Major Flagg, who had just been released from the hospital on Hilton Head. He spoke critically of the hospital management, remarking that "the arrangements *might* be improved and the patients be better fed without positive injury to *their* digestive organs." His words perked Clara up, but "I cannot learn from him that I can probably be of any service to them, by attempts to visit them."

Indeed, the hospital was off-limits to her. When she spoke about it with Dr. Marsh of the Sanitary Commission, who had become her "esteemed friend," the doctor said that the hospital was entirely supplied by his commission, and he advised Clara not to go near it. He said that she "should never be allowed to do so," that "between the surgical regulations and the supreme authority of Miss Dix, what failed of being done must go undone." This was honest advice, she conceded, but it made her feel depressed again.

One evening, after taking tea with Elwell and Miss Mary Baldwin, who was visiting Hilton Head with her father, a Cleveland banker, Clara went for a walk in the open square of the village. At the far end, she encountered a Mrs. Dorman, wife of the army paymaster, who also must have talked with Flagg about the hospital situation. She spoke with great excitement about the deplorable conditions in the Sea Island hospitals, pointing out that the men were not being adequately fed. Did Miss Barton know that all they ever got was milkless tea, dipped toast, and meat cooked dry? Mrs. Dorman said she intended to set up a diet kitchen that would serve those poor men healthy, properly cooked meals. She expected opposition from the surgeons in charge and the hospital matron, who had been appointed and sent by Miss Dix. But Mrs. Dorman thought she could commence "by littles and work herself in." She might report to Washington through her "influential friends," and secure carte blanche from Secretary of War Stanton to operate independently of Dix's matron and the surgeons. Did Clara think it possible for her to procure sufficient supplies and people to cook and serve the food once the operation were established? Mrs. Dorman said that General Gillmore took tea with her the evening before and asked after the patients: "*How are my poor Boys?*"

At that point, Mrs. Dorman's husband joined them, and they discussed the matter generally. Clara said little, but what she thought was "quite another thing." Back in her quarters that evening, she poured into her journal all her pent-up anger and bitterness: "No doubt but the stately stupendous and magnificent indolence of the officers in charge embitters the days of the poor sufferers who have become mere machines in the hands of the Government to be ruled and oppressed by puffed up conceited, and self-sufficient superiors in position. No doubt but a good well regulated kitchen, presided over with a little good common sense and womanly care would change the whole aspect of things and lengthen the days of some, and brighten the last days of others of the poor suffer[ers] within the thin walls of this hospital. I wish it might be but what can *I* do. First it is not *my* province, I should be out of place there, next Miss Dix is supreme, and her appointed nurse is Matron, next the surgeons will not brook any interference, and will in my opinion resent and resist the smallest effort to break over their own arrangements. What *others* may be able to do I am unable to conjecture, but I feel that *my* guns are effectually silenced."

This notation revived the painful memories of Dr. Green and Gillmore's actions against her on Morris Island, events that she recalled in furious detail in her journal. She concluded: "I *went* with all I had, to work where I thought I saw greatest need. . . . My *sympathy* is not destroyed, by any means, but my *confidence* in my ability to accomplish anything of an alleviating character in *this* Dept is completely annihilated."

"I must seek a freer atmosphere," she wrote a couple of nights later, "where one can be allowed to work for a needy soldier without committing an indiscretion meriting disgrace."

December 10 brought still another blow to Clara: a letter from Mr. Upperman concerning their special arrangement in the Patent Office, according to which he did Clara's work for half her salary and gave her the other half. Commissioner Holloway had approved the arrangement, promising Clara that he would hold her position while she was in the field. She used her half of the salary to pay the rent on her Washington apartment and to buy supplies for the soldiers. Now Upperman informed Clara that the arrangement had been terminated. "Mr. Holloway," she wrote in her journal, paraphrasing Upperman's letter, "had ordered my writing to be dropped in consequence of the representation of some twenty ladies that I was in receipt of [a] large salary from the Government here, for my services in the army."

Clara was hurt and baffled by the behavior of those female ingrates—and *twenty* of them no less. The Patent Office had hired a lot more women since she had gone to the field, in no small part, she believed, because of her own pioneering efforts there in behalf of her sex. And what did she get as thanks? A "representation" that Clara's name be removed from the books, on the utterly fallacious grounds that the army was paying her and hence she didn't need her Patent Office job. Obviously the malcontents wanted it for themselves. And Commissioner Holloway, who was supposed to be her friend, had gone along with them. How could they treat her this way after all she had done for the country? She was so upset she started to cry.

Later in the day, Elwell called on Clara and invited her to spend the evening with him and Captain Lamb. Clara hid her feelings and mumbled that she would come. But after he left, she changed her mind and sent him a note: "Dear Col., I said I would come, but a moments reflection tells me I *must not*,—I was glad to see you, and forgot how bruised and sore my heart was. I have been struggling with my tears all day—every thing has gone rough, and the corners have hit and the briers scratched me every minute—Please excuse me, for I *cannot* be company for any one to night. I will come some time when I am *better natured.*" She signed it: "Yours Clara."

The next day she wrote a letter to Commissioner Holloway setting the record straight. First, Clara said, the claim that she received a government salary for her war work was "utterly and entirely" and "willfully and maliciously false." She pointed out that she had served in the field without any remuneration and had lived on the same rations as the troops: "hard crackers, often mouldy and wormy, salt meat, and water, and from no *person* or *persons*, or *Society* or *Commission*, or *Corporation* or *Bureau* or any other conceivable source have I ever received one dollar of salary or reward." If she lost her half salary from the Patent Office, her chief regret would be "the loss of the few dollars to the needy soldiers I meet in my rounds, but if the ladies who write for you need it more than our troops in the field, I have nothing to say in opposition. . . . It has been part of the work of my lifetime to aid in opening every avenue to honorable employment for my own sex. I hope these ladies are equally generous with me."

She beseeched Holloway not to misconstrue her motives in writing this letter. "*It is not to complain* of the decision which has been made, it is not in my nature to complain. . . . My only object is," she insisted, "to thoroughly and flatly contradict as I do, the assertion or insinuation, that I *do now, ever have*, or *ever shall*, receive the least equivalent for time and money expended, upon or services rendered to the soldiers of our Armies." The protest of the female office workers was "niggardly in its nature, and derogatory to every feeling of humanity and patriotism and as such I reject and scorn it."

Once her letter was in the mail, Clara felt better. In fact, her mood swung all the way from angry despair to soaring self-confidence. She dashed off a letter to Mary Norton, telling her friend how much she, Clara, had changed since the old days in New Jersey: "I was not certain of my ground as I am now, and you would find me much more accessible and easy *now* than I was then. I am more open and 'dont care' and all in all I am better and happier, and you would find me more comfortable, and would like me better than you could then. I travel along easily and dont fret in the harness, and you would enjoy me more now than then, because I enjoy myself better. I used to think I must be very cautious and keep much to myself. I tell all I know now if I please, say what I like and *stand by it to the death*, so I am not sorry that I am growing old and gray. I have grown happier."

Clara *traveled along easily* and *didn't care or fret in the harness*? Such remarks betrayed the delusions that the high end of depression fastened upon its victim, for Clara was extremely sensitive and quickly hurt, and fretted terribly when she was mistreated, as her own journal and her letter to Holloway demonstrated.

Equally remarkable was Clara's assertion that she was "not sorry" to be "growing old and gray." When she wrote that, she had not had a "monthly turn" in four months. She had no history of irregular menstrual cycles in her adult years, and she was definitely not pregnant (there is no evidence that she feared she was pregnant when she started missing her menstrual cycles). Therefore, she could only conclude that she was entering the woman's "change of life," menopause, even though she was only forty-one years old. In Clara's day, it was not unusual for the change to occur in a woman that age, and in fact that was exactly what was happening to her. Twelve years later, in private notes to a trusted physician, Clara reported that during her bout with dysentery in August 1863, "menstruation ceased suddenly and never returned or made further sign or symptom." Her remark suggests that she was not bothered by the idea of menopause and the end of her reproductive capacity. She never wanted children anyway. In truth, Clara appears to have regarded menopause with relief, since it freed her from menstruation and the risk of pregnancy. With that behind her now, she probably did feel that she had "grown happier."

Despite what she told Mary, Clara dreaded growing old and gray, which was why she dyed the strands of gray in her hair and fretted about the physical toll of her work in the field: the bags under her eyes, the lines in her face, the loss of weight. Clara was so sensitive to her appearance that she had thrown away two photographs of herself that she considered unflattering, regardless of the expense of having them taken at Mathew Brady's studio. In later years, as her best biographer points out, she would sometimes lie about her age, telling reporters and census takers that she was younger than she was. Thus, as she went through menopause, Clara could not have been cheered by the reminder of the inevitability of aging.

When Clara wrote Mary Norton, however, her mood was upbeat, her spirits soaring. For the moment, she was able to sweep aside confusion and doubt and reach a decision about her immediate future. "And now if you think you can bear it," she wrote Mary, "I will tell you a *great* secret—What is it? say you. Am I going to get married? No not that,—is Charleston going to be taken with a mixture of Greek fire and humbugs? no not that—Is the 'great Rebellion' going to cave in? No I guess not yet, well what upon earth is it?—Well, if I must tell, I'm *coming home*!! There, has it affected you any? I dont know just when but I think perhaps by the next trip of the 'Arago,' say about sixteen days, unless I am prevented."

Clara felt even happier when she received an encouraging letter from a Washington-based friend, who had had a long talk with Commissioner Holloway in her behalf. "I set the whole matter in a strong & emphatic light I can assure you," the friend said. "He [Holloway] was glad to learn the facts in the case & admitted that you was entitled to special consideration for your devotion to the army—I told him he would have all the Mass delegation down on him if he disturbed you . . . you need not fear the thing is all right & shall remain so while I am here." A couple of weeks later came a letter from Commissioner Holloway himself confirming what her friend had written. In her journal, Clara noted with satisfaction that Holloway guaranteed her position for as long as he was commissioner of patents.

*   *   *

After sunset on December 15, Elwell dropped by Clara's room and asked, "How would you like to go to Morris Island tonight?" The colonel was to inspect the quartermaster operations there and was taking a few guests along, among them, Mary Baldwin and Dr. Craven and his wife, and he wanted the pleasure of Clara's company, too. Clara had hoped "for an explosion of the present monotony," and she gladly accepted. She intended to inspect Morris Island herself and decide whether she wanted to return there as a nurse. She doubted that she would ever do so, but resolved to keep an open mind about the possibility.

The party departed that night on the steamer *Ben Deford*. Mary Baldwin, as cheery and bright as always, played the piano all evening, and the others sang in accompaniment. The sea was rough, though, and the ship rolled and pitched so much that Clara felt nauseated and retired to her quarters. "I lay very still till morning," she wrote in her journal, "determined I *would not* be sick."

When day broke, Clara leaped up, dressed, and commenced her toilet. But then the ship gave two or three violent lurches "and I was done." A little later, trying to be "a good sailor," she staggered to the deck and found herself the first lady in the drawing room. Soon Miss Baldwin appeared—"looking rather pale," Clara thought. Both women refused to admit they were feeling poorly, and when breakfast was announced they filed into the dining room with other members of the party. Clara seated herself and stared at a piece of toast in her plate, resisting the urge to retch. Miss Baldwin bravely dabbed at her food, then rose suddenly, announced that "it would suit her convenience best to retire from the table," and hurried off to her stateroom. "I considered myself 'relieved' and followed suit," Clara wrote later. In her own room, she fell so ill that she lost all track of time. Finally, she pulled herself to her desk and scribbled a note to Elwell. "I cant date it but it is *this* morning," the note said. "Colonel Elwell, I think you will have either to take or send me home on the Hunter this morning. I believe I am too sick to remain."

But she remained anyway, determined that seasickness was not going to best her. Indeed, she was feeling better when the *Ben Deford* reached Stono Inlet at the southern end of Folly Island. Here some of the party went ashore with Elwell to pay their respects to General Gillmore at his comfortable, tree-sheltered headquarters. Clara had no desire whatever to see the general, particularly when she learned that he had Mrs. Lander in his charge, the young busybody who had joined forces with Miss Dix. Clara thought Mrs. Lander insufferably arrogant. So Clara and the Cravens disembarked farther up, at Paunee Landing, and took an ambulance across the pontoon bridge to Morris Island and up to the tents of the U.S. Sanitary Commission. "This was the first moment I had felt at home since I left," Clara noted in her journal. "I was almost happy inside those tents." She was touched when she saw that the ground had been cleared for her own tents, should she decide to return under Dr. Marsh's auspices and do for the sick and dying "what men could not do."

She learned that Dr. Kittinger was now chief medical officer of the island and that he had been talking about her, saying that he would "give more" to see Clara Barton "than all the surgeons on the island." That cheered Clara immensely. For a moment, it did seem possible for her to resume her work on Morris Island and "be useful and happy."

Told that Dr. Kittinger was sick in the hospital, Clara hurried off to the cluster of hospital tents in the dunes, with the wintry ocean washing along the shore. Ahead, against a silvery sky, loomed the battered ramparts of Wagner, now renamed Fort Strong, in honor of the brigade commander who had been fatally wounded during the assaults of July 18. At the hospital, Clara was glad to find Dr. Kittinger better now and back at work, though he still was coughing. An arrow of pain pierced her when she saw her two wall tents, the ones Dr. Green had confiscated for "the benefit of the hospital." Dr. Kittinger and his colleagues did urge Clara to remain with them, but the sight of those tents reminded her of how sadly she had been "abused" last summer. If that had not happened, if General Gillmore were not in overall command, if Dr. Green were not still around—maybe then she would have returned. As it was, "I could not quite decide to do it," she told her journal.

She and the Cravens rejoined the rest of their party at Paunee Landing and moved to a new ship, *The Dictator*. To Clara's dismay, Gillmore and Mrs. Lander came on board for the evening meal. Unable to tolerate them, Clara skipped "supper, wine and company" and escaped to her stateroom. Presently Miss Baldwin knocked at her door, saying that the commanding general desired her presence at the table. Clara sent her excuses. "I do not prefer to go up," she confided in her journal, "am more happy to remain alone, to sum up the whole matter of my trip I should say that it has been most unsatisfactory[.] I have not enjoyed a moment of it save the little time spent on Morris Island, and am homesick at this instant."

The next morning, she was so hungry that she had to go to breakfast. Alas, Mrs. Lander came in with Elwell and Miss Baldwin, and then Gillmore himself marched in. He wasn't a bad-looking man, despite his balding forehead and thick brows, but Clara thought he put on airs, acting with excessive courtesy to the other women. He took his seat at the head of the table, "with Mrs. Lander and Miss Baldwin on either arm," Clara noted angrily. Colonel Elwell sat beside Clara, looking "the very ghost of a man," she thought, "pale, sad and dispirited— *discouraged.*" Clara apparently remarked on his appearance, but Mrs. Lander contradicted her, saying that he looked "better" than he had earlier. After Clara finished eating and returned to her stateroom, Elwell came to her and said he was having a terrible time with the men in command here; he "expressed himself in quite expressive terms," Clara recorded, "had done some fighting, could not bear much more, was past being troubled."

Elwell's remarks put Clara into a worse mood. Telling herself that she had had quite enough of these people, she transferred to the *Philadelphia,* "thus bidding adieu to a company which I hope was not more weary of me than I was of them." By the time she was settled on the *Philadelphia,* she was seething at Gillmore and his disingenuous efforts to be the "ladies man," to act so "urbane" and "gallant." She couldn't stand him or the officious Mrs. Lander. "Can there ever come a day to me when I would not strike a blow of honest open indignation in memory of them," she declared in her journal. "I am *not* by nature revengeful, but I thank Heaven that I *can* feel proper resentment, it's slow to come to me I know, but lives long."

As it turned out, the *Philadelphia* wasn't scheduled to depart for a while. Anxious to get away, Clara transferred to a troop ship that would leave for Hilton Head in half an hour. Somebody warned her that it "would not be pleasant" traveling on a crowded ship, but Clara went anyway. "True, there was a crowd of soldiers," she said, "but the Capt. (Crowel) resigned his room to me, and I made the whole trip perfectly comfortably, not sick at all."

It was late at night, December 20, when the ship whistled its arrival at Port Royal Sound and steamed up to the wharf at Hilton Head. Clara disembarked on a long, narrow gangplank that rose up steeply to the dock. As she climbed it "in the midnight moonlight," a strong hand reached down to pull her up, and she recognized the face of Captain Lamb, her "faithful friend." At her rooms, she found a large box from Annie Childs containing "the nicest ostrich plume" hat Clara had ever seen, plus letters from various friends. Reading them and trying on the hat eased her stormy feelings. "I am glad to find me at *home* and quiet once more," she confided in her journal.

*   *   *

Friday, December 25, was rainy, windy, and cold. "One more Birth day," Clara told her journal. That was all she wrote about turning forty-two years old, about being a menopausal woman who had no apparent future or purpose in this war. Not a word in her journal this day about how she had grown happier.

The next day she finally reached a decision: She would go back to Washington City and try to find a place there to serve. But first she would take a trip home to visit her friends and family. She booked passage on the steamer *Fulton*, scheduled to depart once the stormy weather cleared, and arranged for her huge quantity of stores to be shipped with her—dozens of boxes of delicacies and clothing that had piled up in her storehouse. She was glad to be leaving this "miserable" department, and hoped that Elwell, Lamb, and brother David, who was back from his furlough, could get out as well.

On December 27, in the midst of her preparations, she was surprised to see Lieutenant Colonel Leggett approaching her house on crutches. He wanted to say good-bye and thank her again for saving his life. He had a new artificial leg, and Clara thought he walked "very gracefully" with the help of his crutches.

By now, Elwell had returned from the front, and was brave and gracious about her decision to leave, even though it hurt him. Clara Barton was the great love of his life, and he would always cherish his memories of her and their time together, their carriage and horseback rides, their conversations and laughter, and their lovemaking. He gave her a going-away present—"a colored photograph" of himself, Clara told her journal, "very natural and fine."

Then it was time for her to go, time to leave this quiet island and the mixed memories it held for her. She sent a box of 300 shirts to Columbus Simonds for the blacks on St. Helena, and a similar box to a woman named Betsy Jenkins for the destitute at Mitchellville, a black settlement on Hilton Head. Then, with a final good-bye to Elwell, Mary Gage, Captain Lamb, and David, Clara boarded the *Fulton* and sailed north toward home and an uncertain future.

PART FOUR

The Wilderness

Januany 1864 found Clara back in Massachusetts, where she had a loving reunion with Annie Childs and Elvira Stone. Clara admitted that she wasn't in the best physical condition to withstand the intense New England cold. Indeed, she hadn't realized how tired and run-down she was. She visited David's family in North Oxford and was amazed at how much the children had grown since she'd seen them last. If there were hard feelings between Clara and David's wife, Julia, Clara did not record them. "I never saw the old place looking so well," she said of the Barton homestead, so full of memories of her "dear, departed" father. She missed him more than words could convey.

In mid-February she headed south by train, stopping off in New York long enough to hear Henry Ward Beecher preach in Brooklyn's Plymouth Church. Fifty years old now, with graying hair and protruding eyes, Beecher was one of the most famous ministers in America. Speaking in his hypnotic style and gesturing dramatically, he preached on "unwritten heroism," citing as an example a hard-working Irish servant "girl" who in "giving up of her little earnings" was truly magnanimous and brave. The sermon reactivated Clara's self-doubts. "How forcibly *I* felt that my bravery if I ever had any had not been exhibited in the field," she wrote in her journal. "I have nothing to dare or endure in these days."

Then she headed home to Washington City, where her supplies awaited her. She had stored some of them in her rooms, the rest elsewhere—perhaps at her sister Sally's place. As she took stock of her situation in Washington, she found that much had changed while she had been away. The gleaming new dome of the Capitol was completed and crowned by a statue with spectacular white wings and a sword and shield. Washington was bigger and busier, too, its population swelled to 180,000 by an ever-expanding wartime bureaucracy. One of the most startling sights was the number of "government girls" now toiling in Federal offices. Before the war, Clara and a handful of other "temporary" female workers in the Patent Office were the only women employed in government buildings in Washington, and they were regarded as a novelty. But with the outbreak of war, the Republicans officially opened government employment to women, first hiring them as clerks and money counters in the Treasury Department (no women worked there before the war). By 1864, several hundred "government girls" labored in the Treasury Department alone, and others had jobs in the War Office and the Department of the Interior.

While Clara shopped in the markets for her empty pantry at home, army officers in horse-drawn carriages clattered by, and vendors plied their wares among the soldiers and sailors in town on furloughs or passes. Couples promenaded on the sidewalks, the gentlemen wearing stovepipe hats and embroidered waistcoats and the ladies dressed in large hoops and frocks, with their hair worn in chignons. The streets teemed with thousands of blacks, more than Clara had ever seen in Washington before; most of them were former slaves who had escaped there in response to the Emancipation Proclamation. Pigs and cows, too, roamed freely on the sidewalks and in the streets, and here and there "dead horses lay stinking in the winter sun."

The city had a huge population of prostitutes—some 5,000 of them, according to the *Washington Star*, not to mention another 2,500 in Alexandria. With 25,000 soldiers stationed in fifty forts around Washington, enterprising madams sensed a business bonanza. With their harems, they descended on the capital and opened up scores of houses in the red-light districts, offering soldiers and politicians "horizontal refreshments." One section of brothels serviced so many soldiers that it was nicknamed "Hooker's Division." There were "fancy houses" that catered to army officers, whose horses could be seen tied up in a straight line in front of the buildings. By contrast, low-class strumpets solicited on the sidewalks and did their business in alleyway shanties.

Among Washington's better sort, dancing was "the rage" that winter. The National Hotel and Willard's held "monster hops" at which whirling couples did the polka and the lancers. A new theater, built by a pro-war Democrat named John T. Ford, now stood on Tenth Street, only a few blocks from Clara's rooming house. On Saturday nights, "pleasure-seekers" flocked to Ford's and Grover's theaters, or strolled on the sidewalks of Pennsylvania Avenue, where brass bands paraded to the boom of tubas and the trill of cornets.

Once she was settled in her rooms, Clara headed for quartermaster headquarters, to let Daniel Rucker know that she was back in town and looking for a way and a place to resume her war work. During her absence, she discovered, major changes in command had occurred in the Medical Department. The feud between Surgeon General Hammond and Secretary of War Stanton had come to a climax the previous November, when Stanton had summarily dismissed his irascible chief surgeon and named Joseph K. Barnes, Stanton's friend, as acting surgeon general. Hammond had alienated a sizable segment of the medical profession when he'd banned the use of calomel in government hospitals, arguing that its harmful side effects did not justify its benefits. He'd also clashed with Stanton over the choice of medical inspectors, and the secretary of war had finally had enough of him. He was now being tried by court-martial for "conduct unbecoming an officer and a gentleman." Meanwhile, Jonathan Letterman, who had modernized the army's ambulance and hospital system, had asked to be relieved as medical director of the Potomac Army, and Thomas A. McParlin had taken his place.

At the quartermaster offices, Clara found Rucker at his desk, as brusque and busy as always. Now a brigadier general and chief of the Quartermaster Department, he told her that Colonel Elwell had been there inquiring after her, and the possibility that she might see John Elwell again lifted her spirits a little. But she heard nothing more from Elwell until early spring, when she received a letter saying that he was now stationed at the Union prison in Elmira, New York, and that he felt "pretty well" and was getting plenty of rest. Clara remembered that he "used to think he could sleep six months if released from his burdens." She was amazed that he had strength "to go on at all." She still worried about his health but was glad he was out of that "miserable" Department of the South.

Clara's own prospects looked distressingly bleak that March. The Army of the Potomac was now in winter quarters north of the Rapidan in Virginia, but the long arm of Miss Dix extended to its divisional field hospitals, which were staffed in part by her nurses. One Dix appointee, Mary Morris Husband, was matron of a field hospital at Brandy Station, which meant that she supervised its diet kitchen and nursing personnel. It was a painful irony that Clara had cleared the way for other women to serve in Virginia field hospitals, only to find herself excluded from them now.

To make matters worse, the Potomac Army did not need her stores, for the U.S. Sanitary Commission and the Commissary and

Quartermaster departments kept it plentifully supplied. Sanitary agents had their own tents in the army camps, from which they disseminated food, spirits, clothing, and blankets from thousands of affiliated Soldiers' Aid Societies. Having harnessed the collective energy of women across the North, the Sanitary Commission had become so large and powerful that independent relief workers like Clara appeared to be obsolete. Nor was the Sanitary Commission the only relief organization in the field that winter. Agents of the Christian Commission also visited the army camps, distributing supplies as well as religious literature.

Feeling cruelly and unfairly cut off from her work and her army, Clara became severely depressed again. For one who thrived on duty, on being useful, the idle days were maddening. At night, her mind raced in such a "current" that she couldn't sleep, which in turn fueled her despondency in a vicious cycle. At the same time, in this depressed and vulnerable state, she had to cope with whatever physical symptoms (joint pain, hot flashes, cold sweats) and attendant anxiety the changes in her body caused. If she consulted the contemporary medical literature on menopause, she would have been even more distressed. The doctors warned that menopausal women could expect to go through "a period of depression," melancholia, "severe emotional withdrawal," even hysteria and insanity.

Nevertheless, despite how dark everything appeared to her in Washington, Clara did not give up. She fought a brave, daily battle to overcome her external and internal stresses, to find something to give her hope that she could continue, that her life wasn't over. At one point, she thought about emulating Fanny Gage and joining the lecture circuit, using the platform to exhort men to enlist in the army instead of waiting to be drafted. "I could speak from experience and only urge men to go where I would go myself," she wrote in her journal. Unsure of her "ability to speak," however, she abandoned the idea.

She even contemplated becoming a writer and using "the power of pen to move men and women to wider, deeper thought, and sterner actions." But she feared she lacked literary skill. "I sometimes think I might have if I had cultivated it more assiduously, but it seems too late. . . . I know it is useless to regret, but 'of all sad words of tongue or pen, The saddest are these,—It might have been.'"

One thing she knew for certain: she wasn't going back to the Department of the South. "It is not *home*," she wrote Mary Norton, "and I gave them time enough." She was troubled, however, to read that Gillmore's command had scored another failure. According to reports, the general withdrew several thousand troops from the Charleston front, including the Fifty-fourth Massachusetts, and sent them into northeastern Florida under the field command of Brigadier General Truman Seymour. After occupying Jacksonville, Seymour advanced toward the Suwanee River with the idea of wrecking the rebel railroad bridge there and severing communications between east and west Florida, only to suffer a humiliating defeat at the hands of about 5,000 Confederates near Olustee. Gillmore made haste to inform Washington that Seymour had moved from Jacksonville without orders, which prompted the Joint Committee on the Conduct of the War, chaired by gruff Ben Wade, to launch a congressional investigation. From what Clara read, the Fifty-fourth had again fought courageously, striking "a salient blow for the honor of down trodden and long despised Africa," as she put it in her journal. Even so, the expedition did appear to have been "badly planned and rashly led," and Clara, who despised Gillmore anyway, thought he was to blame for the Olustee debacle, just as he was to blame for the rash and costly assaults on Battery Wagner. Her fear, as she told Henry Wilson, was that Congress would condemn poor Seymour and let Gillmore off the hook. She sent Wilson a note urging that the committee summon Colonel Elwell "to look into the Florida matter." She took it upon herself to write Elwell about it—but "I am sure I failed to express all my indignation and contempt," she told her journal.

Meanwhile she learned that Cornelius Welles had died of acute heart disease in California, where he had gone the previous summer. Clara wrote a mutual friend that she was "blinded with tears of wonder and regret" that a man who did such "good works," and was such a friend of "Freedman and Bondman," should be called away so early in his life; he was only about thirty-five. His death reminded her of their great service together at Second Bull Run, Antietam, and Fredericksburg, and her heart ached for him and the useful, exhilarating days of 1862.

On March 8, Clara recorded an electrifying event that had all Washington astir: "Genl Grant arrived in town at 5 to take command as Lt. Genr. of the US Army." In a major shakeup in command, Lincoln had called Grant from the West and appointed him general-in-chief of all Union armies. That evening, Clara attended a huge reception for Grant at the White House, with Lincoln and his gracious wife in attendance. Tall and sad looking, with unruly black hair, the president shook hands as if he were sawing wood. General Grant turned up at 9:30 P.M. and gave Mrs. Lincoln the courtesy of asking for a dance. Going on forty-two, he was a short, slight, shy man with stooped shoulders and mild blue eyes. At first glance, he appeared so unprepossessing that it seemed impossible that the fate of the Union rested on his shoulders.

The next day, the general-in-chief conferred with Lincoln in the White House, leaving Washingtonians to speculate about what strategy the two would work out. On March 10, Grant visited Meade's head-quarters at Brandy Station and then headed west for a conference with General William Tecumseh Sherman, now in command of the Union's western armies. Clearly something momentous was afoot, some con-certed action involving both the Eastern and Western theaters.

On March 18, Clara read in the papers that Grant would return to the East and likely campaign with the Army of the Potomac once warmer weather came. The news set her mind to racing with renewed hope. With Grant in command, the campaign promised to be "san-guinary and final," she thought, which meant that the casualties were likely to be enormous and the Potomac Army would surely have need of her and her stores. But to take the field again, she had to find a trust-worthy male assistant to go with her, someone like Cornie Welles. "It seems impossible for me to go forward all alone," as she put it. "I lack a counsellor always by me, a helping hand, a heart and head ready to act in concert with me." Her thoughts fixed on her cousin, Leander Poor, who was still at Hilton Head and whom she loved and trusted. If she could get Leander promoted to an important rank and transferred to her, he could protect her against the kind of "buffoonery" she had encountered on Morris Island. Perhaps he could also secure govern-ment space in which to store her supplies, which she was "holding back from all quarters" until she could take the field again. Once she had a government storehouse, she would ask an old friend of hers, Mrs. E. M. Rich, to take charge of it. Clara considered Mrs. Rich "the most compe-tent and ladylike business woman" she had ever known. With her man-aging Clara's operation in Washington, Clara and Leander would be free to rejoin her "*own*" Army of the Potomac at last.

Aroused to action, Clara prevailed again on Henry Wilson, asking him to arrange for Leander to be appointed assistant quartermaster and detailed to her. Wilson listened patiently and said "he thought he could do it," and Clara went home feeling hopeful. Wilson was such "an excellent friend," she wrote David, "and no one knows how much I esteem and prize him—*as a friend*. He always listens patiently to my wants and goes straight off and does what I require if he can."

But a few days later, her mood swung back to crippling despair. "Had no courage to get up," she confided in her diary; "all seemed so dark and I laid quiet and heard the raps come and the footsteps go and said not[hing]." On March 29, she found the strength to lobby in behalf of Captain Lamb, who wanted an appointment in the regular army service and a transfer out of the Department of the South. She took the matter to the War Department, hoping to get Lamb reassigned to Washington. General Rucker told Clara that he liked the idea, that Lamb was "just the man he wanted." As for an appointment to the regular army, an assistant quartermaster advised Clara to take the matter to Congressman Samuel Hooper of Boston, who had been instrumental in securing Lamb's original commission. But Hooper refused to act on her request, on the grounds that Lamb did not belong to his district and that in any case the congressman lacked the time to pursue the matter. His rudeness left Clara hurt, angry, and more dejected than ever. Later that day, writing in her journal, she exploded at Massachusetts politicians in general: "With the exception of Henry Wilson, I cannot recal[l] a single instance where any person from my state of Massachusetts has ever lent me aid of a straws strength to help me in my purpose of attempting to care for the soldiers."

By the end of March, she felt so low that she seriously considered returning to the Patent Office and forgetting about the war altogether: "If I could only succeed in reinstating myself in my old position in the office I would be willing to withdraw within myself and never attempt any thing more, so I commenced to look over old letters for copies, and tried to settle down and be content."

But she couldn't "settle down and be content." She wanted to care for the soldiers and couldn't, and the pain of frustration was tearing her apart. She felt even worse when she read that Grant, after returning from the West, had established his field headquarters at Culpeper Court House and was riding back to Washington once a week to confer with Lincoln about the projected spring offensive. On April 6, exhausted from lack of sleep, Clara wrote Henry Wilson a long, disconnected letter that betrayed her distraught emotional state. First, she said, it seemed impossible to get Leander assigned to her for work in the field. Therefore his promotion to assistant quartermaster was "valueless" to her. This subject in turn "woke up the recollection of a train of ills & wrongs," and she found herself reporting how useless David was to her on Hilton Head, how he had remained there in comfort while she "went alone" to do her work on Morris Island, where she endured wretched conditions for the sake of her "employment," which was the only "bright spot" in this sordid tale. Then she had suffered the humiliation of having her tents confiscated by the "worthless" and "greedy"

Dr. Green. Had David been with her, that sorry episode might never have occurred. Frankly, she was tired of trying to help relatives and personal friends, in whose behalf she guessed she had spent seven-tenths of her time, labor, and strength. "I write all this, not for effect,—not for vanity—oh no, *not that*, but simply to show you of how little use is a friend in the service, unless I can command his services myself." And without such a friend, "alone, in constant danger from rank and buffoonery and selfishness," she could accomplish nothing. As a consequence, "I have to give it up, and school my patience to endure and I will do it."

What was more, she told Wilson, her war service had left her in a "perfectly insolvent condition." Her sole "pecuniary" dependence was "the little divided, robbed and insulted salary" from the Patent Office. Feeling more and more aggrieved as she wrote, she recounted what to her was a long history of abuse against her in that office. She accused the Buchanan administration of releasing her because she had been "a Republican," thus robbing her of a lucrative salary. She recalled how the Republicans, when they came to power, "mortified" her by refusing to restore her to her previous position; instead, "my name was simply allowed in a negative list of temporary writers, not with the stipulation that I should receive $50. per month, but with a protest against my receiving any more than that." Now she averaged about twenty-five dollars per month, she told Wilson, and the only way she got that was by "allowing one of the very men who helped to raise the cry of Black Republican at my heels"—Mr. Upperman—"to do my writing at one half the proceeds, making it for his interest to make my Bill up to the maximum $50. dollars." But she was convinced that if she reclaimed her post, her copying assignments would fall off so sharply that her salary in three months would be less than twenty dollars per month, on which she would somehow have to live with the current inflated prices.

She insisted that this was not "a complaining letter" and begged Wilson not to misunderstand her. "And now do me this last favor, withdraw the name proposed [Leander's], destroy this letter, forgive me for writing it, and forget it."

That letter was an appeal for sympathy and help. To make sure Wilson got it, Clara delivered it to the Capitol herself, sending it into the Senate chamber by a messenger. She took a seat in the galleries and watched as Wilson opened the letter, read it between many interruptions, and finally put it in his coat pocket. Then Clara left and waited all day for Wilson to come to her. When he finally arrived, at eleven o'clock that night, he looked perplexed and worried. Could something be done to "make her situation better?" he asked. Did she need money? He had no idea, of course, how acutely depressed she was, and she couldn't tell him either. Instead, she tried to explain "the shameful evils" existing at the Patent Office and implored him "as a friend of the country" to try to remedy them. Then she fell silent. He asked her what she wanted him to do, and it was "a civil, kindly, sensible question," Clara conceded, "and like a spoiled child, I looked down, winked fast, bit my nails, drummed with my foot on the floor and wouldn't answer."

The following day, she was filled with remorse. How could she have treated her friend that way? She promptly wrote Wilson that she was "ashamed" of her behavior. "If it would extenuate the fault of it all, I could offer the excuse of my not having slept for some forty hours previous but as I have not subsequently, there is no very reasonable hope of improvement." Wilson had asked what she wanted him to do. "I thank you for your kindly solicitude," she said and for the first time explained in detail her "plan" to rejoin the army, telling him why she wanted Leander assigned to her and pointing out that she would need passes from Stanton permitting them to take the field. Then "I will find employment, satisfactory to myself, serviceable to my country and beneficial to mankind."

Confiding in Wilson proved wonderfully therapeutic. She fell asleep that night and did not wake until ten o'clock the next morning.

On April 12, Dr. Marsh of the Sanitary Commission visited Clara in her rooms. He had just arrived from the Sea Islands, and he shared her distrust of the official version of the Florida fiasco, which exonerated Gillmore and faulted Seymour for acting without orders in undertaking the forward movement that resulted in defeat. What Dr. Marsh said convinced Clara that Gillmore had directed the campaign with the idea of claiming "the honor of victory," or putting "the disgrace of defeat" on Seymour. Although there was no hard evidence that this was so, Clara was prepared to believe the worst about Quincy Gillmore. Now, she feared, the luckless Seymour was to be sacrificed. "Is there no manly justice in the world?" she demanded of her journal.

She felt miserable again. "Had the most sad down spirited day," she recorded on April 14. "All the world appeared selfish and treacherous. I can get no hold on a good noble sentiment *anywhere*—I have scanned over and over the whole moral horizon and it is all dark—the night clouds seem to have shut down, so stagnant, so dead, so selfish, so calculating. Is there no right? are there no consequences attending wrong, how shall the world move on in all this weight of dead morbid meanness—shall lies prevail for evermore—look at the state of things both civil and military that curse our Government. The pomp[o]us air with which little dishonest pimps lord it over their betters. Contractors ruining the nation, and oppressing the poor, and no one rebukes them. See a monkey faced official not twenty rods from me oppressing and degrading poor women who come up to his stall to feed their children—that he may steal with better grace and show to the Government how much his economy saves it each month. Poor blind Government never feels inside his pockets, pouching with ill gotten gain heavy with sin." Finally she railed against the "ambitious, dishonest Genl" who "lays a political plot to be executed with human life" and when it fails is exonerated while his subordinate takes the blame. "And so my day has been weary with these thoughts, and my heart heavy and I cannot raise it—I doubt the justice of *almost* all I see."

That evening, Wilson came to see her, and she asked if the Florida investigation was closed. Yes, he said, and "General Seymour would leave the Department in disgrace." "This," Clara wrote later, "was too much for my fretted soul, and I poured out the vials of my indignation in no stinted measure. I told him the facts, and what I thought of a committee that was too imbecile to listen to the truth when it was presented to them, that they had made themselves a laughing stock for even the privates in the service by their stupendous inactivity and gullibility, that they were all a set of dupes, not to say knaves." When she finished, Wilson looked at her in amazement. Then, attempting to mollify her, he asked her to prepare a written statement about her knowledge of the Florida expedition.

She spent the next four days compiling testimony from Dr. Marsh and others impugning the official version of the Florida affair, and presented it to Wilson in the form of a handwritten paper. But "he was very busy," she noted, "and could not stop to speak." Suddenly, it dawned on her that Wilson wasn't going to pursue the matter. He accepted the official version of the Florida affair, and it was indeed closed. Her efforts had been in vain.

She went spiraling to the depths, even to the point of wanting to die. "I cannot raise my spirits, the old temptation to go from all the world. I think it will come to that some day. It is a struggle to keep in society at all. I want to leave all." Nothing seemed to cheer her, not even the news that Leander's appointment as assistant quartermaster had been approved. What difference did that make? She was sure that he would never be assigned to her and that she would be "left alone as ever."

When Wilson next called, he said he could not support her efforts to gain War Department approval to take the field. Grant himself had recently ordered all women and civilians to leave the Army of the Potomac, and the War Department wasn't likely to override Grant's order for Clara's benefit and issue her a pass. Wilson admitted that he had little "heart" to contest Stanton's certain objections to her request.

Clara took Wilson's statement as a personal rejection of all her work and worth. After he left, she wrote him a letter "relieving him from all further duty."

> My dear friend, I have been thinking deeply, and I believe candidly, of your remarks. I see that you disapprove what I have done, and seek to do. It all seems worse than useless to you, & I cannot consent that you take upon yourself the burden of presenting that request,—the Sect'y [of War] will oppose it sternly, and perhaps sharply, and you could have no confidence, no 'heart' with which to meet his objections. After all your kind acts, I have neither the right or desire to ask this.

Then she surrendered herself to sarcasm and bitter resignation:

> I know *how worthless a* woman's *life is, and what a* pity *it is to wear* one,—few persons ever felt this more keenly or bitterly than I, few more ready than I for years to resign the useless bauble. I have striven, (against the fearful odds) to make my life worth something to mankind, but realize that it has been, and must be, a failure. I am ready to call it so, and I will stop where I am. I know that others can do better. *I will leave it to them. I did not know that you had been called upon excepting by myself. I did not intend to trouble you.* I was earnest in what I had previously written. Do not ask anything for me, I will remain quiet where I am.

She did not send the letter because that very day, April 25,
Burnside's Ninth Corps reached Washington en route to the Potomac
army, and the sight of her old pet corps restored her fighting spirit.
Arriving from Annapolis, where it had reassembled after returning
from Tennessee, the Ninth Corps marched up Pennsylvania Avenue
past Willard's Hotel, where Lincoln and Burnside reviewed it from a
balcony. On they came that rain-swept day, 19,000 of them in columns
five miles long, white veterans of Antietam, Fredericksburg, and
Chancellorsville who snapped along in booted cadences and black
recruits of a new all-black division who cheered and waved their hats
when they saw Lincoln on the balcony. He refused to go inside out of
the rain, saying, "If *they* can stand it, I guess I can," as the bullet-torn
flags whipped by in the street below.

Clara watched them in awe, thinking what an impressive display of
military force they were: "for it has come that man has no longer an
individual existence, but is counted in thousands, and measured in
miles." She followed the Ninth Corps down to Alexandria, hoping to
find encouragement and support from the Massachusetts troops. She
searched out the Fifty-seventh Massachusetts, a new white outfit from
Worcester and Fitchburg. Her cousin, George Edward, the son of
Judge Ira Barton of Worcester, was a second lieutenant in the regiment. He was a congenial young man, and Clara had fond memories of
him and his brother, Edmund "Ned" Barton, who was a Sanitary
Commission field agent with the Fifth Corps, for she had often stayed
with them in their Worcester home, the famous Barton "palace." She
spoke with Colonel William F. "Frank" Bartlett; she was doubtless
seeking the regiment's help in going to the front. She then visited her
favorite regiment of all, the "Brave old" Twenty-first Massachusetts, of
which she was a "daughter." She had a joyful reunion with old Dr.
Cutter and many of her "boys" who had survived the Tennessee campaign. Then she returned to the Fifty-seventh and "went over the
ground again." Just as the sun was setting, a courier rode up with the
order that the entire corps was to "move to the front at daybreak."

Clara's visit to the camps was a powerful antidote to her depression.
It was uplifting to mingle with soldiers who admired her, to sit at their
campfires and reminisce about their experiences together. The
Massachusetts troops clearly urged her to serve with them again, and
she returned to Washington with awakened resolution. She didn't need
Wilson to intercede with Stanton in her behalf. She wrote the secretary
of war herself, asking for a pass to join the army. As a measure of her
returning confidence, she enclosed a draft of such a pass for him to sign.

"In requesting this pass," Clara told him, "I have no intention or desire to use it unnecessarily or at an improper time, and I have no object but to aid in relieving the sufferings of our soldiery after battle.

"To disabuse your mind of the probable impression that I am some patriotic young lady suddenly seized with a spirit of adventure, I shall perhaps be pardoned a word of explanation,—I am not young,—a native of Worcester, Mass. I have long been a resident of this city. When the 'old Sixth' Mass. Regt., my early school mates were stricken down in Baltimore April 19 1861, I met and cared for them and from that day to the present, my time, labor, strength, thought and such means as I could command, I have used among our wounded men where they fell.

"I have regarded it as a sacred duty (and I believed I have wrought conscientiously),—all the more sacred that my father was a soldier, following Mad Anthony Wayne through his wild career of war and victory, fighting side by side with Harrison and Johnson whose friendship he always retained, and when scarce two years ago, feeble and old, he tottered to his grave, he charged me with a dying patriots love to serve and sacrifice for my country in its peril and strengthen and comfort the brave men who stood for its defence. I have tried to obey."

She answered in advance the question of why she was needed, when the U.S. Sanitary Commission and Christian Commission were doing so much to service the army: "It would *seem* that the two enormous commissions that are driving the charitable world mad of late, must be equal to every contingency. If they only prove as faithful and efficient as they have grown powerful and wealthy we may all rest, quietly, but if the old time cry of wretchedness and suffering without our gates is again to pierce our hearts, I might again wish to reach the scene. Holding your honored pass for such emergency, I will pledge my honor as a lady never to abuse it."

The next day, Sunday, May 1, Clara reeled off a long letter to Frances Gage, who had written her from Ohio, saying that she was on her way to St. Louis to see one of her soldier sons. Clara's reply was one of the most inspired and beautiful letters she ever wrote, without a hint of the inner storms that had beset her for the past few months. She began by remembering another May a year before, when she had visited Fanny on Parris Island: "It seems but yesterday that I walked with you through that sea of bloom and fragrance everywhere surrounding you. . . . And this was a year ago! And one is expected to live only a few such years in a life time." Now Fanny was "in the War stricken West," and Clara was back in Washington, "looking a great soul shaking battle full in the face." For weeks, she said, regiments, brigades, and then an entire corps had marched through Washington heading for the front in Virginia. "I am holding my breath in awe at the vastness of the shadow that floats like a pall above our heads. What numbers! What concentration! *Can* the earth hold up under the shock that is to come? *Can* the Heavens look on and rent not? *Can* God behold and smite not! Ay, but he *is* smiting,—and this is his terrible retribution!"

Clara had given a great deal of thought to this last point. Like Lincoln, like the slaves, like so many other people North and South, she saw the hand of God in this terrible war, shaping and controlling events to suit His own design. In her own search for the meaning of the war, Clara came to see it as divine punishment for the sin of slavery, thus anticipating what Lincoln himself would say almost a year later. "Is this war never to end," she told Fanny, "till for every African slave that ever dragged his chain an Anglo-Saxon shall have suffered? Shall it blight till we take up his old 'shout' and chant with him, 'Oh Lord remember me?' "

As for Lincoln, she realized how unpopular he was in the North, even within his own party. It was a presidential election year, and many Radical Republicans had already spoken out against his reelection on the grounds that he couldn't win the war. Clara, however, intended to stick with Lincoln. "Who am I going to vote for?" she asked Fanny rhetorically. "Why I thought for president Lincoln, to be sure. I *have* been voting for him for the last three years. I thought him honest, and true, and I believe that he sought the right with all his power, and would do it as fast as he saw it clearly, and I still think so." Yes, she saw "a strong tide" setting in for General John Charles Frémont, who had tried to free the slaves in Missouri in 1861, only to be overruled by the president. "It is true," Clara went on, "he did see more clearly than Mr. Lincoln the great drift of this war, and to what it tended and did proclaim it, and did suffer for it. If the Presidency is to be his reward I must not complain." Still, "I *honor* Mr. Lincoln and have believed, and still do, that his election was ordained, that he was raised up to meet this crisis, but it may also be that *no one* man could be constituted who should be equal to both the beginning and ending of this vast, this mighty change, the same mind that could guide safely in the outset may be too slow now, for war has had its effects upon us, and our temper as a people, wiped out our conservativeness and touched us with the fire of the old nations. We have grown enthusiastic, and shout loud and long, where once we should have looked on in silence. I have said from the first that I believed this whole thing was directly in the hands of Providence, and that so it would continue, and that if we had *need* of our present ruler, whom I have always contended was *appointed* and not elected, that if we had further need of him we should have him." Should the Republicans nominate another man in his stead, she would, of course, support him. But she hoped the nominee would be Lincoln, whose "care worn face" had become "very dear" to her.

In May, word came of an intensive buildup at Fort Monroe, where more than one hundred troop transports and gunboats were gathering. Fort Monroe was the headquarters of the newly created Army of the James, under the command of Benjamin F. Butler of Baltimore and New Orleans fame. Butler's patchwork army comprised a cavalry division, the Eighteenth Corps under William F. "Baldy" Smith, and Quincy Gillmore's Tenth Corps, which had been transferred from the South Carolina Sea Islands, a fact that did not escape Clara's notice. The talk in Washington was that Butler would operate against Richmond from the south while the Army of the Potomac pressed Lee north of the rebel capital.

At the Union camps around Brandy Station, Grant whipped the Army of the Potomac into a superb fighting machine, comprising more than 113,000 effectives and 274 pieces of artillery. Parked in neat rows in the fields were 634 supply wagons and 619 ambulances, the latter manned by 2,300 drivers and stretcher-bearers. They were now organized into an independent Ambulance Corps, which Congress authorized in March. In addition, the army's field medical service boasted nearly 700 medical officers organized on a divisional basis. The divisional field hospitals, well supplied and equipped, were to follow the army into action and were the best it ever had.

In the early morning hours of May 4, the army marched out of Brandy Station and headed south toward the Rapidan and Lee's army. "I know pretty nearly that the Army of the Potomac is in motion," Clara wrote in her diary that day, "although no rumor to that effect is out, all seems as quiet as the grave, but still I think I know it must be so." She added: "I feel depressed and dissatisfied with myself," because she sensed that a battle was near, and yet she had heard nothing from the War Department about her request for a pass. She had heard nothing more about Leander either, but she had resolved a few days before to ask that he be assigned to General Rucker, if agreeable to him. "This may do as well as to have him assigned wholly to me. I will see how satisfactory I can make it appear." All night, May 4–5, she lay awake in her Washington apartment, her mind on the march with the soldiers of the Potomac Army. "Like everything else of a soldierly character," she mused, her mind had "gone to the front."

Three days passed. By Saturday, May 7, the capital was in terrible suspense about the fate of the Potomac Army. "Everyone supposes that the army is in motion and fighting but no one professes to know," Clara wrote in her journal. "Our army under Genl Grant seems like 'that bourne from whence no traveller returns.' " As best she could tell, the army had descended into the Wilderness south of the Rapidan, an area of dense underbrush and second-growth trees. Rushing to Rucker's office to get the latest news, Clara found the general sitting on the door step of his office. He knew little more about what was happening than she did. In fact, he had just seen Stanton at the War Office "and was concerned that the Sect did not know the recent results."

When Clara inquired about medical preparations for the campaign, Rucker said that the wounded would first be treated in the field divisional hospitals, which were following in the wake of the advancing army. Ambulance trains would transport the wounded from the divisional field hospitals to an evacuation hospital at Brandy Station on the Orange & Alexandria Railroad, and Haupt's trains would bring them back to Alexandria and Washington.

As Clara and Rucker talked, she raised the matter of cousin Leander. Would Rucker accept Leander if he were assigned to the general here in Washington? "Yes, certainly," Rucker said. What was more, he would lend Leander to Clara as she needed him. "There is no end to his goodness," Clara thought, vastly relieved.

Later that day, Wilson brought her momentous news from the Wilderness. Grant and Lee had fought a terrible battle there on Thursday and Friday, and the Union casualties were said to be severe. To make matters worse, intense musketry fire had ignited the thickets, and the flames had swept over the Union lines, incinerating hundreds of wounded men who were unable to escape. Even so, "the first day's doings," Wilson said, "were very successful for us." But little had been gained since then and "no one knew anything."

Wilson also said he would try to secure a pass for Clara after all. He did not explain why he had changed his mind but merely told her that he would take her request to Stanton. At that, all her harsh feelings toward Wilson evaporated. She remained unsettled, though, for there was no guarantee that Stanton would grant her a pass even if Wilson did plead in her behalf.

The next day, Sunday, brought a whirlwind of rumors that the two armies were fighting at Spotsylvania Court House, some forty miles north of Richmond. A worried Lincoln was seen hurrying to the War Department telegraph office, and there was speculation that this was the start of "the great Battle" that might decide the war. Clara was beside herself with anxiety about the soldiers, her comrades. She could picture the grotesque scenes at Spotsylvania, bodies exploding in shell bursts, wounded men lying helplessly in their own blood. It was maddening to be trapped in Washington, unable to go to the army until Stanton gave her permission to do so. She hated being dependent on a man—on two men, if she counted Wilson—for the right to do her work. Frankly, she doubted that Wilson or anybody else thought it "of much consequence." She summed up her feelings with one word: "Unhappy."

On Tuesday, May 10, came disturbing reports from Fredericksburg. With Grant moving by his left flank, away from Brandy Station and the Orange & Alexandria Railroad, McParlin had elected to send the wounded to Fredericksburg on the Rappahannock, making it the army's evacuation hospital instead of Brandy Station. The trouble was, the army had made no hospital preparations at Fredericksburg. As one authority described it, "There were stretchers and ambulances at the front, trains and boats in the rear, but for this mid section of the route there was neither personnel nor equipment." Already the situation in Fredericksburg was desperate: only thirty to forty surgeons were there to care for 7,000 to 8,000 wounded, with thousands more on the way, and they suffered from dire shortages of medical stores, food, tents, and virtually everything else. Once again, the Medical Department was ill prepared to deal with the emergency. As a result, McParlin and General George Gordon Meade, the titular commander of the Potomac Army, issued frantic appeals for supplies and for volunteer surgeons and nurses to help at Fredericksburg. The Sanitary Commission swung promptly into action, dispatching a team of surgeons and nurses down the Potomac and organizing a wagon train of supplies to follow from its huge storehouse on F Street. The Christian Commission also planned to send tents and agents.

Here was Clara's chance to get back into the war. She couldn't wait for Leander. Resolved to take the field alone and let the buffoons be damned, she rushed to the various war offices and knocked on doors up and down the halls in a valiant effort to secure a pass. She saw General Augurs, a Major Telvici, all to no avail. "No passes," she scribbled in her diary; "went home in despair." Back she came to try another tack. She persuaded General Rucker to write Acting Surgeon General Barnes, asking him to grant Clara a pass. Then Clara took the request to Barnes herself. But the acting surgeon general referred her to a Captain Allen, who was apparently noncommittal. At this juncture, Gardner Tufts of the Massachusetts state agency told Clara he was going down to Fredericksburg and asked her to accompany him. Fed up with War Department equivocations, she made up her mind to accompany Tufts, with or without a pass.

The next day, to her surprise, a pass came for her by special messenger from General Rucker's office. It was signed by Acting Surgeon General Barnes. Later she claimed that it had come "through Mr. Wilson's power with the highest authorities." In fact, the emergency was so great that Stanton and Barnes were handing out passes to anybody who might help at Fredericksburg.

Clara strode to the Seventh Street wharf, where the steamer *Wenonah* was soon to embark for Fredericksburg. She was in such a hurry to get off that she brought only coffee and two kettles. She would return later for the balance of her stores, which she had entrusted to the Massachusetts State Agency. A crowd of other volunteers stood on the wharf, too. There were several army officers, agents of the Sanitary and Christian commissions, and three women of the Michigan State Relief Association—Julia Wheelock, a Mrs. Johnson, and a Mrs. Brainard. While they awaited the *Wenonah*, three hospital ships steamed up to the wharf with the first shipment of wounded from Fredericksburg. The vessels were packed from their holds to their upper decks, and a hellish discord of groans and cries rose from them. At least the Sanitary and Christian commissions were on hand to serve hot coffee, crackers, and milk punch to those who could swallow.

At last the *Wenonah* arrived. The crowd of volunteers boarded, and the steamer headed downriver at four o'clock in the afternoon. Underway at last, Clara must have felt a surge of exhilaration. She was free of the shackles of doubt and depression, free of the paralyzing anxiety, that had plagued her these past few months. She had not just survived a terrible, inactive period in her life. She had prevailed, had overcome the fearful odds against her. And now she was on her way to the field again, to help her comrades again, to serve the country again. Her life was worth something to mankind.

*   *   *

It was raining when the *Wenonah* steamed passed Aquia Creek, rounded Marlborough Point, droned up Potomac Creek to a crowded landing called Belle Plain, and dropped anchor among numerous supply ships and troop and hospital transports. It was about one o'clock in the afternoon, May 12. Because the railroad from Falmouth Station to Aquia Creek had been wrecked, Belle Plain was now the supply base for the army and the debarkation point for the wounded from Fredericksburg. The water at the wharf was too shallow for steamers to reach it, and barges had to carry all traffic to and from the shore.

The rain fell "fearfully" all that day, forcing Clara and the other passengers to remain in their cabins on the *Wenonah*. During the afternoon, Clara befriended Mrs. Brainard of the Michigan State Relief Committee, and they agreed to go to Fredericksburg together. The next morning, the rain slackened enough for the passengers to take a large barge to the landing, where a single, improvised wharf served a dual purpose: it was used to unload troops and supplies bound for the Army of the Potomac, and to evacuate the wounded from Fredericksburg, who lay in wagons stacked up in single file. One by one, the wagons rolled up to the wharf, unloaded their human cargo, took on supplies lifted by gangs of blacks, and headed back down the muddy road for Fredericksburg and the army beyond. As the wounded lay on one side of the dock, awaiting transportation to the hospital ships, a steady stream of troops, horses, and mules passed on the other side. By mid-morning, said one observer, "Mules, stretchers, army wagons, prisoners, dead men, and officials as good as dead are tumbled and jumbled on the wretched dock which falls in every little while and keeps the trains waiting for hours."

Clara made her way through the traffic and crossed a muddy basin to a nearby ridge, from which she gazed on a wrenching spectacle: nearly 400 six-mule army wagons, loaded with wounded men awaiting evacuation to Washington, stood in the basin at various angles, some sunk in the mud to the hubs of their wheels. As it happened, this was an ambulance train from the Spotsylvania battlefield, which had departed the day before with some 2,500 wounded. After waiting four rain-drenched hours for a guard to accompany it, the train had reached Fredericksburg at dawn on May 12, only to find the town already inundated with wounded and dying soldiers. The wagon train unloaded 600 of its worst wounded in Fredericksburg and brought the rest directly to Belle Plain, where many of the vehicles became stuck in the rain. The evacuation of the wounded from Belle Plain did not begin until the morning of May 13, when Clara came ashore. This meant that the suffering wretches in the wagons had gone without food, water, or proper medical attention for thirty-four hours or longer.

As Clara surveyed the scene from the ridge, a frail, intelligent-looking young man approached her. He was a clergyman with the Christian Commission, he said, and he and his colleagues had arrived here on an earlier boat. Unable to get transportation to Fredericksburg, they had erected a tent on the ridge and were trying to decide how they could help at Belle Plain. He admitted that they were inexperienced at relief work and asked Clara what they ought to do.

"You can start by feeding those poor men down there," she said.

"What a pity," he said. "We have a great deal of clothing, and reading matter, but no food in any quantity except crackers."

Clara said that she had some coffee and two kettles, and that hot coffee and crackers would have to suffice. They built a fire on the hill and made coffee, and then, each carrying a kettle and wearing an apron rolled up with crackers, they made their way back down the slope to the edge of the muddy basin. Here the young clergyman balked. "How are we to get to them?" he asked, looking at the oozing red clay.

"There is no way but to walk to them," Clara said. He looked at her as if to say, Are you going to walk in *that*? Clara almost laughed out loud. To think that, before the war, clergymen like him had almost universally contended that women were not suited for "the practical life." Wading into the ankle-deep mud, she glanced back and smiled when she saw the clergyman grasp his apron and take "his first step in military life."

They slogged out to the wagons and set about feeding the "mutilated, starving sufferers" inside. Clara was horrified to find that many of the wagons were the springless variety, pressed into ambulance service because of the sheer numbers of wounded. Inside the springless wagons, Clara saw, the injured were held in place by straps hanging from the framework, and she could not imagine their agony on the hard, bruising ride from the battlefield.

In one wagon Clara found a captain in the Fifty-sixth Massachusetts, who was shot in the neck. He recognized her name and told her, despite his wound, that General Thomas G. Stevenson of Boston, commander of the First Division of the Ninth Corps, had been killed at Spotsylvania. Clara remembered him well; he had been at Morris Island, in command of the brigade held in reserve during the

July 18 assaults, and had joined Burnside after suffering a bout of malaria. Now he was dead of a sniper's bullet before he was thirty years old. This cruel war was taking a dreadful toll on the young men, a whole generation of them.

The Sanitary Commission had established a feeding station at Belle Plain, and the Sanitary agents and the three Michigan women also waded out to the wagons in the basin, handing out coffee, crackers, and slices of bread with apple butter dabbed on them. Clara spent the night in one of the tents at Belle Plain, and the next morning she and Mrs. Brainard and the delicate young clergyman found a ride to Fredericksburg in an ambulance driven by a young lieutenant. They passed several thousand rebel prisoners being held in the woods and set out over a broken corduroy road that led to Fredericksburg, some ten miles to the southwest. They went at their peril, since rebel guerrillas were operating in the area, often attacking the supply trains after they left Belle Plain. The road was treacherous, winding up and down hills and twisting through fields and swamps with exposed tree stumps. Here and there along the roadside lay bodies of Union dead that had been thrown out of the ambulance train. About four miles from town, Clara noted in her diary, they met a group of ambulances "full of wounded, with the tongue broken or wheels crushed in the middle of a hill, in mud from one to two feet deep—what was to be done with the moaning suffering occupants God only knew."

Within the hour, they rode by the Lacy House on the barren plateau and crossed the pontoon bridge into old Fredericksburg, which for Clara awakened memories of the great battle of 1862: the infantry assaults against the heights, the ceaseless racket of the guns, the macabre, makeshift hospitals where she had worked, surgeons at the amputating tables crying "next." Now, as the wagon rattled over the cobbled street, Clara saw a familiar sight. Once again all the churches and public buildings—even crude stables, the old warehouse, and similar structures—were full of shattered men. Hundreds of wounded fellows lay in the streets, too, waiting to take the places of those who died inside or were removed to Belle Plain. Some of the wounded outside had died from lack of proper medical treatment, and their maggot-covered bodies lay rotting in plain sight. A soldier who wandered through town said that "he had no idea what suffering was until he came to Fredericksburg."

The team of Sanitary Commission surgeons and volunteer nurses had reached the city two days before and with the army surgeons were doing all they could to alleviate the suffering, but the sheer numbers of wounded overwhelmed them. One young Sanitary volunteer, Cornelia Hancock, estimated that 14,000 wounded were packed into a town whose prewar population numbered a little more than 5,000. Because of the severe shortage of rations, a patient in the hospitals was lucky to get a single cracker and a cup of coffee a day.

Clara leaped from the ambulance and went off with a Worcester soldier to find where the Massachusetts men were hospitalized. At the hospital of the First Division, Ninth Corps, she found eight hungry officers of the Fifty-seventh Massachusetts, who told her that the regiment had only about 200 men left. The two days of fighting in the Wilderness had been a bloody inferno, with both sides alternately attacking and repelling attacks, as McParlin put it, "swaying back and forth" in a flaming stretch of woods from a mile to two hundred yards wide. On the second day of fighting, the Fifty-seventh Massachusetts had lost 262 men *before* 9 A.M. "The slain and wounded had every imaginable part of their bodies shot off," wrote the best regimental historian, "and heads, arms, legs, hands, feet, fingers, toes, ears, noses, genitals, entrails, and brains were scattered and splattered everywhere." It had been just as bad at Spotsylvania, where for twenty-three hours Union infantrymen had hurled themselves against rebel earthworks, against a continual storm of bullets, shells, and whirling canister. Grant had now lost about 31,000 men all told, and still the fighting raged on at Spotsylvania, just eight miles southwest of Fredericksburg. As she left the officers' hospital that May 13, Clara could hear the thunder of artillery on the wind.

Clara was accustomed to misery, yet what she found in Fredericksburg this day shocked her. In the warehouses, injured soldiers lay in rows on muddy blankets soaked with their own blood, while male and female volunteers walked up and down the rows, ladling out water from pails. It was apparently all the nourishment they had. In other buildings, Clara complained, men lay on bare floors, crowded so close together "that gangrene was setting in." To compound their misery, they had had nothing to eat since their army rations had run out. They were starving. When Clara entered "one old sunken hotel," she was aghast. "I saw . . . lying helpless upon its *bare, wet, bloody* floors, 500 fainting men hold up their cold, dingy, bloodless hands as I passed, and beg me in Heaven's name for crackers to keep them from starving—*and I had none.*" She returned to the hotel that night, but they still had not been fed; "a great number of them were to undergo amputation sometime," Clara wrote in her diary, "but no surgeons yet, they had not dippers for one in ten."

One surgeon admitted to Clara that many of the wounded would die without food, "better air," and more space. "The surgeons do *all* they *can*," she noted, "but no provision had been made for such a wholesale slaughter on the part of anyone, and I believe it would be impossible to comprehend the magnitude of the necessity without witnessing it." Clara promised to return to Washington on the morrow and rush down her own supplies.

The next morning, she discovered hundreds of ambulances and springless wagons waiting in the streets and out on the road beyond Fredericksburg. It was another ambulance train from Spotsylvania, bearing 3,560 more wounded men. Since the hospitals in town had no room for them, they were obliged to lie in the wagons all night without food or water. Many of them had died, Clara wrote on a fragment of paper, "and their companions, where they had sufficient strength, had raised up and thrown them out into the street. I saw them lying there." She saw, too, "the dark spot in the mud under many a wagon," which "told only too plainly where some poor fellow's life had dripped out in those hours of dreadful darkness." "The city is full of houses," she noted, "and this morning broad parlors were thrown open, and displayed to the view of the rebel occupants the bodies of the dead Union soldiers lying beside the wagons in which they had perished."

Clara was furious. Why weren't the Union wounded quartered in the private residences in town and fed the food stored in their cellars? She did some investigating and found that rebel homes and grocery stores alike were shut tight, "the haughty occupants holding barricade within." Sanitary volunteer Georgeanna Woolsey also reported that the townsfolk refused to sell or surrender anything to the hated Yankees. According to Clara, the fault lay with certain "improper, heartless, unfaithful officers" in immediate command of the city, "upon whose action and decisions depended entirely the *care—shelter—food—comfort* and *lives*—of that whole city of wounded men." A "dapper captain of 21," who was billeted in one of the great mansions in town, told Clara that "it was in fact a pretty hard thing for refined people like the citizens of Fredericksburg to be compelled to open their houses and admit these dirty, lousy, common soldiers, *and he was not going to compel it.*"

To Clara this was unspeakable. No, it was worse than that; it was treason. She knew one man who would set this right if he knew about it, Senator Henry Wilson, and she meant to tell him. Marching to the Federal provost marshal's office, she requested an ambulance for the ride to Belle Plain but found herself treated with "plenty of duplicity &

pomposity." She persisted, though, and finally found a friendly quarter-master officer, who not only furnished her a light army wagon drawn by four strong horses but gave her his personal testimony to the wretched conditions in Fredericksburg. With a Mr. Goodrich, Clara raced up to Belle Plain "at an unbroken gallop." At the wharf, an assistant quartermaster secured transportation for her on the *Silver Star*, which left for Washington immediately.

When the steamer landed at dusk, Clara took her story of "suffering and faithlessness" straight to Henry Wilson, who listened with his lips compressed, believing every passionate word of it. Profoundly distressed, he hurried away to the War Department. As Clara learned later, he found that no official report of unusual suffering had reached Stanton or his staff. Wilson assured them that he had irrefutable proof that medical conditions in Fredericksburg were appalling and that the officers in charge were unreliable. When Stanton was not inclined to believe it, the senator issued an ultimatum: either the War Department send somebody tonight to investigate and correct the abuses in Fredericksburg, or the Senate would dispatch someone the next day.

That threat got some action. By ten the next morning, May 16, Quartermaster General Montgomery Meigs and his staff were in Fredericksburg, and "at noon," Clara later noted with satisfaction, "the wounded were fed from the food of the city and the houses were opened to the *dirty, lousy soldiers* of the Union army." Shocked by the chaos at Belle Plain, Meigs also ordered Union engineers to start repairing the railroad from Falmouth Station to Aquia Creek, so that the wounded could be evacuated from Fredericksburg by train. Without Clara's testimony and Wilson's ultimatum based on it, the decision to open the railroad would not have been made, and the unmitigated suffering on the wagon trains out of Fredericksburg would have continued unabated.

After sleeping for twelve straight hours, Clara rose late on the morning of May 16 and went to the Massachusetts state relief agency, where she had left her own supplies. Going through her stock of medical stores, canned food, and clothing, she realized how hopelessly inadequate it was to meet the needs at Fredericksburg. Up to now, she had relied on a large circle mostly of friends and acquaintances for her supplies, but "the necessities of the present campaign," she said, forced her to broaden her appeal, even if that meant shouting "alone to strangers."

After talking the matter over with her old friend, William M. Ferguson of the Treasury Department, she sat down at his desk and wrote her first public appeal to the entire nation: "TO THE CLERGY AND SOLDIERS' FRIENDS: A CALL TO YOU FROM OUR SUFFERING WOUNDED. For the first time in the history of the war, the magnitude and intensity of suffering and want are so appalling as to wring from me a public call for aid." She had just returned from Fredericksburg, she said. "Would it be pardonable if I ask you to aid in filling my hands that I may help meet the distress crowded within the dingy streets of that city of suffering and death[?]" Clara asked that all contributions be sent to her in care of the Rev. William M. Ferguson at the Treasurer's Office in Washington, and then had 500 copies of the appeal printed and distributed to the press.

Summoning Mrs. Rich to oversee her base of operations in Washington, Clara prepared to return to Fredericksburg with the supplies she had. After talking with Gardner Tufts of the Massachusetts state relief agency, which had sent its own delegation to Fredericksburg, she agreed to join the delegation and operate as an affiliate. General Rucker furnished her official "transportation of supplies to Fred. via Belle Plain," just in case some rule-bound officer tried to detain her.

Before she left Washington, Clara heard what had befallen Benjamin F. Butler and the Army of the James, which included her many friends in the old Tenth Corps. At the same time that Grant advanced into the Wilderness, Butler's forces swooped up the James River on troop transports and seized City Point; then they crossed onto Bermuda Hundred, a narrow stretch of land between the Appomattox and the James, and drove to within about eight miles of Richmond, only to be turned back by a stiff rebel counterattack. Because Butler had neglected to seize Petersburg south of the James, he found himself threatened by a rebel force from that direction as well. Accordingly, he fell back to a defensive line across Bermuda Hundred, where the rebels promptly dug entrenchments along his front and effectively cut off his approach to Richmond west of the James.

The general absolved himself of any blame, instead pointing a finger at Quincy Gillmore, Clara's old nemesis. In a remarkable letter to Henry Wilson, Butler asked that Gillmore's name be brought before the Senate Committee on Military Affairs on grounds of gross incompetence. "Gen. Gilmore may be a very good engineer," Butler told Wilson, "but he is wholly inept in the treatment of troops. He has been behind in every movement." On the other hand, Butler's other corps commander, William F. "Baldy" Smith, blamed Butler for the Bermuda

Hundred fiasco, charging him with inexcusable mismanagement in the field. Smith, of course, thought that he ought to command the Army of the James. When Grant learned what had happened on the James, he grumbled that Butler had not accomplished any of his objectives: had not penned down any rebels in Richmond, or seized Petersburg, or severed the railroad lifelines running through there to the rebel port at Wilmington, North Carolina, and to the Deep South. Now, Grant feared, the rebels would concentrate "everything" against the Army of the Potomac, which, by May 21, was racing toward the North Anna River in another effort to turn Lee's right flank.

On that day, Clara was on her way back to Fredericksburg with her supplies. On the boat trip downriver, she befriended a Mrs. Myers of Worcester, whose husband, a captain in the Fifth Corps, had been shot through the lungs and was in a hospital in Fredericksburg. Mrs. Myers was suffering "exceedingly," Clara noted in her diary, fearful that her husband would die before she could reach him. The boat arrived at Belle Plain in the afternoon, and the two women headed for Fredericksburg in an army spring wagon "piled almost to the top" with Clara's boxes. The load proved too much for the horses to pull, and the women had to get out and follow the wagon on foot all the way to town, which they reached after dark.

Mrs. Myers went to find her husband, and Clara stored her supplies at the headquarters of the Massachusetts state relief agency. Thanks to the intercession of an army captain, as she wrote in her diary, she found lodging with a "Secesh" family in town and retired to "an old lumber chamber riddled through & through with Burnside's shot of 1862." Then "a little negro woman came to my room and insisted on taking off my boots and rubbing my feet which she did most perfectly." The next morning, Clara tipped the "little negress" fifteen cents for the foot rub. To show that Yankees were not misers, she paid the "Secesh" woman fifty cents for her lodging.

At the Massachusetts state agency headquarters, Clara struck up a conversation with an elderly gentleman from Worcester, who turned out to be Captain Lamb's father, the surgeon who had once treated her family. Clara shook his hand with tears in her eyes. "Oh how much he was like the Capt," she noted in her diary. He said he had been in town for ten days and was in charge of a hospital. She promised to make him supper that evening and then set to work distributing her supplies to the hospitals.

A new hospital of 300 tents had been erected on the other side of the Rappahannock, and small river steamers were evacuating the wounded down stream to larger transports waiting at Tappahannock on the Potomac. Since the railroad was still being repaired, the ambulance trains continued the dreadful trek to Belle Plain, in order to make room in Fredericksburg for fresh allotments of wounded from the front.

"The number of wounded has exceeded any thing in history," Clara wrote David. But at least they were better cared for than they had been the week before. Some 42 contract surgeons were in town now, plus 194 "reserve surgeons" from sixteen states and 775 medical students and nurses, male and female alike. Dix sent several of her nurses to Fredericksburg. One of them, Ellen Mitchell, had studied surgical nursing at Bellevue before becoming an army nurse. Georgeanna Woolsey, Helen Gilson, Arabella Barlow, Mary Morris Husband, Mrs. R. H. Spencer, and Anna Holstein and her husband were all working in Fredericksburg under the auspices of the Sanitary Commission; Gilson, Barlow, and several of the others supervised the "special diet kitchens" of their respective hospitals. Isabella Fogg was here, too, toiling day and night without sleep, and Irish-born Mary W. Lee was in charge of the special diet kitchen of a Second Corps hospital. Thanks in large measure to Clara's pioneering work, the day had long since passed when women were proscribed from the battlefront. The constant shortages of nurses and relief workers allowed Clara and her Northern sisterhood to tear down such barriers.

As Clara made her rounds that morning, she found Mrs. Myers in an improvised hospital in a private home near the Baptist Church. Alas, Clara recorded, her friend's husband was "sinking fast," and "*she, poor woman, was almost distracted.*" After doing what she could to console Mrs. Myers, Clara saw to the other wounded in the house and came across a man she knew, Major Dexter T. Parker, a prominent citizen of Worcester. The major's left arm had been amputated, and she thought the poor fellow was dying.

In the front parlor, Clara found her cousin Ned Barton sick with rheumatic fever. A Sanitary agent with the Fifth Corps, Ned was a garrulous young chap with much to tell Clara. He had come down with rheumatic fever on the third day of the Wilderness and had been put on the first huge ambulance train leaving for the rear. The train, he said, had no water, morphine, food, medicines, or nurses; all it had were two surgeons for some 1,200 wounded, and plenty of "maggots, flies, chills and fever." Sharing his ambulance was a Massachusetts soldier named Murphy, who had a gaping, three-inch wound in his upper right arm. When the wound began to "mortify," Ned himself amputated Murphy's arm, and Murphy apparently lived. But many others died and "were put off by the roadside," Ned said; "now and then an ambulance tipped over with its precious freight and at all times the shrieks of the wounded and dying as they passed over these cut up roads were fearful to hear."

At last the train reached Fredericksburg, rumbling past "the famous heights" and the stone wall attacked by Burnside in December 1862. For the next eleven days, Ned languished in town, too sick to be evacuated. The surgeons prescribed "bicarbonate of soda" and morphine powder (to help him sleep), to little effect. He kept wishing that he had a wound, "that I were minus a leg or an arm that I might have a bit of glory with my suffering." On May 13, he had a "happy meeting" with his brother George, who was currently detached from his regiment, the Fifty-seventh Massachusetts, and in command of a divisional ambulance train. Ned had nothing but praise for the Sanitary Commission, which sent down fifteen wagons loaded with supplies— "We have literally been kept alive by the U.S.S.C.," he wrote his mother; "many of our wounded would have starved to death if it had not been for them & the Christian Com—." He was extremely critical of some of the contract and volunteer surgeons in town, insisting that they did not know how to do amputations properly. "The vols from home do as well as they know how," he said, "but though they be professors in colleges of pharmacy they are 'greenhorns' in this work. Both amputations in our house have done badly under volunteer treatment. Then again we change doctors about once in twenty-four hours and the wounded suffer accordingly." For the past few evenings, he said, a band had tried to soothe them by playing "Rock Me to Sleep, Mother."

As Clara and her cousin talked, guards patrolled the streets outside, passing and repassing the windows of the parlor, for Fredericksburg was garrisoned and under martial law. Promising to visit Ned again, she set off to locate another Barton cousin, an orderly sergeant in the Nineteenth Maine, who was reported to be in another hospital in Fredericksburg. A soldier in the outfit took Clara to him, and she found her Maine cousin "a splendid looking fellow almost a giant, straight & noble, shot through the upper lungs, but walking about."

Back at the headquarters of the Massachusetts state agency, Clara prepared a supper of toast, crackers, and boiled eggs for Dr. Lamb and others. Afterward, as she was clearing away the dishes, they heard the whistle of a locomotive across the Rappahannock, signaling that the railroad to Aquia Creek was now open. The whistle "sent a thrill of joy

through us all," Clara wrote triumphantly in her diary. "No more cart-
ing wounded men to Belle Plain."

Evacuations by train began that same day. The walking wounded
were the first to go, followed by the more seriously injured. The
amputees, the critically ill, and men with the worst wounds, in the
belly and chest, would be taken off last. Clara devoted herself to the
latter group. Clad in a blue dress and a white apron, she marched into
the wards singing "Rally 'Round the Flag Boys" and cheerfully fed and
bathed her patients.

On May 23, orders came to remove all the wounded remaining in
Fredericksburg. The "evacuation hospital" was to be transferred downriver to Port Royal, which was closer to the fighting front. Ned Barton
was scheduled to depart by train right away, but he elected to remain
behind and travel with Captain Myers. On the night of May 23, however, the captain died, with his brave wife at his side.

The next morning, Clara saw Ned off on a hospital transport down
the Rappahannock, then took a train to Aquia Creek and returned to
Washington on a boatload of "terribly wounded soldiers." It seemed
impossible "to hold body and soul together," she said, until the transport docked at the Sixth Street wharf, where a crowd of onlookers
greeted them. The sight of the mutilated young men moved some people to weep, others to turn their heads and walk away in anguish. The
boats brought up the bodies of the dead, too, and burial parties were
constantly at work along the green ridge below the Custis-Lee mansion in Arlington.

"We have been having a series of terrible battles," Clara wrote
brother David, "and I hope some victories, but it has been at a fearful
cost." The cost was fearful indeed: in two and a half weeks of campaigning, Grant had lost more than 33,000 men, yet Lee's army was
still intact and fighting harder than ever. Because it was the malarial
season, Clara didn't think she should "go much out of Washington" and
expose herself to sickness. She had never fully recovered from her
bout with dysentery and felt exhausted from her trips to
Fredericksburg. Still, she told David, she couldn't "keep quite still,"
not with the Army of the Potomac fighting on in Virginia. "I suppose I
should feel about as much benefitted as my gold fish would if some
kind hearted person should take him out of his vase when he looks so
wet and cold and wrap him up in a warm dry flannel. Cant live out of
our natural elements can we?"

On May 28, a Dr. Bates and a Mr. Fitch, both friends of Clara, told her that Major Parker of Worcester, the man whose left arm had been amputated in Fredericksburg, had come up on the last hospital boat and was now lying in bed at the Clarendon Hotel. Dr. Bates said he was reluctant to take charge of Parker, who fell under the jurisdiction of the post surgeon in Washington. Clara went at once to his bedside while Bates headed for a telegraph office to wire Parker's wife. The major was "very low," and Clara remained with him all night, nursing him with beef tea and her special brand of urgent solicitude, which had rallied so many others from the brink of death. Her magic worked again, for Parker regained consciousness and recognized her immediately. He asked her many questions, took his nourishment, and by morning appeared to be so much improved that Clara thought he would recover completely. At 11:00 A.M., his wife arrived, and she was hopeful, too.

At noon, however, the post surgeon, a Dr. Antsell, called on Parker and insisted on taking charge of the case. To Clara's horror, this army quack prescribed hourly doses of "whiskey, egg punch, quinine, amonia & opium." Both Mrs. Parker and Dr. Bates protested that this lethal combination could be fatal. Besides, thanks to Clara, Parker was doing very well without medication. But the post surgeon argued that Parker "must have" exactly what he ordered and, as Clara noted, "it was got and given."

With Antsell in charge, Clara went home to rest for a while. Later, on her way back to the hotel, she encountered Henry Wilson, who had heard that Parker was better; Wilson couldn't believe it, considering the way he looked the night before. When they reached Parker's room, however, they found him "excited, full of dreadful dreams," Clara wrote in her diary; he "thought he was dead and lost, could scarce be recalled. I remonstrated against his treatment with Dr Bates, he concurred with me, but dared not interfere. Parker still raved in his fever & delirium and at 8 I left and came home."

She was back again at daylight, May 30. "Poor P in a horrible condition," she noted in her diary. "Crazy as a bear . . . and still taking whiskey quinine amonia & opium hourly. I begged that the dosing be stopped for humanitarian sake and Dr. Bates sent for—I knew he must die, but could not tolerate that torture. I have seldom felt so indignant as at the uncalled for interference of the Post Surgeon[.] No one wanted him or his advice, he forced himself upon the case, and ruined it. Dr B came slowly—cautiously—and the P[ost] S[urgeon] had some words with Mr. Fitch. Poor P continued to be quiet and sink, till finally at 2 1/2 he died." They took his body to the embalmer, leaving Mrs.

Parker to the privacy of her grief. Clara wrote her a note of condolence and went home feeling "weary and heart-sick" and "in strange confusion." She gave no explanation why they did not bring a charge of incompetence against Dr. Antsell. Perhaps they believed that his position made him immune to punishment.

The day after Parker died, Clara found herself in a Washington hospital, kneeling beside other friends who had been mortally wounded and brought here to die. "We are waiting at the cotside and closing their eyes one by one as they pass away," she wrote a friend. "I cannot but think that we shall win at last, but *oh the cost*—a regiment reduced to a score and a corporal commanding. Still God demands the sacrifice, and we have only to obey."

To a Mrs. Alling, who had sent her a bank draft for $147, Clara wrote a public letter explaining why she chose to labor independently of the Sanitary and Christian commissions. Long before either took the field, Clara said, she had toiled by herself to help the cause, gathering such helpers as she could and hauling her supplies to the battlefield. She had worked independently to the present time, and it did not seem "wise or desirable" to change her course now. If she had acquired any skill, it belonged to her to use "untrammeled" by any other authority. "I might not work as efficiently, or labor as happily under the direction of those of less experience than myself—it is simply just to all parties that I retain my present position."

This letter appeared in various newspapers (the *American Baptist*, the *Rochester Evening Express*) as part of Clara's ongoing campaign to broaden her support. An editorial coda in the *Express* exhorted its readers: "By all means let her have assistance." Frances Gage lent her help, too, sending a letter to the Washington *Anti-Slavery Standard* that praised Clara's exceptional work. "No woman, perhaps, in the Union has done more than Miss B. on the battlefields and in the front since the war began," Fanny asserted. "I hope she will be generously aided."

She was generously aided, as boxes of supplies poured in from towns in Massachusetts and Pennsylvania, and Mrs. Rich set to work sorting through them. Leander Poor was now stationed in Washington and helping out, but apparently Clara no longer believed it necessary to have him assigned to her for work in the field. She was, after all, perfectly capable of taking care of herself. Feeling well enough to return to duty, she made preparations to leave for White House Landing on the Pamunkey River, Grant's newest supply and hospital base, where other women were already nursing.

Before Clara could secure a pass and take the field, however, the two armies met again at a little-known crossroads called Cold Harbor, situated about ten miles northeast of Richmond. Certain that they were going to die, some Union soldiers pinned strips of paper to their coats that gave their names and addresses, so that their bodies could be identified. On June 3 Grant unleashed all-out frontal assaults against 59,000 rebels well entrenched in zigzag lines. Baldy Smith's Corps, transferred up from Butler's army, charged into the very center of the enemy line, where the rebels caught them in a deadly crossfire from three directions. A New Hampshire captain likened it to "a volcanic blast." Again and again, 40,000 Yankees rushed at the rebel earthworks in doomed assaults reminiscent of Fredericksburg and Battery Wagner. When would Union generals ever learn? In less than twenty minutes of combat, 7,000 to 8,000 Federals lay dead or wounded on that fire-scarred field. Soon a chorus of voices across the North would damn Grant as a butcher and rage at Lincoln for putting him in command. After a month of continual fighting, Grant was stalled northeast of Richmond, and his total casualties for the campaign stood at 54,000 killed, wounded, and missing. "The immense slaughter of our brave men," said Navy Secretary Gideon Welles, "chills and sickens us all."

A week later, Butler came alive on the Bermuda Hundred front and sent 5,300 infantry under Gillmore to attack Petersburg, hub of the railroads that supplied Richmond and Lee's army from the south. Gillmore advanced to the rebel trenches guarding the city but elected to withdraw when the rebels offered resistance. Butler was so enraged that he relieved Gillmore of command and ordered a court of inquiry. Grant, however, overruled Butler and relieved Gillmore by his own request, thus avoiding an embarrassing investigation. As far as Grant was concerned, though, Butler was to blame for the "ill advised" attack against Petersburg, which had gone forth without Grant's approval.

Clara was hardly sorry about Gillmore's fate. "Genl. Gillmore has made his retreat from an old Secesh woman in front of Petersburg," she wrote sarcastically, "and the report is that he has been relieved by Genl. Butler and sent forward by Grant to Washington." That removed a huge impediment to an option Clara was considering, which was to join Butler's Army of the James on Bermuda Hundred. She admired Butler and longed to serve again with her friends in the "old Tenth Corps." Yet developments on the Richmond front were so confusing that Clara hesitated to take the field.

Three days after Gillmore's abortive attack against Petersburg, Grant had the Army of the Potomac on the move again somewhere east of Richmond. On June 14, the army turned up on the banks of the James, crossed the river on giant pontoon bridges, and raced toward Petersburg. A flotilla containing most of the field medical service from White House Landing steamed up the James in the wake of the advancing army. At the same time, Baldy Smith's Eighteenth Corps descended on Petersburg by way of Bermuda Hundred, where Smith picked up reinforcements from Butler. It seemed clear now that Grant hoped to sever Lee's railroad lifeline through Petersburg to Wilmington and the Deep South and force him to fight for his communications in a climactic battle.

For four straight days in mid-June, Union infantry assaulted the rebel lines in front of Petersburg. Clara's cousin George Barton, back with the Fifty-seventh Massachusetts, commanded two squads during those attacks. A feisty lad with blue eyes, long sideburns, and a mustache, Lieutenant Barton left a graphic record of one day's action. While he and his men lay on their arms, awaiting the order to charge, rebel shot and shell flew about them "in good style." Warning his men to lie low, he glanced to his left and saw a cannonball bouncing straight at him. "I had just enough time to whirl over to the left side when it struck just in the place where I sat, grazing my right arm and leaving my coat sleeve almost entirely off, smashed a musket [in two] and covering my 1st sergt up with sand." When the order came to charge, he and his men did so "with a regular *Yankee* yell." They carried part of the rebel works and held it until they ran out of ammunition, which forced them to fall back.

In the end, the Petersburg defenses held off the Potomac Army long enough for Lee to hurry there with the Army of Northern Virginia, which dug in behind a labyrinth of trenches and redoubts. Failing to carry Petersburg by frontal assault, Grant elected to put the city under siege. He informed Washington that he would bombard Lee with heavy artillery and extend Union lines to the east and south of the city in an effort to cut off Lee's railroad communications, thus flushing him out for a showdown battle.

The Petersburg campaign played out in the Washington newspapers under screaming headlines, and Clara winced at the casualties reported on the Black List. Almost 10,000 more of her comrades fell in the Petersburg assaults, and it began to seem that the war might drag on in a hurricane of violence until no one was left on either side. To accommodate the wounded and sick on the Petersburg front, the field medical service erected an emergency evacuation hospital near Grant's headquarters at City Point, between the James and Appomattox rivers.

But everything was pandemonium there, as the troop transports tried to take off the wounded at the same time that long wagon trains were being loaded with supplies for the troops at the front. All this caused "great trouble and delays" in getting the wounded aboard the hospital ships, McParlin reported, "and at first it seemed probable that the scenes of Belle Plain were to be repeated at City Point."

Clara might have gone to the hospital near City Point save for one thing: a Sanitary Commission feeding station was already there, and a Sanitary supply train was on its way with Cornelia Hancock and other female nurses. The Christian Commission and various state relief agencies had delegations on the way as well. From Clara's view, Butler's line on Bermuda Hundred was a more promising field of endeavor for her independent nursing and relief operation, and that was where she decided to go.

On June 21, she left on the steamer *Charlotte Vanderbilt* in the company of a Colonel Phillips. The ever loyal Wilson had given her a glowing letter of introduction for General Butler. "Miss Barton, of Worcester, Massachusetts, goes to your Department with articles for the benefit of the soldiers, sick and wounded," the letter stated. "General Rucker gives her all the aid he can, and I ask you to allow her any means you can to accomplish her work of charity. . . . She understands all about the work, has large quantities of supplies, and will go wherever danger and suffering can be found."

As the *Charlotte Vanderbilt* steamed down the Virginia coast toward the James River, Clara knew she was heading for a deadly field of suffering on the vast Petersburg–Bermuda Hundred line. Yet she faced her newest challenge with absolutely no fear for her own safety. She was a soldier after all, a veteran of siege warfare on Morris Island, and she felt strong and confident. She would make the Army of the James her own army before the summer was out.

PART FIVE

Before Richmond

The *Charlotte Vanderbilt* droned up the storied James and docked at City Point at five o'clock in the afternoon on June 22. The point was a barren neck of land overlooking a wide crook in the James where it converged with the Appomattox River. Here a sprawling military city was under construction—wharves, railroad facilities, and commissary and quartermaster storehouses, all necessary to sustain a sieging army. The Union flag fluttered over a cluster of tents near a white frame house. The tents were Grant's headquarters.

Clara went ashore and sought out a captain she knew, who provided her with an ambulance for the ride to the main evacuation hospital around the bend. The driver, Clara noted in her diary, was "a wee bit" of a fellow, only twelve years old, "who knew nothing of the way but by chance we hit the spot." This Depot Hospital, as it was called, consisted of neat rows of tents pitched on a high bluff on the south side of the Appomattox, less than a mile southwest of City Point. The wounded and sick, after being treated in field dressing stations at the front, were brought here by ambulance trains for evacuation to the north. By the time Clara arrived, the hospital had its own wharf, and hospital transports with shallow draughts—the *State of Maine* and the *Connecticut*— were able to pull right up to the dock. Indeed, the Depot Hospital appeared to be in excellent working order, so that another Belle Plain, with its chaos and needless suffering, would be avoided.

Clara conferred with a few surgeons and that night shared a tent with "two sleepy Ohio women Mrs. Greenwood & Miss Semens," as she wrote in her diary. The next day she and Colonel Phillips took a narrow "black wheel boat" five or six miles upriver to Point of Rocks, on the north side of the Appomattox. On nearby Cobb's Hill stood a Union signal station called Butler's Tower. One hundred and twenty feet high, it afforded a spectacular view of Petersburg off to the southwest, with its rival trench lines and fortifications. To the northwest, across a lovely stretch of country, stood Richmond, whose church spires could be seen on a clear day.

From Point of Rocks, Clara walked the mile to Butler's headquarters on the Bermuda Hundred line. She was anxious to meet the general, after reading so much about his wartime exploits at Baltimore, Fort Monroe, and New Orleans, all of which had made him the most controversial political general in Lincoln's army. As commander of the Department of the Gulf, Butler had dealt with "traitorous" New Orleans even more harshly than he had treated secessionist Baltimore: he had imposed martial law, outlawed public assemblies, jailed prominent secessionists, executed a resident for tearing down a U.S. flag, and enraged Confederates everywhere when he announced that any woman resident who insulted U.S. soldiers would be treated as a common whore "plying her vocation." He issued that order after a woman had emptied her chamber pot on the heads of two Union officers as they passed by her house. Enraged by Butler's harsh measures, Confederate president Jefferson Davis issued a proclamation declaring him "a felon deserving of capital punishment . . . an outlaw and common enemy of mankind."

Relieved of command in December 1862, Butler enjoyed a protracted leave from the army and was much in Washington, hobnobbing with Wilson, Sumner, and other Radical Republicans. He remained on excellent terms with Lincoln, too, who invited him to dinner in the White House. The general shocked Lincoln when he asserted that every deserter from the army ought to be shot. "You may be right," Lincoln said, "but God help me, how can I have a butcher's day every Friday in the Army of the Potomac?" Genuinely admiring Butler's patriotism and administrative abilities, Lincoln approved appointing him to command the Department of Virginia and North Carolina and the Army of the James. But he warned Butler, "Don't let Davis catch you; he has put a price on your head; he will hang you sure." "That's a game two can play at," Butler retorted; "if I get hold of him I shall give him the law of the outlaw after a reasonable time to say his prayers." Because of Butler's influence with Radical Republicans, Lincoln asked him to be his vice-presidential running mate in the presidential canvass of 1864, but Butler turned the president down because he wanted to remain in the army. Even so, he promised to do everything he could to help Lincoln win reelection. After the Bermuda Hundred fiasco in May 1864, Grant wrote Butler off as an effective field commander but left him at the head of the Army of the James in part because of his powerful political connections.

Butler's headquarters at Bermuda Hundred appeared "like a little village," Clara thought, with a flag flying over the general's tent, which was shaded by a few scraggly bushes. When Clara introduced herself, she found Butler "dignified, wise, and princely, and still, perhaps, the most kindly and approachable personage on the grounds." In truth, he hardly resembled the fat and ugly Butler depicted in the illustrated weeklies. Certainly he was not the "lobster-eyed" beast that Southerners called him. "He is stoutish but not clumsily so," reported one sympathetic Union soldier; "he squints badly, but his eyes are very clear and bright; his complexion is fair, smooth and delicately flushed; his teeth are white and his smile is ingratiating. You need not understand that he is pretty; only that he is better looking than his published portraits." He was something of a political chameleon. Before the war, he had been a Democrat and a champion of the working class in Lowell, Massachusetts, and had even favored Jefferson Davis for president in 1860. He was also a brilliant and belligerent lawyer, and extraordinarily successful. By 1860, his annual income was $18,000, an impressive sum in antebellum America.

Clara explained her intentions and handed him Henry Wilson's letter. *Yes, yes*, the general said, reading it rapidly. He motioned for her to sit down. So she was the famous Clara Barton, whom people called the angel of the battlefield. He knew about her achievements, of course. She wanted to work in his field hospitals, did she? He smiled a good deal—a platonic smile, for the general was happily married and faithful to his elegant Sarah.

Even so, Butler and Clara liked one another immediately. Both were from Massachusetts, both were strong-willed mavericks in their forties, and both nursed an intense dislike for Quincy Gillmore. What was more, Clara felt that Butler respected her and welcomed her presence; she could trust him, if necessary, to support her against the buffoons. "Need not note the interview," she scribbled in her diary, "for I shall never forget it. I am satisfied with my success with Genl Butler."

The general wrote out an order directing that his medical directors, surgeons, and other officers give her every aid and assistance in her efforts to provide "relief of the sick in this Department." Then she rode in his carriage to the headquarters of General William T. H. Brooks, acting commander of the Tenth Corps. Here, to her delight, she found Dr. Craven, who had run the hospitals and medical service

on Morris Island. He was genuinely glad to see her, for he respected
the brave work she had done there. Now medical director of the Tenth
Corps, he invited her to serve in the corps hospital and had her escorted to the hospital site at Point of Rocks, at the southern end of Butler's
line of trenches on Bermuda Hundred. Clara discovered that while it
was called a "corps" hospital, it was "only an over burdened and well
conducted field hospital," situated on an abandoned rebel plantation
overlooking the Appomattox River. She noted that "six miles on, where
you hear a great deal of noise, and see a great deal of smoke, is
Petersburg."

She introduced herself to the surgeon in charge, Dr. Horace P.
Porter, a good-natured young man who had originally served as regimental surgeon of the Tenth Connecticut, Lieutenant Colonel
Leggett's command. Dr. Porter welcomed Clara and treated her so
"kindly and nobly" that she proclaimed him "one of the most humane
men I ever met." She had seldom seen anything surpassing "the zeal
and industry" with which he conducted his hospital and looked after
his patients. Since Clara was not one to gush about male surgeons, not
after her experience on Morris Island, her accolades for Dr. Porter
were a measure of her esteem for him.

Clara was also impressed with Dr. Dodge of the Nineteenth
Wisconsin, who functioned as assistant surgeon and executive officer of
the hospital. "No better could have been desired," Clara said. Most of
all, she liked ward master Thomas Don Carlos, who was sixty-eight
years old and "clear, true, warm hearted & dignified." She referred to
him affectionately as "Uncle Don," and he treated her with a protective warmth and regard that endeared him to Clara. "What a friend he
has been to me," she wrote a few weeks later.

The hospital at Point of Rocks consisted of twenty lines of long,
white tents, where from 400 to 500 "used up, wounded, worn-out men"
convalesced at any given time. They lay on cots or straw bags on the
ground, forty men to each tent, with "a waiting tenant for every spare
sack of straw," as Clara put it. There was a segregated section for black
patients, who belonged to the Third Division of the Eighteenth Corps,
which had figured prominently in the assaults on Petersburg the week
before. The Eighteenth Corps held the northern end of the Union
trenches on the Petersburg front, and many of its sick and wounded
were brought to Point of Rocks, just across the Appomattox, because its
own hospital was either full or not yet completely established. Patients
of either corps who were unable to rejoin their units in a few days
were evacuated by boat to the big hospital at Fort Monroe, so that

there was a constant turnover in the hospital population. According to Clara, they were "brought in daily by the scores and shipped away weekly by hundreds."

On June 30, Clara visited the Bermuda Hundred line, which ran from Point of Rocks north to the James River. Passing regiment after regiment of "sunburnt veterans," she was distressed to find so few of her friends left among them. The soldiers faced a parallel line of rebel trenches, and there was a fair amount of sniper fire between the two sides. At the last battery on the southern end of the Union trenches, Clara sat down with a colonel for a cup of coffee. At that moment, in soldier parlance, "the ball opened" at Petersburg downriver, with rebel artillery there blasting the Union trenches held by the Eighteenth Corps. The rate of enemy cannon fire was faster than Clara had ever heard; she counted thirty-six salvoes in a single minute. As she and the colonel sipped coffee and watched, the shells fell on the Eighteenth Corps positions with a distant *thump, thump*, doubtless taking their toll on the poor fellows in the trenches. Many of the wounded would be streaming into Clara's hospital soon enough.

At this time, Clara was evidently the only Northern woman serving at Point of Rocks. She was in charge of nursing and diet for one section of the hospital, which included the black wards, and had soldier nurses and former slave women as her assistants. The women not only did the hospital laundry but helped Clara prepare meals on the hospital's single stove. Because the lines of responsibility were fluid and flexible, she and her helpers often fed the entire hospital population, patients and staff alike.

It was dreadfully hot, the temperature soaring above one hundred degrees in the daytime and scarcely cooling off at night. "Hot . . . am tired," she recorded in her diary on July 1. "I have cooked ten dozen eggs," she explained to Ferguson, "made cracker toast, corn starch blanc mange, milk punch, arrow-root, washed faces and hands, put ice on hot heads, mustard on cold feet, written six soldiers' letters home, stood beside three death-beds—and now, at this hour, midnight, I am too sleepy and stupid to write even you a tolerably readable scrap."

The day before, two boxes and thirty barrels of stores had arrived from Ferguson and Mrs. Rich; the supplies came from donors in New York as well as New England. Sleepy or not, Clara chose her words carefully in her letter to Ferguson, which was intended for publication in order to inspire more support. "Please tell the noble ladies of New York, our Watkins and Reading friends, that less than an hour ago I blistered my hands spreading their hard, sweet, yellow butter on to sliced bread for five hundred and fifty men's suppers."

For the next two weeks, Clara was swept up in a vortex of work that seemed never to let up. Late at night, in rare moments of leisure, she made notes in her campaign diary or wrote letters to Ferguson and other friends, with a candle lantern silhouetting her form on the walls of the tent. Her jottings afford rare glimpses into the "sunshine and dust and toil and confusion" of life in a field hospital on a siege line, with "the mercury above a hundred, the atmosphere and every thing about one black with flies, the dust rolling away in clouds as far as the eye can penetrate, the ashy ground covered with scores of hospital tents shielding nearly all conceivable maladies that *soldier* flesh is heir to, and stretching on beyond the miles of bristling fortifications, entrenchments and batteries encircling Petersburg—all ready to *blaze*."

The searing heat was worse than anything she had ever experienced, even on Morris Island. "July 2," she wrote. "One of the hottest days I ever knew. The whole country is parched like a heap of ashes; there is not even dew; the fields are crisp, and the corn leaves curling, as if under flame." For her patients, the heat was "terribly oppressive" and "painful." She noted that "Capt. Wm Webb 130 O[hio] Kellys Island came to put one of his men with measles in my care—very ill, died at 3." That same day a colonel, two majors, and another man "came in wounded." The colonel was shot in the hip, and the ball had to be "taken out at the back, taking pieces of bone in both instances."

The colonel and the three other wounded men belonged to General August V. Kautz's cavalry division of the Army of the James, and they had just returned from a cavalry raid south and west of Petersburg with General James H. Wilson's cavalry division of the Army of the Potomac. Their story of the raid held Clara rapt with attention. Starting off in the middle of the night, the Union riders, 7,400 strong, had dashed around the southern end of the rebel lines, burned Reams Station and torn up part of the Petersburg & Weldon Railroad, raced west and north to strike the South Side Railroad and torch thirty railroad cars, and then headed back toward the Union lines, with rebel units in hot pursuit. On June 29, threatened by enemy forces closing in from three directions, the raiders broke up, abandoning their wounded and more than 300 slaves who had deserted rebel homesteads to join them. Wilson and most of his division managed to get away in the direction of Jarrett's Station and the James River. Kautz with part of his division and fragments of Wilson's—some 1,000 in all—escaped to the east through tangled swampland and then headed for Bermuda Hundred. For two days, Clara said, "ragged, bareheaded, bleeding, sunstruck, and fainting" and leading "the remnant of jaded horses and mules," groups of Kautz's men staggered into camp near her hospital. "These men," she wrote Ferguson, "with weeks of toil and starvation, days of peril and fighting to the hilt, without sleep or water, shot through and through, rested an hour under the shade of a tent by the road side, ate supper like other men, mounted their horses and rode away."

"The same hot glare," Clara wrote in her diary on July 3, "not a ripple on the river, not a leaf stirs, and to add to the discomfort, two shells have just burst a few rods to the right of us, in a dry, ploughed field and have thrown up such quantities of dust, that it was at first difficult to inhale air enough to sustain us." Exposed day after day to the broiling sun, many soldiers fell victim to sunstroke. According to Surgeon J. S. Billings, the "cases" of sunstroke ranged from "slight dizziness, with inability to walk straight, to violent epileptiform convulsions and almost immediate death." Standard treatment called for the victims to be carried into the shade, doused with cold water, and given shots of whiskey. If that didn't bring them around, they went to the hospital for further treatment, which might include an application of lint saturated with chloroform, which was placed on the victim's abdomen to produce what Billings called "rapid and severe counter irritation."

One day a brigade marched by the Tenth Corps Hospital in the shimmering heat and dust, but before it had gone far, the men started collapsing from exhaustion and sunstroke. Clara took whiskey and water to them, and one fellow was so delirious that she told her assistants to carry him to a hospital tent, where she bound his head with ice packs before turning to her other duties. The man looked familiar, but she couldn't quite place him. Perhaps the heat was playing tricks on her memory.

Because there was little significant fighting in July, both sides settled into the grinding tedium of siege warfare, of deadly sniper fire and incessant cannonades. In his letters home, Lieutenant George Barton vividly described the soldiers' lot in the trenches before Petersburg. He and his men burrowed into "little pits about the size of a common grave," he said. "Here we lay and every time a man Show his head *Zip* would come a Minnie[.] The bullets would just skim the top of the pit that I occupied warning me to keep close to my mother earth, which I did you may be sure." One of his men didn't do that and paid the price. "He raised his head to take a look at the rebs when Zip goes a Minnie through his temple."

Every night there were spectacular artillery barrages by both sides, and Clara could see the blazing fuses of the shells as they arced overhead and then plunged to the earth, exploding in brilliant bursts of yellow and red. The daytime duels were no less grand. The shells followed one another as if demonically synchronized and could be seen along both trench lines for miles. The Union soldiers could always spot an enemy mortar shell. First would come a puff of smoke from the rebel works, then the report, then "a black speck would dart into the sky" with a shriek, "hang a moment, increasing in size, rolling over and over lazily," and then fall on the Union trenches with a *whoosh*, blowing up men, equipment, and barricades in a shower of debris. Lieutenant Barton saw a fragment of a mortar shell strike a man nearby, tearing his face open and almost ripping his left arm off. The Union guns responded with equal ferocity. "We can see the sand fly from their works at every discharge of our rifled guns & 'mortars,' " George reported.

Lying in their embattled trenches day after day, the soldiers "lived and ate and looked like troglodytes," a New Yorker said. They were exposed to summer thunder showers, which turned their rifle pits into mudholes. They battled swarms of mosquitoes and flies, endured scalding summer winds and swirling dust. To a man, they were infested with lice, which they nicknamed "gray backs" in honor of their gray-clad foe. Never without humor, they joked that they had to deal with two enemies at once: the "Johnnies" in their front and the "graybacks" on their rear.

Inevitably, diseases swept through the sieging army, with diarrhea and dysentery leading the list. Because the army diet lacked vitamin C, there were outbreaks of scurvy, too, which turned the afflicted into prostrate, frightful-looking specimens, with swollen legs, discolored skin, and puffy, bleeding gums. Their hair fell out, too, and they suffered from what was described as "subconjunctival" hemorrhaging. The government managed to check scurvy by rushing in enormous quantities of fresh vegetables, "raw potatoes in vinegar," and pickles and kraut. Because of the incessant shelling and sniper fire, some men suffered from what would be termed shellshock in a later day. But Civil War physicians had almost no understanding of the psychological toll of warfare. When a soldier's nerves broke down, they dismissed it as "nostalgia."

To ease their nerves, the men might sing their favorite songs, from the patriotic lyrics of "Battle Cry of Freedom" to the mournful refrains

of "Weeping Sad and Lonely; or When this Cruel War Is Over." In
1864, the latter ballad was the favorite of Union soldiers everywhere.

Dearest love, do you remember,
When we last did meet,
How you told me that you loved me,
Kneeling at my feet?

When they reached the chorus, the men sang from the heart:

Weeping, sad and lonely,
Hopes and fears how vain.
Yet praying, when this cruel war is over,
Praying that we meet again.

For her part, Clara opened her arms to the sick and filthy men
brought in from the trenches, where the burning sun of summer, she
said, dried the mud on them "to the hardness of brick." She found special pleasure in bathing and feeding such soldiers and laying them
down on clean sheets. Because the hospital had plenty of supplies (the
City Point warehouses were just downriver and regular allotments
arrived from Clara's own supporters), the patients were well fed and
cared for by Civil War standards. Cards attached to the foot of their
cots or straw bags indicated their ailment and treatment and designated which diet Clara was to prepare for them. The seriously sick and
wounded received a "low diet" of rice, toast, milk, tea, or farina. This
was standard fare for those afflicted with acute or chronic diarrhea-
dysentery, for Civil War surgeons understood the importance of diet in
treating that tenacious malady. One doctor argued that the best treatment was a restricted diet of plain bread, although most other physicians prescribed broths and soups as well. Almost everyone agreed that
diarrhetic patients should avoid eating fats. Unfortunately for the
patients, much of the medication they received—especially the purgatives—offset the positive effects of a protected diet.

Convalescents, on the other hand, enjoyed a "full diet," which, in
the words of one specialist, "covered the spectrum of the period's
nutritional ideas"—pork, beef, beans, cabbage, lettuce, lemons if available, bread and butter, some kind of pudding, and coffee or punch. All
other patients were on a half diet of soup, bread and butter, potatoes,
and tea or coffee.

Early each morning, Clara would visit the patients with the ward surgeon, who stopped at each cot to ask the patient questions and write out orders for his medication and care. A tag pinned to his hospital shirt gave his name, rank, and unit. During the day, Clara and her assistant nurses changed the patients' bedding and clothing and tried to maintain a measure of sanitation, which was difficult to do in this fly-infested, dust-blown environment. The tents had no floors, and the plumbing was primitive, with outdoor latrines for those who could walk to them and cotside buckets in which the incapacitated relieved themselves. The buckets only added to the foul odors that hung in the air from gangrenous wounds and other effluvia. Daily exposure to "twisted bodies, splintered bones, raw flesh, burning fevers, and fetid air" might have demoralized a lesser mortal than Clara. But she resolved to "keep cheerful, & toil on."

She wrote Ferguson that she was truly "happy being here." Like other women who had extended "woman's sphere" to the wartime hospitals, Clara referred to her patients as her family and the hospital as her home. Indeed, she had never felt more needed and at home than at Point of Rocks, where she loved "old Uncle Don" and got along splendidly with Dr. Porter and his assistants. Thus far, she had not met a single buffoon.

Of all her patients, Clara had a special affection for the black soldiers and gave them extra care. She thought them "so patient and cheerful, so uniformly polite and soldierly. They are brave men and make no complaints." Most of them were former slaves who had enlisted in the Union army to fight their former masters and help free their brothers and sisters still in bondage. Clara said that the blacks made "excellent nurses," too, and took "kind care" of one another. "I am well satisfied that they are not a class of men that an enemy would desire to meet on a charge."

One day, while passing through a "colored" ward, she stopped beside the cot of a sergeant who appeared weak to her but who did not complain.

"How are you feeling?" Clara asked.

He looked up at her. "Thank you, Miss, a little better I hope."

"Can I do any thing for you?"

"A little water if you please," he said, hardly above a whisper.

She turned to get him a dipper of water and at that instant he gasped and died.

One day an elderly, silver-headed black man, a civilian, arrived at the hospital with a fever and severely blistered feet. He had escaped from the rebels one night and had walked barefoot across thirty miles of burning landscape to inform the Yankees of a pending rebel attack. Then he had collapsed. In his hospital tent, he lay moaning with fever, his feet so crippled that the surgeons doubted he would ever walk again.

Clara also met a large number of other neighborhood blacks, most of them women and children. Their masters had taken the able-bodied men with them when they had escaped upcountry. Those left behind were deplorably destitute, having suffered at the hands of both armies. "What one army left them the other has taken," Clara said. On the plantation where the hospital was situated, she found a woman with eight children; five others, including her oldest, had been taken away. According to the woman, rebel troops had confiscated her clothing and bedding, and the Yankees had taken her money—forty dollars in gold, which she had saved, probably from "hiring her own time"—working for others for pay and sharing it with her master. Clara tried to find army employment for the woman and did all she could to help her and the children.

Somebody complained to General Butler about the Tenth Corps Hospital, which resulted in an inspection by elderly Dr. McCormick, medical director of the Army of the James. The complaint was not about Clara. McCormick made that clear, saying that he valued her service and wanted her to stay. Indeed, he sought her opinion about "the direction of the hospital," and they agreed that it would help if there were more nurses to assist her. As it happened, Sarah P. Edson of the New York City Masonic Mission was then in camp; she hoped to send down some young female nurses she was instructing under the mission's auspices. She had talked with Clara, and Clara, despite misgivings about sharing her duties and "family" with young white women from the North, had agreed to put her request before General Butler. Thus, when Dr. McCormick conducted his inspection, the subject of Mrs. Edson's nurses came up, and he "decided with me," Clara wrote, "to allow four nurses of Mrs. Edson's to come to our hospital upon Dr. Porter's request." It was Clara's understanding, however, that the new nurses were to work under her supervision. Otherwise she would never have agreed to let them come.

Since Clara was the daughter of a Mason, she and Sarah Edson had much in common, for Sarah's husband was "an advanced member of the order," and she had taken the "Adoptive Degrees." On the evening after the inspection, Clara held a Masonic meeting in her tent, with Sarah Edson, Dr. Porter, "Uncle Don" Carlos, and others in attendance. There was nothing in Mrs. Edson's manner to indicate that there was any misunderstanding about the role her four nurses were to play at Point of Rocks.

In mid-July, Clara heard "great reports" of a rebel raid on Washington. Led by Jubal Early, the enemy had evidently penetrated as far as the end of Seventh Street, *her* street. As she found out later, the raid was designed to draw off Yankee strength on the Petersburg front by threatening the Union capital. That ploy worked, since Grant dispatched a crack corps against the rebel raiders. Before Grant's troops reached Washington, the rebels skirmished with Union garrison troops at Fort Stevens, where Lincoln himself stood under fire, and burned the "country house" of the loyal Maryland governor. By July 13, Early was gone, having fallen back somewhere toward the Shenandoah. To put an end to such raids, Grant finally sent Philip Sheridan, cavalry leader of the Army of the Potomac, to take field command of all troops in the capital area and follow Early "to the death."

In mid-July Clara left the Tenth Corps Hospital for a quick trip to Washington. She saw the "relics of the fight up 7th St." and then sent the *Worcester Spy* an open letter of thanks to the Soldiers' Aid Society of Oxford, Massachusetts, for its contribution of a "valuable box of supplies." Her letter was vintage Clara—both caring and shrewd, with tender observations calculated to keep the donations coming forward. Of the gifts from the Oxford women, she maintained that she had distributed *"every article"* herself. "I speak distinctly, for I can recall nearly every one as I gave them out, or put them on to the poor sufferers who received them. You will smile at my confession, but it is true. I felt a kind of exclusive—perhaps selfish, right to apply every piece of them myself, and why not? were they not from my own home—had they not been contributed by the very hands I should grasp in friendship if I were near them."

Of course, she continued, her Oxford friends would want to know specifically how their gifts had helped the men under her care. "One feather pillow," she said, "is under the head of a little lad dying of quick consumption, the other [under] a lad of seventeen, broken down in Wilson's cavalry raid, raising blood, and will never stand on his feet again. The lint and bandages are dressing the wounds gained in that fearful raid and fight—the fourteen sheets dressed almost as many beds, (with some quilts I had) and enabled us to take the coarse but woolen clothes from twelve men in raving fevers, growing delirious in their torments, have them bathed, and placed comfortably in bed, with a good cool sheet over them, and clean handkerchief and towel—with a tumbler of jelly and some gruel by their bedsides—you will fail to comprehend the magnitude of the change, because it will be impossible for you to realize the depths of the misery they were taken from." She also mentioned the elderly black man who had walked thirty miles to bring military intelligence to the Union lines. "A pair of your slippers," she reported, were on his crippled feet, which would never walk again.

"If I were to attempt to tell you how hard we had wrought during the last four or five weeks in the sun and dust, to make a comfortable homelike resting place for the poor sufferers who fell back into our hands, you would only think me egotistical but, if I tell you that I try to see that every one of the many hundreds has the proper nourishment each day, and to answer every want that reaches me—stand beside the three or four death beds which number themselves with us each day— and stand by each lonely grave as the earth is thrown in, where some weeping mother, wife, or sister would stand if she might, you will say with great justice, that it is my duty to do these things."

By July 29, Clara was back at City Point with a new load of supplies for her hospital. The Union base at City Point had grown into a sprawling military complex, with seven wharves that serviced as many as 200 ships a day. The ships brought supplies and ordnance from the North that were stored in waterfront warehouses. A huge bakery produced 100,000 loaves of bread a day for Grant's vast and hungry army. There were slaughterhouses, army repair and blacksmith shops, a post office, coffin shops, and parlors for embalming. The U.S. Military Railroad Construction Corps rebuilt the City Point railroad track, and whistling military trains came right up to the wharves on railroad spurs, so that the army's black workers could load supplies on boxcars and flatcars for the troops at the front. In time, twenty-five locomotives pulling 275 cars would run back and forth on the military railroad, which extended south to the siege lines.

Clara rode a tug around the bend to Depot Hospital, where she found lodging for the night at the Massachusetts state relief agency. The hospital was plagued with flies, mosquitoes, and dense clouds of dust that settled on the wards from constant wagon trains and troops passing on the main road. Even so, it was the most impressive evacuation and convalescent hospital of the war, comprising the Second, Fifth, Sixth, and Ninth corps hospitals, which were divided into divisions and laid out with streets and avenues. At its peak, the hospital had 1,200 tents capable of accommodating 12,000 patients. Across the road was Agency Row, which consisted of the stations of the U.S. Sanitary Commission and Christian Commission and the tents of various state relief agencies, not to mention the New York City Masonic Mission. There was a separate hospital for the blacks, which was ably run by Helen Gilson, a pretty, gentle woman in her late twenties, who served as hospital superintendent; she enlisted refugee black women as cooks, nursing assistants, and laundresses and made her diet kitchen a model of discipline and careful management. According to the Sanitary Commission, she raised the "colored" hospital "from a disgrace to an object of pride." "Not only was its standard the highest," said one observer, "but it was the most cheerfully picturesque hospital at City Point." When she came down with malaria, her friends urged her to leave this miserable climate before it killed her. "I couldn't die in a better cause" was her firm reply.

There were many other female volunteers at Depot Hospital, some working under the auspices of the two great commissions, others sent by Miss Dix. Mary Morris Husband, Mrs. R. H. Spencer, Isabella Fogg, and Mary W. Lee were all serving at "the Depot." Cornelia Hancock, a Sanitary volunteer who had served at Fredericksburg, ran the diet kitchen for the First Division hospital of the Second Corps, with the help of a black woman, an Irish woman, a soldier, and a "jewel of a little" black boy. She wrote her mother that "if it were not for the sea breeze from the James River we should die here; the dust is shoe top deep, the sun just pours down, the smell is almost intolerable, and we have had no rain for nearly three weeks." She added: "Our ladies in camp are being reduced considerably by sickness and indisposition to stay. I pray for health. I can stand all other hardships but sickness."

As Clara settled in for the night at the Depot Hospital, there was talk that a great battle was to begin before Petersburg early the next morning. Union soldiers and engineers had dug a mine under the rebel works in front of Burnside's Ninth Corps and placed 320 kegs of gunpowder in it, with the idea of blowing a hole in the enemy defenses large enough for Union infantry to charge through and threaten the city. Three divisions of the Ninth Corps, including the Twenty-first and Fifty-seventh Massachusetts regiments, were to make the attack. That meant that Clara's cousin George would go in, along with Colonel Clark and many of her other comrades.

At about 4:45 the next morning, July 30, a dull, muffled explosion shook the ground like an earthquake. The mine had exploded, sending up a huge column of reddish earth 200 feet high with flashes of fire dancing in it like lightning. Then 110 federal artillery pieces and 44 mortars opened up along the entire two mile line, with concussions so deafening that they bruised ears all the way to City Point. The smoke of the guns and the dust of the exploded mine drifted upward against the rising sun, turning it the color of blood. When the guns at last fell silent, it meant that the infantry was attacking through the hole in the rebel lines, and Depot Hospital on the Appomattox braced itself for the worst.

While the battle of the Crater raged eight miles to the south, Clara returned to her own hospital at Point of Rocks and sent for her stores at City Point. She recorded that her "sick family" was somewhat larger now and that everyone was glad to see her. To her sorrow, she learned that "Uncle Don" Carlos, the old ward master, had left Point of Rocks, perhaps transferred to another hospital.

During her absence, the four female nurses from the New York Masonic Mission had arrived at Point of Rocks and were already at work in Clara's wards. Their leader, young Adelaide "Ada" Smith, had nursed sick soldiers at the Long Island College Hospital in 1862 and had studied nursing with Mrs. Edson. Upon reaching the Tenth Corps Hospital, she informed Dr. Porter that the Masonic Mission had sent her to replace Clara Barton as nurse and manager of the diet kitchen. The young doctor said that there must be some misunderstanding, since Clara was "already in charge of this work." Congenial fellow that he was, however, Dr. Porter invited Ada Smith and her three assistants to stay on anyway.

When Clara heard what Miss Smith had said, she was furious. The nerve of that young upstart, trying to usurp her authority! This was *Clara's* hospital; she had come here first, had won the support of the entire medical staff by dint of her courage, experience, and hard work, and it upset her profoundly that while she was away gathering stores, a tyro should march brazenly into her hospital and try to have her thrown out. Clara reprimanded herself for ever agreeing to let Miss Smith and her assistants invade her domain. To tell the truth, she couldn't bear the sight of them ministering to her patients, her *family*, and ingratiating themselves with her surgeons. Clara feared losing her

work and her position of power over the men of the hospital. She felt
threatened and did not know what to do.

The next day, July 31, word reached Point of Rocks that the battle of
the Crater was an irreversible Union disaster. Further details were not
long in coming. The explosion of the mine had left a huge hole in the
rebel line 30 feet deep, 60 feet wide, and 178 feet long. Into this smoking pit, filled with huge chunks of clay, broken carriages, and pieces of
timber, charged two white divisions and Edward Ferraro's all-black
Fourth Division. No one had thought to supply them with ladders, and
a Union observer reported that the units piling into the crater "melted
away into a mass of human beings clinging by toes and heels to the
almost perpendicular sides." The rebels opened an annihilating fire on
the trapped Federals, raking the hole with musketry and lobbing lethal
mortar shells on top of them. Before it was over, 504 Yankees lay dead,
with 1,881 wounded and 1,413 missing. A third of the losses was suffered by Ferraro's black troops, many of whom had fought to the death,
knowing that the rebels would show them no quarter. In fact, the
rebels shot blacks when they tried to surrender. To exacerbate matters,
Lee refused a truce that day, and the wounded lay under the blazing
sun without food, water, or medical aid.

Lee did consent to a truce the next day, July 31, and ambulance and
burial parties filed out to the battlefield. Among the wounded brought
back that day was Lieutenant George Barton, who had fallen when a
piece of shell glanced off the side of his head. On August 1, a visitor to
Point of Rocks told Clara about other Bay State casualties: Colonel
Jacob Gould lost a leg, Captain William H. Clark was wounded,
Sergeant Horace Gardner was killed . . . Clara turned away, too distressed to hear more, for Horace Gardner was one of her dearest comrades. She had first met him in the old infirmary in Washington in
April 1861, after he had been wounded in the Baltimore riot. Once he
recovered, he called on her at her apartment, and she thought him
such a "handsome," "splendid" young man. When the Sixth
Massachusetts mustered out of service, he joined the Twenty-first
Massachusetts, was wounded again, and was sent back to Washington,
where Clara found him, lonely and frightened. "He had no friends, no
relatives," she remembered. "He seemed to cling to me as he would a
sister or brother." The last time she saw him he was on his way to
Kentucky and Tennessee with Burnside. She heard that he'd met and
married a young schoolteacher in Kentucky and brought her back with
him when the corps returned to the East. He had survived the
Wilderness, Spotsylvania, Cold Harbor, and the June assaults on

Petersburg. But now Horace was dead, and Clara grieved for him as if he were her blood brother.

Later that day of August 1, Clara went to City Point to visit Captain Clark and the other Massachusetts wounded. That night she and a party of nurses and a cavalryman decided to visit the Crater and set out on horseback during a rainstorm. "It was a fearful night and late," Clara recalled. "The thunder was terrific and the lightning fearful. When the lightning came we were able to distinguish one another and see where we were going." The racket and pelting rain so frightened the horses that they refused to go on, and the party had to sit them until the storm cleared at daybreak. When they finally reached the battlefield, Clara dismounted and stood on the edge of a gaping wound in the earth. Burial parties were still at work, and she saw a great many corpses in the crater. They were infested with flies and maggots—the stench was overpowering—and so blackened and bloated that Negroes and whites could be distinguished only by their hair.

"All that I feared so long have transpired," Clara wrote in her diary on August 3. She no longer felt "free" or "at home" at Point of Rocks and complained that "things combine to grieve me." What grieved her was Ada Smith. Young and spirited, Ada had plainly caught the attention of the men at Point of Rocks, and Clara was jealous and hurt. "Miss Smith is taking special care of her officers," Clara noted with palpable sarcasm. "I hear but dare not say much." To make matters worse, Ada treated Clara as if she were a dolt and even complained to the medical officers about her. "I saw very little of her work," Ada later huffed, "but her extreme deliberation, when one day I had run to her quite breathless from the operating tent for bandages, etc., for the surgeons who were waiting, was very irritating. She asked about my health, urged me to take a seat, and very slowly rummaged about for the necessary supplies. The only time I saw her actively engaged was on a day when there had been a skirmish at the front, and she started for the field with the ambulance and an orderly, and a small box of bandages, condensed milk, etc."

In a few days, Sarah Edson arrived from New York and informed Ada that the Masonic Mission had made an error in sending her to Point of Rocks to replace Clara Barton. The mission, Sarah admitted, had acted "quite without authority" in doing so. Before she left, Mrs. Edson advised that Ada move to the Masonic Mission headquarters at

Depot Hospital near City Point. To Clara's consternation, however, Ada remained right where she was, as obnoxious as ever. "Cramped & unhappy," Clara confided in her diary. "Miss old Uncle Don. . . . Miss S still domineering. Still regret Mrs. Edson's visit and do not believe in missions." The next day, Ada sat down on the porch of a tent and proceeded to criticize Clara in front of a group of surgeons. "I both saw and heard her," Clara fumed in her diary. She was so offended that she went straight to Dr. Porter and told him she was leaving Point of Rocks "at once." Dr. Porter, however, "vetoed" the idea. He asked her "some pertinent questions" about her conflict with Ada, and Clara obviously did not mince her words. Dr. Porter left her with the impression that she would "find less objectional society." "Certainly," Clara added, "one of us will leave."

A short while later, Ada Smith left. That disposed of Clara's chief rival, but the other mission nurses remained at Point of Rocks, and additional female volunteers came there as well.

In mid-August, Clara received a note from Colonel Alvin C. Voris, commander of the Sixty-seventh Ohio, the same Colonel Voris she had found bleeding and unconscious after the disastrous assaults on Battery Wagner. He had not forgotten that Clara had bandaged his wound and sent the stretcher-bearers to fetch him, and he considered her his "dear friend." He reported that his regiment, which was in the First Brigade of Terry's First Division, Tenth Corps, was pulling out for "the Lord only knows where." What he said next warmed Clara's heart:

> If fortune should bring you into the vicinity of my regt. I hope you will take the pains to find us out. I shall take pleasure in aiding you and your good work and shall take no less pleasure in aiding you personally.
> I admit to being somewhat selfish in this for if it should be my misfortune to be disabled in the field I shall be ever so glad to have some kind angel of mercy to look after me.

As it turned out, the Tenth Corps took part in a Union expedition against the Richmond defenses near Deep Bottom, situated on the northern tip of a loop in the James across from Bermuda Hundred. Under orders from Grant, the Tenth Corps and Hancock's Second

Corps of the Potomac Army launched attacks against the rebel line, but ultimately they accomplished nothing. On August 20, after suffering almost 3,000 casualties, many of them to the terrible heat, the Tenth Corps fell back to Bermuda Hundred, and the Second Corps returned to the Petersburg front. Hospital transports evacuated the wounded from a landing on the James opposite Jones Neck and carried them to Depot Hospital near City Point.

The war was going better for Grant on the Petersburg front, where the Fifth Corps and two detachments of Kautz's cavalry division captured a segment of the Weldon Railroad near Globe Tavern; the railroad was Lee's crucial supply line down to the blockade-running port of Wilmington, North Carolina. The "little" Twenty-first Massachusetts fought in the Weldon Railroad battle, Clara learned, but its numbers were so reduced by hard campaigning that it was consolidated into a battalion of three companies. Clara tried to keep apprised of the whereabouts of "the dear old regiment" and yet regretted that she knew so few of its new men and officers. "I am a stranger to them now, I know, after all their changes," she wrote Annie Childs. "Few of them ever heard of me, and yet even mention of the number calls up all the love and pride I ever had. I would divide the last half of my last loaf, with any soldier in that regiment, tho I had never met him."

By now, Clara was functioning as unofficial matron of the Tenth Corps Hospital—unofficial because she had no government appointment and received no pay. Even so, with the unequivocal backing of Dr. Porter, she felt more secure against other women trying to usurp her hard-won authority. As volunteer matron, she not only had charge of the soldier and female nurses and the black female assistants but supervised the hospital's diet kitchen and appointed a chief cook and an assistant cook as well. Her "sick family" now numbered 1,200 men, including 500 additional patients recently transferred to Point of Rocks from another hospital.

In late August, an order came for the Tenth Corps Hospital to change places with the Eighteenth Corps Hospital, situated at Broadway Landing on the south side of the Appomattox. The move meant transporting the 1,200 patients and all the tents and equipment by ambulance and wagon. As luck would have it, the chief cook—an elderly gentleman—and his assistant both came down sick the very morning the hospital was to leave Point of Rocks. "It was all the surgeons stewards & clerks could do to keep the names [of the patients] straight," Clara wrote cousin Fannie, "and would you believe it I stepped into the gap and assumed the responsibility of the kitchen and feeding of over 1200." She baked all the gingerbread and puddings she could and then accompanied the long ambulance and wagon train as it rolled a half-mile downriver and crossed a pontoon bridge to Broadway Landing, situated on the south side of the river a little more than a mile west of City Point and about four miles from the northern end of the Union trenches before Petersburg.

Once the Tenth Corps hospital tents were in place and the patients in their proper wards, Clara saw to the feeding of the entire hospital population, which was a staggering undertaking. For breakfast alone, she and her helpers baked 700 loaves of bread (obviously she had more than one stove now), made 170 gallons of hot coffee and two large "wash-boilers" of tea, and cooked a barrel full of sliced pork and thirty hams. For dinner, they served more than 200 gallons of soup made with three barrels of potatoes, two barrels of turnips, two barrels of onions, and two barrels of squash; they also served a wash-boiler full of whiskey sauce for 100 gallons of minute pudding and 150 gallons of "nice home codfish" made by cooking the fish in a batter in a large washtub. Her charges were nothing if not well fed. Supper called for 200 gallons of rice with sauce, 200 gallons of tea, and "toast for a thousand." Clara her-self made 90 apple pies, a dessert that was her specialty.

At length, as she wrote Fannie, she appointed "a new Boss cook and got him regularly installed and then helped him all the time." "Oh what a volume it would make if I could only write you what I have seen, known, heard, done since I first came to this Dept. . . . The most surprising of all of which is (tell Sally) that I should have *turned cook*. Who would have 'thunk it'?"

Clara's sleeping tent had a dirt floor, a narrow straw bed, and a three-legged stand fashioned out of cracker boxes, on which she wrote letters. Beyond her tent, to the south and southwest, lay a lunarscape, denuded, shell torn, and scarred with irregular trenches stretching toward the horizon. The rebel works formed a defensive perimeter around the eastern side of Petersburg, and between them and the Yankee lines was a no-man's-land "bristling with tangles of abatis and sinister sharpened stakes," as one writer described it. At night, the front glowed red from one end to the other, as the two armies contin-ued to bombard one another with mortars and field artillery.

One damp night shortly after the hospital had relocated, forty wounded men arrived from the front, "one with the shoulder gone," Clara said, "a number of legs off[;] one with both arms gone, some blown up with shell & terribly burned, some in the breast." At the request of the surgeons, Clara made eggnog seasoned with brandy and served it to the forty men to help them sleep. One "little fellow" from the Eleventh Maine lay dying, his groans echoing throughout the camp.

A "noble Swiss boy," who was brought to her that night, appeared to be dying from a frightful wound in the right shoulder. Speaking in broken English, he gave his name as Jules Golay, said he would not live until morning, and made Clara promise to stay at his side until he died. She ministered to him in her loving way, urging him to hang on to his life, to hang on to her; she wouldn't let him die. His suffering caught the attention of the surgeons, too, who did everything they could for him medically. They sutured and bandaged his wound, applied an unsanitized cold water sponge to it, and gave him morphine to ease his pain, perhaps rubbing or injecting morphine sulfate directly into the injury. He did recover in the end, but he could scarcely move his right arm and hand.

Jules had no doubt who had saved his life. "I would have died had it not been for you," he told Clara, as he lay "weak and frail in his little army couch." He explained with great effort, searching for the right words, that he was the youngest son of one of the oldest judges of the Geneva Supreme Court. He had been educated in the finest schools in Germany and France, and Clara thought him "a perfect master of French, German and Italian languages." Without telling his father, he had left for America to enlist in the Union army. "All Republicans should fight when a Republic is in danger," he said.

Clara loved this bright, refined young man and was grateful to him for what he had done "and suffered" for her country. She called him "my Swiss boy" and worried about him when he said that his mangled arm might prevent him from ever holding a job. It made her sad that he had no family in America, but Jules himself rectified that, asking her one day if he could be her "younger brother." This touched Clara more deeply than Jules could have known, for Clara, the baby of her family, the tot of the Barton farm, had never been an older sister. Why not? she said of his offer. "The place has been always vacant." But she warned him, with a gleam in her eye, that he must always obey her.

So Clara became Jules Golay's "American older sister," his "Dear sister Clara." Later, when she received an affectionate letter from his real sister, Eliza, Clara responded at great length, trying to convey some sense of the war. "It would be impossible for me to give you any adequate idea of the vastness and terribleness of our great national struggle—so much space—so many armies—such countless battle

fields—such painful marches—and such terrible conflicts, and it is my
pride and joy that my countrymen have been found equal to the sacrifice." As for Jules, he had "fought bravely and well," and she had
agreed to be his American sister; "but when I promised that I did not
realize how much I was to be the gainer, that not only had I found a
brother but a lovely and loving sister. You my dear sister, I do love you
and I will always love you."

When Jules was well enough, he was transferred to a convalescent
hospital in another sector. He wrote Clara that his arm was better, but
his hand was so stiff and sore that he could hardly write. "With my
books I learn many words, but I do not [make] any progress for the
prononciation." On his own, he taught himself what he could of the
language of his "new country," and he thought a great deal about his
future and what work he might be able to do. He promised, "I shall do
nothing without the advice of my dear sister. . . . I shall write my
farewell with my right hand and pray my sister to accept the true love
of her younger brother."

By mid-September, there were two Tenth Corps hospitals: the "base"
or main convalescent hospital at Broadway Landing and a "flying" hospital located three miles farther up on Bermuda Hundred, "in the rear
of the front line of works," as Clara described it. The flying hospital
was so named because it was peripatetic; in the event of an attack or a
change of position on the part of the Tenth Corps, it could move at an
hour's notice in order to remain as close to the troops as possible. The
sick and wounded first went to the flying hospital for treatment. Those
requiring convalescence were transported back to the base hospital,
where Clara stored the supplies from her support groups in the North,
to whom she sent appeals for winter clothing and blankets. This new
hospital organization signaled the willingness of the Army of the James
to adapt its field hospitals to the demands of thrust-and-parry warfare
along a more or less fixed line.

The "most skillful operators," Clara said, were stationed at the flying
hospital, and all were her personal friends. She specifically mentioned
a Dr. Barlow, with whom she had worked at Cedar Mountain, Second
Bull Run, and Morris Island. Evidently Clara divided her time
between the two facilities and relished the double responsibility and
the sense of power that came with it. "*You* know that my range here is
very extended," she wrote Annie; "this department is large, and I am

invited by General Butler to visit every part of it, and all medical and other officers within the department are directed to afford me every facility in their power." She had "stood by" Dr. Porter all summer, both at Point of Rocks and at Broadway Landing, and he agreed to share her some with the upper hospital but insisted that she must not leave the base hospital "on any condition." By now, her reputation had spread to City Point too. The surgeon in charge of one of Grant's largest corps called on Clara and invited her to help him run his hospital. "I begin to think I can 'keep a hotel,' " she wrote Annie in triumph, "but I didn't think so a year ago."

At the base hospital, she now lived in a former slave cabin with one room on the bottom floor, another room above, and a tent across the front. The little house was filthy when they first came to the Landing, but ten men with brooms and water cleaned it up and moved Clara in one night when she was ill, from some disease she perhaps had contracted from her patients. It was the rainy season, she wrote Annie Childs, "and here I have lain and the winds have blown and the rains descended and beat upon my house . . . and for hours in the dark night I have listened to the guy ropes snapping and the tent flies flapping in the wind and rain, and thunder and lightning."

One stormy night, as Clara made her rounds at the base hospital, she found lying at the end of a dark tent "a darling little Massachusetts boy, sick of fever and chronic diarrhea, a mere skeleton." As she told Annie, he was such a "delicate little fellow, about fifteen," that "I couldn't withstand the desire to shield him, and sent through the storm and had him brought, bed and all, and stored in my lower room, and there he lay like a little kitten, so happy, till about noon the next day, when his father, one of the wealthy merchants of Suffolk, came for him." Clara was startled when the boy introduced her to him. "Father," he said, "this is *my* Auntie; doesnt she look like mother?" At that the father started to cry. "It was *too much*," Clara said. "Women's and children's tears amount to little, but the convulsive sobs of a strong man are not forgotten in an hour."

A few days later, Ned Barton called on Clara at the Broadway Landing hospital. It was the second time she had seen him since he returned to active duty as sanitary agent with the Fifth Corps. As he no doubt told her, George had recovered from his wound and was back with his regiment on the Petersburg front. Clara took time off from her duties, and they went for a horseback ride across the Appomattox and along a back road on Bermuda Hundred, heading north for the far end of the Bermuda Hundred line, opposite Dutch Gap on the James. When cavalry pickets warned them that they were on the wrong road, they set "off upon a romantic ride through the woods," Ned said later, and came at last to a signal station opposite Dutch Gap, a narrow isthmus formed by a loop in the James River. From the signal station, Clara and Ned could see the Howlett House, which bristled with the guns of an enemy battery, and the whole line of rebel works extending southward down Bermuda Hundred. From what they could gather, the southern exterior line of Richmond's defenses ran from Chaffin's Bluff on the James River northeast to the Charles City Road, a distance of some thirty miles.

As Clara and Ned discovered, Butler's troops were busily digging a canal across Dutch Gap, a project that grew out of the general's inability to break through the strong rebel line in his front and on his right flank. According to a Union engineer, rebel artillery commanded "a wide, shallow part of the James River on the north flank of the contending armies," thus preventing Union monitors from advancing against Richmond by the river. So Butler conceived the idea of digging a canal across Dutch Gap, which would enable the ships to bypass the rebel guns. But constant enemy mortar fire impeded the excavations, forcing the Union diggers, mostly black troops, to take shelter in earthen dugouts covering the canal site. The project was a measure of Butler's frustration, for he was anxious to move against the enemy capital and recoup his military reputation. Because of sundry delays, however, the canal would not be completed until the end of the year.

Ten days after the outing with Ned, Clara was attending to her duties at the base hospital when orders came to move the entire facility up to Jones Neck, a narrow stretch of land in a loop of the James opposite Deep Bottom. The Tenth and Eighteenth corps were on the march, heading for the pontoon bridges at Deep Bottom, possibly to attack Richmond's outer defenses by that route. The base hospital scrambled into action, and by the next day, September 29, all the tents, surgeons, and nurses were relocated at Jones Neck. The flying hospital, meanwhile, was on the move with the troops. Clara took a monitor upriver to Jones Neck and then walked across a desolate meadow to the base hospital, where wounded were already arriving from the front. She could hear the boom of artillery and rattle of musketry in the direction of Richmond, which lay only ten miles to the northwest. In coming to this theater, she had scarcely dreamed that she would find herself stationed so close to the enemy capital itself. "I gave out rations all the pm," she wrote in her diary; "reports of a great battle & that the 10th corps very near Richmond."

At dawn that day, under orders from Grant, Butler had launched a carefully prepared attack against the city's exterior line of fortifications. His infantry forces stormed and captured rebel entrenchments along New Market Heights and seized Fort Harrison. At the same time, Kautz's cavalry division rode to the "very gates" of the rebel capital and fired on it with artillery. The next day, eight rebel infantry brigades tried to recapture Fort Harrison, but Butler's troops drove them off. To the general's great joy, he now held a new Federal line just southeast of Richmond, which extended from Fort Brady on the James east to Fort Harrison, then north across the New Market road, then back toward the southeast, with cavalry guarding the right flank to the Darbytown road. Rebel prisoners and fleeing civilians reported great panic in Richmond, where church bells tolled and provost marshals pressed all available clerks and citizens into military service.

By dusk, September 30, the Jones Neck hospital was full of wounded from Butler's front, where more than 3,000 soldiers had fallen. It "rained very hard at night," Clara scribbled in her diary, "and such firing at Petersburg, I fear the cost." The firing was probably connected to the Peebles Farm fight, in which elements of the Potomac Army, striking Lee's far right flank southeast of Petersburg, captured two redoubts and a line of rifle pits west of the Weldon Railroad and stretched the Federal siege line ever closer to the South Side Railroad, Lee's vital supply link to the interior of the Confederacy. Just as Grant planned, the Federals had given Lee "another shake" by attacking both of his extreme flanks and extending his depleted army farther than ever.

Mid-October found Clara at the flying hospital, near Butler's line on the Richmond front. One day Dr. Martin S. Kittinger visited the hospital, and Clara was delighted to see her "especial friend" from Morris Island days. Still suffering from chronic bronchitis, he was now chief operating surgeon of the Tenth Corps. Clara accompanied him back to the base hospital at Jones Neck, where she got a rude shock: The wife of an army lieutenant had taken possession of Clara's tent. Evidently Dr. Porter could do nothing about it, perhaps because the woman's husband held an official rank and Clara did not. Furious and frustrated, Clara resigned her post at the base hospital and returned to the flying hospital, where she intended to remain. "She is very welcome to my rooms," Clara wrote of "Mrs." Lieutenant, "but not my companionship."

Clara felt far more secure at the flying hospital, because she was evidently the only woman stationed there. In charge of the diet kitchen and the male nurses, she felt "free" and at home. A few days after she settled in, fighting broke out on Butler's new line above the James, and many wounded came back to the flying hospital. It was a dismal, smoky day, Clara remembered; as the stretcher men laid the injured on the ground, she spotted a lieutenant with a bullet wound in his lungs, strangling on his own blood. She sprang to his side, raised him partly up, and then seated herself on a large coil of tent rope so that she could support him upright until a surgeon could tend to him.

She was sitting thus, "with hands and arms bare and bloody to the elbows," as she said later, when an orderly dashed up and handed her a letter, which she tore open with one hand and her teeth. It was from her nephew Samuel, with a letter enclosed from brother Stephen! Addressed to "C.H. Barton, S.R. Barton, or Vester Vassall all of Washington, D.C.," Stephen's letter pleaded for help, saying that he was sick and in a Union prison in occupied Norfolk, Virginia, apparently charged with having illegally traded cotton between the lines. According to his letter, government detectives had arrested him while he was traveling from Elizabeth City in a wagon with some cotton and $3,000 on his person and in his trunk. He reported that he had been authorized to sell cotton within Federal lines and that his business had "prospered beyond all account." In his accompanying letter, Samuel asked Clara to see General Butler in his father's behalf. ("She can talk pretty to the Genl.," Samuel explained to his mother, "and I think can get him released." Samuel added, in reference to his father's trading in cotton: "I am glad if some of us can make something out of the war. But we must figure large to get him clear.")

After the surgeons came for the wounded lieutenant, Clara washed the blood from her arms and hands, fully intending to see Butler about Stephen forthwith. But she postponed her visit when an order came for the flying hospital to move to Aiken's Landing on the James, less than a mile southeast of Fort Brady. The hospital transferred to the new site on October 15, relocating on a swell of land that had once been an impressive plantation. The surgeons and assistant surgeons occupied the mansion, and Clara took possession of an old slave hut for her quarters. Later that day, worried about Stephen's health, she rode to Butler's headquarters in an ambulance. Agitated and busy as always, the general took time to read Stephen's letter, then turned to Clara.

"This is hard," he said. "What can I do for you?"

"My brother is a Union man," Clara began.

"Yes! yes!" Butler cut in. "I understand it all. What shall I do?"

"He is very ill," Clara said. "Allow me to go to him, General."

"Surely!" Butler said. "But can we not do better? he can come here. You have shelter for him?"

"I have an old negro hut with ground floor," Clara said.

Butler rang for his clerk and wrote out a confidential order to the commander at Norfolk, directing that Stephen Barton be sent to Butler's headquarters with copies of the charges against him and an inventory of all his confiscated property.

"Now go and get ready for him," Butler told Clara. "As soon as he comes I will send him to you."

When she returned to Aiken's Landing, Dr. Craven and another surgeon were there "trying to arrange the Medical Corps." Dr. Barlow was transferred and her friend Dr. Kittinger put in charge of the flying hospital. She felt completely secure with Kittinger in command. "I seem to be a fixture here," she rejoiced. Her kitchen consisted of two large, well-furnished tents with wood floors and a huge stove. The floors were crowded with boxes and barrels of supplies brought up by wagons from the base hospital on the river. By now, Clara was skilled in "the art of scientific cooking." Under her supervision, her cooks piled eggs on a long table, struck each one with the edge of a knife to determine its quality, and divided them into four categories: the best eggs were made into omelets, the second best into custards, and the third into cornstarch puddings. The worst were thrown away.

The hospital wards were now housed in five stockades, each fifty feet long and covered with canvas, with the wards organized by military divisions. As Clara noted, the hospital was just six miles or so from "the entrenchments of Richmond." To the northeast of the hospital, from five to sixteen miles away, were the battlegrounds of Malvern Hill, White Oak Swamp, and Cold Harbor, "names that I would ever breathe with all gentleness and reverence," she said later, "for fall where they may, in our broad ever scathed land, they have a knell for some loving ear, a probe for some aching heart, a shadow for some desolate home."

In preparation for Stephen's arrival, Clara's male assistants renovated her one-room slave cabin, a crude little log dwelling without a floor or windows, which stood on the hospital grounds. Going to work with hammers and saws, the men installed windows and a wooden floor, carpeted it with blankets, added a chimney, knocked together a flight of stairs, and built a loft to serve as Stephen's bedroom. They papered the walls with newspapers and furnished the place with a lounge, a straw bunk on each floor, two tables, a stuffed rocking chair, a wood box, and an oilcloth hearth rug before the fireplace.

When two days passed with no sign of Stephen, Clara was afraid that her fifty-eight-year-old brother might have died in that prison in Norfolk. Three days later, on October 20, as she sat before a fire in her cabin, the door opened, and Dr. Kittinger stepped inside. "Don't be disturbed," he said, "we bring you some one." He moved aside, and there stood her dear brother, leaning on a cane. His appearance shocked her. When she had last seen him, six years before, he weighed 220 pounds and was "strong, muscular, erect," with iron-gray hair. Now he was pale, bent, and emaciated—he couldn't have weighed 130 pounds—with thin, white hair hanging to his shoulders. He limped to her with his cane, and they embraced. She was so glad and relieved to see him, she said. She had been so worried about him.

Stephen was extremely ill with malaria and chronic diarrhea, so much so that he had to be helped upstairs to his straw bunk. Dr. Kittinger took personal charge of his case and started him on quinine for the malaria. The standard treatment for "chronic fluxes" called for morning doses of castor oil or Epsom salts and an evening dose of paregoric or tincture of opium. Unable to talk much or sit up at all, Stephen shook with fever and chills and raised a great deal of phlegm when he coughed; his feet and ankles were swollen, and he was pale and languid. According to Clara, he could not digest any food; the only nourishment he could take was a mixture of wine and water and sips of "good French and madira Brandy." He was "in every way in critical condition," she wrote Sammy; "it seems impossible to control his diarrhea and restore his health." She added, somewhat defensively, that she was trying to make Stephen as comfortable as her "limited facilities" permitted. The family could not expect her to furnish "all the luxuries of a city in the point of an army four miles from Richmond constantly moving and continually fortifying." Stephen himself had no complaints, writing David that Clara was a devoted nurse who gave him "every attention. . . . that is possible for mortal to receive."

As Clara fussed over him, Stephen pointed out that his malaria could not have been treated in impoverished eastern North Carolina. He thought it "providential" that he had left, was sure that "the hand of Divine Mercy" had compelled him to pass through the lines so that ultimately he could be sent to his "dear sister" for nursing and treatment. He was, he said, "very happy in the reflection" and could not feel discontented for a second. "When I awake from my slumbers," he told David, "I imagine that I have been dreaming and it is some minutes before I can realize with certainty that I am here with Clara."

On October 27, Butler's army went into action again along the Richmond line, and the flying hospital moved with the troops, bringing all its patients along. It was one of Stephen's "sickest days," Clara wrote Sammy; "he had a chill and did not realize much about it" as the stretcher-bearers carried him to the new hospital site. Yet Stephen wrote his wife that he could distinctly hear volleys of small arms and the shouts of soldiers and that it was an "obstinate engagement." As it turned out, the battle was a reversal for Butler's ill-starred Army of the James. Hoping to seize Richmond on the very eve of the presidential election, Butler had exceeded his orders from Grant ("you are not to attack entrenched and defended lines") and allowed his forces to assault the enemy works. The rebels hurled the Federals back with blasts of grape and canister, killing, wounding, or capturing more than 1,600 of Butler's men. With that, the Army of the James and its flying hospital fell back to the lines they had left. Meanwhile, on the Petersburg front, a Federal advance against the South Side Railroad fared little better, thus ending active campaigning for the winter.

Clara was inundated with wounded from the Richmond front and spent long hours nursing the badly injured and giving directions for the care of the sick. Butler himself later claimed that he saw Clara with her "beautiful arms red with human blood to the shoulders." Although Stephen praised her for doing so much to relieve her patients, Clara was not satisfied. "I leave *so much* undone," she complained to Elvira; "night comes, and I chide me that I have done so little and morning returns and I feel that I should not have spent so many hours in sleep when so many about me perhaps could not sleep at all,—but one thing I am certain of. I have labored up to the full measure of my strength all summer."

There were times, she confessed, when she could not bear the killing and mangling of so many young men. She saw no end to the war but believed that God had His own designs in letting it continue. "I do not bother my poor head about the end but plod on day by day, trying to perform my round of duty faithfully. . . . We are only laborers, the Great Master who laid out the work will say when it is finished."

By now, Clara's reputation as a battlefield nurse and "the soldiers' friend" had spread far and wide on the Richmond-Petersburg line. Stephen wrote his wife that "no day since I have been here that I have not been introduced to officers, many of them high in rank, who call to pay their respects to Clara, not a few of them having received her care and attention when wounded, and on the field of battle."

*   *   *

When Stephen was strong enough to talk and when Clara's duties permitted, he broached the subject of his imprisonment, assuring her that
he had done nothing wrong, that he was and had always been "an open
Union man, and not only that but a Republican." Then he told her his
story, an extraordinary tale of the trials and exploits of a Yankee businessman in rebel territory.

After the war began, Stephen said, he went to the rebel authorities
and told them that he had to remain at Bartonsville on account of his
asthmatic condition (he was also afraid that if he left, his estate and
everything on it would be seized). They agreed that he could stay
there, on the condition that he promise not to pass intelligence to the
Union bases in eastern North Carolina. He gave his promise. After the
Union capture of Roanoke Island in 1862, Union gunboats patrolling
the Chowan River often stopped at Bartonsville, which was situated on
the west bank in Hertford County, and Stephen went on board to dine
with the officers and converse about the war. This much Clara knew
from the naval officers she had talked to on Hilton Head.

By mid-1863, the Union controlled the area east of the Chowan
River, which included Elizabeth City and South Mills, and the rebels
held the territory west of it, with a Georgia cavalry regiment under
Colonel Joel R. Griffin manning the rebels' Chowan River line.
Finding himself in a precarious position in between the two lines,
Stephen assumed "a neutral position," he said, and both armies
respected his neutrality.

But some of his neighbors, those who energetically supported the
rebel cause, despised this Yankee in their midst and threatened to
"burn him out." Twice Griffin's subordinates arrested him, and Griffin
himself came to have a talk. Thinking Stephen an honest man and a
gentleman, the colonel stationed rebel troops at Bartonsville for
Stephen's own protection. But he forbade Stephen to have any further
communication with Union gunboats, which explained why Clara had
heard nothing more from him after the summer of 1863.

By then, the families of rebel soldiers living in the neighborhood
suffered terribly from hunger: the pay of a rebel private, fixed at eleven
dollars a month at a time of runaway inflation in the Confederacy,
would not feed a soldier's family more than a few days. Stephen
claimed that some of his "conservative" neighbors, Unionists who
opposed secession and were not responsible for "the mischief of this
war," were the "first, and only, men" to offer the starving families

"material aid." Since the men had large quantities of baled cotton on hand, they came to Stephen with a plan. Why not secure permission from the rival military authorities to trade the cotton within Union lines? Some of the cotton could be exchanged for Northern flour and corn, which could then be given "gratuitously" to the famished families. The rest could be sold to Yankee traders for profit.

By 1864, such trading between the lines had become a regular feature of the war. While both the Union and the Confederacy officially banned trading with the enemy, the two governments allowed it to go on for practical reasons: the hungry Southerners needed the food offered by Yankee traders, and the Northern textile industry was desperate for Southern cotton. In an effort to regulate trade in occupied rebel territory, Lincoln's Treasury Department issued trading permits to Yankee merchants and Southern planters in occupied Dixie who took an oath of allegiance. The permit system, however, opened the way for a booming illegal trade, as hordes of war profiteers flocked to occupied Dixie in search of easy money. Some bought permits on the streets of New York City. Others bribed treasury agents and soldiers alike to turn their backs while they traded for rebel cotton and sold it in the North for as much as two dollars per pound. In 1863 and early 1864, the Federal government took steps to end the illicit cotton trade, directing Federal authorities to seize all rebel cotton and issuing stricter regulations for the purchase of cotton from Southerners who had taken the oath of allegiance. The illegal trade, however, continued unabated because the Lincoln administration made no real effort to suppress it. The president thought it better for Northerners to buy rebel cotton than for rebels to sell it abroad through the blockade.

Thus, when Stephen's Unionist neighbors proposed that they capitalize on the cotton trade, Stephen thought it a compelling idea. With the tacit consent of both belligerents, he sought out Yankee agents in occupied North Carolina and traded them cotton and tobacco for corn, flour, and lard. Many of the traders came down from occupied Norfolk, a hub of the commerce between the lines, apparently armed with Treasury Department permits or letters from Lincoln allowing them to operate as long as the army considered it harmless.

Stephen admitted to David and Clara that his activities "may appear strange," but there was a good explanation for them. "All livables," he said, were scarce and too expensive for most of his neighbors. "They had much cotton which they had no use for which the Federals wanted so I was tacitly encouraged in the operation by all." He insisted that his baled cotton "was sold on Government account" and that he had "never been able to obtain any more than half the Northern market price for any cotton." Even so, he conceded that his records indicated "much profit" (in fact, in March 1864 alone, a Petersburg firm had paid him a total of $330,000 for what must have been a large quantity of cotton). The money, however, was inflated Confederate paper currency, which, as Stephen pointed out, "greatly reduced" his actual profit, which was true. In January 1864, a Confederate paper dollar was worth about four and a half cents in gold; thus, the Petersburg firm paid Stephen the equivalent of about $14,850 in gold. Stephen's profit was further reduced by "the interest which the Federal Government claimed" on all the cotton he sold. In a year, he said, "I think I have moved near or quite 100 bales of cotton to the lower counties which was all that was baled." Most of the cotton, he believed, "found its way to the Northern markets."

When Stephen and his neighbors ran out of baled cotton, they faced a dilemma: They had a lot of loose, raw cotton on their homesteads but couldn't bale it for lack of cloth binding. At this point, Stephen struck a deal with William A. Harney of Norfolk, who held a Union permit to trade goods out of South Mills, North Carolina, which was situated northeast of Bartonsville and about halfway between Elizabeth City, North Carolina, and Norfolk. Harney agreed to give Stephen cloth and money in return for Stephen's unbaled cotton. The first time Stephen took cotton to South Mills, Harney wasn't there. When Stephen returned a second time, he learned that Union officers had arrested Harney "for alleged abuse of his trading permit." Harney's agent, however, took Stephen's cotton, gave him $2,000 in Southern paper money and a note for $600, and promised to acquire cloth for him and his neighbors if he would bring another load of raw cotton.

A day after Stephen returned to Bartonsville, three Union gunboats steamed up to his wharf. The officers said they wanted to "buy cotton," having heard from a rebel deserter that there were "great quantities" of it in the Bartonsville area. Stephen replied that that was so, but that it was almost entirely loose, unbaled cotton and couldn't be moved in that condition. When the Union officers asserted that they would "pay a fairer price for it," Stephen agreed to procure some cloth, bale a quantity of local cotton, and send it down to Albemarle Sound, where the Union gunboats could pick it up.

"They took me at my word and left," Stephen said in a letter to David. "My anxiety was now much increased to procure the cloth." To complicate matters, he was suffering from fever and chronic diarrhea, which left him weak and miserable. Even so, he was determined to get the cotton bagging at South Mills and consummate his agreement with the Union officers. In early September 1864, he set out for South Mills lying in the bed of a four-mule wagon. In it were two bales of cotton, which he apparently intended to trade, and a trunk containing Harney's $600 note and some $2,300 in North Carolina bank money, which could not have been worth much in gold. With him was a seventeen-year-old black teamster and an ex-rebel soldier named James Fulford, "who seeing the error of his ways, repented, and was willing to take the oath, and come under our flag again," as Stephen explained it.

Near Elizabeth City, Federal cavalry overtook them in a cloud of dust. In command was a Lieutenant Budd, who explained that he and his men, assisted by government detective I. B. Hutchens, were searching for witnesses to testify against Harney, whose trial was coming up at Fort Monroe. Budd's eye fell suspiciously on the cotton in Stephen's wagon.

"Where are you going with that?" he asked from his horse.

Stephen explained that he hoped to trade it to Harney's agent for baling cloth.

"Have you ever sold cotton to Harney?" Budd demanded.

"I carried cotton to him twice before expecting each time to get the bagging, but always failed," Stephen said.

"But you did get money for it," Budd said.

"Yes, old N.C. money and a note."

"Show it," Budd demanded.

When Stephen produced the money from his trunk, Budd grabbed it, saying that it wasn't safe for Stephen to be carrying so much money and that he, Budd, would hold it for him.

"Can I have a receipt?" Stephen asked.

"There's no time for that," Budd said. Then he ordered a sergeant to confiscate the rest of Stephen's property; the sergeant even took twenty to twenty-five dollars in coveted Union "greenbacks," or treasury notes, Stephen was carrying in his pocket. Worse still, detective Hutchens announced that it was "their duty" to take him to Norfolk as a witness in Harney's trial. When Stephen protested, Budd became "rough and abusive," threatening him with violence if he did not come with them. Stephen agreed to do as he was told.

When they reached Norfolk, Budd took Stephen to the adjutant general's office, where a Captain Thornton interrogated him about his "past history and present business." Stephen insisted that he had always been "true, and loyal to the federal government" and demanded to be treated as such "until some evidence could be produced to the contrary." Budd whispered something to Thornton, and the captain sent Stephen to Colonel H. Sanders, the provost marshal, who promptly locked Stephen in the guardhouse and confiscated his team, wagon, trunk, and blankets. "I was compelled to lay on the naked floor," Stephen remembered, "being denied the use of my own bunk and the medicine that was in my trunk, prescribed by the doctor for my disease." He could not believe that Federal officers would treat him so cruelly. Later he heard that one of them had called him "a notorious rebel."

The next morning, Budd came to take Stephen before the provost marshal. On the way, the lieutenant advised Stephen, "as a friend," to admit that he was "a blockade runner." Stephen was astounded. "I told him that I *would deny it to any body in all places and on all occasions* and that it was a *wicked* and *cruel calumny* for him or any other person to accuse me of such a crime." Budd left him at Sanders's office, and Stephen told the provost marshal what Budd had advised him to say. Why would he give you such advice? Sanders asked. Stephen said he didn't know, unless he was "calculating" to accuse him of blockade running. After questioning him at length about his business papers and his ex-rebel companion, the provost marshal produced a sealed package and said it contained about $1,400 in Southern money that Budd and his men had taken from Stephen.

"They took much more than that," Stephen exclaimed.

This was all he had received, Sanders said. When Stephen asked Sanders "to admit" him to bail, the provost marshal sent him to Brigadier General George Foster Shepley, the commander at Norfolk and a political crony of General Butler. Shepley asked if Fulford, the ex-rebel soldier, was an enemy agent; without waiting for an answer, he summoned a guard to take Stephen away.

The soldier threw Stephen back into the guardhouse, where Fulford and Stephen's young black teamster were also confined. The guards had seized the black man's shoes and coat and were extremely abusive to all three prisoners. To make matters worse, the window panes had been removed from the guardhouse, which "left us much to the misery of the winter and storms," Stephen said later. The guards did not care that Stephen's diarrhea was so severe that he could not control himself.

Later, he saw a notice in a newspaper that described his arrest. Reprinted from the *New York Herald*, the story reported that Union troops had captured, "a blockade runner" with "a Confederate agent" at Elizabeth City, North Carolina. The "blockade runner" had a four-mule team and "a rebel wagon with two bales of cotton, and $3,000 in N.C. Bank money all of which they confiscated." It was clear to Stephen that Budd and Hutchens were the *Herald's* "sources" and that they were spreading the lie about his being a blockade runner in order to justify their actions, particularly their pocketing the rest of his money. "Those wicked men," he said, "wanted to show to the public that they had incurred great risks and were entitled to much credit for invading those Rebel counties and bringing out this property." But how could Stephen convince the Norfolk authorities that Budd and Hutchens were lying about him?

He took heart when he learned that the Federal gunboat *Massasoit* was in dock at Norfolk. The *Massasoit* was one of the boats that had visited Bartonsville, and Stephen recalled the captain well. At once, Stephen wrote a note to Provost Marshal Sanders asking permission to see the captain and get "a certificate that would confirm my statement and establish my loyalty in their estimation." But the lieutenant of the guards refused to take the note to Sanders.

"Humanity and justice demand that I have a chance to prove my innocence and loyalty," Stephen cried.

"There is nothing that the Captain of the boat could say that would do you any good," the lieutenant replied.

And so Stephen languished in the guardhouse. The provost marshal refused to let him buy medicine for his diarrhea, which grew worse. He begged the guards to take him to the hospital, but they ignored him. "I despaired of ever getting a fair trial, if I lived long enough to get any," he said later. In desperation, he wrote frantic appeals to Clara and Samuel and to other "friends in Washington." He also sent a letter to General Butler, who, he claimed, had long been his "political friend."

One day, detective Hutchens stopped by the guardhouse and advised Stephen to see the provost marshal and "don't go to lying but tell the truth." Raising his cane overhead, Stephen exploded: "You damned impudent scoundrel! I enjoy a better character for truth and veracity than you ever did." Hutchens leaped back, crying, "I have done with you forever." "It was well for him he had," Stephen recalled, "unless he wanted his damned head broke."

At last came the order from Butler directing that Stephen be released and sent to the general's headquarters. On his way to the wharf, Stephen saw Hutchens approaching. "Old man," the detective said, "I have been making inquiries about you, and know all that you have done since the commencement of the war, and I don't care how many Brothers, Sons, Sisters and Daughters you have in the Army. They all cant save you."

A gentleman came up to Stephen and inquired about his departure for General Butler's headquarters. According to Stephen, Hutchens overheard the reference to Butler, and his manner changed instantly "from the defiant and insolent to the affable and friendly." He even offered to have Stephen's "property" ready for him when he returned.

The trip to Butler's headquarters "quite exhausted me," Stephen said. The general promised to examine the case personally. But seeing that Stephen was too sick for an interview, Butler accepted Stephen's "parole of honor" and sent him off to Clara in the general's personal carriage. Butler told Stephen to come back when he was well, and they would talk then about his arrest and imprisonment.

That was the story Stephen told Clara. When she thought it over, she was "pretty certain" that he had been dealt with unjustly, even dishonestly. Yet "I was *slow* to give expression to any such suspicion," she wrote Judge Ira Barton a few weeks later, "willing and anxious as I always have been to strengthen the hands of my government in any effort to suppress the growth and strength of our enemies. This sense of almost blind loyalty has entered into and biased every investigation I have made . . . of the course with Stephen, still I cannot to save my life make that course look right, straightforward and honest."

Indeed, the more she thought about the case, the more upset she became. Her poor brother had languished eighteen days in "a common filthy guard house, lying on bare floor without covering, means of cleanliness, proper food or medicine of any kind and all this for a man only professedly held 'as a witness.' " She tried to be charitable, tried to believe that it was "love of country alone" that had impelled "these young officers" to adopt such cruel measures toward her brother. But here were the facts: Stephen "was to all appearance an old man—weak and sick, failing every day, and in case he should die in their hands it was doubtful if any successful claimant would appear for the moneys taken from him" or for the team and cotton, worth $3,500 to $4,000, she reckoned. If their object was to keep all this, they did it "skillfully." Three more weeks in jail and Stephen would have been dead. "Genl Butler's prompt and humane order," Clara wrote Judge Barton, "called him from the jaws of death."

At the same time, she was convinced that Stephen had done nothing wrong and that he really was a patriot. "I need not tell you that your father is one of the strongest Union men you ever saw," she wrote Sammy, "that he is an unconditional Administration man, a Republican, and prays for the election of Pres. Lincoln, says that McClellan must not be elected for the South are building their whole hopes upon that issue. I was astonished, but he seems to have thought out his own conclusion alone by himself. When the guns are heaviest he tells me they are hammering off the shackles from both black and white. He prays for the fall of Richmond & that the Union may be restored."

Stephen's support for Lincoln was genuine. Indeed, he applauded the president's vow to fight the war through to an unconditional Union victory and an end to slavery. As far as the approaching election was concerned, Stephen was right when he said that a great many rebels were pinning all their hopes on George McClellan, the Democratic nominee; they believed that the Democrats would stop the war and invite the seceded states to return to the Union with slavery guaranteed and that the ensuing negotiations would result in Southern victory. But Lincoln's reelection seemed increasingly probable, thanks to recent military developments: Sherman had captured Atlanta, queen city of the Deep South, and Sheridan had destroyed Early's rebel force in the Shenandoah Valley.

Election day, November 8, brought inclement weather to the Richmond front. The skies were overcast, and a mist drifted over the trenches and the flying hospital where Clara worked. When the news reached the Army of the James that Lincoln had won, the soldiers cheered and bands played. Indeed, the soldiers in the Union army had voted for Lincoln by a margin of four to one. As the Yankees celebrated, the rebels on the siege lines fell into despair. "Don't you know that Abe Lincoln is reelected and has called for a million men," one rebel said to another, "and that Jeff Davis says war to the knife?"

According to Clara, Stephen wept with happiness at the news of Lincoln's reelection. Clara, for her part, saw the hand of Providence at work in that salutary event. Earlier that year she had doubted that any one man "could be constituted who should be equal to both the beginning and ending of this vast, this mighty change," but perhaps she had been wrong to doubt the tall and haunted man in the White House. Perhaps he *was* equal to the mighty changes wrought by the war—was the right ruler to see it through to a total Union victory and a triumph of freedom and popular government.

*   *   *

When and if his health returned, Stephen told Clara, he planned to attend to business in Washington and Baltimore and then retrieve his money, wagon, and mule team in Norfolk. Then he hoped to return to Bartonsville. He believed that a great many folk in northeastern North Carolina were disillusioned with the Confederacy and hostile to its war policies, particularly conscription. What was more, he said, "they realize that their institution [of slavery] is worthless and that the sympathy of the world is against them and with the Negroes." Because of their change in attitude, he felt that he would be safe at Bartonsville.

Clara was appalled that Stephen wanted to return to North Carolina and the "traitor" Confederacy, and she expressed her feelings in a letter to Sammy. She recommended nothing, however, and proposed nothing. You know your father, she told Sammy: he wouldn't listen to "ordinary or written advice." Consequently, "I can simply tell other members of the family as nearly as I can the condition of things and hold up the load here as long as it needs holding—the rest of you must act for yourselves." She would do her best to make Stephen well enough to travel to Sammy and his mother; "if I fail, God's will not mine be done."

Clara said nothing when Stephen announced that he intended to put before General Butler a plan for "operating under the new laws of trade with insurrectionary districts." As a loyal Union man, he thought he could do a great deal to help redeem his part of North Carolina for the Union. First, however, he must clear his name before General Butler and get passes for the trip to Washington and Norfolk. The general agreed to talk with him on December 4.

Still too sick to walk, Stephen was carried to Butler's headquarters in a stretcher, accompanied by Clara. When Stephen said that the authorities in Norfolk had not yet returned his money, Butler struck his bell and ordered communiqués sent to Norfolk commanding Budd and Hutchens "to report to him *here* without delay." Butler expressed no opinion about the case, simply telling Stephen to "wait." The general would summon him for his "trial" when Budd and Hutchens arrived.

Back at the hospital, Clara wrote Ira Barton of Worcester about Stephen's case and asked for the judge's help. "Of his loyalty I scarce need speak to you, who have known him so well—you know it is not in his nature to be unfaithful to his country. . . . I am certain that you will rejoice to know that we have no disloyal blood in our family." She came bluntly to the point: "There are plenty of men from whom a word to Genl Butler would be worth every thing to Stephen just now—for instance your own honored self, Col. Davis, Col. Philips, Mr. Dickinson, Col. De Witt etc." General Butler was "disposed to deal kindly" with Stephen, she felt certain, "and would like the intelligent encouragement of his old friends to support his decision."

Butler might be "disposed to deal kindly" with Stephen because the general's own name had often been linked to the cotton trade with the enemy. While he was commander in New Orleans, his brother Andrew and other Yankee speculators had made fortunes from illegal commerce in medicine, cotton, and sugar. These traders had bribed treasury and army officials so that they could conduct their nefarious activities. There were rumors that General Butler shared in his brother's profiteering, but nobody turned up any evidence that this was so. Since coming to the Department of Virginia and North Carolina, Butler had been accused of letting a Baltimore man engage in illegal trade with the rebels in the Chowan River country. As a subsequent investigation was to prove, Butler had done nothing illegal: he had secured permission from Lincoln himself for the Baltimore agent to trade with the Confederates. Because Butler, like Lincoln, took a lenient view of the trade between the lines, he might indeed find Stephen innocent of any wrongdoing.

Clara was worn out from nursing and worrying about Stephen in the midst of all her other duties, and she confessed to Judge Barton that caring for her brother in addition to all her male patients sorely tried her spirit. "For six weeks of such labor, anxiety, weariness alternating hope and fear, dealing with strangers upon delicate matters, standing over Stephen's sick bed day & night, picking him up bed & all and carrying him to Head Quarters, soothing him under all his perplexities, cheering him under his despondency, and no earthly friend of his to lean upon for aid or counsel—all this added to the cares of a hospital in the front of a fighting army, liable to break up at any moment, so singularly situated, for I have not seen the face of a woman, white or black for months, walking on blistered feet every day and falling asleep any hour, per sheer necessity some time in the night—all these things have made me a little earnest and sometimes I have wickedly or foolishly felt that it was time I was relieved by other friends. But I know the true soldier stands patiently at his post, no matter what betide, and I will try to, and hold out faithfully to the end."

She added, "Do you know I think this is my reward for coming and nursing other people's brothers: that I should be able to save my own from dying a felon's death in a prisoner's cell,—with the brand of false suspicion on his brow."

The summons from Butler came on a crisp December morning. Clara and Stephen rode an ambulance to Butler's headquarters, but so many other people were there that they had to wait outside. Clara put her cloak and shawl around Stephen as he sat shivering in the cold. At last, Butler called them inside and rang his bell for Lieutenant Budd and detective Hutchens. With Butler serving as judge and jury, Stephen testified first, telling how the two officers had robbed him of his money and ordered him to Norfolk. They told him, Stephen said, that "Gen. Butler had plenty of places for such as he." At Norfolk, he continued, an officer called him "a notorious rebel," and the provost marshal had him thrown in the guardhouse.

When Butler interrogated Budd and Hutchens, they refrained from accusing Stephen of anything "but indulged in mutual accusation and recrimination" about the money taken from him. They counted out all the money they had brought with them, which fell short $700 in North Carolina bank money. Where was that sum? Butler demanded. When Budd gave an evasive answer, Butler had heard enough. "Gentlemen! this money must be restored, and all of it. I hold you equally responsible. You will divide the responsibility between you." Butler wrote out an order directing Colonel Sanders, the provost marshal, to collect the $700 from Budd and Hutchens and pay it to Stephen upon demand, and to return the rest of his property as well. "This is a bad business," the general asserted; "you are dismissed." Then he stopped them and turned to Clara. Did she have anything to tell them?

She certainly did. She told them that it was as "difficult to acquit themselves of the charge of barbarities with intent to kill" as it was "to exonerate themselves from the charge of robbery and theft."

The "interview," Stephen wrote David's children, was "most interesting, happy and amusing to all present except the officers who commanded the raid."

Early in December, the Army of the James underwent a major reorganization. The Tenth Corps and all the white troops of the Eighteenth

Corps were combined into the new Twenty-fourth Corps under the command of Brigadier General Alfred H. Terry. Butler's black troops and their white officers formed the new Twenty-fifth Corps, the largest force of black soldiers in the war. Their commander was Brigadier General Godfrey Weitzel of Ohio, a respected engineer who had graduated second in his class at West Point.

With military operations apparently suspended for the winter, Clara promised to accompany Stephen to Washington once he was well enough to travel. He talked obsessively about returning to North Carolina and attending to his business. He was worried about Clara, too, fearing that she was working "beyond her power of endurance." He insisted that she needed to return home for a long rest.

During the second week of December, troop movements and the appearance of Federal gunboats at Dutch Gap seemed to signal that a battle was at hand. Clara told Stephen that he must leave before the fighting broke out, but that her duty bound her to the hospital. So it was that Stephen, sick and shivering, returned to Washington alone. Clara made herself "a great deal of 'worriment' " until she learned that he was safely back in the capital and under Sammy's care.

As it turned out, there was no battle at Dutch Gap. But word of another campaign threw Clara's hospital and the surrounding army camps into great excitement. It seemed that General Butler was to lead an expedition against Fort Fisher, which guarded the approach to Wilmington, North Carolina, the rebels' last major blockade-running port, which supplied Lee's army at Petersburg. One division from each corps of the Army of the James would take part in Butler's campaign, which was to include a powerful fleet of fifty-six warships under Rear Admiral David Dixon Porter, commander of the North Atlantic Blockading Squadron. Working from an idea of General Butler, Union engineers intended to annihilate Fort Fisher by blowing up a "Monster Torpedo" close to the rebel stronghold. As Grant said, the "torpedo" was to be an old steamer "loaded with 400 tons of gunpowder." Although Stanton objected to the plan as a waste of "the people's money," Grant thought it might work, and Lincoln decided to give it a try. Grant designated General Godfrey Weitzel to command the two divisions from Butler's army, but Butler never showed the order to Weitzel. In his capacity as commander of the Department of Virginia and North Carolina, Butler elected to direct field operations himself. Grant did not know about this until the evening of Butler's departure. "I rather formed the idea that Gn. Butler was actuated by a desire to witness the effect of his pet *Gunpowder plot*," Grant said later. The general-in-chief forthwith ordered Butler to hold a beachhead once he had effected a landing. His ultimate goal was to reduce and seize Fort Fisher and then to capture Wilmington.

When Butler set off for North Carolina with 6,500 troops, Clara elected to remain at the flying hospital in case the general ordered it to follow. A few days before Christmas, word came that Butler's troop transports and the Union flotilla had rendezvoused off New Inlet, North Carolina, and the flying hospital awaited developments in a state of high tension. On Christmas, Clara's forty-third birthday, a group of soldiers serenaded her, and she felt "especially honored." A few days later, a letter came from Stephen reporting that he was in Norfolk, trying to collect his money from Budd and Hutchens. Clara wrote him that she was "astonished and *frightened*" that he had gone to Norfolk by himself. She was certain he was still sick, and yet she could do nothing to help him: "I know you want me to come home, and I mean to come but I must not leave my post in the present uncertain state of affairs." If General Butler captured Wilmington, he would probably move his headquarters to North Carolina and order the rest of his army, including the flying hospital, to join him there. In that event, she had to be on hand or risk losing all her "effects" and her entire "field operations." Surely Stephen understood her predicament: "I hope you can content yourself to wait till you are strong and I will come home just as soon as I can leave here with any safety to my own interests or the welfare of those I am here to serve." She added that it had been so long since she'd seen a woman's face that "I have almost forgotten how we look."

On January 4, 1865, Clara wrote in her diary that Butler's force had "failed" to capture Fort Fisher and had returned. *Failed* was hardly the word for what was a fiasco from first to last. The navy started it by detonating the "Monster Torpedo" too far from the fort to do any damage. Porter's warships did bombard the fort, and General Weitzel did put 2,500 of his men ashore. But when he saw that the fort was virtually unscathed, Weitzel informed Butler that it was suicidal to throw infantry against it, which was surely the case, and Butler promptly suspended operations and returned with his forces to Fort Monroe. Butler and Porter indulged in mutual accusations, Porter wailing to the press that the army had abandoned him, Butler arguing that the admiral "*did not intend that the attack of the army should succeed.*"

When Grant learned that Porter was still off Fort Fisher with his fleet, the general-in-chief ordered a second expedition to set forth under the command of General Terry. Clara wanted to go along so badly that she wrote the staff surgeon asking for permission. "No one but myself knows or ever can how much I desired to go," she wrote in her diary, but she could not quite bring herself to send the letter, perhaps because she was concerned about Butler's fate. In any case, Terry was gone by morning. "We felt confident of the success of the second expedition," Clara declared, "for we knew that every exertion would be made by the Navy as well as the Army to bring success, and victory."

On January 7, as Clara feared, the ax fell on General Butler. After reviewing the various reports of the first expedition, Grant concluded that Butler had violated his "nondiscretionary orders to hold any beach-head he might gain." As a consequence, Benjamin Butler, the last political general in the field, found himself relieved of command and ordered home to Lowell. In a desperate bid to defend himself, Butler asked Lincoln for permission to publish his report of the expedition, but the president refused. "While the newspapers of the country were filled with extracts from Porter's reports and abusive criticisms of my conduct," Butler said angrily, "I could not say one word as to what that conduct had been."

Thus the war career of Clara's friend and patron ended in disgrace. The day after Butler's dismissal, Clara received another blow when Dr. Kittinger resigned from the service because of his deteriorating health and turned the Twenty-fourth Corps hospital over to Dr. Richardson. Kittinger's resignation left Clara in despair. "No one can fully take the place of an old true and tried friend like D K.," she wrote in her diary; "in all my trials for the past years (almost) he has stood faithfully by me, endorsing every act, willing to cover and forget every fault."

Meanwhile, another friend, Reverend Nathan Brown, the editor of the *American Baptist*, arrived in camp with a letter from Stephen, who was now back in Washington. Stephen had failed to collect any money from Budd and Hutchens and was "very anxious" that Clara come to him: "I want much to see you but would not have you sacrifice your business to come home on my account but had hoped that if you should be here that you would join me in what I suppose you all consider a visionary scheme," which meant that, sick though he was, he still entertained notions of returning to North Carolina.

Since her brother needed her and since she'd lost her two patrons, Butler and Kittinger, and everything in the department was in a state of flux, Clara decided to return to Washington City with Brown. She could take pride in her accomplishments on the Richmond-Petersburg line, where she had nursed and operated diet kitchens in field hospitals averaging from 200 to 1,600 patients each. She calculated that they had "removed some eight or ten times" that number from the flying and base hospitals of the old Tenth Corps (now the Twenty-fourth Corps). As she told a woman's group a few weeks later, it had been "a most interesting field of labor" for her, all the more so because of the help of her soldier assistants. "You would probably think a uniformed Soldier, who lays down his gun and knapsack and turns to making tea and toast rather an unskilled domestic; but I have had scores of such . . . and they have all worked for, or with me, kindly, patiently, and faithfully."

On January 10 she took a final ride along the lines with Brown and a Captain Baker, an Englishman who had served in the Crimean war and claimed to be "one of the famous six hundred that made the gallant charge of death" at Balaclava. Clara's party came across a squad of soldiers, all former slaves, who were putting up a foundation for a church and a schoolhouse. "This was a most remarkable sight," Clara scribbled in her diary, "not 100 yards off stood the front line of rebel pickets facing ours within [a] stones throw. [A] little to the right frowned a rebel fort, and here in full view a company of freed slaves erecting a school house right on the very walls of the fort they had captured and held. Talk no more of fiction—truth is far more striking and strange. Work on poor fellows, God is with you."

On January 12, departure day, Clara distributed her stores in the wards and said good-bye to every patient. Dr. Richardson asked her to come back and promised her "every protection." Clara did agree to return when she was able to do so. Then, in company with Brown and Kittinger, who was going home to his family in New York, Clara boarded the steamer *James T. Brady* for the two-day trip back to Washington.

A few days after her return to the capital, word came that General Terry had captured Fort Fisher, thus sealing off the great blockade-running port of Wilmington and causing worse hardships for Lee's hungry troops in the trenches of Petersburg. "*It is coming spring,*" Clara wrote the Soldiers' Aid Society of Fitchburg, Massachusetts. "Three more months opens the campaign of isles,—there is little rest for our fighting armies, so ladies there is little rest for you, and me."

PART SIX

Andersonville

For Clara, it was strange to be home after almost six and a half months in the field. To her relief, Stephen was holding his own at Sally's and Vester's place on N Street. Irving was living there, too, and working days as chief clerk at the Massachusetts state relief agency, his consumption apparently in remission. She found Henry Wilson in excellent spirits. Up for reelection by the Massachusetts legislature, he expected to sail through, and he was much involved with wartime reconstruction.

On January 16, General Butler turned up in Washington to testify before the Joint Committee on the Conduct of the War concerning the first Fort Fisher expedition. In the committee's hearing room the next day, Butler argued that he had not violated Grant's "nondiscretionary orders" because no beachhead had been achieved. He had withdrawn, he said, when he learned that the fort was "uninjured" and heavily armed with seventeen guns trained "on the beach" and that an attack was doomed. Once again he blamed Rear Admiral Porter for the fiasco, asserting that Porter should have "silenced" the fort with the monster torpedo boat and his huge fleet of warships. Why had Butler been relieved of command? Because he was the last high-ranking civilian general in the army, he argued, and the West Pointers wanted to get rid of him. He also took a swipe at Grant for siding with Porter in the controversy. Grant, Butler said, is "as unjust as he is reckless of other men's lives and reputations."

When Porter responded to Butler in the press, repeating his allegations that Butler had deliberately abandoned the navy when he withdrew, Clara thought that "no man except Genl. Butler could stand such charges." Indeed, Butler had many powerful political friends in both Washington and Massachusetts. When he returned home to consider his next move, Lowell gave him "a hero's welcome," and Clara

was certain that he would come back to Washington in some significant capacity.

Indeed, when she learned that Congress was debating a freedmen's
bureau to help the former slaves, she wrote Wilson recommending
Butler to run it. "I had thought of him as eminently fitted for other
positions," Clara said, "but I am not certain that this is not the link in
the great chain of human progress for which God has shaped and fitted
him." Clara then returned to a theme that had haunted her since the
opening guns. "This is God's war,—its very thunders sound the key
notes of human advancement. He has selected his material, rough
hewn, and shaped it to his purposes." She thought Butler "a peculiar
piece of timber" and believed that "the Great Architect *has* designed
and *scored* him for a main brace" in "the whole structure." As it turned
out, though, her recommendation was in vain. When the Bureau of
Refugees, Freedmen, and Abandoned Lands was created in early
March, one-armed General O. O. Howard became its head.

Meanwhile, at Stephen's behest, Clara went down to Norfolk to see
the authorities about his missing money. Traveling with her was Dr.
Sidney and his wife, the same Dr. Sidney who used to accompany her
to the military camps and the target ranges back in 1861. In Norfolk,
Lieutenant Colonel O. L. Mann, now provost marshal, made her his
guest in "a very fine suite of rooms" in the National Hotel and conferred with her at length about Stephen's arrest and imprisonment
and about the money Budd and Hutchens owed him. After investigating the matter, Mann reported that "all parties" acknowledged
Stephen's claim and promised to pay when they could. Mann was
deeply troubled about "the case of Stephen's arrest," Clara recorded,
and he promised to write it up if Stephen would furnish him a full
account of it.

When Clara reported that to Stephen, he set immediately to work
on a statement, although the entire matter tired and vexed him. To
Clara's alarm, he had grown conspicuously weaker. His diarrhea was so
bad that she feared he might never recover.

To make matters worse, Irving had begun coughing up blood. Clara
stayed an entire day and night with her nephew and looked in on him
almost every day after that. Feeble as he felt, he was soon back at work,
for he loved his job at the Massachusetts state relief agency and
refused to give it up, even though it was an ordeal for him to walk the
single block to catch the streetcar. He realized that he might be dying
from the ravages of consumption but resolved "to make the most of the
little life allotted him." "I am wearing out," he wrote a friend. "One

bolt after another in the machine gives way. Yet as a mechanic repairs a piece of machinery, so I am patching up to run a little longer. I have all the blessings and comforts of home and friends, and a position where everything is pleasant. Ought I to be happy? I believe I am."

It broke Clara's heart to see Irving grow paler and thinner with the passing days. He had suffered so much over the years; she couldn't bear the idea that his life might soon be ending.

Away from the field, Clara felt "dull" and disoriented but knew she could not return as long as Stephen and Irving were both in precarious health. She did take cheer from the war news. Sherman had made his legendary march through Georgia, knocking that state out of the war, and was now burning his way across South Carolina, apparently heading for Virginia and a potential linkup with Grant's huge army before Petersburg. On February 20, cannon boomed at the navy yard in Washington, announcing the capture of Charleston at long last. Two days later, Wilmington surrendered to General Terry, and the Army of the James could claim another measure of exoneration. In Washington, Clara heard rumors that the Confederacy was on the verge of surrendering, that this terrible war was nearing its destined end.

Meanwhile, she and Irving discussed the Union soldiers now returning to the North from prisons in the Confederacy. The practice of exchanging prisoners, suspended in 1863 because the Confederacy had refused to release black prisoners, had recently resumed. The two sides exchanged prisoners on a man-for-man basis and paroled the extra men if they promised not to fight again until other prisoners became available for exchange. A general hospital at Annapolis, Maryland, served as "general rendezvous" for thousands of Federals who had been paroled from Libby, Belle Isle, Salisbury, and Andersonville, macabre prisons all. Irving suggested that Clara ought to go to Annapolis and see if she could help there, and Clara thought it a splendid idea.

Back in her rooms, she pondered what role she might play at Annapolis. Since Union prisoners had begun arriving there, Clara had received many letters from women across the North, asking for her help in their search for missing husbands and sons, "whom they had reason to know or fear had languished or died in southern prisons." They wrote Clara because of her national reputation as "the soldiers' friend" and as the person to contact for information about missing men. Indeed, Clara had long been concerned about such soldiers and recorded facts about them in her campaign diaries. She was struck, she said, by "the intense anxiety and excitement amounting in many instances nearly to insanity which characterized those letters" asking after menfolk who might have died in rebel prisons. The more she thought about it, the more she was convinced that discovering their fate was "the most pressing necessity" of the hour. It was her "imperative duty," she decided, to go to Annapolis and inform the public that she would henceforth receive and answer all letters sent to her there by "the friends of the prisoners."

There were obstacles, of course. She would need government approval and the assistance of the military authorities at Annapolis. But she didn't think that would be a problem, not with all her experience in dealing with politicians and army bureaucrats. Quickly she developed a plan of action: With the help of the military, she would conduct her search among the camps and records of returning prisoners at Annapolis. She would compile a list of the names sent to her and post them in the barracks there, with requests that all returning prisoners examine the lists and send Clara whatever information they might have. Clara would then forward that information to the correspondents who had made the inquiries, "thus placing in communication the friends of the missing man, and the person professing to have knowledge of him."

With Nathan Brown, Clara hurried up to Annapolis to discuss her plan with the officers in charge. The buildings of the Naval Academy had been converted into a hospital under the charge of Surgeon Vanderkieft, and additional hospital tents had been erected on the parade ground, with Maria M. C. Hall of Washington serving as superintendent of them. More than thirty other women had been employed at the facility since July 1863. Two of them, a Miss Young and a Miss Billing, had died from diseases contracted in the wards. When Clara arrived at Annapolis, the hospital was full of freed prisoners stricken with typhoid fever; five of the female nurses also were sick with that deadly disease.

Clara spoke to a Captain Davis in College Green Barracks, which was part of what was called Camp Parole. "I find the captain needs promotion and I will ask for it at once," Clara jotted in her diary, hoping to trade that favor for support of her project. The next day she and Brown stood at the wharves as four ships from Fort Monroe took turns unloading "poor wrecks of humanity" from the "prison pens" of the crumbling Confederacy. As the parolees lay dockside, a military band played cheery tunes in the cold ocean breeze, and male and female nurses washed and fed the soldiers and covered them with fresh blankets. Teams of stretcher-bearers then removed them one after another to Camp Parole at the Naval Academy.

For several months, this ritual went on at the Annapolis landing, and the appearance of the released prisoners shocked everybody who saw them. One and all, they were proof of unimaginable cruelty, neglect, and starvation. Many were little more than living skeletons, with sunken cheeks and a dreamy, "idiotic stare" in their cavernous eyes; some could not even remember their names. A few of them were mad, babbling and choking with clenched teeth and wild eyes as they were led ashore. "You at the North will never be able to conceive or believe the true condition of our prisoners," said Harriet Foote Hawley, Clara's friend from Hilton Head days, who helped ship them to Annapolis from captured Wilmington. "You may see all the pictures," she said, "and read all the accounts, and believe, or think you believe, every word of them, and then you have but a faint idea." The worst were the prisoners from Andersonville in southwest Georgia, the most notorious prison of the war. "No human tongue or pen can describe the horrible condition which they were in," Hawley wrote of one group. "*Starving to death*, covered with vermin, with no clothing but the filthy rags they had worn during their whole imprisonment—a period of from five to twenty months; cramped by long sitting in one position, so that they could not straighten their limbs. . . . Men who had once been educated and cultivated, with fine minds, were reduced to idiocy—to utter and hopeless imbecility." She saw forty men from Andersonville "whose feet, or portions of them, had rotted off. . . . Think of it! feet so rotted away that the surgeons cut them off with the scissors above the ankle! Has God any retribution for those who inflicted such suffering?"

The released prisoners Clara saw upset her terribly. But emaciated and forlorn as they were, they were not her primary concern; her object was to find out what they knew about missing soldiers. Toward that end, she sought out the officer in charge of the new arrivals at Annapolis, a Colonel Root, and explained her plan to him. The colonel, however, declared himself unimpressed and disapproved of her work. He did so "from prejudice," Clara said, which meant that in his estimation a woman was not capable of such work. The next day, Clara met Dorothea Dix, who was in town on army nursing business, but Clara left no record of what they said, how they got along, or what she thought of seeing her old adversary in person. The absence of any recorded impression might well indicate the strength of Clara's aversion to Dix.

Back in Washington, Clara sought Wilson's advice and support. The senator "cordially approved" of her new plan of action and suggested that she lay it before Secretary of War Stanton. "I laughed at him," Clara wrote in her diary, since she was certain that Stanton would have the same prejudiced attitude as Colonel Root. She thought it better to get the approval of President Lincoln himself; that way nobody would dare interfere with her. Wilson agreed to introduce her to the president, and they made plans to meet at the White House at five o'clock the following afternoon. Clara promptly wrote out a formal request, asking Lincoln for permission to serve as "General Correspondent" for missing prisoners at Annapolis, where she would strive to "obtain and furnish all possible information in regard to those that have died during their confinement."

That she was going to meet Lincoln excited her extravagantly. But what would she wear? Her closet was virtually bare save for her field dress. Nathan Brown's wife was "in some anxiety" about Clara's thin wardrobe, too. To help out, she bought Clara a dress skirt and went with her to see a Mrs. Ambrose, who fixed Clara's hair and loaned her a fur coat and a hat.

The next afternoon, February 27, Clara donned her new outfit and pulled on a pair of gloves. She was still petite, shapely, and attractive, with her luxurious brown hair put up in curls and curlets and her cheeks subtly rouged. At four o'clock she hurried off to the White House to meet the president of the United States, whose "care-worn face" meant so much to her.

To her dismay, the guard at the White House door told her that nobody could be admitted after three o'clock. When Wilson walked up, Clara gave him her letter to Lincoln and waited for the guard to admit them. But the guard refused, saying that the president was out. Wilson hurried back to Capitol Hill with her letter, and Clara returned home so disappointed she could have wept. To make matters worse, she had house guests who demanded her attention: Jules Golay, her adopted Swiss brother, was out of the army and looking for a job in Washington, and he desperately needed her help. The other guest was Mary A. Baker, the widow of Brigadier General Edward D. Baker, who had been killed at Ball's Bluff in 1862; Mary was seeking an invalid pension, which required a congressional act of approval. Clara had "loaned" Henry Wilson to her, and he was now promoting her invalid pension bill in the Senate.

The next day, Wilson was too busy to accompany Clara to the White House. Peeved at him, Clara retrieved her letter to Lincoln and tried a different tack: she put her plan before Massachusetts Congressman W. G. Washburn and asked him to introduce her to Lincoln. Washburn was so impressed that he wrote her a letter of introduction, praising her as "one of the most useful, devoted, *valuable* ladies in the country." Later that same day, he met her at the White House. Once again Clara asked to see Lincoln, and once again the guard declined to admit her. The president, he said, was in a cabinet meeting, and it was likely to last all day. She was welcome to try again tomorrow, he said, but the president was extraordinarily busy, what with his inauguration only five days away.

Disappointed though she was, Clara did not write the day off completely. If she couldn't see Lincoln, then she would call on the proper military authorities and seek their help. With Washburn tagging dutifully along, she strode to the War Department and knocked on the door of General William Hoffman, commissary general of prisoners, who had himself been a prisoner earlier in the war. She explained her plan to him and confided her fears that the officers at Annapolis would not cooperate with her. Hoffman refused to endorse her project. If she wanted to go to Annapolis, he said, she should just go. But, he added, he "would not take offence" if she appealed.

She appealed to Major General Ethan Allen Hitchcock, commissioner for the exchange of war prisoners and grandson of Revolutionary War hero Ethan Allen. A gruff old West Pointer, he nodded appreciatively as Clara outlined her plan in her melodious voice. Obviously smitten by her, he pronounced himself "delighted" with her idea, said "it must be carried out," and offered to take her to see Lincoln forthwith. Clara pointed out that the president was tied up in a protracted cabinet meeting, but Hitchcock insisted on escorting her to the White House. There, just as she had warned, they found that the cabinet was still in session. Undaunted, Hitchcock took Clara's letters and promised to handle the matter himself.

On her way home, Clara stopped off at Sally's to check on Stephen and Irving. To her despair, both were worse. Stephen was so feeble that Clara feared he would never recover. He seemed "crushed in spirit" from the physical abuse he had suffered and worried about his unprotected property in North Carolina and the money Budd and Hutchens owed him. "Alternately hoping and despairing," he had almost completed his long statement for Colonel Mann.

When Clara reached her apartment, she found a note from General Hitchcock. It said that as far as Annapolis was concerned, she ought to "go on without anything more," meaning that she should forget about

seeing Lincoln. But without the president's support, she feared her
work was doomed to fail. She was quite certain that if she went to
Annapolis and announced her intentions, Secretary of War Stanton
would send her a card stating that she was "acting without authority."
She knew how jealous male bureaucrats could be about their prerogatives. "I dare not and do not feel it my duty to bring myself to public
mortification in order to do a public charity," she indignantly told her
diary. She wanted to talk with Wilson and get his advice, but Wilson
was too engrossed with Mary Baker's bill to help Clara. God, how she
regretted ever loaning him to her and surrendering "all my power."

The next day, March 1, she could find nobody to escort her to the
White House. In desperation, she decided to go by herself and convention be damned. But she couldn't find her gloves. It would be bad
enough to show up without a male escort; she didn't dare call at the
White House without gloves. "Could not go," she confided in her
diary; "tried hard not to be discouraged . . . could not reconcile my
poor success, I feel that some hand above mine rules and is staying my
progress. I cannot understand but try to be patient, still it is hard. I
was never more tempted to break down from disappointment."

March 2 found Clara and Nathan Brown sitting in the office of Indian
Commissioner William P. Dole. Seeing him was Brown's idea. He
thought that Dole had access to the president that others did not.
When Clara outlined her Annapolis plan, the commissioner thanked
her "very kindly for . . . offering to assume such work" and agreed to
accompany them to the White House later the same day. Clara purchased a new pair of gloves for the visit and at the prescribed hour set
off for the White House with Brown. It was raining "fearfully," but that
did not dampen the enthusiasm of the crowds streaming into
Washington for the Inaugural. Special trains whistled their arrival at
the B&O Railroad depot, which was decorated and painted for the
occasion. Willard's hotel was so full of visitors that the management set
up cots in the halls and lounges to accommodate them.

At the White House, Clara and Brown waited impatiently in the
rain for Commissioner Dole. There was a double guard at the door—a
bad sign. Presently a scowling Stanton arrived, shook the rain off his
coat, and entered the White House. Clara and Brown paced back and
forth, but gave up when 5:00 P.M. came with no sign of Dole. Returning
home, Clara found Mary Baker in a joyous mood. Her "bill" had

passed the Senate the night before and was expected to be cleared in the House forthwith, maybe this very night. "I do not tell her how much I am inconvenienced by her using all my power," Clara confided in her diary. "I have no helper left, and I am discouraged. I could not restrain the tears. . . . I am little profited by the acquaintance and am somewhat annoyed and if my resolution holds good I shall speak my mind the first opportunity."

When Clara and Brown called on Dole the next day, he apologized for his absence the previous day, explaining that a delegation of Indians had detained him. Although he could not meet her at the White House, he did promise to do all "in his power" to help Clara. Once again, she and Brown went to the White House in the rain, passing out-of-town visitors who were wrapped in blankets and looking in vain for rooms. This time the White House guard told Clara that there was no admittance until after the inauguration tomorrow. More discouraged than ever, she "decided to leave my papers with Comm Dole and my cause to God."

That night, bands of serenaders wandered through fog-bound Washington, and a procession of torch-bearing firemen marched down Pennsylvania Avenue. Roof lights on the Capitol "threw a white halo" high into the swirling mist, and the lamps burned late in the Capitol, whose galleries were filled with crowds of sightseers, come to witness the last scenes of the session. Among the visitors was the prominent Shakespearean actor, John Wilkes Booth.

On Saturday, Inauguration day, a violent windstorm struck Washington, blowing rain and particles of mud through the city with hurricane force. The wind ripped the signs off Clara's building and broke one of her windows, spattering the sill and wall with muddy rain. After she had cleaned up and had the window repaired, she received an unexpected visitor. It was Dr. Richardson, surgeon in charge of the Twenty-fourth Corps hospital, who was in town on a twenty-day furlough and asked Clara to return to the front with him. His request was a great tribute to Clara's skill and experience as hospital matron. If her missing-soldier project did not work out, she could always resume her duties on the Richmond line.

Evidently Clara did not attend the Inauguration, perhaps because she expected the foul weather to continue. As it turned out, the rain stopped at noon, when Lincoln made the traditional carriage ride up Pennsylvania Avenue, which teemed with bands, spectators, and clattering cavalry. Just as Lincoln rose to speak at the east front of the Capitol, the sun broke through the clouds, flooding the entire gathering with brilliant light. Then the clouds closed in again. In a terse and lyrical speech, delivered in his shrill voice, Lincoln repeated what Clara had said the year before. Perhaps God had willed this "mighty scourge of war" on a guilty land, he declared, "until all the wealth piled by the bond-man's two hundred and fifty years of unrequited toil shall be sunk, and until every drop of blood drawn with the lash, shall be paid by another drawn with the sword." (Clara had written Fanny Gage: "Is this war never to end, till for every African slave that ever dragged his chain an Anglo Saxon shall have suffered?") When he finished, Lincoln bowed and kissed an open Bible. Cannon exploded in the wind. Then Federal marshals escorted Lincoln and his son Tad back to the White House, bleak against the moving clouds.

That evening, Clara tried to attend the president's public reception, which began at eight o'clock. She arrived with a party of friends and was stunned to find several thousand people crowding through the White House gates and over the grounds in a screaming "free-for-all." It was estimated that Lincoln shook hands with 6,000 people that night, with many others, including Clara Barton, unable to get near him. Once again she felt that some unseen hand prevented her from meeting the president.

On the night of March 6, Clara attended the Inaugural Ball in the great Patent Office, where she was still theoretically employed. Her escort was John Bigelow, editor of the *New York Evening Post* and consul to Paris. Clara wore a green silk dress, which she had borrowed, and a white lace bodice. When she and Bigelow arrived around 10:00 P.M., a ballroom band was playing polkas and waltzes, and couples were sashaying across the marble floor of the flag-covered room. About 4,000 people were in attendance, including all the prominent politicians and high military brass. Among them Clara spotted General Nathaniel Banks and his wife; Admiral David Farragut, the hero of Mobile Bay; and of course Henry Wilson, toward whom Clara felt decidedly cool. At 10:30, Lincoln arrived and made his way to the dais as the band struck up "Hail to the Chief." Mary Lincoln, elegantly dressed in a satin dress and white lace and holding a fan trimmed with silver spangles and ermine, arrived with Senator Charles Sumner, the Lincolns' close personal friend. At midnight, an army of waiters brought forth an enormous supper of poultry, beef, veal, terrapin, oysters, smoked meats, game, ices, jellies, cakes, fruits, nuts, and salads, all served up on a long, flag-draped table. It was "a great crowd," Clara said afterward, "and rush for supper of which I saw only the crowd—

no supper for any of us—the Party was brilliant, and I returned at 1 o'clock having been to Inauguration Ball."

Four days after the ball, Stephen took a turn for the worse. When Clara reached Sally's place, he was coughing up "large mouthfuls of coagulated blood," she said, and they had to change his clothing often. When he grew faint and restless, they summoned the family doctor, but he did not understand Stephen's condition and sent for a Dr. Sheldon of Campbell Hospital. Sheldon said there was nothing he could do; Stephen was dying. With Clara and Sally at his bedside, Stephen spoke of his business affairs—he had finished the account of his arrest for Lieutenant Colonel Mann—and said that when his money was retrieved and Bartonsville made safe, all his debts should be "faithfully paid." He was so weak that he had to pause frequently as he spoke. He turned to Clara. "This war is near its end," he murmured. "God bless Abraham Lincoln and the Union armies." He closed his eyes.

Clara was afraid he was gone, her dear oldest brother, her poor Stephen. She bent over and kissed him. "Stephen," she said, "do you know me?"

He opened his eyes. "Yes," he whispered.

"And do you love me?"

He reached out and clasped her hand. "God knows how much," he said. "*Oh, God,*" he whispered. Then "a dark shade" spread over his face, and he was gone. "I trust to meet the loved ones on the other side," Clara wrote in her diary. "Did our mother welcome him. Oh; the thin, strong veil, when shall it fall that we may see?"

Before the embalmers came, Clara tried to memorize Stephen's "noble handsome features" so well that she would never forget them. After he was taken away, she sat thinking about him, and her thoughts drifted to her missing-soldier project at Annapolis. Suddenly she had a revelation: "I think I can see why I could not go before—think that I was humanly withheld, that I might do the last for my dear sick & dead brother—feel now that the obstacles will be removed and that I can go after this, do not know how but some way will open."

On March 12, a Sunday, she went to the embalmer's parlor to see Stephen for the last time. Staring at him in the coffin, she thought, "God has called his anxious spirit and left us this peaceful clay." In the evening, Wilson arrived at her apartment to express his condolences. He was so "kind and gentle," Clara said, that she was sorry she had ever felt cool toward him. He "asked to take the place as nearly as possible of the dear brother I had lost," Clara recorded in her diary. "Said

he should be proud to do so and to have me for a real sister, so I adopted another brother."

Before Clara left for North Oxford, where Stephen was to be
buried, she and Brown went to Commissioner Dole's office to inquire
about "the fate" of her Annapolis project. The commissioner handed
Clara her papers and a note from Lincoln, written across a note from
General Hitchcock. "As it is a matter pertaining to prisoners," Lincoln
said, "Gen. Hitchcock is authorized to do as he thinks fit in this matter
of Miss Barton." Dole's interpretation was that Lincoln had endorsed
Clara's project, subject to the general's approval.

Delighted with the signs, Clara sought out Hitchcock at his home.
Escorting her to his parlor, the gruff old general gave her "a most
delightful interview." Not only did he heartily endorse her projected
mission to Annapolis; he also wrote out a notice about it for the newspapers, saying that Clara would operate by his authority with the
approval of the president. Hitchcock "encouraged me," Clara wrote
later, "said it would be hard, but I should be sustained through such a
work he felt—and that no person in the U.S. would oppose me in my
work and that he should stand between me and all harm and the
President was there too."

The president was indeed there for Clara, providing her with a
memorable letter of support. "To the friends of missing persons: Miss
Clara Barton has kindly offered to search for the missing prisoners of
War. Please address her at Annapolis, Maryland giving name, regiment, and company of any missing prisoner." The letter was signed: "A.
Lincoln." Clara's premonition had come true; now that she had done
"the last" for her brother, the obstacles against her Annapolis plan had
suddenly evaporated.

After Stephen's funeral in North Oxford, Clara and Sammy,
Stephen's only son, made plans to secure the property at Bartonsville,
which was valued at $30,000. But they never did. In early April, Union
cavalry burned Bartonsville during a raid through the Chowan River
country. Much later, Clara learned that a Federal officer had put
Bartonsville to the torch as a signal to Union gunboats. Bitterly, she
wrote that her brother had prayed "for the success of the Union
armies, and died without knowing—and God be praised for this—that
the reckless torches of that same Union army would lay in ashes and
ruins, the results of the hard labor of his worn out life, and wreck the
fortunes of his only child." Although Clara and Sammy would present
their case to the government, they would never receive recompense

for the burned-out estate or collect a cent of the money owed Stephen by Lieutenant Budd and detective Hutchens.

On March 23, the president and his family left for City Point to visit Grant and the Army of the Potomac. By then, Union forces were smashing up the Confederacy in all directions. Sherman had whipped a makeshift rebel force in North Carolina and was advancing relentlessly on Raleigh; Sheridan had wrecked the Virginia Central Railroad on his way to join Grant; and in northwest Alabama 13,000 Union horsemen under General James Wilson struck southward toward Selma, in what would become the biggest and most destructive cavalry raid of the war.

That same March 23, Clara went to Camp Parole in Annapolis to begin her search for missing soldiers. While she had been in Massachusetts, General Hitchcock's notice of her intentions had appeared in the *Washington Chronicle* and other papers, and the response exceeded Clara's wildest expectations. Three hundred and sixty letters of inquiry awaited her at Camp Parole, each wanting information regarding a missing husband, son, or brother thought to have perished in rebel prisons. Soon the letters of inquiry were flowing in at a rate of one hundred a day, and Clara was overwhelmed. How could she ever reply to so many correspondents, let alone search for their missing relatives and friends? Clearly she had identified one of the war's most pressing necessities. How was one woman to solve it?

Worse still, she ran up against her old adversary: military red tape. When she introduced herself to the commander of Camp Parole, a Colonel Sewell, he and his colleagues did not know what to do with her. She had no military rank or government position—only letters from Hitchcock and Hoffman recommending that Sewell cooperate with her, "if it is practicable." In their view, it wasn't practicable. Every government building in Annapolis was bursting with released prisoners, and there was no facility available for Clara. At her urging, Sewell did put in a request to Washington for a tent, but until his superiors responded, there was nothing he could do for her. Unable to find private lodging, said one soldier, Clara "had to force herself as a scarce wanted guest upon someone for a few days while her baggage stood out in the snow."

In early April, in response to a desperate note from Irving to "come once more and the last," Clara hurried back to Washington. According to Sally, Irving had come home carrying his papers and personal effects from his office at the Massachusetts state agency. He calmly told Sally "he had *finished his work*" and collapsed in bed, admitting that he had been "bleeding at the lungs" for several days.

In the Vassals' house on N Street, Clara and Sally kept a death vigil by Irving's bedside. All that week he fought for his young life, refusing to die quietly. Beyond the windows, the two sisters could hear people cheering in the streets and brass bands playing "Rally 'Round the Flag" and "Yankee Doodle," for Richmond had fallen and Lee's army was in flight along the Appomattox River with Grant in pursuit. The war was almost over now, the Confederacy all but dead.

Early on Palm Sunday, April 9, after a night of great restlessness, Irving died. He was only twenty-four years old. Sally "had learned to be resigned and was calm," Clara said, but Clara could hardly stand the pain in her heart. "He was to me the tenderest earthly tie," she said of Bubby. He had been such a bright young man, with a wry wit and a love for politics. Now he, too, was on the other side of the veil, beyond the pain and suffering of this world.

That night Lincoln returned from the front on the *River Queen*. The next morning, April 10, newspapers and official proclamations announced the momentous news that Lee had surrendered at Appomattox Court House the day before. The news threw Washington into bedlam. A 500-gun salute rocked the capital, breaking out windows on Lafayette Square, and hurrahing crowds and raucous brass bands marched up and down the streets. At the White House window, Tad Lincoln waved a captured rebel flag, and his father summoned a band to strike up "Dixie," saying it was always one of his favorite tunes and was now "our lawful property."

In mourning over the loss of Irving, Clara refrained from joining the celebrations or recording her impressions of the spectacular events of Holy Week. On the evening of April 11, Lincoln stood at a "lamp-lighted window" of the White House and told a large crowd about his reconstruction efforts in Louisiana, after which a band played "Battle Cry of Freedom." Beyond the White House, Washington blazed with illuminations. Some 6,000 candles burned in the windows of the Patent Office alone. Transparencies proclaimed "Union" and "Grant" and "Victory brings peace." Across the Potomac, at Lee's former estate, hundreds of liberated blacks sang "The Year of Jubilee" as rockets exploded in the night.

General Samuel D. Sturgis of Pennsylvania commanded an infantry division of the Ninth Corps at Fredericksburg, December 1862. He gallantly offered Clara his "protection" against those who objected to her presence in the field. *Library of Congress.*

The Lacy House, known locally as Chatham, was Clara's headquarters and a Union field hospital during the battle of Fredericksburg, December 1862. *Library of Congress.*

On December 11, 1862, Clara watched from the Lacy House veranda as Union engineers tried to lay a pontoon bridge across the Rappahannock. This "pencil and Chinese white drawing" by Alfred R. Waud shows the engineers under deadly rebel sniper fire from Fredericksburg. *Library of Congress.*

After the assaults on Marye's Heights, December 13, 1862, Clara tended to the injured and the dying in numerous dressing stations in shell-blasted Fredericksburg. Federal wounded filled up the courthouse and every church, warehouse, school, store, house, and street. *Library of Congress.*

Hilton Head army post, seen here from a signal station atop a manor, was the headquarters and ordnance and supply depots for the Department of the South. The post, Clara said, was "decidedly *fashionable*, and *splendidly gay*," with "ladies and girls" riding horseback on the beach. *U.S. Army Military History Institute.*

Lieutenant Colonel John J. Elwell had an affair with Clara on Hilton Head. They exchanged intimate notes, read poetry together, took romantic horseback rides and walks along the beach, and engaged in conversation, Clara's favorite pastime. *Library of Congress.*

General Quincy A. Gillmore, commander of the Department of the South, led Union forces on the Morris Island campaign in the summer of 1863. After the capture of Battery Wagner, he ordered Clara off the island, despite her brilliant work as a nurse. *Library of Congress.*

Frances Dana Gage became Clara's "dear *womanly* friend" on the Sea Islands. They wrote affectionate poems to one another and conversed about the meaning of the war. "Aunt Fanny" not only converted Clara to the cause of women's suffrage but made her more sensitive to the plight of the former slaves. *Library of Congress.*

Federal field hospitals were swamped with casualties during Grant's spring 1864 offensive against Lee. The wounded here are gathered on Marye's Heights above Fredericksburg. The soldier sitting on the left and the soldier lying on the litter have undergone amputations. *U.S. Army Military History Institute.*

General Benjamin F. Butler, commander of the Army of the James, respected Clara and welcomed her presence in his field hospitals on the Richmond-Bermuda Hundred line, 1864. *Library of Congress.*

Federal earthworks on the southern end of the Bermuda Hundred line near Point of Rocks. This bleak landscape greeted Clara when she visited the "sunburnt veterans" on Butler's line. It was dreadfully hot, Clara wrote in her diary. The countryside was "parched like a heap of ashes," and many soldiers fell victim to sunstroke. *Library of Congress.*

This woodcut, which appeared in *Harper's Weekly*, shows Clara Barton raising the flag over the newly planted head-boards at the Andersonville cemetery, where nearly 13,000 Union dead were buried. When the little crowd sang "The Star Spangled Banner," Clara covered her face and wept. *Ohio Historical Society.*

Dorence Atwater survived the horrors of Andersonville. His secret death register helped the postwar Federal expedition identify the Union dead there. Clara arranged for the *New York Tribune* to publish his register for the benefit of the families and friends of the Andersonville dead. *Library of Congress.*

Clara sent this postwar Brady photograph to one of her "little" namesakes. *Library of Congress.*

For the rest of Clara's long life, it was the Civil War that fired her imagination, the Civil War to which she kept returning in her lectures, her reminiscences, and her dreams. *Library of Congress.*

On Thursday, Grant arrived in Washington. On Good Friday, the papers reported that the Lincolns and Grants would attend Ford's Theater that night (the Grants, however, sent their apologies). That evening, Clara called on Mr. Upperman, the fellow who shared her work and salary at the Patent Office. It was a foggy night, and gas lights on the corners glimmered eerily in the drifting mist. On her way home, Clara heard a rumor that Lincoln had been shot at Ford's Theater. Stunned, incredulous, she hurried on to her apartment. All that night, crazed mobs roamed the streets, and soldiers and police fired on people who looked suspicious. One soldier killed a man for saying, "It served Lincoln right." Secretary of War Stanton put the city under martial law and organized dragnets to bring in suspects. Rumors flew about that it was a monstrous Confederate plot to seize Washington and murder all the heads of the government.

At 7:30 the next morning, with a heavy rain falling on Washington, a church bell began tolling somewhere in the city. The afternoon newspapers confirmed what Clara already suspected: Abraham Lincoln, sixteenth president of the United States, had been shot and killed in Washington, one of the final casualties of a war that had claimed some 620,000 of his countrymen. "History has on its record," asserted the *Washington Star*, "no suicidal act as terrible as that committed by the conquered South yesterday, through its representative, the assassin of President Lincoln."

"The whole city in gloom," Clara wrote in her diary. "No one knows what to do." Dr. Sidney came to see her and brought the news that Andrew Johnson had been sworn in as president. Like her neighbors, Clara wandered through the streets in a daze, trying to comprehend an event that defied belief. Abraham Lincoln was dead? How could it have happened? It was too large, too terrible, too unspeakable, to be understood. Unable to return to Annapolis or think about anything else, Clara went into self-imposed seclusion, keeping track of events in terse diary entries.

April 16, Easter Sunday: "Assassins not detected. Known to be J Wilkes Booth. The attempted murder of Mr. Seward was supposed to be by one Surrat[t]. I was quiet all day." *April 17, Monday*: "The President embalmed & preparing to be laid in state tomorrow." *April 18, Tuesday*: "President Lincoln laid in State—Depts went in bodies to see him. Resolution passed at Mass [state agency] rooms in honor of the President and [in] consideration of poor Irving." *April 19, Wednesday*: "Funeral of President Lincoln. I remained in doors all day." *April 20, Thursday*: "President lain in state at the capitol." Clara apparently paid her respects on this day, joining the long lines of mourners at the Capitol. When she came to Lincoln's casket in the rotunda, she gazed on his face one last time.

April 21, Friday, 8 P.M. "President Lincoln's remains taken on to Baltimore," Clara wrote in her diary. "Great Search for Booth." Lincoln's coffin rode on a nine-car funeral train, which would take him back to Illinois on a circuitous, 1,600-mile journey, with stops in many cities. A second coffin rode side by side with Lincoln's—that of his son Willie, who had died in February 1862 in the terrible early days of the war. The spectacle of that flag-draped train, carrying father and son home together, would haunt an entire generation.

Sunday, April 23: "I had a most distressed day in seclusion," Clara wrote in her diary. On that day, Lincoln's coffin lay in state in Philadelphia, resting in the East Wing of Independence Hall, where Jefferson and his colleagues had signed the Declaration of Independence. Perhaps 300,000 pilgrims filed past Lincoln's coffin that Sunday, some trying to kiss his face in their grief. From Philadelphia, the funeral train sped north to New York City, thence to Albany, and then headed west across Ohio and Indiana. All along the route, bonfires blazed, and mute crowds watched as the train thundered by with a shriek of its whistle.

"That was the grandest funeral that ever passed on earth," Clara wrote later, and tried to capture it in verse:

> *From city to city, the silent train passed on*
> *bearing the sable, shrouded casket.*
> *The nation's emblem for a pall*
> *And ever, the crowding, clinging mourners*
> *between the head and feet.*
> *From the northern ocean to the southern seas was only this.*
> *A silence born of grief too mighty for words; too deep for moans*
> *And thus they bore him on*
> *And laid him in the quiet grave among his own.*

For the next month, the pace of momentous events continued unabated. On April 27, the papers reported that Lincoln's assassin, John Wilkes Booth, had been cornered and mortally wounded in a Virginia tobacco barn. On May 10, Federal cavalry apprehended Jefferson

Davis at Irwinville, Georgia, and President Johnson proclaimed that "armed resistance to the authority of the Government in the said insurrectionary States may be regarded as virtually at an end." On that same day, eight of Booth's alleged conspirators went on trial in the third-floor room of the Old Penitentiary on the arsenal grounds; four of them would be hanged. On May 23, Clara's beloved Army of the Potomac staged a grand review up Pennsylvania Avenue, with Sheridan's cavalry in the lead, followed by brigades of engineers, then Clara's pet Ninth Corps and the Fifth and Second corps, all bearing their shell-torn flags in measured cadences, their guns gleaming in the brilliant sunlight. As the soldiers tramped proudly by, bands played and the huge crowds wept and sang "When This Cruel War Is Over" and "When Johnny Comes Marching Home." The next day, Sherman's army also passed in review, with Mary Ann "Mother" Bickerdyke, the great Sanitary Commission nurse and "field agent" of the western theater, leading Sherman's old Fifteenth Corps astride a magnificent horse, her uniform a bonnet and a calico dress. Then the pageant was over, and the Union's great army, said journalist Noah Brooks, "melted back into the heart of the people from whence it came."

The cruel war was over. Some 260,000 rebels and 360,000 Federals had died in it. On the Union side, about 110,000 perished in combat or from mortal battle wounds and 224,586 from disease. Diarrhea and dysentery alone killed 44,500. Typhoid claimed 27,000 and malaria 4,000. According to Union medical records, a total of 246,712 men were wounded and 29,980 amputations and 6 million "cases" of disease reported. But raw statistics could not convey the emotional and psychological scars left by the conflict. Who knew what damage it had done to the American spirit? Who could calculate the mental anguish and human suffering that continued long after the guns were silent, with so many amputees and scarred veterans in both sections, and so many households without men?

Clara had identified a major cause of anguish: Half the known Union dead were unidentified and thousands more were missing and presumed dead. But who could be certain, who among the survivors could rest, until the missing were found and the unknown dead identified? It was to locate a portion of the missing soldiers, those thought to have died in Southern prison stockades, that Clara now devoted herself with characteristic zeal and commitment to the "stern realities." In late April, the army finally produced a tent for her at Annapolis, after the directive had worked its way down the pecking order from Washington. "To my exceeding astonishment," Clara said in a sardonic letter to Henry Wilson, "I receid. ponderous papers informing me that the Secty. of War had 'directed' the Commissary Genl. of prisons, and the Comm. Genl. of prisons had '*directed*' the col commanding the post of Annapolis and the Col. Comdg. the post of Annapolis had 'directed' the Capt. in charge of College Green Barracks to provide me with all I had ever asked. . . . Like Davy Copperfield I felt about four years old and wanted some one to tell me the story of 'Going over London Bridge and finding a half penny.' "

In her tent, Clara set to work reading the hundreds of letters that had piled up in her absence. It was immediately clear that she could not handle the work alone. Out of her own funds, she hired several assistants and bought her own stationery for what she called "Office of Correspondence with the Friends of the Missing Men of the United States Army." She fully expected Congress to reimburse her for her expenses. Since they exceeded her modest monthly income from the Patent Office, she was obliged to raid her inheritance from her father, which the executor of the estate had profitably invested for her in Oxford. According to a relative, this now amounted to "quite a little money." Anxious not to exhaust her life's savings, though, Clara asked the Patent Office to return her "old time $1400 clerkship" in order to help relieve the financial burden of her work. But nothing came of her request that spring.

With her assistants, Clara made a list of names of missing prisoners of war, tacked up notices about them in the barracks at the Naval Academy, pored over camp records, and forwarded to her correspondents whatever information she turned up. It was frustrating work. Of all the names of missing men on her lists, she found only about one name in thirty on the roles at Annapolis. She felt a pressing responsibility for the other "twenty-nine thirtieth," she said. Meanwhile, word about her work had spread far and wide, and hundreds of additional letters of inquiry fell on her desk from all across the Union.

When Camp Parole was closed and all the released prisoners ordered home, Clara's work at Annapolis came to an end. She had the choice, she said later, of abandoning her search or changing her plan of operation. "I thought my duty plain and determined to continue my search by means of printed rolls circulated among the entire loyal states," she said later. "Under this enlarged system there was no longer necessity for confining my labors to prisoners and I decided to include in my search all missing men of the army." But to print rolls containing their names, she needed a great deal more money. Accordingly, on May

31, she issued an appeal, "To the People of the United States," pointing out that she had received thousands of letters of inquiry about missing soldiers, that even the U.S. Sanitary Commission had referred letters to her, and that she had decided to expand her operation to search for information about all missing men. The trouble was, she lacked the resources for such a vast enterprise. "You, too, must cooperate," she told the American people, "or the work cannot be done. You will excuse me for speaking very frankly on this point, for the work is yours. . . . It has fallen into my hands almost without my seeking, and it is for you to say whether it is worth doing. If it costs the United States four thousand dollars to kill an enemy in battle, is it worth five dollars or ten dollars to discover the fate of a citizen who has been reported missing? . . . If then you approve of my work I ask you to give your abundance for its support."

At the same time, Clara wrote President Johnson for help, explaining the purpose of her work and observing that she had thus far received "no assistance either from the Government or from individuals." What did she want from the government at this juncture? Only this, she told the president: would he authorize the Government Printing Office to publish her rolls of missing soldiers' names? Johnson's private secretary "offered very pleasantly to secure the name of the President to my paper if I would add to it the name of Genl. Hoffman or Genl Hitchcock," Clara wrote in her diary. She did better than that. Skillful at manipulating the military establishment, she secured the endorsement of Hoffman, Hitchcock, Rucker, and Grant. With that kind of backing and the recommendation of his secretary, the president readily approved of Clara's operation and directed the Government Printing Office to publish her rolls. The president's secretary was "exceedingly cordial," Clara noted in her diary, and urged her to "call always" when she needed anything. "I had a hard week's work," she said happily.

When Henry Wilson offered to pay for her postage, Clara went to work in earnest. She and her staff devised an initial roll containing 1,500 names with a request for information about each and had 20,000 copies published and distributed to every post office in the North and circulated throughout the army. Her lists generated an avalanche of letters, as many as 150 a day. As Clara wrote Elvira, all brought "either useful information of some missing soldier or asking for some. My plan is a perfect success, and is growing popular I think—at least no one condemns it that I know of." Already she and her staff were preparing a second roll of 1,500 names. At the same time, Clara kept a master list on which she noted all the pertinent data for each missing man: his unit, the names and addresses of those inquiring about him, and the names and addresses of those responding with information about his whereabouts.

Clara's correspondents, almost all of them women, poured out their suffering to her. An Illinois mother wrote that her "darling boy" had been killed in the battle of the Wilderness but that his body had never been found. Desperately hoping that Clara might discover where her son was buried, she even enclosed a photograph of him, pointing out that he had "dark hazel eyes, hair almost black." A Mrs. Upton wrote that her son had been imprisoned for two years—she didn't know where—and that she had finally learned of his death from a fellow prisoner. Those two years of "waiting, waiting, waiting," she said, "were too terrible to imagine." Clara tried to answer as many such inquiries as she could, reaching out to her correspondents with care and compassion. She replied to Mrs. Upton that "I have placed the fatal check myself beside the dear name so loved, so lost."

One day Clara got a rude surprise: a letter from one of the "missing" soldiers on her list, who happened to be in Springfield, Illinois. He declared himself "mortified" to see his name in the papers. "I would like to know what I have done, so that I am worthy to have my name Blazoned all over the Country," he told Clara. "If my friends in New York wish to know where I am let them wait until I see fit to write them. As you are anxious to my welfare, I would say that I am just from New Orleans, discharged, on my way North but unluckily taken with chills and fever and could proceed no farther for some time at least. I shall remain here for a month."

Clara replied: "The cause of your name having been 'blazoned all over the country' was your unnatural concealment from your nearest relatives, and the great distress it caused them. What you have done to render this necessary I certainly do not know. It seems to have been the misfortune of your family to think more of you than you do of them. . . . *Your mother died waiting* and the results of your sister's faithful efforts to comply with her dying request 'mortify' you. . . . You are mistaken in supposing that I am 'anxious for your welfare.' I assure you I have no interest in it, but your accomplished sister, for whom I entertain the deepest respect and sympathy I shall inform of your existence lest you should not 'see fit' to do so yourself. I have the honor to be, sir, Clara Barton."

* * *

In late June, a Dorence Atwater wrote Clara from a hotel in Washington, reporting that he had seen a copy of her list of missing soldiers in a post office and that he could inform her about a great many of them. "I brought a copy of the Death Register from the Rebel Prison at Andersonville Ga. containing the names of 12,658," he said. "Can you grant me an interview if so I think I can give you some information that would be beneficial to the great cause you are engaged in."

When Clara called on Atwater in his hotel room, she found him shy and subdued to the point of diffidence. A slender lad of twenty, he had a sad smile, blue eyes, light brown hair, and a beardless face. His face was so emaciated and prematurely wrinkled that it made him look older than he was. As Clara sat with this damaged young man, smiling and nodding sympathetically, he told his remarkable story. He had grown up in Terryville, Connecticut, the third in a family of eight children. He had attended the public schools and impressed everybody with his outstanding penmanship. Only sixteen when the war broke out, he had to get his parents' consent to enlist in a squadron of Connecticut cavalry, which was later attached to the Second New York Cavalry under Lieutenant Colonel Judson Kilpatrick, who went on to become a famous general. Three days after Gettysburg, the rebels captured Atwater at Boonsboro, Maryland, while he was carrying military dispatches. Stricken with chronic diarrhea, he spent five months in the prison on Belle Isle, an island in the James River across from Richmond.

When Andersonville prison opened in February 1864, Atwater was among the first detachment of Richmond prisoners transferred there. Inside the Andersonville stockade, living in ragged tents and holes dug in the sloping ground, he and his comrades suffered from "fever, scurvy, and starvation," and many of them died. Atwater blamed the cruel treatment on Captain Henry Wirz, the commander of the prison's interior and a nervous little man who spoke in broken English, cursing his guards for not "vatching dem dam Yankees glose enough!" All the prisoners hated the "Flying Dutchman," and they hated General John H. Winder, too, a harsh disciplinarian sent to command the prison in June 1864. Because of Atwater's superior penmanship, Winder detailed him to the rebel surgeon's office, with orders to keep an official record of all the Union prisoners who died. According to Atwater, the rebels said that when the war ended, the record would be turned over to the U.S. government, even if the Confederacy won. Atwater toiled in the surgeon's office by day and slept in the foul and crowded stockade by night. The mortality rate at Andersonville shocked him: by September 1864, he was registering one hundred names a day, and he watched as "the naked skeleton forms" of his dead comrades were carted off to a common burial ground beyond the stockade.

"The appalling mortality," he told Clara, made him suspicious; he thought the rebels were deliberately killing and crippling prisoners to prevent them from fighting again. Convinced that the rebels would never reveal their death records, Atwater began keeping a secret register on coarse buff paper, copying data from the official records when the rebel surgeons were not around and concealing his paper inside his coat lining when they returned. In his register, he listed the name, unit, disease, cause and date of death, and grave number of every Union mortality. By February 1, 1865, his list contained 12,636 names (and more would be added). If he survived this hellish prison, he vowed to publish his rolls for the benefit of the surviving families.

When he was transferred to Columbia, South Carolina, he smuggled his register out in a little bundle of belongings; none of his guards bothered to search him. In late February, the rebels paroled him to the Union lines at Wilmington, North Carolina, and in mid-March he found himself at Camp Parole in Annapolis, in a barrack full of sick, dull-eyed skeletons from other rebel prisons. At once he wrote the secretary of war that he had a copy of the Andersonville death register. Sick with typhoid fever and diphtheria and emotionally devastated, he got a furlough from the commander at Annapolis and went home to Terryville, where he learned that his mother had died shortly after he had enlisted. He spent a month in bed, nursed by his ailing father.

In mid-April, he received a telegram from Colonel Samuel Breck of the adjutant general's office, ordering him to report at once and to bring his death register. Against the advice of his physician and his family, Atwater entrained for Washington and presented himself and his register at Breck's office. To Atwater's astonishment, the colonel offered him $300 for his death rolls by authority of Secretary of War Stanton. Atwater told him that making money was not his object. If it was, he could probably sell his list for $10,000. But he didn't want to sell it, he told Breck; he simply wanted to publish his rolls so that the families of the dead soldiers would finally know what had happened to them.

"If you go to publish them," Breck warned, "we can call it contraband matter and confiscate them."

After thinking the matter over, Atwater made Breck a counteroffer: if the colonel would give him $300 and a clerkship, he would loan his rolls to the government long enough for a copy to be made. Then he wanted his register back, so that the families of the dead could be properly notified.

As Atwater told the story, Breck agreed to his terms. In exchange for the loan of his rolls, he received a clerkship in "the final statement and disability bureau" of the War Department. Before assuming his duties, he told Clara, he returned home just in time to witness his father's death. To Clara, he seemed so lonely, hurt, and vulnerable that she could only think of him as an orphan, even though he had an older brother, Eugene, who lived in Connecticut.

While working in the War Department, Atwater continued, he asked Colonel Breck several times if his rolls had been copied, and each time Breck said "no" or "not yet." Afraid that the government would never return his register or make it public, Atwater asked if he could at least make a copy of it after work. Breck said he would have to ask General Edward D. Townsend, acting head of the Adjutant General's Department. Townsend, however, refused to let Atwater make a copy of his rolls. The truth was, both officers thought that Atwater was scheming to sell his register to a publisher for a handsome profit.

There the matter stood, Atwater told Clara, when he saw her list of missing soldiers and plea for information in the post office. With her connections, he hoped that she might help him get his register back. Then she could use it to identify missing prisoners. He showed her a drawing he had made of the Andersonville graveyard, where the Union dead had been buried in trenches, with each man's position marked by a numbered stick. Each name on his register, he said, had a number assigned to it that was keyed to the numbered stick in the cemetery.

Clara perceived right away what he was suggesting. If she and Atwater went to Andersonville with his death register, they could identify the graves with proper head markers and notify the families of exactly where their "loved ones" were buried. It was an exciting prospect. With one expedition, she could establish the fate of almost 13,000 missing Union prisoners of war.

Such an expedition required government approval, of course. How was the best way to get it? She dared not approach Secretary of War Stanton directly; she still feared he did not approve of women serving in the war. Her thoughts turned to General Hoffman, commissary general for prisoners, a kind man who had endorsed her recent plea to

President Johnson. If she could get Hoffman's support, perhaps he would secure Stanton's approval. Toward that end, she wrote General Hoffman about Atwater and his register and asked for permission to take it to Andersonville, for the purpose of marking each grave with a proper headboard and aiding "some sorrow burdened families in identifying the spot which contains all that barbarity, treason and crime have left to them of their loved and lost."

"At first," she said later, "the idea was regarded as entirely visionary and I was admonished to abandon it." But Clara refused to give up. It was her duty to go to Andersonville. The ghosts of 13,000 Union dead were calling her there. "By dint of perseverance," she said, she convinced Hoffman that her plan was practical and that Atwater and an army contingent ought to be sent to Andersonville with her. Hoffman sent her proposal to Stanton with an enthusiastic endorsement.

Shortly afterward a summons came from the secretary of war himself. When she entered his office, he met her halfway across the room with his hand extended. He was a short, thick-chested man with a prodigious beard that hung down to his chest. Peering at Clara through round, rimless little spectacles, he allowed himself a smile, saying that he had been anxious to meet her. As he praised her for her war work, Clara could scarcely believe that this was the intimidating Stanton who screamed at his subordinates, kicked unscrupulous contractors out of his office, drove himself and others so hard that he sometimes collapsed at his desk and wept. Brusque, efficient, and brutally honest, he had made many implacable enemies in and out of government. But he had run his department with great energy and competence, and he had been a loyal supporter of Abraham Lincoln, whose assassination had left him inconsolable with grief.

He agreed with Clara that the dead at Andersonville should be remembered and their graves properly identified. Inspired by her proposal, he had ordered a corps of forty workmen and clerks to leave for Andersonville forthwith on the steamer *Virginia*. Captain James M. Moore, an assistant quartermaster in charge of military burials in the Washington area, was to command the expedition, and Atwater was to go along to help identify and mark the Union graves. The graveyard, Stanton said, was to be designated as a national cemetery.

According to Clara, Stanton thanked her profusely for suggesting the expedition. He could not, he said, think of everything that was for the general welfare, and "no one knew how grateful he was to the person who put forth—among all the impracticable, interested, wild and selfish schemes which were continually crowded upon him—one good, sensible, practical, *unselfish* idea that he could take up and act upon with safety and credit." He said he could not order Clara to accompany the expedition, so he asked her to do so, to see that her suggestions were carried out to her "entire satisfaction."

Clara was elated. Clearly she had been wrong about Stanton's attitude toward women serving in the war. With barely restrained excitement, she reported her interview to Atwater, who then went to see Captain Moore for a clarification as to the status of his death register. To Atwater's surprise, Moore now possessed the official death rolls Atwater had made for the rebel authorities at Andersonville. After slashing across Alabama into southwestern Georgia, James Wilson's cavalry had overrun Andersonville and captured the prison records, including the official death rolls. The rolls had been sent to Washington and turned over to Captain Moore. When Atwater examined the books, however, he found that many of the sheets were blurred and that one segment containing 2,500 names was missing altogether. Not to fear, he told Moore: his own secret record would supply the deficiency. Moore promptly acquired it from the adjutant general's office, so that both the incomplete official register and Atwater's secret record would guide Moore and his men in their task of marking the Union graves.

The expedition was scheduled to depart for Savannah on July 8. According to Moore's itinerary, the party would travel on the Georgia Central Railroad up to Macon, some 175 miles northwest of Savannah, and take another train back southwest to Andersonville. It would be a circuitous and demanding journey, but Clara anticipated a great adventure into the heart of the Deep South. What was more, she felt an almost spiritual calling from Andersonville. "If it once shall be my privilege to gaze over that crowded field of hidden graves where sleep the 13,000 dead of my country's loved and lost," she wrote a friend at the *New York Tribune*, "and witness the fast fading mounds giving place to the lettered tablet which shall tell something of the tale the prison-sealed lips beneath could not utter, and feel that the hallowed earth which covers these remains may yet receive a mother's tear or a sister's kiss, it will be one of the happiest and saddest hours of my whole life."

Clara's euphoria was short-lived. From the outset of the expedition, Captain Moore objected "violently" to her going along. Twenty-eight years old, with a full beard and a mildly receding hairline, he was regu-

lar army—a hard-boiled, spit-and-polish sort who could not tolerate a
woman intruding on a man's work. When Clara was late in boarding
the *Virginia* on departure day, Moore rushed on deck and shouted in
the presence of his workmen: "God damn it to hell! Some people don't
deserve to go anywhere, and what in Hell does she want to go for?"

That set the mood for the entire voyage down to Savannah. Many
of the workmen made sarcastic remarks about Clara and repeated
Moore's abusive language within her hearing. God damn it, they
would say, what in hell does *she* want to go for? Moore himself simply shunned her. "I cannot understand Capt Moore," she wrote in
her diary; "he does not seem friendly, is silent, and abstract as if I
were an intruder, and yet I cannot understand how this can be his
feeling as long as the arrangement from the first was mine and not
his. I will use any means in my power to render myself unobtrusive
to him, and hope he may not dislike me. How alone I am on such a
trip—how little people at home can realize my situation, and what it
will cost me."

On the second day at sea, Clara fell sick and retired to her cabin
below deck. She stayed there for the rest of the journey, suffering miserably from the intense heat—her berth was situated near the boil-
ers—and the infernal racket of the engines. On July 12, the *Virginia*
steamed into the mouth of the Savannah River, and Atwater helped
Clara on deck as the ship approached the wharves of Savannah. Stores
and warehouses lined the street along the river, and the main part of
town could be seen on a sandy plateau above it. When the river pilot
learned of their destination, he reported that the Georgia Central
Railroad, which connected Savannah and Macon, was closed. Sherman
had wrecked it on his march to the sea, and it had not been repaired.
Moore inquired about wagon transportation, but learned that there
were not enough wagons in the whole state of Georgia to haul his crew
and materials. Informed that all other railroad routes were closed, too,
Moore telegraphed Quartermaster General Meigs that the expedition
ought to be canceled. He asked permission to store his equipment and
materials, including 7,000 unlettered headboards, and return to
Washington with his men.

The party spent almost a week in Savannah, awaiting orders from
Meigs. Since nobody told her anything, Clara at first had no idea what
was going on. She remained in her hot cabin without "one social or
sympathizing spirit on board," she complained. Yes, she had Atwater,
who adored her, but he was "a mere boy & bashful." She longed for the
companionship of a mature gentleman.

One evening, Edward R. Clement, the *Savannah Herald* correspondent and an old acquaintance of Clara, paid her a visit. She told him about Atwater and the mission and gave him a copy of her roll of missing soldiers. Clement in turn published in the *Herald* a notice of the expedition that featured Clara Barton, crediting her for the idea of the expedition and praising her war work effusively. She was, Clement said, "one of the most efficient and earnest of the volunteer-laborers in the Hospitals and on the battle-fields of the War, one of those noble women whose heroic devotion has added a new glory to American womanhood."

Clement also introduced Clara to William Lane, a wealthy, aristocratic gentleman and an "old friend" of General Sherman; Lane invited Clara to stay with him and his family for the remainder of her time in Savannah. Though usually cool toward Southerners, Clara said she had rarely encountered "so much intelligence in one family home." Lane and his friends took Clara on carriage rides through historic Savannah, which had figured prominently in Sherman's march. After cutting his swath through Georgia, Sherman had seized Savannah and presented it to Lincoln as a Christmas present. Trenches still scarred the earth along the outskirts of the city, and mounds of earth still obstructed its streets. Even so, it was a lovely old city, with many fine brick homes, parks with fountains, and groves of evergreens and live oaks draped with hanging moss.

At some point, Clara learned that Moore was inclined to abandon the expedition, and she was furious. In her view, this was one of the most significant undertakings of the war, a sacred pilgrimage to memorialize thousands of dead Union boys and to ease the hurt of their friends and kinfolk. Why would Moore want to forsake them? Was it because of her? She refused to believe that her presence "constituted the only obstruction over the route."

Her anger grew when an army clerk told her that the route to Andersonville overland from Augusta was "perfect"; he had traveled that way eight weeks before. When Atwater fetched Clara a map, she traced the route suggested by the clerk: they could take a riverboat up the Savannah River to Augusta, then make rail connections west to Atlanta, southeast to Macon, and then southwest to Andersonville. It was a long, roundabout route, a distance of some 460 miles, but it was open and it would get them to Andersonville.

Clara went forthwith to Captain Moore. "*I informed* Capt. M.," she wrote in her diary, "*that I was aware of the perfect condition* of the road from Augusta to And[ersonville] via Atlanta." As it happened,

Moore had received a telegram from Augusta officials telling him that the railroad was now open to Atlanta. All he told Clara, though, was that it was "best" to telegraph the news to Washington and let Meigs decide what should be done. Clara was convinced that Moore was determined to abort the mission and return to Washington. Well, let him do as he wished. She resolved to proceed to Andersonville without him and await another expedition. She hoped to take Atwater with her but had to abandon that idea when Moore or somebody else warned her that Atwater could be charged with desertion if he went with her.

At this critical juncture a dispatch arrived from Meigs containing "peremptory orders" for Moore to proceed by the alternate route through Augusta and Atlanta. Moore appeared less than thrilled. "It was tauntingly remarked," Clara wrote a friend, "that the matter could have been evaded but for me. And still I could not feel like doing penance for this sin." Moore was indeed put out with Clara. When he arranged for river passage on the *Hellen*, he told the captain that it was to leave at the prescribed hour whether Clara was on board or not.

On July 19, the expedition headed up the "crooked, muddy" Savannah River and reached Augusta two days later. Forced to wait another two days for train connections to Atlanta, the party found lodging at the Augusta House. During their stay, Clara expected Captain Moore to treat her like a lady regardless of the difficulties between them. Were they not traveling together on a military assignment from the War Department? Throughout the war, officers and common soldiers alike had shown her courtesy and respect, had even been politely flirtatious. She felt entitled to such attention from men.

To her mortification, however, Moore treated her with studied disrespect. This from a man fifteen years her junior! When the bell rang for mealtimes, the captain would walk into the dining room without waiting for Clara, forcing her to enter unescorted. "Today I went without my dinner rather than go alone," she complained to her diary; "he told me after he came out that he waited near *five* minutes, but he sent no servant to my room. He sort of apologizes for seeing me so little by professing to be *distracted* with business every minute and vexed to death with poor transportation and slack quartermasters. He does not know that my room is precisely over the front door and that I see him sitting in the shade, smoking with other gentlemen by the hours without getting off his feet."

Late one night, someone tried to enter Clara's hotel room; she could

hear a key turning in the lock. Luckily for her, the door was bolted
from the inside. She lay awake for the rest of the night, alert to the
slightest noise. "I am all alone," she wrote in her diary, "none of the
rest of the party near me and Capt. Moore does not know what part of
the house I am in. I might be killed and buried and he would never
know it."

At last, they were off for Atlanta, traveling west on a makeshift train,
with Clara, Moore, and his workmen riding together in the same old-
time coach, whose top, she said, was "punched with rebel bayonets." It
was a hot, dusty trip across a countryside ravaged by war. The rails
were in such poor condition that the train seldom went faster than
twelve miles an hour. There were stops and delays, too, for the railroad, contrary to what Clara and Moore had been told, was still being
repaired. "We literally waited for the roads to be completed to pass
over," Clara said.

It was after dark, July 23, when the train pulled into Atlanta and the
party found rooms at the Bell House. "Atlanta is in terrible condition,"
Clara jotted in her diary the next day. "One mass of ruins. It really
looks as if Sherman's army had quartered in it, Ay! and fought in it too!
shattered and burned." The emotional scars left by the invading
Yankees were much in evidence, too. When Moore's party arrived at
the depot, the Southern railroad officials gave him "great trouble,"
Clara said, refusing to let the Yankees board the train until the captain
secured a military order forcing them to do so. Clara later learned that
the conductor had been a rebel officer.

Soon they were on their way again, heading south for Macon in
sweltering summer heat. All that day Clara subsisted on a wonderful
discovery—sweet Georgia peaches. At Macon, James Wilson detailed a
white cavalry company and a company of black troops to reinforce the
expedition. The next day, July 25, they entrained for Andersonville,
sixty miles to the southwest. From the window of her coach, Clara
looked out on a region of thick pine forests, low hills, swamps, and
marshes interspersed with corn and cotton fields. At about half-past
noon, the train passed a crude stockade off to the left—this was
Andersonville prison—and pulled into Anderson Station with a blast of
its whistle.

There wasn't much in this remote, forested neighborhood beyond
the depot and an old house or two. The nearest town was Americas, sit-

uated some eleven miles to the southwest. It was unbearably hot, and
the few residents moved and talked slowly in apparent deference to
the heat.

A kindly looking gentleman—a native Georgian by the sound of his
drawl—invited Clara to his quarters, out of the blazing sun. His name
was William Griffin; he hailed from Fort Valley, Georgia, and he was
trying to improve the grounds of the prison cemetery. While passing
through Anderson one day, he had learned from local blacks that animals were rooting on exposed bodies at the graveyard. With the help of
the blacks, Griffin had reburied them and started building a fence
around the site. When General Wilson inspected the prison grounds,
he named Griffin temporary superintendent and furnished him with
rations and materials.

Clara was impressed with Griffin. With the blacks, he "had set
bravely to work by himself in the face of a prejudiced community to
care for and protect the neglected graves of our isolated dead," she
wrote a friend. It was all the more astonishing because this "noble philanthropist" was a *Georgian*. Clearly not everyone down here was like
the monstrous rebel fiends depicted in Northern propaganda.

Clara wanted to visit the cemetery, so they climbed into an ambulance, rode up a dirt road past the stockade, and entered a graveyard
surrounded by stunted, scraggly trees and taller pines. The sight of this
hallowed ground, of the vast and silent formations of almost 13,000
crudely numbered identification sticks, moved Clara to tears. The dead
had been buried in mass graves, placed side by side without coffins.
There appeared to be from 100 to 150 bodies to a trench, with the
identification stick at the head of each man serving as the only connection between him and total oblivion. The numbers of dead were staggering. More Union men had died in Andersonville than had been
killed at Second Bull Run, South Mountain, Antietam, Fredericksburg,
Chancellorsville, Gettysburg, Battery Wagner, and the Wilderness all
put together. Andersonville alone accounted for more than a third of
the 30,218 Northern deaths in rebel prisons.

No other Georgian was more contrite about Andersonville than
William Griffin, who hoped it would be made into a prominent
national cemetery. Clara shared that hope. "The original plan for identifying the graves is capable of being carried out to the letter," she
wrote Stanton, "and the field is wide and ample for much more in the
future. If *desirable*, the grounds of Andersonville can be made into a
National Cemetery of great beauty and interest. Be assured Mr.
Stanton that for this prompt and humane action of yours the American

people will bless you long after your willing hands and mind have ceased to toil for them."

Moore's workmen pitched camp within a hundred yards of the stockade, a rectangular structure that dominated the grounds and served as a grisly point of reference for Clara. She knew that at some point she must go inside and witness its "haunts of misery." As she stored her large trunk inside her tent, she realized how glad she was to be in the field again. It seemed so natural to her. She had thought that her camp days were over—that she'd tied her last canvas and sat by her last campfire. Not that there was physical comfort in living in a remote wild, with only twelve square feet of canvas standing between her and the summer sun. Clara, however, thrived on such hardship and eagerly anticipated the work of establishing a national cemetery.

On July 27, with the help of Atwater's death rolls, Moore and his men set to work fashioning a white headboard for each of the Andersonville dead; the slab gave his unit and date of death in black letters. To Clara's despair, however, Captain Moore never once invited her to help with the lettering and the identification of graves, never even asked her to accompany him and his men to the cemetery. Indeed, he went about as if she did not exist. When she did go to the graveyard, she told Stanton later, it was in the evening when the workmen were finished for the day, "for I did not choose to expose myself to their remarks." She was reasonably certain that jealousy accounted for their behavior; they couldn't stand the fact that a woman had proposed the expedition, that a woman had come along to make certain they did the work correctly. With the single exception of Atwater, she felt "entirely alone here" and was extremely cautious; "I know I stand on slippery ground." Even so, Clara found a way to retaliate: She assumed the role of camp nurse for those who came down with chills and fever. In that capacity, she exercised real power over the very men who alternately taunted and ignored her.

Moore shunned Atwater, too, making Atwater feel so much in the way that he never offered to help. To make matters worse, Moore ordered a sick clerk to be moved into Atwater's tent without Atwater's consent. Yet Atwater did not complain. Showing himself "manly beyond his years," as Clara said, he made himself "the constant nurse and attendant of the poor suffering [man] by his side." The man was Edward Watts of Georgetown, a young clerk in the Quartermaster Department. He had taken sick on the trip up the Savannah River and had grown progressively worse. Clara thought he had a dangerous "malignant fever," which she treated with what medicine there was.

When Watts grew steadily weaker, she secured the services of a local physician. After examining the young man, the physician asserted that his fever would probably break soon. Clara made custard and black tea for him and kept him covered when a violent storm struck the area, with blasts of thunder like artillery and wind-whipped rain that pounded the tents and the nearby stockade.

On July 26, the day Watts was moved into Atwater's tent, Clara and Atwater made a pilgrimage to the stockade. He showed her the hospital sheds, situated just beyond the southeast wall, which had been built only a few months before Andersonville closed as a functioning prison. The old hospital, in which Atwater had kept most of his death register, had consisted of a collection of ragged tents enclosed by a rickety board fence and protected by a guard. "Confused heaps of rubbish alone mark the place it occupied," Clara wrote in her notes. Here fifteen or so surgeons had treated only the most critically ill prisoners, as many as 2,000 at a time, most of them afflicted with the killer diseases of the camp: diarrhea, dysentery, hospital gangrene, and scurvy. One scurvy victim left a vivid record of the ravages of that disease at Andersonville: "My legs had begun to twist wrongside out, and feet to change front, and troublesome otherways, my gums swollen and rotting, sloughing off, leaving the teeth almost ready to fall out. My limbs, from the knees to toes, were swollen nearly to bursting, black purple in color, holes in which the finger could be inserted over an inch, putrid, disgusting to look at, while from the knees, torso to head, the body was skin and bone—the skin drawn like parchment on a frame."

When Dr. Joseph Jones, a Georgia professor of medicine, visited Andersonville in the late summer of 1864, he found hospital patients lying two in a bunk or on the bare ground, many without blankets or clothing; flies were crawling all over them, even into their mouths, and laying eggs in their open sores or wounds. Many of them, Jones said, were "literally incrusted with dirt and filth and covered with vermin." Patients too sick to walk relieved themselves in wooden boxes just outside the tents, but the boxes were seldom emptied. Some men were so weak that they defecated and urinated inside the tents. "The whole soil appeared to be saturated with urine and filth of all kinds," Professor Jones reported. "The air of the tents was foul and disagreeable in the extreme, and in fact the entire grounds emitted a most nauseous and disgusting smell." Because of severe medical shortages, hospital attendants often used the same filthy bandages over and over, which spread infection, particularly hospital gangrene, in epidemic proportions. Because of the all-pervasive filth and the poor health of the prisoners, even the most innocuous wound—a splinter in the hand, a scratched mosquito bite, a popped blister—often turned gangrenous. If the wound was on the limbs or fingers and toes, it usually required amputation. Yet amputations seldom arrested the gangrene, so that "almost every amputation was followed finally by death," Professor Jones said, "either from the effects of gangrene or from the prevailing diarrhea and dysentery." When patients died, black prisoners carted the bodies to the "dead-house," where they awaited transportation in open wagons to the graveyard north of the stockade.

One young patient, confined in "the gangrene hospital" with "swamp fever," scurvy, and gangrenous feet and ankles, fought desperately for his life, begging the rebel surgeons to amputate. But they refused on the grounds that he couldn't possibly live anyhow. So the man, whose name was John January, borrowed a pocket knife and cut off his own feet at the ankle joints. "No blood flowed from the amputation whatever," said a comrade, "just a serum of the color of weak vinegar and sticky in consistency." The bones were left "protruding without a covering of flesh for five inches," January said. Somehow he survived, although his weight dropped from 165 to 45 pounds.

From the hospital site, Clara and Atwater walked around to the front of the stockade and entered by the south gate, Clara taking copious notes on what she saw and what Atwater told her. The walls were made of pine logs fifteen feet high and hewn to fit closely together, with roofed sentry boxes standing at about eighty-foot intervals. In the boxes, Georgia reserves had kept close watch on the seething mass of humanity below, ready to shoot anyone who crossed the infamous deadline, a rail running around inside the entire length of the stockade, about eighteen feet from the wall. When gunshots rang out, the inmates knew that some comrade had wandered beyond the deadline or simply strayed too close to it. A member of the Georgia reserves admitted that many of his comrades were trigger happy. "We have many thoughtless boys here who think the killing of a Yankee will make them great men," he said; "every day or two there are prisoners shot."

Inside the gate, Clara gazed over a twenty-six-and-a-half-acre enclosure, consisting of two treeless slopes divided by a sluggish little stream called Stockade Creek. At its peak in August, 1864, this "shelterless, pitiful spot of earth," originally designed for 10,000 prisoners of war, had held 33,000, including white soldiers of the Twenty-first

Massachusetts and black soldiers of the Fifty-fourth Massachusetts. As Atwater recalled his own experiences on the gullied slopes, Clara could envision them teeming with thousands of men clad in rags or wearing nothing at all, their matted hair infested with vermin, their eyes sunken in their skulls, their faces and hands blackened from the pitch-pine smoke of their little campfires. To protect themselves from the sun and storms, some erected meager little shrub huts, or improvised tents from whatever they had carried with them—coats or blankets, which they stretched over sticks. Others dug caves and burrowed into them, Clara thought, "like rabbits or reptiles." Along the face of the northern slope, she found caves arched in the form of ovens, with floors and ceilings made of sticks and pieces of boards; some even had fireplaces and chimneys. During a heavy rain, a few caves had apparently collapsed and become the graves of their occupants. In some of the caves, she found the remnants of crude utensils: "drinking cups made of sections of horns, platters and spoons wrought from parts of old canteens, kettles and pans made, without solder, from stray pieces of old tin or sheet iron."

In other caves, the inmates had dug horizontal galleries—evidence of frantic efforts to escape. To avoid detection, Atwater said, they hid the dirt in their pockets and sprinkled it on the ground above. Some prisoners escaped by underground tunnels, but most were chased down by patrols with hunting dogs and returned to the prison or shot. Atwater showed Clara the kennels for the bloodhounds and the stocks and chains used to torture runaways and others who defied authority.

For food, most inmates subsisted on whatever their captors gave them. Officially, the prisoners' daily rations were supposed to be the same as those issued to Confederate field soldiers: salt beef or fat bacon ("sowbelly" in soldier parlance) and cornmeal, with occasional servings of molasses, rice, and peas. But because of the food shortages plaguing the entire Confederacy in 1864, the prisoners seldom received anything like that. On some days, they got nothing but a half pint of raw meal, or indigestible cornbread with chunks of the cob still in it, or a repelling mixture of swamp water and coarse cornmeal. Atwater described a brackish soup served up with pea pods and dirt in it. On many days, the prisoners got no rations at all and either went hungry or killed swallows and devoured them raw. The human skeletons who survived the camp testified to its famine-like conditions.

To add insult to injury, the commanders of Andersonville allowed a post sutler to sell additional food from a little market *inside* the prison. The few lucky inmates with money could buy pies, cakes, eggs, and vegetables, all at exorbitant prices. The others could only stare at the cornucopia of food on cruel display.

The prisoners' principal source of water was the miserable little stream, a tributary of Sweet Water Creek, that meandered through camp. They not only drank from it but used it for washing and cooking as well. Thanks to the gross mismanagement and lack of system that characterized Andersonville, Stockade Creek was entirely contaminated. The prisoners' latrines, or sinks, were laid out parallel to the stream and overflowed into it during heavy rains. The cookhouse and bakery were situated on the banks of the creek, *upstream* from the stockade, so that its grease and refuse were dumped into the very water the prisoners drank and cooked with. "Not half watter enough to drink," complained a Vermont prisoner, "& what we do get isn't fit for a Hog for it runs through the camp & every night & morning the cooks empty their greasy watter & filth in the Brook & the stench that arises from the watter is enough to suffocate aney comman man god help us." To make matters worse, the camps of the rebel garrison stood on the banks of the stream farther up, and from 2,000 to 3,000 soldiers bathed and washed clothes in it and relieved themselves in latrines that also overflowed into the creek when it rained.

Nobody could drink from this polluted rivulet without risking his life. As Clara walked along Stockade Creek, she saw grease and refuse matter from the cooking kitchens still clinging to the banks. Dear God, she wondered, what manner of men would allow such conditions to exist, when within "rifle shot" of the stockade flowed Sweet Water Creek? Why wasn't its "pure, delicious" water brought to the prisoners? Atwater said that they had often complained to Captain Wirz about the water problem, but Wirz never did anything about it.

In a desperate search for drinkable water, the prisoners dug wells into the ground with whatever they had—canteen halves, spoons, knives, and sticks. Clara found wells that were fifty to eighty feet deep. The well water, alas, was not much of an improvement over Stockade Creek; one man complained that it "appears impregnated with sulfur, or some mineral, looks blue, and induces diarrhea."

According to Atwater and others, a good part of the enclosed draw along Stockade Creek was a foul-smelling swamp, buzzing with flies and mosquitoes. This "poison sink of putrid mud and water," as one prisoner described it, teemed with the excrement of thousands of sick men and with "billions" of maggots, including big, white, long-tailed ones. The maggots, said another captive, would slither out onto the hot, red dirt and, sprouting wings, would swarm about, stinging the inmates and laying eggs in their open sores. Of this "mass pollution," a prisoner said, "We could not get away from it—we ate it, drank it and slept in it." When heavy rains fell, water swept down the slopes into the fetid creek and swamp, creating a flood of filth and excrement. Clara thought it must have been impossible for the inmates to keep their footing on the slippery slopes during a rainstorm. The stronger ones, she learned, had gathered at the tops of the hills, "massed togeth-er like cattle in a storm." Many others, she supposed, slid into the vile waters below and drowned.

Later Clara tried to capture all this in a report to Stanton, her empa-thy for the prisoners heightened by personal observation. "The treach-erous nature of the soil, parching to seams in the sun, and gullying and sliding under their feet with every shower, must have augmented their ills almost beyond conception. I watched the effect of a heavy fall of rain upon the enclosed grounds, and in thirty minutes the entire hill-sides, which had constituted their sole abiding-place, were one rolling mass of slippery mud, and this the effect of a mere summer shower. What of the continued rains of autumn? Think of thirty thousand men penned by [a] close[d] stockade upon twenty-six acres of ground, from which every tree and shrub had been uprooted for fuel to cook their scanty food, huddled like cattle, without shelter or blanket, half-clad and hungry, with the dreary night setting in, after a day of autumn rain. The hill-tops would not hold them all, the valley was filled with the swollen brook; seventeen feet from the stockade ran the fatal dead line, beyond which no man might step and live. What did they do? I need not ask where did they go, for on the face of the whole green earth there was no place but this for them; but where did they place them-selves? how did they live? Ay! how did they die! But this is only one feature of their suffering; and perhaps the lightest. Of the long dazzling months when gaunt famine stalked at noon-day, and pestilence walked by night; and upon the seamed and parching earth the cooling rains fell not, I will not trust me to speak."

Confined in massive numbers in the filthy stockade and hospital, deprived of proper food, water, and shelter, crawling with lice and tor-tured by mosquitoes and flies, bloated from dropsy, stricken by epi-demics of diarrhea, scurvy, and infectious disease, the wretches of Andersonville had died by the hundreds every week. On a single day in August 1864, a prisoner "counted 235 corpses lying at the south gate or about it." Some men went mad from hunger and disease and in their hallucinations talked aloud to members of their families; others regressed into "whining, childish creatures." Many were so demoralized and hopeless that they simply stopped living—death for them was a relief. Others were so brutalized that they turned on their comrades, stole their rations and pitiful possessions, and even maimed or murdered them. Roving gangs of thugs, called raiders, terrorized the entire compound until the leaders were finally seized, hanged, and buried in the graveyard by themselves, apart from the other Union dead.

How, Clara wondered, had Dorence Atwater survived this hellhole of human misery? One thing she knew for certain: that this "mere boy" had defied death and the ravages of disease, had wrenched "from oblivion the last record of 13000 martyred dead" and brought it out to lay at the feet of mourning thousands, made him one of the war's great heroes.

As Clara stood brooding inside the stockade, she sensed that the souls of its victims were hovering near. At last, having seen all she could bear, she turned and with Atwater walked out the gate and into the freedom of open country, of fields and forests that stretched to the distant horizons and the limitless skies beyond.

Her pilgrimage to the stockade would haunt her for the rest of her life. Who was responsible for the atrocities committed there? Local white residents to whom she addressed that question acknowledged "the magnitude and enormity" of the crimes but strongly denied any complicity in them. Indeed, hearing gruesome stories about the scurvy-stricken inmates, some neighborhood women had taken fresh vegetables to the stockade, only to be turned away by General Winder, who questioned their loyalty to the Confederacy. A surgeon who had served at Andersonville told Clara that General Winder, overall prison commander, was responsible for the cruelties and atrocities, and most of the local whites agreed with him. On the other hand, Atwater and others blamed Captain Wirz, who had charge of the inside of the stockade. Profane and irritable, suffering constant pain from an arm wound, the Swiss-born Wirz had cursed and threatened the prisoners, once deploying artillery outside the stockade and vowing to blast the grounds with grape and canister if any more of the Yankees attempted to escape. Atwater himself accused Wirz of various sadistic acts. When one escaped prisoner was caught, Atwater said, Wirz shot him in the leg as punishment. He also had "a chain-gang there," Atwater later testified, "which had at one time twelve men attached to it, with a large ball in the centre and a chain running from that large ball to the leg of each prisoner, with a small ball and chain attached to the other leg. . . . Each time a new man was put in they had to walk a mile to the blacksmith's shop, having to drag this ball and chain through the hot sand.

One man died with the chain upon him." Atwater also testified that Wirz "used to have men put up in the stocks, where they would have to stand with their heads through the stocks for two hours; then they would change positions and lie on their backs with their feet up in the stocks, in the sun, without any shade."

If such reports were true, Clara wrote a friend, then Wirz "would have been a 'Star' in the days of the Spanish Inquisition." Many other survivors also accused Wirz of torturing and murdering prisoners. Even if their claims were exaggerated, the mass graves alone convicted him and Winder of gross and unforgivable negligence, of what medical professor Jones described as "the almost total absence of system, government, and rigid but wholesome sanitary regulations."

Winder himself was beyond mortal punishment—he had died of a heart attack before the war ended—but Wirz had been arrested at the prison and taken to Washington to stand trial for murder, with newspapers calling him "a fiend incarnate," "the Andersonville savage." One day, an officer on General Wilson's staff came to Moore's camp and took the official death register away in a box; the government wanted it for Wirz's upcoming trial. Clara hoped she would be called to testify, for she believed she could proffer damning evidence of cruelty and neglect at Andersonville. Anticipating that possibility, she returned to the stockade and collected some relics of captivity—a makeshift spoon, sieves made of punctured oyster cans, three cattle-horn drinking cups, a turtle shell used as a soup bowl, pieces of boards from the deadline, and a cannonball—and hired a black man to carry them back to her tent.

Clara found herself something of a celebrity in the Andersonville neighborhood, as a steady stream of folk came to see her at the camp. A white lady invited her to tea, and other women called in parties of threes and fours. They "were very neighborly, very bland," Clara said later, and were careful to disassociate themselves from the prison. Some had missing sons, members of the now-defunct rebel army. When they learned about Clara's work on behalf of missing soldiers, they begged her to search for information about their own lost boys, and she promised to do what she could.

One day William Griffin, the prison's "temporary" superintendent, brought his brother Joel to meet Clara. She recognized his name instantly: he was the Confederate Colonel Griffin who had commanded the Chowan River line in North Carolina and whom "Stephen had loved so much" for his kindness and protection during Stephen's exile. Clara was overwhelmed. "How can it be?" she asked her diary; "how has this thing happened, who has directed, does poor old brother Ste look down on this meeting and smile?" She couldn't believe that "here in this desolation, in this *strange* spot, the last in creation, is this meeting. Oh God knows if he have not dedicated this spot to the spirits of the martyred prisoners, and here their souls hover and congregate to work their earthly missions—am I crazy? but both God and that old brother seem very near tonight."

Blacks, too, came from miles around to meet "Miss Clara," the "Yankee woman." Many had never seen a Northern woman before and were excited by the sight of her. One group brought her gifts of chickens, peaches, and tomatoes. In return, she gave them oil for a sick baby and "procured" a woman named Rosa to do the camp washing and help nurse Watts, who showed no sign of recovering.

By August, the blacks were flocking to see Clara, for the word had spread that she liked black people and could be trusted to deal with them truthfully. It was not uncommon, she said, for her to open her tent on a given morning and find eighty to a hundred former slaves standing there. They came from miles around just to meet Clara and to ask whether Lincoln really was dead and whether they really were free. White folks, they said, told them that Lincoln had been killed and that they were all slaves again. That sort of talk made the blacks suspicious that Lincoln was not dead and that whites said so as "a hoax to hold them in slavery." If Miss Clara could set the matter straight and tell them they were free, they said, they could believe it.

Clara said that Lincoln had been shot, that she had seen him dead, and that they were as free as she was. She told them about the Emancipation Proclamation, and they wanted to know how it read. Reassured by her remarks, they sought her advice. The local whites told them that General Wilson had issued an order commanding the blacks to "work six days in the week hard, and half a day on Sunday," and to do so without pay. Was this so? they asked Clara. Others had heard that they were supposed to get a share of the crops. But when they told the white folks that, the whites had run them off. Since they were illiterate, they asked Clara if she would read the new rules and regulations to them.

Clara acquired a copy of Wilson's order and read it to all the blacks who came to see her. As she described it, the order urged them to remain on the estates of their former masters until Christmas, gathering the crops they had planted and awaiting further arrangements by the government. At the same time, he encouraged the whites to give them a share of the crops as wages. Clara understood that General Rufus Saxton, assistant commissioner of the Freedmen's Bureau in Georgia, South Carolina, and Florida, had published regulations specifying exactly what portion of the crops the blacks should get and that those regulations were published in the Macon papers. The blacks were vastly relieved, for they were afraid that they were supposed to work hard for nothing, like slaves. As Clara read Wilson's order, she would pause from time to time to ask if the blacks understood a particular passage. "Yes," they would say, "we understand that." "What do you understand by it?" she would ask, in her former schoolteacher style. They would rephrase it in their own words, demonstrating that they understood it very well indeed. When the lesson was over, she would urge them to return to their home estates and work faithfully until Christmas, and to take their share of the crops, since white Southerners had no money to pay them. After Christmas, the government would advise them what to do. "I think they never failed to follow my advice," she said later.

One morning, the camp cook woke Clara saying that a man wished to see her. She dressed and found a handsome mulatto, about forty-five years old, standing in front of her tent. His name was Arnold Cater, and he had come to see Miss Clara about a problem concerning his wife. As he explained it, he was born and raised as a house slave of former Georgia governor William Rabon. To pay their debts, the Rabon family had been obliged to sell him a few years ago, separating him from his wife and five children. He said that slave traders took him to southwestern Georgia, 200 miles away from the Rabon place, and sold him to Nick Wylie, owner of many slaves and a large plantation. Despairing of ever seeing his family again, Cater took another wife, a young Wylie slave, and they had a child. One day in early 1865, when his wife was pregnant with their second child, she was unable to finish an assigned task, which was to tie yarn into knots. The overseer, a vicious man named Jim Bird, was so furious that he bucked and gagged her as punishment.

Bucked and gagged? Clara asked. What was that?

The overseer stripped her clothing off, Cater explained, and made her sit on the ground with her knees drawn up like so, and her hands put under them. He rammed a stick over her arms and under her knees, tied her hands in front, and gagged her. Then he threw her over on her face, kicked her, and took the lash to her bare back, striking her hard, again and again. Then he untied her and left her lying on the floor of the Caters' cabin, her back "a gore of blood," which was the way Cater found her when he came home from work. He was a slave and didn't dare complain. The next day, Bird ordered Cater's wife to finish her task of tying yarn in knots. So lame and hurt she could scarcely stand, she was unable to finish all eight knots. When Bird found out, he thundered that he would come by for her at seven the next morning and whip her again. That night the Caters escaped, leaving their baby behind. They made their way to Americas, in Southwestern Georgia, where friendly blacks took them in and found him work as a blacksmith for a dollar a day. Soon the war ended, and he heard of Clara Barton at Andersonville and of a Yankee settlement going up there, so he came to ask her help and advice. Did he dare go back to the Wylie plantation and get his baby? Could he and his family live at Andersonville? Would they be safe?

Clara wrote the Union commander at Americas, asking him to dispatch a sergeant and a wagon team to fetch the Caters' baby and belongings (Cater had mentioned that they owned some chickens and a little bedroom furniture), and Cater took her letter to Americas himself. "Two days after," Clara recalled, "the whole assemblage drove up in front of my tent—Cater, his wife and the baby, the chickens, and the bed and bedding." The wife was a young mulatto, round with child, with a pretty, patient face, and Clara thought there was nothing "sulky" about her at all. Her back was so sore that she couldn't stand anything to touch it; she wore a piece of clothing draped loosely over her shoulder. When Clara examined her back, she found it covered with twelve gashes, eight to ten inches long, some cut clear to the bone. The young woman said she had been punished with a "curling whip," one that curled about her arms and back when it struck.

From what other blacks told Clara, such cruelty was not uncommon. Of course, she had no way of knowing whether they were exaggerating. "They might magnify their wrongs," she said later; "but they told me a great deal of them. I believed what I saw."

She referred the Caters to William Griffin, temporary superintendent of Andersonville, who provided them with a house and engaged Cater as a blacksmith and his wife as "a waiting girl." Clara wanted to take them back to Washington with her but guessed that that was impossible. In any case, they seemed content and safe enough with Griffin. Clara did agree to let Rosa, the nurse and washerwoman, and her husband Jarret return with her, and promised to help the couple find employment in Washington.

* * *

On August 8, the sun rose on 6,000 newly lettered, "snow-white" head-boards at Andersonville cemetery, and Clara thought it truly looked "like the city of the dead." She felt terrible that Moore had excluded her and Atwater from the sacred work at the graveyard, where Moore and his men used Atwater's death register to mark the graves. She was more certain than ever that the captain's behavior toward her stemmed from prejudice and jealousy.

The next day, Watts was dramatically worse: he suffered from chills, a high fever, severe abdominal pain, and bloody diarrhea. Clara was sure he had typhoid fever. Atwater went for the doctor and returned with a blister application; he put it to Watts's chest and abdomen, which was then standard treatment for abdominal pain. When the doctor showed up the following day, Watts appeared to be calmer, and the doctor decided that the young man had just been "frightened." There is no evidence that the doctor administered quinine to combat Watts's fever, or Dover's powders or other opiates to fight his diarrhea. Perhaps the doctor had none to give.

By August 11, Watts was so sick that Clara despaired of his recovering. Captain Moore contemplated moving him to Macon, but he was too weak to travel. Sadly, Clara and Atwater began a death vigil, taking turns sitting by Watts's cot. Clara thought what a *poor poor* boy" he was, having to die in such a wretched place as Andersonville, and she was moved by Atwater's devotion to him. "I never saw such faithful-ness," she wrote in her diary, "and how poor Watts loves him."

When the work at the cemetery was almost done, Captain Moore left for Macon to arrange the journey home. While he was gone, Clara and Atwater visited the graveyard to check the lettered slabs for accuracy. Just as they expected, they found "hosts of errors," Clara said later, the result of "indecent" and "criminal haste" on Moore's part, which would never have happened had she and Atwater not been shunted aside. They had the errant headboards pulled up, corrected, and reset.

Nevertheless, the cemetery looked impressive. In addition to the lettered tablets planted on the mass graves, Moore and his men had laid out streets and walkways, erected appropriate inscriptions and whitewashed fences, and put up an arch across the entrance with the inscription: "National Cemetery, Andersonville, Georgia." Additional plans called for the arch to be surmounted by a large gilded eagle, the graves to be raised, leveled, and planted with Bermuda grass, and the entire cemetery to be improved "in a rural landscape gardening style," as Clara put it, complete with paved oval walks.

The next day, August 15, Eddy Watts began to slip away. By the evening, Clara said, he was "praying for his mother in heaven with his poor white cold hands upraised, and poor Atwater with his griefs and losses was weeping at his bedside. I was overcome by the scene. There in that little impoverished tent those two poor orphan boys weeping for their mothers gone to heaven and left them, one on the verge of the grave and the other just escaped it." In a desperate effort to stimulate Watts's circulation, Atwater rubbed Watts's hands, and Clara wrapped her blanket around his feet and rubbed them vigorously, and then she gave him whiskey and water, and Atwater spoke to him, kindly and gently, with tears in his eyes.

"Miss Barton," Watts said with great effort, "is it almost time for me to go home?"

"Almost," she said.

He died at dawn the next morning, after a night of terrible suffering. Clara sent Atwater away and performed "the last little offices" herself. Later she and Captain Moore, who had returned from Macon, put Watts in a coffin "under charcoal" for the trip back to Washington, where he was to be properly buried.

By August 16, the last tablet was in place in the cemetery. Thanks to Atwater's secret death register and the identification sticks, 12,461 Union dead were now properly identified by their names, ranks, units, and dates of death. According to Moore, 451 headboards carried the inscription, "Unknown U.S. Soldier," in memory of the "unknown" entries in Atwater's rolls.

To commemorate the occasion, Captain Moore arranged for a flag-raising ceremony to be held at the cemetery and, with uncustomary magnanimity, gave Clara the honor of raising the colors. "This at Andersonville!" she said, astounded. On the morning of August 17, the entire group assembled at the graveyard: Clara, Captain Moore, William Griffin and his wife, the workmen and soldiers, and presumably Dorence Atwater, plus reporters for the *Washington Chronicle* and *Harper's Weekly*. When everything was in order, Clara advanced to the flagpole with a soldier, and together they raised Old Glory over the cemetery to the cheers of the others. When the flag unfurled in the wind, the little crowd sang "The Star Spangled Banner," and Clara covered her face and cried. "The work was done," she wrote in her diary. "My own hands have helped to run up the old flag on our great *and* holy ground—and I ought to be satisfied—*I* believe I am."

They returned to camp and struck their tents for the long, arduous trip back to Washington. According to the itinerary Moore worked out, they would travel by way of Atlanta, Resaca, Dalton, Lookout Mountain, Chattanooga—all memorable battlefields—Louisville, and Cincinnati. Before boarding the train, Clara took a last look at the stockade, looming "sad and terrible" against the wooded landscape. Later she penned a memorable description of Andersonville that served as a benediction to the Civil War itself: "I have looked over its 25 acres of pitiless stockade, its burrows in the earth, its stinted stream, its turfless hillsides, shadeless in summer and shelterless in winter—its wells and tunnels and caves—its 7 forts of death—its ball and chains— its stocks for torture—its kennels for blood-hounds—its sentry boxes and its deadline—and my heart sickened and stood still—my brain whirled—and the light of my eyes went out. And I said, 'Surely this was not the gate of hell, but hell itself.' And for comfort I turned away to the acres of crowded graves and I said, here at last was rest, and this to them was the gate of heaven."

PART SEVEN

The Trial

$\mathbf{I}$f Clara thought that Captain Moore had softened toward her, she was sadly mistaken. On the journey home, he continued to snub her, and his workmen, no doubt echoing him, cursed her and complained that she was "too much trouble." Worse still, they subjected Rosa, Clara's black companion, to such vile language and rough treatment that it made Rosa sick. When the expedition reached Washington at last, both women were relieved to be free of the workmen's unseemly behavior.

It was August 24, and the capital was abuzz over the trial of Henry Wirz, then in its second day at the Old Capitol Prison on First Street. In antebellum days, Old Capitol had been a boardinghouse for various politicians. During the war, it was converted into a makeshift jail, with boards nailed across its windows and sentries pacing back and forth on First Street. Its crumbling walls and murky rooms had held an assortment of offenders, from blockade runners and rebel prisoners of war to enemy spies like Mrs. Rose O'Neal Greenhow, with whom Henry Wilson had been wrongly accused of having an affair. But the most sensational inmate by far was Henry Wirz, whom Northerners, reading about his alleged crimes in their newspapers, perceived as "the most bloodthirsty monster which this or any other age has produced."

Charged with murder and with conspiring with other prison officials to injure and kill prisoners "in violation of the laws and customs of war," Wirz stood trial before a military tribunal presided over by General Lew Wallace. In the days that followed, a procession of Andersonville survivors took the stand against him. Several claimed that Wirz had shot and killed prisoners in cold blood. Another said that he had stomped one inmate to death with his boot heels. Others testified that he had killed prisoners with vicious dogs, still others that he had meted out cruel and vindictive punishment—had tied prisoners up by their thumbs, had confined them to the stocks and forced them to stand, sit, or lie for hours without changing position, had bound others together on chain gangs and made them carry "large balls" chained to their feet. Such torture, the prosecution argued, had killed about 130 men. Other survivors described the brutal conditions at the hospital, the putrid food doled out in the stockade, the killings along the deadline, the polluted stream "reeking with the filth and garbage of the prison and prison guard," the inadequate shelter, the horrendous stench that hung over the camp like a pall, and the endless deaths—all of which the witnesses blamed on Wirz. On the basis of such evidence, the prosecution argued that Wirz deserved to hang.

Clara hoped that she and Atwater would be called to testify. She could support the claims of the prisoners, describe what her own eyes had seen inside Wirz's stockade, retell what local whites had said about him and General Winder, display the relics she had collected inside the stockade. Awaiting a summons, she busied herself with a detailed report of the Andersonville expedition for Secretary of War Stanton. She also gave interviews about it to the *Washington Chronicle*. Reporting in back-to-back issues, the *Chronicle* attributed the mission's success to Atwater and Clara Barton. "She has seen with her own eyes the fruition of her glorious work," it said. As for Andersonville, "This monument of demoniac cruelty, of worse than fiendish atrocity, will never be destroyed by the hand of man."

Shortly after returning to Washington, Clara learned that her position at the Patent Office had been eliminated. This was the work of James Harlan, Johnson's new secretary of the interior. It was nothing personal; Harlan removed most of the women workers in the Interior Department. Even so, Clara took it as a rejection and plunged into despair. Her "crumb" of a salary from the Patent Office—actually only half a crumb, since she split it with Upperman—was her only income. She could scarcely believe that President Johnson, who had been so kindly disposed to her in the spring, had abolished her "crumb board" and swept her table clear, so that she had not "a scrap or morsel upon it." Now she would have to live entirely on her inheritance from her father.

By casting her off, the government imperiled her missing-soldier work, too. While she was away, her clerks had released a second roll of

1,500 names and were now working on a third. How was she to contin-ue this crucial enterprise without an income?

Then came another piece of bad news: Atwater had been arrested and thrown in jail. The day after returning to Washington, "Dorr" had reported for duty to Colonel Breck at the War Department, and Breck demanded that Atwater either return the $300 the government had paid him for the loan of his secret death register, or give up the register itself. Atwater refused to do either one, on the grounds that he had honored his part of the agreement: he had loaned the register to the War Department so that it could make copies, which it had, and he felt entitled to keep the $300 and the rolls. Did he have them in his posses-sion? Breck demanded. Atwater confessed that he did and added that he intended to publish them "for the benefit of the friends of the deceased." At that, Breck arrested him on a charge of larceny—of stealing his own death register—and confined Atwater in the guard-house of the Veteran Reserve Corps near the War Department; two days later he was transferred to Old Capitol Prison where Wirz was incarcerated.

This was a staggering irony, which Atwater himself was quick to point out. "I am confined here in the same prison with Capt. Henry Wirz, the Andersonville jailer," he said in a letter that appeared in the *New York Citizen*. "He is being tried by a Military Commission for being one of the murderers of 13,000 of our men, and I am being tried for keeping and wishing to publish the names of these same 13,000 men, that the people may know where their dead are buried and of what they died."

Clara was appalled. Breck was not going to get away with such a travesty of justice, not if she could help it. She would see Mr. Stanton and demand that "Dorr" be released at once. Informed that Stanton was at West Point, she took a train there forthwith and secured an interview with him on September 5. At the interview, she told him bluntly what had happened.

"What do you desire me to do in the case?" he asked, and evidently told her to reply in writing.

She did so in her hotel room, setting forth in a letter what she wished of Stanton. "Simply this, Sir,—do nothing, believe nothing, sanction nothing in this present procedure against Dorence Atwater, until all the facts with their antecedents and bearings shall have been placed before you, and this upon your return (if no one more worthy offer) I promise to do, with all the fairness, truthfulness, and judgment that in me lie." She blamed the arrest on those who desired "to gratify a jealous whim, or serve a personal ambition" and who cared nothing about what "unmerited public criticism they might thus draw upon you, while young Atwater, honest and simple-hearted, both loving and trusting you has more need of your protection than your censure."

Then she hurried back to Washington, where she consulted with various friends about what to do. Atwater's trial was scheduled for Monday, September 11. If Stanton was not in town by then, she doubted that Dorr stood a chance of being acquitted. Even so, she helped his defense counsel, H. H. Mason, write a statement Atwater would present to the court, which gave the full story of the death register and his experiences with Breck and Moore. The following lines were in Clara's handwriting: "I have called no witnesses, made no appeal, adduced no evidence. A soldier, a prisoner, an orphan, and a minor, I have little with which to employ counsel to oppose the Government of the United States. . . . I deny the charge of theft. I took my rolls home with me that they might be preserved; I considered them mine; it had never been told or even hinted to me that they were not my own rightful, lawful property. . . . My offense consists in an attempt to make known to the relatives and friends, the fate of unfortunate men who died in Andersonville Prison, and if this be a crime I am guilty to the fullest extent of the law, for to accomplish it I have risked my life among my enemies and my liberty among my friends. . . . I wish it to be known that I am not sentenced to a penitentiary as a common thief, but for attempting to appeal from the trickery of a clique of petty officers."

The next day, in a display of leniency, the War Department allowed Atwater to visit Clara with a guard, and they had dinner together. Then this lad of twenty went off to his trial by court-martial. The War Department charged him with "conduct prejudicial to good military discipline" and with "unlawfully and feloniously" stealing from Captain Moore's quarters at Andersonville "certain property of the United States," namely, his secret death register. Colonel Breck and Captain Moore testified against him, in what Atwater later described as "perjury of the blackest kind." Breck accused Atwater of swindling the government, of wanting to publish the death register for profit. In his testimony, Moore claimed that Clara and Atwater had "had nothing to do with the expedition" to Andersonville, that she had gone along merely to search for missing soldiers and that Atwater had been her assistant, and that he had indeed "stolen" the register from Moore's quarters on or about August 16.

Atwater's only defense was his six-page statement, which contended that the secret death rolls belonged to him, that Moore had given him permission to keep them in his tent during their stay at Andersonville, that he had returned to Washington with them, and that he would not give them up. He declined to call Clara or other friends to testify in his behalf because, he said, "the court hinted that my *doom* was settled." The testimony finished, the court sent Atwater back to Old Capitol Prison to await its verdict.

Moore's testimony infuriated Clara. She was even more upset when the captain released a press statement a few days later. In response to a "large number of letters" he had received, Moore announced that he intended to publish "the record of burials, as well as such other information as he can obtain," next October 1. To Clara, this was outrageous. If Moore published the death register under his name, Clara feared that Atwater's name would be lost to history. Nobody would ever know what that boy had done for his country. It appeared to her that Moore was trying to claim all the glory for himself. In fact, in his official report of the expedition, submitted to General Meigs on September 20, Moore did take the credit for the Andersonville enterprise. He called it "my mission" and boasted of his accomplishments at the Andersonville cemetery. Not once did he mention Clara Barton, Dorence Atwater, or Atwater's death register. When Moore's report later appeared in the *Washington Chronicle*, Clara was aghast. "How can Capt Moore sleep and know what he has done?" she asked her diary.

Meanwhile *Harper's Weekly* published a story about the expedition, which closely followed Moore's own report. True, there was a woodcut of Clara's raising the flag at Andersonville, which she thought was "stately." What distressed her was the way the story featured Moore. "I am mentioned once," she fumed, "his own name 5 times in caplets, poor Atwater not at all, and even his role denied as accompanying us."

Furious at being denied her place in the spotlight, Clara perceived an evil design in all this: she believed that Moore, in league with "tricky little officers" in the Adjutant General's Office, had accused and imprisoned Atwater as a way of hurting Clara, of deprecating her role at Andersonville, so that Moore could claim all the credit for the expedition and thereby win a promotion. "The deeper he can bury his rivals," she'd told a friend, "the more prominent he stands himself, the more likely to gather *fame* out of a visit to a grave yard, and increase the chances for a brevet—and finally become the great country man of the age."

"God will require something at the hands of 'Capt James M. Moore, A. QM,' " she raged; "justice is slow but sure, he will one day make up for all this inhumanity and injustice; it can not be avoided—his name will yet be execrated in proportion as he is known."

After Atwater's trial, Clara had turned to Henry Wilson for help, telling him about Atwater's imprisonment and Moore's plans to publish the death register himself. Wilson admitted that the treatment of Atwater was "high handed," but he wasn't sure what could be done about it. In truth, he was preoccupied with another matter: He and many other Republicans were worried about the condition of the blacks in Dixie. There were reports that many local Southern communities had adopted measures that severely restricted the freed people and that President Johnson, in charge of reconstructing the conquered rebel states, intended to leave race relations in the hands of their ex-Confederate leaders. Wilson was contemplating a trip through the South, to investigate conditions for himself. Even so, he was concerned about Clara, too, and troubled by her allegations about Moore. He told William Griffin that he had known Clara too long and well to see her harmed, that "*no* man could do that without striking through him," and he promised to see Stanton upon his return and "set the matter right" about her role in the expedition.

On September 20, Clara was shocked to read in the *New York Herald* that Atwater had been convicted of theft and sentenced to eighteen months at hard labor in Auburn State Prison in New York State. He had also been fined $300 and dishonorably discharged from the service, with the loss of all emoluments and claims on the government.

The news shook Clara. The injustice of such a sentence was too much to comprehend, too much to bear. Because of Moore and his cabal of officers, poor Atwater would be marked for life. It made her so "exceedingly depressed," she said, that she broke down and cried.

While she was weeping, there was a rap at her door. It was Mrs. Peck, "a poor woman" from Pennsylvania, whom Clara had met a few days before. She had come to town seeking information on her missing son, and General Hoffman had referred her to Clara. As it turned out, Mrs. Peck's son had died at Andersonville; his name was registered on Atwater's rolls. The news left Mrs. Peck "almost beside herself," for she had "waited and mourned so long." Now she returned to Clara for comfort; she was so miserable she didn't know where else to turn. A tearful Clara invited her in at once. "I thought a person whom I in my hopeless condition could comfort must be indeed wretched, and so she was, poor woman. I forgot my own embarrassments in her greater grief and grew more cheerful."

Clara now had quite a little "family" in Washington City. Jules Golay, her "little disabled brother," had moved into one of her rooms and was looking for a job with her help. It was a bold flouting of convention for an unmarried woman to "keep house" with a young, unmarried man, but Clara seemed to think nothing of it, apparently secure in her reputation in Washington as a woman of rectitude. Drawing on a military metaphor, she told her diary that Jules was "a good trusty staff in time of need" and that he gave her "comfort." "He has one of the sweetest dispositions in the world. I wish I could get more time to spend with him in both a social and a literary way."

Rosa and Jarret, the black couple from Georgia, had found a place to live, and Rosa was working for Clara as cook and housekeeper, which "excused" Clara from domestic duties "for the present at least." She thought that Rosa had been "completely metamorphosed" from diffidence to uninhibited garrulity and now talked "like a steamboat." Even so, she couldn't do anything without orders and supervision, and sometimes she complained so much that Clara would get angry at her, thinking her "worse than nothing." At one point she considered releasing her. But they worked things out between them, and on the whole Clara thought her a good, faithful housekeeper, and was glad she had brought her up from Dixie.

On September 24, when the papers reported that Stanton was back in town, Clara put the finishing touches on her report of the Andersonville expedition. In it, she attempted to correct the misinformation Moore had been spreading around Washington. She recounted the genesis of the expedition, which had grown out of her missing-soldier work and Atwater's rolls, and described in detail the way Moore had snubbed her throughout the trip, never telling her anything or asking her opinion. She accused him of attempting to abandon the expedition at Savannah until "peremptory orders" came from General Meigs to proceed, and she complained that after they reached Andersonville, Moore had not once invited her to the cemetery. Since their return, she said, Moore had accredited only himself for the success of the expedition, quite as though she and Atwater had never been present.

She also included a detailed account of what she had seen inside the Andersonville stockade and recommended that it "be preserved as one of the sanctuaries of the nation, and be in due time decorated with appropriate honors."

On September 25, she took her report to Stanton in person. As he peered at her through his spectacles, she warned him that part of it was "personal."

Stanton: Who does it concern?

Clara: Captain Moore.

Stanton: You had best not enter into a controversy, Miss Barton.

Clara: I don't want to do that. That is why I'm submitting my report to you, in private.

She told him what had happened to Atwater. The secretary promised to read the minutes of his court-martial and then decide whether anything should be done for him.

Clara returned home feeling extremely sad. Her heart "ached," she told her diary. "I could scarce breathe and could not account for it all. I thought some terrible thing was about to take place."

Her premonition came true. Jules Golay brought her the terrible news that "Dorr had just left on the train for Auburn state prison." Jules had found him standing at the depot, in irons, with a soldier and captain as his guard. When he saw Jules, Atwater broke down and wept. Jules gave him four dollars—all the money he had—and escorted Atwater to the gate, where Atwater said to give Clara his love.

Clara was devastated. "It seemed that the very Heavens would fall upon me," she wrote later. That poor boy was dragged through the streets like a common convict, "in open daylight, and in the face of his acquaintances," and placed on the train to Baltimore and sent off to serve a year and a half at hard labor, "thus exchanging Belle Isle & Andersonville for Old Capitol and Auburn and for nearly the same period of time, and no crime in either case." She did not understand how such a monstrous iniquity could happen, or what she could do to rectify it. But she must try to think of something.

The Andersonville Survivors' Association, formed in Washington that September, made Clara an honorary member in appreciation of her work "in ameliorating the condition of those who suffered in southern prisons, in her noble plans for helping the widows and orphans of them who have filled the prisoners grave and especially her great work of

marking the graves [of those] who lie buried in the sands of Georgia."
That resolution cheered Clara considerably. At least the *survivors* of
Andersonville appreciated her efforts.

So, too, did the families of missing soldiers. Indeed, letters of
inquiry and follow-up requests continued to pile up by the hundreds.
One such letter, from Hannah N. Nash of Quincy, Massachusetts,
wrenched at Clara's heart. Clara had reported that Hannah's brother,
Bryant Newcomb, of the Thirty-second Massachusetts, had died at
Andersonville. "And is that all that we can ever know?" Hannah wrote
Clara in reply. "Is there no one that can give us any information with
regard to his death and sufferings. His dear mother is heart broken
since the news [was] received. She has raised a great deal of blood and
I fear it will cause her death. But she feels that it would be a great
relief if she could hear the particulars." She added, "I fear trespassing
on your patience. But if there is anyone that knows anything of my darling brother please do all you can for us. And you will ever be remembered with the deepest love and gratitude."

Clara wanted to do more for women like Hannah and her mother.
But now that she had lost her job, she was running dangerously low on
money with which to continue her missing-soldier work. By her
account, she had already spent $7,533 of her own money on clerks, sta-
tionery, and other expenses, and most of it had come out of her savings.
By October, there were 3,500 letters on hand that couldn't be
answered for lack of adequate "clerical force." Desperate for money,
she thought about writing a book about the expedition to
Andersonville. If it sold well, she could use the profits to continue her
search for missing soldiers. She even went so far as to draft a book proposal, which she thought to show Henry Wilson. "It is scarcely necessary for me to explain to you the position of my personal affairs," she
wrote. "I know you have long been pained at the sight of me with my
great burden of missing soldiers and want some one to help me bear
it." She admitted that after eight months of "costly labor," she really
needed help. Hence, the idea for a book. It would clarify her work in
the eyes of the public—"at present not one in twenty who write me
have any clear idea of its nature." She could relate the eight months'
history of her search for information about missing men, show how the
expedition grew out of that, "how inseparably connected the two were;
and how Dorence Atwater's roll led directly to the whole work of identifying the graves of the thirteen thousand sleeping in that city of the
dead." It would point out "that it was due to me that anyone went or
that the work of recovering the graves and erecting that cemetery has

even been done." She would also recount her experiences with "the colored people" who had come from miles around to ask if Lincoln were dead and if they were free. "This," she believed, "if well told, is a little book of itself."

She had doubts that she could write a book, but why not try? Several other women had already published their war experiences. Louisa May Alcott's *Hospital Sketches*, published in 1863, vividly described her work as a Dix nurse in a dingy, dilapidated hospital in Washington. Emily Solder's *Leaves from the Battle-Field at Gettysburg*, appeared in 1864, and Mrs. E. C. Kent's *Four Years in Secessia: A Narrative of a Residence at the South Previous to and During the Southern Rebellion* had also come out in 1864. Why not the Andersonville pilgrimage of Clara Barton? Then she discovered that it would cost her $10,000 to have such a book published, with no guarantees that it would ever earn that much in sales. Unable to find a benefactor who would put up such a sum, she had to abandon the project.

Meanwhile, she fell back on a second and more practical idea: getting government funding for her operation. She couldn't turn to Wilson right away; he had gone home to Massachusetts and would not return until Congress convened in early December. So she sought the support of her other prominent political friend, Benjamin Butler, when he came to town in early October. She had a long talk with him at Willard's Hotel, bringing him up to date on her search for missing men and pointing out her dire need for government assistance if it was to continue. He listened to her carefully, his face flushed, his hands on his ample belly, his eyes squinting. To her delight, Butler declared himself firmly behind her, offered to see Stanton and President Johnson "and show them the necessity of sustaining this work, its importance to the Government & where money could be gotten for it." He observed, however, that her search was mainly for missing white soldiers. He thought she ought to broaden it to include missing "colored" soldiers, too. Clara agreed. With government relief and suitable assistants, she said, her search for information about both would be eminently successful.

Two days later Butler came to her rooms with splendid news. He had seen Stanton and Johnson about her "business," he said, and both "fully approved." According to him, it was to be made a part of the Adjutant General's Office, complete with clerks and expenses—"a Bureau by itself," he said, with Clara as its chief. Butler was going home for a while but told Clara to write out a "programme" of what she required. When he returned to Washington, he would see that she got it, and she could "enter at once" upon her labors.

Clara was ecstatic. With her own bureau, clerks, and expense account, she believed she could trace down the tens of thousands of missing soldiers, Union and Confederate alike. Such a bureau would also strike a major blow for the liberation of her sex, since she would be the first woman in America to run an entire government bureau. "Whoever heard of anything like this," she wrote in her diary, "who but Genl Butler. . . . Of all my days this I suspect has been my greatest and I hope best."

Then she had second thoughts. Moore's allies were in the Adjutant General's Office; she didn't want to be thrown in with those malicious officers. Accordingly, she wrote Butler a "private" letter requesting that, "in the final arrangement" of her position, she be kept entirely away from the Adjutant General's Office and its "petty" subordinates, "as it was through a league with them that Capt. Moore was able to accuse and imprison Dorence Atwater, which blow was intended to harm him less than me." It would be far better for her and her work if she reported "to some distant head of the Government."

When October 1 passed without a sign of the death register in the Washington newspapers, Clara was galvanized into action, embarking on a behind-the-scenes campaign to get Atwater released from prison, so that he could publish his copy before Moore released the official version. She wrote the chaplain of Auburn prison, whom she'd heard was sympathetic to Atwater, that he was no "villain" and that it was her solemn duty to raise her voice against "this great wrong" perpetrated against him. She sought the support of influential newspaper editors like Charles G. Halpine of the *New York Citizen*, who had served with her on Hilton Head. She sent him a full statement of "the facts" in Atwater's case and of Moore's plot against Atwater and her. She also wrote important personages in Connecticut about Atwater's imprisonment, telling them that "the country should at least rebuke the unprincipled who deceived and now punish him" and asking them to "please lend a hand in the right cause." In addition, she joined forces with Atwater's brother, Eugene, who, with the backing of the governor of Connecticut, was getting up a petition demanding Dorr's release.

She called, too, on her old friend and supporter, General Rucker of the Quartermaster Department, to see what he might be able to do about Moore, who was Rucker's subordinate. She had encountered Rucker in the streets a few weeks before, and he had praised her so lavishly it had embarrassed her. During the war, he said, he had helped her because he knew that she was not "a humbug," that she meant what she said and did what she promised. He said that "of all the ladies who had gone to the field," Clara "had done the most and best." If she ever needed "endorsing," he told her, she should come to him.

So she came to him now, and as they sat together in the quartermaster offices she told him "many things" about Captain Moore. Incredulous, Rucker said he "could not see how it was possible for a man of the Capt position to do any such things," but Clara insisted that everything she told him was true. At that moment, Captain Moore himself entered the room and strode past Clara without, apparently, a nod of recognition. Finally, Rucker assured her of his "aid" and "kindness," and she went home feeling "sad" because she feared that Rucker did not entirely believe her.

Filled with misgivings about her future, she suddenly missed Frances Gage, missed her fiercely. Her mind trailed back to those halcyon days on Hilton Head and Parris Island, when they had exchanged poetry and walked together on the wave-washed beaches. She longed for Fanny's company, for her support in this hour of trouble and uncertainty. Clara knew nothing about Fanny's situation, or even where she was, but if Fanny could join her in Washington, Clara thought she could make her comfortable. Since Fanny had often contributed pieces to the *Anti-Slavery Standard*, Clara wrote the editors inquiring about her whereabouts.

The next day, October 16, marked the end of witnesses in the Wirz trial. When the military tribunal refused to grant the defense two weeks to make its case, Wirz's attorney announced that he would not offer a closing argument, and Wirz made a passionate plea himself, pointing out that the vast majority of the 146 witnesses had not seen him commit murder and insisting that there had been no Confederate conspiracy to exterminate Union prisoners. In his summation, the prosecutor reiterated the manifold atrocities attested to by the witnesses and invoked the specter of 13,000 dead prisoners, holding Wirz responsible for "at least" 10,000 of them.

Clara was upset that neither she nor Atwater was called to testify. Colonel Norton P. Chipman, the judge-advocate, had Atwater's name and should have considered him a crucial witness. And what about Clara and her prison relics, which she had on display in a cabinet in her little parlor? The crude, makeshift cutlery, the pieces of board from the deadline, the cannonball from one of the guns that had guarded the stockade—all, she thought, were powerful pieces of evidence. By now more than a little paranoiac, she blamed Moore and his lackeys at the Adjutant General's Office for keeping her and her relics out of court, so that her own role in the expedition would be hidden from the public eye: "*studied measures* to have them, and myself ignored, were taken by those whose *object* and *interest* it is, to bury me, so far as possible, in all connection with the Expedition," she wrote Henry Wilson.

Well, it was too late for her to testify against Wirz. But she heard that Jefferson Davis was to be brought to Washington for trial, and she beseeched Wilson to act as her "friend in that court" and see to it that she was called as a witness against the former rebel president. "My collection of relics from Andersonville should be placed before Davis and his defenders," she told Wilson. "They would tend to carry swift conviction where words fall powerless for want of appreciation." What was more, her testimony in such a trial, which was bound to be sensational, would enable her to "establish the true, and discard the false," about Atwater's death register and her role in the Andersonville expedition, all the while strengthening the government's case against Davis. "I believe I have acted nobly, and well for my *country*, and *humanity* in this last eight months labor at least, and why the jealousy of a little *worthless* petty officer should be allowed to trample me *speechless* in the *dust*, I *cannot* understand—please open *some* way for me to *commence* a vindication."

In the meantime, when Butler came to town and then left without seeing her, Clara thought he was trying to avoid her, and her confidence in him and her projected bureau evaporated. She could just imagine "the feelings" that reference to her had undoubtedly engendered at the Adjutant General's Office. "I see now that the calumny has assumed a fixed form," she told her diary, and even friends like Butler were part of it. "I know that my condition is hopeless and my business and financial ruin complete."

Yes, she was at the end of the line as far as her search for missing soldiers was concerned. Although she had received some 6,000 letters of inquiry and had a total of 7,500 names of missing men on her master list, enough for three more rolls of 1,500 each, she had to suspend her operation for lack of money, and it plunged her into black despair. At one point, her spirits were so low that she contemplated leaving the country, as she had "no interest" in staying here when she could no longer be useful.

Her male friends—Ferguson, Tufts, and Brown—tried to buoy her spirits, but it was no use. She who thrived on duty, on meeting the stern realities, was out of work, out of money, and out of possibilities. "There is no hope, no point," she told her diary, "and I know I am to die so far as usefulness is concerned."

On October 25, Tufts burst into her room with what he thought was "triumphant" news: a report in the *Boston Journal* that Butler was to get a cabinet post. Don't you see, Tufts said; this explains his sudden departure without seeing you—he had to hurry home to prepare for the move to Washington. That Butler was in line for a cabinet position was certainly plausible. He often met with the president about various matters and tried to ward off a rift between Johnson and the Republicans over his lenient reconstruction policy, which allowed former rebels to seize control of their state governments and local white communities to adopt the antiblack measures that so upset Henry Wilson and the other Radical Republicans. There was a strong rumor that Butler was to be appointed secretary of war; if so, he could be counted on to silence Moore and establish a bureau for Clara, enabling her to resume her work.

Clara pronounced herself "greatly relieved." Even so, she had no money on hand and feared that her savings at home were completely exhausted. How was she to pay her rent and buy food? She felt worse than useless; she felt like a pauper. To check on her finances and also solicit support for Atwater, she caught a train for New England, stopping over in New York long enough to visit a spiritualist. During the session, Stephen and Bubby spoke to her from the other side of the veil, with the medium writing down what they said. Stephen was so "excited" he had trouble expressing himself; he promised to talk "next time." Bubby, however, "wrote beautifully," saying that he was often with Clara and his mother in sleep. "Ah me!" Clara wrote in her diary.

Then it was on to New Haven, where she met with Eugene Atwater and many influential men and women who might help get Dorr released. She also persuaded a prominent judge and attorney named Joseph Sheldon to take his case. A Yale graduate and "a radical abolitionist of the Wendell Phillips order," as Clara described him, he declared himself a man of moral principles and appeared to appreciate Clara's own position, both of which convinced her that he was the perfect jurist to "take hold of this matter." He did, however, desire a fee. That was not a problem for Clara. She went to the family for help and in the end Atwater's uncle, a Mr. Terry, agreed to "meet the money part of Dorr's case."

On November 6, when Clara was in New Haven, the military court in Washington found Henry Wirz guilty of murdering and conspiring to kill Union prisoners of war. Four days later he was hanged in the yard of the Old Capitol Prison while four military companies chanted "Remember Andersonville."

On the day Wirz was hanged, Clara took a train to North Oxford, where she found brother David "working like a slave." He had left the army, after less-than-illustrious service on Hilton Head. The next day Clara got the bad news that only $228 remained of her inheritance, which Colonel DeWitt had invested for her. She withdrew the money, thinking, "It is not the first time in my life that I have come to the bottom of the bag—I guess I shall die a pauper, but I haven't been either stingy or lazy, and if I starve I shall not be alone; others have." Then she hastened off to Boston to see Butler. On the way to his office, the heel on one of her boots broke off and she twisted her ankle badly; she had to limp there in considerable pain. She showed Butler the program she had drafted for her projected bureau, and he said she needed no advice from him. He intended to return to Washington within a few days and would arrange an interview with Stanton about her projected bureau.

That made Clara feel better. Later, when she and Butler were both back in Washington, they met again at Willard's Hotel, and he was so encouraging that she left "with the same reliant kindly feeling" she always had in his presence. "He is so kind and genial towards me—I hope I shall always like him as I do now."

On November 27, Butler met Clara at the War Department for an interview with Stanton. The secretary, his mouth turned down sourly at the corners, first invited Butler into his office, alone. Waiting outside his door, Clara was extremely ill at ease, thinking that the officers were watching her every movement "with great sharpness." At last, summoned into Stanton's office, she nervously handed him her proposal for her own government bureau. He glanced over the lengthy document and said her missing-soldier operation might be assumed by one of the offices in the War Department. Butler spoke up that this wasn't fair, that Clara ought to have control of her own work through an independent office. But Stanton would only say that the matter appeared to fall within the jurisdiction of General Hitchcock, now commissary general of prisoners, and that he would forward her proposal to him.

When Clara and Butler left, she feared that she was getting the runaround, that Stanton intended to bury her proposal. If he did, Butler promised her, he would "resuscitate it." Even so, Clara was "half paralyzed by the agony of impending danger." Determined to leave nothing to chance, she called on General Hitchcock and told him what she wanted and where matters stood with Stanton. The old general seemed to like the idea of her proposal—indeed, he expressed himself amazed that she had done all that work for missing soldiers by herself, without government support. Certainly, he said, he would give her proposal every consideration when it came from Stanton.

Clara asked if he wished to speak to Butler about it. No, Hitchcock said. He had "a difficulty" with Butler, which stemmed from some contretemps over a matter relating to the exchange of prisoners; Hitchcock thought Butler acted from "selfish or ambitious motives." For Clara, this was a bad omen, inasmuch as Butler was her strongest advocate for her own bureau. She went home feeling "tired, cold, and faint."

On December 1, the *Washington Chronicle* carried a shocking announcement: "Major J. M. Moore Chief of the United States Burial Bureau has prepared a report of the number of deaths and burials of the soldiers of the Union," which he would soon be releasing. Moore was now a brevet major? (In fact, he had been made a brevet lieutenant colonel.) Brevet ranks were ceremonial, but it galled Clara that Moore was so honored. Worse still, he had his own Burial Bureau, which seemed similar to what Clara had proposed for herself. She had heard rumors about Moore's bureau, and now it was a *fait accompli.* This, she thought, sealed her doom. She reeled off a letter to Butler, releasing him "from further labors" in her behalf and enclosing a copy of the announcement. The existence of Moore's Bureau, she told Butler, proved how useless it would be to continue trying to make her work "a part of the government." Then her fury at Moore burst forth. "This officer with his undeserved rank, his meanness, his tricks, his falsehoods . . . and his crimes black upon him, is purposely elevated to a position where he can thwart every effort and throw contumely upon me every hour of my life." Her complaint was not, she insisted, "the wail of a woman who hopes to win by tears, but a fair, candid expression of my convictions, the timely acknowledgment of defeated purposes, and my heart aching sigh over the artful, heartless destruction of my labors."

As it turned out, Butler could not have helped her anyway because he never got a cabinet post. She wrote in her diary: "I must be and do by myself and alone."

* * *

December 2: incredible news from Attorney Sheldon. Dorence Atwater was free and in New Haven. He had been released from prison by a general order of President Johnson pardoning all prisoners convicted by court-martial of crimes less than murder.

"God is so merciful and knowing and *just*," Clara rejoiced. Yet poor Dorr, having served two months at hard labor, remained a convicted felon with a dishonorable discharge. His life was ruined unless the judgment of his court-martial could be reversed. As she thought about that, a plan of action formed in her mind. His own exoneration hinged on the publication of his death register under his name. It was safe to assume that nobody in Washington knew about Atwater's release under the president's blanket pardon. There was still a chance that he could get his register to the newspapers before Moore released his copy and his report based on it. But Atwater must hurry.

Clara telegraphed him to stay away from Washington at all costs, to "play possum, act dead" and "prepare that roll for publication." Then she outlined her strategy in a long letter to Sheldon. "The utmost *haste* is necessary and *secrecy*," she cautioned him; "can I sufficiently impress the *importance* of *this*—secrecy!!" Once Atwater had his records in publishable form, he should write an "Address to the people to whom the roll is presented," giving the history of how he had kept it, had smuggled it out of Andersonville "at the risk of his life," had been imprisoned on a trumped-up charge of stealing it from his own government, and had only now been able to get the register out to the public. "This will vindicate him before the country and give him a hold on the hearts of the people that will always be more than gold to him." As for Sheldon, "here is your part, my lawyer friend—*help him write* of course—or *write for him* just such things as will touch the people." To do that, she warned, Atwater should not belabor his own grievances and sufferings and must not appear bitter; he must aim his remarks at the Northern people, stressing "the great grief *they* had been subjected to *by these long delays*—not pitying *himself*, but *them*." If this were "well done," she believed, "he will carry all hearts, and move Congress." Then Clara and Sheldon could draft a memorial to Congress, which was scheduled to convene within a few days, "praying it to grant an honorable discharge to Dorence Atwater, and place it in the hands of such men as will ask with it that a note of thanks be rendered and the suitable remuneration,—this is his only chance of reward," Clara said. "I think it requires wise management."

Clara was also motivated by self-interest, with an eye on congressional assistance for her own work. She told Sheldon that Atwater need not hesitate to use her name in his statement. If he did refer to her, it should be to connect her "with the *origin* of the *expedition*," thus countering Moore's "false account" that she and Atwater had had nothing to do with it. She hoped that her connection with the enterprise would impress Congress and convince it to fund her current labors.

She confided her strategy in her friend, Charles Halpine of the *New York Citizen*, asking him to stand by her and Atwater when they went public with his death register. She also found a new supporter on Capitol Hill, her cousin Robert Hale, now a congressman. When Hale, a jolly gentleman, called to pay his respects, she told him everything (Atwater, the death record, Moore and Andersonville), and he vowed to launch an investigation into Moore's conduct and the treatment of Atwater. He also promised to seek a government appropriation for her missing-soldier enterprise. He had "no axes of his own to grind," he told her, so he would grind hers. "What a provision to be made for a poor weak little crushed down woman," Clara wrote, not without sarcasm.

She thought Hale such "a splendid cousin," so kind and noble and easily the peer of any man in Congress. "I felt," she told her diary, "that an angel had been sent to roll the stone away from the door of my sepulchre from the grave of my hopes." At his request, she furnished him a copy of her report of the Andersonville expedition, her proposal for a government bureau for missing soldiers, and Atwater's court-martial proceedings, which a friend had managed to acquire from the War Department.

Clara also introduced Hale to Henry Wilson. Although Wilson was busy drafting a civil rights bill for the former slaves, he too promised to help Clara, so that she had two "friends at court" after Congress convened on December 4. Even so, she was impatient with the political process, knowing that the workings of government were slow and unpredictable. "Oh when can I go on with my work again," she asked her diary; "how long must I wait? when can I have the means to proceed?"

On December 14, she received an official notice from the War Department that there would be no government bureau for her. This came in the form of a report to Stanton written by Adjutant General Townsend, who had conspired with Breck to deprive Atwater of his secret death register even before the Andersonville expedition. "Miss Barton's labors are such as a philanthropist might undertake for the benefit of relatives and friends of soldiers, but they are not such as the War Dept can assume to carry out," Townsend told Stanton. Then he got nasty: "Experience has never failed to demonstrate the fateful effects of allowing irresponsible agents, for whatever purpose, to have access to information contained on the records of this office, and it is most strenuously recommended that it not be granted to Miss Barton, since it would be sure to place persons, through her agency, in possession of official data which they ought not to have." Finally, there was no need for a missing-person bureau to be added to the War Department, since the Adjutant General's Office was already handling "an immense mass of correspondence" and carrying on "investigations similar to Miss Barton's."

"It was of course a cold cutting refusal," Clara wrote in her diary, "just what I expected from that quarter—'they are doing all such work themselves.' of *course* they are. I[t] hurt me of course but not so much as if I had not considered so well where it came from."

Even so, the rejection sent her spinning into "the deepest feeling of depression." She lost confidence in everyone and in every promise made to her. When her friends called to console her, she could not respond; it seemed "such a mockery for people to come and condole and promise when of them all there was not one who could set right so fearsome a wrong" as the one that deprived her of her work, her duty. Then cousin Robert visited her, and she told him all she could "put into words." He said she "must have faith in him" to set all this right. She "promised under protest."

Clara's most pressing problem was money. Mr. Upperman had brought her $138 in "back pay" from the Patent Office, which with the last of her savings would see her through the winter. But what would she do after that? Even if Congress did appropriate money for her missing-soldier work, she still had to have a personal income, a job of some sort, with which to pay her rent and stock her pantry. In desperation, she implored Henry Wilson to get her reinstated at the Patent Office. "I could not but feel," she told Wilson, "that if Secretary Harlan had understood my past connection with the Office, and present occupation, and the expenses I was so continually meeting for others, that with the generous patriotism which has characterized his whole public career he would have increased rather than crippled my means, if not for my own, for the sake of the afflicted and bereaved who have learned to appeal to me for aid and comfort." She was certain that when Wilson set the facts before him, Harlan's "quick sense of justice" would restore her to her old position.

Wilson did speak to Harlan, but it was no use: Harlan rejected her application. Wilson said he was sorry, but she assured him that she had expected this and wasn't really disappointed. Suspecting that she badly needed money, the senator took twenty dollars from his purse and handed it to her, saying that he often felt "troubled" about her and feared she was too proud to tell him about her needs. Clara promptly returned the money. She didn't need it, she said proudly, and couldn't take it. He tried to make it a Christmas present, but she still said no.

After he departed, she felt "discouraged and tearful." Unless she found a means of income, how was she to keep her apartment, with its little parlor, Jules's room, and her own "nice little warm room" with its fireplace and light? Would she have to return to North Oxford a failure? What a terrible curtain that would be to her war career.

Attorney Sheldon, visiting her in mid-December, had suggested a way out of her dilemma. Why not give public lectures on her war experiences? He brought up the example of Anna Dickinson, an attractive young Quaker with a lovely voice, who had mesmerized audiences for years and made a great national reputation for herself on the platform. She had even addressed the House of Representatives in 1864. Look, Sheldon told Clara, the people of New Haven, men and women alike, would like nothing better than to hear you speak about your war-time exploits. They had made comparisons, he said, and "decided upon the three women who had distinguished themselves and gained a name and fame since the commencement of the war. Miss [Mary Abigail] Dodge the writer, Miss Dickinson, the speaker, and Clara Barton, the *worker*."

When a formal invitation arrived, Clara was both impressed and alarmed by the formidable collection of signatures on it. How could she, with all her "deficiencies," presume to address such a worthy and literate group? Struck with premature stage fright, she was nevertheless attracted to the idea of telling them about her work in the war. True, she might be severely criticized in the press, for there was still a lot of popular objection to women speaking to audiences of both sexes. One journalist called it an example of "Gynaekokracy," a disease "which manifests itself in absurd endeavors of women to usurp the places and execute the functions of the male sex." Even so, other

women had defied the barriers to women speaking in public. Frances
Gage had done so, delivering lectures on freed blacks across the North
in 1864. Sarah Jane Clarke Lippincott, using the nom de plume Grace
Greenwood, had spoken for the Sanitary Commission and championed
Abraham Lincoln against the antiwar Democrats. They had opened the
door for Clara to follow. Why not try the platform? "I don't know if
ever my day will ever come," she wrote in her diary. Still, "can it be
that all of this travail and pain and despair is the bursting of the nut—
and I to find light and meat some day yet?"

With considerable trepidation, she accepted the New Haven invitation and started writing notes for a lecture, warmed by memories of
her great service on the battlefield.

December 25: Another Christmas, ushered in by firecrackers and
salutes of artillery. Clara was now forty-four years old, cut off from her
work, unemployed, *idle*. She couldn't stand it. Somehow she must find
a way to resume her missing-soldier work and earn a living. She spent
the day alone, reflecting that a year ago she was in front of Richmond,
cooking for "crowded hospital wards which lay about me," and
Stephen and Bubby were still alive. "Two in a year," she thought, "at
this rate we cannot last long." It was a dull Christmas, "not merry," she
told her diary, "not even happy, not decidedly wretched, but like all
these days so much to wish for, so much to be done so little aid, so
much disappointment and vexation."

She devoted the last days of 1865 to her lecture. Sometimes her
ideas would flow with the electricity of inspiration, but before she
could get them on paper, they would dart away and her mind become a
vacuum. To make matters worse, there were endless interruptions,
Jules wanting affection and assurance from her, others wanting this or
that. "Oh what friends, what friends," she complained. Finally, she
decided that her writing block stemmed from trying to cram all her
ideas into one lecture. "I must write two if not three lectures," she told
herself. "I shall spoil all if I attempt to crowd all into one." "Oh if I was
certain that I could speak."

No sign of Atwater's death record yet. The last she heard, he was
sequestered in the Eagle Hotel in New Haven, working in secret.
Sheldon said he had the names listed alphabetically by state and
lacked only those for Pennsylvania. "If only once I can see Dorr
Atwater's roll coming before the people under his own name," she

wrote her sister-in-law, "I shall, I believe experience such a relaxation of nerve that I cant stand upon my feet. If the War Dept. or Moore had the least idea that any such thing was in the wind, they would bring it out in two days, but the thing has been managed so quietly, I have not even breathed it to Brown, nor any person."

"Dorr" had asked Clara to let him visit her for Christmas—he was lonely and missed her—but she told him no, it could not be risked. "I am so anxious," she wrote in her diary.

Clara wanted the death register to appear in all the major New York papers, but cousin Robert preferred that it be given exclusively to the *New York Times*, whose editor, Henry J. Raymond, was Hale's friend, classmate, and fellow congressman. Hale did talk with Raymond about the register, and Raymond assured him that he wanted it for the *Times* and even promised to run "the proper editorials" with it. But Henry Wilson objected to the idea altogether. He disliked Raymond, thought him "the Marplot of the Republican party" because he took a conservative course on Reconstruction, and in all said so many harsh things about the editor that "it cut Robert," Clara said. "I was sorry from the bottom of my heart."

As it turned out, Raymond decided not to publish the death register after all, and the year ended with it in limbo as far as making it public was concerned. "This is the close of a weary year," Clara sighed. Yet she faced 1866 with awakened resolution, determined to "wipe out" all traces of "weakness" in herself, all the depression and thoughts of failure that had beset her, and to make it a better year on all counts. "I am strong and able and not afraid," she wrote in her diary. "I have commenced a new life, determined to follow closely my own purposes, strive to accomplish something for myself."

Clara spent the initial days of 1866 working on her first lecture, writing an especially vivid description of her experiences at Fairfax Station after Second Bull Run. Jules brought her apples and sweet butter for nourishment, and she promised when possible to go to Switzerland with him. She feared that she had neglected him too much, what with all her woes and worries this past autumn, and that he was becoming "habitually unhappy." Therefore she had made another New Year's resolution: "I must draw him more tenderly and lovingly to me and *never* pain him again if I can help it."

On January 5, Congress reconvened after the holiday recess, and the Hill soon rang with debates and resolutions concerning Johnson's reconstruction program and the plight of the blacks in occupied Dixie. With the president's apparent approval, Mississippi and South Carolina had adopted notorious Black Codes that virtually reenslaved their black populations, and the Republicans were up in arms. Wilson himself was so involved with a civil rights bill for the former slaves, one that would override the Black Codes, that he could do little for Clara or Atwater, and Hale, too, was caught up in raucous congressional politicking over Reconstruction matters.

With her two allies thus involved, Clara took the matter of the death register into her own hands: she wrote Horace Greeley, powerful editor of the *New York Tribune*, the country's most influential Republican paper, telling him about Atwater and formally asking "that this record so sadly earned by the waiting, mourning, wondering people, be given them, and that, by him, who, through toil, pain, loss, persecution, danger & disgrace has so richly earned the right of presenting it to them in his own name." Greeley replied that he would be delighted to publish the record, along with whatever Clara and Atwater wished to add, and said he would like to talk to her. "This is the most cheering news I have met," she told her diary. "Oh if I could know that this record & report would all come out right."

She caught a train to New York, riding in one of Pullman's new sleeping cars, which she found delightfully comfortable, with its gas chandeliers, lush carpets, and black walnut woodwork. Atwater met her in New York with the death register, which was all set for publication, and together they took it to Greeley. An eccentric fellow with a balding head, white throat whiskers, and a pale, round, baby face, Greeley suggested that the *Tribune* publish Atwater's roll as a pamphlet, which would be priced just to cover cost, and Clara thought it a marvelous idea. The pamphlet, as she said, would be Atwater's "free gift" to the people and would place his motives above suspicion, giving the lie to Breck's allegations that he hoped to make money from it.

At long last, Dorr's work would reach the public, and Dorr himself would earn a proper place in history. Yet Clara was deeply worried about him. He looked "pale & sober," she thought, "no laugh, no jest but sad serious & thoughtful." He had a cough, complained of a pain in his side, and suffered from a debilitating nervous depression; he doubted that he would ever be well again. His imprisonment at Auburn, Clara said, "wore upon him more than all of Belle Isle & Andersonville."

In the twilight of a January evening, Clara answered a knock at her door, and there stood Frances Gage, her dear friend. Mary Gage had written that her mother might be calling on Clara, and she had hoped against hope that it was true. And now here she was, looking "quite as well" as when Clara had parted with her in 1863. Clara built a fire in the little front parlor, and she and Fanny took tea together. Her older friend, so warm and self-assured, talked at length about her lecturing experiences in behalf of the "freedmen," recalling how she had addressed Soldier's Aid Societies and other groups through New York, Pennsylvania, Ohio, Illinois, and Missouri. Gage had also worked for a time in a Vicksburg soldiers' home run by the Western Sanitary Commission. Once again Clara was struck by Fanny's "superior mind" and remarkable sympathies. The next day, Clara told her about her own lecture plans, and Fanny urged her by all means to "tell the world as you tell me the story of the battlefield—the story of soldiers' suffering."

Clara also recounted the Atwater story and then raised the issue of her now-moribund search for missing soldiers. Hale and Wilson, she said, had talked about getting her a congressional appropriation for that enterprise. But nothing had happened thus far, and Clara was worried that nothing would ever come of their efforts, that Congress was so busy with Reconstruction that it would forget the missing soldiers of the war.

Fanny agreed to help, and the two women worked together to prod an appropriation out of Capitol Hill. Fanny published in the *Washington Independent* an article about Clara's "great work," reminding the politicians' constituents what Clara had done for the country entirely on her own. At the same time, Clara submitted a memorial to Congress, which formally requested funds to resurrect her missing-soldier operation. She described in detail how she had forged "a well organized" and "successful system" at a cost of $7,533 out of her own pocket. "That it should not be permitted to cease would seem to be a proposition on which all right-minded persons must agree," Clara wrote with Fanny's help. "The Government owes it no less to the brave men who lie in unknown graves, than to the anxious and longing friends in whom hope is not yet wholly dead, to see that no stone is left unturned to complete the personal record of all its bereavers."

Attached to the memorial was a supporting letter from Frances Gage. It was a cleverly worded document designed to play on congressional heartstrings. "As a wife and mother, as one having had sons and kindred in the army, as one who has . . . seen her relatives and those near and dear in hospitals, or wounded on the battle-field and even called upon to suffer the far deeper and more terrible sorrow of knowing they were crippled for life, or dead," Gage now joined with Clara Barton "to aid those still more deeply bereaved, more terribly stricken in this great cause; in that they gave their dearest, and too often their only stay and support to their country's service, and now that the war is over . . . they cannot know what has been done with their loved ones by the power that took them from their hearts and homes. . . . Six thousand letters from wives, mothers, and friends and still they come! And Clara Barton who offered to help them, now stands ready and can do nothing, because she has exhausted her own resources and can give nothing more." What sum did Clara need to resume her search? "30,000 would be a small estimate of those who have gone nameless down amid the wild uproar of the billows of war, during the fearful storm of the last four years. Oh! fathers and husbands, cannot this great nation spare two dollars from its magnificent treasury to ascertain the fate of each of these brave men and brothers."

The two women saw that the documents were circulated on Capitol Hill. Hale promoted them in the House, and Wilson took them before his Senate Committee on Military Affairs, which set about investigating Clara's records and expense vouchers. With luck, she should have an answer before the session ended.

On February 14, 1866, Atwater's death register rolled off the *Tribune*'s presses in the form of a seventy-four-page pamphlet, *A List of the Union Soldiers Buried at Andersonville*, which sold for twenty five cents. Readers of the *Tribune* that day found the word *Andersonville* inserted a great many times throughout the paper, which, said Clara, was Greeley's "peculiar manner of advertising it." In the pamphlet, the dead of Andersonville were arranged alphabetically by states, with their grave numbers beside their names. The pamphlet featured an introduction by Atwater, "To the Surviving Relatives and Friends of the

Martyred 'Dead' at Andersonville, Georgia," which recounted his harrowing sojourn at Andersonville, his contretemps with the War
Department over the death register, and his court-martial and subsequent imprisonment, which accounted for the delay in getting the list
to the public. Just as Clara had advised, the statement was a restrained
rehearsal of all the wrongs perpetrated against Atwater by the War
Department. Because Atwater emphasized that those wrongs were also
inflicted on the aggrieved and waiting families of the dead, his statement was all the more effective.

The pamphlet included Clara's report of the Andersonville expedition, which she had submitted to Stanton the previous year. The report
also appeared in the issue of the *Tribune* advertising Atwater's *List*.
Here Clara got in her blows against Moore: She told how she had met
Atwater, how she had suggested to Stanton that he send an expedition
to Georgia, and how he had invited her to accompany it. She also gave
a graphic description of what she had seen inside the Andersonville
stockade. Still, she made it plain that this was Atwater's show. "For the
record of your dead, you are indebted to the forethought, courage, and
perseverance of Dorence Atwater, a young man not yet twenty-one
years of age; an orphan; four years a soldier; one tenth part of his whole
life a prisoner, with broken health and ruined hopes, he seeks to repre-
sent to your acceptance the sad gift he has in store for you."

The pamphlet created a sensation. Thanks to Clara's careful nurturing, Halpine's *New York Citizen* ran a three-column story under the
headline, "GREATEST OUTRAGE OF THE WAR." Young Atwater
"is one of the unquestionable heroes of our recent war," editorialized
Halpine. "And it is one of the most disgraceful facts connected with the
closing of our war, that young Atwater was sent from the Old Capitol to
Auburn in irons . . . and that there was not then, nor has been since,
any voice of public indignation raised against the vile and outrageous
character of his trial, sentence and treatment. It is true he was released
after some two months of incarceration; but that makes no difference
whatever in a review of the cruelty and gross injustice of his treatment. . . . Before the high court of the people in Congress now assembled, can the men who have had part in this outrage escape the brand
of shame?"

The *New York Independent* was equally damning. The pamphlet, it
said, not only vindicated "the boy-patriot" but condemned Moore and
other military authorities for failing to release their own records after
Moore had promised to do so. The *Independent* also published a pro-

file of Atwater by Frances Gage: "There he sits before me—a slender youth. . . . Sorrow, suffering, and wrong have marked his beardless face with lines that are painful to see; a flow of joy pervades the hearts of the little group of true friends who have rushed in to clasp his hands and thank God, oh, so fervently! that he has escaped his prison walls and is once more among them. . . . Dorence Atwater does not laugh; a smile only answers the wittiest jest—a smile so sad, so full of painful memories."

Stung by this onslaught, Quartermaster General Meigs insisted that Moore's office had actually completed its own list of Andersonville dead but that an accumulation of orders at the public printer had delayed its publication (this was Moore's excuse). Meigs grumbled to Stanton that bureaucratic red tape and an overworked public printer had brought "unfounded" allegations of "remissness" against the War Department.

Clara, of course, maintained that no such government record would ever have come forth, and in any case such a list would be redundant now. She was grimly satisfied that justice had at last been done. She and "Dorr" had outwitted the army officers, exonerated him, and served the public in the process. Atwater's pamphlet enjoyed a huge circulation and relieved the families and friends of the men who had perished at Andersonville. The pain of knowing what had happened to them was preferable to the pain of not knowing anything at all, of nurturing some faint and fleeting hope that somehow, somewhere, a missing husband, son, or brother would turn up again. Now their search could end and they could weep over imagined headboards in a silent graveyard in southwest Georgia.

As Clara hoped, the pamphlet also alerted thousands of readers, including influential politicos in Washington, to her important role in the grave-marking expedition to Andersonville. As a consequence, the Joint Committee on Reconstruction, set up the previous December to investigate conditions in occupied Dixie, summoned her to appear before it. One writer speculated that she was "perhaps the first American woman to testify before Congress." Certainly she was the only woman to appear before the Joint Committee on Reconstruction, which consisted of twelve Republicans under William Pitt Fessenden of Maine, Lincoln's last secretary of the treasury. As she sat before the committeemen, her dark eyes shining, her small hands folded in her lap, she gave witness to what she had seen inside the stockade, described the whites who had called on her, and recalled her experiences with the blacks. She made a point of telling the story of Arnold Cater and his wife, whom the cruel overseer had bucked and gagged.

Clara's was important testimony, for the joint committee was to report whether the former Confederate states ought to be readmitted under the Johnson reconstruction program. To that end, it was gathering evidence on the lot of black folk there, on the Black Codes that oppressed and discriminated against them, on the fitness of blacks for free labor, and on white attitudes toward the U.S. government.

How did white Georgians feel about the government? the questioner asked her.

"I think they have no respect for it," Clara said.

How did they feel about blacks?

"I think far less kindly than when they owned them themselves."

Were the whites trying to reenslave the blacks?

"That I cannot say; but I should not want to take the chance of being a slave there."

How did the blacks feel about the U.S. government and the North?

"The very best of feeling—friendly, full of confidence in the United States government, loving the northern people."

"You have had a good deal of intercourse with the blacks," the questioner said; "what is your idea about their capacity to acquire knowledge?"

"In their present condition they can hardly be compared with the whites; still, to a certain extent they learn as easily, as readily."

What about their morals and truthfulness?

They were no more untruthful than what white people would be in "similar circumstances," Clara replied. "Naturally, I think the negro not less moral, not less religious, not less truthful than any other race, only as his condition has made him so."

Thanks to testimony like Clara's, the joint committee concluded that the conquered South was too unrepentant, too hostile to the North, and too cruel and oppressive to blacks to be readmitted into the Union under the Johnson reconstruction program, and that Congress ought to assume control of the restoration process. This was a repudiation of the president's lenient approach to restoring civilian rule in the conquered South, an approach that had allowed former rebels to return to power there and threaten the fruits of the war. The stage was set for a dramatic showdown between the president and congressional Republicans, which would ultimately lead to Johnson's impeachment trial.

* * *

The publicity surrounding Atwater's pamphlet and Clara's appearance before the joint committee virtually guaranteed that Congress would award her funds to continue her missing-soldier operation. In March, Wilson moved for a $15,000 appropriation, in the form of a joint resolution, which sum was to reimburse her for expenses already incurred and to aid her "in the further prosecution" of her work. Speaking in his slipshod style, his face flushed, Wilson showed the Senate the two lists of missing men Clara had already circulated across the country and defended her with the sympathy and understanding born of their fruitful wartime friendship. Senator Grimes of Iowa also spoke in her defense, saying that her work "was performed faithfully and well."

While Clara basked in all the accolades, the amount of the appropriation was disappointing. Some of her supporters had advocated a good deal more; Clara and Fanny had hoped for at least $30,000. Wilson's committee did agree that if $15,000 wasn't enough for Clara to finish her work, "a small additional appropriation might be made," but Wilson thought the sum proposed was adequate. With that, the Senate unanimously endorsed his resolution; the House also approved; and Clara was back in the business of tracking down missing soldiers.

In terms of the art of the possible, Clara won a considerable victory in getting $15,000 out of a Congress faced with a huge war debt and with reconstructing a war-torn country. "By voting $15,000 to Miss Clara Barton," the *New York Citizen* asserted, "Congress has performed a noble duty in acknowledging, even to that limited extent, our country's obligations to a true heroine."

The *Citizen* went on to urge that Wilson and his colleagues now "take up this case of Atwater, and see that reparation shall be made to him for his wasted youth and undeserved stigma of incarceration in a state prison." But Atwater was not so fortunate as Clara. Although he too appeared before the Joint Committee on Reconstruction, to which he told his entire story, the present Congress did not make any reparation to him or reverse his dishonorable discharge. Clara did hire him as her assistant, yet there was nothing she could do to erase the deep hurt he felt. "Do you wonder his soul was embittered and that he damned the government and his country?" a relative asked one of Clara's cousins. "The word soldier makes me mad," he once complained, "while the sight of a uniform makes me froth at the mouth."

Clara meanwhile hired a staff and reopened her Office of

Correspondence with the Friends of the Missing Men of the United States Army, which continued in operation until 1868. She put little brother Jules on her payroll and was delighted for him when he married a girl named Mattie, who later bore him a daughter. Jules thanked her for allowing him to participate in such "honorable" work and credited her with making his life whole and happy.

In a final report to Congress, Clara recounted her record with justifiable satisfaction: all told her office had received 63,182 inquiries, written 41,855 letters, mailed 58,693 printed circulars, distributed 99,057 copies of her printed rolls, and identified 22,000 men, including those on Atwater's death register. She assumed that those not accounted for at that date—some 40,000 men—were dead and that their graves, if they had any, were not likely to be found. Only then, satisfied that she had done her duty, did Clara close her office and bring an end to her Civil War career.

It was a spectacular career by all counts. Had she been a soldier, as she had wanted most of all to be, her résumé of wartime accomplishments might have won her a congressional Medal of Honor. A great many of her contemporaries considered her the outstanding battlefield nurse and relief worker of either sex in the showcase eastern theater, perhaps of the entire war. Her pioneering efforts, in fact, had opened the way for other women to serve in battlefield hospitals in the East. Though frequently called an American Florence Nightingale, Clara had gone beyond Miss Nightingale, who had performed her great Crimean War service in the Barrack Hospital in Scutari, Turkey, 350 miles behind the lines on the Crimea. True, Miss Nightingale had gone to the hospitals in Balaclava near the close of the war, but she had never toiled on the battlefield itself and been under fire as had Clara Barton.

An efficient and effective "Sanitary Commission of one," Clara had also raised impressive quantities of supplies through her network of women's support groups and had personally taken those supplies to the army in the field, thanks to the wagons she had persuaded the Quartermaster Department to give to her. While Clara's individual operation hardly matched the collective efforts of the thousands of Soldiers' Aid Societies and the U.S. Sanitary Commission, her stores had comforted many a regiment and supplied several hard-pressed battlefield hospitals, whose surgeons were forever in her debt. The soldiers and surgeons would have challenged anyone who contended that

Clara's contributions hadn't made a difference. Certainly nobody else had done as much as she in acting as an individual conduit between the home front and the needy soldier on the battlefield. If Reid Mitchell is right, if the war's outcome owed much to the perseverance of the Union's common soldiers, then credit Clara Barton and the other women of the war for reinforcing their resolve.

Add to all this Clara's work as unofficial matron of a field hospital on the Richmond-Petersburg front in 1864 and her role in the grave-marking pilgrimage to Andersonville in 1865, not to mention her search for missing soldiers, which she had conducted through her own office with energy and skill, and it was clear why Clara could view her career with pride. Even more remarkable, Clara had attained all this independently, without institutional affiliation or official government appointment. By dint of her driving will and her ability to exploit the male military and political bureaucracies, she had overcome "the fearful odds" against a woman serving in the field in wartime and had cared for wounded and infected male strangers without compromising her reputation as a respectable "lady."

By nursing shattered men in the hell of combat, standing under fire with only her will as a shield, Clara Barton offered her generation, and all succeeding generations, a profound measure of valor.

The Circuit

Clara's exploits made her perhaps the most famous eastern woman of the war. "I appear to be known by reputation by every person in every train I enter and everywhere," she wrote in her diary. Because she needed a personal income, she did take to the lecture circuit in 1866, giving variations of an address called "Work and Incidents of Army Life," which enabled her to relive her war experiences in front of an audience. To her surprise, she discovered that she was a gifted platform speaker, with a soft, melodious voice and a poetic cast to her descriptions that enthralled her audiences. Her newspaper notices were almost universally favorable, describing her talks as "animated," "instructive and enjoyable." One journalist stated flatly: "We have never seen an audience more interested or attentive." Lyceums, literary societies, and veterans' organizations affiliated with the Grand Army of the Republic all vied for her services. One GAR post named itself after her, which pleased Clara enormously, since she regarded herself as a war veteran.

She was so good that she was able to demand, and get, the same fees that Ralph Waldo Emerson, Thomas Wentworth Higginson, and other popular male lecturers received. She commanded $75 to $100 per performance, sometimes plus expenses. Such fees enabled her to earn a handsome net income, as much as $900 in a single month. Occasionally she donated all or part of her proceeds to charities for the poor or to soldiers' funds for widows and orphans, but most of the money she kept.

For two years after the war, Clara crisscrossed the country, speaking in cities and remote towns from Boston and New Haven to Milwaukee and Washington, Iowa. Her grueling schedule found her riding in smoky, monotonous trains by day and often by night, giving a lecture to strangers in a packed auditorium and grabbing what sleep she could in a railroad hotel before setting off again. Sometimes her accommodations were terrible. "Fearfully dirty room," she wrote in Dixon, Illinois, "filthy, the whole house so, could not sleep for filth and stench." She survived a winter train wreck between Decatur and Jacksonville, Illinois. When the train jumped the track, Clara found herself on the ceiling of an upside-down coach, pinned down by a hot stove, with coals scattered all over her. Atwater, who accompanied Clara as her assistant, helped her out of the smoking wreckage into the icy wind. Bruised, burned, and visibly shaken, she nevertheless proceeded to the next town, where a railroad superintendent gave her $50 for her loss.

Those who attended a Clara Barton lecture saw a small, slender, feminine woman, dressed perhaps in her light blue traveling dress, still looking younger than she was. She would stride to the podium to read her speech from a carefully prepared text, written in large, round script. At first her voice would be low and gentle, but then it would swell into singsong eloquence.

She spoke candidly about the inhibitions that had kept her from the field in 1861 and early 1862. "I struggled long and hard with my sense of propriety," she said, "with the appalling fact that I was a woman, whispering in one ear, and groans of suffering men, dying like dogs, unfed and unsheltered, for the life of the very institutions which had protected and educated me, thundering in the other. I said that I struggled with my sense of propriety, and I say it with shame before God and before you, I am ashamed that I thought of such a thing."

Then she transported her listeners back to Fairfax Station just after Second Bull Run, where she and her colleagues had labored among the wounded for three straight days and nights. She brought tears to many an eye when she told how she had found Hugh Johnson dying of an abdominal wound, had pretended to be his sister, and held him all night before putting him on the train. She took her readers on to Antietam, where a soldier had been shot dead while she cradled him in her arms ... to the Lacy House, where the wounded lad of four words kept telling her "you saved my life" ... to the bloody plain before Marye's Heights, where Sergeant Plunkett had saved the flag even though both of his arms had been blown away. As she moved from point to point in her narrative, there were often "outbursts of laughter over some ludicrous picture she was holding up before them," as one listener said. Perhaps it was the story of how she had shamed into submission the hardened mule drivers who had challenged her authority in 1862. "But when some brave scene poured forth in words of masterly eloquence," the listener said, "the applause was deafening." She recalled Belle Plain, too, and Fredericksburg in 1864, and the macabre stockade at Andersonville—"that eternal blot on the pages of humanity." When she spoke in Connecticut, she added a section on Atwater, "the keeper of the death records," who still stood "unpardoned, a prison convict at large, deprived of his hard earned record as a soldier by dishonorable discharge, unrewarded for his services, disgraced," a boy "ruined in health, maligned, abused and persecuted, but still, unbroken in principle."

Why, she liked to say, had she talked so long about her "own little personal doings in the war"? "It is for this," she said: "to show you that from first to last I have been the soldiers' friend and have an honest right to speak for him." She was indeed "the soldiers' friend," having won the undying love, respect, and gratitude of countless thousands of veterans with whom she had served in the Army of the Potomac and the Army of the James. Wherever she spoke, the veterans turned out to cheer her and listen, transfixed, as she recalled their experiences together and their shared sacrifices. She praised the hard-working army surgeons who had served with her, and she exhorted everyone to look after the widows and orphans of the Union dead. When she spoke in the Midwest, she described meeting a destitute widow, with three small children, who had lost a husband and three sons in the war; one of the sons had starved to death at Andersonville. Clara reminded her audiences that the work of the Civil War remained unfinished as long as there were widows and orphans in need.

She was generous in praising the other women of the war, with whom, on the lecture platform at least, she felt bonded in a powerful sisterhood. During the war, she had stopped taking female assistants with her to the battlefront and hated sharing her patients and hospital—her power and her glory—with other women. In one lecture draft, speaking of the women of the war in the singular, she described how the Union woman had stood up "on the power" of her femininity and declared that the dangers to the country were her dangers, the perils to its armies her perils, the suffering of its defenders her suffering, the ruin of its government her ruin. She had bade her husband and sons to go fight in the army while she worked in her husband's place "in the field or the workshop or plied her needle day and night, took the covering from her bed, the carpet from her floor, the last curtain from her window, to send to some far away field, a hospital where perchance his wasted wounded form was lying." The woman of the Union had also organized relief societies in every town and village. She had "supplied the material" for the work of the U.S. Sanitary Commission and the Christian Commission, which had earned her the wonder and admiration of every civilized nation on earth and had enabled her to "set the world an example easy to follow but hard to surpass through all future time and generations." Too, breaking the restraints of military etiquette, the Union woman had "made her way into every hospital" and even followed marching armies "far out upon the dusty road and on to the fighting field." As she labored for "liberty" and "humankind," Clara said, "she forgot even the argument which had always met her advancing footstep whichever way she turned—women are well enough in their places—wives and mothers and nurses at home—kind and tender but weak and unreliable and worth nothing in an emergency."

Clara did not say so, but the women of the war had done more, much more. Breaking the shackles of strict domesticity in unprecedented numbers, they had entered government service, secured retail jobs, and toiled in war-related industry; they had replaced male teachers who had joined the army and had run farms in the absence of army husbands. They had taken to the stump in support of emancipation and the Union war effort, had campaigned for Lincoln and Republican candidates, and had formed the National Women's Loyal League, which gathered 400,000 signatures in support of the Thirteenth Amendment and which taught women invaluable lessons in organization for the postwar years. On top of all that, some 400 uninhibited women had even enlisted in the Union army disguised as men.

Women, black and white alike, had made equally impressive gains in the male realm of military nursing. According to Jane E. Schultz, more than 18,200 women had worked in Northern military hospitals as paid matrons, nurses, laundresses, and cooks. Their service eroded the popular idea that women's war work ought to be strictly voluntary, an extension of the home. Approximately 3,214 women had served in Dix's department alone. Among the laundresses and cooks, as Schultz points out, were some 2,000 black women, many of them escaped slaves. An estimated 2,000 other women had toiled in army hospitals as unpaid volunteers and independents like Clara. In sheer numbers alone—more than 20,000 all told—women hospital workers had made an indispensable contribution to the Federal cause.

By invading a hitherto male domain and proving that they could function ably there, Union women helped bring about a profound change in American nursing itself. Impressed by their wartime record, the president of the American Medical Association, Samuel Gross, urged the United States to train a corps of women nurses equal to that produced by the Nightingale Training School in England. Toward that end, several women who had served in the 1862 hospital transport service led postwar efforts to set up women's nursing schools in the United States, the first of which opened in the 1870s. Regarded as "a menial service" before the war, nursing became a trained, paid profession for women after the conflict.

In no comparable previous period had American women demanded and won so many new opportunities in the field of nursing and medicine, teaching, retail sales, government employment, and political activity. Even if such gains did not fundamentally alter what one author called "the gender hierarchy of northern society," they did offer women more options for employment and chances for personal fulfillment than they had had when the war began. While it was true that Clara and other women actually lost their government jobs in the year immediately following the war, the number of women wage-earners in the 1860s rose by 60 percent or more. By war's end, Clara told a group in Boston, the American woman was at least "fifty years in advance of the normal position which continued peace and existing conditions would have assigned her."

What was more, the war had given Clara and her entire generation of women a new sense of worth. "Only an opportunity was wanting for woman to prove to man that she could be in earnest," Clara declared, "that she had character, and firmness of purpose—that she *was* good for something in an emergency." The women of the war had not only demonstrated their competence to men, Clara believed, they had also proved it to themselves. By expanding the limits of what was possible, they had "dug grand and deep and laid firm and forever the cornerstone of future womanhood."

Clara also took a bold feminist stance on the platform, in the process revealing the ways the war had shaped her political views. She had always, she said, been "at heart and long before the idea took shape in words a firm and indignant supporter of women's right to all privilege that any rational beings could enjoy." But her wartime friendship with Frances Gage, plus her own liberating achievements, transformed Clara's quiet beliefs into open advocacy. At the lecture podium, she proclaimed her emphatic support for "perfectly equal rights" for women, including the right to vote, and she shared the platform with Susan B. Anthony and other feminist leaders at women's conventions.

On one postwar issue, however, Clara clashed bitterly with some established leaders of the woman's rights movement. That issue concerned the political rights of the former slaves, the "three millions of

God's poor neglected, long-abandoned, late-remembered, down-trod-
den children of the dust," as Clara called them, whose cause she
ardently defended. Her friendship with Fanny Gage and her contact
with blacks at Port Royal and Andersonville had made her acutely sensitive to the plight of the freed people, so much so that Clara asserted
that black men ought to have the vote even before women did. Clara
said as much at a convention of the Equal Rights Association, held in
New York in 1869. Invited to speak on the war, her sphere of work, she
defended black suffrage as "a part of the war," an extension of emancipation, pointing out how much Southern blacks needed the ballot to
protect themselves from their former masters. In effect, as she said
later, she told the convention, "Finish my work first, then I am ready
with heart and soul for yours."

With that, Clara took sides in a fierce debate within feminist ranks
about the timing of women's suffrage demands. The debate focused on
the projected Fifteenth Amendment, which sought to protect the former slaves by enfranchising black men. The amendment did not
include women, black or white. One women's rights group, led by Julia
Ward Howe, endorsed the amendment, agreeing with its Republican
framers that black suffrage was already controversial enough and
would go down to defeat if women's suffrage were linked to it. Better,
they believed, to get the blacks enfranchised first. Clara's friend, Fanny
Gage, agreed with this position. Another feminist group, led by
Anthony and Elizabeth Cady Stanton, opposed the amendment as "an
open, deliberate insult to American womanhood." Anthony and
Stanton considered it extremely unfair that uneducated black males
should gain the elective franchise while educated white women were
denied it. The struggle between the two women's groups reached a climax at the 1869 convention, where Anthony and Stanton tried but
failed to unite the delegates behind a projected Sixteenth Amendment
that would enfranchise women. Shortly after that, the Anthony-Stanton
faction formed the National Women's Suffrage Association, whose leaders and members were mostly women and whose goal was to rally
national support for a woman's suffrage amendment. The rival group,
with the endorsement of well-known Republicans and reformers like
Thomas Wentworth Higginson and Frederick Douglass, then founded
the American Woman Suffrage Association, which made a point of
seeking male support.

Word reached Clara that some feminist leaders thought her speech
at the 1869 convention had degraded their sex. She fervently disagreed. How, she asked, could she, who was "well fed, warmed &

clothed with the privilege at least of appealing to the law" if she were in danger, put herself before "the thousands of hungry Negroes"—she had seen many of them in southwest Georgia—"waiting in fear, trembling and uncertainty all through the South, surrounded by an enemy as implacable as death"? Their need for the ballot was urgent. "I only meant to be understood like this," she told Mary Norton: "no person in that house would or could be more rejoiced than I to see the franchise bestowed upon every person capable of using it without regard to race, color, or sex, but if the door was not wide enough for all at once—and one must wait, or all must wait, then I for one was willing that the old scarred slave limp through before me. . . . I had no heart to pull or thrust him back in spite because he was already in advance of me, but I should claim the right to go next, and immediately. This might have been all very unwise, but it was like me, and I could not take any other ground. Heaven knows I have no desire to degrade my sex . . . but the cause is not to be hastened by quarreling with men as men, nor with races nor with anyone."

The last line underscored another crucial element in Clara's feminism. Because she had "identified with men" since childhood, she refused to quarrel "with men as men" and rejected an antimale stance of any kind. Indeed, she expressed her sympathy for men and believed that they would one day accept women as their equals. "Man is trying to carry the burdens of the world alone," she insisted. "When he has the efficient help of woman he should be glad, and he will be."

Even so, she was not going to beg men for rights that ought to have been hers at birth. Once, when asked to sign a petition asking for women's suffrage, Clara indignantly refused. "Of whom should I ask this privilege?" she demanded. "Who possessed the right to confer it? Who had greater right than woman herself? Was it man and, if so, how did he get it? Who conferred it on him? He depended upon woman for his being, his very existence, nature and rearing. More fitting that she should have conferred it upon him."

For Clara, the lecture circuit had its moments of genuine surprise, which made all the controversies and arduous traveling worthwhile. In Cleveland, where she lectured to "a splendid house," John Elwell called on her—with his wife. Four times breveted for bravery in the war, he still walked with a limp. He had hurt himself again in back-to-back accidents at Elmira in 1864: first a carriage in which he was riding had overturned, hurling him against a stone step and breaking many bones; not long after that he had stumbled while descending the steps from his office and had fallen head forward, refracturing the leg he had broken on Hilton Head. When the war ended, he had come home to Cleveland and had taken up law and medicine again. He was delighted to see Clara, and over the years wrote her passionate and tender letters recalling their love affair in 1863.

During one address in a town west of the Mississippi, as she recalled Antietam and the bullet-ridden farmhouse hospital to which she had brought desperately needed supplies, Clara told how the surgeon in charge had toiled among the dead and dying all that bloody day, and how she found him at night slumped at a table, in despair because the single candle burning beside him was all the light he had for a thousand wounded men. Clara told how she took him to the door and pointed at a lantern glowing in the barn, saying that she had brought four boxes of them. The surgeon, she said, was too overwhelmed to tell her thanks. As she spoke, a gentleman sprang from his chair, leaped on the stage, and told the audience: "Ladies and gentlemen, if I never have acknowledged that favor, I will do it now. I am that surgeon."

In another lecture, held in the hall of a local YMCA, Clara's audience was especially enthusiastic. When she reached the end with a poetic tribute to the "dead on the field of battle," people were amazed to discover that she had spoken for an hour and a half. Afterward, as Clara shook hands with well wishers, she noticed a man approach the platform with his arm around a little girl; he wore a light blue soldier coat and walked with a limp. Something about his manner, and his lined, weather-beaten face, jarred Clara's memory. She excused herself and strode to him with her hand extended.

"Have we met before?" she asked.

"Yes," he said, "three times."

Still clasping his hand, Clara said quietly, "Well, tell me."

"At the battle of 2nd Bull Run when I was shot through the body and had lain on the field for days with nothing to eat, you came out of the woods and met the wagon that was taking me off and climbed up onto the wheel and fed me."

"I remember," Clara said softly, and waited for him to continue.

"Before my wound had entirely healed," he said, "I rejoined my regiment at Falmouth—and the next day went to the battle of Old Fredericksburg, had this leg shattered in the charge of Saturday and lay out on the field in the cold till Monday night—my hands and feet were frozen. When we got over the river there were so many wounded there was no shelter for us. And you had the men scrape the snow off the ground and gave us warm drink and kept hot bricks about us all night—you had them heated in the camp fires."

"I remember," Clara said, her lips trembling a little.

"I lost you then for nearly two years—when one terribly hot day in front of Petersburg, when from our marching nearly our whole brigade fell with exhaustion and sunstroke, I among the first—for I hadn't the strength I had at Bull Run—and while I lay there on the ground you came with whiskey & water for us all and had me taken to the hospital tents and you bound my head in ice and I was too crazy to tell you that I knew you but I did—and your care saved my life."

When it was clear that he was done, Clara withdrew her hand from his and touched the cheek of the child standing next to him. "And is this your little girl?"

"Yes," he said, running his hand through her hair. "She is almost three years old and we call her Clara Barton."

Scores of other veterans also named their daughters after Clara. There was Clara Barton Leggett, daughter of Lieutenant Colonel Robert Leggett, who had lost his leg on Morris Island and credited Clara with saving his life. There was a Clara Barton Whitaker, a Clara Barton Thompson, a Clara Barton Hoffman, a Clara Barton Clausson, and a Clara Barton Bergh. Sally Gardner, wife of the splendid young man whom Clara had nursed after the Baltimore riot and who had been killed at the Crater, wrote Clara that a daughter had been born after his death and that she was named Clara Horace Gardner. Harry and Mary Barnard, the young lovers of Antietam fame, had married after Clara had left them in Frederick, Maryland; their first child, Clara Barton Barnard, was born in 1864. Before long, there were young Clara Bartons all over the United States, from Massachusetts to California. In these young women who bore her name, the spirit of childless, spouseless Clara lived on.

According to Union army surgeon F. H. Harwood, Harry Barnard retained a romantic, sentimental view of war, once telling his young children: "War is the scourge of tyrants, the shield of the oppressed, the nurseling of brave men and lofty deeds; the theatre where heroes enact melo-dramas on the world's stage to the thunderous music of bursting artillery." Clara disagreed with that view, emphatically. The unprece-

dented violence and ghastly human suffering she had witnessed in the Civil War made her a confirmed hater of "the war side of war" and an eloquent critic of men for waging it. "Men have worshipped war," she asserted, "till it has cost a million times more than the whole world is worth, poured out the best blood and crushed the fairest forms the good God has ever created.—Deck it as you will, war is—'Hell.' . . . All through and through, thought, and act, body and soul—I hate it. . . . Only the desire to soften some of its hardships and allay some of its miseries ever induced me, and I presume all other women who have taken similar steps, to dare its pestilence and unholy breath."

Even so, for the rest of Clara's long life, it was the Civil War that fired her imagination, the Civil War to which she kept returning in her lectures, her reminiscences, her correspondence, and her dreams. As with millions of others in her generation, the Civil War was the central, defining event of Clara's life. She discovered in nursing and the relief of suffering a real purpose to her existence; after years of searching, she had found her calling. After the war, she became a "professional angel" and humanitarian whose relentless will, ambition, and sense of duty took her to war fronts in foreign lands. She went on to found and become first president of the American Association of the Red Cross, thus institutionalizing the nursing and relief work she had begun in the Civil War. At the age of seventy-seven she was still in the field, serving in hospitals in Cuba during the Spanish-American War. As she lay dying in 1912 at the age of ninety, her thoughts perhaps leaped back to the war in which her life's work had begun—back to that troubling time in 1861 and early 1862 when she had wanted desperately to serve her country but had been held back by societal restrictions on women going to the battlefield. Her last words were: "Let me go; let me go!"

Afterword and Acknowledgments

The literature of the Civil War has never given Clara the attention she deserves. She is rarely mentioned in the textbooks and general histories; their focus is almost exclusively on the men, anyway. The studies of the campaigns in which Clara participated largely ignore her. So do the biographies of the men who served with her. Even Ken Burns's superlative documentary, "The Civil War," overlooks Clara's contributions, although she is quoted a few times.

While the early biographies of Clara do cover her war years, I found their treatments perfunctory and inaccurate. Some of them, like Blanche Colton Williams's *Clara Barton, Daughter of Destiny* (1941), are an unhappy mixture of fact and fiction. William E. Barton's two-volume *The Life of Clara Barton: Founder of the American Red Cross* (1922) is less a biography than a compendium of letters, other documents, and not always assimilated factual matter.

Of all the biographies, Elizabeth Brown Pryor's *Clara Barton, Professional Angel* (1987), offers the most original scholarly account of Clara's Civil War career, and I learned much from it. Overall, the book is brilliant portraiture, by far the best full-scale biography of Clara yet written. Pryor's real emphasis, however, is the postwar years, to which she devotes almost two-thirds of her book. I can appreciate that, since nearly everyone associates Clara's historical significance with the Red Cross. But when I plunged into the records relating to the Civil War and saw how much the biographical literature had left out, I knew for certain that Clara's wartime achievements merited book-length treatment. As I have tried to show, her great service to the Union cause was an act of momentous self-discovery and self-empowerment and the foundation of the rest of her life. I wanted, moreover, to use Clara's war years as a way of illuminating *her* Civil War—the brutal medical side of the conflict and the inferno of combat as she experienced it. She was my witness to a larger, more universal story about war itself.

In electing to write about Clara Barton, I hoped that my experience as a biographer would enable me to be properly empathetic and to offer new insights into her character and personality. I walked many a mile in her footsteps, visiting all of her Civil War sites, from Antietam to Andersonville. I tried to view the world through her eyes, think her thoughts, and feel her feelings. It was one of the most liberating and enlightening adventures of my writing life.

I also hoped that my experience as a student of the Civil War—I've studied and written about it for thirty-five years—would help me describe the nature and importance of Clara's actions within the war's military context. As my references indicate, I have corrected the published record of her war career on many points. Even so, I am deeply indebted to Elizabeth Pryor, William E. Barton, Ishbel Ross, and Percy Epler for breaking the ground ahead of me.

In preparing A Woman of Valor, I've accumulated a great debt to many authors and scholars. Carolyn G. Heilbrun's Writing a Woman's Life (1988) taught me "what a woman's biography" should entail. Moreover, her discussions of the lives of other intelligent, independent, and ambitious women helped me understand Clara Barton. Bettina Aptheker's Tapestries of Life: Women's Work, Women's Consciousness, and the Meaning of Daily Experience (1991) introduced me to the teachings of Adrienne Rich and the idea that the best thing women can do for one another is to enlarge their sense of possibilities. Aptheker's observation that "women's resistance . . . comes out of women's subordinated status to men, institutionalized in society and lived through every day in countless personal ways," gave me insight into the struggle of Clara Barton and her Northern sisters to overcome societal restrictions against women serving at the battlefront. Poet Michelle Murray, who says that she "created" herself "from scratch through language," helped me realize that Clara created herself through action.

But perhaps the most important influence on A Woman of Valor was Joyce Carol Oates's fiction—particularly Them (1969), Solstice (1985), Marya (1986), Because It is Bitter, and Because It Is My Heart (1990), and Black Water (1991)—whose richly complex and fully realized female characters not only helped me comprehend woman's experience but showed me the wondrous possibilities of illuminating that experience through the narrative form. Jane Smiley's A Thousand Acres (1991), about the complex relationships of a father and his daughters, of sisters and husbands, enhanced my understanding of Clara's relationships with her father and family. One line of Smiley's story stands out in my mind: "It was exhilarating," Ginny said, "talking to my father as if he were my child, more than exhilarating to see him as my child." Clara felt a similar sense of exhilaration, of real power, when she nursed sick and dying men as though they were *her* children. Mary McGarry Morris's *A Dangerous Woman* (1991), so elegantly written, made me aware of the extent to which rejection can damage the spirit and personality of a sensitive woman. The strong, original female characters in Larry McMurtry's novels showed me that a man can write intelligently and sympathetically about women.

I also benefited enormously from Professor Jane E. Schultz's scholarly articles about Northern female nurses and hospital workers; from Catherine Clinton's *The Other Civil War: American Women in the Nineteenth Century* (1984) and *Divided Houses: Gender and the Civil War* (coedited, with Nina Silber, 1992); from Mary Elizabeth Massey's pioneering *Bonnet Brigades* (1966); from Marilyn Mayer Culpepper's *Trials and Triumphs: The Women of the American Civil War* (1991); from Carl N. Degler's *At Odds: Women and the Family in America from the Revolution to the Present* (1980); from Nancy F. Cott's *The Bonds of Womanhood: 'Woman's Sphere' in New England* (1977); from Frank R. Freemon's *Microbes and Minie Balls: An Annotated Bibliography of Civil War Medicine* (1993), an obvious labor of love and an indispensable reference tool; and from other works on women's history and on the Civil War too numerous to list. Indeed, we are in the midst of a renaissance of writing about the Civil War, with new studies of politics, campaigns, and the leading players—almost all of them men—tumbling off the presses every week. My references show my specific indebtedness to the modern studies of the political, military, and medical side of the war, to many older works, and to other writings about women, medicine, and nursing.

Words cannot express my gratitude to four creative scholars who took time out from their own projects and busy lives to read *A Woman of Valor* in manuscript and to offer cogent, constructive criticism: Dr. Karen Manners Smith, a specialist in women's history and biography; Dr. Betty L. Mitchell, a feminist and Civil War scholar at the University of Massachusetts, Dartmouth; Dr. Sandra L. Katz, a specialist in women's biography and professor of English at the University of Hartford; and Dr. Gary W. Gallagher, a Civil War expert and chairman of the Department of History, Pennsylvania State University. Their critiques made my story far better than it otherwise would have been. I am most grateful to my editor, Joyce Seltzer, for her own careful reading of the manuscript, her perceptive comments, and her enthusiastic support of the project from the beginning. Members of the Amherst Creative Biography Group—Linda Davis, Dr. Sandra Katz, Dr. William Kimbrel, Elizabeth Lloyd-Kimbrel, Dr. Ann Meeropol, Helen Sheehy, and Dr. Harriet Sigerman, accomplished biographers all— heard segments of the work during our monthly meetings and offered excellent advice about narrative voice, interpretation of character, and the art of composition. Michael Meeropol of Western New England College joined our discussions and made suggestions that were most helpful. My enduring thanks go to my agent, Gerry McCauley, and to my assistants, Liang He, Dan Costello, Lisa May, Susanna Yurich, Rebecca Watson, Beth Weston, Glendyne Wergland, and Anne-Marie Taylor, who performed myriad duties with skill and alacrity.

A number of folk offered generous help during my research stage. I am indebted to Ted Alexander, historian, and Paul Chiles, chief interpreter, of the Antietam National Battlefield, U.S. National Park Service, for providing me with scholarly papers about the battle of Antietam and Clara's role in it and for helping me locate her whereabouts there. The National Park Service historians and staffs at the Lacy House (or Chatham), the Fredericksburg battlefield site, and the Appomattox Manor on City Point also gave me valuable information. James H. Blankenship, Jr., historian, Petersburg National Battlefield, gave me valuable information and sources on Depot Hospital and the hospital at Point of Rocks. I owe a considerable debt to the entire staff at the Andersonville National Historic Site in Georgia, particularly to park historian Mark Ragan, superintendent Fred Boyles, and ranger Bill Burnett, who made my visit there both profitable and pleasurable. In Washington, D.C., archivist Michael Pilgrim helped me locate pertinent records in the manuscript and microfilm collections of the National Archives. While I worked my way through the Library of Congress's immense Clara Barton collection, I was fortunate to have the assistance of Jeffrey M. Flannery, reference librarian of the Manuscripts Division. I spent two enjoyable days in the Prints and Photographs Division of the Library of Congress, where Mary M. Ison, division head and reference specialist for the Civil War Collections, gave me the benefit of her considerable expertise. At the American Antiquarian Society, Thomas Knowles, Curator of Manuscripts, was generous with his time and counsel while I examined the rich Clara Barton collection there. The Interlibrary Loan Office of the University of Massachusetts, Amherst, found obscure sources for me in all corners of the country, and I am most grateful to Edla Holm, head of the Interlibrary Loan office, and her entire staff—particularly Nancy McAvoy and Marion Grader—for their enthusiastic efforts in my behalf. To the officers and staffs of all the other repositories listed at the beginning of my references, I offer my sincere thanks for the professional services they rendered. My thanks, too, to William Clipson for drawing the fine maps that accompany my text.

References

ABBREVIATIONS OF MANUSCRIPT SOURCES
(LISTED APHABETICALLY BY ABBREVIATIONS)

AC Papers MHS	Austin Craig and Family Papers, Minnesota Historical Society, St. Paul, Minnesota
AL Collection SLRC	Alma Lutz Collection, Schlesinger Library, Radcliffe College, Cambridge, Massachusetts
BB Papers LC	Benjamin F. Butler Papers, Library of Congress, Washington, D.C.
CB Collection AHL	Clara Barton Collection, Universalist Historical Society, Andover-Harvard Library, Cambridge, Massachusetts
CB File ANHS	Clara Barton File, Andersonville National Historic Site, Andersonville, Georgia
CB Papers AAS	Clara Barton Papers, American Antiquarian Society, Worcester, Massachusetts
CB Papers DU	Clara Barton Papers, Duke University, Durham, North Carolina
CB Papers HL	Clara Barton Papers, Huntington Library, San Marino, California
CB Papers LC	Clara Barton Papers, Library of Congress, Washington, D.C.
CB Papers NYPL	Clara Barton Papers, New York Public Library, New York, New York
CB Papers SC	Clara Barton Papers, Sophia Smith Collection, Smith College, Northampton, Massachusetts

CB Papers SLRC — Clara Barton Papers, Arthur and Elizabeth Schlesinger Library on the History of Women in America, Radcliffe College, Cambridge, Massachusetts

DA Diary CBPLC — Dorence Atwater Diary, Clara Barton Papers, Library of Congress, Washington, D.C.

DA File ANHS — Dorence Atwater File, Andersonville National Historic Site, Andersonville, Georgia

EMB Letters AAS — Edmund Mills Barton Letters and Diary, 1863–1865, American Antiquarian Society, Worcester, Massachusetts

FGC Papers SC — Frank G. Carpenter Papers, Smith College, Northampton, Massachusetts

GEB Letters AAS — George Edward Barton Letters, 1862–1865, American Antiquarian Society, Worcester, Massachusetts

HW Papers LC — Henry Wilson Papers, Library of Congress, Washington, D.C.

IMB Papers AAS — Ira and Maria Barton Family Papers, American Antiquarian Society, Worcester, Massachusetts

JD Papers UVA — James L. Dunn Papers, Manuscripts Division, Special Collections Department, University of Virginia, Charlottesville, Virginia

JE Papers WRHS — John J. Elwell Papers, Western Reserve Historical Society, Cleveland, Ohio

LMS Papers OHS — Lilly Martin Spencer Papers, microfilmed by the Archives of American Art, Smithsonian Institution, through the courtesy of Campus Maritus Museum of the Ohio Historical Society, Marietta, Ohio

MLS Papers MHS — Marion Louisa Sloan Papers, Minnesota Historical Society, St. Paul, Minnesota

MN Papers DU — Mary Norton Papers, Duke University, Durham, North Carolina

MS Papers OCHS — Marion Sloan Papers, Olmsted County Historical Society, Rochester, Minnesota

NARA — U.S. National Archives and Records Administration, Washington, D.C.

Cemeterial Quartermaster Notifications, 1863–1866

Compiled Military Service Records (Record Group 94)

Commissary General of Prisoners, Letters Received

Department of the South, Letters Received, 1863

Department of the South, Letters Sent (old volume 21)

Pension Records (Record Group 15)

NARA AGO   U.S. National Archives and Records
                          Administration
                          Letters Received by the Appointment,
                          Commission, and Personal Branch of the
                          Adjutant General's Office (Record Group 94)

NARA QMG   U.S. National Archives and Records
                          Administration, Records of the Office of
                          Quartermaster General Consolidated
                          Correspondence File, 1794–1915

NEWAA Papers MHS   New England Women's Auxiliary Association
                          Papers, Massachusetts Historical Society, Boston,
                          Massachusetts

SRB Papers DU   Samuel R. Barton Papers, Duke University,
                          Durham, North Carolina

WR Collection SLRC   Women's Rights Collection, Schlesinger Library,
                          Radcliffe College, Cambridge, Massachusetts

p. iv   *opening quotation*: Percy H. Epler, *The Life of Clara Barton*
                          (New York: Macmillan, 1915), viii.

PART ONE: THE SEARCH

p. 3   *"indignant, excited"*: CB interview in the *National
                          Repository* 5 (Feb. 1879), 159; Elizabeth Brown Pryor,
                          Clara Barton, Professional Angel (Philadelphia: University
                          of Pennsylvania Press, 1987), 78; Ishbel Ross, *Angel of the
                          Battlefield: The Life of Clara Barton* (New York: Harper &
                          Bros., 1956), 78.

p. 3   *CB description*: William E. Barton, *The Life of Clara Barton,
                          Founder of the American Red Cross* (2 vols., Boston:
                          Houghton Mifflin Co., 1922), 2:326–28; "Miss CB," newspa-
                          per clipping (circa 1886), CB Papers LC; "Biographical
                          Department: Clara H. Barton," newspaper clipping, ibid.

p. 3   *"from the bottom"*: CB to Judge Ira Barton, Apr. 14, 1861,
                          CB Papers AAS.

p. 4   *arrival of the Sixth Massachusetts and "schoolmates"*: CB
                          undated notes for a lecture, CB Papers LC; CB to Elvira
                          Stone, Apr. 29, 1861, ibid.; and Margaret Leech, *Reveille in
                          Washington: 1860–1865* (New York: Harper & Brothers,
                          1941), 60.

p. 4   *"Men need guns"*: quoted in William Q. Maxwell, *Lincoln's
                          Fifth Wheel: The Political History of the U.S. Sanitary
                          Commission* (New York: Longman's, Green & Co., 1956),
                          50; see also Hannah Ropes, *Civil War Nurse: The Diary
                          and Letters of Hannah Ropes*, ed. John R. Brumgardt
                          (Knoxville: University of Tennessee Press, 1980), 39.

p. 4   *Clara helps wounded*: Barton, *Life of Clara Barton*, 1:109;
        Epler, *Life of Clara Barton*, 29. Edward F. Jones, a mem-
        ber of the Sixth Massachusetts, recalled CB and other
        women caring for the men wounded in the Baltimore riot.
        See undated newspaper clipping, CB Papers LC.

p. 5   *Baltimore riot: New York Times*, Apr. 29, 30, 1861; Henry
        Steele Commager (ed.), *The Blue and the Gray: The Story
        of the Civil War as Told by Participants* (Indianapolis:
        Bobbs-Merrill Co., 1950), 79–83; P.C. Headley,
        Massachusetts in the Rebellion . . . (Boston: Walker, Fuller,
        and Co., 1866), 108–15.

p. 5   *"great national calamity"*: CB letter fragment [circa Apr.
        1861], CB Papers LC.

p. 5   *Washington isolated*: Leech, *Reveille in Washington*, 64;
        Howard P. Nash, Jr., *Stormy Petrel: The Life and Times of
        General Benjamin F. Butler, 1818–1893* (Rutherford, N.J.:
        Fairleigh Dickinson University Press, 1969), 79.

p. 5   *"the battlements"*: Tyler Dennett (ed.), *Lincoln and the Civil
        War in the Diaries and Letters of John Hay* (reprint 1939
        ed., Westport, Conn.: Negro Universities Press, 1972), 6.

p. 5   *"little spruce clerks"*: CB to Annie Childs, Apr. 14, 18, 1861,
        CB Papers AAS; also "A Woman Clerk," *Washington
        Sunday Chronicle*, March 11, 1863, clipping, CB Papers
        LC; Alice Stone Blackwell, "Clara Barton Kept a Secret,"
        Woman's Journal, Feb. 24, 1883.

p. 6   *"largest market basket," "you would have smiled"*: CB to
        Will Childs, Apr. 25, 1861, in Barton, *Life of Clara Barton*,
        1:110; CB, "Work and Incidents of Army Life," circa 1866,
        CB Papers SC; "Biographical Department: Clara Barton,"
        Soldier's Weekly Messenger, May 8, 1867, clipping CB
        Papers LC; L. B. Halstead interview, July 29, 1890, ibid.

p. 6   *"if it must be"*: CB to Will Childs, Apr. 25, 1861, in Barton,
        Life of Clara Barton, 1:110; also CB to Elvira Stone, Apr.
        29, May 5, 14, 1861, CB Papers LC.

p. 6   *troops in Washington*: CB to Elvira Stone, Apr. 29, 1861,
        CB Papers LC; Leech, *Reveille in Washington*, 66–69.

p. 6   *"we are now an armed city," "thirty thousand soldiers"*: CB
        to Elvira Stone, Apr. 29, May 14, 1861, respectively, CB
        Papers LC.

p. 7   *"I don't know how long"*: CB to Stephen Barton, Sr., May
        19, 1861, ibid. Quoted also in Pryor, *Clara Barton*, 79, and
        in Ellen Langenheim Henle, "Against the Fearful Odds:
        Clara Barton and American Philanthropy" (Ph.D. disserta-
        tion, Case Western Reserve University, 1977), 35.

p. 7   *CB's poem*: CB Papers LC.

p. 7   *CB's opposition to sexual discrimination*: CB to Mary
        Norton, Oct. 15, 1859, AL Collection SLRC; CB, *The
        Story of My Childhood* (New York: Baker & Taylor, 1907),
        90.

p. 7   *CB's views of marriage*: In a letter to Bernard Vassall, July
              28, 1860, CB Papers LC, Clara associated marriage with
              death, saying of some female friends, "Don't know if they
              are all dead or married, as for myself I am neither, entire,
              about half of the former, and not a bit of the latter, haven't
              taken the first step." She was then thirty-eight years old.
              Clara appears to have entertained the same opinion of mar-
              riage as her contemporary, Dr. Elizabeth Blackwell, who,
              in the words of Margaret Forster, managed "to separate the
              attractions of the flesh from the reality of the marital condi-
              tion." Blackwell wrote that she saw "what a life association
              might mean and I shrank from the prospect, disappointed
              or repelled." Forster, *Significant Sisters: The Grassroots of
              Active Feminism, 1839–1939* (New York: Alfred A. Knopf,
              1985), 63.

p. 7   *"more boy than girl"*: CB Journal, Apr. 23, 1907, CB Papers
              LC; quoted first in Pryor, *Clara Barton*, 13, without italics.
              In the journal entry, CB claimed that her long-dead moth-
              er, speaking to her in a recent seance, reminded her of
              Stephen Barton's observation.

pp. 7–8   *CB and her father*: Pryor, *Clara Barton*, 18, 21–23; CB,
              "Black Book," CB Papers SC; Ross, *Angel of the Battlefield*,
              4. Pryor, *Clara Barton*, 13, also says that CB "idolized" her
              father. Stephen Barton, Sr., was called "Captain" because
              he had been elected captain of the local militia after his ser-
              vice in the Indian wars.

p. 8   *"we marshalled large armies"*: file 81, p. 4, CB Papers SC.

p. 8   *"I had no end of camp material"*: quoted in George F.
              Daniels, *History of the Town of Oxford Massachusetts . . .*
              (Oxford: published by the author, 1892), 391.

p. 8   *"Where other little girls listened," "I early learned"*: CB to
              Captain I.W. Denny, Mar. 30, 1862, CB Papers LC; copy
              in CB Papers AAS.

p. 8   *"The patriot blood of my father"*: Epler, *Life of Clara
              Barton*, 32, and Barton, *Life of Clara Barton*, 1:128–29.

p. 8   *female soldiers impersonating men*: Agatha Young, *The
              Women and the Crisis: Women of the North in the Civil
              War* (New York: McDowell, Obolensky, 1959), 43, esti-
              mates the number at 400. See also Ann Douglas Wood,
              "The War within a War: Women Nurses in the Union
              Army," *Civil War History* (Sept. 1972), 202, and Richard
              Hall, *Patriots in Disguise: Women Warriors of the Civil War*
              (New York: Paragon House, 1993), 20–45.

p. 8   *CB must be "a proper little lady"*: CB, *Story of My
              Childhood*, 62–66.

p. 8   *Clara's identification with men*: Pryor, *Clara Barton*, 13–15.
              Clara later remarked of her identification with men: "I . . .
              have spent the strength of my life for *men*, working always
              to all *appearances* at least in their behalf and receiving their

thanks." CB's notes for postwar speech on woman's rights [undated], CB Papers SC.

p. 8   *morning ritual of facial creams, rouge, hair dye*: Henle, "Against the Fearful Odds," 204; Pryor, *Clara Barton*, x. In the antebellum era, as Lois Banner points out, Victorian ladies identified cosmetics with prostitution. But in the American cities in the 1850s, fashionable and respectable women adopted the new styles from Paris, which included heavy use of cosmetics. By the Civil War, as Banner says, the earlier Victorian prohibitions against the use of cosmetics had ended, and "fashionable women not only creamed and powdered their faces, but they also used rouge, lipstick, and mascara." See Banner, *American Beauty* (Chicago: University of Chicago Press, 1983), 42, 44.

p. 9   *"battle flag of humanity"*: Francis Tiffany, *Life of Dorothea Lynde Dix* (Boston and New York: Houghton Mifflin, 1890), 145.

p. 9   *"I propose to organize"*: quoted in Dorothy Clarke Wilson, *Stranger and Traveler: The Story of Dorothea Dix, American Reformer* (Boston: Little, Brown, 1975), 266.

p. 9   *"General Superintendent of the Female Nursing Establishment"*: Cecil Woodham-Smith, *Florence Nightingale, A Biography* (reprint of 1951 ed., New York: Atheneum, 1983), 174.

p. 9   *Dix's efforts*: Helen Marshall, *Dorothea Dix: Forgotten Samaritan* (reprint of 1937 ed., New York: Russell and Russell, 1967), 219; Marjorie Barstow Greenbie, *Lincoln's Daughters of Mercy* (New York: G. P. Putnam's Sons, 1944), 63.

p. 9   *Cameron's directive Apr. 23, 1861*: U.S. War Department, *The War of the Rebellion: A Compilation of the Official Records of the Union and Confederate Armies* (70 vols. in 128; Washington, D.C.: Government Printing Office, 1880–1901), ser. 3, 1:107; hereafter cited as *OR*. Acting Surgeon General Wood issued a follow-up directive on May 20, 1861, ibid., 217, asserting that Dix was "authorized to exercise a general supervision of the assignment of nurses to the hospitals, general and regimental, occupied by the troops of Washington and its vicinity."

p. 9   *"No young ladies"*: quoted in Sylvia G. Dannett, (ed.), *Noble Women of the North* (New York: Thomas Yoseloff, 1959), 62–63; Wilson, *Stranger and Traveler*, 270. For Dix's connection with the Women's Central Association of Relief, see Elizabeth Blackwell, *Pioneer Work in Opening the Medical Profession to Women: Autobiographical Sketches* (reprint of 1895 ed., New York: Source Book Press, 1970), 235–36; Maxwell, *Lincoln's Fifth Wheel*, 3, 66, 68; George Washington Adams, *Doctors in Blue: The Medical History of the Union Army in the Civil War* (New York: Henry Schuman, 1952), 5, 7; Anne L. Austin, *The Woolsey Sisters of New York: A Family's Involvement in the Civil War and a New Profession (1860–1890)* (Philadelphia: American Philosophical Society, 1971), 34–42. According to Kristie Ross, "Arranging a Doll's House: Refined Women As Union Nurses," in Catherine Clinton and Nina Silber (eds.), *Divided Houses: Gender and the Civil War* (New York: Oxford University Press, 1992), 99, the Women's Central stopped sending nurses to Dix in Oct. 1861, on the grounds that Dix wasn't using them properly. For the significance of the Soldiers' Aid Societies, see Jeanie Attie, "Warwork and the Crisis of Domesticity in the North," in ibid., 247–59.

p. 10   *"Oh that I may have a hand"*: quoted in Greenbie, *Lincoln's Daughters of Mercy*, 23. See also Dannett, *Noble Women of the North*, 45–46; and Mary Elizabeth Massey, *Bonnet Brigades: American Women and the Civil War* (New York: Alfred A. Knopf, 1966), 28–31.

p. 10   *"horde of eager women"*: Adams, *Doctors in Blue*, 153.

p. 10   *extending women's experience to the hospitals*: See Wood, "The War within a War: Women Nurses in the Union Army," *Civil War History* (Sept. 1972), 197–206. Jane E. Schultz, "The Inhospitable Hospital: Gender and Professionalism in Civil War Medicine," *Signs* (Winter 1992), 389, observes that Northern women felt that they had a "special suitability for nursing sick and wounded soldiers" and offered a "maternal and comforting presence in the otherwise austere hospital environment." As Susan M. Reverby points out, nursing before the Civil War was generally regarded as a menial service. Most nurses worked in the home as "the patient's servant," occupying an "ambiguous position" between the cook and the lowly domestics. Women were also hired on a daily basis in the country's rudimentary hospitals. Susan M. Reverby, *Ordered to Care: The Dilemma of American Nursing, 1850–1945* (Cambridge and New York: Cambridge University Press, 1985), 1–15, 23–35. This otherwise excellent work manages not to mention Clara Barton or the American Civil War.

p. 10   *"No woman under thirty"*: quoted in Marshall, *Dix*, 206, and Wilson, *Stranger and Traveler*, 206.

p. 10   *"stern woman," "Dragon Dix"*: quoted, respectively, in Wilson, *Stranger and Traveler*, 293, and Massey, *Bonnet Brigades*, 47.

p. 11   *"stuffed birds"*: CB to Frank Clinton, Oct. 4, 1854 [typescript], CB Papers AAS.

p. 11   *"bold round record"*: quoted in Blanche Colton Williams, *Clara Barton: Daughter of Destiny* (Philadelphia: J. P. Lippincott, 1941), 55.

p. 11   *Clara's job at Patent Office:* Laura Sellers, "Commissioner
             Charles Mason and Clara Barton," *Journal of the Patent
             Office Society* (Nov. 1948), 803–22; CB to Henry Wilson,
             Dec. 19, 1865, CB Papers LC; "A Woman Clerk,"
             Washington Sunday Chronicle, Mar. 11, 1883, ibid.;
             Halstead interview, ibid.; Blackwell, "Clara Barton Kept a
             Secret," *Woman's Journal*, Feb. 24, 1888; CB's 1886 state-
             ment in Epler, *Life of Clara Barton*, 25–26; Pryor, *Clara
             Barton*, 57–58. Information on comparative women's
             salaries from Barbara Mayer Wertheimer, *We Were There:
             The Story of Working Women in America* (New York:
             Pantheon, 1977), 90–101, 156–89.

p. 11   *sexual harassment,* "*Yankee blood,*" "*principle involved,*"
             Mason and malcontent: Blackwell, "Clara Barton Kept a
             Secret," *Woman's Journal*, Feb. 24, 1888; "A Woman
             Clerk," *Washington Sunday Chronicle*, Mar. 11 1883; Pryor,
             Clara Barton, 61.

p. 12   *CB released from Patent Office*: CB to Henry Wilson, Apr.
             7, 1864, CB Journal, Apr. 11, 1864, CB Papers LC; CB to
             Wilson, Sept. 29, Dec. 19, 1864, ibid.; Sellers,
             "Commissioner Charles Mason and Clara Barton," *Journal
             of the Patent Office Society* (Nov. 1948), 822–23. In the
             Dec. 19, 1864, letter, Clara claimed, "My books were
             demanded, three hundred and eighty dollars of undrawn
             salary withheld from me, on settlement, and I returned to
             New England to wonder in silence if God ruled and
             reigned."

p. 12   *CB's inaptitude for painting*: CB to Mary Norton, Mar. 8
             1859, MN Papers DU.

p. 12   *vortex of household duties and deepening despair*: chroni-
             cled in CB Diary entries of June–Aug. 1859, CB Papers
             LC. For example, June 23: "Ironed nearly all day; do not
             feel very well either mentally or physically." July 7:
             "Ironed and washed floors, the first day of haying, cut the
             clover, Julia has sick head ache—have felt low spirited and
             discontented all day." See also CB to Bernard Vassall, Feb.
             7, 1860, ibid.

p. 12   "*something somewhere*": CB to Bernard Vassall, Jan. 26,
             1860, ibid.

p. 12   "*no room for ladies*": CB to Bernard Vassall, Mar. [Apr. ?]
             4, 1860, ibid.

p. 12   *school committee*: Pryor, *Clara Barton*, 72. Clara had also
             suffered from gender discrimination in connection with her
             public school in Bordentown, New Jersey. See ibid.,
             52–53.

p. 12   "*were you in my place*": CB to Bernard Vassall, Feb. 13,
             1860, CB Papers LC.

p. 12   "*outgrown that*": CB to Bernard Vassall, Jan. 26, 1860, ibid.

p. 13   *"tired of doing nothing," "cried half the night"*: CB to Bernard Vassall, Apr. 22, Feb. 10, 1860, ibid.

p. 13   *CB's collapse*: CB to Bernard Vassall, June 17, July 28, Aug. 9, 1860, and CB to Elvira Stone, June 14, 1860, CB Papers LC.

p. 13   *"the sweetest hour"*: CB to Bernard Vassall, July 28, 1861, ibid.

p. 13   *reinstatement at Patent Office*: Sellers, "Commissioner Charles Mason and Clara Barton," *Journal of the Patent Office Society* (Nov. 1948), 825; CB to Wilson, Dec. 19, 1865, CB Papers LC; CB to Mary Norton, Mar. 24, 1861, MN Papers DU. The unnamed friends who got her reinstated must have included former congressman Alexander DeWitt of Oxford, who had helped get Clara her initial appointment at the Patent Office.

p. 13   *"mortifying," "crumb"*: CB to Henry Wilson, Apr. 7, 1864, in CB Journal, Apr. 7, 1864, CB Papers LC; CB to Wilson, Sept. 29, 1864, ibid.

p. 13   *CB's political connections*: CB to Elvira Stone, Feb. 7, Apr. 5, 1861, CB Papers LC; CB to Annie Childs, Apr. 14, 18, 1861, CB Papers AAS. "Mr. Sumner has become my advocate," Clara wrote Bernard Vassall, Apr. 7, 1861, "and from the efficient manner he has thus far proceeded I am confident that he intends to serve my cause to the best of his ability." CB Papers LC. Once back in Washington, Clara also made important friends in the Post Office. See CB to Elvira Stone, Apr. 5, 7, 1861, ibid.; CB to Annie Childs, Apr. 14, 18, 1861, CB Papers AAS.

p. 13   *"friend at court"*: phrase derives from CB to Wilson, Oct. 27, 1864, CB Papers LC.

p. 13   *"settled himself"*: CB to Elvira Stone, Mar. 29, 1861, CB Papers LC. Description of the Capitol from Leech, *Reveille in Washington*, 5; William Howard Russell, *My Diary North and South*, ed. Fletcher Pratt (New York: Harper & Brothers, 1954), 17.

pp. 13–14   *Wilson portrait*: Dolphone to CB [circa 1865], CB Papers LC; Noah Brooks, *Washington, D.C., in Lincoln's Time*, ed. Herbert Mitgang (Chicago: Quadrangle, 1971), 32–33; Richard H. Abbott, *Cobbler in Congress: The Life of Henry Wilson, 1812–1875* (Lexington: University Press of Kentucky, 1972), 3, 5, 13, 40, 54–114; Ernest McKay, *Henry Wilson, Practical Radical: A Portrait of a Politician* (Washington, N.Y.: Kennikat Press, 1971), 8–123, 180; Elias Nason and Thomas Russell, *The Life and Public Services of Henry Wilson* (Boston: B. B. Russell, 1876), 29–123. Pryor, *Clara Barton*, 75–76, has a brief sketch of Wilson.

p. 14   *"greatest faculty"*: quoted in CB to Elvira Stone, June 26, 1861, CB Papers LC.

p. 14　　　　　　*"some laughable apologies," "did not object," "called on me every day"*: CB to Elvira Stone, Mar. 29, Apr. 5, 1861, ibid.

p. 14　　　　　　*"Oh I was so glad," "almost wild"*: CB to Annie Childs, Apr. 14, 18, 1861, CB papers AAS; CB to Elvira Stone, Apr. 29, 1861, CB Papers LC.

p. 14–15　　　　*CB and Horace Gardner*: undated newspaper clipping [circa 1905], CB Scrapbook, CB Papers LC.

p. 15　　　　　　*"let them go"*: CB to Elvira Stone, May 14, 1861, ibid.

p. 15　　　　　　*Butler occupation of Baltimore*: "bag the whole nest" in Dannett, *Noble Women of the North*, 11–12; Hans L. Trefousse, *Ben Butler: The South Called Him BEAST!* (reprint 1957 ed., New York: Octagonal Books, 1974), 65–76; Nash, *Stormy Petrel*, 98–100.

p. 15　　　　　　*"I wept for joy," "laurels"*: CB, respectively, to Annie Childs, May 19, 1861, CB Papers AAS; and CB to Elvira Stone, May 14, 1861, CB Papers LC.

p. 16　　　　　　*SB and Bartonsville*: Colonel Joel Griffin to CB, Aug. 1865, ibid.; CB affidavit, Oct. 10, 1885, ibid. (copy of affidavit in SRB Papers DU); Thomas C. Parramore, "The Bartons of Bartonsville," *North Carolina Historical Review* (Jan. 1974), 25–29.

p. 16　　　　　　*"a weary band . . . helped them home,"* Tribune *story*: CB affidavit, Oct. 10, 1885, CB Papers LC (copy in SRB Papers DU).

p. 17　　　　　　*"picture book war"*: Bruce Catton, *Mr. Lincoln's Army* (Garden City, N.Y.: Doubleday & Co., 1951), 1.

p. 17　　　　　　*"you couldn't discover"*: Helen Nicolay, *Lincoln's Secretary: A Biography of John G. Nicolay* (New York: Longman's, Green and Co. 1949), 98.

p. 17　　　　　　*sickness in the army*: Joseph K. Barnes et al., *The Medical and Surgical History of the War of the Rebellion (1861–65)* (two vols. in six, Washington, D.C.: Government Printing Office, 1875–1883), 1: pt. 1, 17, 29–31; Adams, *Doctors in Blue*, 14–23; Paul E. Steiner, *Disease in the Civil War: Natural Biological Warfare in 1861–1865* (Springfield, Ill.: Charles C. Thomas, Pub., 1968), 102–11; Charles J. Stillé, *History of the United States Sanitary Commission: Being the General Report of Its Work During the War of the Rebellion* (Philadelphia: J. B. Lippincott, 1866), 93–124 (hereafter cited as *History of the Sanitary Commission*).

p. 17　　　　　　*if she could not be a soldier*: CB to Stephen Barton, Sr., May 19, 1861, CB Papers LC; and CB to General Quincy A. Gillmore, Sept. 18, 1863, Department of the South, Letters Received, 1863, NARA.

p. 17　　　　　　*"Our men's nerves"*: CB to Elvira Stone, May 14, 1861, CB Papers LC; also CB to Stephen Barton, Sr., May 19, 1861, ibid.; Pryor, *Clara Barton*, 80.

p. 18　　　　　　*"I have no time"*: CB to Bernard Vassall, May 29, 1861, CB Papers LC.

p. 18   *R. O. Sidney portrait*: CB to Elvira Stone, Apr. 7, May 14, June 26, 1861, ibid.; CB to Ira M. Barton, July 21, 1861, CB Papers AAS; CB to Elvira Stone, Sept. 22, 1861, CB Papers LC.

pp. 18–19   *CB's supporting friends*: CB to Mary Norton, June 11, 1861, MN Papers DU; CB army pass to camps, July 3, 1861, CB Papers SC; CB to Elvira Stone, Sept. 16, 1861, CB Papers LC; Barton, *Life of Clara Barton*, 1:128–129. I am summarizing here from the many letters CB would write her supporters during the war; these are in the CB Papers LC.

p. 19   *Edward Shaw*: Sellers, "Commissioner Charles Mason and Clara Barton," *Journal of the Patent Office Society* (Nov. 1948), 822.

p. 19   *"nothing but the fear"*: CB to Mary Norton, June 11, 1861, MN Papers DU.

p. 19   *Lowe's balloon*: Leech, *Reveille in Washington*, 84; E. B. Long, *Civil War Day by Day: An Almanac* (Garden City, N.Y.: Doubleday & Co., 1971), 86–87. Haunted by all the military activity, Clara reflected on "the strange confusion and unrest that heaves us like a mighty billow, and the broad dark sweeping wing of war hovering over our heads, whose flap and crash is so soon to blacken our fair land." CB to Elvira Stone, June 9, 1861, CB Papers LC.

p. 20   *"constant explosion," New York soldiers' parade*: William Howard Russell, *My Diary North and South*, ed. Fletcher Pratt (New York: Harper & Bros., 1954), 191; Leech, *Reveille in Washington*, 88.

p. 20   *"folly of being the beginners"*: Abraham Lincoln, *Collected Works*, ed. Roy P. Basler et al. (9 vols.; New Brunswick: Rutgers University Press, 1953–1955), 4:439.

p. 20   *"firing serpents"*: CB to Elvira Stone, July 4, 1861, CB Papers LC.

p. 20   *"noble, gallant handsome"*: CB to Stephen Barton, Sr., July 22, 26, 1861, CB Papers LC (typescript in CB Papers AAS); slightly different version in Barton, *Life of Clara Barton*, 1:120–21.

p. 20   *Wilson to Bull Run*: Abbott, *Cobbler in Congress*, 119, 149; McKay, *Henry Wilson*, 146.

p. 20   *"rumors of* intended *battle," "blood ran cold"*: CB to Stephen Barton, Sr., July 22, 26, 1861, CB Papers LC (typescript in CB Papers AAS)

p. 20   *"our city was jubilant," "all is quiet and sad"*: CB to I. M. Barton, July 21, 1861, CB Papers AAS.

p. 21   *"forming a most fantastic"*: Russell, *My Diary*, 231.

p. 21   *"streets of woe," clustered together*: Maxwell, *Lincoln's Fifth Wheel*, 20. See also Russell, *My Diary*, 231–32.

p. 21   *"memorable display"*: James G. Randall, *Lincoln the President: Midstream* (New York, 1953), 9.

p. 21   *"We want more men"*: quoted in Nason and Russell, *Life
          and Public Services of Henry Wilson*, 308.

p. 21   *"no plans, no organization"*: Captain Louis C. Duncan,
          "The Battle of Bull Run," in Duncan, *The Medical
          Department of the United States in the Civil War*
          (Washington, D.C.: Government Printing Office, n.d.), 20.
          My account of the performance of the Union field medical
          system at Bull Run derives from ibid., 4–21; Stewart
          Brooks, *Civil War Medicine* (Springfield, Ill.: C. C.
          Thomas, 1966), 13; Horace C. Cunningham, *Field Medical
          Services at the Battles of Manassas* (Athens: University of
          Georgia Press, 1968), 1–22; Adams, *Doctors in Blue*, 24–27.
          As Cunningham points out, other field hospitals were
          improvised during the fighting, only to be abandoned
          when the army fled to Washington.

p. 21   *wounded walk and crawl back to Washington*: Brooks, *Civil
          War Medicine*, 13; Duncan, "The Battle of Bull Run," in
          Duncan, *The Medical Department of the United States in
          the Civil War*, 20.

p. 22   *"painful duty," "a hard day"*: CB to Stephen Barton, Sr.,
          July 22, 26, 1861, CB Papers LC (typescript in CB Papers
          AAS).

p. 22   *CB's offer to Holloway*: CB to Henry Wilson, Dec. 19,
          1865, CB Papers LC; Halstead interview, ibid,; Blackwell,
          "Clara Barton Kept a Secret"; *Woman's Journal*, Feb. 24,
          1883; "A Woman Clerk"; *Washington Sunday Chronicle*,
          Mar. 11, 1883; CB statement in Barton, *Life of Clara
          Barton*, 1:129. In the latter source, CB claimed that she
          now "resigned and went into direct service of the sick and
          wounded troops wherever found." Actually, she didn't
          begin such work until the battle of Cedar Mountain, and
          she never resigned from the Patent Office. She kept her
          position there, thanks to a special arrangement with
          Holloway (described later in my story), until she was
          released from the office after the war.

p. 22   *train of ambulances*: Cunningham, *Field Medical Services
          at the Battles of Manassas*, 18; Duncan, "The Battle of Bull
          Run," in Duncan, *The Medical Department of the United
          States in the Civil War*, 18–20.

p. 22   *"knocked together," "any time"*: Dannett, *Noble Women of
          the North*, 81, 82.

p. 22   *nurses' pay*: See Julia C. Stimson and Ethel C. Thompson,
          "Women Nurses with the Union Forces during the Civil
          War," *Military Medicine* (Feb. 1928), 227–28; and Wilson,
          Stranger and Traveler, 283.

p. 22   *"Madam, who are you"*: quoted in Marshall, *Dorothea Dix*,
          220. For Dix's battle to control her domain, see ibid., 219;
          Young, *Women of the Crisis*, 55–63; and Wilson, *Stranger
          and Traveler*, 286–92. Schultz, "Inhospitable Hospital,"

Signs (Winter 1992), 373–89, has an insightful discussion of the conflict between female hospital nurses and army surgeons.

p. 23   "*go to the rescue*": quoted in Barton, *Life of Clara Barton*, 1:128–29.

p. 24   "the *power of the land*": George B. McClellan, *The Civil War Papers of George B. McClellan: Selected Correspondence, 1860–1865*, ed. Stephen W. Sears (New York: Ticknor & Fields, 1989), 70; quoted in Stephen W. Sears, *George B. McClellan, the Young Napoleon* (New York: Ticknor & Fields, 1988), 95.

p. 24   *CB at depot, associates*: CB to Elvira Stone, Sept. 16, 1861, CB Papers LC; CB statement in Barton, *Life of Clara Barton*, 1:128.

p. 24   *CB at Liberal Institute*: Halstead interview, CB Papers LC; reminiscences of unidentified woman, AC Papers MHS. For a full account, see Pryor, *Clara Barton*, 31–39. CB resumed her education after teaching for many years while living at home. In going off to Clinton, she said, she wanted to "break the shackles" of living at home and prepare for her own advancement. Barton, *Life of Clara Barton*, 1:59.

p. 24   *CB was perhaps unwanted*, "*she muttered and cursed*": Henle, "Against the Fearful Odds," 214, 211, also 4. See also Pryor, *Clara Barton*, 3–10. In her notes to Dr. Foote (circa 1875), CB Papers SC, CB remembered her mother as a "nervous" and "splendid physical specimen of a woman, of extreme vigor who always did two days work in one never time to sleep."

p. 25   *CB's troubled childhood*: CB, *Story of My Childhood*, 15, 42–43, 112, 114; CB Diary, Jan. 8, 1882, CB Papers LC; CB to Mary Norton, Dec. 12, 1863, MN Papers DU.

p. 25   *wished herself dead, "less and less to live for"*: CB to Bernard Vassall, Mar. 14, 1852, CB Papers LC; CB Diary, Mar. 11, 1852, ibid.; also Mar. 1, 2, 23, 1852, ibid.

p. 25   "*Clara Barton had many admirers*": quoted in Barton, *Life of Clara Barton*, 1:83–84. For CB's prewar suitors, see Pryor, *Clara Barton*, 25–26, 43–44.

p. 26   "*entirely different in temperament*": CB's notes to Dr. Foote (circa 1875), CB Papers SC; also CB to Julia Barton, Dec. 29, 1860, CB Papers LC.

p. 26   *older siblings as teachers*: CB, *Story of My Childhood*, 17–20, 95; CB in folder 81, Box 4, CB Papers SC; Barton, *Life of Clara Barton*, 1:22, 26.

p. 26   "*a funny way*": Irving Vassall to Uncle Stephen Barton, Mar. 23, 1857, CB Papers HL; also Irving Vassall to Stephen Barton, Feb. 3, 1857, CB Papers LC.

p. 26   "*unmanned me*," "*poor dear child*," "*None but our Heavenly Father*": CB to Elvira Stone, Mar. 11, 1859, ibid; CB to Mary Norton, Mar. 8, Apr. 3, 1859, MN Papers DU; CB

Diary, Mar. 7–13, 1859, CB Papers LC. See also Irving Vassall to Uncle Stephen Barton, Mar. 23, 1857, CB Papers HL.

p. 27   "he must not give up": CB to Elvira Stone, Mar. 11, 1859, CB Papers LC. CB's female charge: CB to Mary Norton, Jan. 3, 1860, MN Papers DU.

p. 27   "clear, bracing air": "Personal Recollections of Clara Barton," Housekeeper's Weekly, Apr. 16, 1892, CB Collection AHL; CB to Bernard Vassall, Aug. 4, 21, 1861, and CB to Irving Vassall, Aug. 21, 1859, CB Papers LC; CB Diary, Sept. 8–Dec. 18, 1859, ibid. For anecdotes about CB's stay in Minnesota, see Marion Sloan's reminiscences in MLS Papers MHS.

p. 27   "excepting male friends": CB to Mary Norton, Jan. 30, 1860, MN Papers DU; CB Diary, Dec. 13–19, 1859, Jan. 3, 1860, CB Papers LC.

p. 27   "still we must hope": CB to Mary Norton, Mar. 21, 1861, MN Papers DU; also CB to Bernard Vassall, Dec. 29, 1859, Jan. 1, 15, 26, Mar. 1, 1860, CB Papers LC.

p. 27   "In thought and spirit": CB to "Dear Sister" [Julia Barton], Dec. 29, 1860, ibid.

p. 27   "I am so glad": CB to David Barton, Feb. 2, 1861, in Barton, Life of Clara Barton, 1:113.

p. 27   "His recovery": CB to "My Dear Cousin," Feb. 6, 1861, CB Papers AAS.

p. 27   "I think of him": CB to Elvira Stone, Sept. 16, 1861, CB Papers LC.

p. 28   "necessities," "useful articles": CB to Mrs. Miller, Secretary, Ladies' Relief Committee, Worcester, Dec. 16, 1861 [typescript], CB Papers AAS; see also Barton, Life of Clara Barton, 1:121–22, 128.

p. 28   McClellan: Sears, McClellan, 135–46; T. Harry Williams, Lincoln and His Generals (New York: Alfred A. Knopf, 1952), 29–32.

p. 28   Wilson's regiment: McKay, Henry Wilson, 148–50; Abbott, Cobbler in Congress, 118–20.

pp. 28–29   CB's trip home: CB to "My Darling Cousin" [Lucy Bigelow], Dec. 24, 1861, CB Papers LC.

p. 29   "worthy ladies," "Are our labors": CB to Mrs. Miller, Secretary, Ladies' Relief Committee, Worcester, Dec. 16, 1861 [typescript], CB Papers AAS. The original, housed in CB Papers LC, is largely unreadable on microfilm. The letter appears in Barton, Life of Clara Barton, 1:136–40.

p. 29   CB's visit with Twenty-first Massachusetts: CB to "My Darling Cousin" [Lucy Bigelow], Dec. 24, 1861, CB Papers LC. For a historical sketch of the regiment, see Headley, Massachusetts in the Rebellion, 275–76.

p. 30   "patriotic ladies," CB's warehouse: CB to Mrs. Miller, Secretary, Ladies' Relief Committee, Worcester, Dec. 16,

1861 [typescript], CB Papers AAS; Halstead interview, CB
Papers LC: Epler, *Life of Clara Barton*, 30; Barton, *Life of Clara Barton*, 1:122.

p. 30   *"link between home and the soldier"*: Young, *Women of the War*, 191.

p. 30   "more *than busy," "the most happily situated"*: CB to Mrs.
Miller, Secretary, Ladies' Relief Committee, Worcester,
Dec. 16, 1861 [typescript], CB Papers AAS; CB to Lucy
Bigelow, Dec. 21, 1861, CB Papers LC.

p. 30   *"proper authority," "male or female," Private Pollard*: CB to
Mrs. Miller, Secretary, Ladies' Relief Committee,
Worcester, Dec. 16, 1861 [typescript], CB Papers AAS.

p. 31   *"an anomalous civil element"*: Jane Stuart Woolsey in
Dannett, *Noble Women of the North*, 98–99. For pavilion
hospitals, see Maxwell, *Lincoln's Fifth Wheel*, 54, and
Adams, *Doctors in Blue*, 152.

p. 31   *seniority system*: Adams, *Doctors in Blue*, 27; Leech,
Reveille in Washington, 212.

p. 31   *Clement Alexander Finley*: Maxwell, *Lincoln's Fifth Wheel*,
53, 95, 107–43, 331.

p. 32   *"criminal weakness," "self satisfied, supercilious"*: quoted in
Adams, *Doctors in Blue*, 27.

p. 32   *"ossified," calls for reform*: Maxwell, *Lincoln's Fifth Wheel*,
95; Adams, *Doctors in Blue*, 29; McKay, *Henry Wilson*,
151; Stillé, *History of the Sanitary Commission*, 93–124.

p. 32   *CB's health, habits, hygiene*: CB's notes to Dr. Foote [circa
1875] and Dr. Foote to CB, Mar. 12, 1875, CB Papers SC;
Barton, *Life of Clara Barton*, 2:329. Butchered ox episode
from CB, *Story of My Childhood*, 72–74.

p. 33   *typhoid outbreak AOP*: Barnes, *Medical and Surgical
History*, 1: pt. 1, 31.

p. 33   *"The rebel army"*: quoted in James V. Murfin, *The Gleam of
Bayonets: The Battle of Antietam and Robert E. Lee's
Maryland Campaign of 1862* (reprint 1965 ed., Baton
Rouge: Louisiana State University Press, 1982), 42–43.

p. 33   *Burnside in Washington, "amphibious division"*: William
Marvel, *Burnside* (Chapel Hill: University of North
Carolina Press, 1991), 32, 37, 40.

pp. 33–34   *"pet expedition," "upwards of forty," "You know how foolishly"*: CB to "Dear Sis Fannie [Childs]," Jan. 9, 1862, CB
Papers LC, and in Barton, *Life of Clara Barton*, 1:141, 142.
New army uniforms from Leech, *Reveille in Washington*,
128.

p. 34   *"harbor was full," "My head is just this moment," "Southern
Sands," "common trench"*: CB to "Dear Sis Fannie
[Childs]," Jan. 9, 1862, CB Papers LC, and in Barton, *Life
of Clara Barton*, 1:142. CB's line "uncoffined and
unknown" is from Byron's *Childe Harold's Pilgrimage*,
canto IV, stanza 179.

p. 34   *"no private returns," "tedious labor," "a great deal* more *than busy"*: CB to Dear Sis Fannie [Childs]," Jan. 29, 1862 (a continuation of Jan. 9, 1862, letter), CB Papers LC, and in Barton, *Life of Clara Barton*, 1:142–43.

p. 35   *"a general nightmare"*: Dannett, *Noble Women of the North*, 82.

p. 35   *"a fine young man," "bought him a grave," "Poor Fellow"*: CB to "Dear Sis Fannie [Childs]," Jan. 9, 1862, CB Papers LC, and in Barton, *Life of Clara Barton*, 1:144.

p. 35   *wartime Washington*: Leech, *Reveille in Washington*, 121; A. Howard Meneely, *War Department, 1861* (New York: Columbia University Press, 1928), 252–69; Fred A. Shannon, *The Organization and Administration of the Union Army* (2 vols., Cleveland: Arthur H. Clark, 1928), 1:61–62; CB to brother Stephen Barton, Mar. 1, 1862, CB Papers LC.

p. 36   *Twenty-first at Roanoke*: Charles F. Walcott, *History of the Twenty-first Regiment Massachusetts Volunteers in the War for the Preservation of the Union, 1861–1865* (Boston: Houghton Mifflin, 1882), 19–55; Headley, *Massachusetts in the Rebellion*, 275.

p. 36   *"appalling fact"*: CB lecture draft [undated], CB Papers LC.

p. 36   *"sat up with Grandpa"*: Barton, *Life of Clara Barton*, 1:145, also 143, 146; Pryor, *Clara Barton*, 83, for CB's arrangements at the Patent Office.

p. 37   *"not a morsel of food"*: CB to Leander Poor, Mar. 27, 1862, CB Papers LC.

p. 37   *Winton, N.C., burned*: John G. Barrett, *The Civil War in North Carolina* (Chapel Hill: University of North Carolina Press, 1963), 92–94; Irving Vassall to CB, Mar. 16, 1862, CB Papers LC.

p. 37   *"I am generally"*: Stephen Barton, Jr., to CB, Feb. 26 [?], 1862, ibid.

pp. 37–39   *CB to Stephen Barton, Jr.*: Mar. 1, 1862, ibid. Parramore, "Bartons of Bartonsville," *North Carolina Historical Review* 51, 32–33, also discusses CB's reply to Stephen.

p. 39   *"I think it the best"*: David Barton to Stephen Barton, Jr., Mar. 3, 1862, CB Papers LC; Irving Vassal to CB, Mar. 16, 1862, ibid.

p. 39   *CB sees Gov. Andrew*: CB to Andrew, Mar. 20, 1862, ibid.; Barton, *Life of Clara Barton*, 1:156; CB to Mrs. Miller, Secretary, Ladies Relief Committee, Worcester, Dec. 16, 1861 [typescript], CB Papers AAS, argues in detail in favor of a Massachusetts state agency. Description of Andrew from Peleg W. Chandler, *Memoir of Governor Andrew, with Personal Reminiscences* (Boston: Roberts Bros., 1880), 15; also Henry Greenleaf Pearson, *The Life of John A. Andrew: Governor of Massachusetts, 1861–1865* (2 vols., Boston: Houghton Mifflin, 1904), 1:3.

p. 40   *"lived and moved"*: CB to Leander Poor, Mar. 27, 1862, CB Papers LC.

pp. 40–41   *CB's talk with her father*: scene derives from CB to I. W. Denney [circa Mar. 30, 1862], ibid.; CB to General Quincy A. Gillmore, Sept. 18, 1863, Department of the South, Letters Received, 1863, NARA; Epler, *Life of Clara Barton*, 34; Barton, *Life of Clara Barton*, 1:157; Pryor, *Clara Barton*, 84; CB to Edwin Stanton, Apr. 29, 1864 [typescript], CB Papers AAS.

p. 41   *"I desire Your Excellency"*: CB to Gov. Andrew, Mar. 20, 1862, CB Papers LC.

p. 41   *father's death and funeral*: CB to Gillmore, Sept. 18, 1863, Department of the South, Letters Received, 1863, NARA (in this letter CB called her father her "last earthly guide"); Stanton, Apr. 29, 1864 [typescript], CB Papers AAS; CB to Leander Poor, Mar. 27, 1862, CB Papers LC; CB Diary, Mar. 25, 1862, CB Papers LC; CB to I. W. Denney [circa Mar. 30, 1862], ibid.; Daniels, *History of the Town of Oxford*, 391. Pryor, *Clara Barton*, 84, also describes CB's loneliness as she watched her father, "her mentor," being buried.

p. 42   *"with my hearty approval"*: Andrew to CB, Mar. 24, 1862, CB Papers LC; CB Diary, Mar. 25, 1862, ibid.

p. 42   *"I do not think"*: J. W. Fletcher to Dr. Alfred Hitchcock, Mar. 25, 1862, ibid.

p. 42   *"ludicrous opinions," "I am a daughter"*: CB to I. W. Denney [circa Mar. 30, 1862], ibid.

p. 42   *"no hope of proceeding"*: Irving Vassall to CB, Mar. 16, 1862, ibid.

p. 43   *"didn't feel ready"*: CB to Leander Poor, May 2, 1862, ibid.

p. 43   *Judge Ira Barton and family*: undated newspaper obituaries, ibid.; IMB Family Papers index, AAS; CB to Dr. Samuel L. Bigelow [Lucy's husband], May 2, 1862, CB Papers LC, was written from Worcester.

p. 43   *Irving's letters to CB and Elvira Stone*: Mar. 5, 13, 16, April 13, 1862, CB Papers LC.

p. 44   *"the heart, the brain"*: quoted in Abbott, *Cobbler in Congress*, 145. See also Henry Wilson, *History of the Antislavery Measures of the Thirty-seventh and Thirty-eighth United-States Congresses, 1861–1864* (Boston: Walker, Wise, & Co., 1864), 38–78, 92–109, 198–202.

p. 44   *Medical Department reform, Surgeon General Hammond*: Stillé, *History of the Sanitary Commission*, 125–33; Adams, *Doctors in Blue*, 29–30; McKay, *Henry Wilson*, 151, 156; Maxwell, *Lincoln's Fifth Wheel*, 194, 332; Captain Louis C. Duncan, "Evolution of the Ambulance Corps and Field Hospital," in Duncan, *The Medical Department of the United States Army in the Civil War*, 8.

p. 45   *"I am greatly disappointed"*: Irving Vassall to CB, Apr. 13, 1862, CB Papers LC.

p. 45   *Olmsted and hospital transport service*: Maxwell, *Lincoln's Fifth Wheel*, 10, 162, 191; Greenbie, *Lincoln's Daughters of Mercy*, 80, 128; Stillé, *History of the Sanitary Commission*, 75–78, 153–62.

p. 45   *women of the hospital transport service*: Ross, "Arranging a Doll's House: Refined Women as Union Nurses," in Clinton and Silber (eds.), *Divided Houses*, 100–105; Austin, *Woolsey Sisters of New York*, 54–68.

p. 45   *profiles of "lady superintendents"*: Greenbie, *Lincoln's Daughters of Mercy*, 125–37, 160; Dannett, *Noble Women of the North*, 160–62; Brockett and Vaughan, *Women's Work*, 279–83, 300–301.

p. 46   *"We all know in our hearts"*: quoted in Greenbie, *Lincoln's Daughters of Mercy*, 130; Ross "Arranging a Doll's House," Refined Women as Union Nurses," in Clinton and Silber (eds.), *Divided Houses*, 104–5, for the women superintendents' "self-reliance," "self-confidence and mutual support."

p. 46   *"come and have a tent"*: CB to Leander Poor, May 2, 1862, CB Papers LC; also CB to Dr. Sam L. Bigelow, May 2, 1862, ibid.

p. 47   *"a frightful scene"*: Brockett and Vaughan, *Woman's Work*, 308, also 309–10; Maxwell, *Lincoln's Fifth Wheel*, 155–56.

p. 47   *"There were eight hundred"*: Brockett and Vaughan, *Woman's Work*, 151. The best account of the military aspects of the Peninsula Campaign is Stephen W. Sears, *To the Gates of Richmond* (New York: Ticknor & Fields, 1992).

p. 47   *"treasures" from Mary Norton*: CB Diary, June 10, 1862, CB Papers LC; CB to Mary Norton, June 28, 1872, MN Papers DU. Also CB to Julia Barton [circa summer 1862], CB Papers AAS.

p. 47   *10,000 sick cases*: see Barnes, *Medical and Surgical History*, 1:pt. 1, 31–32.

p. 48   *"hot fomentations," "turpentine stupes," leeches*: Barnes, *Medical and Surgical History*, vol. 1, pt. 1, 809–10; Adams, *Doctors in Blue*, 196.

p. 48   *treatment of diarrhea-dysentery*: Barnes, *Medical and Surgical History*, 1:pt. 2, 43–52, 71, 265, 709–19, 747–83, 805, 818; Brooks, *Civil War Medicine*, 65, 117; Adams, *Doctors in Blue*, 226–27; Charles Beneulyn Johnson, *Muskets and Medicine, or Army Life in the Sixties* (Philadelphia: F. A. Davis Co., 1917), 62.

p. 48   *calomel's side effects*: Adams, *Doctors in Blue*, 38–39. Surgeon General Hammond banned the use of calomel in May 1863.

p. 48   *treatment of malaria, the second most common "camp disease" in the war*: Barnes, *Medical and Surgical History*, 1:pt, I, 129–84; Brooks, *Civil War Medicine*, 65, 119;

Adams, *Doctors in Blue*, 227–28; Paul E. Steiner, *Disease in the Civil War: Natural Biological Warfare in 1861–1865* (Springfield, Ill.: Charles C. Thomas, 1968), 20–21. Nobody in the period knew that the infection was carried by the Anopheles mosquito.

pp. 48–49   *symptoms of malaria*: Barnes, *Medical and Surgical History*, 1:pt. 1, 129–30.

p. 49   *treatment of typhoid*: ibid., 275–324; Brooks, *Civil War Medicine*, 118; Steiner, *Disease in the Civil War*, 22–25; Adams, *Doctors in Blue*, 227. As Brooks points out, among "specific microorganisms," or "a *specific* infectious disease," typhoid fever was "the chief single cause of death in both armies," killing 30,000 Federals alone. Only diarrhea and dysentery killed more in the Union army. Their toll: 37,313. Other sources put the figure as high as 44,500.

p. 49   *"turpentine as little short," "no care whatever"*: Johnson, *Muskets and Medicine*, 159–60.

p. 49   *typhoid sickness in AOP*: Barnes, *Medical and Surgical History*, 1:pt. 1, 31–32.

p. 49   *"I cannot make a pleasant letter"*: CB to Julia Barton, June 26, 1862, CB Papers AAS.

p. 49   *burials, Judiciary Square Hospital embalming*: Leech, *Reveille in Washington*, 207.

p. 49   *"tender" boy*: CB to Julia Barton, June 26, 1862, CB Papers AAS.

p. 50   *Seven Days Campaign and Washington*: CB to Mary Norton, July 4, 1862, MN Papers DU; Leech, *Reveille in Washington*, 205–9.

p. 50   *"Oh these terrible days"*: CB to Mary Norton, July 4, 1862, MN Papers DU.

p. 50   *Size of Army of Virginia*: John J. Hennessy, *Return to Bull Run: The Campaign and Battle of Second Manassas* (New York: Simon & Schuster, 1993), 6.

pp. 51–52   *CB at Rucker's office*: scene put together from Halstead interview, July 29, 1890, CB Papers LC; "Clara Barton and the International Red Cross Association" (circa 1891), ibid.; Epler, *Life of Clara Barton*, 34; information on Rucker from Rucker's Military Service Records, NARA AGO, and from materials provided by Nancy G. Garmazin, Grosse Ile Historical Society, Grosse Ile, Michigan. The passes of July 11, 1862, are in CB Papers SC. Previous CB biographies are vague or wrong about which army and which front CB wished to visit in July 1862. In the Halstead interview, Clara remembered that Rucker in this meeting "wrote out an order for six wagons & the men to work them," but there is no other evidence to support this. She was assigned her first wagon from the Quartermaster Department during the South Mountain–Antietam campaign.

p. 52   *"Miss Barton proposes"*: letter of introduction from the
               Assistant Secretary of the Sanitary Commission, July 11,
               1862, CB Papers SC.

p. 52   *whirlwind tour*: CB Diary, July 18–28, 1862, CB Papers LC.

p. 53   *Anna Carver*: I could find out little about her. She is men-
               tioned in Brockett and Vaughan, *Woman's Work in the
               Civil War*, 647.

p. 53   *Cornelius Welles*: obituary of Welles, *American Baptist*,
               clipping, CB Papers LC; CB to Mary Norton, Sept. 26,
               1862, MN Papers DU.

p. 53   *"we are whipping them"*: CB to Leander Poor, Aug. 2, 1862,
               CB Papers LC.

p. 53   *CB to Fredericksburg*: CB Diary, Aug. 2, 1862, ibid.

p. 54   *"Our reign is over"*: quoted in Dannett, *Noble Women of
               the North*, 195.

                          PART TWO: THE FIELD

p. 57   *Alexandria and Mt. Vernon*: Julia S. Wheelock, *The Boys in
               White: The Experience of a Hospital Agent in and Around
               Washington* (New York: Lange & Hillman, 1870), 47.

p. 57   *CB in Fredericksburg*: CB Diary, Aug. 2–5 1862, CB Papers
               LC; Barton, *Life of Clara Barton*, 1:168. Information on
               Lacy and Lacy House, or Chatham, from Ralph Happel,
               Chatham: The Life of a House (Philadelphia: Eastern
               National Park & Monument Association 1984), 36–51; and
               A. Wilson Greene, *J. Horace Lacy: The Most Dangerous
               Rebel of the County* (Richmond: Owens Publishing Co.,
               1988), 7–10.

p. 58   *"truly named"*: James Dunn to his wife, Aug. 11, 1862, JD
               Papers UVA.

p. 58   *McParlin's medical arrangements*: Duncan, "Pope's Virginia
               Campaign," in Duncan, *Medical Department of the United
               States in the Civil War*, 10–13.

p. 58   *"in all probability," "I fail to see"*: CB to Soldiers' Relief
               Society of Hightstown, Aug. 1862, in *Bordentown Register*,
               Sept. 12, 1862, CB Papers LC.

p. 58   *Pope's harsh measures*: Hennessy, *Return to Bull Run*,
               14–16; Douglas Southall Freeman, *R. E. Lee, a Biography*
               (4 vols., New York: Scribner's, 1947), 2:263–64.

p. 58   *"a campaign of indescriminate robbery and murder"*: OR,
               ser. 2, 4:329; Hennessy, *Return to Bull Run*, 21.

p. 59   *CB's pass*: Aug. 12, 1862, CB Papers SC; also in Barton,
               Life of Clara Barton, 1:166, 174.

p. 59   *CB's preparations, "precious freights"*: CB Diary, Aug. 13,
               1862, and CB to "Dear Old Time Friend" [undated], CB
               Papers LC.

p. 59   *Culpeper "relief" station and hospitals*: Duncan, "Pope's
             Virginia Campaign," in Duncan, *Medical Department of the
             United States in the Civil War*, 11–13.

p. 59   *wounded at Culpeper: Boston Traveller*, undated clipping,
             CB Papers LC; Pryor, *Clara Barton*, 89.

p. 59   *"shattering, splintering"*: Brooks, *Civil War Medicine*, 75;
             Thomas F. Cullen, "Observations on the Influence of the
             Present War upon American Medicine and Surgery,"
             Medical Society of New Jersey Transactions 118 (1864),
             21–44.

p. 60   *ignorance of infection*: Dr. William W. Keen as quoted in
             Sister Mary Denis Maher, *To Bind Up the Wounds:
             Catholic Sister Nurses in the U.S. Civil War* (Westport,
             Conn.: Greenwood Press; 1984), 49; and in Brooks, *Civil
             War Medicine*, 79, 94.

p. 61   *mortality rate for wounds*: Barnes, *Medical and Surgical
             History*, 2:pt. 2, 202, 501; pt. 1, 307, 606. Somewhat differ-
             ent figures are given in Brooks, *Civil War Medicine*, 74.
             See also Richard Harrison Shryock, *Medicine in America:
             Historical Essays* (Baltimore: Johns Hopkins University
             Press, 1966), 92.

p. 61   *amputations*: Johnson, *Muskets and Medicine*, 97, 130;
             Brooks, *Civil War Medicine*, 92, 97–99, 100–101; Barnes,
             Medical and Surgical History, 2:pt. 3, 412, 609.

p. 62   *fatality rate for amputations*: Barnes, *Medical and Surgical
             History*, 2:pt. 1, 614; pt. 2, 655, 697, 805, 824; pt. 3, 127,
             175, 367, 432. Of 174,200 cases of gunshot wounds in the
             limbs, Brooks says, 29,980 involved amputations and 7,096
             resulted in death, "almost always of surgical fevers." The
             average mortality rate for amputations was 26 percent.
             Brooks, *Civil War Medicine*, 99. Soldiers who underwent
             excision, or the removal of bone and tissue in place of
             amputation, fared little better than those who had amputa-
             tions. The fatality rate for excision at the shoulder was about
             35 percent; in the upper arm, 28.5 percent; in the leg, 26
             percent; at the ankle joint, 29.6 percent. The survivors,
             many of them, were left with limbs that were grotesquely
             deformed. Barnes, *Medical and Surgical History*, 2:pt. 2,
             655, 696–97; pt. 3, 575, 578, plus the revealing photographs.
             Another alternative to amputation was "resection," or "the
             removal of joints with preservation of the extremities,"
             which some rebel physicians thought for the most part was
             "reprehensible surgery." See H. H. Cunningham, *Doctors
             in Gray: The Confederate Medical Service* (Baton Rouge:
             Louisiana State University Press, 1958), 224–25.

p. 62   *"odorless creamy pus," "laudable pus"*: Brooks, *Civil War
             Medicine*, 81; George W. Adams, "Caring for the Men," in
             William C. Davis (ed.), *The Image of War* (6 vols., Garden
             City, N.Y.: Doubleday, 1981–1984), 4:237.

p. 62   *hospital gangrene*: Barnes, *Medical and Surgical History*, 2:pt. 3, 287, 291, 437, and picture of gangrenous foot opposite p. 18; Brooks, *Civil War Medicine*, 84. Also see Abraham Coles, "On Hospital Gangrene," *Medical Society of New Jersey Transactions* 98 (1864), 45–49; Frank R. Freemon, *Microbes and Minie Balls: An Annotated Bibliography of Civil War Medicine* (Rutherford, N.J. Fairleigh Dickinson University Press, 1993), 60–61; Shryock, *Medicine in America*, 94; Adams, *Doctors in Blue*, 129. Freemon, *Microbes*, 94, points out that in 1864 a Union surgeon in the Atlanta campaign found that iodine effectively checked hospital gangrene. Cunningham, *Doctors in Gray*, 234, has a brief discussion of how maggots arrested gangrene; he calls it "larval therapy."

p. 62   *CB's cleaning*: *Boston Traveller*, undated clipping, CB Papers LC.

p. 62   *"Miss Barton"*: Ross, *Angel of the Battlefield*, 35.

p. 63   *Dr. Dunn profile*: Dunn to his wife, June, Aug. 11, 15, 1862, JD Papers UVA; James Dunn's Military Service Records, NARA; physical description of Dunn in John W. Schildt, *Antietam Hospitals* (Chewsville, Md.: Antietam Publications, 1987), 45.

p. 63   *"covered with blood"*: Dunn to his wife, Aug. 15, 1862, JD Papers UVA.

p. 63   *"I thought that night"*: Dunn to his wife in *Conneautville* (Penn.) *Reporter*, undated newspaper clipping, CB Papers LC.

p. 63   *"I am from Massachusetts"*: *Boston Traveller*, undated clipping, CB Papers LC; also CB Diary, Aug. 15, 1862, ibid.

p. 63   *"unoccupied place"*: CB Notes for a Lecture [undated], CB Papers LC.

p. 63   *"a course of labor"*: CB to Soldiers' Relief Society, Hightstown, N.J. Aug. 19, 1862, in *Bordentown Register*, Sept. 12, 1862, CB Papers LC; also in Pryor, *Clara Barton*, 89.

p. 64   *"Oh for time to breathe"*: CB to Mary Norton [Aug. 19, 1862], MN Papers DU; CB Diary, Aug. 16, 1862, CB Papers LC; CB to Leander Poor in Barton, *Life of Clara Barton*, 1:174.

p. 64   *CB's spurious letter*: newspaper clipping, CB Papers LC. See also Pryor, *Clara Barton*, 90–91.

p. 65   *"minute, intuitive," "such blessings"*: CB Notes for a Lecture [undated], CB Papers LC. In an undated war lecture, ibid., Clara said she was ashamed that her "sense of propriety" had held her back from the battlefield.

p. 65   *Patent Office salary arrangement*: CB to Henry Wilson, Apr. 7, 1864, Dec. 19, 1865, CB Papers LC; CB Journal, Dec. 10, 11, 1863, ibid.; CB to Holloway, Dec. 11, 1863, in ibid.; Sellers, "Commissioner Charles Mason and Clara

Barton," *Journal of the Patent Office Society* (Nov. 1948), 826–27. Pryor, *Clara Barton*, 91, and Barton, *Life of Clara Barton*, 1:259, give somewhat different versions.

p. 65   *military movements*: see Hennessy, *Return to Bull Run*, 60–200; Duncan, "Pope's Virginia Campaign," in Duncan, *Medical Department of the United States in the Civil War*, 10–17. Brooks, *Civil War Medicine*, 15, says that Jackson captured "thousands of cases of chloroform." Stillé, *History of the Sanitary Commission*, 262, makes a general reference to "forty wagon loads of medical supplies" captured by the rebels during Pope's campaign.

p. 66   *"Genl Pope was fighting"*: CB Notes for a Lecture [undated], CB Papers LC.

p. 66   *"terrific battle"*: Stephen W. Sears, *Landscape Turned Red: The Battle of Antietam* (New Haven and New York: Ticknor & Fields, 1983), 10.

p. 66   *hacks, buckboard wagons*: Leach, *Reveille in Washington*, 190.

p. 66   *"There is pressing need"*: quoted in Duncan, "Pope's Virginia Campaign," in Duncan, *Medical Department of the United States in the Civil War*, 34.

p. 66   *drunken "rabble"*: Sears, *Landscape Turned Red*, 10; Leach, *Reveille in Washington*, 189–92.

p. 67   *"Dear Brother & Sister"*: CB letter, Aug. 31, 1862, CB Papers LC.

p. 67   *Second BR battlefield*: Brooks, *Civil War Medicine*, 15–16; C.F.H. Campbell's report in Barnes, *Medical and Surgical History*, 1:pt. 1, 119.

p. 67   *"As I looked over the scene"*: McParlin's report in Barnes, *Medical and Surgical History*, 1:pt. 1, 116; also quoted in Cunningham, *Field Medical Service at the Battle of Manassas*, 60.

p. 67   *civilian ambulance train*: Cunningham, *Field Medical Service at the Battle of Manassas*, 63.

p. 67   *Medical Inspector Coolidge*: Coolidge's report, Sept. 11, 1862, *National Republican* (Washington, D.C.), Sept. 19, 1862; Duncan, "Pope's Virginia Campaign," in Duncan, *Medical Department of the United States in the Civil War*, 32, 35; Cunningham, *Field Medical Service at the Battle of Manassas*, 63.

p. 67   *CB at depot*: CB to Elvira Stone, Aug. 31, 1862, CB Papers LC.

p. 68   *CB's assistants*: CB to "Dear Friends," Sept. 4, 1862, ibid. (typescript in CB Papers AAS and copy in CB Papers NYPL); CB, "Work and Incidents of Army Life," CB Papers LC, CB Papers SC.

p. 68   *"I heard you were off"*: Ross, *Angel of the Battlefield*, 35–36.

p. 68   *"if by any chance"*: CB to Elvira Stone, Aug. 31, 1862, CB Papers LC.

p. 68   *CB reaches Fairfax Station*: CB Lecture [undated] and
                Notes for a Lecture [undated], ibid.; CB, "Work and
                Incidents," ibid., and CB Papers SC; CB to "Dear
                Friends," Sept. 4, 1862, CB Papers LC. The latter letter
                and lengthy passages of CB's war lectures dealing with
                Fairfax Station are quoted in Barton, *Life of Clara Barton*,
                1:176–90. My quotations are from the original documents.

p. 68   *"ghastly heaps"*: Pryor, *Clara Barton*, 93.

pp. 68–69   *Dr. Dunn in Second BR battle*: Dunn to his wife, Sept. 6,
                1862, JD Papers UVA.

p. 69   *"supply us with bandages"*: Dunn to his wife, undated
                newspaper clipping, CB Papers LC; also quoted in Pryor,
                Clara Barton, 93.

p. 69   *"I never realized"*: CB, "Work and Incidents," CB Papers
                LC and CB Papers SC; CB to "Dear Friends," Sept. 4,
                1862, CB Papers LC.

p. 69   *CB's nursing*: ibid.

p. 70   *CB and Charley Hamilton*: CB, "Work and Incidents," CB
                Papers LC, CB Papers SC; CB Lecture [undated], CB
                Papers LC.

p. 70   *"wept and worked," "some poor mangled fellow," "a little
                band"*: ibid.

pp. 70–72   *CB and Hugh Johnson*: this scene derives from ibid.; CB
                Notes for a Lecture [undated], CB Papers LC; CB "Black
                Book," CB Papers SC.

p. 72   *"fearful emergency," meat from sandwiches*: ibid.; CB
                "Work and Incidents," CB Papers LC; CB to "Dear
                Friends," Sept. 4, 1862, ibid.

p. 72   "Seven times": CB to Mary Norton, Sept. 4, 1862, MN
                Papers DU; also quoted in Pryor, *Clara Barton*, 95. My
                quotation is from the original document.

p. 72   *rebel cavalry in woods*: CB to "Dear Friends," Sept. 4,
                1862, CB Papers LC.

p. 72   *medical personnel as noncombatants*: Samuel E. Lewis,
                "General T. J. Jackson (Stonewall) and His Medical
                Director, Hunter McGuire, M.D., at Winchester, May,
                1862," *Southern Historical Society Papers*, 30 (1902),
                226–36; Edward L. Munson, "The Army Surgeon and His
                Work," in Francis Trevelyan Miller (ed.), *The Photographic
                History of the Civil War* (10 vols., reprint ed., New York:
                Castle Books, n.d.), "Prisons and Hospitals," 228. The
                Union formally responded to Stonewall Jackson's "uncon-
                ditional" release of Federal surgeons in what became
                known as the "Lieber Code," devised by Columbia profes-
                sor Francis Lieber and promulgated in General Orders No.
                100, on Apr. 24, 1863. Article LII stated: "The enemy's
                chaplains, officers of the medical staff, apothecaries, hospi-
                tal nurses and servants, if they fall into the hands of the
                American Army, are not prisoners of war, unless the com-

mander has reasons to retain them. In the latter case, or if, at their own desire, they are allowed to remain with their captured companions, they are treated as prisoners of war, and may be exchanged if the commander sees fit." In 1864 in Europe, the Geneva Convention "established protective principles for Red Cross personnel and others engaged in helping the wounded." Leon Friedman (ed.), *The Law of War: A Documentary History—Volume I* (New York: Random House, 1972), 168–69. Even so, medical personnel continued to be captured and incarcerated during the Civil War. Dr. Mary Walker, an assistant surgeon in the Union army, was seized in Tennessee in 1864 and sent to Castle Thunder in Richmond. See Edward T. James et al. (eds.), *Notable American Women* (3 vols., Cambridge: Harvard University Press, 1971), 3:532, and Mary Elizabeth Massey, *Bonnet Brigades: American Women in the Civil War* (New York: Alfred A. Knopf, 1966), 62–63.

p. 73   *"going for stores," "begged to be excused"*: CB to "Dear Friends," Sept. 4, 1862, CB Papers LC.

p. 73   *thunderstorm, Chantilly*: CB, "Work and Incidents," CB Papers LC and CB Papers SC; CB Black Book, CB Papers SC; CB Notes for a Lecture [undated], CB Papers LC.

p. 73   *"no man knew," "fire from its plunging engines," CB's tent*: CB, "Work and Incidents," CB Papers SC; also CB Notes for a Lecture [undated], CB Papers LC.

p. 74   *"a distant corner"*: CB Lecture [undated], CB Papers LC.

p. 74   *"ceaseless rumbling"*: CB, "Work and Incidents," CB Papers SC.

p. 74   *AOP soldiers at Fairfax, "We knew this was the last"*: CB to "Dear Friends," Sept. 4, 1862, CB Papers LC.

p. 74   *"Miss Barton . . . Can you ride" to "Now is the time"*: CB, "Work and Incidents," CB Papers LC and CB Papers SC; CB Lecture [undated], CB Papers LC; CB to "Dear Friends," Sept. 4, 1862, ibid.

p. 75   *"Oh! the repast"*: CB to "Dear Friends," Sept. 4, 1862, CB Papers LC.

p. 75   *Hugh Johnson's death*: CB, "Work and Incidents," CB Papers SC.

p. 75   *"head, heart, and hands"*: Leander Poor to Elvira Stone, Sept. 3, 6, 1862, CB Papers LC.

pp. 75–76   *CB letter to Lizzie Shaver*: addressed to "Dear Friends," Sept. 4, 1862, CB Papers LC.

p. 76   *convalescent soldiers sent to Philadelphia*: Cunningham, *Field Medical Services at the Battle of Manassas*, 56.

p. 76   *"absent secessionists"*: ibid., 68.

p. 76   *hospital in Capitol*: Duncan, "Pope's Virginia Campaign," in Duncan, *Medical Department of the United States in the Civil War*, 49; Adams, *Doctors in Blue*, 154.

p. 76   *need for ambulance corps, civilian teamsters*: Duncan, "Pope's Virginia Campaign," in Duncan, *Medical Department of the United States in the Civil War*, 48; McParlin's report in Barnes, *Surgical and Medical History*, 1:pt. 1, 116–17; Coolidge's report, Sept. 11, 1862, *National Republican* (Washington, D.C.), Sept. 19, 1862; Cunningham, *Field Medical Services at the Battles of Manassas*, 68.

p. 77   *"the frightful state"*: Hammond's letter is quoted in full in Edward L. Munson, "Transportation of Federal Sick and Wounded," in Miller (ed.), *Photographic History of the Civil War*, "Prisons and Hospitals," 304, 306.

p. 77   *"effeminating comforts"*: quoted in Maxwell, *Lincoln's Fifth Wheel*, 177. See also Adams, *Doctors in Blue*, 33.

p. 77   *improvised ambulance train*: Maxwell, *Lincoln's Fifth Wheel*, 168; Assistant Surgeon J. J. Woodward's report in Barnes, *Medical and Surgical History*, 1:pt. 1, 127.

p. 77   *"I am almost discouraged"*: Dunn to his wife, Sept. 6, 1862, JD Papers UVA.

p. 77   *AOP on the march*: Leach, *Reveille in Washington*, 198; Robert Underwood Johnson and Clarence Clough Buel (eds.), *Battles and Leaders of the Civil War* (4 vols., reprint ed., New York: Thomas Yoseloff, 1956), 2:59; Sears, *Landscape Turned Red*, 102; Duncan, "Antietam," in Duncan, *Medical Department of the United States in the Civil War*, 6.

p. 78   *Letterman preparations*: Letterman report to Gen. S. Williams, March 1, 1863, *OR*, ser. 1, vol. 19, pt. 1, 107–10; Jonathan Letterman, *Medical Recollections of the Army of the Potomac* (New York: D. Appleton and Co., 1866), 34; Duncan, "Antietam," in Duncan, *Medical Department of the United States in the Civil War*, 13.

p. 78   *"the folly and wickedness"*: CB, "Work and Incidents," CB Papers SC.

p. 78   *CB's preparations and illness*: CB to Mary Norton, Sept. 9, 26, 1862, MN Papers DU.

p. 78   *"Harper's Ferry"*: CB Lecture [undated], CB Papers LC; CB, "Work and Incidents," ibid. and CB Papers SC; also quoted in Barton, *Life of Clara Barton*, 1:194.

p. 78   *"I have all the plans," "cut the enemy"*: McClellan, *Civil War Papers* (ed. Stephen W. Sears), 453, 455.

p. 79   *CB at Colonel Rucker's*: CB lecture [undated], CB Papers LC; CB, "Work and Incidents," ibid. and CB Papers SC; Halstead interview, CB Papers LC. In her lectures after the war, ibid., Clara incorrectly recalled that Rucker provided her with four wagons and teams for what became the Antietam campaign; Pryor, *Clara Barton*, 97, reports that number as well. In an interview [circa 1891] CB put the figure at six wagons ("Clara Barton and the International Red Cross Association," CB Papers LC). But Welles to Dear Brethren, Sept. 22,

1862, newspaper clipping, CB Papers LC, states that Clara had only one wagon drawn by four horses; and CB to the Soldiers' Friend Society of Hightstown, N.J., Feb. 14, 1863, also says that the Quartermaster Department furnished her just one wagon, presumably with a driver. I have used the number given in the latter two documents, which were written closest to the time of the event. It was after Antietam that Rucker gave CB four wagons and the teamsters to man them.

p. 79   *CB departure*: CB Lecture [undated] and Notes for a Lecture [undated], CB Papers LC; CB, "Work and Incidents," CB Papers SC; Agatha Young, *The Women and the Crisis: Women of the North in the Civil War* (New York: McDowell, Obolensky, 1959), 211.

p. 79   *CB's first day and night on road*: CB to Mary Norton, Sept. 26, 1862, MN Papers DU; CB, "Work and Incidents," CB Papers LC and CB Papers SC; CB Lecture [undated] and Notes for a Lecture [undated], CB Papers LC.

p. 80   *"glorious victory"*: McClellan, *The Civil War Papers of George B. McClellan*, 461; also quoted in Sears, *Landscape Turned Red*, 143.

p. 80   *Letterman's ambulances and traffic jam*: Letterman report *OR*, ser. 1, vol. 19, pt. 1, 107; Letterman, *Medical Recollections*, 35; Duncan, "Antietam," in Duncan, *Medical Department of the United States in the Civil War*, 9, 14, 20–21, 43; Maxwell, *Lincoln's Fifth Wheel*, 171.

p. 80   *"I told them"*: CB to Mary Norton, Sept. 26, 1862, MN Papers DU.

p. 80   *"stretched on boards"*: F. H. Harwood, "An Army Surgeon's Story," *St. Louis Illustrated Magazine* (Apr. 1883), 144, copy in CB Papers LC.

p. 80   *"solid moving mass"*: Halstead interview, ibid.; CB Notes for a Lecture [undated] and Lecture [undated], ibid.; "Clara Barton and the International Red Cross Association," ibid.; CB, "Work and Incidents," ibid. and CB Papers SC; Johnson and Buel, *Battles and Leaders*, 2:557.

p. 80   *"pale haggard wrecks"*: CB Notes for a Lecture [undated], CB Papers LC; also CB, "Work and Incidents," ibid. and CB Papers SC; also quoted in Barton, *Life of Clara Barton*, 1:195–96.

p. 81   *"a mingled mass"*: CB to Soldiers' Friend Society, Hightstown, N.J., Feb. 14, 1862, newspaper clipping, CB Papers LC; also quoted in Pryor, *Clara Barton*, 97. My quotation is from the original document.

p. 81   *"Shocked and sick"*: CB Notes for a Lecture [undated], CB Papers LC; also CB Lecture [undated], ibid.; CB, "Work and Incidents," CB Papers LC and CB Papers SC; Welles to "Dear Brethren," Sept. 22, 1862, newspaper clipping, CB Papers LC.

p. 81   *"That house" ox episode*: CB Notes for a Lecture [undated], CB Papers LC.

p. 81   *stragglers*: CB, "Work and Incidents," CB Papers SC.

p. 82   *"bridge that chasm"*: "Clara Barton and the International Red Cross Association," CB Papers LC; Halstead interview, ibid.

p. 82   *CB around the wagon train*: ibid.; CB Lecture [undated], ibid.; CB, "Work and Incidents," ibid. and CB Papers SC; CB Lecture quoted in Barton, *Life of Clara Barton*, 1:198.

p. 82   *CB at Ninth Corps bivouac*: CB, "Work and Incidents" and Halstead interview, CB Papers LC; "Clara Barton and the International Red Cross Association," ibid.; CB Lecture quoted in Barton, *Life of Clara Barton*, 1:198–99.

p. 82   *general note on CB in Antietam battle*: My details about Clara's whereabouts and activities derive almost entirely from manuscripts, which are cited in the following notes. Barton, *Life of Clara Barton*, 1:200–205, quotes passages from CB's war lectures about Antietam, lectures I have also used. Since Barton's book is here acknowledged, I won't cite it in my specific references to Antietam. Pryor, *Clara Barton*, 98–99, presents an excellent summary of Clara's work at Antietam but incorrectly identifies the farmhouse hospital in which she served as the Joseph Poffenberger farm. It was the Sam Poffenberger farmhouse, as National Park historian James R. Atkinson demonstrated in a scholarly and persuasive paper, "The Location of the 'Clara Barton Hospital' at Antietam" (Antietam National Battlefield, March 1971), copy provided by Ted Alexander, historian, Antietam National Battlefield. In an effort to prepare a full and accurate account of Clara at Antietam, I used detailed battlefield maps furnished by the National Park Service to trace Clara's movements from the far left to the far right of the Union line, where she posted herself at the Sam Poffenberger farm, which still stands today. My details of the battle itself come from the specific manuscripts and sources cited below and from Sears, *Landscape Turned Red*, 180–300; Murfin, *The Gleam of Bayonets*, 211–91; Johnson and Buel, *Battles and Leaders*, 2:630–694; and Joseph Mills Hanson, "A Report of the Employment of the Artillery at the Battle of Antietam, Md." (National Park Service, Feb. 14, 1940), copy provided by Ted Alexander, Antietam National Battlefield.

p. 83   *CB predawn, Sept. 17*: "Clara Barton and the International Red Cross Association," CB Papers LC; CB, "Work and Incidents," CB Papers SC.

p. 83   *Artillery bombardment*: Johnson and Buel, *Battles and Leaders*, 2:682–83; Hanson, "Artillery at Antietam," 20.

p. 84   *CB's party to Sam Poffenberger farm*: CB said they traveled "about 8 miles" to reach the farmhouse hospital in which

they served during the battle (she did not name the farm). I
traced her route with battlefield maps, using information in
CB Lectures [undated], Notes for Lectures [undated],
"Work and Incidents," Halstead Interview, and "Clara
Barton and the International Red Cross Association," all in
CB Papers LC; CB, "Work and Incidents," and CB, "Black
Book," CB Papers SC; and Atkinson, "Location of the
'Clara Barton Hospital' at Antietam." Like Atkinson, I considered several other farms as possible sites of the "Clara
Barton hospital" but concluded that Atkinson is right: the
evidence in CB's own accounts and that of Dr. Dunn point
to the Sam Poffenberger farm as the location of the improvised hospital in which they served. Poffenberger, who
rented the farm, had fled when the armies approached. For
the field hospital arrangements on the Union right, see
Duncan, "Antietam," in Duncan, *Medical Department of
the United States in the Civil War*, 21–25; and Schildt,
Antietam Hospitals, 10–24.

p. 84   *CB party at Cornfield*: CB to Soldiers' Friend Society,
Hightstown, N.J., Feb. 14, 1863, CB Papers LC, said they
reached here at 9:00 A.M. In her war lectures, she says it was
"scarce ten o'clock." Atkinson, "Location of the 'Clara Barton
Hospital' at Antietam," identified the Union battery as Capt.
J. T. Pettit's, which held the lower end of the Federal
artillery line "on a hill west of the Poffenberger farm."

p. 84   *"We were entirely surrounded"*: Welles to "Dear Brethren,"
Sept. 22, 1862, newspaper clipping, CB Papers LC.

p. 84   *"they are there"*: CB, "Work and Incidents," CB Papers SC.

p. 84   *"slight hollow," "under the lee," farmhouse description*:
"Clara Barton and the International Red Cross
Association," CB Papers LC; CB, "Work and Incidents,"
ibid. and CB Papers SC; CB Lecture [undated], CB Papers
LC. Also quoted in Atkinson, "Location of the 'Clara
Barton Hospital' at Antietam."

p. 84   *"God has indeed remembered us," "We have nothing"*: CB,
"Work and Incidents," CB Papers SC and CB Papers LC;
CB Notes for a Lecture [undated], CB Papers LC. For dif-
ferent versions of what Dunn told CB, see Halstead inter-
view, ibid.; "Clara Barton and the International Red Cross
Association," ibid.; and Dunn to his wife, Oct. 25, 1862,
newspaper clipping, "The Angel of the Battle Field," ibid.
Dunn described his going into combat earlier that morning
in Dunn to his wife, Oct. 1, 1862, JD Papers UVA. See also
Atkinson, "Location of the 'Clara Barton Hospital' at
Antietam."

p. 85   *"never before"*: CB Notes for a Lecture [undated], CB
Papers LC.

p. 85   *"toiled as few men"*: clipping from "The Philanthropic
Results of the War in America," 15, CB Scrapbooks, ibid.;

Welles to Dear Brethren, Sept. 22, 1862, newspaper clipping, ibid.

p. 85   *bullet-riddled farmhouse*: Halstead interview, ibid.

p. 85   *soldier shot in CB's arms*: CB, "Work and Incidents," CB Papers SC.

p. 86   *"You can't hurt me," "I will help," "I do not suppose," CB's operation*: ibid.; CB Notes for a Lecture [undated], CB Papers LC; CB Fragment of a Lecture, ibid.

p. 86   *"Oh no, no, madam"*: CB Fragment of a Lecture, ibid.

p. 86   *"savage continual thunder"*: so said a New York man quoted in Sears, *Landscape Turned Red*, 241.

p. 86   *description of fighting at sunken road*: *New York Tribune* correspondent quoted in ibid.; Johnson and Buel, *Battles and Leaders*, 2:684; Murfin, *Gleam of Bayonets*, 253–57.

p. 86   *improvised hospitals bursting with wounded*: Duncan, "Antietam," in Duncan, *Medical Department of the United States in the Civil War*, 21–24.

p. 86   *"stretched out"*: Halstead interview, CB Papers LC. Duncan, "Antietam," 24, estimated that 1,400 wounded men were ultimately brought to the Sam Poffenberger hospital.

p. 87   *"Open the wine," search in the cellar*: CB, "Work and Incidents," ibid.; CB Notes for a Lecture [undated], ibid.

p. 87   *"gruel, gruel, gruel," CB disheveled*: Halstead interview, ibid.; also "Clara Barton and the International Red Cross Association," ibid. Pryor, *Clara Barton*, 99, using the same sources, also states that CB's hair was "astray" and "her face covered with gunpowder."

p. 87   *"quite a number," "They were amazed"*: Welles to Dear Brethren, Sept. 22, 1862, newspaper clipping, CB Papers LC.

p. 87   *Dunn's departure*: Dunn to his wife, Oct. 1, 1862, JD Papers UVA.

p. 87   *"I wish I could pay you"*: Welles to Dear Brethren, Sept. 22, 1862, newspaper clipping, CB Papers LC.

p. 87   *rebel artillery bombardment*: Sears, *Landscape*, 290–91, said that it began at about mid-afternoon and was part of Jeb Stuart's attempt to carry out a Lee order to turn the extreme right of the Federal line. Union surgeon A. Hashberger reported that "a terrific cannonading of shell and shot" commenced at 4:00 P.M. (Hashberger letter, Jan. 8, 1863, newspaper clipping, CB Papers LC). In her postwar lectures (CB Papers LC), CB recalled that the artillery barrage occurred a little after noon, but in interviews in later years, she thought the bombardment began near sunset (Halstead interview, ibid.; "Clara Barton and the International Red Cross Association," ibid.).

p. 87   *It was "the most terrific"*: "Clara Barton and the

International Red Cross Association," ibid. See also CB Lecture [undated] and Notes for a Lecture [undated], ibid.

p. 87   *"The tables jarred and rolled," surgeons and nurses fled*: Halstead interview, ibid.; "Clara Barton and the International Red Cross Association," ibid. Pryor, *Clara Barton*, 104, also reports that the male medical assistants fled and that CB remained behind to assist in an operation.

p. 87   *"Can I assist you?" "frightful firing," CB helps with the operation*: Halstead interview; "Clara Barton and the International Red Cross Association," ibid.

p. 88   *"smoke became so dense"*: CB Lecture [undated], ibid.; CB Notes for a Lecture [undated], ibid.

p. 88   *"blood-red"*: Sears, *Landscape Turned Red*, 293. Charles Carleton Coffin, "Antietam Scenes," in Johnson and Buel, *Battles and Leaders*, 2:684, described the sun's disc as "red and large as seen through the murky battle-cloud." My assertion that Antietam was "the bloodiest single day of combat in American military history" is common knowledge.

pp. 88–89   *CB, the chief surgeon, and the lanterns*: this scene was put together from several CB recollections. They comprise CB Lecture [undated] and Notes for a Lecture [undated], CB Papers LC; Halstead interview, ibid.; "Clara Barton and the International Red Cross Association," ibid. Ross, *Angel of the Battlefield*, 47, also describes it, as does Williams, *Clara Barton*, 79–80.

p. 89   *"We could not think of rest"*: Welles to Dear Brethren, Sept. 22, 1862, newspaper clipping, CB Papers LC; also CB to the Soldiers' Friend Society, Hightstown, N.J., Feb. 14, 1862, newspaper clipping, ibid.

p. 89   *half the soldiers died*: Welles to Dear Brethren, Sept. 22, 1862, newspaper clipping, ibid.

p. 89   *"storm of bloody hail"*: Confederate Colonel John B. Gordon in Richard Wheeler, *Voices of the Civil War* (reprint 1976 ed., New York: New American Library, 1990), 87.

p. 89   *"fearful cost"*: CB to Soldiers' Friend Society, Hightstown, N.J., Feb. 14, 1862, newspaper clipping, CB Papers LC.

p. 89   *"hundreds of horses"*: [Samuel Fiske], *Mr. Dunn Browne's Experiences in the Army* (Boston: Nichols and Noyes, 1866), 49–50. "Dunn Browne" was Fiske's *nom de plume*; Fiske was a member of the Fourteenth Connecticut. The quotation beginning with "hundreds of horses" is also in Sears, *Landscape Turned Red*, 314. A similar description is in William Child, *A History of the Fifth Regiment New Hampshire Volunteers in the American Civil War, 1861–1865* (Bristol N.H.: R. W. Musgrave, 1893), 130. See also Johnson and Buel, *Battles and Leaders*, 2:685.

p. 90   *smell and vomit*: Sears, *Landscape Turned Red*, 314; [Fiske], *Mr. Dunn Browne's Experiences in the Army*, 49; Child, *A History of the Fifth Regiment New Hampshire Volunteers*, 130.

p. 90   *"a dozen of the same company"*: Welles to Dear Brethren, Sept. 22, 1862, CB Papers LC.

p. 90   *Letterman ambulance system at Antietam*: Duncan, "Antietam," in Duncan, *Medical Department of the United States in the Civil War*, 17–18; Adams, *Doctors in Blue*, 78; Maxwell, *Lincoln's Fifth Wheel*, 172–75. See also Letterman's report, *OR*, ser. I, vol. 19, pt. 1, 109–10, and Letterman, *Medical Recollections*, 43–44.

p. 90   *"If we had followed up"*: Dr. Dunn to his wife, Oct. 1, 1862, JD Papers UVA.

p. 91   *Union's seventy-one field hospitals*: Adams, *Doctors in Blue*, 78; Duncan, "Antietam," in Duncan, *Medical Department of the United States in the Civil War*, 72.

p. 91   *"In my feeble estimation"*: Dunn's letter to his wife in "The Angel of the Battle Field," newspaper clipping, CB Papers LC; also quoted in Pryor, *Clara Barton*, 99.

p. 91   *F. H. Harwood and CB*: Harwood, "A Soldier's Story," *St. Louis Illustrated Magazine* (Apr. 1883), 136–37, 143.

p. 91   *CB and Mary Hartwell*: ibid., 137, 135–36, 139–45.

pp. 91–92   *scene with CB, Harwood, and Mary Hartwell*: ibid., 137–38.

pp. 92–93   *Mary and Harry Barnard*: ibid., 139–46.

p. 93   *William Platt and Sanitary Commission at Antietam*: Stillé, *History of the Sanitary Commission*, 269. Dr. Cornelius R. Agnew of the commission was already with the army. Duncan, "Antietam," in Duncan, *Medical Department of the United States in the Civil War*, 43, and Maxwell, *Lincoln's Fifth Wheel*, 171, state that the commission's first wagon train reached Antietam on September 19, a day ahead of the government's stores. It was at Antietam that the commission first used its field relief system.

pp. 93–94   *Mary W. Lee, Eliza Harris, Anna Holstein*: L. P. Brockett and Mary C. Vaughan, *Woman's Work in the Civil War: A Record of Heroism, Patriotism and Patience* (Philadelphia: Zeigler, McCurdy & Co., 1867), 484, 156–57, 252–53. In *Nurse and Spy* (1864), Sarah Emma Edmonds claimed that she served with a medical team at Antietam while masquerading as a man.

p. 94   *"jogged," "color of gunpowder"*: Halstead interview, CB Papers LC; "Clara Barton and the International Red Cross Association," ibid.

p. 94   *"Have I told you"*: CB to Mary Norton, Sept. 26, 1862, MN Papers DU.

p. 95   *"remorseless revolutionary struggle"*: Lincoln, *CW*, 5:49.

p. 95   *"obstinate and prolonged"*: CB to Stephen, Mar. 1, 1862, CB Papers LC.

p. 95   *"appointed"* him to *"meet this crisis"*: CB to Frances Gage, May 1, 1864, ibid.

p. 95   *CB to Alexandria*: CB to Mary Norton, Oct. 10, 1862, MN Papers DU.

p. 95   "*a sort of pen*": quoted in Adams, *Doctors in Blue*, 190. For other descriptions of Camp Misery, see Noah Brooks, *Washington, D.C., in Lincoln's Time*, ed. Herbert Mitgang (Chicago: Quandrangle Books, 1971), 18–19; and Mary Livermore, *My Story of the War* (reprint of 1887 ed., Williamstown, Mass.: Corner House Publishers, 1978), 253.

p. 95   "*a most laborious day*," "*I don't know how*": CB to Mary Norton, Oct. 10, 1862, MN Papers DU.

p. 96   "*They will fight again*": CB Lecture [undated] and Lecture [typescript], CB Papers LC.

p. 96   *four wagons and an ambulance, CB's stores*: CB Diary [undated], ibid., said that Rucker furnished her with four wagons, teamsters, and an ambulance driver. Rucker's order of Oct. 18, 1862, CB Papers SC, provided her with an ambulance. Welles to Dear Brethren, Dec. 14, 1862, newspaper clipping, ibid., said they took along "the largest quantity of stores we have ever taken at any one time to the army." In her postwar lectures, ibid., CB incorrectly recalled that the Quartermaster Department gave her six army wagons and an ambulance.

p. 96   "*in the sun and dust*": CB Lecture [undated] and Lecture [typescript], ibid.

pp. 96–97   *CB's trouble with her teamsters*: CB Lecture [typescript], CB Papers LC; CB "Black Book," CB Papers SC.

p. 97   *medical personnel at Frederick*: Letterman report, *OR*, ser. 1, vol. 19, pt. 1, 111.

pp. 97–98   *Harry Barnard story and quotations*: Harwood, "An Army Surgeon's Story," *St. Louis Illustrated Magazine* (April 1883), 147–48.

p. 98   *CB's linkup with AOP*: CB Diary [undated entry], CB Papers LC; CB Lecture [undated], ibid.; Barton, *Life of Clara Barton*, 1:206.

p. 98   *McClellan*: Sears, *McClellan*, 328–38; Bruce Catton, *Mr. Lincoln's Army* (Garden City: Doubleday & Co., 1951), 333.

p. 98   *CB's love for the marching army*: CB, "Black Book," CB Papers SC; CB Lecture [typescript], CB Papers LC; CB to Soldiers' Relief Society, Watkins, N.Y., Dec. 3, 1863, ibid; information on Burnside from Marvel, *Burnside*, 1, 7, 90–91, 112–13, 157, 173.

pp. 98–99   *John Brown's Body*: CB, "Black Book," CB Papers SC; CB, Lecture [typescript], CB Papers LC. There were many versions of this popular song, which originated as a sarcastic jibe at a Massachusetts sergeant named John Brown, but which Union soldiers soon associated with John Brown of Harpers Ferry fame. The version I quote is from Boyd B.

Stutler, "John Brown's Body," *Civil War History* (Sept. 1958), 256–57. The last two verses are from CB, Lecture [typescript], CB Papers LC. In the version in Frank Moore, *The Civil War in Song and Story, 1860–1865* ([no place] P. F. Collier, 1889), 509, each verse is repeated three times, then the chorus three times.

p. 99   *"something sublime"*: CB, "Work and Incidents," CB Papers LC; also quoted in Pryor, *Clara Barton*, 103.

p. 99   *"I am a* U.S. soldier": CB to T. W. Meighan, June 24, 1863, CB Papers LC.

p. 99   *"womanly dignity"*: Walcott, *History of the Twenty-first Regiment Massachusetts Volunteers*, 213–14.

p. 99   *dress parade*: Pryor, *Clara Barton*, 103.

p. 99   *daughter Twenty-first Massachusetts, "21st woman"*: Charles F. Walcott, "Extract from the Official History of the Twenty-first Regiment," CB Papers AAS; Walcott, *History of the Twenty-first Regiment Massachusetts Volunteers*, 213–14.

p. 99   *CB's "selfish" right to nurse soldiers*: CB to Soldiers' Aid Society, Oxford, Mass., July 20, 1864, CB Papers LC. My interpretation of CB in this paragraph was influenced by Carolyn G. Heilbrun, *Writing a Woman's Life* (New York: W. W. Norton, 1988), 18, 23.

pp. 99–100   *CB's inflamed finger*: CB to Soldiers' Relief Society, Dec. 3, 1863, CB Papers LC.

p. 100   *Dr. Dunn*: James Dunn's Military Service Records, NARA.

p. 100   *"on the field"*: CB to Soldiers' Relief Society, Dec. 3, 1863, CB Papers LC.

p. 100   *McClellan relieved*: Sears, *Landscape Turned Red*, 337–45; Sears, *McClellan*, 337–43.

p. 100   *"Good bye, lads"*: quoted in Sears, *Landscape Turned Red*, 345.

p. 100   *Burnside in command, "Old Burny"*: Marvel, *Burnside*, 154, 163, 165; Catton, *Glory Road*, 30–31; T. Harry Williams, *Lincoln and His Generals* (New York: Alfred A. Knopf, 1952), 177, 180–82. Grand Division organization: Johnson and Buel, *Battles and Leaders*, 3:107, 143–47.

p. 100   *CB and Sam return to Washington*: CB to Soldiers' Relief Society, Watkins, N.Y., Dec. 3, 1863, CB Papers LC; Sam Barton to Elvira Stone, Dec. 8, 1862, ibid.

p. 101   *"I have no word"*: quoted in Dannett, *Noble Women of the North*, 224.

p. 101   *"We need more liquors:"* quoted in Ross, *Angel of the Battlefield*, 50.

p. 101   *CB to Aquia Creek*: Sam Barton to Elvira Stone, Dec. 8, 1862, CB Papers LC; CB to Soldiers' Relief Society, Watkins, N.Y., Dec. 3, 1863; CB Diary, Dec. 11, 1862, ibid.

p. 101   *cold and snow*: Johnson and Buel, *Battles and Leaders*, 3:107.

p. 101   *Aquia Creek description*: Leach, *Reveille in Washington*, 229.

p. 101   *"great joy"*: CB to Messrs. Brown & Co., Dec. 8, 1862, CB Papers LC; the letter is also in Barton, *Life of Clara Barton*, 1:210–11.

p. 101   *desolate countryside*: Catton, *Glory Road*, 27.

p. 102   *"canvas city"*: CB, "Black Book," CB Papers SC.

p. 102   *AOP at Fredericksburg*: Marvel, *Burnside*, 177, 179; Johnson and Buel, *Battles and Leaders*, 107, 121–26, 128–30; Catton, *Glory Road*, 28.

p. 102   *Burnside's balloons*: Shelby Foote, *The Civil War: A Narrative* (3 vols., New York: Random House, 1958–1974), 2:25.

p. 102   *CB to Sturgis HQ*: CB to Brown & Co., Dec. 8, 1862, CB Papers LC. Internal evidence in this letter implies that the general's tent was pitched on the Lacy House grounds.

p. 102   *Sturgis's "protection"*: CB to Sturgis, April 1881, ibid.

p. 102   *Sturgis profile, "I don't care"*: Stewart Sifakis, *Who Was Who in the Civil War* (New York: Facts on File, 1988), 632–33; Samuel Sturgis's Military Service Records, NARA AGO; Murfin, *Gleam of Bayonets*, 274–76.

p. 102   *"splendid serenade," Miss "G.," "very neighborly"*: CB to Brown & Co., Dec. 8, 1862, CB Papers LC.

pp. 102–103   *Sumner's headquarters and Lacy House (Chatham) portrait*: Ralph Happel, *Chatham: The Life of a House* (Philadelphia: Eastern National Park & Monument Assoc., 1984), 9–49, 55, including an excellent map of the area, which helped me immeasurably. I visited the Lacy House, a national historical site, and studied where CB stayed and worked as a nurse. Happel, 59, says that Sumner's headquarters was at the Phillips House, but General Darius Couch in Johnson and Buel, *Battles and Leaders*, 3:107; *OR*, ser. 1, vol. 21, 315, *History of the Twelfth Regiment Rhode Island Volunteers in the Civil War, 1862–1863* (prepared by the Committee of the Survivors, Providence: Snow and Farnham, 1901–1904), 32; and Marvel, *Burnside*, 171, state that Sumner's headquarters was in the Lacy House. *History of the Twelfth Regiment Rhode Island Volunteers*, 27, and General Rush C. Hawkins, in Johnson and Buel, *Battles and Leaders*, 3:126, both state that Burnside's headquarters was at the Phillips House.

p. 103   *"honest heart:"* CB, "Black Book," CB Papers SC; also in Barton, *Life of Clara Barton*, 1:214; and quoted in Happel, *Chatham*, 59.

p. 103   *"future programme" and "to my astonishment"*: CB to Brown & Co., Dec. 8, 1862, CB Papers LC.

p. 103   *CB visits regiments*: ibid.

p. 104   *Federal band*: Johnson and Buel, *Battles and Leaders*, 3:86.

p. 104   *"in spicy repartee," "how they liked," "supposed"*: Walcott, *History of the Twenty-first Regiment Massachusetts Volunteers*, 230–31.

p. 104   *divisional tent hospitals*: Letterman's report, *OR*, ser. 1, vol. 19, pt. 1, 114–17; Letterman, *Medical Recollections*, 58–68; Duncan, "Campaign of Fredericksburg," in Duncan, *Medical Department of the United States in the Civil War*, 6–8, 20–22, 39–40; Adams, *Doctors in Blue*, 88; Welles to Dear Brethren, Dec. 14, 27, 1862, newspaper clipping, CB Papers LC. Sanitary Commission presence from Duncan, 34, and Stillé, *History of the Sanitary Commission*, 371. The commission sent three wagons loaded with supplies, which the agents handed out on Dec. 11 and 12.

p. 104   *Letterman's ambulance system*: Duncan, "Campaign of Fredericksburg," in Duncan, *Medical Department of the United States in the Civil War*, 8, 39, 40; Letterman's report, *OR*, ser. 1, vol. 19, pt. 1, 115–16; also Letterman's report ibid., ser. 1, vol. 11, pt. 1, 210–20.

p. 105   *meetings of the generals*: Johnson and Buel, *Battles and Leaders*, 3:126, 107–8; Marvel, *Burnside*, 170–74; Catton, *Glory Road*, 45.

p. 105   *"Thy will O God be done," CB in Lacy House yard*: CB to Elvira Stone, Dec. 12 [Dec. 11], 1862, CB Papers LC. CB incorrectly dated this epistle. In CB to Elvira, Mar. 2, 1863, ibid., CB says that she wrote the letter in the early morning dark before the cannonade, which occurred on Dec. 11, 1862. She did not send this letter in December but enclosed it with the letter of Mar. 2, 1863. The letter is also in Barton, *Life of Clara Barton*, 1:212–13, with the grammar tidied up.

p. 105   *CB to Elvira Stone*: Dec. 12 [Dec 11], 1862, CB Papers LC.

p. 106   *CB on Lacy House veranda*: CB, "Black Book," CB Papers SC; CB Lecture [typescript] and CB, "Work and Incidents," CB Papers LC and SC; CB to Soldiers' Relief Society Watkins, N.Y., Dec. 3, 1863, CB Papers LC. A portion of CB's "Black Book" and of a lecture dealing with the battle for Fredericksburg is in Barton, *Life of Clara Barton*, 1:213–16.

p. 106   *sniper firing on Union engineers*: ibid.; *History of the Twelfth Regiment Rhode Island Volunteers*, 26–31; Marvel, *Burnside*, 175–76; Catton, *Glory Road*, 46–47; Freeman, *Lee*, 2:444–46; Foote, *Civil War*, 2:27. Couch description from Andrew E. Ford, *The Story of the Fifteenth Regiment Massachusetts Volunteer Infantry in the Civil War, 1861–1864* (Clinton: Press of W. J. Coulter, 1898), 219. See also Walcott, *History of the Twenty-first Regiment Massachusetts Volunteers*, 236–37.

p. 106   *"great solid squares," "most impressive exhibition"*: E. Porter Alexander, *Fighting for the Confederacy: The Personal Recollections of General Edward Porter Alexander*, ed. Gary W. Gallagher (Chapel Hill: University of North Carolina Press, 1989), 170–71.

p. 106   *CB under fire*: CB, "Black Book," CB Papers SC; CB Lecture [typescript] and CB, "Work and Incidents," CB Papers LC and SC; CB to Soldiers' Relief Society Watkins, N.Y., Dec. 3, 1863, CB Papers LC.

p. 107   *"Bring the guns to bear"*: CB, "Black Book," CB Papers SC. CB maintained that she saw General Burnside on the riverfront that morning and that he uttered the words quoted here, but he was actually at the Phillips House (see *OR*, ser. 1, vol. 21, 107, and *History of the Twentieth Regiment Rhode Island Volunteers*, 27). The words she heard came from General Hunt.

p. 107   *179 guns opened fire*: The figure is from *History of the Twelfth Regiment Rhode Island Volunteers*, 28. The Parrotts were on Falmouth Heights. Other sources put the figure at about 150 guns.

p. 107   *"cyclone of fiery metal"*: James Longstreet in Johnson and Buel, *Battles and Leaders*, 3:75. My description of the bombardment of Fredericksburg derives from CB, "Black Book," CB Papers SC; CB Lecture [typescript], CB Papers LC; Marvel, *Burnside*, 177; Foote, *Civil War*, 2:28; Johnson and Buel, *Battles and Leaders*, 3:75, 87; Catton, *Glory Road*, 48–49; Freeman, *Lee*, 2:446–47.

p. 107   *"like two great spirits"*: Alexander, *Fighting for the Confederacy*, 171.

p. 107   *"in every quarter," "cellars are filled," "Man the boats," "Row! Row!"*: CB "Black Book," CB Papers SC; CB Lecture [typescript] and "Work and Incidents," CB Papers LC and SC.

p. 107   *"tearing, whirling"*: Freemon, *Microbes and Minie Balls*, 49.

pp. 107–108   *battle for Fredericksburg*: CB, "Black Book," CB Papers SC; CB Lecture [typescript], CB Papers LC; CB to Soldiers' Relief Society, Watkins, N.Y., Dec. 3, 1863, ibid.; Johnson and Buel, *Battles and Leaders*, 3:108, 121; Catton, *Glory Road*, 49; Freeman, *Lee*, 2:447–48.

p. 108   *"flushed with indignation," "Come to me"*: CB, "Black Book," CB Papers SC; CB Lecture [typescript], CB Papers LC. Ross, *Angel of the Battlefield*, 51–52, identified the surgeon who sent CB the note as J. Clarence Cutter.

p. 108   *"Lady, you have been very kind"*: "Biographical Department: Clara H. Barton," *Soldiers Weekly Messenger*, clipping, CB Papers LC. For other versions of this story, see "Miss Barton in the Field," *Des Moines* (Iowa) *Daily State Register*, clipping, ibid., and Capt. Joseph Hamilton, "Clara Barton: A Story of Her Heroism on the Battlefield of Fredericksburg," clipping, CB Collection AHL.

p. 108   *"water hissing," "like a harmless pebble"*: CB, "Black Book," CB Papers SC; CB Lecture [typescript], CB Papers LC. See also CB, "Work and Incidents," CB Papers LC and SC.

p. 109   *"gallant rider"*: ibid.

p. 109   *CB's soup kitchen*: Welles to Dear Brethren, Dec. 27, 1862, newspaper clipping, CB Papers LC; Pryor, *Clara Barton*, 106.

p. 109   *"Oh what a days work," dead Union officer*: CB Notes for a Lecture [undated], CB Papers LC: CB Lecture [typescript], ibid.

p. 109   *looting of Fredericksburg*: Foote, *Civil War*, 2:30; Marvel, *Burnside*, 178–79; Catton, *Glory Road*, 61; Couch in Johnson and Buel, *Battles and Leaders*, 3:108.

p. 109   *"fully equipped"*: Ford, *The Story of the Fifteenth Regiment Massachusetts Volunteer Infantry*, 225.

p. 109   *"sadly wounded"*: CB to Mrs. Carslake, Mar. 29, 1863, CB Papers LC.

p. 109   *CB's records of dying and wounded*: CB Diary [undated], CB Papers LC.

p. 110   *Wiley Faulkner*: ibid.; CB "Black Book" SC; CB Lecture [typescript], CB Papers LC. CB sometimes called him Wriley Faulkner.

p. 110   *"Old Bull" Sumner*: Sifakis, *Who Was Who in the Civil War*, 634; Sears, *Landscape Turned Red*, 239.

p. 110   *Burnside's plan of attack*: Marvel, *Burnside*, 179–80; Johnson and Buel, *Battles and Leaders*, 3:133; Catton, *Glory Road*, 51–52.

p. 110   *J. Horace Lacy*: Greene, *Lacy*, 11–12.

p. 110   *"gayly dressed women," "authorize the fire"*: quoted in ibid., 12–13.

p. 111   *CB at Lacy House dawn, Dec. 13*: CB "Black Book," CB Papers SC; CB Lecture [typescript], CB Papers LC. CB's uniform from Barton, *Life of Clara Barton*, 1:221.

p. 111   *"an indistinct murmur"*: quoted in Foote, *Civil War*, 2:30.

p. 111   *artillery duel, Lacy House struck*: CB "Black Book," CB Papers SC; CB to Mrs. Carslake, Mar. 29, 1863, CB Papers LC; CB Notes for a Lecture [undated], ibid; Freemen, *Lee*, 2:457–58.

p. 111   *"while the house"*: CB to Mrs. Carslake, Mar. 29, 1863, CB Papers LC.

p. 112   *"You saved my life"*: episode told in CB "Black Book," CB Papers SC; and CB Lecture [typescript] and other lectures and Notes for a Lecture, CB Papers LC.

p. 112   *CB into town, "You are alone," "best-protected woman"*:

ibid.; also Welles to Dear Brethren, Dec. 14, 1862, newspaper clipping, CB Papers LC; CB to Soldiers' Relief
Society, Watkins, N.Y., Dec. 3, 1863, ibid.

p. 112   *battle description*: scores of books describe the assaults on
Marye's Heights, including those by Foote, Catton,
Freeman, Marvel, Wolcott, and Johnson and Buel, all cited
in previous notes. I acknowledge my debt for my sentences
about the battle to all the previous books that describe it.

p. 113   *"Oh, great God!"*: Johnson and Buel, *Battles and Leaders*,
3:113.

p. 113   *"While the horrid red fountain," Sergeant Plunkett story*:
Wolcott, *History of the Twenty-first Massachusetts*,
241–42, 255; CB to members of the Senate Committee on
Military Affairs, Feb. 22, 1863, CB Papers LC (the letter is
also in Barton, *Life of Clara Barton*, 1:228–230); CB
Lecture [undated], ibid.

p. 113   *Federal casualties*: OR, ser. 1, vol. 21, 129–42.

pp. 113–114   *improvised Fredericksburg hospitals*: Duncan, "Campaign
of Fredericksburg," in Duncan, *Medical Department of the
United States in the Civil War*, 13–14. [Fiske], *Mr. Dunn
Browne's Experiences in the Army*, 107; Johnson and Buel,
Battles and Leaders, 3:125.

p. 114   *CB a ubiquitous presence*: Welles to Dear Brethren, Dec.
14, 1862, newspaper clipping, CB Papers LC; CB Lecture
[typescript], ibid.; CB "Black Book," CB Papers SC. Pryor,
Clara Barton, 107, also writes that Clara "was everywhere
in that pinched and unhappy town."

p. 114   *"She did not flinch"*: Welles to Dear Brethren, Dec. 14,
1862, newspaper clipping, CB Papers LC.

p. 114   *"obliterated the stripes"*: CB to members of the Senate
Committee on Military Affairs, Feb. 22, 1863, ibid.; CB
Lecture [undated], ibid.

p. 114   *"every conceivable posture"*: quoted in Freeman, *Lee*,
2:470–71.

p. 114   *"cacophony" of groans*: quoted in Alice Rains Trulock, *In
the Hands of Providence: Joshua L. Chamberlain and the
American Civil War* (Chapel Hill: University of North
Carolina Press, 1992), 97.

p. 114   *"a wail so far and deep"*: Joshua Chamberlain, "Night on
the Field of Fredericksburg," in W. C. King and W. P.
Derby, *Camp-Fire Sketches and Battle-Field Echoes*
(Springfield, Mass.: W. C. King & Co., 1887), 128.

p. 114   *"Never—forever"*: quoted in Trulock, *In the Hands of
Providence*, 98.

p. 114   *"through the murk the dusky forms"*: Quoted in Duncan,
"Campaign of Fredericksburg," in Duncan, *Medical
Department of the United States in the Civil War*, 14–15. A
similar description is in Chamberlain, "Night on the Field
of Fredericksburg," in King and Derby, *Camp-Fire*

Sketches and Battle-Field Echoes, 129. See also Letterman, *Medical Recollections*, 72–73.

p. 115   *Fredericksburg at night*: Johnson and Buel, *Battles and Leaders*, 3:125; Duncan, "Campaign of Fredericksburg," in Duncan, *Medical Department of the United States in the Civil War*, 18–19;

p. 115   *"almost frozen"*: "Clara Barton: A Story of Her Heroism on the Battlefield of Fredericksburg," newspaper clipping, CB Collection AHL.

p. 115   *CB and Nathan Rice*: CB "Black Book," CB Papers SC; CB Diary [undated entry], CB Papers LC; CB Lecture [typescript], and Notes for a Lecture [undated], ibid.

pp. 115–116   *Burnside quotations*: Johnson and Buel, *Battles and Leaders*, 3:127, 138; also 117–18. Burnside's location during battle from Marvel, *Burnside*, 187.

p. 116   *"limbs flung from their bodies"*: Chamberlain, "The Last Night at Fredericksburg," in King and Derby, *Camp-Fire Sketches and Battle-Field Echoes*, 134–35. Casualty figures from *OR*, ser. 1, vol. 21, 142, 562.

p. 116   *AOP withdrawal*: Johnson and Buel, *Battles and Leaders*, 3:117–18; Foote, *Civil War*, 2:44.

p. 116   *Letterman's medical service*: Maxwell, *Lincoln's Fifth Wheel*, 182; Adams, *Doctors in Blue*, 82; Duncan, "Campaign of Fredericksburg," in Duncan, *Medical Department of the United States in the Civil War*, 14–15.

p. 116   *Second Corps casualties*: *OR*, ser. 1, vol. 21, 129–30, 228; Duncan, "Campaign of Fredericksburg," in Duncan, *Medical Department of the United States in the Civil War*, 20, gives a lower casualty figure.

p. 116   *CB's return to Lacy House*: CB to Soldiers' Relief Society, Watkins, N.Y., Dec. 3, 1863, CB Papers LC.

p. 116   *"I cannot tell you," "covered every foot," "A man who could find," five men on common cupboard*: ibid., CB Lecture [typescript] and Notes for a Lecture [undated], ibid.; CB "Black Book," CB Papers SC. Pryor, *Clara Barton*, 107, also describes CB in the Lacy House hospital.

pp. 116–117   *CB's caring for late arrivals, Second Bull Run veteran*: "Clara Barton's Lesson," newspaper clipping, CB Papers LC; CB Diary, Mar. 7–27, 1866, ibid.

p. 117   *"at the foot of a tree"*: Charles I. Glicksberg (ed.), *Walt Whitman and the Civil War* (reprint 1933 ed., New York: A. S. Barnes, [n. d.]), 69–70; Walt Whitman, *Correspondence*, ed. Edwin Haviland (6 vols., New York: New York University Press, 1961–1977), 1:590.

p. 117   *CB's pillows for amputees*: Welles to Dear Brethren, Dec. 27, 1862, newspaper clipping, CB Papers LC.

p. 117   *haunting scenes in Lacy House, Edgar Newcomb, Wiley Faulkner*: CB "Black Book," CB Papers SC; CB Lecture [typescript], Lecture [undated], and Notes for a Lecture [undated], CB Papers LC; CB to Henry Wilson, Jan. 18, 1863, ibid.; Halstead interview, ibid.; "Clara H. Barton," newspaper clipping, ibid. Scene with Edgar M. Newcomb from Margaret Hamilton to CB, Feb. 15, 1903, and CB to Hamilton, Feb. 24, 1903, ibid.; A. B. Weymouth to CB, Dec. 20, 1882, ibid. Pryor, *Clara Barton*, 107, and Ross, *Angel of the Battlefield*, 54, also quote CB's remarks about her blood-soaked clothing.

p. 118   *other women at Fredericksburg*: Brockett and Vaughan, *Woman's Work in the Civil War*, 119, 157, 254, 445. Marie Tebe, a *vivandière* with the 114th Pennsylvania, was reported to have followed the regiment into battle and to have helped some of its men set up a field hospital on December 13 (Hall, *Patriots in Disguise*, 7). But CB appears to have been the only volunteer Northern female nurse and relief worker in Fredericksburg during the battles of Dec. 11 and 13.

p. 118   *Wilson's visit, "draft every man"*: CB to Mary Norton, Jan. 19, 21, 1863, MN Papers DU; Abbott, *Cobbler in Congress*, 129, 147; McKay, *Wilson*, 160; Henry Villard, *Memoirs* (2 vols., Boston: Houghton Mifflin, 1904), 1:388–90.

p. 119   *evacuations began*: Letterman, *Medical Recollections*, 87; Duncan, "Campaign of Fredericksburg," in Duncan, *Medical Department of the United States in the Civil War*, 30–35.

p. 119   *CB's hot toddies, "you saved my life," Wiley Faulkner, "mere little white bundle"*: "Clara H. Barton," newspaper clipping, CB Papers LC; CB Lecture [typescript], ibid.; CB "Black Book," CB Papers SC; CB to P.M. [H?] Watson [circa Mar. 1863], CB Papers LC. The recipe for milk punch is in Marion Harland, *Breakfast, Luncheon and Tea* (New York: Scribner, Armstrong and Co., 1875), 367.

p. 119   *Sgt. Plunkett*: CB Lecture [undated], CB Papers LC; CB to Senate Committee on Military Affairs, Feb. 22, 1863, ibid., and also in Barton, *Life of Clara Barton*, 1:229.

p. 119   *CB's return to Washington*: CB's pass from Gen. Sturgis, CB Papers SC; CB Diary, Jan. 1, 1863, CB Papers LC.

p. 119   *"fires of Fredericksburg," scene in CB's apartment, CB's pledge*: CB to Annie Childs, May 28, 1863, CB Papers AAS. An edited version of the letter is in Barton, *Life of Clara Barton*, 1:221–24. My quotations are from the original.

p. 120   *Wilson's response, "more joy"*: Nason and Russell, *Life and Public Services of Henry Wilson*, 324; Abbott, *Cobbler in Congress*, 146. Wilson attacked slavery in the border by getting blacks there enrolled in the military, with the promise of freedom to follow (ibid., 147). For Andrew and what became the Fifty-fourth Massachusetts Regiment, see Louis F. Emilio, *A Brave Black Regiment: History of the Fifty-fourth Regiment of Massachusetts Volunteer Infantry, 1863–1865* (3d ed., Salem, N.H.: Ayer Co., 1990), 2–5.

p. 120   *"vast"* and *"mighty" change*: CB to Frances Gage, May 1, 1864, CB Papers LC.

p. 120   *"seeing and answering everybody"*: CB to Mary Norton,
              Jan. 19, 21, 1863, MN Papers DU.

p. 120   "our cause ought not to fail": CB to Mary Norton, Jan. 19,
              21, 1863, ibid.; Pryor, *Clara Barton*, 109. Pryor, 110, incor-
              rectly states that, after Fredericksburg, CB never again
              served under fire. In fact, as this study shows, she served
              under fire on Morris Island in the summer of 1863. I would
              also dispute Pryor's assertion that by Jan. 1863 CB "had
              already given her greatest service and seen her most direct
              action." My study argues that she continued to give "great
              service" despite the obstacles against her.

p. 121   *"I had only to lay aside," "Oh, the crowd,"* CB's kitten:
              Ross, *Angel of the Battlefield*, 54–55.

p. 121   *CB's Brady photograph*: CB to Mary Norton, June 26, 1863,
              MN Papers DU; information on Brady's studio from
              Dorothy Meserve Kunhardt and Philip B. Kunhardt, Jr.,
              Mathew Brady and His World (Alexandria, Va.: Time-Life
              Books, 1977), 52–53.

p. 121   *CB's "campaign diary" entries*: [no dates], CB Papers LC.
              On Jan. 7, 1863, CB wrote Annie Childs that she had tried
              to keep "a record, a *campaign diary*" of her war experi-
              ences but had found it difficult to do so in the field (CB
              Papers AAS).

p. 121   *CB's visit to Lincoln Hospital*: CB Diary [undated], CB
              Papers LC; CB Lecture [typescript], ibid; CB "Black
              Book," CB Papers SC.

p. 121   *"hero of the* four words": ibid.

p. 122   *Plunkett brothers, CB, and Wilson*: My scene derives from
              CB to "My dear Friend," Apr. 1885, CB Papers LC; CB
              Notes for a Lecture [undated], ibid.; CB to Senate
              Committee on Military Affairs, Feb. 22, 1863, ibid., and
              quoted in Barton, *Life of Clara Barton*, 1:228–30.

p. 123   *Medical Department performance*: Duncan, "Campaign of
              Fredericksburg," in Duncan, *Medical Department of the
              United States in the Civil War*, 37–40.

p. 123   *efforts at Medical Department reform*: Adams, *Doctors in
              Blue*, 36–39, 89–90. See also Maxwell, *Lincoln's Fifth
              Wheel*, 195–96.

p. 123   *"the imperfect system"*: CB to Wilson, Jan. 8, 1863, CB
              Papers AAS.

p. 124   *Rucker and CB*: Sam Barton to Dear Cousin Mary, Jan. 18,
              1863, Barton, *Life of Clara Barton*, 1:227; CB to Mary
              Norton, Jan. 19, 21, 1863, MN Papers DU.

p. 124   *CB prevailed on Wilson*: CB to Wilson, Jan. 18, 1863, CB
              Papers LC.

p. 124   *CB and Welles back with AOP*: Sam Barton to Dear Cousin
              Mary, Jan. 18, 1863; Barton, *Life of Clara Barton*, 1:227.
              Catton, *Glory Road*, 103, and Foote, *Civil War*, 2:129, for
              the start of the new campaign.

p. 124   *"surely the stormiest," "little chimney," "I have no idea"*: CB to Mary Norton Jan. 21, 25, MN Papers DU.

p. 125   *"rivers of deep mire," "free-for-all"*: Catton, *Glory Road*, 103, 105.

p. 125   *"THIS WAY TO RICHMOND"*: Foote, *Civil War*, 2:130.

p. 125   *AOP back at Falmouth*: CB to Mary Norton, Jan. 21, 25, 1863, MN Papers DU.

p. 125   *"some destructive fate"*: Catton, *Glory Road*, 107.

p. 125   *"I do not believe"*: Duncan, "Campaign of Fredericksburg," in Duncan, *Medical Department of the United States in the Civil War*, 36. Foote, *Civil War*, 2:130, reports that desertions rose to an "all-time high."

p. 125   *Dix nurses at Aquia Creek, "drank water from holes"*: Dannett, *Noble Women of the North*, 217.

p. 125   *Dix's campaign against unaffiliated nurses*: Young, *Women of the Crisis*, 55–63.

p. 125   *"the most gifted"*: Brockett and Vaughan, *Woman's Work in the Civil War*, 553. Lisa May, "Justice to the Women's Work: The New England Women's Auxiliary Association, 1861–66" (May 26, 1990), 8, quotes Louisa Schuyler as saying that Abby May was "the mainspring of that branch and the originator of everything good and new in it." May's paper is an excellent, well-documented account of the NEWAA. The roster of officers in Dec. 1862, and a list of Massachusetts towns and villages sending supplies to the organization is in the NEWAA Papers MHS. For the Sanitary Commission's field relief agents, see Stillé, *History of the Sanitary Commission*, 251–62.

p. 125   *"loyal women of our land"*: Miss Isa Gray to Dear Madam, Dec. 22, 1862, NEWAA Papers MHS.

p. 126   *"overflowed with plentiousness"*: Livermore, *My Story of the War*, 233, 248.

p. 126   *"independent Sanitary Commission of one"*: Harwood, "Army Surgeon's Story," *St. Louis Illustrated Magazine* (Apr. 1883), 136.

p. 126   *CB's return to Washington*: CB to Mary Norton, Jan. 25, Feb. 12, 1863, MN Papers DU.

p. 126   *"large colony of the fragments," "I find that my scholars"*: Welles to Dear Brethren, Dec. 27, 1862, newspaper clipping, and obituary for Welles in the *American Baptist*, newspaper clipping, CB Papers LC. The documents I consulted do not specifically state that Clara lost Welles as her assistant, but this must have been the case, since she now sought to make David Barton her assistant. Welles would die of acute heart disease in Nov. 1863.

p. 126   *CB's need for a male companion*: this was hardly unusual for her time. Mary Kelley's *Private Woman Public Stage: Literary Domesticity in Nineteenth-Century America* (New York: Oxford University Press, 1984), 180–216 ("A Man's

Clothing"), points out that women writers of the mid-nineteenth century, feeling obliged to hide or deny their "unwomanly" career aspirations, often used male relatives or friends to handle their business arrangements (most states at that time did not allow women to sign contracts, for instance), or to accompany the women when they sought to conduct business matters in their own behalf.

p. 127   *"companion and protector"*: CB to "My dear cousin" [Elvira Stone], Feb. 20, 1863, CB Papers AAS; CB's Henry Wilson, Jan. 27, 1863, CB Papers LC. Pryor, *Clara Barton*, 110–11, relates the story of David's appointment and Wilson's involvement in it somewhat differently.

p. 127   *"I know how my brother's name"*: ibid.

p. 127   *"I have only to beg you"*: CB to David Barton, Feb. 20, 1863, ibid.

p. 127   *"Your rank, a Capt."*: CB to David, Feb. 20 [21?], CB Diary [typescript version], ibid.

p. 128   *"without hesitation"*: CB to "My dear cousin" [Elvira Stone], Feb. 20, 1863, CB Papers AAS.

p. 128   *David's acceptance*: CB to David Barton, Feb. 25, Mar. 8, 1863, and CB's draft of David's letter to Rucker, Mar. 8, 1863, CB Papers LC. The latter is in CB's handwriting. David's commission as assistant quartermaster of volunteers with rank of captain was signed by Lincoln Mar. 12, 1863; the appointment was retroactive, dating from Nov. 26, 1862. The commission is in ibid.

p. 128   *"The Army of the Potomac"*: Helen Nicolay, *Lincoln's Secretary: A Biography of John G. Nicolay* (New York: Longmans, Green and Co., 1949), 166.

p. 128   *"I am buried"*: CB to Elvira Stone, Mar. 2, 1863, CB Papers LC.

p. 129   *"the broad platform," "not only opens"*: CB to Mrs. A. C. Thomas, Mar. 9, 1863, CB Diary [typescript version], ibid. See also CB to Mrs. Lamb, undated, ibid.

p. 129   *the gown from Mrs. Stout*: CB to Mrs. Stout, Mar. 17, 1863, ibid.

pp. 129–130   *CB and Mary Norton in Hightstown*: "How Clara Barton Taught the First Public School in New Jersey," ms., CB Papers LC; CB to Bernard Vassall, Oct. 19, Nov. 30, Dec. 31, 1851, Jan. 24, Mar. 14, 26, 1852, ibid.; CB Diary, Feb. 12–May 25, 1852, ibid. CB referred to Mary as "a good Republican abolitionist Quaker girl" (CB to Mary Norton, Oct. 15, 1855, copy AL Collection SLRC). See Pryor, *Clara Barton*, 40–45, for a brilliant description of CB's stay with the Nortons, her courtship with Charley, and her teaching experiences.

p. 130   *"I am so weary," "am more and more certain"*: CB Diary, Mar. 2, 23, 1852. Pryor, *Clara Barton*, 44, identifies Joshua Ely, "a farmer who lived near Philadelphia," as CB's romantic interest at this time. She was also attracted to a Hightstown farmer named Edgar Ely, whose daughter attended CB's school. A self-taught man who could read Latin, French, German, Italian, Greek, Hebrew, and Arabic, he struck CB as "one of the most impressive men I ever met." He invited her to visit his home and library and often walked with her to and from school. "I could cite curiosities about him all day," CB wrote her nephew Bernard. CB's depression seems to have begun on Feb. 12, 1852, when she recorded in her diary: "rather melancholy don't know why I receive no intelligence from certain quarters." It isn't clear if this was a reference to Joshua Ely or another suitor or potential suitor. A former pupil who had gone West to hunt for gold entertained notions of marrying CB and may well have written her. In fact, after CB moved to Bordentown, N.J., he returned from the West and begged her to marry him, but she turned him down. They remained friends, however. See Barton, *Life of Clara Barton*, 1: 78.

p. 130

"True I laugh and joke," "I will indulge": CB Diary, Mar. 11, 1852, CB Papers LC. CB's depression had steadily worsened since Feb. 1852, and it seemed to be fueled by more than simply a deteriorating relationship, though that certainly played its part. On March 2 she wrote in her diary: "[I] cannot but think it will be a quiet resting time when all these cares and vexations and anxieties are past and I no longer give nor take offence I am badly organized to live in the world, or among society I have participated in too many of its unpleasant scenes have always looked on its most unhappy features and have grown weary of life at an age when other people are enjoying it most." On Mar. 13 she wrote in her diary: "evening tried to write again, but felt too much depressed cannot think what has been the matter with me for the last two or three days could not feel worse if I had heard some sad inteligence [*sic*] from my best friends. . . . Laid my head on the piano until 8 in the evening, and went to bed in the dark." On Mar. 31 she confided in her diary: "no letters and do not care to receive any, have grown indifferent and do not care to hear or write don't know what has come over me am somewhat surprised that I do not hear from J.L.E. [Joshua Ely]. think must be sick or worse but fear to imagine I am thinking tonight of the future and what my next move must be wish I had some one to advise me or that I could speak to some one of it had ever one poor girl so many strange wild thoughts and no one to listen or share one of them or even realize that my head contains an idea beyond the present foolish moment. I know how it will be at length I shall take a strange sudden start and be off somewhere and all will

wonder at and judge and condemn, but I like the past I shall survive it all and go on working at some trifling, unsatisfactory thing and half paid at that how foolish to think and who can help it but I will not allow myself in any more such grumbling." Here clearly was a woman who longed for independence, meaningful, fulfilling work, and responsibility over her own life. As she wrote her nephew Bernard, she had felt this way before, when, without employment, she had been forced to live at home and had felt trapped. "I have lived on years wishing myself dead all the time," she wrote. "I could feel no other way at home and how could I get away. I had no where to go no one to go [to] nothing to go with and no way of earning my living if I did go anywhere. . . . I had no employment" (letter of Mar. 14, 1852, ibid.). In New Jersey, at least, she had that, even if she was living with the Norton family. Thanks to her fierce will and go-ahead spirit, CB pulled herself out of her depression and in May moved to Bordentown, N.J., where she established its first public school. See Pryor, *Clara Barton*, 45–54.

p. 130   *"Dear Mary, it grieves me"*: Mar. 8, 1859, MN Papers DU.

p. 130   *"dear darling sister"*: in her letters to Mary, in ibid., CB referred to her as "My darling Sister," "dear darling sister," "my darling sis," or "My darling." Their loving friendship and endearing salutations were typical of women of their day.

pp. 130–31   *"a little tiny," "Please do this"*: CB to Mary Norton, Jan. 25, 1863, ibid.

p. 131   *"You dont know"*: CB to Mary Norton, Feb. 12, 1863, ibid.

p. 131   *David appointed to Port Royal*: CB Diary [circa Mar. 1863], CB Papers LC.

p. 132   *"family held me responsible"*: CB to Henry Wilson, Apr. 7, 1864, in CB Journal, Apr. 7, 1864, ibid.

p. 132   *"very particular," CB's decision to accompany David*: CB to Judge Barton, Mar. 31, 1863, CB Papers AAS; CB Diary [circa Mar. 1863], CB Papers LC; Barton, *Life of Clara Barton*, 1: 225–37.

p. 132   *"I believe my services"*: CB to Assistant Secretary of War P. M. [H.?] Watson [circa Mar. 1863], ibid. An undated typescript of the letter is in CB Papers AAS, and it is quoted in Barton, *Life of Clara Barton*, 1: 226. William E. Barton dates the letter early in 1863, but it could not have been written until March, since in early March she was still contemplating serving in Virginia.

p. 132   *"The Quarter Master"*: CB's order from P. M. [H.?] Watson, Assistant Secretary of War, CB Papers SC.

p. 133   *"the bearer Miss Clara H. Barton"*: CB had at least two similar versions of Preston's letter of introduction. I quote the one addressed to Medical Director, St. Helena, Mar. 23

[29?], 1863, ibid. When she reached Morris Island, CB gave a slightly different version to Lt. Col. John Elwell. It is dated Mar. 29, 1863, and is in JE Papers WRHS.

p. 133 *"made great haste"*: CB to Judge Barton, Mar. 31, 1863, CB Papers AAS. Information on Sam Barton from CB to "my dear friend charlie" [Charlie Newcomb], June 15, 1863, CB Papers LC, and CB to Mary Norton, Feb. 12, 1863, MN Papers DU. See also Sam Barton to his mother, June 3, 1863, CB Papers LC.

p. 133 *"horrorgraph," "I was thin"*: CB to Mary Norton, June 26, 1863, MN Papers DU.

p. 133 *Gen. Sturgis's visit*: CB to Judge Barton, Mar. 31, 1863, CB Papers AAS; CB Diary [undated entries], CB Papers LC.

p. 133 *CB and David to New York, "Being out in the field"*: ibid.; CB Diary, Apr. 2, 1863, ibid.

p. 134 *Sgt. Plunkett's visit*: CB Diary [Apr. 3, 1863], CB Papers LC.

p. 134 *voyage to Hilton Head*: CB Diary, Apr. 4, 7, 1863, ibid.

PART THREE: HILTON HEAD AND BATTERY WAGNER

p. 137 *description of Sea Islands and Beaufort*: Charlotte Forten, *A Free Negro in the Slave Era: The Journal of Charlotte L. Forten*, ed. Ray Allen Billington (reprint 1953 ed., New York: Collier Books, 1961), 144; Esther Hill Hawks, *A Woman Doctor's Civil War: Esther Hill Hawks' Diary*, ed. Gerald Schwartz (Columbia: University of South Carolina Press, 1984), 34; Rev. Frederick Denison, *Shot and Shell: The Third Rhode Island Heavy Artillery in the Rebellion, 1861–1865* (Providence: J.A. & R.A. Reid, 1879), 55.

p. 137 *description of Hilton Head military post*: Charles Nordruff, "Two Weeks at Port Royal," *Harper's New Monthly Magazine* (June 1863), 112; photograph of manor with odd-looking signal tower, U.S. Army Military History Institute, Carlisle Barracks, Pa. reproduced in Stephen B. Oates, "Clara Barton's Finest Hour," *Timeline* (Jan.–Feb. 1993), 10.

p. 137 *post heavily fortified, "The whole work"*: Denison, *Shot and Shell*, 63.

p. 137 *"the first gun is to be fired"*: CB Diary, Apr. 7, 1863, CB Papers LC.

p. 138 *John Elwell description*: Thomas Hall Shastid, "A Short Biography of Dr. John J. Elwell," *American Medicine* (Feb. 1909), 95; photographs of Elwell in Oates, "Clara Barton's Finest Hour," *Timeline* (Jan.–Feb. 1993), 10. Barton, *Life of Clara Barton*, 1: 241, incorrectly identifies Captain Samuel T. Lamb as chief quartermaster of the department.

p. 138   *not "in the very best"*: Elwell to "Col. Halpin" [*sic*], Apr. 8,
              1863, CB Papers SC. Major Charles G. Halpine identified
              in *OR*, ser. 1, vol. 28, pt. 1, 191.

p. 138   *JE's broken leg*: Elwell's Pension Records, NARA; CB
              Diary, Apr. 7, 1863, CB Papers LC.

p. 138   *"spoke in the most consoling manner"*: CB Diary, Apr. 7,
              1863, ibid.

p. 138   *CB's letter of introduction, "American Florence
              Nightingale"*: JE Papers WRHS; Elwell to "Col. Halpin"
              [*sic*], Apr. 8, 1863, CB Papers SC.

p. 138   *CB's concerns about Charleston Expedition*: CB to Mary
              Norton, Apr. 9, 1863, MN Papers DU.

p. 139   *Captain Lamb*: CB Diary, Apr. 9, 1863, CB Papers LC;
              Sarah Lamb to CB, Sept. 14, 1863, ibid.

p. 139   "polite *warfare*," *"ladies and girls"*: CB to Mary Norton,
              Apr. 26, 1863, MN Papers DU; CB to Elvira Stone, May
              24, 1863, CB Papers LC; information on Hunter and his
              wife from Peter Burchard, *One Gallant Rush: Robert Gould
              Shaw and His Brave Black Regiment* (New York: St.
              Martin's Press, 1965), 97.

p. 139   *officers' invitations*: CB Diary, Apr. 9, 1863, ibid.; Ross,
              Angel of the Battlefield, 50.

p. 139   *not "quite inclined"*: CB Diary, Apr. 9, 1863, CB Papers
              LC.

p. 139   *"Our fleet is battering"*: CB to Mary Norton, Apr. 9, 1863,
              MN Papers DU.

p. 139   *"much to the consternation," "old soldier times," "A dull
              life"*: CB Diary, Apr. 11, 12, 13, 1863, CB Papers LC.

p. 140   *Hunter sketch*: Nordruff, "Two Weeks at Port Royal,"
              Harper's New Monthly Magazine 27 (Mar., 1863), 112, 118;
              Ray Allen Billington, Introduction to Forten, *Free Negro in
              the Slave Era*, 28; Benjamin Quarles, *The Negro in the Civil
              War* (Boston: Little, Brown, 1953), 109–13; Dudley Taylor
              Cornish, *The Sable Arm: Negro Troops in the Union Army,
              1861–1865* (reprint 1956 ed., New York: W. W. Norton,
              1966), 37–53; Joseph T. Glatthaar, *Forged in Battle: The
              Civil War Alliance of Black Soldiers and White Officers*
              (New York: Free Press, 1990), 6–7; James M. McPherson,
              *The Struggle for Equality: Abolitionists and the Negro in
              the Civil War and Reconstruction* (Princeton: Princeton
              University Press, 1964), 107–8.

p. 140   *Hunter's visit with CB*: CB Diary, Apr. 13, 1863, CB Papers
              LC; other information on du Pont's expedition from
              Johnson and Buel, *Battles and Leaders*, 4: 7–11, 35–42; 54;
              E. Milby Burton, *The Siege of Charleston, 1861–1865*
              (Columbia: University of South Carolina Press, 1970),
              135–49; Richard S. West, *Gideon Welles, Lincoln's Navy
              Department* (Indianapolis: Bobbs-Merrill Co., 1943),
              221–37.

p. 141   *"single brief effort"*: quoted in Burton, *Siege of Charleston*, 143. See also William M. Fowler, Jr., *Under Two Flags: The American Navy in the Civil War* (reprint 1990 ed., New York: Avon Books, 1991), 256–57; and John Niven, *Gideon Welles: Lincoln's Secretary of the Navy* (New York: Oxford University Press, 1973), 438.

p. 141   *"possession of that City," "I thank you darling"*: CB to Mary Norton, Apr. 26, 1863, MN Papers DU.

p. 141   *"a kind of relative"*: CB Diary, Apr. 9, 1863, CB Papers LC.

p. 142   *"old extemporized rig," "alpaca skirt"*: CB to Annie Childs, May 29, 1863, CB Papers AAS.

p. 142   *CB's relationship with Lamb*: CB Diary, Apr. 15, 18, 29, May 7, June 19, 22, 26, Nov. 1, 1863, CB Papers LC; CB to Mary Norton, June 26, 1863, MN Papers DU; CB to Annie Childs, Nov. 1, 1863, CB Papers LC; information on mockingbirds from Nordruff, "Two Weeks at Port Royal," *Harper's New Monthly Magazine* (June 1863), 112.

p. 142   *"We think this rather advanced"*: CB to Mary Norton, June 26, 1863, MN Papers DU.

p. 142   *"only the other side," CB's and David's quarters, "We are most kindly"*: ibid.; CB Diary, Apr. 14, 1863, CB Papers LC.

p. 142   *"grotesque," "of the highest order," "a most refined," "old scraps of poetry"*: CB to Elvira Stone, May 24, 1863, ibid.

p. 143   *"mess" with Lambs, "a nice charcoal range"*: CB to Mary Norton, June 26, 1863, MN Papers DU.

p. 143   *"The white sand"*: CB to Elvira Stone, May 24, 1863, CB Papers LC.

p. 143   *Hilton Head history, Port Royal experiment*: Katherine M. Jones, *Port Royal Under Six Flags* (Indianapolis: Bobbs-Merrill Co., 1960), 245–76; Billington, Introduction, Forten, *Free Negro in the Slave Era*, 28–32; Willie Lee Rose, *Rehearsal for Reconstruction: The Port Royal Experiment* (reprint 1964 ed., New York: Oxford University Press, 1976), 3–198.

p. 143   *blacks on Hilton Head*: Rose, *Rehearsal*, 121–40; Forten, *Free Negro in the Slave Era*, 142; Hawks, *A Woman Doctor's Civil War*, 35, 37.

p. 145   *"in the very heart"*: Forten, *Free Negro in the Slave Era*, 145.

p. 145   *"a charming young lady"*: CB to Mary Norton, June 26, 1863, MN Papers DU; CB Diary, Apr. 25, 1863, CB Papers LC.

p. 145   *"colored boys," CB and black women*: CB Diary, Apr. 15, June 16, 1863, ibid.; Barton, *Life of Clara Barton*, 1: 242.

p. 145–146   *Elwell profile*: Elwell's Pension Records, NARA; Shastid, "A Short Biography of Dr. John J. Elwell," *American Medicine* (Feb. 1909), 94–95; "John Johnson Elwell," *The*

Encyclopedia of Cleveland History, ed. David D. Van Tassel and John G. Grabowski (Bloomington: Indiana University Press, 1987), 373; "Toledo to the Herald," Oct. 6, 1863, newspaper clipping, CB Papers LC.

p. 146   *"manly man"*: CB Diary, Apr. 7, 1863, ibid.

p. 146   *CB's diary entries about Elwell*: Apr. 19, 21, 25, 27, 28, 1863, ibid.; see also CB to Mary Norton, June 26, 1863, MN Papers DU.

p. 146   *CB as Elwell's nurse*: Elwell to CB, June 18, 23, July 1876, Dec. 20, 1883, CB Papers LC; Shastid, "A Short Biography of Dr. John J. Elwell," *American Medicine* (Feb. 1909), 94; CB Diary, Apr. 28, 1863, ibid.

p. 146   *"little paradise of flowers," "excellent judgment"*: CB Diary, Apr. 28, May 4, 1863, ibid. CB paid a one-day visit on Apr. 28 and returned on May 3 for a more extensive stay with Frances Gage.

p. 147   *Frances Gage's background, "waged moral warfare"*: Brockett and Vaughan, *Women's Work in the Civil War*, 684.

p. 147   *"a woman's true province"*: Frances Gage to "My dear Mrs Martin," May 20, 1848, LMS Papers OHS.

p. 147   *Gage's feminist activities, "craziness"*: Clara Cornelia Holtzman, "Frances Dana Gage" (master's thesis, Ohio State University, 1931), 12, 13–38; CB to Mrs. Martin, Feb. 11 [?], Nov. 14 [?], May 20, 1848, LMS Papers OHS.

p. 147   *"better time," "Let the mothers"*: Gage to "Dear Mrs. Martin," Feb. 11 [?], and Gage to "My dear Mrs. Martin," May 20, 1848, ibid.

p. 147   *"the platform amidst hissing," fires, "incendiaries"*: Brockett and Vaughan, *Women's Work in the Civil War*, 688.

p. 147   *Gage and Civil War, Gages to Port Royal*: Holtzman, "Gage," 40–42.

p. 148   *CB's three-day visit, "dense as a black velvet," "sea of bloom"*: CB Diary, May 3–6, 1863, CB Papers LC; "dense" from Ross, *Angel of the Battlefield*, 59; CB to Frances Gage, May 1, 1863, CB Journal, ibid.

p. 148   *"dear womanly friend"*: CB to Mary Norton, June 26, 1863, MN Papers DU.

p. 148   *"Her reading and vigor:"* CB Diary, May 28, 1863, also May 3, 1863, CB Papers LC.

p. 148   *"He is my friend"*: CB to Mary Norton, June 26, 1863, MN Papers DU; also see CB Diary, Apr. 15, 1863, CB Papers LC.

p. 148   *"glow of the eye," "best" friend*: Elwell to CB, June 24 or July 5 and July 1876, CB Papers LC. For Elwell and his wife, see Elwell to CB, Dec. 20, 1883, ibid.; and CB Diary, May 15, June 27, 1863, ibid.

p. 148   *"all the law allows"*: Elwell to CB, July 1876, ibid.; quoted slightly differently in Pryor, *Clara Barton*, 114.

pp. 148–149   *CB and Elwell as lovers*: Pryor, *Clara Barton*, 114, was the first CB biographer to assert that "the intimacy of their letters strongly suggest a relationship of the closest kind." But Henle, "Against the Fearful Odds," argues that the relationship was platonic. I agree with Pryor, yet put a different emphasis on the Elwell-CB romance. Pryor contends that Elwell was the love of CB's life, but I believe the evidence suggests that it was the other way around: that CB was the love of Elwell's life. Long after the Civil War, he wrote her love letters in which he addressed her as his "darling" and recalled their passionate moments together on Hilton Head in 1863. For CB, the romance appears to have been a wartime fling that cooled by the autumn and winter of that year. Elwell's postwar letters to CB are in CB Papers LC. CB's postwar letters to him are in JE Papers WRHS.

p. 149   *"immediately after intercourse"*: An American Physician, *Reproductive Control, or A Rational Guide to Happiness* (Cincinnati: no pub., 1855), 53, as published in Charles Rosenberg and Carroll Smith-Rosenberg (eds.), *Birth Control and Family Planning in Nineteenth-Century America* (New York: Arno Press, 1974); Linda Gordon, *Woman's Body, Woman's Right: A Social History of Birth Control in America* (New York: Grossman Pub., 1976), 66. Pryor, *Clara Barton*, 114, incorrectly states that CB had gone through menopause "a few months earlier" and thus had no worries about pregnancy. In fact, CB entered menopause following a severe bout of dysentery in August 1863, after she and Elwell became lovers. See CB's notes to Dr. Foote (circa 1875), CB Papers SC.

p. 149   *"pessaries," "a weak solution," "upper part," "effective preventive"*: An American Physician, *Reproductive Control*, 67; Dr. J. Soule, *Science of Reproduction and Reproductive Control* (1856), 65–66, in Rosenberg and Smith-Rosenberg, *Birth Control and Family Planning*; James Ashton, *The Book of Nature; Containing Information for Young People Who Think of Getting Married* (New York: Brother Jonathan Office, 1865), 41, in ibid. See also Janet Farrell Brodie, "Family Limitation in American Culture, 1830–1900" (Ph.D. dissertation, University of Chicago, 1982), 98–165.

p. 149   *"French secret," condoms*: Soule, *Science of Reproduction and Reproductive Control* (1856), 65–66, in Rosenberg and Smith-Rosenberg, *Birth Control and Family Planning*; An American Physician, *Reproductive Control, or A Rational Guide to Happiness*, 53, in ibid.; Ashton, *The Book of Nature*, 41, in ibid.; Brodie, "Family Limitation," 73–85, has a detailed, scholarly discussion of condoms and their use and availability in CB's time.

p. 149   *notes, "Birdie," "My Pet," "nest"*: Elwell to CB, May 12, 14, Sept. 1, Oct. 3, 9, 27, 1863, CB Papers SC.

p. 149   *"My Dear Sister"*: Elwell to CB, May 9, 1863, ibid.

p. 150   *"Sunrise at the east window"*: "Birdie" [CB] to Elwell [undated], JE Papers WRHS.

p. 150   *"John Boy"*: Elwell to CB [no date], and Elwell to CB, May 14, Nov. 3, 1863, CB Papers SC; Elwell to CB, July 1876, CB Papers LC.

p. 150   *"My Birdie, I have had"*: Elwell to CB, Oct. 27, 1863, ibid.

pp. 150–151   *"loving hours," "When my life," "darling," "for ever and ever"*: Elwell to CB, July 1876, CB Papers LC; "extract" in Elwell's handwriting [undated], JE Papers WRHS; also Elwell to CB, May 24, 1888, CB Papers LC; and CB Diary, June 1, 1863, ibid.

p. 151   *trip to Port Royal*: CB to Elwell, Feb. 17, 1872, JE Papers WRHS.

p. 151   *"elegant friend"*: CB to Mary Norton, June 26, 1863, MN Papers DU.

p. 151   *"John Boy will be busy"*: Elwell to CB [undated], CB Papers SC; carriage rides in notes in ibid. and CB Diary, entries of May and early June 1863, CB Papers LC.

p. 151   *"Shall we take," "Sister Clara," "My dear brother," "This has been so beautiful"*: Elwell to CB, May 19, 1863, ibid.; Elwell to CB [undated], CB Papers SC; CB to Elwell [undated], JE Papers WRHS; Elwell to CB [undated], CB Papers SC.

p. 151   *"Thus far shall thou go"*: "Birdie" [CB] to Elwell [undated], JE Papers WRHS.

p. 151   *"He is so sensitive"*: CB Diary, June 27, 1863, CB Papers LC.

p. 152   *"object," "All things conspire"*: CB Diary, Apr. 22 and 23, also Apr. 18 and 24, 1863, CB Papers LC.

p. 152   *Leander Poor*, "Hooker was whipped," *"God is great"*: ibid., May 8 and 16, 1863.

p. 152   *"Still unsettled"*: ibid., May 11, 1863.

p. 152   *"a most emphatic no," Captain Griffin, "God's will not mine," "My Dear Sister, shall we"*: ibid., May 14, 15, 16, and 17, 1863: Elwell to CB, May 14, 1863, CB Papers SC.

p. 153   *storm, Frances Gage's departure*: CB Diary, May 27–29, 1863, CB Papers LC.

p. 153   *"I do not deserve such friends"*: quoted in Barton, *Life of Clara Barton*, I, 244. CB describes the gift of the Bible in her diary, June 3, 1863, CB Papers LC, but doesn't make it clear which "Col."—Colonel Elwell, Colonel Davis, or Colonel Littlefield—presented it to her. William E. Barton thinks it was Elwell, but I think it was one of the other colonels present.

p. 153   *the dinner*: CB Diary, June 3, 1863, CB Papers LC.

p. 154   *Colonel Montgomery*: ibid.; Robert Gould Shaw's descriptions in Russell Duncan (ed.), *Blue-Eyed Child of Fortune:*

the Civil War Letters of Robert Gould Shaw, (Athens: University of Georgia Press, 1992), 356, 357.

p. 154   *54th Mass*: ibid., 282–352; Emilio, *Brave Black Regiment*, 1–50.

p. 154   *"There is not a man"*: James Henry Gooding, *On the Altar of Freedom: A Black Soldier's Civil War Letters from the Front,* ed. Virginia M. Adams, (Amherst: University of Massachusetts Press, 1991), 24.

p. 154   *"We saw the most beautiful"*: CB Diary, June 3, 1863, CB Papers LC.

p. 154   *Harriet Tubman, Montgomery's Combahee River raid: Boston Commonwealth,* July 10, 1863, claimed that she conceived and led the raid; see also Earl Conrad, "The Charles P. Wood Manuscripts of Harriet Tubman," *Negro History Bulletin* (Jan. 1950), 92–93; Earl Conrad, *Harriet Tubman: Negro Soldier and Abolitionist* (New York: International Publishers, 1942), 38; Sarah H. Bradford, *Harriet Tubman: The Moses of Her People* (reprint 1886 ed., New York: Corinth Books, 1961), 99–102; and CB Diary, June 3, 1863, CB Papers LC. Forten, *Free Negro in the Slave Era*, 180, records that Tubman was living in Beaufort and keeping "an eating house." Details about the raid itself are in Montgomery's report as quoted in Denison, *Shot and Shell,* 155; see also 156–57.

p. 155   *"fought well"*: CB Diary, June 3, 1863, CB Papers LC.

p. 155   *"negroes were of all ages"*: CB to my dear cousin [Annie], July 3, 1863, CB Papers AAS.

p. 155   *"every mark," "choice entertainment"*: ibid.; contents of Higginson's tent from Forten, *Free Negro in the Slave Era,* 173. Higginson's was "the first American regular army regiment of freed slaves." Howard N. Meyer, Introduction to Thomas Wentworth Higginson, *Army Life in a Black Regiment* (reprint 1869 ed., New York: W. W. Norton, 1984), 163–76.

p. 155   *CB and Susie King Taylor*: Taylor, *Reminiscences of My Life in Camp. . . .* (reprint 1902 ed., New York: Arno Press, 1968), 2, 15–17, 21–30; Quarles, *Negro in the Civil War,* 228; General Hospital Number Ten for Colored Troops identified in Hawks, *A Woman Doctor's Civil War,* 47–50.

p. 156   *Elwell and CB*: CB Diary, June 9, 15 and passim 1863, CB Papers LC; CB to nephew Stephen Barton, June 25, 1863, ibid.; Elwell's affidavit, June 1, 1866, Elwell's Military Service Records, NA; CB to Mary Norton, June 26, 1863, MN Papers DU.

p. 156   *"to little purpose," "eating, sleeping," "It is a great change"*: CB Diary, June 8, 1863, CB Papers LC; CB to Mary Norton, June 26, 1863, MN Papers DU.

p. 156   *CB's leg and ear trouble, siege guns to Folly Island*: CB Diary, June 13–15, 1863, CB Papers LC.

pp. 156–57   *Department of South command changes*: Burton, *Siege of Charleston*, 143; Burchard, *One Gallant Rush*, 111; Lincoln, *CW*, 6:310.

p. 157   *Gillmore profile*: Herbert M. Schiller, *The Bermuda Hundred Campaign* (Dayton: Morningside House, 1988), 16; *OR*, ser. 1, vol. 28, pt. 1, 34; Johnson and Buel, *Battles and Leaders*, 4:20, 54–55; Gillmore's Military Service Records, NARA AGO; Sifakis, *Who Was Who in the Civil War*, 249.

p. 157   *"we are to have"*: CB Diary, June 20, 1863, CB Papers LC.

p. 158   *CB's letter to T. W. Meighan*: June 24, 1863, ibid.; quoted with editorial changes in Barton, *Life of Clara Barton*, 1:245–48. My quotations are from the original letter.

p. 159   *troop movements*: CB to nephew Stephen Barton, June 25, 1863, CB Papers LC; Johnson and Buel, *Battles and Leaders*, 4:56–57.

p. 159   *rebel invasion of Pennsylvania*: CB Diary, June 24, 26, 1863, CB Papers LC; CB to nephew Stephen Barton, June 26, 1863, ibid.

p. 159   *June 28 storm*: CB Diary, June 28, 1863, ibid.; Emilio, *Brave Black Regiment*, 47; Duncan (ed.), *Blue-Eyed Child of Fortune*, 360.

p. 159   *"praying, shooting, burning" Darien raid*: ibid., 355–56, 43–45; Emilio, *Brave Black Regiment*, 41–44.

p. 159   *"He seems anxious"*: quoted in ibid., 48.

p. 159   *"stay late," "he came home"*: CB Diary, June 28, 1863, CB Papers LC.

pp. 159–160   *July 1 horseback ride and quotations*: ibid., July 1, 1863.

p. 160   *"I begin to feel," "pushing his whole dept."*: ibid., July 3, 5–6, 1863; also CB to "my dear Cousin," July 3, 1863, CB Papers AAS.

p. 160   *Gillmore's plan of operations*: *OR*, ser. 1, vol. 28, pt. 1, 8–9; Johnson and Buel, *Battles and Leaders*, 4:22, 54–60; Burton, *Siege of Charleston*, 114, 120, 153–54; Gregory J. W. Urwin, "I Want You to Prove Yourselves Men," *Civil War Times Illustrated* (Nov.–Dec. 1989), 44.

p. 160   *"planned and sent off"*: CB to Elvira Stone, July 11, 1863, CB Papers LC.

pp. 160–61   *CB and Elwell's preparations*: CB Diary, July 5, 9, 1863, ibid.; Elwell to CB, Aug. 23, 1898, ibid.; Leander Poor to Elvira Stone [Sept. 5, 1863], ibid.; Pryor, *Clara Barton*, 115–16, describes CB's ambulance.

p. 161   *"like going into a wilderness"*: Leander Poor to Elvira Stone [Sept. 5, 1863], CB Papers LC; CB Diary, July 9, 1863, ibid. Johnson and Buel, *Battles and Leaders*, 4:706, and Burton, *Siege of Charleston*, 318, identify the *Canonicus* as a monitor. CB merely referred to it as "a steamer" (CB to My dear Cousin, July 11, 1863, CB Papers AAS).

p. 161   *military preparations Folly and James islands*: OR, ser. 1, vol. 28, pt. 1, 9–11, 13, 194–95; Johnson and Buel, *Battles and Leaders*, 4:56–57; Burton, *Siege of Charleston*, 154; Higginson, *Army Life in a Black Regiment*, 163–76.

p. 161   *"quarantine burying-ground"*: OR, ser. 1, vol. 28, pt. 1, 279.

p. 161   *moving troops across the bar, field hospital*: CB to Elvira Stone, July 11, 1863, CB Papers LC; J. J. Craven's report in Barnes, *Medical and Surgical History*, 1:pt. 1, 241.

p. 161   *"one sullen shot," cannonade*: CB to Elvira Stone, July 11, 1863, CB Papers LC; CB Diary, July 10, 1863, ibid.; CB to "My dear Cousin," July 11, 1863, CB Papers AAS; OR, ser. 1, vol. 28, pt. 1, 12, 354–55; Johnson and Buel, *Battles and Leaders*, 4:58, 72; Denison, *Shot and Shell*, 160–66; Daniel Eldredge, *The Third New Hampshire and All About It* (Boston: E. B. Stillings and Co., 1893), 298–302; Burton, *Siege of Charleston*, 155; Burchard, *One Gallant Rush*, 120.

p. 162   *"lay hidden by the lushes," "and lo! our troops," "brave old Fort"*: CB to Elvira Stone, July 11, 1863, CB Papers LC (typescript in CB Papers AAS); also see CB Diary, July 10, 1863, CB Papers LC.

p. 162   *"was sending up columns," floating battery, "one most terrible gun," "tips of the waves"*: CB to "My dear Cousin," July 11, 1863, CB Papers AAS; and CB to Elvira Stone, July 11, 1863, CB Papers LC. See also Eldredge, *Third New Hampshire*, 302–3.

p. 162   *"While all were tired"*: CB to Elvira Stone, July 11, 1863, CB Papers LC.

p. 163   *"a succession of low"*: Johnson and Buel, *Battles and Leaders*, 4:58. See also OR, ser. 1, vol. 28, pt. 1, 15.

p. 163   *Wagner's structure and armament*: Burchard, *One Gallant Rush*, 120; 133, Johnson and Buel, *Battles and Leaders*, 4:23; Emilio, *Brave Black Regiment*, 69–70; Burton, *Siege of Charleston*, 153.

p. 163   *"an enfilading and a cross-fire"*: Johnson and Buel, *Battles and Leaders*, 4:68–69.

pp. 163–164   *first assault on Wagner*: OR, ser. 1, vol. 28, pt. 1, 12, 210, 355–56, 360; Burton, *Siege of Charleston*, 158, 163; Johnson and Buel, *Battles and Leaders*, 4:58; Abraham J. Palmer *The History of the Forty-Eighth Regiment of New York State Volunteers in the War for the Union, 1861–1865* (Brooklyn: The Veterans' Association of the Regiment, 1885), 88–93.

p. 164   *Gillmore's new plan of attack*: OR, ser. 1, vol. 28, pt. 1, 14, 267; Johnson and Buel, *Battles and Leaders*, 23, 59; Cornish, *Sable Arm*, 151–52.

p. 164   *Wagner strengthened*: *Battles and Leaders*, 4: 23; *OR*, ser. 1, vol. 28, pt. 1, 419, 431, and Burton, *Siege of Charleston*, 161, give the peak rebel strength as about 1,300 men.

p. 164   *Craven's field hospital*: Craven's report in Barnes, *Medical and Surgical History*, vol. 1, pt. 1, 242. Dr. Marsh and Sanitary Commission from Stillé, *History of the Sanitary Commission*, 407.

p. 165   *"Miss Barton, Hospital nurse"*: pass from Gillmore, July 11, 1863, CB Papers SC.

p. 165   *"I said yesterday," Elwell's departure*: CB Diary, July 12, 1863, CB Papers LC; Toledo to *New York Herald*, Oct. 6, 1863, newspaper clipping, ibid.

p. 165   *CB's ambulance ride to Morris Island*: CB Diary, July, 13 1863, ibid.

p. 165   *Dr. Kittinger profile*: Kittinger's Military Service and Pension Records, NARA.

p. 165   *"It is a narrow strip"*: CB to Lizzie Shaver, Oct. 1, 1863 [typescript], CB Papers LC.

p. 165   *soldiers' ailments*: CB Diary, July 15, 1863, ibid.; CB to Lizzie Shaver, Oct. 1, 1863, ibid.

p. 165   *"Directly up the beach"*: CB to Judge Ira Barton, July 16, 1863, CB Papers AAS: *Wabash* armament from Johnson and Buel, *Battles and Leaders*, 4:51.

p. 166   *James Island skirmish, first battle as a regiment, "baptism of fire"*: Emilio, *Brave Black Regiment*, 52–63; Gooding, *On the Altar of Freedom*, 36–38; Duncan (ed.), *Blue-Eyed Child of Fortune*, 49–50; CB Diary, July 16, 1863, CB Papers LC; Burchard, *One Gallant Rush*, 125, for "baptism."

p. 167   *"It is not for us"*: Gooding, *On the Altar of Freedom*, 38.

p. 167   *CB's horseback ride*: CB Diary, July 16, 1863, CB Papers LC; data on *Paul Jones* from Johnson and Buel, *Battles and Leaders*, 4:51.

p. 167   *dinner on* Philadelphia, *"I said I* would not go": CB Diary, July 16, 1863, CB Papers LC.

p. 168   *"a little wormy," "almost overwhelmed," "Everything is going"*: CB Diary, July 16, 17, 1863, CB Papers LC; Elwell to CB, July 17, 1863, CB Papers SC.

p. 168   *thunderstorm*: CB Diary, July 18, 1863, CB Papers LC; Emilio, *Brave Black Regiment*, 66.

pp. 168–69   *Union bombardment*: ibid.; *OR*, ser. 1, vol. 28, pt. 1, 15, 76, 417, 572; Burton, *Siege of Charleston*, 162–63; Urwin, "I Want You to Prove Yourselves Men," *Civil War Times Illustrated*, 48; Johnson and Buel, *Battles and Leaders*, 4:16, 59, 63; Emilio, *Brave Black Regiment*, 71; Burchard, *One Gallant Rush*, 132.

p. 169   *rebel flag story*: Wagner commander William B. Taliaferro in *OR*, ser. 1, vol. 28, pt. 1, 418; also in Eldredge, *Third New Hampshire*, 314, 320; Denison, *Shot and Shell*, 168; and Burton, *Siege of Charleston*, 163.

p. 169   *council of commanders on Lookout Hill*: Johnson and Buel, *Battles and Leaders*, 4:59; Ira Berlin et al. (eds.), *Free at Last: A Documentary History of Slavery, Freedom, and the Civil War* (New York: New Press, 1992), 445.

p. 170   *"run right over it"*: ibid.

p. 170   *"I told the General"*: Eldredge, *Third New Hampshire*, 320; also in Burton, *Siege of Charleston*, 170.

p. 170   *CB on Lookout Hill, arrival of Fifth-fourth Massachusetts*: CB Diary, July 18, 1863, CB Papers LC; Emilio, *Brave Black Regiment*, 73.

pp. 170–71   *attack formation, "solid phalanx"*: Johnson and Buel, *Battles and Leaders*, 4:74; Emilio, *Brave Black Regiment*, 77; Duncan (ed.), *Blue-Eyed Child of Fortune*, 52; CB to Dear Friends, Dec. 8, 1865, CB Papers LC.

p. 171   *war's most vigorous barrage*: Urwin, "I Want You to Prove Yourselves Men," *Civil War Times Illustrated*, 48, argues the point. Rebel commander Taliaferro estimated the total Union shells fired on Wager as 9,000 and reported that others thought the figure was higher than that. See *OR*, ser. 1, vol. 28, pt. 1, 417; P. G. T. Beauregard repeated his claim in ibid., 76. Urwin's article and Burton, *Siege of Charleston*, 162, put the figure at 9,000.

p. 171   *"Boys, I am"*: quoted in Emilio, *Brave Black Regiment*, 77, and in Burchard, *One Gallant Rush*, 136.

p. 171   *"Forward!" "a sheet of flame"*: Emilio, *Brave Black Regiment*, 79, 80; Burchard, *One Gallant Rush*, 137.

p. 171   *"scene was grand," "A long line"*: CB Diary, July 18, 1863, CB Papers LC; CB Lecture [undated], ibid.

pp. 171–72   *assault of Fifty-fourth Massachusetts, Shaw's death, hand-to-hand fighting*: Emilio, *Brave Black Regiment*, 80–84; Federal and rebel reports in *OR*, ser. 1, vol. 28, pt. 1, 15–16, 346–47, 362–63, 418–20; Johnson and Buel, *Battles and Leaders*, 4:59; Gooding, *On the Altar of Freedom*, 38–40; Isaiah Price, *History of the Ninety-seventh Regiment, Pennsylvania Volunteer Infantry, During the War of the Rebellion, 1861–1865* (Philadelphia: published by the author, 1875), 167–70; Burchard, *One Gallant Rush*, 137–41; Duncan (ed.), *Blue-Eyed Child of Fortune*, 52; CB quotation ("*Our men are on the parapets*") from CB Diary, July 18, 1863, CB Papers LC.

p. 172   *Strong's and Putnam's assaults*: Burton, *Siege of Charleston*, 165–66; Eldredge, *Third New Hampshire*, 315–16; Price, *History of the Ninety-seventh Pennsylvania*, 170–73; Emilio, *Brave Black Regiment*, 86–87, *OR*, ser. 1, vol. 28, pt. I, 347–49.

p. 173   *"My God, our men"*: Toledo to *New York Herald*, Oct. 6, 1863, clipping, CB Papers LC.

p. 173   *"long hair streaming," Elwell's horseback dash, "More men!"*: Shastid, "A Short Biography of John J. Elwell,"

American Medicine, XV, 94; Toledo to *New York Herald*, Oct. 6, 1863, newspaper clipping, CB Papers LC; CB to Ira M. Barton, Oct. 11, 1863, ibid.; CB Lectures [undated], ibid.

p. 173   *Elwell wounded*: Elwell's account in Barton, *Life of Clara Barton*, 1:251; Epler, *Life of Clara Barton*, 82. CB described the episode in her postwar lectures and notes for lectures, CB Papers LC.

p. 173   *"in a most unmartial manner"*: Elwell quoted in Epler, *Life of Clara Barton*, 82, and Barton, *Life of Clara Barton*, 1:251.

p. 173   *CB helped Elwell*: Pryor, *Clara Barton*, 116, citing "A Noble Woman: What Clara Barton Did for Humanity During the War," *New York Daily Graphic*, Dec. 12, 1884, writes that CB "reached Elwell and bathed his face until he regained consciousness." But the *Daily Graphic* doesn't mention John Elwell; I could find no evidence that CB nursed Elwell on the beach. In his account quoted in Barton, *Life of Clara Barton*, 1:251, Elwell doesn't even mention CB. Yet in another statement (see the "thrilling stories" reference in the next note), he remembered seeing her rescue Colonel Voris on the beach. This and other surviving records suggest that CB did help Elwell back to Union lines. It would have been completely out of character for her to stand by without helping him or to assist Voris without also assisting her lover.

p. 173   *Col. Voris, "dabbling in the sand"*: CB Lecture [undated], CB Papers LC; "Clara Barton: General J. J. Elwell Tells Thrilling Stories of Her Work in the Field during the Civil War," typescript [undated], CB Papers AAS; Barton, *Life of Clara Barton*, 1:249, 250–51.

p. 173   *"insensible to fear"*: "Clara Barton: General J. J. Elwell Tells Thrilling Stories of Her Work in the Field during the Civil War," typescript [undated], CB Papers AAS.

p. 173   *"There, with the shot and shell"*: "Vidette," newspaper clipping, CB Papers LC.

p. 173–74   *"the only woman present"*: "A Noble Woman: What Clara Barton Did for Humanity During the War," *New York Daily Graphic*, Dec. 12, 1884.

p. 174   *"They mowed us down"*: Gooding, *On the Altar of Freedom*, 39; for the role of Stevenson's reserve brigade, see Alfred S. Roe, *The Twenty-fourth Regiment Massachusetts Volunteers 1861–1866* (Worcester: Twenty-fourth Veteran Association, 1907), 205–6. Palmer, *History of the Forty-eighth Regiment of New York State Volunteers*, 118, says that the heavens that night were "black with clouds." Dr. Marsh's Sanitary team from Soulé, *History of the Sanitary Commission*, 410.

p. 174	*continued rebel fire*: Price, *History of the Ninety-seventh Pennsylvania*, 174.
p. 174	*CB and Mary Gage, "Bury me here"*: CB Diary, July 18 1863, CB Papers LC; CB Lectures [undated] and Notes for a Lecture [undated], ibid.
p. 174	*"I can see again"*: quoted in Quarles, *Negro in the Civil War*, 16.
p. 174	*ambulance drivers ran their teams*: Price, *History of the Ninety-Seventh Pennsylvania*, 174.
p. 174	*"The sands about our hospital tents," "They too many for us," "permitted to strike"*: CB Lectures [undated], CB Papers LC.
p. 175	*"that fearful night"*: CB to Dear Friends, Dec. 8, 1865, ibid.
p. 175	*evacuation of wounded*: Craven's report in Barnes, *Medical and Surgical History*, vol. 1, pt. 1, 242.
p. 175	*"a dear, blessed woman"*: quoted in Barton, *Life of Clara Barton*, 1: 252; CB Diary, July 19, 1863, CB Papers LC.
p. 175	*"It seemed as if"*: CB to Dear Friends, Dec. 8, 1865, ibid. CB reported in her diary, July 18, 1863, ibid., that she "did not sleep" during the night after the assaults.
p. 175	*"almost exclusively"*: quoted in Emilio, *Brave Black Regiment*, 98; Burchard, *One Gallant Rush*, 142, and Burton, *Siege of Charleston*, 168, also describe the dead bodies littering the beach.
p. 175	*"We buried him"*: variations of this oft-quoted line in Urwin, "I Want You to Prove Yourselves Men," *Civil War Times Illustrated*, 51; Saunders Redding, "Tonight for Freedom," *American Heritage* (June 1958), 90; Burchard, *One Gallant Rush*, 143. See also Duncan (ed.), *Blue-Eyed Child of Fortune*, 54, 55.
p. 175	*Union casualties: OR*, ser. 1, vol. 28, pt. 1, 210; Johnson and Buel, *Battles and Leaders*, 4: 59–60, 74; Emilio, *Brave Black Regiment*, 88, 95–96, 392, 431.
p. 175–76	*assessment of Gillmore*: I'm persuaded by the cogent analysis in Burton, *Siege of Charleston*, 164, 169–70.
p. 176	*"one of the most terrific"*: quoted in Burton, *Siege of Charleston*, 247. The quotation, however, is not in the source he cites.
p. 176	*"They moved up as gallantly"*: quoted in Emilio, *Brave Black Regiment*, 94. Similar praise by a Confederate is in Eldredge, *Third New Hampshire*, 331.
p. 176	*black man's Bunker Hill, "fighting with clenched teeth"*: Duncan (ed.), *Blue-Eyed Child of Fortune*, 53; Lincoln, *CW*, 6:410.
p. 176	*"I can never forget"*: CB to Brown and Duer, Mar. 13, 1864, CB Papers LC.
p. 176	*evacuations*: Craven's report in Barnes, *Medical and Surgical History*, 1:pt. 1, 242; CB Diary, July 19, 1863, CB Papers LC.

p. 177   *"My Baby as I told him"*: ibid., July 22, 1863.

p. 177   *Gillmore's new strategy, parallel trenches: OR*, ser. 1, vol.
                28, pt. 1, 16–24, 272–303, 317–25; Johnson and Buel,
                Battles and Leaders, 4:60–61; Denison, *Shot and Shell*,
                171–78; Roe, *Twenty-fourth Regiment Massachusetts
                Volunteers*, 210–21.

p. 177   *rebel sharpshooters*: Major T. B. Brooks reports this in *OR*,
                ser. 1, vol. 28, pt. 1, 277; also in Burton, *Siege of
                Charleston*, 174.

p. 177   *rebel mortars*: Emilio, *Brave Black Regiment*, 113; Johnson
                and Buel, *Battles and Leaders*, 4: 61, 62.

p. 177   *temperature, flies, and sand fleas*: Leander Poor to Cousin
                Sam, Aug. 23, 1863, CB Papers LC; Emilio, *Brave Black
                Regiment*, 109.

p. 178   *story of Robert Leggett and quotations*: "A Woman's Work
                on a Battlefield," Bridgeport, Conn., Aug. 28, 1866, news-
                paper clipping, CB Papers LC; "The Soldiers Record,"
                clipping in CB Scrapbook, ibid.; "Clara Barton: General
                J. J. Elwell Tells Thrilling Stories of Her Work in the
                Field During the Civil War," typescript [undated], CB
                Papers AAS; CB to David Barton, Aug. 4 [5?], 1862
                [1863], ibid. *Catalogue of Connecticut Volunteer
                Organizations* . . . (Hartford: Press of Case, Lockwood and
                Co., 1864), gives his full name as Robert Leggett of New
                London. A different version of the Leggett story is in "A
                Noble Woman: What Clara Barton Did for Humanity
                During the War," *New York Daily Graphic*, Dec. 12,
                1884. Pryor, *Clara Barton*, 116, also tells the story of
                Leggett and CB but says that it happened during the
                assaults of July 18. In fact, it occurred a few days and per-
                haps even a week later.

p. 178   *"little army," "of weary siege"*: CB Lecture [undated], CB
                Papers LC. Quoted somewhat differently in Pryor, *Clara
                Barton*, 117.

p. 178   *"You cannot forget"*: CB to Elvira Stone, Aug. 30, 1863, CB
                Papers LC.

p. 178   *wounded men of 100th New York and quotations*: CB
                Diary, July 22, 1863, ibid.

p. 179   *"poor fellow, when carefully"*: CB to Elvira Stone, Aug. 30,
                1863, ibid.

p. 179   *wounded Pennsylvanian, George Peets, and quotations*: CB
                to David Barton, Aug. 4 [5?], 1862 [1863], CB Papers AAS.

pp. 179–80   *Elwell's letter to CB*: July 26, 1863, CB Papers SC.

p. 180   *"salt junk," "old beef," "the mouldiest, wormiest," "a little
                piece of salt meat"*: CB to Elvira Stone [undated], CB
                Papers LC; CB to Wilson, Apr. 7, 1864, ibid.

p. 180   *Mary Gage sent home, "shelterless sands"*: CB to Elvira
                Stone [undated], ibid.; CB to Wilson, April 7, 1864, ibid.
                See also CB to Mary Norton [undated], MN Papers DU.

pp. 180–181 *CB's dispute with Dr. Green, "receipted, and was responsible," "a worthless, pain saving"*: CB to Wilson, Apr. 7, 1864, CB Papers LC; CB Journal, Dec. 5, 1863; Green to Elwell, Aug. 16, 1863, CB Papers SC.

p. 181 *CB and the male principal in New Jersey*: Pryor, *Clara Barton*, 50–54, is the best account of this episode. See also "Clara Barton Opens the First Public School in New Jersey," 12, and Halstead interview, CB Papers LC; Barton, *Life of Clara Barton*, 1:74; and Ross, *Angel of the Battlefield*, 21.

p. 181 *"six weeks of unremitting toil"*: CB Journal, Dec. 5, 1863, CB Papers LC.

p. 181 *CB's dysentery*: CB's notes for Dr. Foote [circa 1875], CB Papers SC; Sam [?] to Cousin Sam, Aug. 23, 1863, CB Papers HL; CB to Annie Childs, Oct. 27, 1863 [typescript], CB Papers LC; CB Journal, Dec. 5, 1863, ibid.

p. 181 *"dead face"*: CB to Wilson, Apr. 7, 1864, ibid.

p. 181 *"almost by force"*: quoted in Epler, *Life of Clara Barton*, 84; date of CB's departure from Morris Island from Sam [?] to Cousin Sam, Aug. 23, 1863, CB Papers HL. Siege of Fort Sumter from Johnson and Buel, *Battles and Leaders*, 4: 61–62.

p. 181 *CB ill on Hilton Head, "that it was the opinion"*: Leander Poor to Elvira Stone, Aug. 27, 1863, CB Papers LC; Sam [?] to Cousin Sam, Aug. 23, 1863, CB Papers HL. I failed to find out who this was. Pryor, *Clara Barton*, 119, says that Leander and another CB cousin were stationed in the Department of the South but doesn't name the other cousin. The Sam who wrote Cousin Sam, in the letter cited above, referred to David Barton as "Uncle David," so he apparently wasn't CB's cousin.

p. 182 *"tenderly," "My slightest suggestion"*: CB's note in Leander Poor to Elvira Stone, Aug. 27, 1863, CB Papers LC.

p. 182 *"a piece of petty spite"*: Lt. Col. James Hall to CB, Nov. 15, 1863, ibid.

p. 182 *"old self," "Happy as I am"*: Leander Poor to Elvira Stone, Aug. 27, 1863, ibid.; CB to Elvira Stone, Aug. 30, 1863, ibid.; also CB to Mary Norton, Aug. 31, 1863, MN Papers DU.

p. 182 *"She is filled with patriotism"*: Elvira Stone to CB, Aug. 21, 1863, CB Papers LC.

p. 183 *CB's letter to Elvira*: circa early Sept. 1863, ibid.

p. 183 *"an intelligent colored woman"*: Leander Poor to Elvira Stone [Sept. 5, 1863], ibid.

p. 183 *Elwell's arrangement, "beautifully supplied," "spacious tents"*: Pryor, *Clara Barton*, 118; Leander Poor to Elvira Stone, Aug. 27, [Sept. 5], 1863, CB Papers LC.

p. 184 *Hall, Green, and location of CB's tents*: Lt. Col. Hall to Capt. Lamb, Sept. 2, 1863, ibid.

p. 184   *"I have just seen"*: Hall to Lamb, Sept. 8, 1863, CB Papers SC.

p. 184   *"in effect that Wagner"*: Sam [?] to Cousin Sam, Sept. 6, 1863, CB Papers HL; *OR*, ser. 1, vol. 28, pt. 1, 268, and Johnson and Buel, *Battles and Leaders*, 4: 63–64, for fifth parallel and siege of Wagner.

p. 185   *"To think of establishing"*: Leander Poor to Elvira Stone [Sept. 5, 1863], CB Papers LC.

p. 185   *bombardment of Wagner*: *OR*, ser. 1, vol. 28, pt. 1, 300–2, 483–89; Johnson and Buel, *Battles and Leaders*, 4: 63–64, 64n; Denison, *Shot and Shell*, 185.

p. 185   *"the most remarkable in history"*: Price, *History of the Ninety-seventh Pennsylvania*, 408.

p. 185   *"like lightning," "mission of death," "every detail of our works"*: quoted in Roe, *Twenty-fourth Regiment Massachusetts Volunteers*, 225.

p. 185   *"As a pyrotechnic achievement"*: Johnson and Buel, *Battles and Leaders*, 4:62.

p. 185   *torpedoes, "edged or bladed hooks"*: Denison, *Shot and Shell*, 186. Also see Price, *History of the Ninety-seventh Pennsylvania*, 200.

p. 185   *"Dead bodies"*: Eldredge, *Third New Hampshire*, 367, quoting Band Master Ingalls; Burton, *Siege of Charleston*, 179. Similar descriptions are in Price, *History of the Ninety-seventh Pennsylvania*, 199; Gooding, *On the Atlar of Freedom*, 58; and Roe, *Twenty-fourth Regiment Massachusetts Volunteers*, 223–24.

p.186   *"Fort Wagner is a work"*: Gillmore to H. W. Halleck, Sept. 7, 1863, *OR*, ser. 1, vol. 28, pt. 1, 93.

p. 186   *casualties and assessment of Gillmore's campaign*: *OR*, ser. 1, vol. 28, pt. 1, 210; Burton, *Siege of Charleston*, 156, 179–80.

p. 186   *"a confused mass"*: Johnson and Buel, *Battles and Leaders*, 4:17.

p. 186   *"It will all come"*: CB to Amelia Barton, Sept. 17, 1863, CB Papers HL; *OR*, ser. 1, vol. 28, pt. 1, 726–27, and Burton, *Siege of Charleston*, 196, for the failed Union naval attack.

p. 186   *CB's Wagner trophies*: CB to Ira Barton, Oct. 14, 1863, CB Papers LC.

p. 186   *skulls*: Susie King Taylor, *Reminiscences*, 31.

p. 186   *"We have captured"*: CB to Mr. Parker, Dec. 9, 1863, CB Journal, CB Papers LC; edited version in Barton, *Life of Clara Barton*, 1:261.

p. 187   *"The Brig. Gen. Commanding"*: E. W. Smith to CB, Sept. 15, 1863, CB Papers LC; copy in Department of the South, Letters Sent (old volume 21), NARA.

p. 187   *"After four weeks," CB in Beaufort, "supremacy over all," "each hospital," "How in reason's name"*: CB Journal, Dec.

5, 1863, ibid. Pryor, *Clara Barton*, 118–19, also describes this episode.

p. 188   *she had never felt so depressed*: In her letter to General Quincy A. Gillmore, Sept. 18, 1863, Department of the South, Letters Received, 1863, NARA, CB said that the episode was "the severest ordeal of my life" and that she intended to return to her "former fields" where she was "both needed and wanted."

p. 188   *fall social functions, "all bright, clear"*: CB to Amelia Barton, Sept. 17, Oct. 6, 8, 1863, CB Papers HL; CB to Mary Norton, Oct. 2, 1863, MN Papers DU.

p. 188   *"all the dust"*: CB to Amelia Barton, Oct. 6, 1863, CB Papers LC.

p. 188   *"There is no war news"*: CB to Mary Norton, Oct. 2, 1863, MN Papers DU.

p. 188   *"Pet," "Dear Birdie," "I not only tell you," her "friend"*: Elwell to CB, Oct. 27, 1863, CB Papers SC; also Elwell to CB, Oct. 9, Nov. 3, 1863, ibid.; CB to Elwell, Nov. 14, 1863, JE Papers WRHS.

p. 189   *"I have an idea"*: CB to Elwell [circa fall 1863], ibid. The context of this note is not known, but the tone of it suggests that CB and Elwell, or CB and someone in his presence, might have had a disagreement about women in war, and this was CB's response.

p. 189   *CB and Frances Gage friendship*: Although my account is based on the original documents and other sources, I am indebted to Elizabeth Pryor for the idea of Fanny Gage's friendship with and extraordinary influence on CB. See Pryor, *Clara Barton*, 120–22.

p. 189   *Gage in Illinois, lectures in East*: F. D. Gage letter in *Anti-Slavery Standard*, May 18, 1864, clipping, CB Papers LC; Holtzman, "Frances Dana Gage," 43.

p. 189   *"Scores of young men," "only for the dying"*: F. D. Gage letter, July 28, 1863, newspaper clipping, CB Papers LC.

p. 190   *Fanny's praise for CB's war work*: Gage letter, May 29, 1864, newspaper clipping, CB Scrapbooks, ibid.

p. 190   *long walks, "pine dew," "O, Lord," "dancing to the shore"*: Gage's verse to CB [circa fall 1863], ibid.

p. 190   *"dear adopted mother," "my dear darling daughter," "to the death"*: CB Diary, Jan. 1, 1877, ibid.; Gage to CB, Sept. 20, Dec. 26, 29, 1867, May 7, 1871, June 12, 1874, July 7, 1876, Aug. 12, 1878, Dec. 26, 1882, ibid.

p. 190   *"Aunt Fanny dear"*: CB to Frances Gage [circa fall 1863], ibid.

pp. 190–191   *"Your kindness & care," "I know not dear Clara"*: Gage to CB, Oct. 22, 1863, ibid.; Gage to CB [circa fall 1863], ibid.

p. 191   *"Think of this noble"*: Gage to CB [circa fall 1863], ibid.; also quoted in Pryor, *Clara Barton*, 122.

p. 191   *Parris Island scene, Bryant's poetry, Gage's poem to CB, "the talent"*: CB to Mary Norton, Nov. 15, 1863, MN Papers DU; Gage's poem in CB Papers LC and in *Anti-Slavery Standard*, newspaper clipping, ibid.

p. 192   *"Justice to the negro"*: Brockett and Vaughan, *Women's Work in the Civil War*, 690.

p. 192   *Gage, abolitionism, and women's rights*: Gage's letters to Mrs. Lilly Martin in LMS Papers OHS; Holtzman, "Frances Dana Gage," 12–35; Brockett and Vaughan, *Women's Work in the Civil War*, 684–88; Eleanor Flexner, *Century of Struggle: The Woman's Rights Movement in the United States* (rev. ed., Cambridge: Harvard University Press, 1975), 41–102.

p. 192   *"Don't let her speak"*: quoted in Holtzman, "Frances Dana Gage," 18.

p. 192   *"Look at me!"*: quoted in Hertha Pauli, *Her Name Was Sojourner Truth* (reprint 1962 ed., New York: Avon Books, 1976), 177.

p. 192   *"with one united voice," "Be bold, be firm"*: quoted in Holtzman, "Frances Dana Gage," 17–18, 58. For Gage's feminist influence on CB, see Pryor, *Clara Barton*, 120.

p. 193   *Gage's concern for blacks*: Holtzman, "Frances Dana Gage," 43–44; Brockett and Vaughan, *Women's Work in the Civil War*, 689.

p. 193   *"thousands of old," "in a state," smallpox epidemic, "some tons of clothing," "I told them," "of the strongest character"*: CB to Brown & Duer, Mar. 13, 1864 [typescript], CB Papers LC. From a modern perspective, Clara's remarks about the character traits of African-Americans sound paternalistic. But in her day, her comments were considered an enlightened white view of blacks.

p. 194   *Wagner "trophies," "rebel 'shell' and 'shot' "*: CB to Ira M. Barton, Oct. 14, 1863, CB Papers AAS; see also CB to Annie Childs, Oct. 2, 14, 1863, ibid., and CB to Ladies of Soldiers' Relief Committee, Worcester, Oct. 10, 1863, CB Papers LC.

p. 194   *Ruffin and John Brown pikes*: Avery O. Craven, *Edmund Ruffin, Southerner: A Study in Secession* (Baton Rouge: Louisiana State University Press, 1932), 178–80; Betty L. Mitchell, *Edmund Ruffin, A Biography* (Bloomington: Indiana University Press, 1981), 145–46.

p. 194   *CB and John Brown*: CB to brother Stephen Barton [circa late 1859], CB Papers LC, quoted in Barton, *Life of Clara Barton*, 1:102–4.

p. 194   *"with the fingers," "for the benefit," "as it occurs"*: CB to Ira M. Barton, Oct. 14, 1863, CB Papers AAS.

p. 194   *"the rebel torpedo"*: Elvira Stone to CB, Oct. 23, 1863, CB Papers LC.

p. 195   *"perhaps they contemplate"*: CB to Annie Childs, Nov. 1,

1863 [typescript], CB Diary, ibid. See also CB to Mary Norton, Nov. 15, 1863, MN Papers DU.

p. 195 *CB's need for a wardrobe*: CB to Annie Childs, Oct. 14, 16, 1863, CB Papers AAS.

p. 195 *"a very pretty"*: CB to Annie Childs, Oct. 16, 1863, ibid.

p. 195 *box of clothes from Annie and CB quotations*: CB to Annie Childs, Nov. 1, 1863, ibid. (typescript in CB Papers LC).

p. 196 *"Oftener than I could wish"*: CB to Annie Childs, Oct. 27, 1863, CB Papers AAS (typescript in CB Papers LC).

p. 196 *"Reply to my question"*: CB to Elwell [circa early Nov. 1863], CB Papers SC.

p. 196 *"I don't know"*: Elwell to CB, Nov. 6, 1863, ibid.

p. 196 *"Don't feel bad," Gillmore's pass*: Elwell to CB, Nov. 8, 1863, ibid.; pass and note to CB from Gillmore, Nov. 9, 1863, ibid.

p. 197 *David Barton, "very light, and without," "creaturely comfort"*: Sam [?] to Cousin Sam, Sept. 6, 1863, CB Papers HL; CB to Henry Wilson, Apr. 7, 1864, CB Papers LC.

p. 197 *Gage and David Barton's departure, "most intimate lady friend"*: CB to Mary Norton, Nov. 15, 1863, MN Papers DU.

p. 197 *"take charge of what they"*: ibid.

p. 197 *Ohio surgeon on woman's special role*: Dannett, *Noble Women of the North*, 252; Nina Bennett Smith, "The Women Who Went to the War: The Union Army Nurse in the Civil War" (Ph.D. dissertation, Northwestern University, 1981), 103.

p. 197 *Elwell and friends v. CB's return to Morris Island, "Folly Island folly"*: CB to Mary Norton, Nov. 15, 1863, MN Papers DU; CB Journal, Dec. 2, 7, 1863, CB Papers LC; CB to Elwell, Dec. 2, 1863, JE Papers WRHS.

p. 197 *"My friends here at the Head"*: CB to Mary Norton, Nov. 15, 1863, MN Papers DU.

p. 198 *"a fine regiment," "the one that led," "splendid little lady"*: CB to Mary Norton, Dec. 12, 1863, ibid.; Harriet Hawley profile from Brockett and Vaughan, *Women's Work in the Civil War*, 416; nickname "Hatty" from Dannett, *Noble Women of the North*, 302.

p. 198 *"Wind and weather permitting"*: CB to Hawley and other wives, Nov. 24, 1863, CB Papers LC.

p. 198 *CB's Thanksgiving on St. Helena Island, "After dinner"*: CB to Sam Barton, Dec. 3, 1863, CB Papers HL; CB to Mary Norton, Dec. 12, 1863, MN Papers DU.

p. 199 *"We have quite a little"*: CB Journal, Dec. 2, 3, 1863, CB Papers LC.

p. 199 *"'tell' to more purpose," "like a huge bar of silver," "the arrangements might be"*: ibid., Dec. 3, 4, 1863.

p. 199 *"esteemed friend," "should never be allowed"*: ibid., Dec. 5, 7, 1863; part of Marsh's quotation is also in Ross, *Angel of the Battlefield*, 65–66.

pp. 199–200   *CB and Mrs. Dorman, CB quotations*: CB Journal, Dec. 6, 1863, CB Papers LC.

p. 200   *Upperman letter, "Mr. Holloway," CB upset*: ibid., Dec. 10, 11, 1863; Pryor, *Clara Barton*, 123; Barton, *Life of Clara Barton*, 1:259.

p. 201   *"Dear Col., I said"*: CB to Dear Col. [Dec. 10, 1863], JE Papers WRHS; CB Journal, Dec. 10, 1863, CB Papers LC.

pp. 201–202   *CB's letter to Holloway*: Dec. 11, 1863, ibid.

p. 202   *CB to Mary Norton*: Dec. 12, 1863, MN Papers DU.

p. 202   *CB's menopause, "menstruation ceased suddenly"*: CB's notes for Dr. Foote [circa 1875], CB Papers SC. My discussion of CB and menopause was influenced by several authoritative studies: Germaine Greer, *The Change: Women, Aging and the Menopause* (New York: Alfred A. Knopf, 1992), which is rich with insight and analysis; Paula Weideger, *Menstruation and Menopause: The Physiology, and Psychology, the Myth and the Reality* (New York: Alfred A. Knopf, 1976), especially chap. 9; Lois W. Banner, *In Full Flower: Aging Women, Power, and Sexuality* (New York: Alfred A. Knopf, 1992), 15, 20, 181–85, 192–93, 258, 273–310, with its magnificent phrase, the "autumnal majesty" of one's middle years (182); Madeline Gray, *The Changing Years: The Menopause Without Fears* (Garden City: Doubleday, 1981); and Carroll Smith-Rosenberg, *Disorderly Conduct: Visions of Gender in Victorian America* (New York: Oxford University Press, 1985), 182–97. I was also influenced by Carolyn Heilburn's inspiring discussion of "what a woman's biography or autobiography should look like" and her account of Dorothy Sayers's "change of direction" in her middle years (Heilburn, *Writing a Woman's Life*, 27–28, 58–59).

p. 203   *CB's dyed hair, lying about her age*: Pryor, *Clara Barton*, x. As Pryor points out, CB boasted that she had never had a strand of gray on her head. As for photographs of her, CB wrote Mary Norton, Dec. 12, 1863, MN Papers DU: "It would be a great gratification to me if my poor face were passable enough so that I could have a copy of it that would not be startling in its ugliness, but I cannot, and I give it up now. I have tried very faithfully—for the sake of my friends—I have tried even here, but it is of no use—I burned a whole day—they were even worse than the original besides not looking at all like me." Clara Barton did pose for Mathew Brady in 1865 and 1866, and those "war" photographs survived.

p. 203   *letter from Washington-based friend*: name indecipherable, Dec. 4 1863, CB Papers SC.

p. 203   *letter from Holloway*: CB Journal, Dec. 26, 1863, CB Papers LC.

p. 204   *"How would you like"*: ibid., Dec. 15, 1863.

p. 205   *trip to Morris Island*: ibid., Dec. 15–21, 1863; CB's note ("*Colonel Elwell, I think*") in JE Papers WRHS; CB's remarks about Gillmore ("*ladies man*") and quotation ("*Can there ever come a day*") in CB to "My dear friend" [Mar. 14, 1864] JE Papers WRHS (CB Diary, Mar. 14, 1864, identifies the date of CB's letter to Elwell). All other quotations are from CB's Journal.

p. 207   "*One more Birth day,*" *CB's preparations, Leggett, Elwell's photograph, CB's departure*: CB Journal, Dec. 25, 27, 28, 30, 1863, CB Papers LC. Identification of Mitchellville from Denison, *Shot and Shell*, 63.

PART FOUR: THE WILDERNESS

p. 211   *CB's trip home, "I never saw the old place"*: CB to Col. Clark, Jan. 28, 1864, CB Papers LC; CB to David Barton, Feb. 25, 1864, CB Papers AAS. Also see CB to Mary Norton, Mar. 23, 1860, MN Papers DU.

p. 211   *CB at Beecher's church and CB quotations*: CB Diary, Feb. 14, 1863, ibid.; profile of Beecher from Milton Rugoff, *The Beechers: An American Family in the Nineteenth Century* (New York: Harper & Row, 1981), 131, 369–70.

p. 211   *Capitol's new dome*: Leech, *Reveille in Washington*, 279.

p. 212   *"government girls" in Washington*: Massey, *Bonnet Brigades*, 131–33.

p. 212   *promenading couples and their dress*: George S. Bryant, *Great American Myth* (New York: Carrick & Evans, 1940), 11.

p. 212   *"dead horses lay stinking"*: Leech, *Reveille in Washington*, 283.

p. 212   *Washington prostitution*: ibid., 261–64; Bell I. Wiley, *The Life of Billy Yank: The Common Soldier of the Union* (reprint of 1952 ed., Garden City: Doubleday, 1971), 257–58; Massey, *Bonnet Brigades*, 263.

p. 212   *"horizontal refreshments"*: James I. Robertson, Jr., *Soldiers Blue and Gray* (Columbia: University of South Carolina Press, 1988), 119.

p. 212   *"Hooker's Division," "fancy houses"*: Leech, *Reveille in Washington*, 264.

p. 212   *"the rage," "monster hops," John T. Ford, "pleasure seekers"*: ibid., 284, 276–78.

p. 213   *Medical Department changes*: Adams, *Doctors in Blue*, 38–40, 92; Louis C. Duncan, "The Strange Case of Surgeon General Hammond," *Military Surgeon* (Jan. and Feb. 1929), 98–114, 252–62; Letterman, *Medical Recollections*, 185.

p. 213   *CB at Rucker's office, Elwell's inquiry*: CB to David Barton,

Feb. 25, 1864, CB Papers AAS; Rucker's rank from his Military Service Records, NARA AGO, and *OR*, ser. 1, vol. 29, pt. 2, 533; vol. 33, 433, 577. In his correspondence in the *OR*, Rucker was addressed as chief quartermaster or as chief of the Quartermaster's Department, although he still commanded the Quartermaster Depot in the capital. He did so throughout the war, as Sifakis points out in *Who Was Who in the Civil War*, 558.

p. 213   *"pretty well," "used to think," "miserable"*: CB Journal, Apr. 2, 1864, CB Papers LC; CB to "My dear friend" [Mar. 14, 1864], JE Papers WRHS; CB Diary, Mar. 14, 1864, CB Papers LC. See also CB to David Barton, Apr. 2, 1864, CB Papers AAS.

p. 213   *Mary Morris Husband*: Brockett and Vaughan, *Women's Work in the Civil War*, 295. As Jane E. Schultz points out in "The Inhospitable Hospital," *Signs* (Winter 1992), 370, *matron* was "a catch-all term" that not only designated women who supervised ward nurses in hospitals but also referred to "the regimental women who nursed, cooked, and did laundry."

p. 214   *Sanitary Commission, CB shut out*: CB Diary, Mar. 7, 1864; Stillé, *History of the Sanitary Commission*, 378–90; Pryor, *Clara Barton*, 123–24.

p. 214   *CB's depression, "current"*: CB Diary, Mar. 8, 19, 20, 24, 1864, CB Papers LC.

p. 214   *whatever physical symptoms*: Greer, *The Change*, 76, 81, 95–98, 115, 245, 247, and Weideger, *Menstruation and Menopause*, 201–2, discuss the physical symptoms ("hot flashes or flushes," crawling skin, "cold sweats") that can accompany menopause and that Greer says may be expressions of "vasomotor disturbance." Both authors also describe "symptoms that might be called psychological": headaches, nervousness, depression, irritability, and insomnia. In her diary, CB did not mention any of the physical symptoms listed above, but she was certainly irritable, nervous, depressed, and insomniac. I think this was due to her circumstances in Washington. Menopause may or may not have contributed to her malaise.

p. 214   *medical literature on menopause*: Smith-Rosenberg, *Disorderly Conduct*, 191–93.

p. 214   *"I could speak," "power of pen"*: CB Diary, Mar. 11, 20, 1864, CB Papers LC; CB Journal, Apr. 1, 1864, ibid. CB's quotation "of all sad words of tongue and pen" comes from John Greenleaf Whittier's *Maud Muller* (1856), stanza 53.

p. 214   *"it is not home"*: CB to Mary Norton, Mar. 23, 1863, MN Papers DU.

p. 215   *Florida expedition, Olustee, congressional investigation*: *OR*, ser. 1, vol. 35, pt. 1, 276–77, 285–92. Total Union casualties were 1,861 (ibid., 298).

p. 215   *"a salient blow," "badly planned"*: CB to Brown and Duer, Mar. 13, 1863, CB Papers LC. Actually, Seymour did disobey his instructions from Gillmore to hold his lines and make no aggressive moves. For the role of the Fifty-fourth Massachusetts in the battle, see Emilio, *Brave Black Regiment*, 155–70.

p. 215   *"to look into the Florida matter"*: CB Diary, Mar. 16, 1864, CB Papers LC.

p. 215   *"I am sure I failed"*: ibid., Mar. 14, 1864.

p. 215   *"blinded with tears"*: CB to Mr. J. Conroy, Mar. 11, 1864 [typescript copy in CB Diary], ibid. Welles had died in Nov. 1863, in California. See his obituary in the *American Baptist*, clipping, ibid.

p. 215   *Grant's White House reception*: CB Diary, Mar. 8, 1864, ibid.; Earl Shenck Miers (editor-in-chief), *Lincoln Day by Day: A Chronology, 1809–1865* (Washington, D.C.: Lincoln Sesquicentennial Commission, 1960), 245.

p. 215   *Lincoln's handshake*: Herman Melville said that Lincoln shook hands "like a man sawing wood at so much per cord." Melville to Elizabeth Melville, Mar. 24, 1861, *Letters of Herman Melville*, ed. Merrell R. Davis and William H. Gilman (New Haven: Yale University Press, 1960), 209–10.

p. 216   *"sanguinary and final"*: CB to Wilson, Apr. 8, 1864, in CB Journal, Apr. 8, 1864, CB Papers LC; CB Diary, Mar. 18, 19, 1864, ibid.

p. 216   *"It seems impossible"*: CB Journal, Apr. 1, 1864, ibid.

p. 216   *plans for Leander, "holding back from all quarters," "the most competent and ladylike"*: ibid., CB Diary, Mar. 19, 22, 31, 1864, ibid.; CB to Wilson, Apr. 8, 1864, in CB Journal, Apr. 8, 1864, ibid.

p. 216   *"he thought he could do it"*: CB Diary, Mar. 18, 1864, ibid. See also Mar. 19, 1864, ibid., and CB Journal, Apr. 1, 1864, ibid., and CB to David Barton, Mar. 24, 1864, CB Papers AAS.

p. 216   *"Had no courage to get up," CB's efforts in Lamb's behalf, "With the exception"*: CB Diary, Mar. 24, 1864, CB Papers LC; CB Journal, Mar. 29, 1864, ibid.

p. 217   *"If I could only succeed"*: ibid., Mar. 31, 1864.

p. 217   *CB's disconnected letter to Wilson*: written Apr. 6, 1864 but dated Apr. 7, 1864, CB Journal, Apr. 7, 1864, ibid.

p. 219   *"make her situation better," "shameful evils," "a friend of the country," "a civil, kindly, sensible question"*: ibid., Apr. 7, 1864. In recounting this scene, Ross, *Angel of the Battlefield*, 70, scolds Clara for being "pettish and difficult."

p. 219   *"ashamed," "If it would extenuate," "I thank you," "I will find employment"*: CB to Wilson, Apr. 8, 1864, in CB Journal, Apr. 8, 1864, CB Papers LC; also Apr. 9, 1864.

p. 219   *Dr. Marsh, Florida fiasco, "the honor of victory," "Is there no manly justice"*: CB Journal, Apr. 12, 13, 1864, ibid. Like Gillmore, Captain Emilio of the Fifty-fourth Massachusetts believed that Seymour was guilty of "disregarding his instructions" from the commanding general. See Emilio, *Brave Black Regiment*, 157.

p. 220   *"Had the most sad down spirited," "All the world appeared"*: CB Diary, Apr. 14, 1864, CB Papers LC; CB Journal, Apr. 14, 1864, ibid. The Journal version is also quoted in Barton, *Life of Clara Barton*, 1: 265–67, with the grammar corrected.

p. 220   *"General Seymour would leave," "This was too much for my fretted soul"*: ibid.

p. 220   *"he was very busy"*: CB Diary, Apr. 18, 1864, ibid.; also entries of Apr. 15–17, and CB Journal, Apr. 15, 1864, ibid.

p. 221   *"I cannot raise my spirits"*: CB Diary, Apr. 19, 1864, ibid. Quoted somewhat differently in Pryor, *Clara Barton*, 124.

p. 221   *Wilson's rejection*: CB Diary, Apr. 25, 1864, ibid.; CB to Wilson Apr. 25, 1864, in CB Journal, Apr. 25, 1864, ibid; Frank Moore, *Women of the War: Their Heroism and Self-Sacrifice* (Hartford: S. S. Scranton & Co., 1866), 327.

p. 221   *CB's letter to Wilson*: CB Journal, Apr. 25, 1864, CB Papers LC; CB Diary, Apr. 25 1864, ibid.

p. 222   *Review of Ninth Corps, "If they can stand it"*: quoted in Carl Sandburg, *Abraham Lincoln: The War Years* (4 vols., New York: Harcourt, Brace & World, 1939), 2: 551–52; Leech, *Reveille in Washington*, 319; George Barton to Mother, Apr. 24, 1864, GEB Letters AAS. Robert G. Scott, *Into the Wilderness with the Army of the Potomac* (Bloomington: University of Indiana Press, 1985), 12, gives the corps's strength as 19,331.

p. 222   *"for it has come that man"*: CB to Frances Gage, May 1, 1864, in CB Journal, May 1, 1864, CB Papers LC.

p. 222   *George Edward and Ned Barton*: information gleaned from their letters home in the GEB Letters and the EMB Letters and Diary AAS.

p. 222   *CB's visit to Ninth Corps, "went over the ground"*: CB Diary, Apr. 26, 1864, CB Papers LC.

p. 222   *"move to the front"*: CB to Frances Gage, May 1, 1864, in CB Journal, May 1, 1864, CB Papers LC.

p. 222   *CB's letter to Stanton*: Apr. 29, 1864, ibid.; CB Diary, Apr. 30, 1864, ibid.

p. 223   *CB's letter to Frances Gage*: May 1, 1864, in CB Journal, May 1, 1864, ibid.

p. 225   *AOP strength, medical personnel, ambulances*: Scott, *Into the Wilderness*, 12; *OR*, ser. 1, vol. 36, 188, 225 (number of ambulances); McParlin report in Barnes, *Medical and Surgical History*, vol. 1, pt. 1, 148, 151; Adams, *Doctors in Blue*, 95–98, 101–02.

p. 225   *"I know pretty nearly"*: CB Journal, May 4, 1864, CB Papers LC.

p. 226   *"This may do as well," "Like everything else"*: ibid., May 1, 5, 1864.

p. 226   *"Everyone supposes," "'that bourne from whence' "*: ibid., May 7, 1864. CB misquotes Shakespeare's *Hamlet*, Act III, scene 1. The line should read: "The undiscover'd country, from whose bourn / No traveller returns."

p. 226   *CB at Rucker's office, "and was concerned," medical preparations*: CB Journal, May 7, 1864, CB Papers LC; McParlin's report in Barnes, *Medical and Surgical History*, vol. 1, pt. 1, 151; Duncan, "Battle of the Wilderness," in Duncan, *Medical Department of the United States in the Civil War*, 8.

p. 226   *"Yes, certainly," "There is no end"*: CB Journal, May 7, 1864, CB Papers LC.

p. 226   *"the first day's doings"*: ibid.; Scott, *Into the Wilderness*, 60, 66.

p. 226   *Wilson and CB's pass*: CB Journal, May 7, 1864, CB Papers LC.

p. 227   *"great Battle," CB's anxiety, "of much consequence," "Unhappy"*: CB Diary [May 8, 10, 1864], ibid.; Leech, *Reveille in Washington*, 320, describes the tension in the capital. Beginning with May 1, 1864, CB's diary is confusing as far as correct dates are concerned. She obviously wrote many entries in haste, often letting one day's happenings fill up the diary space for several days. For example, the events of May 8–13, 1864, are written in the spaces for May 1–6, 1864, without regard for dates. She records her arrival at Fredericksburg as May 7 when it was actually May 14, three days after she received her pass from Dr. Barnes. Her Journal indicates that she was still in Washington on May 7. Thus, the dates of her diary entries about her first trip to Fredericksburg are off by a week. I have worked out the chronology of her efforts to go to Fredericksburg and her two trips there according to the logic of events and to corroborating evidence.

p. 227   *"There were stretchers"*: Duncan, "Battle of the Wilderness," in Duncan, *Medical Department of the United States in the Civil War*, 9; also McParlin's report in Barnes, *Medical and Surgical History*, 1: pt. 1, 153 (McParlin's report is also in *OR*, ser. 1, vol. 36, pt. 1, 210–61).

p. 227   *conditions in Fredericksburg*: Dr. E. B. Dalton's report in Barnes, *Medical and Surgical History*, vol. 1, pt. 1, 191; McParlin's report in ibid., 156; Adams, *Doctors in Blue*, 102; Duncan, "Battle of the Wilderness," in Duncan, *Medical Department of the United States in the Civil War*, 20.

p. 227   *appeals for supplies, USSC, Christian Commission*: Leech, *Reveille in Washington*, 323–24; Maxwell, *Lincoln's Fifth Wheel*, 252.

p. 228   *CB at war offices*, "*No passes*," "*went home in despair*," *Barnes and Allen*: CB Diary [undated], CB Papers LC.

p. 228   *CB's pass from Barnes*, "*through Mr. Wilson's power*": ibid.; CB's pass, dated May 11, 1864, in CB Papers SC; CB Notes for a Lecture [undated], ibid. Many other men and women volunteers—Cornelia Hancock and Julia Wheelock among them—also secured passes and set out for Fredericksburg.

p. 229   *CB on* Wenonah: CB Diary, May 1–6, 1864 [May 11, 1864], ibid.; Wheelock, *Boys in White*, 187. Wheelock gives the departure date as May 11, which fits with the date of CB's pass.

p. 229   Wenonah *at Belle Plain*, "*fearfully*," *CB and Mrs. Brainard*: CB Diary, May 1–6 [May 12], 1864, CB Papers LC; Wheelock, *Boys in White*, 186–87.

p. 229   *description of Belle Plain*: McParlin's and Mackenzie's reports in Barnes, *Medical and Surgical History*, 7:pt. 1, 157, 181–82; CB, "Black Book," CB Papers SC; CB Lecture [typescript], CB Papers LC; Stillé, *History of the Sanitary Commission*, 393; Maxwell, *Lincoln's Fifth Wheel*, 252–53.

p. 229   "*Mules, stretchers*": Jane S. Woolsey, *Hospital Days* (New York: D. Van Nostrand, 1868), 151; quoted also in Maxwell, *Lincoln's Fifth Wheel*, 253; Stillé, *History of the Sanitary Commission*, 393.

p. 229   *CB to the ridge, wagon train from Spotsylvania*: CB, "Black Book," CB Papers SC; CB Lecture [typescript], CB Papers LC; McParlin's report in Barnes, *Medical and Surgical History*, 1:pt. 1, 155.

p. 230   *CB and the Christian Commission clergyman*: CB, "Black Book," CB Papers SC; CB Lecture [typescript], CB Papers LC; CB Diary, May 1–6 [May 13], 1864; Smith, "Women Who Went to the War," 106, reports that clergymen before the war held that women were ill suited for "the practical life." Barton, *Life of Clara Barton*, 1:273–79, quotes a version of CB's lecture recalling this and a subsequent trip to Belle Plain and Fredericksburg in May 1864.

p. 230   "*mutilated, starving sufferers*": CB, "Black Book," CB Papers SC; CB Lecture [typescript], CB Papers LC.

p. 230   *springless wagons, straps hanging from framework*: Maxwell, *Lincoln's Fifth Wheel*, 253, quotes a Sanitary Commission agent who said that the wounded were held by "extemporized straps suspended from the framework of wagons."

p. 230   *captain in Fifty-sixth* Massachusetts: CB Diary, May 1–6 [May 13], 1864, CB Papers LC.

p. 230   *Gen. Stevenson's death*: ibid.; Warren Wilkinson, *Mother, May You Never See the Sights I Have Seen: The Fifty-*

seventh Massachusetts Veteran Volunteers in the Army of the Potomac, 1864–1865 (New York: Harper & Row, 1990), 104.

p. 231   *Sanitary agents and Michigan women handing out food*: Wheelock, *Boys in White*, 189; Stillé, *History of the Sanitary Commission*, 391–94.

p. 231   *CB's trip to Fredericksburg*: CB Diary, May 7 [May 14], 1864, CB Papers LC; Sanitary Commission worker's description of the road and its perils in private letter of May 12, 1864, from Fredericksburg, newspaper clipping, NEWAA Papers MHS; Leech, *Reveille in Washington*, 324.

p. 231   *"full of wounded, with the tongue broken"*: undated fragment in CB Journals and Diaries, CB Papers LC, misfiled in folder of Dec. 1862. This clearly occurred on CB's initial trip to Fredericksburg in May 1864, not in her Dec. 1862 trip to Fredericksburg, when she took the train there from Aquia Creek. Typescript copy in AAS is misdated Dec. 1862.

p. 231   *surgeons crying "next"*: Freemon, *Microbes and Minie Balls*, 7.

p. 231   *wounded in Fredericksburg*: Dalton's report in Barnes, *Medical Surgical History*, 1:pt. 1, 191; John Anderson, *History of the Fifty-seventh Regiment of Massachusetts Volunteers in the War of the Rebellion* (Boston: E. B. Stillings & Co., 1896), 58; CB quoted in Frances Gage's letter of May 29, 1864, newspaper clipping, CB Papers LC; Ned Barton to his mother, May 17, 1864, EMB Letters AAS; Sanitary Commission private letter of May 12, 1864, from Fredericksburg, newspaper clipping, NEWAA Papers MHS; *Daily Advertiser*, June 3, 1864, clipping, ibid.; Cornelia Hancock, *South After Gettysburg: Letters of Cornelia Hancock, 1863–68*, ed. Henrietta Stratton Jaquette (New York: Thomas Y. Crowell Co., 1956), 92–93; Stillé, *History of the Sanitary Commission*, 276; Adams, *Doctors in Blue*, 102; Wheelock, *Boys in White*, 191–92. Miller (ed.), *Photographic History of the Civil War*, "Prisons and Hospitals," 270–71, has a photograph of the Old Warehouse hospital.

p. 231   *"he had no idea"*: quoted in George Barton to his mother, May 19, 1864, GEB Letters AAS.

p. 232   *Hancock's estimate, daily ration*: Brockett and Vaughan, *Women's Work in the Civil War*, 285; Leech, *Reveille in Washington*, 323; CB's fragment [May 1864], CB Papers LC [see note for p. 231 *"full of wounded"*]; CB Diary, May 7 [May 14], 1864, ibid; Georgeanna Woolsey quoted in Dannett, *Noble Women of the North*, 288. Cornelia Hancock claimed that she was the first Northern woman to reach Fredericksburg; she did so about May 12 (Hancock,

South After Gettysburg, 92). Christian Commission agent John Vassar seconded her claim (Brockett and Vaughan, *Women's Work in the Civil War*, 285). Stillé, *History of the Sanitary Commission*, 276, asserts that the Sanitary team numbered 150 agents and volunteers and included Helen Gilson, Arabella Barlow, and several other women. He also claims that more than 20,000 wounded were in Fredericksburg when the team arrived. McParlin insisted that after May 13 "the condition of the wounded in Fredericksburg was comparatively comfortable, and the supply of all necessary articles was abundant" (McParlin's report in Barnes, *Medical and Surgical History*, 1:pt. 1, 157). That statement is refuted by the overwhelming testimony of CB, Wheelock, Woolsey, and other volunteers about the wretched conditions they found in Fredericksburg after that date. "Such scenes of wretchedness and terrible suffering I have never before witnessed," wrote Wheelock, who reached Fredericksburg shortly after CB did. Wheelock, *Boys in White*, 191–92, citing her journal, entry May 10 [*sic*]. She actually arrived on May 13.

p. 232   *CB at First Division hospital, description of Wilderness battle*: CB fragment [May 1864], CB Papers LC [see note for p. 461 *"full of wounded"*]; McParlin's report in Barnes, *Medical and Surgical History*, 1:pt. 1, 151.

p. 232   *57th Mass. in Wilderness, "The slain and wounded had every"* : Wilkinson, *Mother, May You Never See the Sights I Have Seen*, 76.

p. 232   *Spotsylvania*: ibid., 110–14; Bruce Catton, *A Stillness at Appomattox* (Garden City: Doubleday, 1954), 125–28; William D. Matter, *If It Takes All Summer: The Battle of Spotsylvania* (Chapel Hill: University of North Carolina Press, 1988), 99–268. My casualty figures come from Thomas L. Livermore, *Numbers and Losses in the Civil War in America*, 1861–65 (2d ed., Boston: Houghton Mifflin, 1901), 113. Gary Gallagher informs me that the figure was closer to 36,000 total losses by the end of May 12. Matter, 348, states that Federal casualties for the entire Wilderness-Spotsylvania campaign (May 5–21) were reported to be about 36,000.

p. 232   *CB heard artillery on wind*: That the boom of the guns could be heard in Fredericksburg is recorded in Sanitary Commission worker's private letter, May 12, 1864, in NEWAA Papers MHS; and Hancock, *South After Gettysburg*, 93.

p. 232   *warehouses full of wounded*: Anderson, *History of the Fifty-seventh Regiment of Massachusetts Volunteers*, 58, and quoted in Wilkinson, *Mother, May You Never See the Sights I Have Seen*, 96.

p. 232   *"that gangrene was setting in"*: undated fragment in CB

Journals and Diaries, CB Papers LC [see note p. 461 for "*full of wounded*"].

p. 232   "*one old sunken hotel*," "*I saw . . . lying*": CB, "Black Book," CB Papers SC; also CB Lecture [typescript], CB Papers LC. Somewhat different versions in CB Diary, May 7 [May 14], 1864, ibid., and in undated fragment in CB Journals and Diaries, ibid. [see note for "*full of wounded*" p. 461].

p. 232   "*a great number of them*," *wounded would die*, "*better air*," "*The surgeons do* all *they can*": ibid.

p. 233   *another ambulance train from Spotsylvania*, "*and their companions*": McParlin's report in Barnes, *Medical and Surgical History*, 1:pt. 1, 155; undated fragment in CB Journals and Diaries, ibid. (see note p. 461 for "*full of wounded*").

p. 233   "*the dark spot in the mud*": CB, "Black Book," CB Papers SC.

p. 233   "*city is full of houses*": undated fragment in CB Journals and Diaries, CB Papers LC. [see note for "*full of wounded*" p. 461].

p. 233   "*the haughty occupants*," *Woolsey reported*: CB, "Black Book," CB Papers SC; CB Lecture [typescript], CB Papers LC; Woolsey in Dannett, *Noble Women of the North*, 289. Cornelia Hancock likewise reported that "the Secesh help none" (Hancock, *South After Gettysburg*, 92). McParlin stated that at first some Fredericksburg residents "seemed inclined to make trouble," but they did allow Federal *officers* to be billeted in their homes and generally treated the officers "kindly" (McParlin's report in Barnes, *Medical and Surgical History*, 1:pt. 1, 156).

p. 233   "*improper, heartless, unfaithful officers*," "*dapper captain of 21*": CB, "Black Book, CB Papers SC; CB Lecture [typescript], CB Papers LC. Doris Kirkpatrick, *The City and the River* (Fitchburg, Mass.: Fitchburg Historical Society, 1971), 1:287, and Wilkinson, *Mother, May You Never See the Sights I Have Seen*, 96, state that the problem lay with the Federal provost marshal, who refused to coerce rebel families into opening their homes to "dirty common soldiers." Wilkinson further says that senior officers "rapidly" overruled him, but it could not have been too rapidly since CB found rebel homes still closed to "dirty common soldiers" a week after the town was occupied. It was Quartermaster Montgomery Meigs who "overruled" the provost marshal, after Henry Wilson, acting on CB's complaint, put pressure on the War Department.

pp. 233–34   *CB's return to Washington*, "*plenty of duplicity*," "*at an unbroken gallop*": CB Diary, May 8 [15], 1864, CB Papers LC; CB Lecture [typescript], ibid.

p. 234   "*suffering and faithlessness*," *Wilson's threat at the War Department, Meigs and staff to Fredericksburg*, "*the wounded were fed*": CB Diary, May 8 [May 15], 29, 1864, ibid.; CB Lecture [typescript], ibid.; CB, "Black Book," CB Papers SC; *OR*, ser. 1, vol. 36, pt. 2, 829, 854–55. CB also gave Senator Charles Sumner a written "statement of affairs in Fredericksburg" (CB Diary, May 9 [May 16], 1864, CB Papers LC). Leech, *Reveille in Washington*, 325, also tells the story of CB and the opening of rebel homes to Union wounded. Adams, *Doctors in Blue*, 102, reports that "after Clara Barton had aroused her political friends in Washington," Meigs went to Fredericksburg "and directed the opening of the rail service to Aquia Creek."

p. 235   *CB's first public appeal*: the circular was dated May 16, 1864. I quote from the copy that appeared in *American Baptist*, May 24, 1864, clipping, CB Scrapbook, CB Papers LC (another copy of circular in MN Papers DU); CB Diary, May 11 [18], 1864, CB Papers LC. Henle, "Against the Fearful Odds," 31, points out that the circular was CB's "first national public appeal for supplies."

p. 235   *summoning Mrs. Rich, CB and Massachusetts state relief agency delegation, "transportation of supplies"*: CB Diary, May 11 [18], 12 [19], 1864, CB Papers LC.

p. 235   *Butler's Bermuda Hundred campaign*: my paragraph draws from William Glenn Robertson, *Back Door to Richmond: The Bermuda Hundred Campaign, April–June 1864* (Baton Rouge: Louisiana State University Press, 1987), 53–242; Schiller, *Bermuda Hundred Campaign*, 51–334; Nash, *Stormy Petrel*, 191–97; Ulysses S. Grant, *Papers* (18 vols. thus far, ed. John Y. Simon, Carbondale: Southern Illinois University Press, 1967–1991), 14:171–72; Grant, *Personal Memoirs of U.S. Grant and Selected Letters, 1839–1865*, ed. Mary Drake McFeely and William S. McFeely (New York: Library of America, 1990), 1053–54; Trefousse, *Ben Butler*, 145–50. The Bermuda Hundred campaign, states Trefousse, "shattered" Butler's military reputation.

p. 235   *"Gen. Gilmore may be"*: Butler to Wilson, May 7, 1864, HW Papers LC; *OR*, ser. 1, vol. 36, pt. 1, 12.

pp. 235–36 *Smith's criticism of Butler*: Noah Andre Trudeau, *The Last Citadel: Petersburg, Virginia, June 1864–April 1865* (Boston: Little, Brown, 1991), 32.

p. 236   *Grant's criticism of Butler*: Horace Porter, *Campaigning with Grant* (reprint 1961 ed., New York: Bonanza Books, n.d.), 147.

p. 236   *CB's return to Fredericksburg, Mrs. Myers, "piled almost to the top"*: CB Diary, May 14 [21], 1864, CB Papers LC. Ned Barton (Diary, May 12, 1864, EMB Letters AAS) identified Myers [or Myer] as a captain in the Fifty-seventh Massachusetts. But neither Anderson, *History of the Fifty-seventh Regiment of Massachusetts Volunteers*, nor Wilkinson, *Mother, May You Never See the Sights I Have*

Seen, lists a Captain Myers on the regimental roster. CB merely identified him as a captain in the Fifth Corps. She sometimes spelled his name as Myre.

p. 236   *CB's night with the "secesh" family and quotations*: CB Diary, May 14, 15 [21, 22], 1865, CB Papers LC.

p. 236   *CB and Dr. Lamb, "Oh how much"*: ibid., May 15 [22], 1864.

pp. 236–37   *tent hospital, river evacuations*: Duncan, "Battle of the Wilderness," in Duncan, *Medical Department of the United States Army in the Civil War,* 20; Wheelock, *Boys in White,* 211; McParlin's report in Barnes, *Medical and Surgical History,* vol. 1, pt. 1, 157.

p. 237   *"The number of wounded"*: CB to David Barton, May 26, 1864, CB Papers AAS.

p. 237   *medical personnel in Fredericksburg*: Adams, *Doctors in Blue,* 58.

p. 237   *Dix nurses, Ellen Mitchell*: Hancock, *South After Gettysburg,* 92; Brockett and Vaughan, *Women's Work in the Civil War,* 422, 230, 139.

p. 237   *Woolsey, Holstein, Gilson, Barlow, Husband, Spencer*: Dannett, *Noble Women of the North,* 282–88; Brockett and Vaughan, *Women's Work in the Civil War,* 139, 230, 295, 411; Moore, *Women of the War,* 328; Stillé, *History of the Sanitary Commission,* 276–77; Austin, *Woolsey Sisters of New York,* 103–4.

p. 237   *Fogg and Lee*: ibid.; Brockett and Vaughan, *Women's Work in the Civil War,* 486–88, 505–10.

p. 237   *"sinking fast," Major Parker, Ned Barton*: CB Diary, May 18–19 [22], 1864, CB Papers LC; CB to David Barton, May 26, 1864, CB Papers AAS; CB to Mr. Baldwin, May 30, 1864, CB Papers LC. Ned Barton noted in his diary that Parker had arrived in Fredericksburg on May 19, 1864 (EMB Letters AAS).

p. 237   *CB found Ned Barton*: Ned Barton, Diary, May 22, 1864, ibid.; CB Diary, May 18–19 [22], 1864, CB Papers LC.

pp. 237–38   *Ned Barton's illness, ambulance train of 1,200 wounded, "maggots, flies," Murphy's amputation, "were put off by the roadside," "famous heights"*: Ned Barton to his mother, May 15, 1864, EMB Letters AAS.

p. 238   *Ned Barton's convalescence, "that I were minus a leg," "happy meeting," "We have literally been kept alive"*: ibid.; Ned Barton, Diary, May 13, 1864, ibid.; Ned Barton to his mother, May 16, 17, 19, 20, 1864, ibid.

p. 238   *"The vols from home do as well," "Rock Me to Sleep, Mother," guards passing*: Ned Barton to his mother, May 17, 19, 20, 1864, ibid.

p. 238   *CB's Maine cousin, supper with Dr. Lamb, "sent a thrill of joy"*: CB Diary [May 22, 1864], CB Papers LC. See also CB Lecture [typescript], ibid. May 22, 1864, was indeed the

⎧day the railroad began to operate. See McParlin's report in
Barnes, *Medical and Surgical History*, 1:pt. 1, 157.

p. 239 *evacuations*: ibid.; Ned Barton to his mother, May 24, 1864,
EMB Letters AAS; Ned Barton, Diary, May 24, 1864, ibid.;
Leech, *Reveille in Washington*, 325; Adams, *Doctors in
Blue*, 102.

p. 239 *CB's dress, "Rally 'Round the Flag Boys"*: Pryor, *Clara
Barton*, 126.

p. 239 *final evacuations, hospital transferred, Myers's death, Ned
Barton's departure*: Ned Barton to his mother, May 24,
May 25–28, 1864, EMB Letters AAS; Ned Barton, Diary,
May 24–28, 1864, ibid.

p. 239 *CB's departure, "terribly wounded soldiers," "to hold body
and soul"*: CB to Mrs. Alling, May 30, 1864, CB Papers LC.

p. 239 *some people wept, corpses brought up, new cemetery in
Arlington*: Leech, *Reveille in Washington*, 325, 326.

p. 239 *CB's letter to David Barton*: May 26, 1864, CB Papers AAS.
Part of the letter is quoted in Barton, *Life of Clara Barton*,
1, 282.

p. 240 *Major Parker's death*: CB Diary, May 28–30, 1864, CB
Papers LC.

p. 241 *"We are waiting at the cotside"*: CB to Mr. Baldwin, May
30, 1864, ibid.

p. 241 *CB's letter to Mrs. Alling, "By all means let her have"*: May
30, 1864, ibid.; *Rochester Evening Express*, June 14, 1864,
CB Scrapbooks, ibid.; *American Baptist*, clipping, CB
Papers AAS.

p. 241 *"No woman, perhaps, in the Union"*: undated clipping, CB
Scrapbooks, CB Papers LC. Leander's letter to Elvira
Stone, June 20, 1864, ibid., says that Gage's letter appeared
the previous week in the *Anti-Slavery Standard*.

p. 241 *CB's supplies from Northeast*: in late May 1864 a committee
of citizens in Fitchburg, Mass., forwarded three install-
ments of supplies to CB (Report of Alfred Hitchcock, E. B.
Hayward, H. A. Goodrich, May 24, 1864, undated clipping,
CB Scrapbooks, CB Papers LC); CB Diary, June 3, 1864,
ibid., indicates that six boxes of supplies were en route to
her from two Pennsylvania towns.

p. 241 *Mrs. Rich, Leander Poor*: ibid.; Poor to Elvira Stone, June
20, 1864, ibid.

p. 242 *Cold Harbor, "volcanic blast"*: Catton, *Stillness at
Appomattox*, 159–63. Porter, *Campaigning with Grant*, 174,
reports the detail about the soldiers' pinning to their coats
strips of paper giving their names and addresses.

p. 242 *"The immense slaughter"*: Gideon Welles, *Diary*, ed. John
T. Morse (3 vols., Boston: Houghton Mifflin, 1909–1911),
2:44.

p. 242 *Gillmore's advance against Petersburg, Gillmore relieved*:
Trudeau, *Last Citadel*, 11, 153n; Nash, *Stormy Petrel*,

197–98. Gillmore hardly retired from active service. In July 1864 he was put in command of two divisions that were defending Washington; in that capacity he saw action against rebel General Jubal Early. In February 1865 he again assumed command of the Department of the South. Gillmore's Military Service Records, NARA AGO.

p. 242   "ill advised": Grant's report, June 20, 1865, in Grant, *Papers*, 14:179. See also Grant, *Personal Memoirs and Selected Letters*, 1058–59.

p. 242   "Genl. Gillmore has made": CB Diary, June 20, 1864, CB Papers LC.

pp. 242–43   *AOP across the James, field medical service*: McParlin's and Dalton's reports in Barnes, *Medical and Surgical History*, 1:pt. 1, 162–63, 192; Grant, *Personal Memoirs and Selected Letters*, 559–602; Porter, *Campaigning with Grant*, 194–98.

p. 243   "in good style," "I had just enough," "regular Yankee yell": George Barton to his mother, June 20, 1864, GEB Letters AAS. See also, Anderson, *Fifty-seventh Regiment of Massachusetts Volunteers*, 138.

p. 243   *Grant laid siege*: Grant, *Personal Memoirs and Selected Letters*, 601–2; Porter, *Campaigning with Grant*, 206–9; Trudeau, *Last Citadel*, 48–65.

pp. 243–44   *emergency evacuation hospital near City Point*, "great trouble," "at first it seemed probable": McParlin's report in Barnes, *Medical and Surgical History*, 1:pt. 1, 165–66; Dalton's report in ibid., 192. See also Hancock, *South After Gettysburg*, 114–24; Wheelock, *Boys in White*, 274–75, 277, 281; and Maxwell, *Lincoln's Fifth Wheel*, 256.

p. 244   "Miss Barton, of Worcester": Wilson to Butler, June 20, 1864, in Benjamin F. Butler, *Private and Official Correspondence* (5 vols., Norwood, Mass.: Plimton Press, 1917), 4:423.

p. 244   *CB to James River*: CB Diary, June 20, 1864, CB Papers LC.

PART FIVE: BEFORE RICHMOND

p. 247   *City Point*: information provided by park ranger, Appomattox Manor, City Point, Virginia; Wilkinson, *Mother, May You Never See the Sights I Have Seen*, 209–10; Trudeau, *Last Citadel*, 131–32.

p. 247   *CB to Depot Hospital*, "who knew nothing of the way": CB Diary, June 22–23, 1864, CB Papers LC.

p. 247   *description Depot Hospital*: McParlin's and Dalton's reports in Barnes, *Medical and Surgical History*, 1:pt. 1, 165–66, 192; Adelaide Smith, *Reminiscences of an Army Nurse During the Civil War* (New York: Greaves Publishing Co.,

1911), 96–100; Hancock, *South After Gettysburg*, 138–39; Maxwell, *Lincoln's Fifth Wheel*, 258; Adams, *Doctors in Blue*, 110.

p. 247   *"two sleepy Ohio women"*: CB Diary, June 22, 23, 1864, CB Papers LC.

p. 247   *"black wheel boat," Cobb's Hill and Butler's Tower*: Smith, *Reminiscences*, 80; Charlotte E. McKay, *Stories of Hospital and Camp* (reprint 1876 ed., Freeport, N.Y.: Books for Libraries Press, 1971), 110–11.

p. 248   *Butler's Louisiana exploits*: Nash, *Stormy Petrel*, 144–72; Trefousse, *Ben Butler*, 108–14; David M. Nellis, "Between a Crown and a Gibbet: Benjamin F. Butler and the Early War Years" (Master's thesis, University of Massachusetts, Amherst, 1973), 32–50. Butler's "woman order" is in Butler, *Private and Official Correspondence*, 1:490.

p. 248   *"a felon deserving"*: Jefferson Davis, *Messages and Papers of Jefferson Davis and the Confederacy*, ed. James D. Richardson (2 vols., New York: Chelsea House . . . in association with R.R. Bowler, 1966), 1:217–20.

p. 248   *Butler in Washington*: Lincoln, *CW*, 6:76–77; Butler, *Private and Official Correspondence*, 3:13; T. Harry Williams, *Lincoln and the Radicals* (Madison: University of Wisconsin Press, 1941), 278.

p. 248   *"You may be right," "Don't let Davis," "That's a game"*: Butler in Allen Thorndike Rice, *Reminiscences of Abraham Lincoln by Distinguished Men of His Time* (reprint 1888 ed., New York: Haskell House, 1971), 143–44, 145–46. See also Lincoln, *CW*, 7:207, 207n.

p. 248   *Butler and vice-presidency*: J. G. Randall and Richard N. Current, *Lincoln the President: Last Full Measure* (New York: Dodd, Mead, 1955), 134–36; Butler in Rice, *Reminiscences*, 158–59; Lincoln, *CW*, 7:290n.

p. 249   *"like a little village," "dignified, wise, and princely"*: CB to Ferguson, July 3, 1864, *New York Evening Express*, clipping, CB Scrapbooks, CB Papers LC.

p. 249   *"he squints badly"*: John William De Forest, *A Volunteer's Adventures: A Union Captain's Record of the Civil War*, ed. James H. Croushore (New Haven: Yale University Press, 1946), 9.

p. 249   *Butler's prewar career*: Nash, *Stormy Petrel*, 23–26, 33, 39–66; Nellis, "Between a Crown and a Gibbet," 8–13. By 1853, according to Trefousse, *Ben Butler*, 27, Butler had $140,000 in the bank.

p. 249   *CB's interview with BFB, "Need not note"*: CB Diary, June 23, 1864, CB Papers LC. For BFB's elegant Sarah, see Nellis, "Between a Crown and a Gibbet," 10.

p. 249   *"relief of the sick in this Department"*: Butler's order dated June 23, 1864, CB Papers SC. As Pryor points out (*Clara Barton*, 126–27), CB in later years erroneously claimed that Butler had appointed her superintendent of nursing for the Army of the James.

p. 250   *CB assigned to Tenth Corps Hospital*: CB Diary, June 23, 1864, CB Papers LC; CB to Ferguson, July 3, 1864, ibid.

p. 250   *hospital location, "only an over burdened"*: fragment of CB letter [circa June or July 1864], ibid.; Sophronia E. Bucklin, *In Hospital and Camp: A Woman's Record of Thrilling Incidents Among the Wounded in the Late War* (Philadelphia: John E. Potter and Co., 1869), 332; CB to Esteemed and Dear Friend [Ferguson], July 5, 1864, CB Papers LC.

p. 250   *"six miles on"*: CB to Ferguson, July 3, 1864, ibid.; see also CB to Mary Norton, July 24, 1864, MN Papers DU.

p. 250   *CB and Dr. Porter*: CB Diary, July 2–8, 1864, CB Papers LC; CB to Soldiers' Aid Society, Oxford, Mass., July 20, 1864, *Worcester Spy*, clipping, CB Scrapbooks, ibid.; fragment of CB letter [circa June or July 1864], ibid.

p. 250   *"No better could have been desired," "Uncle Don," "What a friend"*: CB Diary, July 2–8, 1864, ibid.

p. 250   *"used up, wounded," description Tenth Corps Hospital, "brought in daily"*: CB to Ferguson, July 1, 1864, *New York Evening Express*, clipping, CB Scrapbooks, ibid.; CB to Soldeirs' Aid Society, Oxford, Mass., *Worcester Spy*, clipping, CB Scrapbooks, ibid.; fragment of CB letter [circa June or July 1864], ibid. Adelaide Smith, *Reminiscences of an Army Nurse*, 84, claimed that the hospital consisted of about twelve long tents, each holding about forty patients.

p. 251   *"sunburnt veterans," "the ball opened," rebel cannonade*: CB to Ferguson, July 1, 1864, *New York Evening Express*, clipping, CB Scrapbooks, CB Papers LC.

p. 251   *CB's hospital duties, single stove, "Hot . . . am tired," "I have cooked ten dozen eggs," "Please tell the noble ladies"*: ibid; CB Diary, July 1, 2–4, 1864, ibid.

p. 252   *"sunshine and dust," "mercury above a hundred"*: CB to Esteemed and Dear Friend [Ferguson], July 5, 1864, ibid.

p. 252   *"July 2," "One of the hottest days," "Capt. Wm Webb," "came in wounded," "taken out at the back"*: CB Diary, July 2, 1864, ibid.; CB to Ferguson, July 2, 1864, *New York Evening Express*, clipping, CB Scrapbooks, ibid. Union soldier Elisha Hunt Rhodes, *All for the Union: A History of the 2nd Rhode Island Volunteer Infantry in the War of the Great Rebellion*, ed. Robert Hunt Rhodes (Lincoln, R.I.: Andrew Mowbray Incorp., 1985), 166, claimed that on July 2, 1864, the temperature in the trenches stood at 124 degrees. Another Union soldier wrote that he had never experienced such heat, that "it seems already to have reached about as high a point as human nature can stand." Wilbur Fisk, *Hard Marching Every Day: The Civil War Letters of Private Wilbur Fisk, 1861–1865*, ed. Emil and Ruth Rosenblatt (Lawrence: University of Kansas Press, 1992), 234.

p. 252   *Wilson and Kautz's cavalry raid*: CB Diary, July 1, 2, 1864,
                ibid.; *OR*, ser. 1, vol. 40, pt. 1, 731–33; Trudeau, *Last
                Citadel*, 87–90.

p. 253   *"ragged, bareheaded, bleeding," "These men"*: CB Diary,
                July 1, 2, 1864, CB Papers LC; CB to Ferguson, July 2,
                1864, *New York Evening Express*, clipping, CB
                Scrapbooks, CB Papers LC.

p. 253   *"The same hot glare"*: CB Diary, July 3, 1864, ibid.

p. 253   *sunstroke victims, "slight dizziness," treatment, "rapid and
                severe"*: J. S. Billings's report in Barnes, *Medical and
                Surgical History*, 1:pt. 1, 199.

p. 253   *CB and delirious soldier*: CB Diary, Mar. 7–27, 1866, CB
                Papers LC.

p. 253   *"little pits," "Here we lay," "He raised his head"*: George
                Barton to his mother, June 23, 1864, GEB Letters AAS.
                See also his letters of July 3, 11, 14, 20, 1864, ibid.;
                Wheelock, *Reminiscences*, 238; and Wilkinson, *Mother,
                May You Never See the Sights I Have Seen*, 191–96.

p. 254   *spectacular artillery barrages, bursts of yellow and red*:
                ibid., 196; John D. Billings, *Hard Tack and Coffee* (reprint
                1887 ed., Williamstown, Mass.: Corner House Publishers,
                1973), 58–60.

p. 254   *daytime artillery duels, shells followed one another, along
                both trench lines for miles, first a puff of smoke*: McKay,
                Stories of Hospital and Camp, 109.

p. 254   *rebel mortar shells, "a black speck," "hang a moment"*: quot-
                ed in Trudeau, *Last Citadel*, 291; McKay, *Stories of
                Hospital and Camp*, 109; Billings, *Hard Tack and Coffee*,
                59; Anderson, *Fifty-seventh Regiment of Massachusetts
                Volunteers*, 151.

p. 254   *fragment of mortar shell, "We can see the sand fly"*: George
                Barton to his mother, July 14, 20, 1864, GEB Letters AAS.

p. 254   *"lived and ate and looked"*: quoted in Trudeau, *Last
                Citadel*, 289.

p. 254   *life in the trenches, swarms of mosquitoes and flies, "gray
                backs"*: ibid., 289–90; Anderson, *Fifty-seventh Regiment of
                Massachusetts Volunteers*, 157–58.

p. 254   *diseases, scurvy*: McParlin's report in Barnes, *Medical and
                Surgical History*, 1:pt. 1, 164; Anderson, *Fifty-seventh
                Regiment of Massachusetts Volunteers*, 157; Wilkinson,
                Mother, May You Never See the Sights I Have Seen, 206, 228.

p. 254   *scurvy symptoms, "subconjunctival" hemorrhaging*:
                Freemon, *Microbes and Minie Balls*, 184, 230; Robert E.
                Hodges and others, "Clinical Manifestations of Ascorbic
                Acid Deficiency in Man," *American Journal of Clinical
                Nutrition* (Apr. 1971), 432–43.

p. 254   *enormous quantities of vegetables, "raw potatoes in vine-
                gar"*: Wilkinson, *Mother, May You Never See the Sights I
                Have Seen*, 206.

p. 254   *shellshock, "nostalgia"*: Adams, *Doctors in Blue*, 228.

p. 255   *singing, "Weeping Sad and Lonely"*: Bell I. Wiley, *Life of Billy Yank: The Common Soldier of the Union* (reprint 1952 ed., Garden City, N.Y.: Doubleday, 1971), 160–61; Will and Allison Heaps, *The Singing Sixties* (Norman: University of Oklahoma Press, 1960), 224; Miller, *Photographic History of the Civil War*, "Poetry and Eloquence from the Blue and the Gray," 351. Lyrics from Lois Hill (ed.), *Poems and Songs of the Civil War* (New York: Fairfax Press, 1990), 232–33.

p. 255   *"to the hardness of brick"*: CB, "Black Book," CB Papers SC.

p. 255   *CB's special pleasure in nursing such soldiers*: Pryor, *Clara Barton*, 128. Pryor, 127, incorrectly identified CB's hospital as "a receiving and convalescent center located on the James River." It was a corps field hospital on the Appomattox, on the Bermuda Hundred line.

p. 255   *CB and hospital routine, "covered the spectrum"*: my description is adapted from Brooks, *Civil War Medicine*, 58–59; also CB Diary, July 2–8, 1864, CB Papers LC.

p. 256   *"twisted bodies, splintered bones," "keep cheerful, & toil on"*: Brooks, *Civil War Medicine*, 59; CB Diary, July 2–8, 1864, CB Papers LC.

p. 256   *"happy being here"*: CB to Ferguson, July 1, 1864, *New York Evening Express*, clipping, CB Scrapbooks, ibid. The soldiers were happy to have Clara there. "Her devotion to her work," said Isaiah Price of the Ninety-seventh Pennsylvania, "was unabated and unwavering." Price, *History of the Ninety-seventh Pennsylvania*, 408.

p. 256   *"so patient and cheerful," "excellent nurses," "kind care," "I am well satisfied"*: CB to Ferguson, July 3, 1863, *New York Evening Express*, clipping, CB Papers LC.

p. 256   *scene with black sergeant, CB and local blacks, quotations*: CB to Esteemed and Dear Friend [Ferguson], July 5, 1864, ibid.

p. 257   *CB and Sarah Edson, "decided with me,"* CB Diary, July 2–8, 1864, ibid..

pp. 257–58   *"an advanced member" and "Adoptive Degrees," Masonic meeting*: Brockett and Vaughan, *Women's Work in the Civil War*, 445; "General Items," CB Diary [typescript], CB Papers AAS.

p. 258   *"great reports," Early's raid*: CB Diary, July 13–14, 1864, CB Papers LC; Charles C. Osborne, *Jubal: The Life and Times of General Jubal A. Early, CSA* (Chapel Hill: Algonquin Books, 1992), 277–293; Williams, *Lincoln and His Generals*, 326.

p. 258   *"to the death"*: ibid., 331.

p. 258   *CB's trip to Washington, "relics of the fight"*: CB Diary, July
                  15–17, 1864, CB Papers LC.

p. 258   *CB's open letter to Soldiers' Aid Society, Oxford*, Mass.: July
                  20, 1864, *Worcester Spy*, clipping, CB Scrapbooks, ibid.

p. 259   *CB back at City Point, military base there*: CB Diary, July 29,
                  1864, ibid.; informational brochure provided by park ranger,
                  Appomattox Manor, City Point; Wilkinson, *Mother, May
                  You Never See the Sights I Have Seen*, 209–10; Fisk, *Hard
                  Marching Every Day*, 294; Trudeau, *Last Citadel*, 132.

pp. 259–260   *description Depot Hospital*: McParlin's and Dalton's reports
                  in Barnes, *Medical and Surgical History*, 1:pt. 1, 166–67,
                  193; Wheelock, *Boys in White*, 238, 240; Smith,
                  Reminiscences, 96–99; Hancock, *South After Gettysburg*,
                  125, 139; Adams, *Doctors in Blue*, 110; Maxwell, *Lincoln's
                  Fifth Wheel*, 258. The fullest description is Donald C.
                  Pfanz, "The Depot Field Hospital at City Point" (unpub-
                  lished, 1988), copy at Petersburg National Battlefield.

p. 260   *Helen Gilson's black hospital, "from a disgrace"*: Brockett and
                  Vaughan, *Women's Work in the Civil War*, 145; Maxwell,
                  Lincoln's Fifth Wheel, 258. Smith, *Reminiscences*, 107–8, says
                  that Gilson was "a dainty young woman" who wore "a short
                  pretty dress" in the hospital. "She had a pure soprano voice,
                  and frequently sang army songs and hymns to the men."

p. 260   *"Not only was its standard," "I couldn't die"*: quoted in
                  Greenbie, *Lincoln's Daughters of Mercy*, 183.

p. 260   *other female volunteers at Depot Hospital*: Pfanz, "Depot
                  Field Hospital," 17–23, 79–82; Brockett and Vaughan,
                  Women's Work in the Civil War, 328, 412–14, 507–10,
                  484–88; Marshall, *Dix*, 229.

p. 260   *Hancock at City Point, "jewel of a little," "if it were not for,"
                  "Our ladies in camp"*: Hancock, *South After Gettysburg*,
                  131, 125, 127.

p. 260   *mine at Petersburg trenches*: see Trudeau, *Last Citadel*,
                  105–9; Johnson and Buel, *Battles and Leaders*, 4:545–50.

p. 261   *description of explosion, Federal artillery barrage*: Porter,
                  Campaigning with Grant, 263; Johnson and Buel, *Battles and
                  Leaders*, 4:551; Price, *History of the Ninety-seventh
                  Pennsylvania*, 307–8; Trudeau, *Last Citadel*, 109; Wilkinson,
                  Mother, May You Never See the Sights I Have Seen, 245.

p. 261   *CB to Point of Rocks, "sick family," Uncle Don's departure*;
                  CB Diary, July 30, 31, 1864, CB Diary, CB Papers LC; CB
                  to Sister Fannie, Sept. 3, 1864, CB Papers AAS, and quot-
                  ed in Barton, *Life of Clara Barton*, 1: 207.

p. 261   *Adelaide Smith at Point of Rocks, "already in charge"*:
                  Smith, *Reminiscences*, 21, 81–82; CB Diary, July 30, 1864,
                  CB Papers LC. Dannett, *Noble Women of the North*, 306,
                  says that Adelaide went by "Ada."

p. 261   *CB's unhappiness about Ada Smith*: deduced from CB's
                  Diary, Aug. 3, 6–8, 1864, CB Papers LC.

p. 262   *news of Crater*: ibid., July 31, Aug. 1, 1864.

p. 262   *"melted away"*: Johnson and Buel, *Battles and Leaders*,
              4:553–62. Other details of the battle derive from Anderson,
              Fifty-seventh Regiment of Massachusetts Volunteers,
              167–227; Trudeau, *Last Citadel*, 110–27; Catton, *Stillness
              at Appomattox*, 251; Livermore, *Numbers and Losses in the
              Civil War* 116; Wilkinson, *Mother, May You Never See the
              Sights I Have Seen*, 245–64; George Barton to his mother,
              Aug. 3, 1864, GEB Letters AAS.

p. 262   *Twenty-first Massachusetts at Crater, Gould and Clark
              wounded*: CB Diary, Aug. 1, 1864, CB Papers LC.

p. 262   *Gardner's death, "handsome," "splendid," "He had no
              friends," "He seemed to cling to me"*: ibid.; newspaper clip-
              ping [circa 1905], CB Scrapbooks, ibid.

p. 263   *CB to City Point*: CB Diary, Aug. 1, 2, 1864, ibid.

p. 263   *"It was a fearful night," "The thunder was terrific," CB at
              Crater*: newspaper clipping [circa 1905], CB Scrapbooks, ibid.
              CB Journal, Jan. 12, 1866, ibid., says that Cornelia Hancock
              was "one of the party who constituted our famous night ride
              in front of Petersburg a year 1/2 ago when our necks all
              escaped as if by miracle."

p. 263   *description of corpses at Crater*: Wilkinson, *Mother, May
              You Never See the Sights I Have Seen*, 262–63.

p. 263   *"All that I feared," "things combine to grieve me," "I hear but
              dare not say much"*: CB Diary, Aug. 3, 6, 1864, CB Papers LC.

p. 263   *"I saw very little"*: Smith, *Reminiscences*, 90.

p. 263   *"quite without authority," Mrs. Edson's advice to Ada*: ibid.,
              81–82, 91.

p. 264   *"Cramped & unhappy," "Miss old Uncle Don," "I both saw
              and heard," "some pertinent questions," "find less objection-
              al," "one of us will leave"*: CB Diary, Aug. 7, 8, 1864, CB
              Papers LC. For a different discussion of CB's relationships
              with the new nurses, see Pryor, *Clara Barton*, 128–29.

p. 264   *Ada Smith's departure*: Smith went to Depot Hospital and
              attached herself to the Ninth Corps hospital there. Smith,
              Reminiscences, 94–100.

p. 264   *Voris's note to CB*: Aug. 13, 1864, CB Papers SC.

p. 264   *Deep Bottom action* Trudeau, *Last Citadel*, 146–58, 160–61,
              170; McParlin's report in Barnes, *Medical and Surgical
              History*, 1:pt. 1, 173.

p. 265   *Weldon Railroad battle*: Trudeau, *Last Citadel*, 160–69,
              173–77, 188; Walcott, *History of the Twenty-first
              Massachusetts*, 353; Johnson and Buel, *Battles and Leaders*,
              4:568–73.

p. 265   *"dear old regiment," "I am a stranger"*: CB to Annie Childs,
              Sept. 14, 1864, *Worcester Sunday Telegram*, Sept. 16,
              1917, CB Papers LC; quoted in Barton, *Life of Clara
              Barton*, 1:290–96.

p. 265   *CB as unofficial matron Tenth Corps Hospital*: deduced from CB Diary entries, July–Sept. 1864, CB Papers LC; CB to darling sis Fannie, Sept. 3, 1864, CB Papers AAS (quoted in Barton, *Life of Clara Barton*, 1: 287–88); CB to Soldiers' Aid Society, West Fitchburg, Mass., Jan. 26 [1865], CB Papers LC. As Freemon, *Microbes and Minie Balls*, 12 points out, Civil War hospital matrons functioned "as supervisors, cooks, and laundresses."

p. 265   *CB's "sick family"*: CB to darling sis Fannie, Sept. 3, 1864, CB Papers AAS.

pp. 265–66 *to Broadway Landing, "It was all the surgeons," feeding the entire hospital population, "a new Boss cook," CB's sleeping tent*: ibid. See also CB to Annie Childs, Sept. 14, 1864, *Worcester Sunday Telegram*, (Sept. 16, 1917), CB Papers LC; and CB to Soldiers' Aid Society, West Fitchburg, Mass., Jan. 26 [1865], ibid. The Eighteenth Corps "Base Hospital" relocated at Point of Rocks. See *Moses Greeley Parker, M.D.* (Lowell: Privately printed,1921[?]), 59–81.

p. 266   *denuded lunarscape, irregular trenches, "bristling with tangles of abatis"*: Catton, *Stillness at Appomattox*, 319–20; George B. Davis and others, *Atlas to Accompany the Official Records of the Union and Confederate Armies* (Washington, D.C.: Government Printing Office, 1891–1895), republished as *The Official Military Atlas of the Civil War* (New York: Arno Press, 1978), plates LXVII (8, 9), LXXVII (2), LXXIX (1), C (1, 2), CXVIII (3). Hereafter cited as *OMA*. For a vivid description of the rival works, abatis, and *chevaux de frise* ("a beam of wood through which rows of pointed rods about six feet in length are driven"), see Anderson, *Fifty-seventh Regiment of Massachusetts Volunteers*, 134–35.

pp. 266–67 *"one with the shoulder gone," "little fellow," "noble Swiss boy" apparently dying*: CB to darling sis Fannie, Sept. 3, 1864, CB Papers AAS; CB to Henry Wilson, May 18, 1865, CB Papers LC.

p. 267   *Jules Golay saved*: CB to Eliza Golay, March 5, 7, 1865, ibid.

p. 267   *"I would have died"*: Jules Golay to CB, Nov. 10, 1867, ibid.

p. 267   *"a perfect master," "All Republicans should fight"*: CB to Henry Wilson, May 18, 1865, ibid.

p. 267   *"and suffered," "my Swiss boy," "younger brother," "the place has been always"*: CB to Eliza Golay, Mar. 5, 7, 1865, ibid.; CB Diary, Dec. 18, 1864, ibid.; CB to Isaac Golay [circa 1865], ibid.; Jules Golay to CB, Nov. 10, 1867, ibid. See also CB Diary, Dec. 8, 1864, ibid.

p. 267   *"American older sister," "Dear sister Clara," "It would be impossible"*: CB to Eliza Golay, Mar. 5, 7, 1865, ibid.; Jules Golay to CB, Nov. 10, 1867, ibid.

p. 268   *"With my books I learn"*: Jules Golay to CB, Dec. 4, 1864, ibid.

p. 268   *base and "flying" hospitals, "in the rear of the front line," "most skillful operators"*: CB to Annie Childs, Sept. 14,

1864, CB Papers AAS (quoted in Barton, *Life of Clara Barton*, 1:293); CB Diary, Oct. 5, 1864.

pp. 268–69   *"You know that my range," "stood by," "on any condition," "I begin to think,"* CB's slave cabin, *"and here I have lain"*: CB to Annie Childs, Sept. 14, 1864, CB Papers AAS.

p. 269   *"a darling little Massachusetts boy," "delicate little fellow," "Father, this is my Auntie"*: ibid.

p. 269   *CB's horseback trip with Ned Barton, "off upon a romantic ride," signal station, rebel works*: Ned Barton to his mother, Sept. 18, 1864, EMB Letters and Diary, AAS; Ned Barton, Diary, Sept. 18, 1864, ibid.; *OMA*, plates XVII (1), LXXIV (1), LXXVII (1,3), C (1, 2).

p. 270   *Dutch Gap canal, "a wide, shallow part"*: Johnson and Buel, *Battles and Leaders*, 4:575.

p. 270   *base hospital to Jones Neck, "I gave out rations all the pm"*: CB Diary, Sept. 28–29, 1864 CB Papers LC.

pp. 270–71   *Butler's attack against Richmond defenses, Butler's new line*: Porter, *Campaigning with Grant*, 299–304; Trudeau, *Last Citadel*, 211–24; Lossing, *Numbers and Losses in the Civil War*, 128; Johnson and Buel, *Battles and Leaders*, 4:577–78; Grant, *Personal Memoirs and Selected Letters*, 625–26.

p. 271   *"rained very hard"*: CB Diary, Sept. 30, 1864, CB Papers LC.

p. 271   *Peebles Farm fight*: Porter, *Campaigning with Grant*, 303; Grant, *Personal Memoirs and Selected Letters*, 626; Trudeau, *Last Citadel*, 212–14.

p. 271   *"another shake"*: Grant quoted in Porter, *Campaigning with Grant*, 299.

p. 271   *Dr. Kittinger, "especial friend"*: Kittinger's Pension Records, NARA; CB to Samuel Barton, Oct. 30, 1864, CB Papers HL.

p. 271   *CB's resignation from base hospital, "She is very welcome"*: CB Diary, Oct. 12, 1864, CB Papers LC.

p. 272   *CB at flying hospital, felt "free" and at home*: my interpretation based on the evidence. When Ada Smith competed with CB at Point of Rocks, CB complained that she no longer felt "free" and at home there (CB Diary, Aug. 3, 7, 1864, CB Papers LC). But, as her diary entries and letters indicate, she felt "free" at the flying hospital, "a fixture here," because she was the only woman present and thus had no competition from other females. See CB to Samuel R. Barton, Oct. 30, 1864, CB Papers HL; CB Diary, Oct. 17, 1864, CB Papers LC; Stephen Barton to "my own wife," Nov. 16, 1864, CB Papers HL; CB to Stephen Barton, Dec. 29, 1864, ibid. See also William P. Scott to CB, May 21, 1888, CB Papers LC.

p. 272   *fighting on Butler's new line, CB and wounded lieutenant, "with hands and arms"*: CB Diary, Oct. 13, 1864, ibid.; CB affidavit, Oct. 10, 1885, CB Papers LC.

p. 272   *Stephen Barton's letter, "She can talk pretty"*: Samuel Barton to his mother, Oct. 9, 1864, SRB Papers DU.

p.272   *hospital on plantation at Aiken's Landing*: CB Diary, Oct. 14, 15, 17, 1864, CB Papers LC; Stephen Barton to his nieces and nephew, Dec. 11, 1864 [typescript], ibid.

pp. 272–73   *CB at Butler's headquarters, dialogue*: CB Diary, Oct. 15, 1864, ibid; CB affidavit, Oct. 10, 1885, ibid. Butler's confidential order regarding Stephen is in Butler, *Private and Official Correspondence*, 5:265. CB paraphrases it in CB Diary, Oct. 15, 1864, ibid.

p. 273   *"trying to arrange," Dr. Kittinger in charge*: CB Diary, Oct. 16, 1864, ibid.

p. 273   *"I seem to be a fixture"*: CB to Samuel Barton, Oct. 30, 1864, CB Papers HL.

p. 273   *CB's kitchen, "art of scientific cooking," eggs*: Stephen Barton to his nieces and nephew, Dec. 11, 1864 [typescript], CB Papers LC.

p. 273   *hospital wards, "entrenchments," "names that I would ever breathe"*: CB to Soldiers' Aid Society, West Fitchburg, Mass., Jan. 26 [1865], CB Papers LC.

p. 273   *renovation CB's cabin*: CB to Elvira Stone, Oct. 30, 1864, CB Papers LC; CB affidavit, Oct. 10, 1885, ibid.; Stephen Barton to nieces and nephew [typescript], Dec. 11, 1864, ibid.

p. 274   *"Don't be disturbed," Stephen's arrival, "strong, muscular, erect:"* CB affidavit, Oct. 10, 1885, ibid.; CB to Judge Barton, Dec. 5, 1864, CB Papers AAS. Date of Stephen's arrival calculated from his letter of Oct. 23, 1864, to his son Sammy (CB Papers LC). In it, Stephen reported that he reached Clara three days earlier—that is, on Oct. 20.

p. 274   *Kittinger in charge of Stephen, standard treatment for "chronic fluxes"*: CB to Judge Barton, Dec. 5, 1864, CB Papers LC; CB to Samuel Barton, Oct. 30, Nov. 1, 1864, CB Papers HL; Adams, *Doctors in Blue*, 226; Brooks, *Civil War Medicine*, 117.

p. 274   *Stephen's sickness and symptoms, "good French and madira Brandy," "in every way"*: CB to Elvira Stone, Oct. 30, Nov. 1864, CB Papers LC; CB to Samuel Barton, Oct. 30, Nov. 1, 1864, CB Papers HL.

p. 274   *"every attention ... that is possible"*: Stephen Barton to David Barton, Oct. 23 1864 [typescript], CB Papers AAS.

p. 274   *"hand of Divine Mercy," "dear sister," "very happy," "I imagine that I have been"*: CB to Samuel Barton, Oct. 30, 1864, CB Papers LC; Stephen Barton to David Barton, Oct. 23, 1864 [typescript], CB Papers AAS.

p. 275   *"sickest days," "obstinate engagement"*: CB to Samuel Barton, Oct. 30, Nov. 1, 1864, CB Papers HL; Stephen to "my own wife," Nov. 16, 1864, ibid. See also CB to Elvira Stone, Oct. 30, 1864, CB Papers LC.

p. 275   *Butler's reversal, "you are not to attack," casualties*: Trudeau, *Last Citadel*, 241–51; Porter, *Campaigning with Grant*, 309–13. The Federal advance south of the James resulted in the battle of Hatcher's Run.

p. 275   *wounded from Richmond front, CB's labors*: CB to Elvira Stone, Oct. 30, 1864, CB Papers LC; Stephen to "my own wife," Nov. 16, 1864, CB Papers HL.

p. 275   *"beautiful arms red with blood"*: Butler quoted in *Worcester Sunday Telegram*, Sept. 16, 1917, clipping, CB Papers LC.

p. 275   *"I leave so much undone," "I do not bother"*: CB to Elvira Stone, Oct. 30, 1864, CB Papers LC; Stephen to "my own wife," Nov. 16, 1864, CB Papers HL.

p. 275   *"no day since I have been here"*: ibid.

p. 276   *"an open Union man"*: CB to Elvira Stone, Oct. 30, 1864, CB Papers LC.

p. 276   *Stephen told CB his story, his situation 1861–1862, Union gunboats*: CB to Judge Barton, Dec. 5, 1864, CB Papers AAS; Joel R. Griffin to CB, Aug. 1865, ibid.; Stephen to David Barton, Oct. 23, 1864, ibid.; Stephen Barton to Lt. Col. O. L. Mann, Mar. 6, 1865, SRB Papers DU.

p. 276   *Union and rebel lines Chowan River country*: Griffin to CB, Aug. 1865, CB Papers LC; Parramore, "The Bartons of Bartonsville," *North Carolina Historical Review* (Jan. 1974), 30–34.

p. 276   *"a neutral position"*: Stephen Barton to David Barton, Oct. 23, 1864 [typescript], CB Papers AAS.

p. 276   *"burn him out," Col. Griffin and Stephen*: Griffin to CB, Aug. 1865, CB Papers LC.

pp. 276–77   *hungry families, "conservative" neighbors, "material aid"*: Stephen Barton to Lt. Col. Mann, Mar. 6, 1865, SRB Papers DU. In June, 1864, the monthly pay for rebel privates went up to $18—still pitifully low for those with families.

p. 277   *trading between the lines, Union Treasury Department permits*: James M. McPherson, *Ordeal by Fire: The Civil War and Reconstruction* (New York: Alfred A. Knopf, 1982), 378–80; Bruce Catton, *Grant Takes Command* (Boston: Little, Brown, 1969), 17.

p. 277   *booming illegal trade*: Ludwell Johnson, *The Red River Campaign: Politics and Cotton in the Civil War* (Baltimore: Johns Hopkins University Press, 1958), 49–50.

p. 277   *Federal efforts to suppress illicit trade, Lincoln's ambivalence*: Lincoln, *CW*, 7:151, 354, and 8:163–64. See also G. S. Boritt, *Lincoln and the Economics of the American*

Dream (Memphis: Memphis State University Press, 1978),
243–49.

p. 277   *Stephen Barton's trading in cotton*: Stephen to David
Barton, Oct. 23, 1864, [typescript], CB Papers AAS;
Stephen Barton to Lt. Col. Mann, Mar. 6, 1865, SRB
Papers DU.

p. 277   *traders from occupied Norfolk, hub of trade*: Catton, *Grant
Takes Command*, 411.

p. 277   *"may appear strange," "All livables," "They had much
cotton"*: Stephen to David Barton, Oct. 23, 1864 [type-
script], CB Papers AAS.

p. 277   *"was sold on Government account"*: Samuel Barton to his
mother Oct. 9, 1864, SRB Papers DU. According to
Sammy, Stephen wrote him that the government had
"made only $30,000 out of his [Stephen's] labors but don't
say what he has made."

p. 278   *"never been able," "much profit"*: Stephen to David Barton,
Oct. 23, 1864 [typescript], CB Papers AAS.

p. 278   *cotton sale to Petersburg firm*: value of Confederate currency from Clement Eaton, *A History of the Southern
Confederacy* (New York: Macmillan, 1956), 239. Stephen
Barton's business records, SRB Papers DU, show that in
March, 1864, the firm of Pachels [?] and Son paid Stephen
$180,000 and $150,000 in Confederate currency for 1,200
pounds of cotton. If taken literally, this meant that
Stephen's cotton sold for the equivalent of $12.38 a pound
in gold, which was impossible. In the summer of 1864, cotton was selling in Boston for $1.90 per pound in Union
paper currency (Johnson, *Red River Campaign*, 50), or the
equivalent of about sixty-five cents per pound in gold. The
1,200 pounds of cotton listed in Stephen's records was
doubtless the first installment in a much larger quantity of
cotton.

p. 278   *"greatly reduced," "interest which the Federal
Government," "I think I have moved"*: Stephen to
David Barton, Oct. 23, 1864 [typescript], CB Papers
AAS.

p. 278   *Stephen Barton's deal with Harney*: Stephen Barton to Lt.
Col. Mann, Mar. 6, 1865, SRB Papers DU.

p. 278   *"for alleged abuse," Union gunboats, "buy cotton," "pay a
fairer price," "They took me at my word"*: ibid.; Stephen to
David Barton, Oct. 23, 1864 [typescript], CB Papers AAS.
Also CB to Judge Barton, Dec. 5, 1864, ibid.

p. 279   *Stephen's party to South Mills*: ibid.; Stephen Barton to
"Dear Friend," Nov. 1, 1864 [typescript], CB Papers AAS
(the manuscript version of this letter, in CB Papers LC, is
mostly unreadable on microfilm); Lt. ADC to Col. H.
Sanders, Sept. 27, 1864, SRB Papers DU; Stephen Barton
to Lt. Col. Mann, Mar. 6, 1865, ibid. Samuel Barton to his

mother, Oct. 8, 1864, ibid., said that his father took $3,000 in "state money and greenbacks."

p. 279   *"who seeing the error"*: Stephen Barton to Dear Friend, Nov. 1, 1864 [typescript], CB Papers AAS; Stephen Barton to Lt. Col. Mann, Mar. 6, 1865, SRB Papers DU.

p. 280   *Stephen Barton's arrest*: the scene derives from ibid.; Stephen Barton to "Dear Friend," Nov. 1, 1864 [typescript], CB Papers AAS; CB to Judge Barton, Dec. 5, 1864, ibid. See also CB affidavit, Oct. 10, 1865, CB Papers LC.

p. 280   *Thornton's interrogation, Stephen jailed, "I was compelled"*: Stephen Barton to Lt. Col. Mann, Mar. 6, 1865, SRB Papers DU. See also CB to Judge Barton, Dec. 5, 1864, CB Papers AAS.

p. 280   *"a notorious rebel"*: CB's letter to family friend "Dear M" in CB affidavit, Oct. 10, 1885, CB Papers LC; CB to Benjamin F. Butler [circa 1885], SRB Papers DU.

p. 280   *"a blockade runner," "I told him," "calculating"*: Stephen Barton to Lt. Col. Mann, Mar. 6, 1865, SRB Papers DU.

p. 280   *"They took much more," "to admit," Shepley interview*: ibid. A fragment, dated Sept. 28, 1864, ibid., states that $1,476.25 in "Confederate and southern" money had been taken from Stephen Barton.

p. 281   *Stephen back in guardhouse, "left us much,"* New York Herald *story, "Those wicked men,"* Massasoit, *"a certificate," "humanity and justice," "there is nothing"*: Stephen Barton to Lt. Col. Mann, Mar. 6, 1865, ibid.

p. 281   *"I despaired of ever," "friends in Washington," "political friend," "don't go to lying," "You damned impudent," "I have done with you," "It was well"*: ibid.

pp. 281–82   *"Old man, I have been," "from the defiant and insolent," "quite exhausted me"*: ibid.

p. 282   *Butler to examine SB's case, "parole of honor"*: CB to Judge Barton, Dec. 5, 1864, CB Papers AAS; Stephen Barton to Lt. Col. Mann, March 6, 1865, SRB Papers DU.

p. 282   *"pretty certain," "I was slow to give"*: CB to Judge Barton, Dec. 5, 1864, CB Papers AAS.

p. 282   *"a common filthy guard house," "love of country alone," "was to all appearance," "Genl Butler's prompt"*: ibid.

p. 283   *"I need not tell you"*: CB to Samuel Barton, Oct. 30, 1864, CB Papers HL. Stephen set forth his views on slavery, Union black troops, Confederate conscription, and other political issues in his letter to Elvira Stone, Nov. 1864, CB Papers LC.

p. 283   *rebels hopes on McClellan*: See Paul D. Escott, *After Secession: Jefferson Davis and the Failure of Confederate Nationalism* (Baton Rouge: Louisiana State University Press, 1978), 207–19; and McPherson, *Battle Cry of Freedom*, 766–72.

p. 283   *election day, inclement weather*: Smith, *Reminiscences*, 116.

p. 283   *soldiers cheered, bands played*: CB to Judge Barton, Dec.
                5, 1864, CB Papers AAS.

p. 283   *soldier vote for Lincoln, "Don't you know that Abe"*:
                Trudeau, *Last Citadel*, 253.

p. 283   *Stephen wept, "could be constituted"*: CB to Judge Barton,
                Dec. 5, 1864, CB Papers AAS; CB to Frances Gage, May 1,
                1864, CB Papers LC.

p. 284   *Stephen's plans, disaffection in Confederacy, "they realize
                that their institution"*: CB to Samuel Barton, Oct. 30, 1864,
                CB Papers HL; CB to Judge Barton, Dec. 5, 1864, CB
                Papers AAS; Stephen to Elvira Stone, Nov. 1864, CB
                Papers LC.

p. 284   *"ordinary or written advice," "I can simply tell other mem-
                bers," "if I fail"*: CB to Samuel Barton, Oct. 30, Nov. 1,
                1864, CB Papers HL.

p. 284   *"operating under the new laws," loyal Union man, help
                redeem North Carolina*: CB to Judge Barton, Dec. 5, 1864,
                CB Papers AAS; Stephen Barton to Benjamin F. Butler,
                Nov. 19, Dec. 1, 1864, CB Papers LC.

p. 284   *"to report to him here," Stephen to "wait," "Of his loyalty"*:
                CB to Judge Barton, Dec. 5, 1865, CB Papers AAS.

p. 285   *Butler in New Orleans, brother's illicit trading*: Nellis,
                "Between a Crown and a Gibbet," 44–46; Gerald M.
                Capers, *Occupied City: New Orleans Under the Federals
                1862–1865* (Lexington: University of Kentucky Press, 1965),
                79–94, 161–67; McPherson, *Battle Cry of Freedom*, 624.

p. 285   *Butler and Baltimore trader in North Carolina*: Nash,
                Stormy Petrel, 215–16. For more on Butler's attitude
                toward the cotton trade, see his testimony, Jan. 17, 1865, in
                Report of the Joint Committee on the Conduct of the War,
                38th Cong., 2d sess., vol. 2 (Washington D.C.: Government
                Printing Office, 1865), 46–47.

p. 285   *"For six weeks of such labor"*: CB to Judge Barton, Dec. 4,
                1864, CB Papers AAS.

p. 286   *Stephen's "trial" at Butler's HQ and quotations*: CB's letter
                to family friend "Dear M" in CB affidavit, Oct. 10, 1885,
                CB Papers LC; CB to Benjamin F. Butler [circa 1885],
                SRB Papers DU; Stephen Barton to Lt. Col. Mann, Mar. 6,
                1865. Butler's directive to Col. Sanders is in SRB Papers
                DU.

p. 286   *"most interesting, happy and amusing"*: Stephen Barton to
                nieces and nephew [typescript], Dec. 11, 1864, CB Papers
                LC.

p. 286   *corps reorganization*: Trudeau, *Last Citadel*, 378, 485. The
                Twenty-fifth Corps also included black troops assigned to
                Butler's army from the AOP's Ninth Corps. Rod Cragg,
                Confederate Goliath: The Battle of Fort Fisher (New York:
                HarperCollins, 1991), 36, observes that this was the largest
                organization of black soldiers in the war.

p. 287   *"beyond her power," potential battle Dutch Gap, CB's duty*: Stephen Barton to "my own wife," Dec. 17, 1864, SRB Papers DU.

p. 287   *"a great deal of 'worriment' "*: CB to Stephen Barton, Dec. 24, 1864, CB Papers HL. See also Stephen Barton to "my own wife," Dec. 17, 1864, SRB Papers DU; and Samuel Barton to his mother, Dec. 15, 1864, ibid.

p. 287   *first Fort Fisher expedition*: Cragg, *Confederate Goliath*, 35–36; Grant, *Personal Memoirs and Selected Letters*, 665–66.

p. 287   *Butler's idea, "Monster Torpedo," "loaded with 400 tons of gunpowder," "the people's money"*: Grant's report in Grant, *Papers*, 14:187–89. See also Nash, *Stormy Petrel*, 206, and Grant, *Personal Memoirs and Selected Letters*, 197.

p. 287   *Butler assumed command*: Nash, *Stormy Petrel*, 208–9; Grant, *Personal Memoirs and Selected Letters*, 665–66; Grant report in Grant, *Papers*, 14:190.

p. 287   *"I rather formed the idea"*: ibid.

p. 288   *Grant's orders to Butler*: Butler, *Private and Official Correspondence*, 5:380–81.

p. 288   *CB at flying hospital, news of Butler, "especially honored"*: CB to Stephen Barton, Dec. 24, 29, 1864, CB Papers HL.

p. 288   *"astonished and* frightened," "*I know you want," "I hope you can," "I have almost forgotten"*: CB to Stephen Barton, Dec. 29, 1864, ibid.

p. 288   *Butler's force "failed"*: CB Diary [Jan. 4], 1865, CB Papers LC. My details of the failed operation derive from Butler's testimony in *Report of the Joint Committee on the Conduct of the War* (1865), 2:3–51; Grant's report in Grant, *Papers*, 14:190; Grant, *Personal Memoirs and Selected Letters*, 667; Cragg, *Confederate Goliath*, 45–98; Nash, *Stormy Petrel*, 211–13.

p. 288   "did not intend that the attack": Benjamin F. Butler, *Butler's Book: Autobiography and Personal Reminiscences* (Boston: A. M. Thayer, 1892), 808.

p. 289   *second Fort Fisher expedition*: Grant's report in Grant, *Papers*, 14:191.

p. 289   *"No one but myself knows," "We felt confident"*: CB Diary [Jan. 4, 5], 1865, CB Papers LC.

p. 289   *"nondiscretionary orders to hold," Butler sacked*: Nash, *Stormy Petrel*, 214; Grant's report in Grant, *Papers*, 14:191; Grant, *Personal Memoirs and Selected Letters*, 668; Butler's testimony in *Report of the Joint Committee on the Conduct of the War* (1865), 2:33. See also Randall and Current, *Last Full Measure*, 291.

p. 289   *Lincoln and Butler, "While the newspapers of the country"*: Lincoln, *CW*, 8:207, 207n; Butler, *Butler's Book*, 830.

p. 289   *Kittinger's resignation, "no one can fully take"*: CB Diary [Jan. 3, 6–8], 1865, CB Papers LC. See also Kittinger's Pension Records, NARA.

p. 289   *Brown in camp, "very anxious," "I want much to see you"*:
          CB Diary [Jan. 7], 1865, CB Papers LC; Stephen Barton to
          CB, CB Papers SC.

p. 290   *"removed some eight or ten times," "a most interesting
          field," "You would probably think"*: CB to Soldiers' Aid
          Society, West Fitchburg, Mass., Jan. 26 1865, CB Papers
          LC.

p. 290   *CB's ride with Brown and Baker, "one of the famous," "This
          was a most remarkable"*: CB Diary, Jan. 10, 11, 1865, ibid.

p. 290   *"every protection," CB's return to Washington*: ibid., Jan.
          12–13, 1865.

p. 290   "It is coming spring": CB to Soldiers' Aid Society, West
          Fitchburg, Mass., Jan. 26 [1865], ibid.

PART SIX: ANDERSONVILLE

p. 293   *Stephen and Irving, Senator Wilson*: CB Diary, Feb. 9–10,
          13, 1865, CB Papers LC; *The Universalist*, May 27, 1865,
          clipping, ibid.; Abbott, *Cobbler in Congress*, 154.

p. 293   *Butler's testimony*: Report of the Joint Committee on the
          Conduct of the War (1865), 2:3–51; Williams, *Lincoln and
          the Radicals*, 366–67.

p. 293   *"no man except Genl. Butler," "hero's welcome"*: CB Diary,
          Jan. 27, 1865, CB Papers LC; Nash, *Stormy Petrel*, 217.

p. 294   *"I had thought of him," "This is God's war," "the Great
          Architect"*: CB to Wilson, Mar. 9, 1865, CB Papers LC.

p. 294   *CB's trip to Norfolk, interview with Mann, "all parties," "the
          case of Stephen's arrest"*: CB Diary, Feb. 2–7, 1865, ibid.;
          also Stephen Barton to Lt. Col. Mann, Mar. 6, 1865, SRB
          Papers DU.

p. 294   *Stephen's condition*: CB Diary, Feb. 9–10, 13, 28, Mar. 3,
          1865, CB Papers LC.

p. 294   *Irving's condition, "I am wearing out"*: CB Diary, Feb. 12,
          17, 1865, ibid.; CB to Col. A. T. Sharp, Dec. 25, 1865 [type-
          script], AAS; *The Universalist*, May 27, 1865, clipping, CB
          Papers LC.

p. 295   *CB "dull" and disoriented, war news, cannon boomed,
          rumors*: CB Diary, Feb. 16–17, 20, 1865, ibid.

p. 295   *prisoner exchange policy*: McPherson, *Battle Cry of
          Freedom*, 567, 650, 791–92, 799–800; William B.
          Hesseltine, *Civil War Prisons: A Study in War Psychology*
          (reprint 1930 ed., New York: Frederick Ungar, 1964),
          69–113.

p. 295   *returning prisoners, Annapolis, "general rendezvous"*: CB
          Diary, CB Papers LC; Feb. 19, 1865; Moore, *Women of the
          War*, 373–74, 405–6.

p. 295   *Irving's suggestion*: CB Diary, Feb. 19, 20, 1865, CB Papers LC.

pp. 295–96   *"whom they had reason," "the intense anxiety and excitement," "most pressing necessity," "imperative duty," "friends of the prisoners"*: CB to Stanton [draft], Sept. 1865, ibid.; CB's Memorial to Congress, Jan. 20, 1866, ibid. Fanny Gage referred to CB as "the soldiers' friend" (Gage's letter in CB's behalf [circa Jan. 1866], ibid.). For CB's earlier concerns for missing soldiers, see for instance CB to Capt. J. B. Proctor, Sept. 9, 1862, CB Collection AHL.

p. 296   *CB's plan of action, "thus placing in communication"*: CB to Stanton [draft], Sept. 1865, ibid.; CB's Memorial to Congress, Jan. 20, 1866, ibid.

p. 296   *CB to Annapolis, description of hospital*: CB Diary, Feb. 21, 1865, ibid.; Moore, *Women of the War*, 373–74, 405–6; Brockett and Vaughan, *Women's Work in the Civil War*, 455–56, 462–63.

p. 296   *"I find the captain needs"*: CB Diary, Feb. 21, 1865, CB Papers LC.

p. 296   *"poor wrecks of humanity," "prison pens,"* unloading ritual, prisoners' appearance, dreamy, *"idiotic stare"*: Brockett and Vaughan, *Women's Work in the Civil War*, 246, 259, 371–72, 455. CB said there were four boatloads of "poor wretched men" from the South (CB Diary, Feb. 22, 1865, CB Papers LC).

p. 297   *Hawley's description*: quoted in Moore, *Women of the War*, 395.

p. 297   *"from prejudice," CB and Dix*: CB Diary, Feb. 22, 23, 1865, CB Papers LC.

p. 298   *"cordially approved," "laughed at him," CB and Lincoln*: ibid., Feb. 24–25, 27, 1865; Barton, *Life of Clara Barton*, 1:335–36.

p. 298   *"General Correspondent," "obtain and furnish"*: CB's request to Lincoln, Feb. 27, 1865, CB Papers LC.

p. 298   *"in some anxiety," Mrs. Brown and CB, Mrs. Ambrose*: CB Diary, Feb. 27, 1865, ibid.

p. 298   *CB's first effort to see Lincoln*: ibid., Feb. 27, 1865.

p. 298   *Jules Golay and Mary A. Baker,* Wilson *"loaned"*: ibid., Feb. 28, Mar. 2, 3, 1865. Barton, *Life of Clara Barton*, 1:337, points out that CB shared her bed with her "friend" but doesn't identify her. CB referred to her house guest as "Miss Baker," but it is clear that she was Mrs. Mary A. Baker. On March 3, according to the *Congressional Globe*, 38th Cong., Special Sess. (Feb. 6–Mar. 11, 1865), 35:1404, Congressman Miller of Pennsylvania reported from the Committee on Invalid Pensions a bill entitled "An Act for the relief of Mary A. Baker, widow of Brigadier General Edward D. Baker," and the House agreed to consider the bill. CB said that Wilson promoted the bill in the Senate (CB Diary, Feb. 28, 1865, CB Papers LC).

p. 299   *CB and Washburn, "one of the most useful," second attempt to see Lincoln*: CB Diary, Feb. 28, 1865, CB Papers LC.

p. 299   *CB's visit with Gen. Hoffman, "would not take offence"*: ibid. Hoffman's position and background from Sifakis, *Who Was Who in the Civil War*, 312.

p. 299   *CB's appeal to Hitchcock, "it must be carried out," third attempt to see Lincoln*: CB Diary, Feb. 28, 1865, CB Papers LC; Sifakis, *Who Was Who in the Civil War*, 311.

p. 299   *Stephen and Irwin, "crushed in spirit," "Alternately hoping and despairing"*: CB Diary, Feb. 28, 1865, CB Papers LC; CB to family friend Dear M in CB affidavit, Oct. 10, 1885, ibid.

pp. 299–300   *"go on without anything," "acting without authority," "I dare not and do not," Wilson engrossed, "all my power"*: CB Diary, Feb. 28, Mar. 2, 1865, ibid.

p. 300   *"Could not go," "tried hard not to be"*: ibid., Mar. 1, 1865.

p. 300   *CB's visit with Dole, "very kindly for," raining "fearfully"*: ibid., Mar. 2, 1865.

p. 300   *crowds streaming in, depot painted and decorated, cots in Willard's halls and parlors*: Leech, *Reveille in Washington*, 366.

p. 300   *CB's fourth attempt to see Lincoln*: CB Diary, Mar. 2, 1865, CB Papers LC.

pp.300–301   *joyous Mary Baker, "I do not tell her"*: ibid. On March 4, the Speaker of the House signed Mary's bill; the Senate approved it, and the president, who had been a good friend of her husband, signed it into law (*Congressional Globe*, 35:1371, 1391).

p. 301   *CB and Dole, "in his power," fifth attempt to see Lincoln, "decided to leave my papers"*: CB Diary, Mar. 3, 1865, CB Papers LC.

p. 301   *bands of serenades, firemen's parade, "threw a white halo," crowded galleries, Booth*: My details are from Leech, *Reveille in Washington*, 366.

p. 301   *March 4 storm*: CB Diary, Mar. 4, 1865, CB Papers LC. CB said it "rained almost a hurricane."

p. 301   *Dr. Richardson's visit*: ibid.

p. 301   *sunburst*: Brooks, *Washington, D.C. in Lincoln's time*, 213.

p. 302   *"mighty scourge of war," "until all the wealth"*: Lincoln, CW, 8:333.

p. 302   *"Is this war never to end"*: CB to Frances Gage, May 1, 1864, CB Papers LC.

p. 302   *CB at Lincoln's reception*: CB Diary, Mar. 4, 1865, ibid.; Leech, *Reveille in Washington*, 370, for "free-for-all"; Miers, *Lincoln Day by Day*, 3:318.

p. 302   *CB and Bigelow to Inaugural Ball*: CB Diary, Mar. 6, 1865,

CB Papers LC; Bigelow's career from Sifakis, *Who Was Who in the Civil War*, 54–55.

p. 302   *sashaying couples, flag-covered room, 4,000 people*: Leech, *Reveille in Washington*, 371.

p. 302   *Banks, Farragut, and Wilson*: CB Diary, Mar. 6, 1865, CB Papers LC.

p. 302   *Lincoln's arrival, Mary Lincoln's dress and arrival, enormous supper*: Sandburg, *Lincoln: The War Years*, 4:119–20; Leech, *Reveille in Washington*, 372. See also Brooks, *Washington, D.C. in Lincoln's Time*, 215.

p. 302   *"great crowd"*: CB Diary, Mar. 6, 1865, CB Papers LC.

p. 303   *"large mouthfuls," family physician, Dr. Sheldon*: ibid., Mar. 10, 1865.

p. 303   *"faithfully paid," "This war is near its end"*: CB to family friend Dear M in CB affidavit, Oct. 10, 1885, ibid.

p. 303   *CB and Stephen's dialogue, Stephen's death, "Did our mother"*: CB Diary, Mar. 10, 1865, ibid.; CB to family friend Dear M in CB affidavit, Oct. 18, 1885, ibid.

p. 303   *"noble handsome features," "I think I can see why"*: CB Diary, Mar. 11, 1865, ibid.

p. 303   *"God has called," "kind and gentle," "asked to take the place"*: ibid., Mar. 12, 1865.

p. 304   *CB at Dole's office*: ibid., Mar. 13, 1865.

p. 304   *"As it is a matter pertaining"*: Lincoln, *Collected Works—Supplement*, ed. Roy P. Basler (Westport, Conn.: Greenwood Press, 1974), 283; CB Diary, Mar. 13, 1865, CB Papers LC.

p. 304   *"a most delightful interview," "encouraged me"*: ibid. Gen. Hitchcock wrote the commanding officer at Annapolis in CB's behalf. See his letter of Mar. 25, 1865, in Barton, *Life of Clara Barton*, 1:306.

p. 304   *"To the friends of missing persons"*: Lincoln, CW 8:423. Also quoted in Ross, *Angel of the Battlefield*, 86, and Pryor, *Clara Barton*, 134.

p. 304   *Bartonsville burned*: Abram Riddick's deposition [Dec. 27, 1865], George W. Lewis's deposition [Jan. 4, 1866], George F. Dern's deposition [July 29, 1886], SRB Papers DU; CB to Wilson, Apr. 22, 1865, CB Papers LC.

p. 304   *"for the success of the Union armies:"* CB to family friend Dear M in CB affidavit, Oct. 10, 1885, ibid.

p. 305   *CB to Annapolis, 360 letters, 100 per day*: CB Diary, Mar. 24, 1865, ibid.; CB, Memorial to Congress, Jan. 20, 1866, ibid.; Frances Gage to Senators and Representatives [circa Jan. 1866], ibid. Barton, *Life of Clara Barton*, 1:306, also states that CB received a hundred letters of inquiry each day.

p. 305   *Colonel Sewell, "if it is practicable"*: CB Diary, Mar. 25, 28, 1865, ibid.; Washington Gardner, "Clara Barton at

Andersonville," and address at the Dedication of a Memorial to CB, Andersonville, Ga., May 31, 1915, Thirty-third National Convention of the Women's Relief Corps, 280, CB Papers SLRC; Gen. Hitchcock to commanding officer, Annapolis, Mar. 25, 1865, in CB to Stanton [draft], Sept. 1865, CB Papers LC.

p. 305   *"had to force herself"*: "Biographical Department: Clara H. Barton," *Soldier's Weekly Messenger* [circa 1867], clipping, ibid.

p. 306   *"come once more and the last"*: CB to Col. A. T. Sharp, Dec. 25, 1865 [typescript], CB Papers AAS.

p. 306   *"he had* finished," *"bleeding at the lungs"*: ibid.

p. 306   *people cheering, brass bands playing*: Leech, *Reveille in Washington*, 377–78.

p. 306   *Irving's death, "He was to me the tenderest"*: CB, Diary, Apr. 9, 1865, CB Papers LC; CB to Col. A. T. Sharp, Dec. 25, 1865 [typescript], CB Papers AAS.

p. 306   *Washington in bedlam, 500-gun salute, "Dixie," "our lawful property"*: Brooks, *Washington, D.C. in Lincoln's Time*, 223–25. See also Welles, *Diary*, 2:278.

p. 306   *"lamp-lighted window," "Battle Cry of Freedom," illuminations, 6,000 candles at Patent Office, "Union," "Victory," "Year of Jubilee"*: Leech, *Reveille in Washington*, 382–84; Brooks, *Washington, D.C. in Lincoln's Time*, 225.

p. 307   *CB with Mr. Upperman*: CB Diary, Apr. 14, 1865, CB Papers LC.

p. 307   *rumors of Lincoln's death, CB to her apartment*: ibid.

p. 307   *"It served Lincoln right"*: quoted in Thomas Reed Turner, *Beware the People Weeping: Public Opinion and the Assassination of Abraham Lincoln* (Baton Rouge: Louisiana State University Press, 1982), 49.

p. 307   *Stanton's dragnets*: Benjamin P. Thomas and Harold M. Hyman, *Stanton: The Life and Times of Lincoln's Secretary of War* (New York: Alfred A. Knopf, 1962), 396–99.

p. 307   *monstrous Confederate plot*: See Turner, *Beware the People Weeping*, 46–52; and Herbert Mitgang (ed.), *Abraham Lincoln: A Press Portrait* (Chicago: Quadrangle Books, 1971), 463, 466.

p. 307   *"History has on its record"*: *Washington Evening Star*, Apr. 15, 1865. The *New York Tribune*, Apr. 17, 1865, and other Northern papers struck a similar note.

p. 307   *"The whole city in gloom"*: CB Diary, Apr. 15, 1865, CB Papers LC.

pp. 307–308   *CB's diary entries*: ibid. When she testified before the Joint Committee on Reconstruction in 1866, CB stated that she had seen Lincoln's remains (her April diary entries do not mention this). This must have been when he lay in state in the Capitol. See U.S. Congress, *Report of the Joint Committee on Reconstruction*, 39th Cong. 1st sess.

(Washington, D.C.: Government Printing Office, 1866), pt. 3, 103. Ross, *Angel of the Battlefield*, 87, states that Grant asked CB to attend the funeral ceremonies in Philadelphia and that she did so. I could find no evidence to support this statement.

p. 308   *Lincoln's funeral train and its journey*: Dorothy Meserve Kunhardt and Philip B. Kunhardt, Jr., *Twenty Days* (New York: Harper & Row, 1965), is the most complete account.

p. 308   *"That was the grandest funeral"*: CB's fragment [undated], CB Papers LC.

p. 309   *"armed resistance to the authority"*: quoted in Long, *Civil War Day by Day*, 687.

p. 309   *army's grand review*: Brooks, *Washington, D.C. in Lincoln's Time*, 271–84; Leech, *Reveille in Washington*, 415–17, particularly for the details about Mother Bickerdyke.

p. 309   *"melted back into the heart"*: Brooks, *Washington, D.C. in Lincoln's Time*, 284.

p. 309   *numbers and losses*: compiled from James M. McPherson, *Ordeal by Fire: The Civil War and Reconstruction* (New York: Alfred A. Knopf, 1982), 488; Livermore, *Numbers and Losses in the Civil War*, 1–20; Brooks, *Civil War Medicine*, 126–29; Steiner, *Disease in the Civil War*, 10–11; Duncan, "The Comparative Mortality of Disease and Battle Casualties in the Historic Wars of the World," in Duncan, *Medical Department of the United States Army in the Civil War*, 27–28; Barnes, *Medical and Surgical History*, 1:pt. 1, passim.

p. 309   *unidentified dead*: Barton, *Life of Clara Barton*, 1:304–5. As CB's relative put it, 200,000 Northern households had lost a kinsman in the war but had no idea where he was buried. See also Pryor, *Clara Barton*, 135.

p. 309   *"To my exceeding astonishment"*: CB to Wilson, Sept. 29, 1865, CB Papers LC.

p. 310   *CB's "Office of Correspondence"*: CB to Brig. Gen. D. C. McCallum, Apr. 16, 1865, Consolidated Correspondence File, 1794–1915, NARA QMG; Frances Gage to Senators and Representatives [circa Jan. 1866], CB Papers LC; CB to Elvira Stone [circa spring 1865], ibid. Barton, *Life of Clara Barton*, 1:306, incorrectly states that the War Department provided CB with a clerk and postal privileges.

p. 310   *"quite a little money"*: ibid., 334; also 333. Barton, 334, also points out that CB expected Congress to reimburse her.

p. 310   *"old time $1400 clerkship"*: CB to Wilson, Dec. 19, 1865, CB Papers LC.

p. 310   *CB's Naval Academy operation, "twenty-nine thirtieth"*: CB, "To the People of the United States," May 31, 1865, CB Papers AAS: also CB to Stanton [draft], Sept. 1865, CB Papers LC.

p. 310   *"I thought my duty plain"*: ibid.

p. 311   *CB's "To the People"*: CB Papers AAS.

p. 311   *"no assistance either from the Government"*: CB to President Johnson, May 31, 1865, CB Papers LC. An edited version of the letter is in Barton, *Life of Clara Barton*, 1:307–8.

p. 311   *"offered very pleasantly,"* endorsement of generals, *"exceedingly cordial," "I had a hard week's work"*: CB Diary, June 1–4 1865, ibid.; Barton, *Life of Clara Barton*, 1:309–10.

p. 311   *Wilson paid her postage*: CB to Stanton [draft], Sept. 1865, CB Papers LC.

p. 311   *CB's initial roll*: ibid.; CB Diary, June 9, 1865, ibid.; CB to C. K. Smith [circa 1865], ibid.

p. 311   *150 letters a day*: ibid. CB told Gen. Hoffman, however, that she received from 80 to 100 letters a day (ibid., June 28, 1865). See also CB to Brig. Gen. D. C. McCallum, Apr. 16, 1865, Consolidated Correspondence File, 1794–1915, NARA QMG.

p. 311   *"either useful information of some missing soldier"*: CB to Elvira Stone [circa June 1865], CB Papers LC.

p. 312   *master list, second roll*: CB to Stanton [draft], Sept. 1865, ibid.

p. 312   *"dark hazel eyes, hair almost black"*: Mrs. T. B. Hurlbut to CB, Sept. 26, 1865, ibid.

p. 312   *"waiting, waiting, waiting," "I have placed"*: Mrs. Martha A. Upton to CB, Sept. 10, 1865, ibid. (also quoted in Massey, *Bonnet Brigades*, 332); CB to Mrs. Upton, Sept. 16, CB Papers LC.

p. 312   *"mortified," "I would like to know," "The cause of your name"*: Joseph H. Hutchins to CB, Oct. 16, 1865, ibid.; CB to Hutchins [circa Oct. 1865], ibid. An edited version is quoted in Barton, *Life of Clara Barton*, 1:312.

p. 313   *"I brought a copy"*: Atwater to CB, June 26, 1865, ibid. An edited version is quoted in Barton, *Life of Clara Barton*, 1:312.

p. 313   *CB to Atwater's room*: CB to Gen. William Hoffman, June 28, 1865, Commissary General of Prisoners, Letters Received, NARA (also in CB Papers LC); CB's testimony, *Report of the Joint Committee on Reconstruction*, pt. 3, 103.

p. 313   *Atwater description*: Frances Gage in *New York Independent*, Feb. 29, 1866, clipping, CB Papers LC; Atwater's Military Service Records, NARA.

p. 313   *Atwater's military career, imprisonment, secret death register, parole, sick at home*: Atwater told his story many times and was remarkably consistent in his details. My account derives from Atwater's Military Service Records, NARA; Atwater's testimony, *Report of the Joint Committee on Reconstruction*, pt. 2, 279–85; typescript biography and Atwater's Statement, CB Papers LC; Atwater's

"Introduction" and CB's "Report" in *A List of the Union Soldiers Buried at Andersonville* (New York: Tribune Association, 1866); Memorial Address, "Dorence Atwater," Congregational Church, Terryville, Conn., May 29, 1911, CB Papers LC; *"Dorence Atwater"* [undated ms.], CB Papers SC; *New York Tribune*, Aug. 3, 1865, report on basis of a letter from CB; affidavits in support of Atwater's wife, Atwater's Pension Records, NARA. Quotation "vatching dem dam Yankees" is from John McElroy, *This Was Andersonville,* ed. Roy Meredith, (reprint 1879 ed., New York: Bonanza Books, 1957), 19 (also quoted in Hesseltine, *Civil War Prisons*, 141); quotation "Flying Dutchman" is from John L. Ransom, *John Ransom's Diary* (reprint 1881 ed., New York: Dell Publishing Co., 1964), 55, 65. See also Adjutant General's Memorandum for the Quartermaster General, Dec. 14, 1914, DA File ANHS. Barton, *Life of Clara Barton*, 1:317, and Pryor, *Clara Barton*, 137–38, also have profiles of Atwater.

pp. 314–15 *Atwater's negotiations with Breck and quotations*: Breck's telegram to Major Dodge, Mar. 23, 1865, and Breck's memo to Commanding Officer, May 2, 1865, Atwater's Military Service Records, NARA; Atwater's "Statement," 3–4, CB Papers LC; Atwater's "Introduction," *List of the Union Soldiers Buried at Andersonville*; Atwater's testimony, *Report of the Joint Committee on Reconstruction*, pt. 11, 285.

p. 315 *Atwater's drawing, description of Andersonville graves, CB's idea of expedition*: CB's notes about Andersonville expedition and letter to Stanton [draft], Sept. 1865, CB Papers LC; CB to Hoffman, June 28, 1865, Commissary General of Prisoners, Letters Received, NARA (also in CB Papers LC).

p. 316 *CB to Gen. Hoffman*: ibid.; CB to Mrs. Albert Dow, Dec. 15, 1865, ibid.

p. 316 *"At first the idea was regarded," "By dint of perseverance"*: CB's notes about Andersonville expedition, ibid.; CB to Gen. Hoffman, June 28, 1865, with Hoffman's endorsement and remarks to Stanton on the back, Commissary General of Prisoners, Letters Received, NARA (also in CB Papers LC).

p. 316 *CB's visit with Stanton*: loose sheets in CB Diary [miscellaneous folder], ibid.; edited version in Barton, *Life of Clara Barton*, 318–19; CB's notes about the Andersonville expedition, CB Papers LC. See also accounts based on letters from CB in *New York Tribune*, Aug. 3, 1865, and in *Savannah Herald*, July 14, 1865, clippings, CB Papers LC.

p. 316 *Stanton profile*: based on Thomas and Hyman, *Stanton*, 143–401, 638; Turner, *Beware the People Weeping*, 55–56, 63, 69–72; and Mark Neely, Jr., "Vindication," *Lincoln Lore* (May 1982).

p. 316   *Stanton's orders for the expedition, Moore as commander, Atwater to go along,*; Stanton to General George H. Thomas, June 29 1865, *OR*, ser. 1, vol. 39, pt. 2, 1051; Stanton to General Montgomery Meigs, June 30, 1865, copy in CB File ANHS; Stanton to Meigs, July 1, 1865, Consolidated Correspondence File, 1794–1915, NARA; CB's notes about the Andersonville expedition, CB Papers LC; CB Diary, July 8, 1865, ibid. That Moore was in charge of military burials in the Washington area derives from documents in Cemeterial Quartermaster Notifications, 1863–1866, NARA.

pp. 316–17   *"no one knew how grateful he was," "entire satisfaction"*: CB Diary, July 8, 1865, CB Papers LC; CB to "My Dear Friend," July 1865, ibid.; CB to Mrs. Albert Dow, Dec. 15, 1865, ibid.; CB's testimony, *Report of the Joint Committee on Reconstruction*, pt. 3, 285; loose sheets in CB Diary [miscellaneous folder], ibid., and quoted in Barton, *Life of Clara Barton*, 1:318–19.

p. 317   *Atwater and Moore, official and secret death registers*: Atwater's "Introduction," *List of the Union Soldiers Buried at Andersonville*; Atwater's testimony in *Report of the Joint Committee on Reconstruction*, pt. 2, 285–86; James Pickett Jones, *Yankee Blitzkrieg: Wilson's Raid Through Alabama and Georgia* (Athens: University of Georgia Press, 1976), 180.

p. 317   *"If it once shall be my privilege"*: CB quoted in *New York Tribune*, Aug. 3, 1865, clipping, CB Papers LC.

pp. 317–18   *"violently," "God damn it to hell"*: CB's "Report" in *List of the Union Soldiers Buried at Andersonville*. My description of Moore, a Pennsylvanian, comes from a photograph of him and his Military Service Records in Letters Received, NARA AGO.

p. 318   *workers' abuse, "I cannot understand Capt Moore"*: ibid.; CB Diary, July 12, 1865, CB Papers LC.

p. 318   *CB retired sick, CB's berth*: ibid., July 9–11, 1865; CB to "My dear Friend," July 1865, ibid. See also CB's notes about Andersonville expedition, ibid.

p. 318   *arrival in Savannah, description of city*: CB Diary, July 12, 1865, ibid.; CB to "My dear Friend," July 1865, ibid.; William Tecumseh Sherman, *Memoirs* (New York: Library of America, 1990), 708, 694.

p. 318   *Georgia Central closed; shortage of wagons*: CB Diary, July 12, 1865, CB Papers LC; Moore's report, *OR*, ser. 3, vol. 5, 319–20.

p. 318   *Moore's telegram to Meigs*: July 16, 1865, copy, CB File ANHS; CB's notes about Andersonville expedition, CB Papers LC; CB's "Report" in *List of the Union Soldiers Buried at Andersonville*. In his official report (*OR*, ser. 3, vol. 5, 320), Moore admitted that he "abandoned all idea of

attempting a route through a country difficult and tedious."
Moore's report should not be used by itself, for it omits a
sizable part of the story, including the fact that CB and
Atwater accompanied the expedition and that Atwater's
death register guided Moore in marking the graves. Moore
claimed all the credit for the mission.

p. 318 *CB in her cabin, "one social or sympathizing spirit," "a mere
boy"*: CB Diary, July 12–13, 1865, CB Papers LC.

p. 319 *Clement's visit, Clement's story*: CB Diary, July 13, 1865,
ibid.; *Savannah Herald*, (July 14, 1865), clipping in ibid.

p. 319 *CB and William Lane, "so much intelligence"*: CB to "My
dear Friend," July 1865, ibid.; CB's notes about the
Andersonville expedition, ibid.

p. 319 *carriage rides, description of Savannah*: CB Diary, July
14–15, 1865, ibid.; Sherman, *Memoirs*, 708.

p. 319 *Moore's inclination to abandon the expedition*: CB's suspi-
cions were aroused on July 13, 1865, when she learned that
Moore had purchased a pair of mockingbirds as a gift for
Stanton's wife. Surely, she thought, he intended to abandon the expedition; otherwise he would never have
attempted "such a delicate undertaking" as buying the
birds. By July 15, she was convinced that he lacked the
"will" to continue with the expedition. "What a pity!" she
exclaimed two days later. "And the country can never be
made to understand the circumstances. I have no witness,
no friend." CB Diary, CB Papers LC.

p. 319 *"constituted the only obstruction"*: CB's "Report" in *List of
the Dead Soldiers Buried at Andersonville*.

p. 319 *overland route was "perfect"*: CB Diary, July 14, 17, 1865,
CB Papers LC.

p. 319 *"I informed Capt. M.," Moore's telegram from Augusta officials, Moore to telegraph Washington*: ibid., July 15, 1865;
Moore's report, *OR*, ser. 3, vol. 5, 320; CB Diary, July 15,
1865, CB Papers LC.

p. 320 *CB's resolution to proceed*: CB Diary, July 17, 1865, ibid.;
CB's notes about the Andersonville expedition, ibid.

p. 320 *"peremptory orders" from Meigs*: CB's notes about the
Andersonville expedition, CB Papers LC; CB Diary, July
17, 1865, ibid.; Moore's telegram to Meigs, July 17, 1865,
copy in CB File ANHS, acknowledging receipt of Meigs's
telegram of July 15, 1865 and assuring Meigs that "I shall
make every effort possible to reach Andersonville," as
Meigs had plainly ordered. Moore's subsequent report of
the expedition does not mention Meig's order or CB's own
determination to push the expedition forward. Moore
claimed that he resolved to proceed as soon as he received
a telegram from Augusta officials, July 18, stating that the
railroad from Augusta to Atlanta had been repaired (*OR*,
ser. 3, vol. 5, 320). A correspondent for the *New York*

Tribune supported CB's version of the story. "When the expedition was at Savannah," he reported, "it was feared that in consequence of the difficulty of transportation, its object might be abandoned for the present, but the devoted energy of Miss Barton and the zealous cooperation of the Government [e.g., officials in Washington] have carried it through" *New York Tribune*, Aug. 3, 1865.

p. 320   *"It was tauntingly remarked"*: CB to "My dear Friend," July 1865, CB Papers LC.

p. 320   *Moore's arrangements, CB to be left if late*: CB Diary, July 18, 19 1865, ibid.

p. 320   *"crooked, muddy" river, stay in Augusta*: ibid., July 19–22, 1865.

p. 320   *Moore's studied disrespect, "Today I went without my dinner"*: ibid., July 21, 1865; also July 22. For a different emphasis on Moore's "snub," see Pryor, *Clara Barton*, 139.

p. 321   *"I am all alone"*: CB Diary, July 22, 1865, CB Papers LC.

p. 321   *journey to Atlanta, top was "punched," "we literally waited"*: ibid., July 23, 1865; CB to T. J. S. Brown, Aug. 7, 1865, ibid.

p. 321   *"Atlanta is in terrible condition," "great trouble", conductor a rebel officer*: CB Diary, July 23, 1865 (typescript version because LC microfilm unreadable), CB Papers AAS; ibid., July 24, 1865, CB Papers LC. CB wrote T. J. S. Brown that Atlanta was *"torn in fragments, a shocking place"* (Aug. 7 1865, ibid.).

p. 321   *sweet Georgia peaches, white and black reinforcements*: CB Diary, July 24, 1865, ibid.; Moore's report, *OR*, ser. 3, vol. 5, 320; Moore to "General," July 30 1865, copy CB File ANHS.

p. 322   *description of countryside*: CB's "Report" in *List of the Union Soldiers Buried at Andersonville*; Ovid L. Futch, *History of Andersonville Prison* (Gainesville: University of Florida Press, 1968), 1, 3; MacKinlay Kantor, *Andersonville* (Cleveland: World Publishing Co., 1955), 11.

p. 322   *arrival at Andersonville, unbearably hot*: CB Diary, July 24, 25, 1865, CB Papers LC; Futch, *History of Andersonville*, 3, gives the population of Anderson as fewer than twenty residents in 1864.

p. 322   *William Griffin profile*: CB Diary, July 25, 1865, CB Papers LC; CB to T. J. S. Brown, Aug. 7, 1865, ibid.; CB's "Report" in *List of the Union Soldiers Buried at Andersonville; Washington Chronicle, Aug. 26, 1865*, clipping, CB Papers LC.

p. 322   *"had set bravely to work," "noble philanthropist"*: CB to T. J. S. Brown, Aug. 7, 1865, ibid.

p. 322   *CB's visit to Andersonville cemetery*: ibid.; CB Diary, July 25, 1865, ibid.; CB's "Report" in *List of the Union Soldiers Buried at Andersonville*; CB's testimony, *Report of the Joint*

Committee on Reconstruction, pt. 3, 107; CB to Stanton [draft], Sept. 1865, ibid.; CB to Edward R. Clement, July 30, 1865, CB Papers LC; CB To T. J. S. Brown, Aug. 7, 1865, ibid.

p. 322   *total Northern deaths in rebel prisons*: McPherson, *Battle Cry of Freedom*, 802. Modern authorities put the total Union deaths at Andersonville at 12,912. See Joseph P. Cangemi and Casimir J. Kowalski (eds.), *Andersonville Prison: Lessons in Organizational Failure* (Lanham Md.: University Press of America, 1992), 34, 41.

p. 322   *"The original plan for identifying"*: CB to Stanton, July 26, 1865, CB Papers LC; edited version in Barton, *Life of Clara Barton*, 1:320. See also CB Diary, July 25, 1865, CB Papers LC.

p. 323   *camp days were over*: CB to T. J. S. Brown, Aug. 7, 1865, ibid.; CB to Edward R. Clement, July 30, 1865, ibid.

p. 323   *location of camp, headboards*: Moore to "General," July 30, 1865, copy in CB File ANHS; CB to Dear Madam, Dec. 30, 1865, CB Papers LC (copy in CB File ANHS).

p. 323   *"for I did not choose"*: CB to Stanton [draft], Sept. 1865, CB Papers LC; also CB Diary, July 27, 1865, ibid.

p. 323   *CB never invited to help, "entirely alone here," "I know I stand"*: CB to Stanton [draft], Sept. 1865, ibid.; CB Diary, Aug. 11, 1865, ibid.

p. 323   *CB as camp nurse*: CB to Stanton [draft], Sept. 1865, ibid.

p. 323   *Atwater shunned*: Atwater to Joseph Sheldon, Nov. 28, 1865, ibid.

p. 323   *"manly beyond his years," Watts's illness, nursed by CB*: CB to Rev. B. I. Ives, Oct. 13, 1865, ibid.; CB's notes about Andersonville expedition, ibid.; CB to Stanton [draft], Sept. 1865, ibid.; CB Diary, July 31, Aug. 1, 1865, ibid.

p. 324   *CB's pilgrimage to stockade, prison hospital, "Confused heaps of rubbish"*: CB Diary, July 26, 1865, ibid.; CB's "Report," *List of the Union Soldiers Buried at Andersonville*; Dr. Joseph Jones's report, *OR*, ser. 2, vol. 8, 604. Dr. Jones said that the hospital was surrounded by "a frail board fence" (ibid.). Futch, *History of Andersonville*, 105, referred to it as "a flimsy board fence."

p. 324   *fifteen surgeons, 2,000 sick prisoners*: ibid., 99; Atwater's testimony, *Report of the Joint Committee on Reconstruction*, pt. 2, 281, 282. Atwater put the figure at 2,500 hospital inmates at a time. Dr. Joseph Jones reported that almost 2,000 sick prisoners and attendants were in the hospital when he visited it in September 1864 (Jones's report, *OR*, ser. 2, vol. 8, 604). In early Aug. says Futch, 99, the hospital "had 1,305 patients."

p. 324   *camp diseases*: Dr. Jones's report, *OR*, sec. 2, vol. 8, 600–2, 621, 616–18, 621–22; Joseph Jones, *Medical and Surgical Memoirs: Containing Investigations on the Geographical Distribution*,

Causes, Nature, Relations and Treatment of Various Diseases, 1855–1890 (3 vols., New Orleans: Clark and Hofeline, 1876-90), 3:400–1; John L. Ransom, *Diary, 56–57*; P.F. Gethings's narrative in Wolcott, *History of the Twenty-first Massachusetts*, 397.

p. 324
scurvy victim's symptoms: Charles Hopkins, *Andersonville Diary & Memoirs*, ed. William B. Styple and John J. Fitzpatrick (Kearny, N.J.: Belle Grove Publishing Co., 1988), 133.

pp. 324–25
Dr. Jones's observations: OR, ser. 2, vol. 8, 604–6, 618–23, 630–32. Futch, *History of Andersonville*, 100, also states that there were two men per bunk and that others lay on the ground; Futch, 105–9, also quotes extensively from Jones's report. See also Jones, *Medical and Surgical Memoirs*, 3:405–7.

p. 325
John January's self-amputation: Hopkins, *Andersonville Diary & Memoirs*, 136, 139.

p. 325
stockade walls, sentry boxes, Georgia reserves, deadline: CB to T. J. S. Brown, Aug. 7, 1865, CB Papers LC; CB's "Report," *List of the Union Soldiers Buried at Andersonville*; George A. Hitchcock's Diary in Wolcott, *History of the Twenty-first Massachusetts*, 402, 404–5, 408–9; Ransom, *Diary*, 55, 94; McElroy, *This Was Andersonville*, 27, 30, 32, 50–51; Hesseltine, *Civil War Prisons*, 135, 143–44; Futch, *History of Andersonville*, 2, 5, 56. Futch says that the walls were about fifteen feet in height.

p. 325
"We have many thoughtless boys": quoted in ibid., 56. "Guards shoot now very often," John Ransom wrote in his diary on July 8, 1864. "Boys, as guards, are the most cruel. It is said that if they kill a Yankee, they are given a thirty days furlough." Ransom, *Diary*, 94.

p. 325
"shelterless, pitiful spot," 33,000 prisoners: CB's "Report," *List of the Union Soldiers Buried at Andersonville*; Atwater's testimony, *Report of the Joint Committee on Reconstruction*, pt. 2, 282; Futch, *History of Andersonville*, 44; Hitchcock's diary in Wolcott, *History of the Twenty-first Massachusetts*, 401–23; Emilio, *Brave Black Regiment*, 173, 183; Ransom, *Diary*, 77.

p. 326
description of prisoners: Ransom, *Diary*, 54, 62, 71; Dr. Jones's report, *OR*, ser. 2. vol. 8, 602–3; Hitchcock's diary in Wolcott, *History of the Twenty-first Massachusetts*, 402–3; Gething's narrative in ibid., 396–97; McElroy, *This Was Andersonville*, 28.

p. 326
shrub huts, improvised tents: Atwater's testimony, *Report of the Joint Committee on Reconstruction*, pt. 2, 281; Dr. Jones's report, *OR*, ser. 2, 8, 599. "I observed men urinating and evacuating their bowels at the very tent doors and around the little vessels in which they were cooking their

food," Dr. Jones reported. "Small pits, not more than a foot or two deep, nearly filled with soft offensive feces, were everywhere seen, and emitted under the hot sun a strong and disgusting odor. Masses of corn bread, bones, old rags, and filth of every description were scattered around or accumulated in large piles" (ibid.). See also Futch, *History of Andersonville*, 18.

p. 326   caves, "like rabbits or reptiles," "drinking cups made of sections": CB to T. J. S. Brown, Aug. 7, 1865, CB Papers LC; CB's "Report," *List of the Union Soldiers Buried at Andersonville.*

p. 326   horizontal galleries, dirt hidden in their pockets: ibid McElroy, *This Was Andersonville*, 45, said that the dirt from the tunnels "was taken up in improvised bags made by tying up the bottoms of pantaloon legs, carried to the swamp [or marsh inside the stockade], and emptied."

p. 326   escaped prisoners, bloodhound kennels, stocks and chains: CB, "Black Book," CB Papers SC; CB Lecture [undated], CB Papers LC; Atwater's testimony, *Report of the Joint Committee on Reconstruction*, pt. 2, 283; Hitchcock's diary in Wolcott, *History of the Twenty-first Massachusetts*, 405; Ransom, *Diary*, 64, 71; J. Holt to President Johnson, *OR*, ser. 1, vol. 8, 777–81, citing testimony of prisoners. See also Futch, *History of Andersonville*, 49–50, 54. Local blacks told CB that "the same blood hounds which had been kept and used to catch runaway slaves in the olden times, were set upon the track to hunt down our own escaped prisoners in later days" (CB to T. J. S. Brown, Aug. 7, 1865, CB Papers LC).

p. 326   prison rations: Atwater's testimony, *Report of the Joint Committee on Reconstruction*, pt. 2, 281–82; Hitchcock's diary in Wolcott, *History of the Twenty-first Massachusetts*, 403–5, 409–10, 415; Ransom, *Diary*, 61, 70 (for eating swallows), 77, 84; Amos E. Stearns, *The Civil War Diary of Amos E. Stearns, a Prisoner at Andersonville*, ed. Leon Basile (Rutherford, N. J.: Fairleigh Dickinson University Press, 1981), 66–74, 78; McElroy, *This Was Andersonville*, 128, 164; Dr. Jones's report, *OR*, ser. 2, vol. 8, 602–3, 617; Hesseltine, *Civil War Prisons*, 147; Futch, *History of Andersonville*, 21, 32, 35, 37. See the engravings and photographs of the "living skeletons" in Hopkins, *Andersonville Diary & Memoirs*, 168, 172, 174. For those who argue that the prisoners received the same rations as rebel soldiers, the caption on p. 174 asks: "Were there any Rebel guards found at Andersonville in this condition?"

p. 326   sutler inside stockade: Stearns, *Civil War Diary*, 77; Hesseltine, *Civil War Prisons*, 149; Futch, *History of Andersonville*, 35.

p. 327   polluted Stockade Creek: CB's "Report," *List of the Dead*

Soldiers Buried at Andersonville; CB's testimony, *Report of the Joint Committee on Reconstruction*, pt. 3, 106; Atwater's testimony, ibid., pt. 2, 282; Dr. Jones's report, *OR*, ser. 2, vol. 8, 598–99, 604; McElroy, *This Was Andersonville*, 53; Futch, *History of Andersonville*, 37–38.

p. 327   *"Not half watter enough"*: quoted in ibid., 37.

p. 327   *rebel camps upstream*: CB's "Report," *List of the Dead Soldiers Buried at Andersonville*; Futch, *History of Andersonville*, 37–38. Dr. Jones, however, said that the rebel camps were too far upstream for their waste to "sensibly affect the constantly flowing waters." Jones's report, *OR*, ser. 2, vol. 8, 593.

p. 327   *nobody could drink*: Futch, *History of Andersonville*, 37–38, states that "Stockade Creek became so contaminated that no one could drink its waters and hope to remain healthy."

p. 327   *CB saw grease and refuse matter, "rifle shot," "pure, delicious"*: CB's testimony, *Report of the Joint Committee on Reconstruction*, pt. 3, 106; CB's "Report," *List of the Union Soldiers Buried at Andersonville*.

p. 327   *complaints to Wirz, nothing ever done*: Atwater's testimony, *Report of the Joint Committee on Reconstruction*, pt. 2, 282. Prisoner Hopkins claimed that when he and his comrades complained about the water, Wirz yelled: "The water of the creek is good enough for you God-damned Yankee sons of ———." Hopkins, *Andersonville Diary & Memoirs*, 100.

p. 327   *wells*: CB's "Report," *List of the Union Soldiers Buried at Andersonville*; Futch, *History of Andersonville*, 37–38.

p. 327   *"appears impregnated with sulfur"*: quoted in ibid., 37.

p. 327   *foul-smelling swamp, "poison sink," maggots, "We could not get away from it"*: Atwater's testimony, *Report of the Joint Committee on Reconstruction*, pt. 2, 282; Hopkins, *Andersonville Diary & Memoirs*, 73, 75; McElroy, *This Was Andersonville*, 53. See also Dr. Jones's report, *OR*, ser. 2, vol. 8, 604; and Futch, *History of Andersonville*, 104. Arch Fredric Blakey, *General John H. Winder, C.S.A.* (Gainesville: University of Florida Press, 1990), 184, says that the swampy cesspool inside the stockade covered some three and a half acres.

p. 328   *heavy rains fell, "massed together"*: CB's "Report," *List of the Union Soldiers Buried at Andersonville*; CB to Stanton [draft], Oct. 1865, CB Papers LC. See also Hitchcock's diary in Wolcott, *History of the Twenty-first Regiment of Massachusetts Volunteers*, 411.

p. 328   *"The treacherous nature of the soil"*: CB's "Report," *List of the Union Soldiers Buried at Andersonville*.

p. 328   *"counted 235 corpses," some went mad, "whining, childish"*: Hopkins, *Andersonville Diary & Memoirs*, 96, 95.

p. 329   *simply stopped living, prisoners turned on one another, raiders*: Ransom, *Diary*, 81, 91–97; Dr. Jones's report, *OR*, ser. 2, vol. 8, 597; Hitchcock's diary in Wolcott, *History of the Twenty-first Massachusetts*, 408. Dr. Jones referred to the prison as "this gigantic mass of human misery" (*OR*, ser. 2, vol. 8, 623)

p. 329   "*mere boy*," "*from oblivion the last record*": CB, "Black Book," CB Papers SC.

p. 329   "*the magnitude and enormity*": CB to T. J. S. Brown, Aug. 7, 1865, CB Papers LC.

p. 329   *neighborhood women, Gen. Winder*: Futch, *History of Andersonville*, 120.

p. 329   *a rebel surgeon told CB, most local whites agreed*: CB Diary, July 26, 1865, CB Papers LC; CB's testimony, *Report of the Joint Committee on Reconstruction*, pt. 3, 105. Blakey's *General John H. Winder*, 175–215, though based on impressive scholarship, unconvincingly exonerates Winder of almost all blame for what happened at Andersonville. Instead, Blakey faults among other things the cruel Yankees for suspending the exchange of prisoners, the Confederacy's chaotic prison system and food and medical shortages, and Winder's own ill-disciplined soldiery (see chaps. 9–19). Futch's assessment, *History of Andersonville*, 119, seems closer to the mark: "General Winder was ill-suited to the task assigned him. He was narrow, unimaginative, and short-sighted."

p. 329   *Atwater blamed Wirz, "a chain-gang," "used to have men put up*": Atwater's testimony, *Report of the Joint Committee on Reconstruction*, pt. 3, 283.

p. 330   "*would have been a 'Star'*": CB to T. J. S. Brown, Aug. 7, 1865, CB Papers LC.

p. 330   *gross and unforgivable negligence, "the almost total absence of system*": Futch, *History of Andersonville*, 25, 89, 106; Dr. Jones's report, *OR*, ser. 2, vol. 8, 605. See also the modern analyses by Capt. Gwynn A. Tucker, Wilburn Clouse, and Carl L. Romanek in Cangemi and Kowalski (eds.), *Andersonville Prison: Lessons in Organizational Failure*, 1–34, 35–40, 41–50.

p. 330   *Winder's death*: Blakey, *General John H. Winder*, 5.

p. 330   "*a fiend incarnate*," "*the Andersonville savage*": *New York Times*, Aug. 12, 16, 1865; *New York Tribune* (Aug. 12, 1865). The *Tribune* is also quoted in Hesseltine, *Civil War Prisons*, 239.

p. 330   *official death register taken to Washington*: Atwater's testimony, *Report of the Joint Committee on Reconstruction*, pt. 2, 287; Atwater's "Introduction," *List of the Union Soldiers Buried at Andersonville*.

p. 330   *CB's Andersonville relics*: CB Diary, Aug. 7, 1865, CB Papers LC; CB's "Report," *List of the Union Soldiers Buried at Andersonville*; "LOAN EXHIBITION" [typescript], CB Papers LC; Frances D. Gage, "Relics of Andersonville," *New York Independent*, clipping, ibid.

p. 330   white visitors, "were very neighborly, very bland," CB promised to help: CB Diary, July 26, 1865, CB Papers LC; CB's testimony, Report of the Joint Committee on Reconstruction, pt. 3, 105.

p. 330–31   Col. Joel Griffin, "Stephen had loved so much," "How can it be?": CB Diary, July 26, 27, 1865, CB Papers LC.

p. 331   black visitors, "Miss Clara," "Yankee woman," Rosa: ibid., July 26, 31, Aug. 13, 1865.

p. 331   eighty to a hundred former slaves, whether Lincoln was dead, "a hoax to hold them": ibid., Aug. 1, 13, 1865; CB to T. J. S. Brown, Aug. 7, 1865, ibid.; CB's "Report," List of the Union Soldiers Buried at Andersonville; CB's testimony, Report of the Joint Committee on Reconstruction, pt. 3, 103.

pp. 331–32   CB's response to black visitors, CB read Wilson's order, "Yes, we understand," "I think they never failed": ibid., 103–4; also CB Diary, Aug. 1, 13, 1865, CB Papers LC; and CB to T. J. S. Brown, Aug. 7, 1865, ibid.

pp. 332–33   Arnold Cater's story, wife's beating, employment at Andersonville, quotations: CB's testimony, Report of the Joint Committee on the Conduct of the War, pt. 3, 104–5. See also CB Diary, Aug. 7, 1865, CB Papers LC. See ibid., Aug. 13, 17, 1865, for Rosa and Jarret.

p. 334   "snow-white" headboards, "like the city of the dead," Moore's behavior: CB Diary, Aug. 7, 11, 1865, ibid.

p. 334   Watts was dramatically worse, local doctor, "frightened," "poor poor boy," "I never saw such": ibid., Aug. 8–14, 1865.

p. 334   "hosts of errors," "criminal haste": ibid., Aug. 14, 1865; see also Ross, Angel of the Battlefield, 91.

p. 334   cemetery looked impressive, "National Cemetery," "in a rural landscape": CB's notes about Andersonville expedition, CB Papers LC; CB to Stanton [draft], Sept. 1865, ibid.; Moore's report, OR, ser. 3, vol. 5, 321; CB's "Report," List of the Union Soldiers Buried at Andersonville; Washington Chronicle, Aug. 26, 1865.

p. 335   Watts's death and quotations: CB Diary, Aug. 15–16, 1865, CB Papers LC. See also Dorence Atwater, "Statement," 5, ibid.

p. 335   last tablet in place, Union dead identified, "Unknown U.S. Soldier": Moore's report, OR, ser. 3, vol. 5, 320–21; CB's "Report," List of the Union Soldiers Buried at Andersonville; CB to Stanton [draft], Sept. 1865, CB Papers LC.

p. 335   "This at Andersonville!" CD Diary, Aug. 17, 1865, ibid.

p. 335   flag-raising ceremony, "The work was done": Washington Chronicle, Aug. 26, 1865; Harper's Weekly, Oct. 7, 1865; CB Diary, Aug. 17, 1865, CB Papers LC.

p. 336   itinerary of return trip: see ibid., Aug. 17–24, 1865.

p. 336   "sad and terrible": ibid., Aug. 17, 1865.

p. 336   "I have looked over its 25 acres": CB, "Black Book," CB

Papers SC; slightly different version in CB Lecture [undated], CB Papers LC.

PART SEVEN: THE TRIAL

p. 339   *"too much trouble," abuse of Rosa*: CB Diary, Aug. 21–22, 1865, CB Papers LC.

p. 339   *description and history Old Capitol Prison*: Leech, *Reveille in Washington*, 141–42, 148–51; Bryan, *Great American Myth*, 5. See Abbott, *Cobbler in Congress*, 117, 117n–118n, and McKay, *Wilson*, 152–54, for the unfounded allegations about Wilson and Rose O'Neal Greenhow.

p. 339   *"most bloodthirsty monster"*: New York Tribune, Aug. 12, 1865; also quoted in Hesseltine, *Civil War Prisons*, 239.

p. 339   *"in violation of the laws and customs of war"*: OR, ser. 2, vol. 8, 785, 786.

p. 339   *testimony of Andersonville survivors, "reeking with the filth"*: ibid., 777–81, 784–91; 785 for quotation.

p. 340   *CB's desire to testify*: CB to Henry Wilson, Oct. 27, 1865, CB Papers LC.

p. 340   *"She has seen"*: Washington Chronicle, Aug. 26, 1865. See also issue of Aug. 27, 1865.

p. 340   *CB's Patent Office job eliminated, "crumb board," "a scrap or morsel"*: CB to Henry Wilson, Dec. 19, Sept. 29, 1865, CB Papers LC. Massey, *Bonnet Brigades*, 133, points out that Harlan removed most of the Interior Department's female employees.

p. 340   *second roll*: CB to Stanton [draft], Nov. 1865, CB Papers LC.

p. 341   *Atwater v. Breck, "for the benefit of the friends," Atwater's arrest and imprisonment*: Atwater's "Statement," 6, ibid. See also Atwater's "Introduction," *List of the Union Soldiers Buried at Andersonville*; and CB to Mrs. Albert Dow, Dec. 15, 1865, CB Papers LC.

p. 341   *"I am confined here"*: Atwater's letter in *New York Citizen*, Mar. 3, 1866, clipping, ibid.

p. 341   *CB's interview with Stanton*: CB Diary, Sept. 3–5, 1865, ibid.

p. 341   *"What do you desire," "Simply this, Sir"*: CB to Stanton, Sept. 5, 1865, ibid. Quoted in Barton, *Life of Clara Barton*, 1:324.

p. 342   *she consulted with various friends*: CB Diary, Sept. 8–10, 1865, CB Papers LC.

p. 342   *"I have called no witnesses"*: "Added Clause of Dorence Atwater's Statement," ibid.; CB Diary, Sept. 10, 1865, ibid. Atwater's statement is quoted in full in Barton, *Life of Clara Barton*, 1:322–23.

p. 342   *CB's dinner with Atwater*: CB Diary, Sept. 11, 1865, CB
                Papers LC.

p. 342   *Atwater's trial, "unlawfully and feloniously," "certain prop-
                erty"*: court-martial proceedings, *Report of the Joint
                Committee on Reconstruction*, pt. 2, 288; Atwater's
                "Introduction," *List of the Union Soldiers Buried at
                Andersonville.*

p. 342   *"perjury of the blackest"*: Atwater to Joseph Sheldon, Nov.
                28, 1865, CB Papers LC.

p. 342   *Breck's and Moore's testimony, had "had nothing to do"*:
                court-martial proceedings, *Report of the Joint Committee
                on Reconstruction*, pt. 2, 288; Atwater's testimony, ibid.,
                287; Judge Advocate General Joseph Holt to Stanton, Sept.
                27, 1865, copy in DA File ANHS; CB to Joseph Sheldon,
                Dec. 3, 1865, CB Papers LC; CB to Mrs. Albert Dow, Dec.
                15, 1865, ibid.

p. 343   *Atwater's statement, "court hinted"*: ibid.; Atwater to Joseph
                Sheldon, Nov. 28, 1865, ibid.

p. 343   *"large number of letters," "the record of burials"*:
                Washington Chronicle, Sept. 14, 1865, and *New York
                Independent*, Feb. 9, 1866, respectively; CB Diary, Sept.
                14, 1865, CB Papers LC.

p. 343   *Moore's report: OR*, ser. 3, vol. 5, 319–22.

p. 343   *"How can Capt Moore sleep"*: CB Diary, Oct. 19, 1865, CB
                Papers LC.

p. 343   *"stately," "I am mentioned once"*: ibid., Oct. 3, 1865. See
                Harper's Weekly, Oct. 7, 1865.

p. 343   *"tricky little officers," "The deeper he can bury his rivals"*: CB
                Diary, Oct. 3, 1865, and CB to Butler [undated],CB Papers
                LC; CB to Charles Graham Halpine, Sept. 27, 1865, ibid.

p. 344   *"God will require something"*: CB Diary, Oct. 3, 1865, ibid.

p. 344   *"high handed"*: CB Diary, Sept. 14, 1865, ibid.

p. 344   *restrictive measures against Southern blacks*: Eric Foner,
                *Reconstruction: America's Unfinished Revolution,
                1863–1877* (New York: Harper & Row, 1988), 198–99.

p. 344   *"no man could do that"*: CB Diary, Sept. 16, 1865, CB
                Papers LC.

p. 344   *Atwater's sentence, CB shocked*: court-martial proceedings,
                Report of the Joint Committee on Reconstruction, pt. 2, 288;
                CB Diary, Sept. 20, 1865, CB Papers LC; CB to Mrs.
                Albert Dow, Dec. 15, 1865, ibid.; Atwater's "Introduction,"
                List of the Union Soldiers Buried at Andersonville. The sen-
                tence is also in Barton, *Life of Clara Barton*, 1:322.

p. 344   *CB "exceedingly depressed," Mrs. Peck, "waited and
                mourned," "I thought a person"*: CB Diary, Sept. 18, 22,
                1865, CB Papers LC.

p. 345   *"little disabled brother," "keep house," "good trusty staff,"
                "He has one of the sweetest dispositions"*: ibid., Sept. 24,
                10, Oct. 20, 1865.

p. 345   *Rosa, "excused," "for the present"*: ibid., Sept. 24, 1865.

p. 345   *CB and Rosa, quotations*: ibid., Oct. 8, 10, 14, 1865.

p. 345   *CB's report to Stanton*: report in *List of the Union Soldiers Buried at Andersonville*; draft in CB Papers LC; CB Diary, Sept. 24, 1865, ibid.

p. 346   *CB's visit with Stanton, "I could scarce breathe"*: ibid., Sept. 25, 1865.

p. 346   *"Dorr had just left"*: ibid. See also CB note, Sept. 25, 1865, ibid., and quoted in Barton, *Life of Clara Barton*, 1:324; CB to Halpine, Sept. 27, 1865, CB Papers LC.

p. 346   *"It seemed that the very Heavens"*: CB to Rev. Mr. Ives, Oct. 13, 1865, ibid.

p. 346   *"in ameliorating the condition"*: Andersonville Survivors' Association, Resolution, Sept. 1865, ibid.

p. 347   *Hannah Nash to CB*: Aug. 27, 1865 [typescript], CB Papers AAS.

p. 347   *$7,533 of her own money*: CB Memorial to Congress, Jan. 20, 1866, CB Papers LC. Frances Gage claimed that CB spent $12,000 of her own money "in her country's service" (Gage to Senators and Representatives [circa Jan. 1866], ibid.).

p. 347   *"clerical force"*: CB to Butler, Oct. 3, 1865, ibid.

p. 347   *CB's book idea and letter to Wilson*: CB wrote two drafts of the letter but probably never sent either of them. A rough manuscript draft (undated) is in CB Papers LC. A cleaner draft (undated) is published in Barton, *Life of Clara Barton*, 1:330–33. My quotations draw on both drafts. CB's Diary first mentions the book idea on Sept. 16, 1865, and refers to it again on Oct. 16, 1865, when Ferguson agreed to help her find a publisher. It was in this period that she probably wrote the letter drafts to Wilson, in which she admitted her self-doubts and said that it would cost $10,000 to have such a book published. On Oct. 22, 1865, she wrote in her diary that she knew her book project would fail, probably because she could never raise $10,000, or convince a publisher to waive that sum and simply share in her profits.

p. 348   *women's books about the war*: see Massey, *Bonnet Brigades*, 178–96, for a discussion of the literature.

p. 348   *CB's meeting with Butler, "and show them the necessity," "colored" soldiers*: CB Diary, Oct. 2, 1865, CB Papers LC; CB to Butler, Oct. 3, 1865, ibid.

p. 348   *"fully approved," "a Bureau by itself," "Whoever heard"*: CB Diary, Oct. 4, 1865, ibid.

p. 349   *"in the final arrangement," "as it was through a league," "some distant head"*: CB to Butler [circa Oct. 5, 1865, or shortly thereafter] [typescript], ibid. Her Diary entry for Oct. 5, 1865, shows that she had second thoughts about what Butler told her.

p. 349   *"this great wrong"*: CB to Rev. Mr. Ives, Oct. 13, 1865, ibid.

p. 349   *CB's campaign in Atwater's behalf*: CB to Halpine, Sept. 27, 1865, ibid.; CB Diary, Oct. 2, 7, 10–12, 1865, ibid.; CB to Connecticut Adjutant General, Oct. 10, 1865, ibid.; CB quoted in letter to Francis Atwater, Aug. 11, 1912, CB Papers SC.

p. 350   *was not "a humbug," "of all the ladies"*: CB Diary, Sept. 18, 1865, CB Papers LC.

p. 350   *CB's meeting with Rucker, "many things," "sad"*: ibid., Oct. 6, 1865.

p. 350   *CB missed Frances Gage*: ibid., Oct. 14–15, 1865.

p. 350   *Wirz trial*: *OR*, ser. 2, vol. 8, 776–81; Hesseltine, *Civil War Prisons*, 244.

pp. 350–51   *CB's desire to be a witness*, "studied measures," *"friend in that court," "My collection of relics," "I believe I have acted"*: CB to Wilson, Oct. 27, 1865, CB Papers LC. Jefferson Davis was never brought to trial for treason. He was finally released from prison at Fort Monroe in May 1867. See William C. Davis, *Jefferson Davis: The Man and His Hour* (New York: HarperCollins 1991), 655–56.

p. 351   *CB's lost confidence in Butler, "I see now that the calumny," "I know that"*: CB Diary, Oct. 19–21, 1865, ibid.

p. 351   *CB's search for missing soldiers suspended*: CB to Stanton [draft], Nov. 1865 and CB Memorial to Congress, Jan. 20, 1866, CB Papers LC.

p. 351   *leaving the country, "no interest"*: CB Diary, Oct. 22, 1865, ibid.

p. 352   *"There is no hope"*: ibid. See also ibid., Oct. 23–24, 1865.

p. 352   *Tufts burst into her room, "greatly relieved"*: ibid., Oct. 25, 1865.

p. 352   *CB's visit with spiritualist, "wrote beautifully," "Ah me!"*: ibid., Oct. 26, 1865.

p. 352   *CB's stay in New Haven, quotations*: ibid., Oct. 31, Nov. 1–8, 16, 1865.

p. 353   *Wirz convicted and hanged, "Remember Andersonville"*: *OR*, ser. 2, vol. 8, 790–91; Sifakis, *Who Was Who in the Civil War*, 725.

p. 353   *"working like a slave," $228 withdrawn, "It is not the first time"*: CB Diary, Nov. 10, 11, 16, 1865, CB Papers LC; Barton, *Life of Clara Barton*, 1:340.

p. 353   *CB and Butler in Boston*: CB Diary, Nov. 18, 1865, CB Papers LC.

p. 353   *"with the same reliant kindly"*: ibid., Nov. 24, 1865.

p. 353   *CB's interview with Stanton, Butler would "resuscitate it"*: ibid., Nov. 1865.

p. 354   *"half paralyzed by the agony"*: CB to Butler, Dec. 1, 1865, ibid.

p. 354   *CB's meeting with Hitchcock*: CB Diary, Nov. 27, 1865, ibid.

p. 354   *Moore's Burial Bureau*: ibid.; Dec. 1, 1865; also Oct. 6, 1865.

p. 354   *Moore's promotions*: he was appointed brevet major and brevet lieutenant colonel in the same month, November 1865. See his Military Service Records, NARA AGO.

p. 354   *"from further labors," "This officer"*: CB to Butler, Dec. 1, 1865, ibid.

p. 355   *Atwater's release*: E. D. Townsend to Atwater, May 2, 1865, ibid; CB to Dear Sister, Dec. 29, 1865, ibid.; CB to Mrs. Dow, Dec. 15, 1865, ibid.; CB to Halpine [circa Dec. 1865], ibid.; Atwater's "Introduction," *List of the Union Soldiers Buried at Andersonville*.

p. 355   *"God is so merciful"*: CB Diary, Dec. 2, 1865, CB Papers LC.

p. 355   *CB's strategy, "play possum"*: ibid., Dec. 4, 1865; CB to Dear Sister, Dec. 29, 1865, ibid.

p. 355   *CB's letter to Sheldon*: Dec. 3, 1865, ibid.

p. 356   *CB confided in Halpine*: CB to Halpine [circa Dec. 1865], ibid .

p. 356   *CB and Robert Hale, "no axes of his own," "What a provision," "splendid cousin," "I felt that an angel"*: CB Diary, Dec. 3–5, 1865, ibid.; CB to Elvira Stone, Dec. 4, 1865, and Apr. 1, 1866, ibid.

p. 356   *"Oh when can I go"*: CB Diary, Dec. 11, 1865, ibid.; McKay, *Wilson*, 199–202, for Wilson's civil rights bill.

p. 356   *Townsend's report to Stanton*: Dec. 8, 1865, CB Papers LC; copy dated Dec. 11 sent to CB, ibid.; she received it on Dec. 14, CB Diary, ibid.

p. 357   *"It was of course"* : ibid.

p. 357   *"deepest feeling of depression," "such a mockery," "put into words," "must have faith," "promised under protest"*: ibid., Dec. 17, 1865.

p. 357   *"back pay"*: ibid., Dec. 8, 1865.

p. 357   *"I could not but feel," "quick sense of justice"*: CB to Wilson, Dec. 19, 1865, ibid. See also CB Diary, Dec. 20, 1865, ibid.

p. 358   *no hope at Patent Office, Wilson's offer of $20, "discouraged and tearful," "nice little warm room"*: ibid., Dec. 21–22, 1865.

p. 358   *Sheldon's suggestion, "decided upon"*: CB Diary, Dec. 18, 1865. For Mary Abigail Dodge, whose pen name was Gail Hamilton, see James et al. (eds.), *Notable American Women*, 1:494.

p. 358   *formal invitation to speak, "deficiencies"*: CB to Mrs. A. G. Shaven, Dec. 23, 1865, ibid.; CB Diary, Dec. 19, 1865, CB Papers LC.

p. 358   *"Gynaekokracy"*: quoted in Massey, *Bonnet Brigades*, 153–54.

p. 359   *Sarah Clarke Lippincott*: James et al.(eds.), *Notable American Women*, 2:408–9.

p. 359   *"I don't know if ever"*: CB Diary, Dec. 18, 1865.

p. 359   *invitation accepted*: CB to Mrs. A. G. Shaven, Dec. 23, 1865, ibid.; CB Diary, Dec. 24, 1865, ibid.

p. 359   *"crowded hospital wards," "Two in a year," "not merry"*: ibid., Dec. 25, 1865.

p. 359   *CB's lecture, interruptions, "what friends," "I must write," "oh if I was certain"*: ibid., Dec. 25, 27, 29, 1865, ibid.

p. 359   *Atwater working in secret, "If only once I can see," no Christmas visit*: CB Diary, Dec. 26, 1865; CB to Dear Sister, Dec. 29, 1865, ibid.

p. 360   *"I am so anxious"*: CB Diary, Dec. 29, 1865, ibid.

p. 360   *negotiations with* New York Times, *"the proper editorials," "the Marplot of the Republican party"*: CB to Dear Sister, Dec. 29, 1865, ibid.; CB Diary, Dec. 18, 30, 1865.

p. 360   *"This is the close of a weary year," "wipe out," "I am strong and able"*: ibid., Dec. 30–31, 1865, Jan. 1, 1866.

p. 360   *CB's lecture writing, apples and sweet butter, "habitually unhappy," "I must draw him"*: ibid., Jan. 1–4, 1866, Dec. 24, 1865.

p. 361   *Mississippi and South Carolina Black Codes*: Robert Self Henry, *The Story of Reconstruction* (reprint 1938 ed., New York: Peter Smith, 1951), 97–98, 107–10; Foner, *Reconstruction*, 199–209; Abbott, *Cobbler in Congress*, 171–72.

p. 361   *"that this record so sadly"*: CB to Greeley, Jan. 8, 1866, CB Papers LC; CB Journal, Jan. 8, 1865, ibid.

p. 361   *CB's and Atwater's meeting with Greeley, "pale & sober," "wore upon him more"*: CB Journal, Jan. 13, Feb. 14, 1866, ibid.; Daniel E. Sutherland, *The Expansion of Everyday Life, 1860–1876* (New York: Harper & Row, 1989), 180–81, for the details about the new Pullman sleeping car.

p. 361   *description of Greeley*: Hodding Carter, *The Angry Scar: The Story of Reconstruction* (Garden City, N.Y.: Doubleday, 1959), 169; William Harlan Hale, *Horace Greeley, Voice of the People* (New York: Harper & Brothers, 1950), 1–2, 4–5, 77–78, 295–96, 340; plus photographs of Greeley.

p. 362   *Gage's arrival, "quite as well"*: CB Diary, Jan. 9, 1866; Holtzman, "Frances Gage," 43–50, for Gage's war work, 1863–1865.

p. 362   *"superior mind," "tell the world"*: CB Journal, Jan. 9–10, 1866, CB Papers LC; Gage to CB, Dec. 28, 1880, ibid.; quoted also in Henle, "Against the Fearful Odds," 38.

p. 362   *"great work," "well organized"*: *Washington Independent*, clipping, CB Papers LC; see also Frances Gage, "Relics of Andersonville: Clara Barton, and Her Work of Mercy," in King and Derby, *Camp-Fire Sketches and Battle-Field*

Echoes, 591–94.

p. 362   *"That it should not be permitted"*: CB's Memorial to Congress, Jan. 20, 1866, CB Papers LC.

p. 363   *"As a wife and mother"*: Gage to Senators and Representatives [circa Jan. 1866], ibid.

pp. 363–64   *Atwater's pamphlet*: copy in ibid.; *New York Tribune*, Feb. 14, 1866, with CB's note on it about Greeley's "peculiar manner of advertising it," in CB Papers SC. See also Barton, *Life of Clara Barton*, 1:326–27.

p. 364   New York Citizen *story*: Mar. 3, 1866, copy in CB Papers LC.

p. 364   New York Independent *story*: Feb. 29, 1866, copy in ibid.

p. 365   *response of Moore and Meigs*: Moore to Meigs, Feb. 12, 1866, copy in DA File ANHS; Meigs to Stanton, Feb. 21, 1866, copy in ibid.

p. 365   *justice had been done*: Pryor, *Clara Barton*, 145, offers a completely different interpretation of CB's involvement with Atwater. As far as I am concerned, the War Department adjutants treated him with cruelty and injustice.

p. 365   *huge circulation*: Barton, *Life of Clara Barton*, 1:327, reported that the pamphlet had "an enormous circulation."

p. 365   *"perhaps the first American woman"*: Henle, "Against the Fearful Odds," 38. Pryor, *Clara Barton*, 147, makes the same point as Henle and also observes that CB's "was the only female testimony during months of hearings," which can be substantiated by examining the committee's *Report*.

pp. 365–66   *CB's testimony before the Joint Committee on Reconstruction*: Feb. 21 1866, *Report of the Joint Committee on Reconstruction*, pt. 3, 102–8.

p. 366   *Radical Republicans v. Johnson*: see ibid., xvi–xxi; Kenneth M. Stampp, *The Era of Reconstruction, 1865–1877* (New York: Alfred A. Knopf, 1966), 83–118, 148–54.

p. 367   *"in the further prosecution," "was performed," "small additional," $15,000 appropriation*: *Congressional Globe*, 36, pt. 2, 1184, and pt. 3, 1184–85; *New York Tribune*, Mar. 6, 1866; CB's Statement to the Senate [typescript], CB Papers LC; Barton, *Life of Clara Barton*, 1:316.

p. 367   *"By voting $15,000," "take up this case"*: *New York Citizen*, Mar. 10, 1865, copy in CB Papers LC.

p. 367   *Atwater as CB's assistant*: CB Ledger Book 1866 and Diary entries 1866, CB Papers LC; Atwater's testimony, *Report of the Joint Committee on Reconstruction*, pt. 2, 279–87. Pryor, *Clara Barton*, also says that Atwater was one of CB's "clerks."

p. 367   *"Do you wonder"*: Frances Atwater to Wm. E. Barton, Aug. 27, 1919, CB Papers SC.

p. 367   *"The word soldier"*: quoted in "Dorence Atwater," Memorial Address, Congregational Church, Terryville,

Conn., May 29 1911, p. 11, CB Papers LC. In a tardy effort
to mollify Atwater, the government in 1868 appointed him
U.S. consul to the Seychelles Islands in the Indian Ocean
and three years later transferred him to the U.S. consulate
on Tahiti Island in the South Pacific. He married a
Tahitian, Moetia Salmon, who was the sister of a queen. In
1898, Congress reversed his court martial verdict and
granted him an honorable discharge, retroactive to Sept. 22
1865. According to the Meriden (Connecticut) *Daily
Journal*, he did not get a pension or receive official recognition for his "great service" in the war. He died and was
buried in Tahiti in 1911. After his death, Moetia Atwater
filed for and won a pension from the U.S. Government. See
the Adjutant General's Memorandum for the
Quartermaster General, Dec. 31, 1914, DA File ANHS;
Washington Chronicle, July 29, 1868, and *Meriden Daily
Journal*, May 29, 1911, clippings, ibid.; John T. Tucker to
Hon. Jean-Paul Pera, Dec. 17, 1962, ibid.; and other rele-
vant documents in ibid.; newspaper clipping, CB
Scrapbooks, CB Papers LC; Frances Atwater to Barton,
Aug. 27 1919, Barton, *Life of Clara Barton*, 1:327; Dorence
Atwater's Pension Records, NARA.

p. 368   *Jules Golay*: CB's Ledger Book, Mar. and Apr. 1866, CB
          Papers LC; Golay to CB, Nov. 10, Dec. 17, 1867, Oct. 15,
          1869, ibid. Pryor, *Clara Barton*, 147, also points out that
          Golay was a CB assistant.

p. 368   *CB's Memorial to Congress*: Doc. 57 in U.S. Senate,
          Miscellaneous Documents, 40th Cong., 3d sess.
          (1868–1869); copy in CB Papers LC. See also Pryor, *Clara
          Barton*, 154, and Barton, *Life of Clara Barton*, 1:316. There
          are documents in MS Papers OCHS relating to CB's miss-
          ing-soldier work in 1866.

p. 368   *Nightingale*: see Woodham-Smith, *Florence Nightingale*,
          96–179.

p. 369   *Reid Mitchell*: Gabor S. Boritt (ed.), *Why the Confederacy
          Lost* (New York: Oxford University Press, 1992), 109–32.

EPILOGUE: THE CIRCUIT

p. 373   *"I appear to be known"*: CB Diary, Apr. 1, 1866, CB Papers
          LC.

p. 373   *"Work and Incidents"*: various drafts and typescript in ibid.

p. 373   *CB's soft voice, poetic descriptions*: Worcester *Spy*, clip-
          ping, ibid.; *Schenectady* (New York) *Republican*, Oct. 27,
          1866, clipping, ibid.; *Peoria* (Illinois) *Transcript*, Dec. 6,
          1867.

p. 373   *"animated," "instructive and enjoyable"*: see, for example,

Davenport (Iowa) *Gazette*, Dec. 7, 1867; *Lincoln* (Illinois) *Herald*, Dec. 5, 1867; *Peoria* (Illinois) *Transcript*, Dec. 6, 1867. Clippings of these and many other newspapers in the West and East are in CB Papers LC.

p. 373   *"We have never seen"*: *Alton* (Illinois) *Telegraph*, Dec. 3, 1867, clipping, ibid.

p. 373   *speaking invitations, GAR post named after CB*: ibid.; CB to Major Seth Hagges, June 10, 1881, ibid. For CB's view of herself as a soldier and veteran, see CB to Gen. Edward W. Whitaker, Jan. 3, 1870, from Corsica, ibid. See also the GAR tribute to CB in 1881, ibid., and the tribute of the Twenty-first Massachusetts' surviving veterans, Sept. 13, 1911, ibid.

p. 373   *CB's speaking fees, profits*: see CB Diary, relevant entries 1866–1867, which record her fees and expenses, ibid; CB Ledger Book, ibid.; and CB's vast correspondence regarding her speaking engagements, ibid. Fees of other lecturers come from a brochure of the Western Lecture Bureau and circular, Sept. 23, 1867 of Association of Western Literary Societies, ibid. Pryor, *Clara Barton*, 149, and Barton, *Life of Clara Barton*, 1:342, state that her rates were $75 to $100. CB gave her fees as $100 to $125 but settled for $75 when speaking to veterans' groups or small audiences. See CB to H. Moore, Nov. 26, 1867, CB Papers LC; see also Frank Brown to CB, July 5, 15, 1867, ibid.; and CB to H. W. Clark, Dec. 20, 1868, CB Papers DU. In one period she was in greater demand than Emerson or Higginson.

p. 373   *CB on smoky, monotonous trains*: derived from CB Diary, entries 1866–1867, CB Papers LC. See also DA Diary CBPLC.

p. 374   *"Fearfully dirty room"*: ibid., Feb. 21, 1867.

p. 374   *train wreck*: ibid., Jan. 25, 1867.

p. 374   *CB's light blue traveling dress, young-looking*: ibid., Oct. 30, Nov. 12, 1866. A *New York Herald* reporter thought her "an unassuming lady of about thirty" (*New York Herald*, Oct. 30, 1866, clipping, ibid.). Said a *New York Mills* reporter: "She appears to be any where between twenty-five and thirty-five." Newspaper clipping, Oct. 26 [no year], ibid.

p. 374   *voice low and gentle to singsong eloquence*: according to a listener quoted in CB Diary, Mar. 7–27, 1866, ibid.

p. 374   *"I struggled long and hard"*: CB Lecture [undated] and Lecture [typescript], ibid.

p. 374   *"outbursts of laughter," "But when some brave scene"*: a listener quoted in CB Diary, Mar. 7–27, 1866, ibid.

p. 375   *"that eternal blot," "keeper of the death records," "unpardoned," "ruined in health"*: CB Notes for a Lecture [undated], ibid.

p. 375   *"own little personal doings"*: ibid.

p. 375   *widows and orphans*: ibid.; CB Lecture [undated], ibid.; CB
                  Lecture [typescript], ibid.

p. 375   *"on the power" of her femininity*: CB "Women in the War,"
                  ibid. See also CB's poem, "The Women Who Went to the
                  Field," ibid. Pryor, *Clara Barton*, also points out that CB
                  stopped using female helpers and competed with other
                  women for the right to nurse men.

pp. 375–76   *women's wartime achievements*: See Massey, *Bonnet
                  Brigades*, 109–22, 130, 132–34, 151–52, 164–66, 343–45;
                  Livermore, *My Story of the War*, 145, 156; Smith, "The
                  Women Who Went to the War," 1; Catherine Clinton, *The
                  Other Civil War: American Women in the Nineteenth
                  Century* (New York: Hill and Wang, 1984), 90–92; Jeanie
                  Attie, "Warwork and the Crisis of Domesticity in the
                  North," in Clinton and Silber, *Divided Houses*, 247–59;
                  Young, *The Women and the Crisis*, 43.

p. 376   *numbers of Union female hospital workers*: Older studies
                  estimate the total at about 9,000, but Professor Jane E.
                  Schultz puts the figure at more than 20,000, including
                  more than 18,200 paid workers. Among the latter group,
                  she says, were 5,600 mostly white nurses and 2,000
                  African-Americans. Her numbers derive from hospital ser-
                  vice records in NARA. Schultz, "Race, Gender, and
                  Bureaucracy: Civil War Army Nurses and the Pension
                  Bureau," 1, 25, forthcoming in *The Journal of Women's
                  History* (manuscript copy generously provided by
                  Professor Schultz); Schultz, "'Seldom Thanked, Never
                  Praised, and Scarcely Recognized': Black and White
                  Women in Civil War Relief Work" (manuscript copy gen-
                  erously provided by Professor Schultz), 3–4, 19; and
                  Schultz to Stephen B. Oates, August 8, 1993. My figure for
                  Dix's department is from Julia C. Stimson and Ethel C.
                  Thompson, "Women Nurses with the Union Forces
                  During the Civil War," *Military Medicine* (Jan. and Feb.
                  1928), 1–17, 208–229; and Sister Mary Denis Maher, *To
                  Bind Up the Wounds: Catholic Sister Nurses in the U.S.
                  Civil War* (Westport, Conn.: Greenwood Press, 1984),
                  51–52, 69. For the significance of the female hospital work-
                  ers, see Schultz, "The Inhospitable Hospital," *Signs*
                  (Winter 1992), 363–92; Smith, "The Women Who Went to
                  the War," 3, 7–8, 103, 150, 156; and Woods, "War Within a
                  War," *Civil War History* (Sept. 1972), 197–212.

pp. 376–77   *Samuel Gross's urging*: Smith, "The Women Who Went to
                  War," 142, reports that he "demanded that America pro-
                  duce a trained corps of female nurses to match England's."

p. 377   *postwar nursing schools and profession*: ibid., 142–44, 150,
                  156; Schultz, "The Inhospitable Hospital," *Signs* (Winter
                  1992), 389–92; and Massey, *Bonnet Brigades*, 351–53. See
                  also Reverby, *Ordered to Care*, 2–4, 15–35, passim. Austin,

Woolsey Sisters of New York, 116–60, discusses how Abby Howland Woolsey, Jane Stuart Woolsey, and Georgeanna Woolsey were "pioneers" in postwar civilian nursing. McPherson, *Battle Cry of Freedom*, 484, notes that "the Civil War marked a milestone in the transformation of nursing from a menial service to a genuine profession." But Barbara Melosh, *"The Physician's Hand": Work Culture and Conflict in American Nursing* (Philadelphia: Temple University Press, 1982), disputes that interpretation, arguing that "nursing is not and cannot be a profession" (p. 15).

p. 377   *"the gender hierarchy"*: Attie, "Warwork and the Crisis of Domesticity in the North," in Clinton and Silber, *Divided Houses*, 251.

p. 377   *so many new opportunities, 60 percent rise in women wage earners*: Massey, *Bonnet Brigades*, 151–52, 339–67. As Massey points out, the figure was slightly higher in the war years than in the postwar years. She also reports that "the greatest increase" of female workers in the 1860s occurred in the area of "personal services," which included hundreds of thousands of domestics, "many of them former slaves." The war, of course, provided job opportunites for Southern black women that they would never have had without it. The 60 percent figure also included teachers, nurses, and government workers. On the other hand, Alice Kessler-Harris, *Out to Work: A History of Wage-Earning Women in the United States* (New York: Oxford University Press, 1982), 76, argues that the war did not expand "job opportunities" for all women; it did so mainly for "educated" and "professional" women, "opening clerical jobs in government to them, legitimizing nursing as a profession, and dramatically increasing the number of female teachers." The impact of the war on "less-skilled women," Kessler-Harris contends, "was more problematic." Perhaps so, but I remain persuaded by Massey's well-substantiated argument (p. 340) that "the economic emancipation of women was the most important single factor in her social, intellectual, and political advancement, and the war did more in four years to change her economic status than had been accomplished in any previous generation."

p. 377   *"fifty years in advance"*: CB Speech in the Boston Music Hall, May 30, 1888, p. 15, CB Papers SC.

p. 377   *"Only an opportunity was wanting," female competence*: CB Lecture [undated] and Notes for a Lecture [undated], CB Papers LC; quoted somewhat differently in Pryor, *Life of Clara Barton*, 151. Pryor also makes the point about "female competence." Massey, *Bonnet Brigades*, 339–40, stresses a similar point.

p. 377   *By expanding the limits of what was possible*: My line was inspired by Adrienne Rich's felicitous phrase "the boundaries of the possible" and her idea that the best thing women can do for one another is to enlarge their sense of possibilities. Certainly that was what the Northern women of the war did for their generation. See the Rich quotations and discussion in Bettina Aptheker, *Tapestries of Life: Women's Work, Women's Consciousness, and the Meaning of Daily Experience* (Amherst: University of Massachusetts Press, 1991), 246.

p. 377 *"dug grand and deep"*: CB "Women in the War," CB Papers LC.

p. 377 *"at heart and long before the idea"*: CB to Mary Norton, Oct. 15, 1869 [typescript], AL Collection SLRC.

p. 377 *"perfectly equal rights"*: "Clara Barton Is 90," *Woman's Journal* (Dec. 30, 1911), clipping, WR Collection SLRC. See also CB Draft of a Lecture on Women's Rights [undated], CB Papers SC. Pryor, *Clara Barton*, 120, 151, first analyzed how Gage's influence and CB's war experiences converted her to feminism. Pryor points out that CB established "a symbiotic relationship" with "more radical feminist leaders" yet "never allied herself too closely with" the feminist movement. See Pryor, 150–53.

pp. 377–78 *"three millions of God's poor"*: CB, "Black Book," CB Papers SC. Pryor, *Clara Barton*, 153, likewise credits "Aunt Fanny's teaching" and CB's stay in Georgia with her "championship of the Negro."

p. 378 *"a part of the war," "Finish my work first"*: CB to Mary Norton, Oct. 15, 1869 [typescript], AL Collection SLRC.

p. 378 *feminists and black vote, 1869 convention, rival suffragist associations*: This paragraph is indebted to Ellen Carol DuBois, *Feminism and Suffrage: The Emergence of an Independent Women's Movement in America, 1848–1869* (Ithaca, N.Y.: Cornell University Press, 1978), 53–78, 162–202.

pp. 378–79 *"well fed, warmed," "thousands of hungry," "I only meant"*: CB to Mary Norton, Oct. 15, 1869 [typescript], AL Collection SLRC.

p. 379 *"identified with men"*: Pryor, *Clara Barton*, 152, used those words, but anyone reading the evidence can discern that CB "always identified" with the masculine world of her father and brothers.

p. 379 *"with men as men"*: CB to Mary Norton, Oct. 15, 1869 [typescript], AL Collection SLRC.

p. 379 *"Man is trying to carry"*: Ida Husted Harper, "The Life and Work of Clara Barton," *North American Review* (May 1912), 712; also quoted in Henle, "Against the Fearful Odds," 146.

p. 379 *"Of whom should I ask this privilege"*: "Clara Barton Is 90," *Woman's Journal*, Dec. 30, 1911, clipping, WR Collection SLRC.

p. 379   *"splendid house," Elwell visit*: CB Diary, Feb. 25, 1867, CB
                Papers LC. Elwell's accidents from his Pension Records,
                NARA; Shastid, "A Short Biography of John J. Elwell,"
                American Medicine (Feb. 1909), 95; Van Tassel and
                Grabowski (eds.), *Encyclopedia of Cleveland History*, 373.

p. 380   *CB's recalling Antietam hospital, "Ladies and gentleman, if I
                never"*: CB Lecture [undated], CB Papers LC.

pp. 380–81   *CB's lecture in local YMCA, episode with soldier, daughter
                named CB*: CB Diary, Mar. 7–27 1866, ibid.

p. 381   *children named after CB*: See entire folder of letters about
                this in CB Papers LC. A county in Kansas was also named
                after her.

p. 381   *"War is the scourge"*: Harwood, "An Army Surgeon's
                Story," *St. Louis Illustrated Magazine* (April 1883), 147

p. 382   *"Men have worshipped war"*: quoted in Epler, *Life of Clara
                Barton*, vii.

p. 382   *Civil War to which she kept returning*: for instance, visiting
                Charleston in 1886, CB stood on "the dismantled dome of
                Charleston Orphan House" and gazed across the bay at
                Morris Island, remembering the assaults of July 18, 1863.
                "I saw the bayonet glistening . . . the fleet thundered its
                cannonade, and the little dark line of blue trailed its way to
                the belching walls of Wagner. . . . Voris and Cumminger
                gasping in their blood. . . . Elwell's gallop on 'Old Sam.' "
                "Miss Clara Barton Writes a Grand Letter to the 'Yates
                Phalanx,' 39th Illinois," *National Tribune*, Oct. 12, 1886,
                clipping, CB Papers LC. She was still giving interviews on
                her role in the Civil War in the 1890s.

p. 382   *"professional angel"*: Pryor's subtitle of her CB biography,
                Clara Barton. Pryor's is by far the best account of CB's
                post–Civil War years, especially her great work with the
                Red Cross.

p. 382   *"Let me go; Let me go!"* Barton, *Life of Clara Barton*, 2:374.
                Pryor, *Clara Barton*, 372, also ends her book with CB's last
                words. But I put a different emphasis on them than do her
                previous biographers.

Afterword and Acknowledgments

p. 384   *Michelle Murray quotation*: Janet Steinburg (ed.), *The
                Writer on Her Work: Contemporary Writers Reflect on
                Their Art and Situation* (New York: W. W. Norton, 1980),
                83.

Index

Books by Stephen B. Oates

Confederate Cavalry West of the River (1961)

Rip Ford's Texas (1963)

The Republic of Texas (1968)

Visions of Glory (1970)

To Purge This Land With Blood: A Biography of John Brown (1970)

The Fires of Jubilee: Nat Turner's Fierce Rebellion (1975)

With Malice Toward None: The Life of Abraham Lincoln (1977)

Our Fiery Trial: Abraham Lincoln, John Brown, and the Civil War Era (1979)

Let the Trumpet Sound: The Life of Martin Luther King, Jr. (1982)

Abraham Lincoln: The Man Behind the Myths (1984)

Biography as High Adventure: Life-Writers Speak on Their Art (1986)

William Faulkner, The Man and the Artist: A Biography (1987)

Portrait of America (2 vols., 6th edition, 1994)

A Woman of Valor: Clara Barton and the Civil War (1994)